RETHINKING PHOTOGRAPHY

Rethinking Photography is an accessible and illuminating critical introduction to the practice and interpretation of photography today.

Peter Smith and Carolyn Lefley closely link critical approaches to photographic practices and present a detailed study of differing historical and contemporary perspectives on social and artistic functions of the medium, including photography as art, documentary forms, advertising and personal narratives.

Richly illustrated with full colour images to connect key concepts to real world examples, the book also includes:

- accessible chapters on key topics, including early photography, photography and industrial society, the rise of photography theory, critical engagement with anti-realist trends in the theory and practice of photography, photography and language, photography education, and photography and the creative economy
- specific case studies on photographic practices, including snapshot and portable box cameras, digital and mobile phone cultures, and computer-generated imagery
- critical summaries of current theoretical studies in the field, displaying how critical theory has been mapped on to working practices of photographers and students
- in-depth profiles of selected key photographers and theorists, and studies of their professional practices
- assessment of photography as a key area of contemporary aesthetic debate
- focused and critical study of the world of working photographers beyond the horizons of the academy.

Rethinking Photography provides readers with an engaging mix of photographic case studies and an accessible exploration of essential theory. It is an essential guide for students of photography, fine art, art history, and graphic design, as well as practitioners from any background wishing to understand the place of photography in global societies today.

Peter Smith is a writer and lecturer with over 30 years of experience in teaching art history and cultural theory. He has written articles and reviews for many journals including *The Oxford Art Journal* and *Kunst und Politik*. Recent publications include chapters in books including *As Radical as Reality Itself: Essays on Marxism for the 21st Century* (2007) and *Renew Marxist Art History* (2013). He is currently teaching at the University of West London, UK.

Carolyn Lefley is Lecturer in Photography at the University of Hertfordshire, UK and a photographic artist. Her research interests include photography and expanded media: moving image, mobile photography and computer generated imagery. Her photographic practice explores notions of home, belonging and folklore.

Praise for this edition:

'*Rethinking Photography* is ideal for stimulating discussions on the critical issues regarding the theory of photography. Smith and Lefley's writing on the historical and contemporary debates of the medium is comprehensive, lucid, and engaging.'

Stephen Chalmers, *Associate Professor of Photography and Digital Imaging, Youngstown State University, USA*

'In this excellent new book *Rethinking Photography: Histories, Theories and Education* Peter Smith and Carolyn Lefley lucidly articulate the distinctive nature and alluring power of photography throughout its history, and also how it continues to influence contemporary visual dialogues.

Its innovative framework provides an accessible blend of critical information and investigative prompts that will make it essential reading for all photography students. The extremely useful summaries of key points for each section, the case studies, key terms and biography boxes provide supportive pedagogic connections between academic lecturing and student understanding. Therefore, I'm confident this book will become an essential guide for all students of photography and also anyone else who has a desire to investigate the fascinating pluralities of the medium.

The most exciting feature of this book for me was its formulation of the importance of photography's critical position in the contemporary art and design context. In particular the sections on Photography Education and its status Beyond the Academy present an innovative reflection on the key dialogues that influence contemporary notions of the photographic. I would imagine most students may initially bypass these sections but however subsequently realise that they provide a critical understanding of the past, current and future contexts of photography.'

Mark Cocks, *Assistant Dean, Swansea College of Art (UWTSD), UK*

'This remarkable book is a unique contribution to rethinking photography's histories, theories and practices. No other study of photography enables us to think about education and look beyond the academy in order to understand what's at stake in photography today.'

Antigoni Memou, *Lecturer in Art History, University of East London, UK*

'Peter Smith and Carolyn Lefley (with photographer Andy Golding) have written a very well-organised and pacey introduction to photography, which ranges from the first developments to mobile phone technology and from art to advertising. It is admirably clear, without over-simplifying the issues and the examples are superbly selected. With an economy of means, key terms are explained, central figures introduced and processes described. Succinct summaries help the reader at every point. The novel focus on photographic education makes this textbook an excellent starting point for students and teachers working with photography. All that is left to say is that this is also a very smart and partisan book.'

Steve Edwards, *Professor of Art-History-Materialism, Open University, UK*

'An excellent contribution to histories and discourses relating to the theory and practice of photography, which though far ranging and complex are very clearly communicated, facilitated by the use of "key term" boxes, box profiles, case studies and section summaries. Of particular note is the perspective on photography education itself as a determining factor in the development of the field's theory and practice, which presented together with significant insights regarding narrative, reportage, commerce and the attendant implications of a changing market, create an important and thought-provoking resource for all serious students of photography.'

Susan Andrews, *Reader in Photography, Cass Faculty of Art, Architecture and Design, London Metropolitan University, UK*

'A detailed and copiously illustrated book – one to return to again and again. Readers, particularly those in photography education, will find much to reward them from *Rethinking Photography*.'

Stephen Bull, *Course Leader BA Photography, University of Brighton, UK*

RETHINKING PHOTOGRAPHY

Histories, Theories and Education

Peter Smith and Carolyn Lefley

NEW YORK AND LONDON

First published 2016
by Routledge
2 Park Square, Milton Park, Abingdon, Oxon OX14 4RN

and by Routledge
711 Third Avenue, New York, NY 10017

Routledge is an imprint of the Taylor & Francis Group, an informa business

© 2016 Peter Smith and Carolyn Lefley; individual contributions, Andrew Golding

The right of Peter Smith and Carolyn Lefley to be identified as authors of this work has been asserted by them in accordance with sections 77 and 78 of the Copyright, Designs and Patents Act 1988.

All rights reserved. No part of this book may be reprinted or reproduced or utilised in any form or by any electronic, mechanical, or other means, now known or hereafter invented, including photocopying and recording, or in any information storage or retrieval system, without permission in writing from the publishers.

Trademark notice: Product or corporate names may be trademarks or registered trademarks, and are used only for identification and explanation without intent to infringe.

British Library Cataloguing in Publication Data
A catalogue record for this book is available from the British Library

Library of Congress Cataloging in Publication Data
Smith, Peter, 1946 December 26-
Rethinking photography : histories, theories, and education / Peter Smith and Carolyn Lefley.
pages cm
Includes bibliographical references and index.
1. Photography--Philosophy--History. 2. Photography--Social aspects--History. 3. Photography--Study and teaching. I. Lefley, Carolyn, 1978- II. Title.
TR183.S58 2015
770--dc23
2014045245

ISBN: 978-0-415-73433-2 (hbk)
ISBN: 978-1-40-820384-2 (pbk)
ISBN: 978-1-315-72241-2 (ebk)

Typeset in Helvetica Neue LT Std Condensed 8/10 pt
by Fakenham Prepress Solutions, Fakenham, Norfolk NR21 8NN
Printed by Bell & Bain Ltd, Glasgow

For my mother Jennie Smith

Peter Smith

For my grandmother Joan Whittaker

Carolyn Lefley

CONTENTS

List of Figures	x
Illustration Acknowledgements	xiv
Acknowledgements	xxi
Introduction	1

PART 1: Histories of Photography — 5

Introduction to Part 1	5
Chapter 1: Histories and Pre-Histories of Photography	7
Chapter 2: Photography in the Nineteenth Century *with Andrew Golding*	43
Chapter 3: Photographic Realism: Straight Photography and Photographic Truth	77
Chapter 4: The Constructed Photograph	112
Case Study 1: Snapshot Photography and the Portable Box Camera	135
Case Study 2: The Digital Camera	141

PART 2: Photography Theories — 149

Introduction to Part 2	149
Chapter 5: The Rise of Photography Theory	151
Case Study 3: Semiology: How Images Make Meanings	171
Chapter 6: Photography and the Written Word	187

PART 3: Photography Education — 219

Introduction to Part 3	219
Chapter 7: Issues and Debates in Photography Education I: New Photography Theory	221
Chapter 8: Issues and Debates in Photography Education II: The Return of the Real	249
Chapter 9: Teaching and Learning Photography *with Andrew Golding*	266
Chapter 10: New Technologies and Photography Education	278

CONTENTS

PART 4: Beyond the Academy 299

Introduction to Part 4 299

Chapter 11: Photography, Advertising and Consumer Cultures 303

Chapter 12: Photography and the Creative Economy 319

Case Study 4: Digital and Mobile Phone Cultures 342

Case Study 5: The Designed Photograph: Computer Generated Imagery (CGI) in
Car Photography 357

Index 369

CONTRIBUTOR

Andrew Golding is Head of the Department of Photography and Film in the Faculty of Media, Arts and Design at the University of Westminster.

FIGURES

1.1	William Henry Fox Talbot, title page of *The Pencil of Nature* (1844–46).	7
1.2	Dress by Madeleine Vionnet, photographed by Man Ray, 1937.	16
1.3	Pink satin corset by Mainbocher, photographed by Horst P. Horst for *Vogue*, 1939.	17
1.4	Eugène Atget, *Cour, 41 rue Broca, Paris 5*, 1912.	19
1.5	Eugène Atget, *Marchand de Parapluies (The Umbrella Man)*, 1899–1900.	20
1.6	Willy Ronis, *Le Depart du Morutier (A Cod Fisherman Takes his Leave)*, Fécamp, 1949.	21
1.7	Robert Doisneau, *Le Baiser de l'Hôtel de Ville (Kiss by the Town Hall)*, 1950.	21
1.8	Annie Leibovitz, *HM Queen Elizabeth II*, 2007.	26
1.9	The British Royal Family at Balmoral: Elizabeth II, Prince Charles, Duke of Edinburgh, Princess Anne, early 1950s.	27
2.1	Roger Fenton, *The Photographer's Van with Marcus Sparling in the Crimea*, 1855.	43
2.2	Camera Obscura. From Athanasius Kircher, *Ars Magna*, Amsterdam, 1671.	47
2.3	Unknown artist, *Camera Lucida in use drawing small figurine*, illustration from the *Scientific American* Supplement, 1879.	48
2.4	Joseph Nicéphore Niépce, *View From the Window at Le Gras*, 1826.	49
2.5	Daguerreotype of young woman about 1860.	54
2.6	Gustave Le Gray, *Tree, Forest of Fontainebleau, c.* 1856.	59
2.7	Gustave Le Gray, *The Great Wave, Sète*, 1856, albumen print from two collodion glass negatives.	60
2.8	Roger Fenton, *The Valley of the Shadow of Death After the Charge of the Light Brigade*, 1855.	61
2.9	Simon Norfolk, *Track of Destroyed Taliban Tank at Farm Hada Military Base near Jalalabad*, from the series *Afghanistan: Chronotopia*, 2002.	62
2.10	Timothy H. O'Sullivan, *A Harvest of Death, Gettysburg, Pennsylvania*, July 4th, 1863.	63
2.11	Alexander Gardner, *Home of a Rebel Sharpshooter, Gettysburg*, July 1863.	64
2.12	Julia Margaret Cameron, *The Echo*, 1868.	66
2.13	A stereograph, Elmer and Bert Elias Underwood, *The Great Pyramid of Giza*, 1905.	68
2.14	André Adolphe-Eugène Disdéri, *Carte-de-visite of Napoleon III*, 1859.	69
2.15	*The Graphic: Arctic Supplement*, 'The Arctic Expedition', 1875, London.	72
3.1	Alexander Gardner, *Abraham Lincoln*, 1863.	77
3.2	Jan van Eyck, *The Arnolfini Portrait*, 1434.	83
3.3	The visual cone, from Brook Taylor, *New Principles of Linear Perspective*, 1719.	84
3.4	Leonardo da Vinci, *Study for the Adoration of the Magi, c.* 1481.	85
3.5	Pere Borrell del Caso, *Escaping Criticism*, 1874.	85
3.6	Jan Vermeer, *View of Delft, c.* 1660–61.	88
3.7	Honoré Daumier, *The Washerwoman (La Blanchisseuse), c.* 1860.	90

3.8	Gustave Caillebotte, *Raboteurs de Parquet*, 1876.	91
3.9	Louis Mandé Daguerre, *The Artist's Studio*, daguerreotype, 1837.	92
3.10	André Adolphe-Eugène Disdéri, *Portraits Sitting 41494: Docteur Magnan and His Son and Daughter, c.* 1861.	93
3.11	Paul Strand, *Wall Street*, 1915.	94
3.12	Margaret Bourke-White, *Workers Leaving Jones & Laughlin Steel Plant at 3 pm Shift*, 1936.	95
3.13	Margaret Bourke-White, *Portrait of a Sharecropper with a Bonnet on Her Head and Her Hands on the Handle of a Plow, Hamilton, Alabama*, 1937.	96
3.14	Edward Weston, *Nude*, 1936.	105
4.1	Hippolyte Bayard, *Autoportrait en noyé (Self Portrait as a Drowned Man)*, 1840.	112
4.2	Typical Victorian-era post-mortem family portrait, private collection.	115
4.3	Oscar Gustave Rejlander, *The Two Ways of Life, c.* 1857.	116
4.4	Henry Peach Robinson, *Fading Away*, 1858.	117
4.5	William H. Martin, *Taking Our Geese to Market*, 1909.	118
4.6	Elsie Wright and Frances Griffiths, *Alice and the Fairies*, July 1917.	119
4.7	Martha Rosler, *Cleaning the Drapes*. From the series *House Beautiful: Bringing the War Home [In Vietnam]*, 1967–72.	121
4.8	Cindy Sherman, *Untitled Film Still #58*, 1980.	123
4.9	Jeff Wall, *Mimic*, 1982.	125
4.10	Gregory Crewdson, *Untitled (Ophelia)*, from the series *Twilight*, 2001.	127
4.11	Tom Hunter, *Anchor and Hope*, from the series *Unheralded Stories*, 2009.	127
4.12	Jeff Wall, *A Sudden Gust of Wind (after Hokusai),* 1993.	129
4.13	Andreas Gursky, *Shanghai*, 2000.	129
4.14	David Levinthal, *Untitled*, from the series *Hitler Moves East*, 1975–77.	130
4.15	James Casebere, *Flooded Hallway*, 1998–99.	131
4.16	Thomas Demand, *Bathroom (Badezimmer)*, 1997.	131
CS1.1	Kodak No. 1 box camera.	135
CS1.2	An 1889 advertisement for the Kodak box camera.	136
CS1.3	Brownie advertisement, *c.* 1900.	137
CS2.1	Prototype digital camera, Steve Sasson, 1975.	141
CS2.2	CCD image sensor.	142
CS2.3	Kodak EasyShare digital camera and dock system *c.* 2001.	144
CS2.4	Teru Kuwayama and Balazs Gardi, collaborative 'Basetrack' photojournalist project using only a mobile phone, southern Afghanistan, 2010.	146
5.1	Hamish Fulton, *A Hollow Lane on the North Downs*, 1971.	151
5.2	John Hilliard, *Camera Recording its Own Condition (7 apertures, 10 speeds, 2 mirrors)*, 1971.	159
5.3	Barbara Kruger, *"Untitled" (I shop therefore I am)*, 1987.	165
5.4	Sherrie Levine, *After Walker Evans: 4 (Allie Mae Burroughs)*, 1981.	167
CS3.1	Jimmy Choo fragrance advertisement, 2014.	183
6.1	*She's Got Your Eyes*, concept by Warren Neily and photograph by Shannon Mendes, 2000.	187

FIGURES

6.2	'Let Us Go Forward Together', World War II propaganda poster.	190
6.3	Raoul Hausmann, *ABCD (self-portrait)*, 1923–24.	190
6.4	Margaret Bourke-White, *At the Time of the Louisville Flood,* 1937.	191
6.5	Couple sitting on a beach together in summer.	196
6.6	Humphrey Spender, *Men Greeting in a Pub*, 1937.	197
6.7	Fabian Cevallos, *French Philosopher Roland Barthes*, 1979.	200
6.8	An Iraqi prisoner allegedly being tortured by American soldiers at Abu Ghraib prison, Iraq, *c.* 2003.	201
6.9	Prime Minister Tony Blair addressing troops in Basra, Iraq, in May 2003.	202
6.10	Eamonn McCabe, *Ascot Racegoers*, 1977.	204
6.11	René Magritte, *The Key to Dreams*, 1930.	206
6.12	Edward Steichen, *Solitude (Portrait of a Man)*, 1901.	207
6.13	Alfred Stieglitz, *The City of Ambition*, 1910.	208
6.14	August Sander, *Handlanger (Bricklayer)*, 1928.	209
6.15	Andres Serrano, *Piss Christ*, 1987.	210
6.16	Portrait of Myra Hindley, 1965.	211
6.17	Henry Hering, *Acute Mania – William Thomas Green*, 1858.	211
6.18	Cover for *Allure*, March 2011.	212
6.19	Walker Evans, *Allie Mae Burroughs, Wife of a Cotton Sharecropper, Hale County, Alabama*, 1936.	213
7.1	James Jarché, *General Wavell Watches His Gardener at Work*, 1941.	221
7.2	Cover of *Camerawork*, November, 1977.	228
7.3	Cover of *Photography/Politics: Two*, 1986.	229
7.4	*Ten.8* Photo Paperback vol. 2, no. 3, Spring 1992.	230
7.5	Diane Arbus, *A Young Brooklyn Family Going for a Sunday Outing, NYC*, 1966.	232
7.6	Victor Burgin, *Possession,* poster, 1976.	234
7.7	Richard Hamilton, *Portrait of Hugh Gaitskell as a Famous Monster of Filmland*, 1964.	237
7.8	John Heartfield, photomontage on the cover of *AIZ*, 24 August 1933.	240
7.9	Jo Spence and Rosy Martin, *How Do I Begin to Take Responsibility for My Body? Creative Camera*, No. 249, 'The Portraitive-Self in Context', September 1985.	240
7.10	Jo Spence and David Roberts, *Not of Our Class*, 1989.	241
7.11	Jo Spence in collaboration with Dr Tim Sheard, *Booby Prize*, 1989. From *Narratives of Disease*.	243
8.1	Mitra Tabrizian with Andy Golding and Zadoc Nava, from the series *Another Country*, 2010.	249
8.2	Bernd and Hilla Becher, *Winding Towers*, Belgium and Germany, 1983.	258
8.3	Martha Rosler, *The Bowery in Two Inadequate Descriptive Systems*, 1974–5.	259
8.4	Allan Sekula, cover for the book *Fish Story*, 1995.	260
8.5	Walker Evans, *Sharecropper Bud Fields and His Family at Home, Hale County, Alabama*, 1935.	261
8.6	Jeff Wall, *A Ventriloquist at a Birthday Party in October 1947*, 1990.	262
9.1	Photography lecturer Nick Galvin teaching BA Photography class at the University of Hertfordshire. The photograph is by Rebecca Thomas, 2013.	266

FIGURES

10.1	Florian Einfalt with Andreas Franke and Thomas Kapzan, *Desert Change*, 2011.	278
10.2	Trevor Coultart (undergraduate student at the University of Hertfordshire 2012–2015), *Retouching*, 2012.	281
10.3	Richard Kolker, *Around a Bodegon – after Juan Sanchez Cotan 1602*, 2012.	286
11.1	Max Factor's creamy Pan-Stik make-up, 1950s.	303
11.2	Edward Steichen, colour photograph for *Vogue*, 1932.	305
11.3	Anton Bruehl, *Art Deco Tobacco Jar, Pitcher, and Inkwell, c.* 1929.	306
11.4	Werner Gräff, *Es kommt der neue Fotograf (Here Comes the New Photographer)*, 1929.	307
11.5	Magazine advertisement for Kodachrome film, 1940s.	308
11.6	RoSPA World War II safety poster, 'Protect your eyes'. Designed by Manfred Reiss and G. R. Morris, 1942.	309
11.7	Robert Freeman (photographer), *With the Beatles*, long playing record sleeve, 1963.	312
11.8	Still from a TV advertisement for Vauxhall, *c.* 2010.	313
11.9	Beck's beer advertisement featuring Tracey Emin (*c.* 1998).	314
11.10	Richard Prince, *Marlboro Man* series: 'Untitled (Cowboy)', 1989.	315
12.1	Businesswoman outdoors using mobile phone, Bart Geerligs.	319
12.2	Burning car advertisement for United Colors of Benetton. Photography by Oliviero Toscani (*c.* 1992).	325
12.3	Walter Van Beirendonck's 'Finally Chesthair' T-shirt, 1996.	325
12.4	Erwin Olaf for *The New York Times*, Christian Lacroix, haute couture, lace ruched blouse over long taffeta and moiré flounced skirt and shoes, 2006.	326
12.5	Stock image, caption: 'View from the top', 2013.	332
12.6	Stock image, caption: 'Pittsburgh, Pennsylvania, USA. Cars parked in front of suburban houses at dusk'.	334
CS4.1	World Press Photo of the Year 2013. John Stanmeyer, VII for *National Geographic*, 26 February 2013.	342
CS4.2	Two mobile phone photographs taken by Ukrainian Instagram user nata_original. Real name: Natalia Ukolova.	349
CS4.3	Penelope Umbrico *5,377,183 Suns from Flickr (Partial) 4/28/09*, 2009.	351
CS4.4	Joachim Schmid, *Another Self*, from the book series *Other People's Photographs*, 2008–11.	351
CS4.5	Erik Kessels, *24HRS IN PHOTOS*. Installation at Photography in Abundance, FOAM, Amsterdam December 2011 – January 2012.	352
CS4.6	Nina Katchadourian, *Lavatory Self-Portrait in the Flemish Style #12,* 2011, from *Seat Assignment* (2010 and ongoing).	353
CS5.1	Press image for Porsche Cayenne. Courtesy of Dr. Ing. h.c. F. Porsche AG.	357
CS5.2	From concept to factory floor – the main stages of car design.	362
CS5.3	Stages in the creation of a CGI 'designed photograph', René Staud.	363
CS5.4	Variations on the make-up of a designed car photograph.	365

ILLUSTRATION ACKNOWLEDGEMENTS

1.1 William Henry Fox Talbot, title page of *The Pencil of Nature*, 1844. By permission of University of Glasgow Library, Special Collections.

1.2 Model wearing Vionnet evening gown with 'Brouette' by Oscar Dominguez, photographed by Man Ray, 1937. Gelatin-silver print © DACS, London/Victoria and Albert Museum, London.

1.3 Pink satin corset by Mainbocher, photographed by Horst P. Horst for *Vogue*, 1939. © Vogue/Horst. P. Horst/Condé Nast.

1.4 Eugène Atget, *Cour, 41 rue Broca, Paris 5*, 1912. New York, Museum of Modern Art (MoMA). Albumen silver print, 6 ⅝ x 8 ¼ in. (16.9 x 21 cm). Abbot-Levy Collection. Partial gift of Shirley C. Burden. © 2014. Digital image, the Museum of Modern Art, New York/Scala, Florence.

1.5 Eugène Atget, *Marchand de Parapluies* from *Photo Album – E. Atget coll. Man Ray 1926*. Albumen print 21.8 x 18.0cm (trimmed). Courtesy of George Eastman House, International Museum of Photography and Film.

1.6 Willy Ronis, *Le Depart du Morutier*, 1949. © Willy Ronis/Gamma Rapho.

1.7 Robert Doisneau, *Le Baiser de l'Hôtel de Ville*, 1950. © Robert Doisneau/Gamma Rapho.

1.8 Annie Leibovitz, *HM Queen Elizabeth II*, 2007. © Annie Leibovitz/NB Pictures. Image courtesy of NB Pictures.

1.9 The British Royal Family at Balmoral – early 1950s with Elizabeth II, Prince Charles, Duke of Edinburgh, Princess Anne. Courtesy of Lebrecht.

2.1 Roger Fenton, *The Photographer's Van with Marcus Sparling in the Crimea* (salt print), 1855. © Sterling and Francine Clark Art Institute, Williamstown, Massachusetts, USA/ Bridgeman Images.

2.2 Camera Obscura. From Athanasius Kircher, *Ars Magna*, Amsterdam, 1671. © Universal History Archive/UIG/Bridgeman Images.

2.3 Unknown artist, *Camera Lucida in use drawing small figurine*, illustration from the *Scientific American* Supplement, 1879.

2.4 Joseph Nicéphore Niépce, *View From the Window at Le Gras*, 1826. Courtesy of the Harry Ransom Center, University of Texas.

2.5 Daguerreotype of young woman about 1860. © Nancy Nehring. Courtesy of iStock.

2.6 Gustave Le Gray, *Tree, Forest of Fontainebleau, c.* 1856 (salted paper print). Courtesy of Museum of Fine Arts, Houston, Texas, USA (Museum purchase funded by the Brown Foundation Accessions Endowment Fund), The Manfred Heiting Collection/Bridgeman Images.

ILLUSTRATION ACKNOWLEDGEMENTS

2.7 Gustave Le Gray, *The Great Wave, Sète*, 1856 © Victoria and Albert Museum, London.

2.8 Roger Fenton, *The Valley of the Shadow of Death After the Charge of the Light Brigade*, (sepia photo), 1855. © Private Collection/Ken Welsh/Bridgeman Images.

2.9 Simon Norfolk, *Track of Destroyed Taliban Tank at Farm Hada Military Base near Jalalabad*, from the series *Afghanistan: Chronotopia*, 2002. © Simon Norfolk/INSTITUTE.

2.10 Timothy H. O'Sullivan, *A Harvest of Death, Gettysburg, Pennsylvania*, July 4th, 1863 (b/w photo). Courtesy of George Eastman House, Rochester, NY, USA, Bridgeman Images.

2.11 Alexander Gardner, *Home of a Rebel Sharpshooter, Gettysburg*, July 1863. New York, Museum of Modern Art (MoMA). Albumen silver print, 7 x 9 in. (17.8 x 22.9 cm). Anonymous gift. © 2014. Digital image, The Museum of Modern Art, New York/Scala, Florence.

2.12 Julia Margaret Cameron, *The Echo*, 1868. The J. Paul Getty Museum, Los Angeles. Albumen silver print, 27.1 x 22.7 cm (10 $^{11}/_{16}$ x 8 $^{15}/_{16}$ in.). Courtesy of The J. Paul Getty Museum, Los Angeles.

2.13 Elmer and Bert Elias Underwood, *The Great Pyramid of Giza, Egypt*, 1905. Courtesy of Getty.

2.14 André Adolphe-Eugène Disdéri, *Carte-de-visite of Emperor Napoléon III*, 1859 (b/w photo). Courtesy of Private Collection/Bridgeman Images.

2.15 *The Graphic: Arctic Supplement,* 'The Arctic Expedition', 1875, London. Courtesy of Private Collection/© Look and Learn/Illustrated Papers Collection/Bridgeman Images.

3.1 Alexander Gardner, *Abraham Lincoln (1809–65)*, 1863. Courtesy of Private Collection/ Bridgeman Images.

3.2 Jan van Eyck, *The Arnolfini Portrait*, 1434. Oil on oak (82.2 x 60cm). © The National Gallery, London 2014.

3.3 The visual cone, from Brook Taylor, *New Principles of Linear Perspective.* Originally published/produced in R. Knaplock: London, 1719. © The British Library Board.

3.4 Leonardo da Vinci, sketch in pen and ink and bistre for *The Adoration of the Magi* (facsimile). Florence, Gabinetto dei Disegni e delle Stampe degli Uffizi. © 2014. Photo Scala, Florence – courtesy of the Ministero Beni e Att. Culturali.

3.5 Pere Borrell del Caso, *Escaping Criticism*, 1874. Courtesy of the Collection of the Bank of Spain.

3.6 Jan Vermeer, *View of Delft, c.* 1660–61. Canvas, 96.5 x 115.7 cm, inv. 92. Courtesy of Mauritshuis, the Hague.

3.7 Honoré Daumier, *The Washerwoman (La Blanchisseuse), c.* 1860. Paris, Musée d'Orsay. Photo © RMN-Grand Palais (Musée d'Orsay)/Hervé Lewandowski.

3.8 Gustave Caillebotte, *Raboteurs de Parquet*, 1876. Paris, Musée d'Orsay. Photo © RMN-Grand Palais (Musée d'Orsay)/Hervé Lewandowski.

3.9 Louis Mandé Daguerre, *The Artist's Studio (Intérieur d'un Cabinet de Curiosités)*, 1837. Courtesy of Collection Société Française de Photographie de Paris.

3.10 André Adolphe-Eugène Disdéri, *Portraits Sitting 41494: Docteur Magnan and His Son and Daughter, c.* 1861 (albumen print (8 uncut *cartes-de-visite*)). Courtesy of Art Gallery of Ontario, Toronto, Canada (purchase with donated funds in memory of Eric Steiner, 2003)/Bridgeman Images.

3.11 Paul Strand, *Wall Street*, 1915 (photogravure). Private Collection. Photo © Christie's Images/Bridgeman Images.

ILLUSTRATION ACKNOWLEDGEMENTS

3.12   Margaret Bourke-White, *Workers Leaving Jones & Laughlin Steel Plant at 3pm Shift*, 1936. Courtesy of The LIFE Picture Collection/Getty Images.

3.13   Margaret Bourke-White, *Portrait of a Sharecropper with a Bonnet on Her Head and Her Hands on the Handle of a Plow, Hamilton, Alabama*, 1937. Courtesy of The LIFE Picture Collection/Getty Images.

3.14   Edward Weston, *Nude*, 1936. Courtesy of Center for Creative Photography.

4.1   Hippolyte Bayard, *Autoportrait en noyé*, 1840. Courtesy of Collection Société Française de Photographie de Paris.

4.2   Victorian post-mortem portrait (private collection).

4.3   Oscar Gustave Rejlander, *The Two Ways of Life, c.* 1857. © Photo: Moderna Museet/Stockholm.

4.4   Henry Peach Robinson, *Fading Away*, 1858. Courtesy of the Royal Photographic Society/National Media Museum/Science and Society Picture Library.

4.5   William H. Martin, *Taking Our Geese to Market*, 1909. Courtesy of Wm. B. Becker Collection/American Museum of Photography.

4.6   Elsie Wright and Frances Griffiths, *Alice and the Fairies*, July 1917. Courtesy of SSPL via Getty Images.

4.7   Martha Rosler, *Cleaning the Drapes*. From the series *House Beautiful: Bringing the War Home [In Vietnam],* 1967–72. Courtesy of Mitchell-Innes and Nash.

4.8   Cindy Sherman, *Untitled Film Still #58*, 1980. Gelatin silver print, 8 x 10 inches, edition of 10. Courtesy of the artist and Metro Pictures, New York.

4.9   Jeff Wall, *Mimic*, 1982. Transparency in lightbox, 198 x 228.6 cm. Courtesy of the artist.

4.10   Gregory Crewdson, *Untitled (Ophelia)*, 2001. Digital C-print 48 x 60 in. (121.92 x 152.4cm) © The artist. Courtesy of White Cube.

4.11   Tom Hunter, *Anchor and Hope*, 2009. C-print, edition of 5, 122 x 152 cm. Courtesy of the artist and Purdy Hicks Gallery, London.

4.12   Jeff Wall, *A Sudden Gust of Wind (after Hokusai)*, 1993. Transparency in lightbox, 229.0 x 377.0. Courtesy of the artist.

4.13   Andreas Gursky, *Shanghai*, 2000. Courtesy of Museo Nacional Centro de Arte Reina Sofia.

4.14   David Levinthal, *Untitled* from the series *Hitler Moves East*, 1975–77. Courtesy of the artist.

4.15   James Casebere, *Flooded Hallway*, 1998–99 © James Casebere. Courtesy of the artist and Sean Kelly, New York.

4.16   Thomas Demand, *Bathroom (Badezimmer)*, 1997. © DACS, London. Courtesy Matthew Marks Gallery.

CS1.1   Kodak No. 1 box camera, 1888. Courtesy of National Media Museum/Bridgeman Images.

CS1.2   1889 advertisement for Kodak box camera. Courtesy of Kodak.

CS1.3   Brownie advertisement, *c.* 1900.

CS2.1   Prototype digital camera, Steve Sasson, 1975. Courtesy of Kodak.

CS2.2   CCD (charge coupled device) image sensor for digital cameras. © David J. Green – technology/Alamy.

CS2.3   Kodak EasyShare digital camera and dock system *c.* 2001. Courtesy of Kodak.

CS2.4   Teru Kuwaya and Balazs Gardi, collaborative 'Basetrack' photojournalist project using only a mobile phone – Helmand, Afghanistan, 2010. Courtesy of the artists.

ILLUSTRATION ACKNOWLEDGEMENTS

5.1   Hamish Fulton, *A Hollow Lane on the North Downs*, 1971. Image courtesy Maureen Paley, London.

5.2   John Hilliard, *Camera Recording its Own Condition (7 Apertures, 10 Speeds, 2 Mirrors)*, 1971. 70 photographs, black and white, on card and Perspex, 2162 x 1832 mm. Presented by Colin St John Wilson, 1980. © 1972 John Hilliard. Digital Image © Tate. London, 2014.

5.3   Barbara Kruger, *"Untitled" (I shop therefore I am)*, 111 x 113 in., photographic silkscreen/vinyl, 1987. MBG#4057. © Barbara Kruger. Image courtesy of Mary Boone Gallery, New York.

5.4   Sherrie Levine, *After Walker Evans: 4 (Allie Mae Burroughs)*, 1981. New York, Metropolitan Museum of Art. Gelatin silver print. 12.8 x 9.8 cm (5 $\frac{1}{16}$ x 3 $\frac{7}{8}$ in.). The Metropolitan Museum of Art, gift of the artist, 1995 (1995.266.4) © Walker Evans Archive, The Metropolitan Museum of Art. © 2014. Image Copyright The Metropolitan Museum of Art/Art Resource/Scala, Florence.

CS3.1   Jimmy Choo fragrance advertisement, 2014. Courtesy of The Advertising Archives.

6.1   *She's Got Your Eyes*. Concept by Warren Neily and photograph by Shannon Mendes. From *Culture Jam: How to Reverse America's Suicidal Consumer Binge – and Why We Must* by Kalle Lasn, New York: Harper Collins, 2000. Courtesy of Adbusters.

6.2   'Let Us Go Forward Together'. Chromo-lithograph photo poster. UK, 1940. © Victoria and Albert Museum, London.

6.3   Raoul Hausmann, *ABCD (self-portrait)*, 1923–24. New York, Metropolitan Museum of Art. Gelatin silver print. 15.1 x 10.1 cm (5 $\frac{15}{16}$ x 4 in.). Ford Motor Company Collection, Gift of Ford Motor Company and John C. Waddell, 1987 (1987.1100.58). © 2014. Image copyright The Metropolitan Museum of Art/Art Resource/Scala, Florence.

6.4   Margaret Bourke-White, *At the Time of the Louisville Flood*, 1937. Courtesy of Time & Life Pictures/Getty Images.

6.5   Couple sitting on a beach together in summer – stock image © Yuri. Courtesy of Getty Images.

6.6   Humphrey Spender, *Men Greeting in a Pub*, Worktown Series, 1937, courtesy of the Mass Observation Archive, Bolton Museum and Art Gallery.

6.7   Fabian Cevallos, *French Philosopher Roland Barthes*, 1979. © Fabian Cevallos/Sygma/Corbis.

6.8   An Iraqi prisoner allegedly being tortured by American soldiers at Abu Ghraib prison, Iraq, between October and December 2003. Image published April 2004. Courtesy of Rex Features.

6.9   Tony Blair visiting Basra and Umm Qasr, Iraq, 29 May 2003. Courtesy of Rex Features.

6.10   Eamonn McCabe, *Ascot Racegoers*, 1977. © Eamonn McCabe/Getty Images.

6.11   René Magritte, *The Key to Dreams*, 1930 (oil on canvas). Courtesy of Private Collection/Bridgeman Images. © DACS London.

6.12   Edward Steichen, *Solitude (Portrait of a Man)* (b/w photo), 1901. Courtesy of Private Collection/Archives Charmet/Bridgeman Images. © DACS London.

6.13   Alfred Stieglitz, *The City of Ambition*, 1910. Courtesy of Mary Evans/Everett Collection.

6.14   August Sander (1876–1964), *Handlanger (Bricklayer)*, 1928. © Die Photographische Sammlung/SK Stiftung Kultur – August Sander Archiv, Cologne/DACS London/Tate, London 2014. Courtesy of Tate, London.

ILLUSTRATION ACKNOWLEDGEMENTS

6.15 Andres Serrano, *Piss Christ*, 1987. Courtesy of the artist/Bridgeman Images.

6.16 Myra Hindley, photographed upon her arrest, 1965. Courtesy of Rex Features.

6.17 Henry Hering, *Acute Mania – William Thomas Green*, 1858. Courtesy of Bethlem Art & History Collections Trust.

6.18 *Allure* magazine cover, March 2011 with cover lines. © Allure Magazine/Michael Thompson/Condé Nast.

6.19 Walker Evans, *Allie Mae Burroughs, Wife of a Cotton Sharecropper, Hale County, Alabama*, 1936 (gelatin silver print). Courtesy of the Museum of Fine Arts, Houston, Texas (museum purchase funded by the Caroline Wiess Law Accessions Endowment Fund, the Manfred Heiting Collection/The Farm Security Administration/Bridgeman Images from *Let Us Now Praise Famous Men*, 1941).

7.1 James Jarché, *General Wavell Watches His Gardener at Work*, 1941.

7.2 *Camerawork*, photography journal, cover, November 1977, Half Moon Photography Workshop.

7.3 *Photography and Politics: Two*, Patricia Holland, Jo Spence and Simon Watney (eds), 1986, London: Comedia. Image courtesy of Patricia Holland.

7.4 *Ten.8* Photo Paperback, vol. 2, no. 3, Spring 1992, 'Critical Decade – Black British Photography in the 1980s', Birmingham: 10.8 Ltd.

7.5 Diane Arbus (1923–1971), from 'A Box of Ten Photographs', *A Young Brooklyn Family Going for a Sunday Outing, NYC,* 1966. © Tate, London 2014.

7.6 Victor Burgin, *Possession*, poster, 1976. © Victor Burgin, courtesy Galerie Thomas Zander, Cologne/Arts Council Collection, South Bank Centre, London.

7.7 Richard Hamilton (1922–2011), *Portrait of Hugh Gaitskell as a Famous Monster of Filmland*, 1964. © The Estate of Richard Hamilton. Courtesy of Arts Council Collection, South Bank Centre, London.

7.8 John Heartfield, 'Mirror, mirror on the wall, who is the strongest of them all? The crisis'. Photomontage on the cover of *AIZ*, 24 August 1933.

7.9 Jo Spence and Rosy Martin, *How Do I Begin to Take Responsibility for my Body?*, 1985. © The Estate of Jo Spence. Courtesy of Richard Saltoun Gallery and Terry Dennett.

7.10 Jo Spence and David Roberts, *Not of Our Class*, 1989. © The Estate of Jo Spence. Courtesy of Terry Dennett.

7.11 Jo Spence and Tim Sheard, *Booby Prize*, 1989. © The Estate of Jo Spence. Courtesy of Terry Dennett.

8.1 Mitra Tabrizian with Andy Golding and Zadoc Nava, from the series *Another Country*, 2010. Courtesy of the artists.

8.2 Bernd and Hilla Becher, *Winding Towers*, Belgium and Germany, 1983. 12 black and white photographs, 20 x 16 in. (51 x 41 cm). Courtesy of Sonnabend Gallery, New York.

8.3 Martha Rosler, b. 1943. *The Bowery in Two Inadequate Descriptive Systems* (1974–75). Forty-five gelatin silver prints of text and image mounted on twenty-four backing boards, each: 11 $^{13}/_{16}$ x 23 $^{5}/_{8}$ in. (30 x 60 cm). Whitney Museum of American Art, New York; purchase, with funds from John L. Steffens 93.4a-x. Photography by Geoffrey Clements.

8.4 Allan Sekula, *Fish Story* (cover), Richter Verlag: 1995. Courtesy of Richter Verlag.

ILLUSTRATION ACKNOWLEDGEMENTS

8.5 Walker Evans, *Sharecropper Bud Fields and His Family at Home, Hale County, Alabama*, 1935 (b/w photo). Courtesy of Private Collection/Universal History Archive/UIG/The Farm Security Administration/Bridgeman Images.

8.6 Jeff Wall, *A Ventriloquist at a Birthday Party in October 1947*, 1990. Transparency in lightbox, 229 x 352 cm. Courtesy of the artist.

9.1 Photography lecturer Nick Galvin teaching BA Photography class at the University of Hertfordshire, 2013. Courtesy of Rebecca Thomas.

10.1 Florian Einfalt with Andreas Franke and Thomas Kapzan, *Desert Change*, 2011. Backplate photography: Andreas Franke (staudinger+franke). CGI and post-production: Florian Einfalt, Thomas Kapzan. Produced at Georg-Simon-Ohm University of Applied Sciences Nuremberg. Courtesy of the artists.

10.2 Trevor Coultart, *Retouching*, 2012. © Trevor Coultart 2012. Courtesy of the artist.

10.3 Richard Kolker, *Around Bodegon – after Juan Sanchez Catun 1602*, 2012. Courtesy of the artist.

11.1 Max Factor's creamy Pan-Stik make-up, 1950s. Image courtesy of The Advertising Archives.

11.2 Edward Steichen, photo for *Vogue* – woman in bathing suit holding a beach ball over her head, 1932. © Vogue/Edward Steichen/Condé Nast.

11.3 Anton Bruehl, *Art Deco Tobacco Jar, Pitcher, and Inkwell*, all in silver and designed by Kay Fisker, *c.* 1929. © Condé Nast Archive/Corbis.

11.4 Werner Gräff, cover for the book *Es kommt der neue Fotograf*, Verlag Hermann Reckendorf, 1929. Courtesy of the Manhattan Rare Book Company.

11.5 Magazine advertisement for Kodachrome film, 1940s. Courtesy of The Advertising Archives.

11.6 The Royal Society for the Prevention of Accidents, World War II poster 'Protect your eyes', designed by Manfred Reiss and G.R. Morris, 1942. Courtesy of Paul and Karen Rennie Collection.

11.7 *With the Beatles* LP by the Beatles – original 1963 mono version – first British pressing, Parlophone PMC 1206. Portrait photography by Robert Freeman. © Marc Tielemans/Alamy.

11.8 Still from a TV advertisement for Vauxhall, *c.* 2010. Image courtesy of The Advertising Archives.

11.9 Beck's beer advertisement featuring Tracey Emin (*c.* 1998). Image courtesy of The Advertising Archives.

11.10 Richard Prince, *Marlboro Man* series: 'Untitled (Cowboy)', 1989 © Richard Prince. Courtesy Gagosian Gallery. Photography by Robert McKeever.

12.1 Businesswoman outdoors using mobile phone. Bart Geerligs. Courtesy of Getty Images.

12.2 Oliviero Toscani, magazine advert for United Colors of Benetton, *c.* 1992. Image courtesy of The Advertising Archives.

12.3 Walter van Beirendonck, 'Finally Chesthair' T-shirt, 1996. Courtesy of Museum Boijmans Van Beuningen, Rotterdam/Photographer: Bob Goedewaagen, Rotterdam.

12.4 Erwin Olaf, Christian Lacroix, haute couture, lace ruched blouse over long taffeta and moiré flounced skirt and shoes from *New York Times* Couture, 2006. Courtesy of Hamiltons Gallery, London, UK/The artist.

12.5 'View from the top' – stock image, 2013 © BeachcottagePhotography. Courtesy of Getty Images.

XIX

ILLUSTRATION ACKNOWLEDGEMENTS

12.6 Stock image, caption: 'Pittsburgh, Pennsylvania, USA. Cars parked in front of suburban houses at dusk'. Photographer: Lynn Saville. Courtesy of Getty Images.

CS4.1 World Press Photo of the Year 2013. John Stanmeyer, Djibouti City, Djibouti. VII for *National Geographic*, 26 February 2013. © ANP/Alamy.

CS4.2 Two mobile phone photographs taken by Ukrainian Instagram user nata_original, real name Natalia Ukolova.

CS4.3 Penelope Umbrico, *5,377,183 Suns from Flickr (Partial)* 4/28/09, 2009. 1440 chromogenic prints; dimensions variable; San Francisco Museum of Modern Art, Members of Foto Forum purchase. Courtesy SF MOMA. © Penelope Umbrico.

CS4.4 Joachim Schmid, *Another Self*, from the book series *Other People's Photographs*, 2008–11. Courtesy of the artist.

CS4.5 Erik Kessels, *24 HRS IN PHOTOS*. Installation at Photography in Abundance, FOAM, Amsterdam, December 2011–January 2012. 4x6 inch prints. Photo: Carsten Rehder. © dpa picture alliance archive/Alamy.

CS4.6 Nina Katchadourian, *Lavatory Self-Portrait in the Flemish Style #12*, 2011 from *Seat Assignment*, 2010 and ongoing. Courtesy of the artist.

CS5.1 Press image for Porsche Cayenne. Courtesy of Dr. Ing. h.c. F. Porsche AG.

CS5.2 From concept to factory floor – the main stages of car design.

CS5.3 René Staud, stages in the creation of a CGI 'designed photograph'. Courtesy of the artist.

CS5.4 Variations on the make-up of a designed photograph.

Disclaimer

Whilst every effort has been made to trace copyright holders and obtain permission, this has not been possible in all cases. Any omissions brought to our attention will be remedied in future editions.

ACKNOWLEDGEMENTS

The authors would like to thank their editors Claire Lipscomb, Holly Gardner, Helen Leech and Natalie Foster. We owe special thanks to Andrew Taylor who commissioned the book and kept faith during its development and Niall Kennedy, Mary Dalton and Anna Callander for their expert guidance through its final stages.

Thanks are due to all the photographers, artists and other copyright holders for permission to reproduce their work in this volume and Paul Brotherston for his valiant work in tracing the images and securing permissions. Many thanks to Fakenham Prepress Solutions for a book design that is in keeping with the aesthetic aims of the authors. We are grateful to reviewers of initiating chapters and recognize how far their criticism helped in shaping the book. The educational environment is a primary resource for creative and critical thought and the authors wish to acknowledge their debt to students and colleagues associated with the MA in Photography at the University of West London. Thanks also to Andy Golding at the University of Westminster for his collaboration in writing two chapters in the book.

Peter Smith: I am very grateful to friends and colleagues whose comradeship and ideas have kept me going during the writing of this book. They are too numerous to list but special thanks to Andrew Hemingway, Steve Edwards, John Parham, John Roberts, Deirdre Robson, Lesley Stevenson and Rob van Beek. My co-author Carolyn Lefley widened the scope of the book and has been a tremendous support and inspiration. I have received invaluable support from the librarians at University of West London including in particular Susan Arthur and Imran Hussein. Finally, I want to express deep gratitude to my wife Rebecca. Without her patience, specialist advice and encouragement this book could not have been written. I also extend a heartfelt thanks to my daughters Romana, Georgia and Ruby. I owe them recompense for tolerating my distractedness and absence during the writing of the book.

Carolyn Lefley: I would like to thank my co-author Peter Smith for inviting me to be involved in this book and for his critical insight and support during the writing process. Along the way there have been many illuminating conversations with friends, colleagues, photography professionals and academics; in particular special thanks to Heike Lowenstein, Jonathan Worth, Conrad Tracy, Eti Wade, Adamina Turek, Kerstin Hacker, Rebecca Thomas, Michael Heilgemeir, Holger Pooten and Florian Einfalt. My teaching duties allowed opportunity to test materials used in this book and I acknowledge the input of teaching staff and students on the BA Photography course at the University of Hertfordshire. Their feedback and suggestions are much valued. My family has been a huge support during the writing of this book. I am grateful to my husband Ralph Tayler-Webb. He has not only been patient with me during the long hours I've spent in my office but a constant source of encouragement. Many thanks to him and also to Cynthia Tayler-Webb for her invaluable help with proof reading. My parents, brother and close friends have always been there to offer support and much needed distractions.

INTRODUCTION

This book is a guide to contemporary issues and debates in the theory and practice of photography. The extensive bibliographic resources we have drawn our ideas from reveal a flourishing academic field related to technical innovation, artistic appropriation of the medium, new social media practices, and an expansion in industrialized commercial photography in the twenty-first century. The book is written from a British perspective but relates to an international context that draws historical materials from European and North American developments in photography. The historical range is from early photography in the 1830s to contemporary issues and ideas. Some of the key themes and ideas are informed by art-historical and photographic practical knowledge. The authors are motivated by the view that photography education at its best produces theoretically informed photographers and theorists with practical knowledge and engagement.

The four main parts of the book are as follows: *Histories of Photography*, *Photography Theories*, *Photography Education*, and a final part entitled *Beyond the Academy* which addresses photography in the workplace. Each part contains chapters with box profiles of prominent figures and key concepts. Each chapter concludes with a summary of key points. The book also includes case studies on camera technologies (Part 1) supporting debates on photography in the early part of the book and an extended introduction to semiology (Part 3) which links with Chapter 6, Photography and the Written Word. The final part of the book (Part 4) includes case studies on 'Digital and Mobile Phone Cultures' and 'The Designed Photograph: Computer Generated Imagery (CGI) in Car Photography'. These two studies are linked to debates on photography and employment and the wider context of photography 'Beyond the Academy'.

Part 1, *Histories of Photography*, begins with a discussion of the various ways historians have approached photography and the diversity of their interpretations. Our main objective is to underline how far particular historical interests and concerns have shaped the way audiences think about the medium. We argue that mainstream literature in photography gives prominence to the great inventors, famous art photographers, and celebrity figures in advertising and fashion and yet neglects important historical and cultural areas. Consequently, *Rethinking Photography* provides an introduction to relatively under-developed subjects of photography education, photography in the workplace and histories of critical writing. We also discuss new kinds of social interaction linked with the Internet and mobile phones and the growing importance of recreational photography. There is no unified history of photography or agreed body of ideas. The subject can easily be mapped onto other fields of art history or the social sciences and yet we have argued that photography stubbornly commands attention as an independent subject and has become a successful and dominant area of practice in the institutions of the visual arts since the 1970s.

An object of central importance in the recent history of photography is the dissolving of older lines of opposition between 'doers' and 'thinkers' in photography education. The strategy of linking of theory and practice was conspicuously evident in the period following the social unrest and adversarial politics of the 1960s. The chapters on theory and education describe how the work and ideas of a new generation of photographers and theorists challenged received ideas about 'art photography' and encouraged students to think more deeply about their everyday experience of photography. We have called this trend New Photography Theory. The book presents a critical assessment of the work and ideas of the New Photography Theorists in the 1970s and 1980s and draws attention to their desire to bridge the gap between scholarly and intuitive modes of knowledge.

In Part 2, 'Photography Theories', we have shown a 'theoretical turn' had powerful influence on photography-centred modes of artistic practice in the period after the publication of Victor Burgin's seminal textbook *Thinking Photography* in 1982. Burgin and his associates identified photography education in the 1970s as an intellectually limiting mixture of self-expression and technical training. Photography was identified as being without a legitimate place in the critical tradition of the humanities. New Photography Theory established a bridge between theory and practice and new ways of writing about photography drawing on cultural theory and identity politics.

Many of the new concepts were drawn from film studies, literary studies, the social sciences and other areas of the curriculum that were intellectually advanced in comparison with photography in the 1970s and 1980s. Photography education was thus involved in catching up with critical debates on the issues of authorship, artistic celebrity, social identity, market forces and a range of contextual factors that influence creative work. Ideas were imported from French structuralism and semiology and applied to the study of photography and new terms entered the studios and lecture rooms. These included naturalism, realism, ideology, denotation and connotation and more broadly the politics of representation. One of the tasks of this book is to explain some of these terms and show how they relate to contemporary debates.

Whilst recognizing what appears to be an epochal shift in ways of thinking about photography in the 1980s we have also provided a breakdown of key issues and ideas that pre-date the moment of New Photography Theory. These include commentary on the classic histories of photography, the importance of historical research in photography education, analysis of photography and the historical avant-garde, and continuing debates around the artistic status of the medium.

The perception of an anti-intellectual malaise in photography education is a central issue discussed in Part 3, *Photography Education*. In this section of the book we address the way New Photography Theory shaped contemporary debates in the theory and practice of photography and also challenge what appears to be an anti-realist orthodoxy that developed out of this intervention. The New Photography Theorists distrusted documentary photography that was thought to rely on naive conceptions of visual evidence. In this view photography is always constrained by language in the form of captions, historical writing, news stories, advertising copy, verbal discourse and so forth. Following this line of thought we have argued that photographs *are* influenced by language and contextual factors and yet they are also resistant to these determinations. Words always influence pictures but equally pictures influence words.

Photographs are more closely related to what they represent than any other kinds of sign. They bring back the past and establish contact with objects and the histories to which they refer. A sense of direct contact with the past is evident in documentary work and the narrative styles of some contemporary art photographers discussed in Part 3. We have contrasted this way of thinking about photography with

INTRODUCTION

postmodern scepticism which denies 'photographic truth'. This leads to a polemical discussion of the 'return of the real' later in the book.

One of the aims of *Rethinking Photography* is to analyse a revival of interest in narrative meanings and reportage. We have noted for example how photography was greeted in the nineteenth century as the culmination of the desire for accurate transcription of the appearance of things and was supported by new systems of knowledge acquisition which were often socially constructive and enlightened. We have selected and discussed examples of contemporary work that connects with empirical and archival trends in earlier practices. Instead of seeing photography as a distorting mirror or a symbol of alienation, we have considered how far it became a useful tool in linking the past with a current climate of productive thinking about the medium. In a strategy to link past and present we present a critical perspective on the historical context in which photography came into being. The birth of photography was convergent with new philosophical and literary trends in the early nineteenth century. As a new medium with special powers it satisfied a psychological need for a type of representation that preserves the past and was born in a period when there was a deep fascination for the experience of time, of memory and place. Inspired by the romantic yearning for contact with past events its vivid powers of recall were an answer to this need. This point is developed in Chapter 3, 'Photographic Realism: Straight Photography and Photographic Truth' which challenges the prejudice that relegates photography to a mechanical or merely descriptive role. The discussion of photographic realism in Part 1 represents an attempt to locate photography in a wider history of pictorial representation.

In contrast with the discussion on reportage we also analyse historical examples of constructed images from early experiments up to contemporary use of visualization software. This historical perspective ranges from convincing views of fairies at the bottom of the garden to the seamless digital compositing in the work of contemporary artists. We argue that the practice of constructing a photograph from multiple negatives or cutting and pasting printed images to form a single image are often playful versions of what we imagine to be real. Constructed photographic images are 'anti-photographic' when they imitate a single snapshot view. They are, nevertheless, dependent on the realist properties of the medium they seek to exploit. The practice of constructing photographs in art and commercial photography and various socio-political uses of constructional techniques is viewed in relation to the wider theoretical aims of the book.

In Part 3 the discussion of photography education engages with issues that relate to contemporary provision and future prospects. We identify four areas of interest. First, photography education is delivered in various ways but the field of study has expanded enormously in the Anglo-American university departments and colleges. Second, the impact of New Photography Theory in the late twentieth century broadened the field of study, elevated its status in the academy and redefined the curriculum at key institutions. Third, there is now a wider recognition that artistic and intellectual skills should co-exist with technical and applied modes of study. Fourth, we have also noted skills shortages and technological change affects photography education more than other areas of humanities and arts provision and this has consequences for graduates entering the workplace. Part 3 concludes with a chapter on new technologies and photography education. This is supported by Case Study 4 on computer-generated imagery in Part 4 (pp. 357–68) in which we discuss how far new technologies have influenced photography education at undergraduate levels.

RETHINKING PHOTOGRAPHY

Part 4 presents an historical study of photography advertising, critical analysis of the contemporary world of photography at work, and study of the relations between photography and commercial culture. The convergence of high art cultural and commercial art has become a defining characteristic of postmodern economies. The ambiguous role of the advertising photographer as both artist and 'hired hand' is explored in the discussion of the creative economy in the final chapter of the book. We have analysed changing conditions of work and the part played by photographers in the formation of a new creative class of workers. The so-called creative industries support a large working population of photographers in a highly competitive marketplace, which has social consequences including long hours of work, low pay, and increasingly diverse skills requirements. In conclusion we have argued that in challenging and difficult circumstances photographers find solidarity and opportunities for self-expression in occupational groups and adapt to new working practices. We also note a prideful opposition to exploitation in the workplace and expressions of commitment to creative practice in photography despite the odds against it.

This book is addressed to readers at a time when photography has a strong presence in contemporary cultural debate. It is hoped that *Rethinking Photography* will be a valuable resource for students, teachers and enthusiasts with an interest in the histories, theories and practices of photography.

PART I
HISTORIES OF PHOTOGRAPHY

INTRODUCTION

In this part of the book we will be analysing different approaches to the history of photography. The use of the plural term 'histories' is intended to show how far historical writing is slanted by the ideas of different historians. Disputed ways of writing about photography are debated in Chapter 1: 'Histories and Pre-Histories of Photography'. Historical writing may have an unreasoned bias or 'agenda' but more commonly historians reflect the shared viewpoints of other specialists in their area of expertise. Some historians are motivated by a desire to correct other interpretations. We have argued there is no single unified history of photography and we may need to be objective and think things through rather than accept a given viewpoint or perspective. There are, nevertheless, key issues and debates that command attention and some 'histories' have greater legitimacy than others.

Chapter 2, 'Photography in the Nineteenth Century', introduces a debate on the birth of photography and the historical context in which the new medium became established. This chapter provides a discussion of earlier inventions and practices that belong to the 'pre-history' of the medium. It includes analysis of socio-cultural and technical factors that relate to the discoveries in the 1820s and 1830s and discussion of various applications of the medium in the middle years of the nineteenth century. We have argued that the major technological innovations that appear in nineteenth-century photography remained largely unchanged until the digital revolution of the late twentieth century.

The central concern in Chapter 3, 'Photographic Realism: Straight Photography and Photographic Truth', is to encourage readers to think more deeply about the specific character of the medium and in particular to address how it compares with other systems of representation. Chapter 3 introduces a discussion of perspective in painting as a quasi-technical method of depiction that sought to eliminate or at least modify what seemed to be arbitrary and selective ways of ordering the visible world. We follow the argument that Western painting developed as a 'quest for reality' reached its fulfilment in the invention of photography. The implications of a causal connection between painting and photography are related to a wider discussion about the concept of realism. This in turn is followed by a discussion of what later came to be known as documentary photography.

This part of the book also maps the production of constructed photographs in the nineteenth century and the various examples of this method in later artistic and political applications. We observe how the

HISTORIES OF PHOTOGRAPHY

constructed photographic image (made from multiple negatives) is a deviation from what may seem to be the vocation of the medium to tell the truth. We also note how this 'deviation' is related to the imperatives of realistic seeing if only as a way of challenging its effects. This part of the book is supported by case studies on camera technologies that provide historical background to the main chapters in Part 1. The case studies are also intended to show how photographic technology became easier to use and more widely available for industrial, artistic and recreational functions before the end of the nineteenth century.

CHAPTER 1
HISTORIES AND PRE-HISTORIES OF PHOTOGRAPHY

The importance of *The Pencil of Nature* lies in its status as the first commercial publication to include photographs – 24 paper prints pasted in by hand. Produced in instalments by the author, William Henry Fox Talbot, in the period between 1844 and 1846, it represents a major event in the history of the book. Talbot was one of the great pioneers of photography and is best known for the invention of the negative-positive process. His invention had the enormous power of making exactly repeatable photographic images he hoped would be financially rewarding. In 1844 Talbot established one of the first photography studios in Reading (about 30 miles from London).

His studio's first project was the publication of *The Pencil of Nature*. It was not a commercial success but had enormous historical influence on the development of photographically illustrated books. *The Pencil of Nature* anticipates the value of photographic documentation of miscellaneous 'things' of scientific and social interest. These include buildings and monuments, botanical specimens, inventories of possessions (including books, china and glass articles etc.), and views of

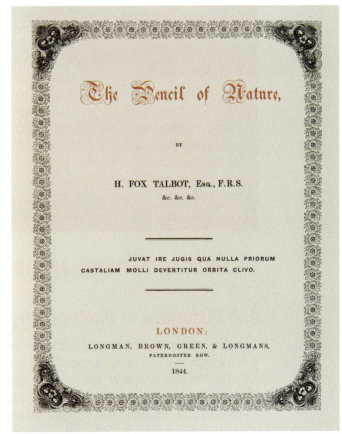

1.1 William Henry Fox Talbot, title page of *The Pencil of Nature*, 1844. By permission of University of Glasgow Library, Special Collections.

Talbot's home at Lacock Abbey in Wiltshire (England). Forty copies of the original book published in London by Longman, Brown, Green and Longmans have survived and facsimile copies have been printed at later dates.

HISTORIES OF PHOTOGRAPHY

INTRODUCTION

The aim of this chapter is to address the question: what is photography history? A short answer would state that photography history is whatever has been said about the practice, or rather what has been said on the subject by historians, scholars, journalists or any other speakers whose voices have been recorded for posterity. We can point to key texts, mostly books, to help readers understand first causes (including the achievements of pioneers like William Henry Fox Talbot) and offer views on the ranking of key figures and deliberations on style, historical context and social attitudes as well as material conditions of the practice at a given time in its development. There is no single story of photography and opinions vary on what should be celebrated; yet there are key themes and dominant debates. The history of any subject is variable and can be designed to further particular interests and ideas at the expense of others. This has led scholars to speculate about the nature of history itself.

DISCUSSION: WHAT IS HISTORY?

We all bring some background knowledge with us. Whatever we make of the subject is determined by this knowledge but having a past is not enough. We should ask questions about and seek to discover what is important in the practice and how others have approached it. Such questions provide a way of approaching the past in a focused and thoughtful way. We wish to show that doing history involves more than merely recording facts. One of the big issues we consider is *which facts are selected and why?* Who chooses? Is one perspective valid when another is not? Is history a random collection of what happened or a structured narrative in which only things of importance are predominant? Again, who chooses and what is their agenda?

HISTORICAL METHODS AND IDEAS

The Historians of Photography

To say that the historical study of photography is important would be stating the obvious. Most people with a professional interest in the medium will have at least a sketchy knowledge of 'key moments' and 'founding fathers'. He or she may be aware of movements, trends, technical innovations, pioneering photography institutions (including museums and schools), overlapping or related developments in other disciplines that influence our understanding of what photography is. There are of course keynote speakers and important documents, famous journals and other essential publications on photography as a mass media phenomenon or as art. The expert and the amateur have perspectives and both seek validation. The history of photography, like any history, is a site of contestation. As the photographer and photography theorist Joan Fontcuberta says: 'Histories, like any other human product, are governed by conventions, beliefs and circumstances of time and place' (Fontcuberta, 2004: 14).

HISTORIES AND PRE-HISTORIES OF PHOTOGRAPHY

Photography history is not only wide ranging but is constantly in dispute. When a photographer asks herself what kind of photographer she is the question is inscribed in history. Fontcuberta notes: 'There can be no real creation without historical consciousness' (ibid.: 12). This might be a useful starting point since questions of genre, function or professional status attaching to the practice take us directly into debates on historical method. If photography has an identity what is it? What is its 'paternity' and where lies its specific field? Is it wrong or misleading to look for a single cause that marks the beginning of photography and determines its subsequent history? In this chapter we argue that photography has no single history and no essence but rather has a plurality of approaches and 'histories' that are time-bound and adaptive to changing circumstances. Rather than constructing specific histories we will indicate some of the ways photography is *historicized* and indicate new approaches and ideas.

Historically photography is something of a Cinderella subject, by which we mean it is overshadowed or looked down upon. It is often seen as a component part of art history or media studies – subjects that were themselves overshadowed in the past by political and social histories. Photography forms a lesser history in the general scheme of things and yet its appearance in the academic curriculum indicates its importance in the humanities and in wider fields of scholarship.

The idea of photography as a lesser art is an old prejudice now superseded by the fashion for art photography as a powerful presence in the art market. The relative status of photography (*qua* art or science) is, nevertheless, a matter that historians of photography still address. The growing literature that we might define as 'photography history' indicates a widening recognition of the importance of a medium largely ignored by scholars in the period before Helmut and Alison Gernsheim's pioneering historical research in the 1950s. Other important contributions to the early history of photography include classic studies such as Josef Maria Eder's *Geschichte der Photographie* (*History of Photography*) first published 1905 (1978), Gisèle Freund's *Photography and Society* of 1936 (1980), Beaumont Newhall's *The History of Photography: From 1839 to the Present Day* which appeared under this title in 1949, Robert Taft's *Photography and the American Scene: A Social History, 1839–1889* of 1939 (1964), Raymond Lécuyer's *Histoire de la Photographie* (1945) and Aaron Scharf's *Art and Photography* of 1968 (1974). Essential histories of photography published more recently include Jean-Claude Lemagny and André Rouillé (1987), Michel Frizot (1998), Geoffrey Batchen (1999), Mary Warner Marien (2002), and Steve Edwards (2006b).

BIOGRAPHY: HELMUT AND ALISON GERNSHEIM

Helmut and Alison Gernsheim co-authored *The History of Photography: From the Earliest Use of the Camera Obscura in the Eleventh Century up to 1914*, published by Oxford University Press in 1955. Later editions were published by Thames and Hudson. Helmut was a German Jewish émigré who became a British citizen in 1946. This huge study became a central text in the historical study of photography. Helmut and Alison's huge collection of photographs, books, research notes and correspondence were sold to the University of Texas in 1963. The Gernsheims' written work, together with the published works of a few other photography historians, gave the subject a more serious standing in the humanities. *A Concise History of Photography* by Helmut, in collaboration with Alison, was published in The World of Art Series by Thames and Hudson in 1965.

HISTORIES OF PHOTOGRAPHY

The slow rise of photography to a higher station in the social view of human occupations is related to its humble origins as a mechanical art. Compared with high cultural practices such as painting or classical music, photography was regarded as a 'lowly carrier of information' (Edwards, 2006a: 14), lacking scholarly content and powers of emotional expression. Histories of photography provide discussions (often disputed) based on studies of the pre-histories of the medium and often dwelling upon what came first (founding images and the mysteries of their creation) before proceeding to reflect on the questions about the identity of the new medium. Broad categories of science, technology and art have been offered in historical writing as the most obvious sites for the early discussions about the new medium of photography. In this chapter we accept the relative autonomy of photography as subject in its own right. The literary scholar Lee Patterson says of literature that it is a practice 'whose difference from other kinds [of writing] is a matter not of its essential being but of its cultural function' (Patterson, 1995: 256). A similar point might be made about photography. If enough people see its products *as* photographs it has a functional existence as a distinctive medium with a legitimate right to its own histories. The related philosophical question of whether photography has 'essential being' is discussed at various stages in this book (see Chapter 3 in particular).

The Making of Photography and its Histories

Photography in the nineteenth century has been characterized by some historians as a technological initiative and, as noted, much has been written about its founding discoveries and innovations in the period before its triumphal launch in the late 1830s. (The scientific and technical apparatus is discussed in Chapter 2 below). Suffice it to say at this point the making of photography and its later histories are infused with a strong sense of their progressive character as a medium often contrasted with the timeless arts of painting and drawing. For example the matter of its 'discovery' is still widely debated. For some historians its inception is strongly connected with industrial capitalism and a growing demand for what the art historian Steve Edwards has called 'cheap mechanical means of producing images' (Edwards, 2006a: 71). Edwards reflects on early industrial societies and notes 'emerging desires' for reproductive techniques capable of supplying 'portraits for the new middle class and the wide range of visual documents required by the new society' (ibid.: 71). The French curator of photography Bernard Marbot (1987: 15) argues, like Edwards, that historical forces in early nineteenth-century Europe were effectively willing photography into life. In both of these accounts the proclaimed need for systematic methods of recording the appearance of things is directly connected to the experiments of pioneer photographers.

Marbot indicates the desire to capture the fleeting effects of light is rooted 'at the deepest levels of the human imagination' (ibid.: 14). By the time of the industrial period, however, stronger influences were at work as a rapidly changing world impatient with the 'arts of drawing' called out for innovation. Marbot argues:

> The rate at which society was changing made it impossible for art to continue to fulfil adequately the descriptive and narrative functions it had hitherto performed. The rapid and unrelenting progress of science and technology called now for an iconographical system of a different kind, one that was capable of carrying it forward (ibid.: 15).

The genesis of photography in this account is underlined by the prospects for its applications in a range of technical, scientific and aesthetic functions. It is a compelling view of the way photography (even before

HISTORIES AND PRE-HISTORIES OF PHOTOGRAPHY

it had a name) was whipped into existence by a world that was suddenly in need of it. It is an argument rooted in the idea that the invention of things relies on a prior need for their usage. The American philosopher Patrick Maynard has, however, challenged this way of thinking about invention. Following the technology historian George Basalla (1988: 139–40), Maynard argues that 'technological inventions usually neither arise nor succeed because of any perceived need for them' (Maynard, 1997: 69). In the Maynard/Bassala view the invention itself is the mother of necessity rather than the other way around.

The pioneers of photography may have felt a need for the kind of practice they were in the process of creating. To what extent they were compelled by historical forces is not, however, clear. Maynard makes the point that Talbot, inventor of the negative-positive method of image duplication, had made lists of possible photographic functions and applications. In connection with this Maynard notes that inventors have two objectives: create the technology and then find something for it to do. Maynard cites an example of this kind of causal effect in Talbot's *The Pencil of Nature*. Hand-mounted photographs in Talbot's book are accompanied by texts describing the pictures and forecasting their future uses (Maynard, 1997: 74; Meggs, 1992: 145).

According to Maynard speculation on what might be done with the new medium followed its discovery and first applications (Maynard, 1997: 77). Whichever came first, the invention or the need for it, it is clear that exponents of early photography had new and extraordinary ways of creating images at their disposal and turned to the task of creating new industries and inventive practices that would exploit its potential. Early modes of disseminating photographic prints yielded great success for some of the early entrepreneurs in the field and, from the 1840s onwards, established conceptions of picture making were irretrievably changed. The photographic image was accepted as a 'norm of truthfulness in representation' (Ivins, 1996: 94) and quickly impacted on all aspects of the visual arts including print culture and later developments in digital technology.

Whichever came first, the 'invention' or the need for it, there is little doubt that photography was quickly adapted to a wide range of applications and functions. Some of these were oriented towards high culture and the arts and others were made to serve the more prosaic functions of illustration.

KEY TERM: Carte-de-visite

The *carte-de-visite* was a photographic portrait pasted on to a card and circulated as a kind of early social media artefact. The studio camera designed for the production of these images had several lenses and was capable of producing several images on one photographic plate. These portraits allowed individuals to fancy themselves up for the shoot and enterprising photographers were able to provide clothes for hire and studio locations with decorative backdrops to enhance the status of the sitter. The *carte-de-visite* was called the card photograph in America (Marien, 2002: 84). Both types were produced in huge numbers in major cities throughout the world. The *carte-de-visite* allowed wealthy social groups and less affluent groups to purchase studio portraits of themselves and their family and friends. The popularity of the format is related to the interest in collecting pictures and celebrity figures were popular with collectors. In some ways the format marks the beginning of media-influenced celebrity culture.

HISTORIES OF PHOTOGRAPHY

Amongst the latter we would include the production of commercial portrait photography (see discussion in Chapter 2). The French photographer and entrepreneur André Adolphe-Eugène Disdéri patented the so-called *carte-de-visite* in November 1854 (fig. 2.14).

The commercial photographic practice of the *carte-de-visite* is in stark contrast with the 'artistic' pursuits of the more leisured amateur photographers such as the Victorian portraitist Julia Margaret Cameron (fig. 2.12) who tried to make photography into an instrument of self-expression. Throughout the early period of photography the separation of 'highbrow' and 'low brow' practices was defined by existing distinctions between the mechanical practices such as printing and the more refined arts of painting. Photography gradually adapted to the fine arts and was accepted by connoisseurs. As we will see this often required concessions to painting in choice of subject matter and technique. This narrative has been widely discussed by photography historians. What is seldom discussed is the degree to which the aesthetic character of photographs plays a part in its commercial and industrial performance. The connections (and antinomies) between photography, industry and commerce are discussed in Edwards (2006b) and in the last part of this book.

The classic histories of photography referred to above (including the Gernsheims, Newhall *et al.*) underlined the importance of pioneers, technical innovators and artistic performers such as Cameron and others. This kind of history has been displaced to some extent by a new generation of writers challenging the romanticized narrative of struggling individual pioneers. Photography is a medium with great aesthetic power. Since its inception it has been used as a medium of self-expression and a revelatory medium that allowed close inspection of both ordinary and exotic things and places. Both of these functions, the expressive and the descriptive, have been assimilated to the history of photography and yet where they stand *qua* art is not clear. We have allowed these approaches to represent an essential part of our understanding of the medium and yet 'art photography' is, in fact, a very restricted and specialist part of the wider field of the practice. Compared with specialist and collectable work the vast numbers of photographs in the world have a deadening familiarity about them. As photography enters mass production its claim to status as a form of creative work in its own right is usually lost.

In the nineteenth century Cameron used portraiture as an expressive medium and yet the social status of the poets and scientists she photographed also added value to the meaning of her work. Portraiture is a way of fixing identity and establishing a sense of place in the world. *Carte-de-visite* photographs had many social functions. They were amusing objects and as a source of pleasure for their users. They also had important social readings that would attract the attention of historians of domestic life and critics of bourgeois family relations in later, critical studies of family albums (Spence and Holland, 1991). The critical literature on photography and family- and peer-group ties is continued in recent studies of new-media technologies such as Facebook and mobile telephones (Larsen and Sandbye, 2014; Rose, 2007).

Portrait photographs often had disciplinary applications when used to classify, and possibly subjugate, indigent and disadvantaged social groups such as prisoners, psychiatric patients and the itinerant poor. Historians in recent times have become sensitive to the way photographs are used as a medium of identity construction. This approach has motivated some historians to focus on the repressive functions of photography as a possible counter-balance to the more purely aesthetic and honorific role of the medium in the history of portraiture. Histories of photography have thus become politicized and even combative in areas of the humanities when scholars have turned a critical eye on the way pictures are used as instruments of social control in mainstream and high culture (Tagg, 1988; Sekula, 1989).

HISTORIES AND PRE-HISTORIES OF PHOTOGRAPHY

Historical writing on photography, just like the photography itself, is an interpretive practice. The writer is never neutral or 'objective' and his or her worldview is often an important influence on the kind of photographs selected and the conclusions that are drawn from them. Whatever the photographer leaves out might be significant and areas of photography practice are routinely marginalized or ignored by historians and critics of the discipline. These include recreational and amateur practices, popular photography journals, photography in the illustrated press, photography and propaganda, and a diverse range of applications and uses of photography within and in support of the creative industries. Advertising, fashion, sport, tourism, news media, music and so forth leave plenty of scope for historical research. Technical and scientific uses of photography have little coverage although there are key developments in anthropological, geographical and ethnographic modes of photography.

Other areas with potential for historical study include pornography, commercial portraiture, mass media and current affairs. Specialist practices such as microsurgery and the exploration of outer space could hardly exist without photographic technology and expertise and yet there is a paucity of research in these fields. There are important publications on all these areas but they are not to be found in the mainstream of academic photography writing.

Photographic histories include studies of the populist and cheap areas of practice (pin-ups and snapshots) and the portentous and challenging areas of life (images of conflict, war zones and atrocity). To what extent does the categorical status of a type of photograph determine its historical legitimacy? Who decides? As the medium diversifies new kinds of histories are being written and attention is given to the way photography merges with specialist image technologies. The changing ways we encounter and use photography in everyday life is an important area of photography research. The old craft-centred art-photography rooted in the museum-type notions of work on paper has been challenged by Internet art, much of which relies on photographic media. If there is a question about where photography begins – the eleventh-century use of the camera obscura is a possible starting point – it is followed by the question of when it ends.

Prospects for a wider trawl of these areas are evident in new areas of historical research that include recreational and social uses of photography (Larsen and Sandbye, 2014), radical and interventionist approaches to photojournalism (Linfield, 2010; Bogre, 2012; Prosser *et al.*, 2012; Memou, 2013), photography history in Eastern Europe (James, 2013) to name a few recent English-language publications. The turn to a wider social field and studies of photography and everyday life suggests convergence with other academic disciplines (including cultural studies, sociology and political science). To some doubters there is danger of assimilation into wider fields of research and yet photography writing has never been more widely available and ambitious in its scholarly aims than it is at present.

All books about photography (including this one) are based on the belief that there is specific object called photography. It has an intrinsic history with founding texts and a developing literature that identify decisive periods of technical and aesthetic innovation, discoveries and ideas that are particular to photography, commercial trends and initiatives that are driven by photography (including fashion and advertising). As a rising field of scholarship it overlaps with related movements in the arts more generally, and particular sites for investigation and critique including art-historical genres such as landscape, portraiture, still life and so forth.

Key debates around the social and artistic values of photography have been conducted in some of the major historical writings on medium. The writing of photography histories against a backdrop of

HISTORIES OF PHOTOGRAPHY

aesthetic trends and movements has linked the subject with the well-known style labels in the arts and wider social and political ideals. The promotion of photography in the past as a kind of 'new vision' with forward-looking and optimistic applications across the social world is a central component in the study of the medium's various functions throughout the last century. Photography in alliance with progressive politics and radical ideals has been central to the study of modernity.

Photography and Modernity

Christopher Phillips notes a turn to 'the intellectual history of photography' in the 1920s and 1930s when photographers and theorists saw the medium as a harbinger of new modes of visualization:

> Although it was a century old, photography was repeatedly described during this time as having only recently been discovered – which is to say, only recently having revealed its social and creative consequences.

(Phillips, 1989: xii)

Phillips notes this moment of optimism with projections into a future when photography would become a new instrument of vision, a modern mode of seeing, with democratic potential as a force for good:

> Photography was grasped as a medium whose images could be multiplied thousands of times by high-speed printing presses, and could by way of illustrated books, newspapers, and magazines, reach a vast and increasingly image-hungry public.

(Ibid.: xiii)

The inter-war generation and its experimental attitude to photography captured the imagination of artists and theorists in the post-war period. Photography was linked with progressive art movements in the 1920s and produced a cross-fertilization between magazines, books and exhibitions. Artists were looking for new audiences beyond the traditional boundaries of photography, art and design. Key European avant-garde movements such as Dada and Constructivism were led by revolutionary artists who were socially minded and extended their efforts beyond artistic innovation for its own sake.

KEY TERM: The concept of the 'avant-garde'

The term 'avant-garde' is a French word with its roots in military discourse. It can be translated into English as 'vanguard'. Both terms suggest the idea of individual troopers moving courageously ahead of their battalion in a spirit of confrontation with the enemy. The combative attitude and visionary outlook indicated by the use of 'avant-gardism' has been adapted to cultural frameworks in which artists, writers and photographers are judged to have challenged established or traditional values. In later coinage the term has been debased by its application to anything that claims to be fashionable or new.

In the 1920s artistic groups such as the Constructivists in the Soviet Union and the Dadaists more widely in Europe deployed photography as a medium that extended their ideas beyond the academies and museums. Photography was an exemplary medium for reaching out to

HISTORIES AND PRE-HISTORIES OF PHOTOGRAPHY

a wider audience with the aim of turning readers or spectators into collaborators (Benjamin, 1982: 27) rather than mere consumers of artistic works. Experimental work associated with these groups was often difficult to understand and ill-suited to its intended socio-political ambitions. The more 'readable' and comically subversive graphics of John Heartfield (in 1920s/1930s Germany) turned 'avant-gardism' towards a prospective working-class audience. The publication of his satirical black and white graphics, printed in affordable journals such as *Arbeiter Illustrierte Zeitung* (*AIZ*) (fig. 7.8), bridged the gap between progressive art-photography and the wider social context. Photography and graphic design were seen as a valid alternative to museum art at a time of political unrest and were calculated to act as propaganda for the revolutionary cause.

Some historians regard the artistic radicalism of the 1920s (in its various forms throughout Europe and elsewhere) as representing the last stand of a politically militant form of cultural avant-gardism.

Political idealism and social commitment were expressed in the anti-Nazi photomontages of the politically motivated German artist John Heartfield (Helmut Herzfelde) and the new formal ideas connected with technological culture and experimental photography. This heroic phase in European culture was extinguished by the end of the 1930s. The English theorist Peter Wollen notes:

Indeed, as is well known, by the mid 1940s there was hardly an avant-garde artist in Europe still working. Those who had not converted or accommodated to conservative or official forms of art, were either dead, in exile, or silent. It was not until the 1960s that anything resembling the richness and energy of the 1920s was able to re-emerge.

(Wollen, 1982: 186)

This statement encapsulates the spirit of avant-garde culture and established a link between generations, including Walter Benjamin's seminal writing on photography in the 1930s and the later Anglophone voices of John Berger and the post-1968 photography theorists. At a time when modern art began to seem familiar and conventional in the 1960s (by this time abstract painting was unexceptional) there was a return to the subversive ideals of the earlier forms of artistic radicalism that had emerged in Soviet Russia and Weimar Germany. In England for example there was growing uneasiness about 'high culture' (such as easel painting, opera and classical art) and a broadening of the field of cultural engagement. Advertising and publicity become fashionable areas of research with vocational prospects for growing numbers of art students and a gradual absorption of photography into the university curriculum. This incorporation of the applied visual arts into the higher education curriculum is also connected with growing demands for a skilled and visually literate workforce.

Technological advances in printing and the resurgence of commerce led to a proliferation of photographic images and their convergence with mass media and the visual arts. Movements like Pop and New Realism in the 1960s signalled an awareness of the inescapable influence of photography in newspapers, ads, as well art magazines and museums. Some of these tendencies were clearly reactionary but for others there was a need to address the wider social effects of photographic

HISTORIES OF PHOTOGRAPHY

representation. The German painter Gerhard Richter, speaking of the early 1970s, noted: 'Photography had to be more relevant to me than art history; it was an image of my, our, present-day reality' (Richter cited in Rugoff, 2007: 10).

By the mid-twentieth century the photograph disappeared down rabbit holes variously labelled as art, advertising, journalism, publicity and so forth. Fashion became especially attractive to photographers and some well-known images were taken by key figures made prominent in the more traditional histories of photography. Progressive styles of modern art such as Surrealism had a radical and heavily politicized agenda in the inter-war period and gradually began to attract photographers who absorbed its interest in psychoanalysis and the unconscious mind. The transition of some key photographer-artists such as the Paris-based American Man Ray into high fashion produced memorable work that was gradually being assimilated into mainstream culture. The alliance of Surrealism with fashion and advertising is especially noticeable after the Second World War (Wood, 2007).

INFLUENCE: SURREALISM AND FASHION PHOTOGRAPHY

The American Surrealist artist and photographer Man Ray is a classic figure in the crossover movement from avant-garde art to fashion photography in the 1920s and 1930s. His fashion pictures are acknowledged as photographs of distinction in their own right as much as fashion documents. Figure 1.2 is a dress designed by Lucien Lelong, which was photographed by Man Ray for the magazine *Harper's Bazaar*, in 1937. Figure 1.3 is by the designer Mainbocher. His pink satin corset was photographed in a Surrealist style by Horst P. Horst for *Vogue*.

1.2 Dress by Madeleine Vionnet, photographed by Man Ray. The model (Lee Miller) is seated in a wheelbarrow designed by the sculptor Oscar Dominguez. 1937. © DACS, London/Victoria and Albert Museum, London.

HISTORIES AND PRE-HISTORIES OF PHOTOGRAPHY

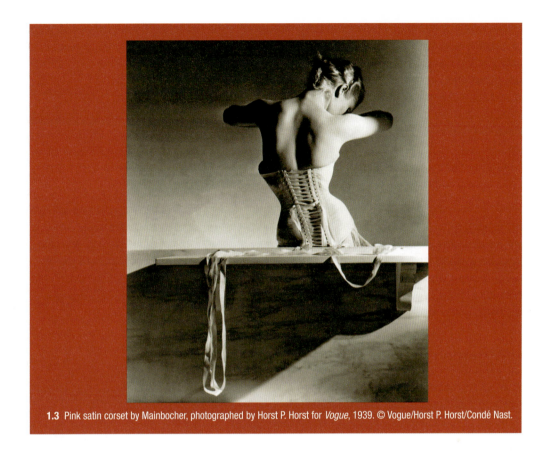

1.3 Pink satin corset by Mainbocher, photographed by Horst P. Horst for *Vogue*, 1939. © Vogue/Horst P. Horst/Condé Nast.

Photography as an Independent Subject of History

As part of a wide range of practices in which it is used as an illustrational medium photography has a central role in a wide range of media practices. Alongside film and graphic design it provides one of the most effective means of transforming visual culture in the modern world. What is less clear is how far photography can be treated as a subject in its own right. Some histories of photography include pen portraits of heroic innovators embroidered into familiar time-lines. We have described these as histories of now famous photographers that are often highly readable, sometimes romanticized, narratives. The strength of this approach is that it provides a range of key figures together with supporting, and sometimes critical, commentaries on their achievements. Its weakness lies in the tendency to give prominence to individuals and emphasize biographical and psychological information as if these things are a key to the meaning of their work. Even when its social content is compelling the photograph is appraised as a token of the photographer's personal vision and self-expression. It is in other words treated as a work of art and its value, measured against a scale of purely artistic performance, is made to fit what the historian Abigail Solomon-Godeau has called 'an all-purpose aesthetic framework' (1997: 43).

Photographs are sensual and poetic objects. Their charms can be enjoyed wherever they appear and yet wider meaning may not be restricted to this. Advertisements and photojournalism are often more compelling than gallery photographs and therefore demand a share of historical attention. Sometimes routine work is upgraded and reclassified as art. Photographs with low aesthetic value can be redefined by selective representation in a museum or glossy magazine. Such pictures might be included in a historical document and redefined by the weighty influence of an expert in the field. The authors Hilde van Gelder and Helen Westgeest have noted: 'The aesthetic of an image might be very low in the immediate moment of the picture's reception, but it always increases as time goes by' (2011: 171). In other words we might say the 'referential function [of a photograph] collapses into the expressive function' (Sekula, cited by van Gelder and Westgeest, 2001: 171). Or we might say the 'expressive function' of the photograph is always constrained by a context that gives it value and meaning. An image is never isolated from a wider context in which it gains its value and meaning. Audiences bring meaning to it and exercise judgement on the basis of past experience and knowledge.

The distinction between art and documentary photography provides a way of thinking about the medium and locating some of its distinctive modes in an historical context. The distinction has always failed to provide absolute categories but it remains a useful way of separating the expressive and descriptive functions of photography. One kind is personal and subjective and the other is impersonal and objective. It is of course a crude opposition and its common sense application to the medium is often limiting and misleading. In the following section we address some of the implications of the historical separation of photography into documentary and art fractions.

DOCUMENTARY INTO ART

When photographic documents designed for social investigation are elevated to the abstract level of purely aesthetic reading they are arguably misused. In the general scheme of things it is not a great crime but there are reasons, sometimes forcefully argued, for resisting this kind of transformation. The case of the early-twentieth-century French documentary photographer Eugène Atget who was adopted by the museum world after his death is a useful test case for this kind of discussion.

We are concerned here with the historical incorporation of documentary photography into the institutional framework of art history and the increasing prestige in the late twentieth century of photography as museum work. The elevation of photography may be good news for aspiring art-photographers and the enormous output of museum-centred photographs in the past few decades confirms this trajectory. It does, however, present difficulties for the historian forced into collusion with the marketing of art. Abigail Solomon-Godeau notes:

> The discipline of art history and its newest offshoot, the history of photography, differs from all other self-contained histories of cultural production (e.g. musicology, architectural history, literary studies, etc.) in that the object of study exists also as a commodity within a market system. Thus the enterprise of scholarship – no matter how disinterested – is inevitably linked to a parallel world of dealers and collectors, investment and speculation.
>
> (Solomon-Godeau, 1997: 4)

The traditional idea of scholarly distance and critical objectivity in the selection and interpretation of photographic data is thus compromised. The problem of art-historical *incorporation* may seem especially acute in the case of 'factual' photographs of street-life or sites of labour snapped up by museums or sold as bona fide works of art. The problem in fact is twofold: the social meaning of the image is

HISTORIES AND PRE-HISTORIES OF PHOTOGRAPHY

BIOGRAPHY: EUGÈNE ATGET

Eugène Atget is a test case for historians. He made thousands of black and white photographs of Paris, a lot of them backstreets, shop fronts, window displays, staircases, interiors, fairs, suburbs, parks and castles. He appears to have been a roving reporter or jobbing photographer. Many of his photographs are unpopulated and to the modern eye (accustomed to busy city streets) they look strangely quiet and poetic (fig. 1.4). He also photographed people in a way that signifies their identity, their occupation and their 'place' in the city. Take *Marchand de Parapluies* (*The Umbrella Man*) (fig. 1.5) for example, photographed in a Paris city street in 1899–1900, or his views of the park attendant, the basket seller and the peddlers.

The jobbing and workman-like character of Atget's photographs were admired for their ordinariness by the German critic Walter Benjamin: 'Atget almost always passed by the "great sights and the so-called landmarks", simply passing them by; but not a long line of boot lasts; not the Parisian courtyards…not the uncleared tables and stacks of washing-up…' (Benjamin, 2009, 185).

1.4 Eugène Atget, *Cour, 41 rue Broca, Paris 5*, 1912. New York, Museum of Modern Art (MoMA). Albumen silver print, 6 ⅝ x 8 ¼ in. (16.9 x 21 cm). Abbot-Levy Collection. Partial gift of Shirley C. Burden. © 2014. Digital image, the Museum of Modern Art, New York/Scala, Florence.

HISTORIES OF PHOTOGRAPHY

Similar work by the German photographer August Sander is described by Benjamin as an 'atlas of practical instruction … shifting the investigation out of the realm of aesthetic distinctions and into social functions' (186–187). The emphasis on social and practical uses of photography should be related to the historical context in which Benjamin was writing about photography. At a time of political upheaval and economic recession there was a feeling that photography should extend its reach to working-class audiences. The work of Atget and Sander seemed to Benjamin to fulfil a need for an informational photography with a social function.

1.5 Eugène Atget, *Marchand de Parapluies (The Umbrella Man)*, 1899–1900, from *Photo-Album – E. Atget coll. Man Ray 1926*. Courtesy of George Eastman House, International Museum of Photography and Film.

distorted or ignored; and the classification of the image is changed as it moves from one historical site to another. Consider the picture *A Cod Fisherman Takes His Leave, Fécamp*, 1949 (fig. 1.6) by the French photographer Willy Ronis. The theme is maritime labour and the hardships of separation, an image with strong social content. On the one hand it is a subjective and personal statement about the world. On the other hand it is an objective statement about parenthood, working life and personal relationships. The photograph's political resonance is just as valid as its poetical and narrative meaning and in fact the two things are related. From the point of view of the socially minded observer an overt art-historical valuation may disguise underlying thoughts we might have about wage labour and exploitation on the high seas. Contextualization of the picture clearly influences the way it is read.

Documentary photography is often used to expose living conditions and has revealed marginalized social groups, poverty, housing crises, class struggle, intimacy in human affairs and the struggle for survival. Humanist photography of this kind focuses on the everyday life of ordinary people and was designed for publication in popular illustrated magazines in mid-twentieth-century France. Peter Hamilton has noted the 'crazy thirst for images' immediately after the Second World War when the French people,

HISTORIES AND PRE-HISTORIES OF PHOTOGRAPHY

he claims, wanted to see their own self-image. After a period of German occupation the quest for a 'quintessential Frenchness' and a sense of communality is in evidence in this kind of imagery. It is material designed for social ends and widely reproduced in journals aimed at working-class audiences (Beaumont-Maillet *et al.*, 2006). The aesthetic category of poetic realism describes post-war Paris in photographs and other media. It is epitomized in the famous kissing couple by the French photographer Robert Doisneau (fig. 1.7) and the genre is now easily divorced from the political milieu that inspired this kind of work (Hamilton, 1997). It is a type of humanist photography traduced by sentimental interpretations of Parisian left-bank counter-culture in the 1950s.

1.6 Willy Ronis, *Le Depart du Morutier (A Cod Fisherman Takes his Leave), Fécamp*, 1949. © Willy Ronis/Gamma Rapho.

1.7 Robert Doisneau, *Le Baiser de L'Hôtel de Ville (Kiss by the Town Hall)*, 1950. © Robert Doisneau/Gamma Rapho.

21

HISTORIES OF PHOTOGRAPHY

> **KEY TERM: Humanist Photography**
> The term 'humanist photography' has been used to describe the black and white photographs that promoted social interest in street-life, factories and the workplace, bars and places of leisure in post-war (that is post 1945) France. The style also generated images of striking workers, itinerant musicians and the homeless. The style is often associated with the rehabilitation of 'a French way of life' after German wartime occupation. The images were both serious and playful and destined for publication in popular journals including the fashionable *Paris Match* and the communist party newspaper *L'Humanité*. Robert Doisneau's well-known kissing couple appeared in the English magazine *Life* in 1950. Humanist photography is a classic example of a street style that was later upgraded and repositioned in fashionable collections of 'art photography'. The art-historical appropriation of humanist photography is, arguably, at odds with its exponents' interest in social change.

The separation of documentary and art into separate kinds of photographic practices denotes the way photographs are made for different kind of audiences. The photographs of Doisneau and Ronis were made for newspapers and magazines and were intended to carry strong informational messages. A more self-consciously aesthetic work made by the American photogapher Edward Steichen (fig. 6.12) was aimed at the kind of audiences who formed part of a growing 'art world' in early twentieth-century New York.

Audiences educated in ways that allowed for an understanding of art might be persuaded to adapt cultural knowledge to the appreciation of photography. Abstract feelings of contemplation reserved for the study of art could be employed in the enjoyment of photography when seen in the expensively produced periodical *Camera Work* (1903–1917) edited by the American photogapher Alfred Stieglitz, the great campaigner for 'art photography', in this period. Humanist photographs made for the popular press were influenced by a different kind of aesthetic based on the un-staged and everyday character of the scenes they represented.

The meditative pose adopted in the Steichen self-portrait is suited to the kind of spectator in possession of the contemplative habits of looking at works of art. The work appeals to somebody with the right kind of attitude. The elevation of photography to the status of art had been a recurrent aim of photographers since the arrival of the medium in the nineteenth century. Photography was not, however, widely accepted as art until progressive artists, critics and curators in the early twentieth century began to promote it. At this point photography was more clearly demarcated by the categories that had dominated the wider fields of culture in the modern world: that is, the divide between high art and popular culture.

The Ascent to Art

Photography's ascent to fine art status was promoted by key figures associated with the institutions of modern art. Stieglitz (an associate of Steichen) ran an art gallery in New York showing work by Cubist painters and other pioneers of avant-garde art. Stieglitz and Steichen co-founded a progressive group called the Photo-Secession in 1902 dedicated to photography as a form advanced pictorial expression, a medium with a capacity for self-expression and personalized camera vision. The established idea

HISTORIES AND PRE-HISTORIES OF PHOTOGRAPHY

that photographs illustrate a text and provide information about the world was gradually displaced by a competing idea that it might equally tell us something important about the photographer. In other words it might give prominence to his or her subjective feeling and artistic interpretations of the world. Insofar as photography was recognized as an expressive medium it was assimilated into the institutional framework of high culture.

The generation associated with the Photo-Secession had experimented with techniques of manipulating photographic prints and ways that simulated the painterly effect of progressive trends in contemporary painting. The next generation, abandoning the idea of simulating art, turned back to the basics of photography and proclaimed its virtues were to be found in sharp-focus realism and the exploitation of its own media-specific properties. The so-called 'straight photographers' such as Paul Strand and Edward Weston exemplified this photographic aesthetic throughout their careers. Their work was influential amongst photographers interested in high levels of technical skill and painstaking attention to the descriptive potential of the medium. It was also a style that came to be fêted by curators and historians who celebrated the reputations of its most revered exponents as original artists rather than documentary observers of the American scene.

We have argued that historians approach the subject in different ways. The Gernsheims for example meticulously diagnosed the importance of technical innovation in the early years before advancing to study the lives of great photographers. Much of what constitutes 'the history of photography' belongs to the lives of the great and good, noble art and exalted ideas (the so-called great tradition) and yet much that has been written also affirms the importance of the 'lives of the people' (rooted in the everyday, the down-to-earth subjects associated with realism in art and literature). It is an opposition that offers only two views of history: history from above or history from below. The two sides are often informed by opposing political ideas and perspectives. All historical writing is fraught with ideological tensions and anxieties and this is acutely evident in the widely varied and fractious areas of photography writing.

Some indication of the tentative and exploratory nature of historicizing photography is in evidence in major textbooks on the subject. Michel Frizot for example concentrates on a 'history of the photograph' that foregrounds the photographic image as the locus of his scholarly interest in the medium:

> Since historical study is always something of a gamble on what the very notion of history will be in the future, we have favoured the content of the photograph *rather than the actual history of photography* ... These have been selected not on the basis of some theoretical aesthetic stand-point, but because, in our view, they best represent the wide variety of photographic images.
>
> (Frizot, 1998: 12; emphasis added)

Ignoring the various categories of photographic practice Frizot's monumental work is governed by a search for the essence of the medium:

> By probing beneath these often simplistic categories [such as art and advertising] whose function is mainly one of professional convenience, we have sought out the essential inner core of photographic unity within which they all form part of 'photography'.
>
> (Ibid.: 13)

What really matters (in Frizot's view) is the 'inner core' of the subject, its real *nature* as medium that connects directly with the object it represents. The idea of an inner core of meaning that defines photography as a unified and self-contained subject has tempted many theorists who believe the essential properties of the medium differentiate it from other models of expression and communication. The concept of something specific or even distinctive in the nature of the photograph is a compelling idea that sustains its future as a discipline with a claim to independent functions.

The disparate practices called 'photography' are often in search of a unifying philosophy and a turn to the idea of an 'essential inner core' is indicative of this kind of thinking. As we have noted there is one thing that singles out the photographic image from other types of image: it is *caused* by what it represents and, therefore, has an unusual link with what it shows. This strange phenomenon is discussed more detail in later chapters since it is tied in with truth claims that attach to photography and explain its strong identity as a medium. Insofar as we might accept that the medium can be defined by its technical and chemical properties we need say little more on this issue at this stage. Indeed, as we have noted, ideas relating to the material and technological nature of the medium are highlighted by some theorists. They have such a profound influence of the way photographs are understood and used. Patrick Maynard for example notes that 'A history of photography could scarcely avoid a history of the technologies of photography' (Maynard, 1997: 15).

Technology and issues around the reproducibility and the wide dissemination of the photographic image contrast significantly with Frizot's focus on the particularity of the photographic image. For Maynard, photography is not so much 'a class of things but a kind of productive process' (ibid.: 9) which forces us back to an investigation of its various uses in the world. For Maynard the product and the process (not the image) are what matters. It is not just a matter of finding its essential being (assuming there is such a thing in photography) but of understanding its *cultural* functions as well.

Perspectives in Photography History

It would perhaps be nice to have a comprehensive and unified history of photography that comprises a coherent collection of facts presented in chronological order. Some histories look like this. Michel Frizot's attempt to find this is, indeed, impressive. Such a history might appear balanced and objective but will reflect standpoints or perspectives that might be challenged by others. New explorations in the history of photography are often driven by political interest in marginalized or neglected social groups. These include 'worker-photography', which is studied in relation to their programmes of militancy, self-education and propaganda objectives, women in relation to repressive modes of photographic representation, and issues around ethnicity and geographical factors that have provided scope for exploration and development in the field. Emerging nations offer considerable opportunities for new histories of photography.

The fact that so much world history of photography is not yet written is symptomatic of the way scholarship in general has been restricted to the study of Western societies. The turn to a global view of the subject is furthered by the rise of network societies with their promise of closer contact and co-operation between social groups. On the other hand the more powerful world cultures are undiminished by the effects of new technology and transnational corporations have increased their control and development of the visual world (see Chapter 12 for discussion of these issues).

New histories are many and varied and are often united by a common interest in the inequalities of power. It is a particular kind of historical writing which addresses the way images classify or stereotype

HISTORIES AND PRE-HISTORIES OF PHOTOGRAPHY

people and ensure their acceptance of social norms that reduce their opportunities in life. The cultural theorist Stuart Hall said stereotyping 'divides the normal and acceptable from the abnormal and the unacceptable' (Hall, 1997: 258) and establishes a way of seeing that favours the interests of particular social groups. Some groups are made highly visible and others are marginalized or excluded. The notion of 'visibility' has many sides to it. It can be used for and against the persons or groups made visible in media representation. Henrietta Lidchi notes, 'being made visible is an ambiguous pleasure, connected to the operation of power' (Lidchi, 1997: 195). New historians and cultural theorist are equally drawn to stereotype reversals which include images of social integration and the more challenging strategies of 'excess' and exaggeration adopted by 'alternative' comedians, artists, film makers and photographers. These are 'counter-strategies' that include gay pride marches, militant expressions of ethnic identity and willingness to address taboo issues such as sexuality, 'race' and gender in confrontational ways. The structural role of photography in forming opinion and generating dominant ways of seeing the world is a major object of interest for historians. Power is sustained in many ways. In some parts of the world it is applied as a coercive force and elsewhere it is expressed indirectly in codified ways of seeing.

'Britishness', for example, expressed as a social code can influence the way people dress, the way they speak and the way they conduct themselves. This in turn might establish social norms against which other people are measured. Identity positions are expressed in iconic images of gender, sexuality, social class, family values, nationhood and so forth. Historical studies of identity construction written by activists are an expression of personal interest in the critical opposition to negative stereotypes and repressive ideologies. In the case of these types of historical studies writers endeavour to make their social ideas explicit.

Photography and Nationhood

We have tried to show that the classification of photography is often complex and that the idea of writing 'a history of photography' invites questions and themes, ideas, and objectives. This is good news and bad news. It is good to enjoy a range of approaches that reflects the diversity of photographic practices. On the other hand a single book containing everything you need is an unlikely prospect. As we have seen, a favoured approach is one that seeks to assimilate photography to a purely aesthetic level of valuation. For example art-historical categories such as national schools play an important part in the structuring of the discipline. We have British, American, German and Hungarian 'schools' of photography, just as we might still have national schools of painting, literature or music. Any other nation (or region) can be added to the list. This of course begs the question of what constitutes a school.

Historians, curators and other cultural gatekeepers, have often used 'nationhood' as a convenient way to classify and organize study materials. Others have sought to focus on marginalized nations outside the northern hemisphere/Western hegemonic framework for the arts. Against this kind of presumption counter-hegemonic projects have given pride of place to 'developing' nations such as South Africa (Garb, 2011). Comparative studies of non-Western photography have been carried out but as an emergent field of study it is still underdeveloped. On the other hand history might be local and person- alized such as in family archives or albums of photographs or more generalized in state institutions that hold repositories of a more collective nature (Merewether, 2006: 10). The family album is notoriously

HISTORIES OF PHOTOGRAPHY

'ordinary' in its nature and content and yet it is a powerful medium for passing on traditional values across the generation divide.

Family Values

The potential areas for historical analysis are variable and extensive and the varieties of methods used in their interpretation are also determining in the production of the meanings we attach to them. The way we single out objects for study influences the way we see them. This applies to individual photographic images as well as the choices historians make when approaching an archive or collection of prints. There is all the difference in the world between the honorific status of, say, The Victoria and Albert Museum's photographic collection and a typical family album. By the same token there is a great difference between the average family album and one belonging to the British royal family.

The institutional framework in which an object of historical interest is framed influences the meaning we attach to it and its ideological effect. A family album is important for the family members. A royal family album is no doubt appreciated in a similar way but it is a different kind of historical document with a potential for wider political representation. Official portraiture is used to reinforce the idea of authority and power (fig. 1.8). The solemn design of Annie Leibovitz's portrait of Queen Elizabeth II presents knowledge of portrait conventions established in painting. These include formal dress codes, sumptuous décor, serious demeanour and facial expression, and strategic use of lighting to create an austere but noble appearance.

1.8 Annie Leibovitz, *HM Queen Elizabeth II*, 2007. © Annie Leibovitz/NB Pictures. Image courtesy of NB Pictures.

HISTORIES AND PRE-HISTORIES OF PHOTOGRAPHY

This example continues a tradition of official portraiture and contrasts with informal styles of photographic representation. At a certain point in its history the British royal family began to make strategic use of the media to reduce the distance between the public perception of royalty and the 'subject' audience. The family portrait in Figure 1.9, for example, is (arguably) a calculated attempt to reverse a trend that saw monarchy as remote or detached from the ordinary lives of people. This example can be used to illustrate how the positioning of a subject in the public mind can be achieved. The royal family in this case may be seen as just like an ordinary family sharing with all families a common sense of parental duty and care. And yet what counts as 'ordinary' when social, sexual and familial relations are changing?

The narrow aesthetic range of the family album provides a comforting sense of familiar social habits but often denies the complexities and interpersonal tensions of everyday life.

The feminist idea that 'the personal is political' gives greater focus to issues of domesticity, intimacy and the everyday. The private and the intimate scale of the domestic environment, the role of still-life and interior spaces have formed a kind of photographic poetics that owes more to literature and psychoanalysis than is normally given recognition in traditional histories (Newton and Rolph, 2005). Portrait photographs are poignant 'keepsakes' that bind people together and form emotional feelings about lost objects and past human contact (Ferres, 2000). The turn to the analysis of personal life and critical evaluation of domestic space is indicative of the greater prominence of women photographers (and women historians) in a field traditionally dominated by men. In some measure the predisposition to

1.9 The British Royal Family at Balmoral: Elizabeth II, Prince Charles, Duke of Edinburgh, Princess Anne, early 1950s. Courtesy of Lebrecht.

27

HISTORIES OF PHOTOGRAPHY

question the dominance of male historians and the selection of predominantly male photographers has led to changes of direction and a more critical engagement with the field of study.

Equally important for feminist historians was the desire to broaden the field of historical interest to women photographers who challenged social stereotyping and the marginalization of women in photography. The work of the English photographer Jo Spence is relevant to this discussion. This is analysed in Chapter 7.

Multi-perspectival Histories

Just as there are personal and subjective standpoints that might influence historical interpretation of a subject there are also disciplinary perspectives. A social history of photography that 'allows the pictures to speak for themselves' has a considerable appeal yet it fails to account for the way photographs relate to the context in which their meaning is established. Photographs are almost never seen without words or other contextualizing influences. The sociological approach might rely on an accumulation of social facts (modes of transport, housing, dress, physical attributes, etc.), and the art-historical approach might be more concerned with the way photographs relate to pictorial styles of the past and present. Both methods could benefit from a reading from another position so that for example art-historical expertise in the analysis of images might supplement a more statistical survey of particular types of images produced in a specific site at a particular time.

Recent writing about photography is marked by a shift towards multi-perspectival approaches and a deliberate use of methods and ideas from different intellectual traditions. This mixing of traditions has always been present in intellectual life but has strong links with radical social theory emerging in the avant-garde movements of the early twentieth century. Terms such as 'representation', 'taste', 'high culture', 'stereotyping', and so forth, are commonly used in all the arts and the social sciences. This suggests two things: first, historians, scholars and others consciously or otherwise borrow methods and ideas from other disciplines, and second, there are advantages in keeping an open mind about the varieties of ways of writing history.

A sociological approach, or one informed by political science, might (for example) broaden the way we see classic documentary images in some of the standard histories of photography. A critical engagement with social or political meanings requires a broadening of the field of study. Photography historians might usefully study a wider field and require new levels and new types of expertise. Knowledge of political economy, or chemistry or optics might prove to be useful or perhaps even necessary. The political-sociological approach to photography, with intellectual roots in the 1920s, which is informed by a commitment to social change, is rearticulated in the historical work of writers and artists such as Martha Rosler and Allan Sekula in North America in the 1970s (and after), and the theorist and historian John Tagg (1988), and others, in England in the same period. A more detailed analysis of this movement is provided in Chapters 5 and 7 below.

All these critics were suspicious of street photographs with their special claims on objective readings of the scenes they represented. The work of this generation represents a backlash against the kind of campaigning photography that claimed to speak for the poor. The historian John Tagg and the artist Martha Rosler have argued that although pictures of the poor invite sympathy they also reinforce stereotypes of suffering and failure associated with marginalized social groups.

HISTORIES AND PRE-HISTORIES OF PHOTOGRAPHY

Martha Rosler focused attention on documentary photography (including images of the poor) being collected by the Museum of Modern Art in New York. The acquisition and display of documentary photographs by MOMANY was, she claimed, 'connoisseurship of the tawdry' (Rosler, 2003: 270). 'Connoisseurship' is a word that defines the kind of refined sensibility associated with the appreciation of art. 'Tawdry', in this illustration, is a word that defines a kind of defiled condition which might signify poverty or social alienation. Rosler's scepticism about 'social concern' photography and its recuperation by the art establishment drew attention to the need to find different ways of thinking about photography. Seeing contradiction in a street photograph, or in the way it is used by the media, is an important way of dealing with it as an historical subject. A multi-perspectival approach requires an open-minded view on the kinds of knowledge that might be brought to the project. Sometimes a moral or political perspective might be useful as a supplementary, or as an alternative, to the institutional preference for a purely aesthetic reading of images. Taking television as a subject for theoretical analysis Steven Best and Douglas Kellner state:

> A multiperspectival position argues that one cannot grasp the full dimensions of television simply by analysing its determination by political economy alone, or its political functions, or its constitution as a cultural form, though all of these aspects are important. Rather one would need to analyse the connections between the political economy of television, its insertion in the political struggles of the day, its changing cultural forms and effects, its use of new technologies, and its diverse use by its audiences in order to produce a comprehensive theory of television.

> (Best and Kellner, 1991: 268)

This statement demonstrates an acceptance that all media forms are endowed with different dimensions of meaning. It invites the reader to consider 'determinations' such as politics, economy and culture. Which comes first in the production process? In the arts we like to focus on the artist but if a TV show depends on ratings and advertising revenue then we might need to re-assess our thinking on this. Replace the word 'television' with 'photography' in this statement and relate it to a range of so-called documentary photographs. Multi-perspectivalism presents a way of avoiding a narrowly specialist reading that might fail to address connections between the thing we are studying and the wider world that gives it meaning. Whatever meanings attach to an individual photograph, they didn't drop from heaven. Their meanings are always framed by the world that gives them currency.

There are drawbacks that might result from widening the disciplinary perspectives beyond what might appear the concerns of photography. We might for example need to address which perspective is relevant in contested and changing areas of photographic work. The old art school idea of self-expression is especially embattled and defensive and the socially engaged approach has its critics. The main point we are making is that art-historical and socio-political discourses are not easily separated. Art's claims on spiritual meaning give it symbolic power that is wielded by state institutions, or wealthy collectors, and the economic status that often attaches to venerated work is very much part of the histories we are considering.

We can, nevertheless, say that some positions might be more valid than others. For example, as a minimum requirement, we might expect historians of photography to be specialists in the field. Rather than being an intellectual jack-of-all-trades we should expect awareness of key issues and debates, critical insight on the constitution of photographic practices and organizations past and present, and

HISTORIES OF PHOTOGRAPHY

a willingness to consider aesthetic ideas as well as applied or 'socio-political' ones. Indeed, we would expect an articulate negotiation of the relation between the art of photography and the world in which it gains aesthetic value and social meaning.

We have noted that photography has no single or unified history, no single cause or agreed body of ideas and yet despite this it stubbornly commands attention as an independent subject. Photography overlaps with other fields, most notably the visual arts, and extends into philosophy, literary studies, anthropology and the academic study of popular culture. As this book demonstrates one of the biggest areas of growth in the academy (colleges, schools and universities) is photography theory. In Chapters 5 and 6 we map the rise of photography theory and the question of how photography and language interrelate. The terms 'modernism' and 'postmodernism' have dominated key histories of late twentieth-century and twenty-first century photography. We therefore include a more detailed discussion of these issues in the next section. Modernism and postmodernism are key terms in the recent historiography of photography.

KEY TERM: Historiography

Historiography is an academic term used to describe the way history is written. It can also be described as a history of historical writing or a study of the methodologies deployed by historians. Readers might note, for example, how far historians are influenced by their own peer group and adopt approaches that show loyalty to historians with whom they have an association. There are various and competing methods of historical research. Some historians might choose to write about great figures in history. Others might take a more inclusive view of history. For example they might choose to write about the role of women in past and present society or other social groups marginalized in previous accounts of world history. 'History from below' focuses on social groups who have worked on the land or in factories. Photography historians focusing on 'worker photography' in the 1920s and 1930s have given an emphasis to the documentation of 'ordinary' life and political struggles for emancipation. These kinds of historical writing mark a shift away from studies of the ruling class or the more exclusive studies of high culture. As we have noted, the social ideas and cultural perspective of the historian are one of the determinants that can influence his or her approach to history. Knowledge of these variables is what historiography is about. This chapter is an example of historiographical writing.

ON THE NATURE OF PHOTOGRAPHY: A CONTEMPORARY DEBATE

Modern and Postmodern Approaches

In this part of the chapter we provide an account of modernist versus postmodernist approaches to the history of photography. Our intention is to show how key practitioners and theorists (sometimes they are both) have been influenced by the shift from the relatively strict acceptance of photography as a uniquely privileged way of visualizing the world to a more expanded view of the practice that allows for overlap with other types of representation. Generally the postmodernist view allows for an expanded field of 'visual culture' in which photography merges with other forms of lens-based media.

The first group, corralled into a particular version of modernism, have tended to accept medium purity (or medium specificity as we called it above) whilst the second group, so-called postmodernists, have accepted that photography is always a hybrid medium that mixes freely with written texts and other forms of representation including different ways of making pictures. One group holds on to the idea of photographic truth whilst the other claims all systems of meaning production (including photography) are mediated by the context in which they circulate. In the postmodernist perspective 'truth' (in journalism, art, literature, photography etc.) is something that is 'produced not discovered, it is not a property of the world but of statements [about the world]' (Patterson, 1995: 257). In this view 'truth' is always relative (never absolute) when it is deferred or passed on to another level of cultural mediation.

According to the more bleak interpretations of late capitalism the world itself is not a source of truth any more than the photographs that represent it. Hence the tendency for postmodernist theorists to doubt the common sense truth claims attaching to documentary photographs and the claims of the photographer to a personalized or subjective interpretation of the scene. What looks like a naturalistic and 'straight' picture of an American scene in a photograph by Walker Evans re-appears in the late twentieth century in a re-photographed version by the artist Sherrie Levine (fig. 5.3). Levine's version is a *representation*, a copy and a simulacrum. It is the kind of work that recognises itself as a constructed reality. The French theorist Jean Baudrillard used the term 'hyper-reality' to describe this kind of construction.

In this perspective all representations (including photographs) might be playful and entertaining but they have little testimonial value. The postmodernist artist abandoning the truth claims of photography (or any other medium with a claim on truth) playfully conjures its appearances in the world of culture. As noted, Sherrie Levine and the artist Barbara Kruger (fig. 5.3) made copies of existing photographs (re-photographs) with an ironic sense of detachment from the conventions of authorship associated with their making. The American artist Richard Prince simulates advertising photography (fig. 11.10) as if to remind us that meaning has no end point where 'truth' or 'reality' comes to rest. The cultural theorist W.J.T. Mitchell says, 'Postmodern culture is often characterised as an era of "hyper-representation"... in which reality itself begins to be experienced as an endless network of representations' (Mitchell, 1995: 16). Postmodernism is the label that applied to key changes in the arts in the late 1960s.

The term Modernism is used by critics and historians to describe a self-consciously critical tradition in the arts. It is often used as a covering term for the progressive movements or styles that challenge the authority of official culture. The term has been used retrospectively as a covering term for artistic

HISTORIES OF PHOTOGRAPHY

radicalism in the period from 1850 to the 1970s. Photography was especially relevant to progressively minded visual artists in the period of its technological ascendancy. Some artists admired the technological efficiency and directness of the camera. This is particularly relevant to the deployment of small hand-held cameras such as the 35mm Leica and the Ermanox in the 1920s. In this period avant-garde photographers admired the anti-aesthetic properties of the documentary image and the vernacular forms of everyday life that express a sense of modernity. The art historian Polly Nesbit notes photography 'was always called upon to furnish a true picture, not an aesthetic version of the truth' (1987: 104). The virtue of the camera was for many to be found in its 'artless' and impersonal qualities.

Two Avant-gardes

According to Steve Edwards (2006a: 50) there were two avant-gardes. First, there was the visionary kind of photographer-artist venerated by establishment critics and assimilated into the formalist aesthetic ideals of museum culture. This was a fraction of the avant-garde that treated photography as a 'precious activity distinct from everyday life' (Edwards, 2006a: 50). Second, there were by the 1920s growing numbers of artists, designers and photographers attracted to advertising, journalism, fashion and other new areas of visual communication. Photographers were encouraged by opportunities to explore new areas of work in mass media publications. This orientation was certainly commercial but it also includes the kind of photography that is defined by its relevance to the wider community. Socially motivated traditions in photography were sustained by the radical and progressive political cultures of the early twentieth century. Modernism had both conservative and radical tendencies represented by both types of avant-garde.

Broadly, postmodern criticism has tended to equate the first kind of avant-garde with 'formalism', a term that connects the 'formal' properties of an artistic practice with the expressive designs of its author. The term formalism has been used to define the heightening of experience enjoyed in the appreciation of art. In its more extremist articulation this kind of aesthetic outlook divorces artistic 'experience' from history, life and *social* meaning. Difficulties attach to the use of the term when applied to photography since contact with the world (with life itself) is a defining property of the medium. The apparent mismatch between what a photograph refers to and what it *is* remains a fascination for aesthetic theorists.

KEY TERM: Formalism

Formalism is a term that has been used in literary and art criticism. It denotes a way of thinking about art and literature that seeks to emphasize specific characteristics of a medium that single it out or make it different from other media. It is in other words a way of saying that each medium in the arts has properties unique to itself and that practitioners achieve higher levels of performance when and if they exclude other properties that it might share with other media. Formalist painting, for example, would exclude any literary references such as biblical or romantic narrative. The painter would concentrate on media attributes such as flatness of the picture plane, colour expression, arrangement of shapes, and sensitivity to the framing edge of the picture. Formalist theory applied to photography leads to questions about the nature of the medium: are there uniquely *photographic* properties?

The French critic Roland Barthes said the photograph 'always carries its referent with itself' (1981: 5) as if the photochemical linkage with an object in the world is what defines the medium. In this view the 'form' actually belongs to the object itself rather than to the image. The photograph's 'reality effect' gives emphasis to the referent rather than the image itself. Since the viewer looks through a photograph there is a sense in which it denies its own reality as a medium and therefore negates its own 'form'. This makes the term 'formalism' rather strange when applied to photography. If the photograph has properties unique to itself they must lie in the direction of its capacity for realistic representation. Insofar as a photograph retains the 'authentic nature of its subject' it is true to its own nature. The so-called 'straight photographers' such as Edward Weston and Paul Strand, in the early twentieth century, and their followers, came nearest to fulfilling this aim. In respecting the founding attributes of the medium (its unique powers of merging object and image) they are the true formalists in photography.

Photo-Formalism: The Photographer as Visual Connoisseur

Two issues arise from the use of the term formalism. First, the idea of the arts in search of their own unique properties is limiting since it fails to account for the interaction between different arts or the possibility of mixed media projects. The postmodernist art photographers of the last century rejected the self-imposed limits of formalist theory in work that wilfully crossed media boundaries. Second, there is confusion about the use of the term formalism in photography since it has been applied to photographers whose interest in the medium is at odds with its capacity for realistic representation. The later work of the American photographer Aaron Siskind, for example, takes on an aesthetic orientation that emphasizes the pictorial properties over its capacity to show the object. Writing in 1956 he said: 'I accept the flat plane of the picture as the primary frame of reference of the picture … the object serves only a personal need and the requirement of the picture' (cited in Wright, 1999: 43). In other words Siskind deserted the idea of photography having its own unique properties and copied the 'formalist' look of contemporary abstract art.

For the formalist the artwork is placed at the centre of things. The work is thought to be aesthetically independent and bound up with its own formal properties as a work of art. For example in painting the viewer might attend to painterly effects such as brushwork, or might be inclined to read the work in terms of composition, scale and colour. The value of the work is measured in relation to the viewer's historical knowledge of these painterly effects. This knowledge is not random or indiscriminate. It derives from experience and engagement with painting. It might be enhanced by art history and frequent museum attendance. It is not an incidental fact that, for example, certain museums have considerable influence on artistic taste because of the way they have selectively formed collections of works including paintings, prints, photographs, and sometimes sketchbooks, letters, and other biographical material.

HISTORIES OF PHOTOGRAPHY

Such collections build archives of information on individual artists. They may be the same institutions that have selectively formed historical collections of photography.

Abstract Expressionist painters such as the American Mark Rothko produced large pictures, stripped down to essentials in what looks like a reflexive examination of the medium. Colour, surface marks and floating abstract shapes remain. Illusionism and narrative meanings are eliminated in this kind of painting. Visual effects shared with other arts are avoided. It is as if the painter sought to discover the *pure essence* of the art: the flatness of the picture, the expressive value of colour and the spatial organization of shapes. According to the American critic Clement Greenberg (1960) these are the defining properties of painting. Abstract painting, for example, having abandoned illustrative content, privileges the 'pure form' (colour etc.). This particular model of formalist criticism gives credence to the tasteful appreciation of the spectator.

In photography the search for 'essence' is arguably less certain and yet the case has been made for transparency as the distinctive and unique property of the medium. This is a singular quality that privileges photography as the provider of 'true realism', a way of seeing that allows us to look through a print or a screen at the world directly in an apparently unmediated way. In some ways this seems to deny the materiality of the photographic image since it takes the viewer's eye to the object. This fact was to prove a difficulty for the formalist theory of photography. The tendency to see through the photograph undermines its aesthetic entitlement to be seen as aesthetic object in its own right.

This difficulty notwithstanding, transparency was seen as a medium-specific condition of photography, as something uniquely 'photographic', and significantly it was a property not shared with painting or drawing and proved to be important in the development of a formalist theory of photography. The photograph's inescapable link with the world outside the image (theorists have called it an indexical link) is, nevertheless, a problem for photographers in search of artistic effect. The author John Roberts notes the solution to this was adopted by critics who devalued the photograph's reference to the world of things: 'In order to do this the photographer or writer has had to upgrade the perceptual poetic powers of the photographer' (Roberts, 1998: 117) and, in doing so, attach greater significance to 'subjective interpretation of the scene' as the American historian of modernist photography, Beaumont Newhall, did in the 1930s and after.

The English cultural theorist Gillian Rose has used the term 'visual connoisseurship' and the principle of the 'good eye'. These are useful ways of thinking about photo-formalism because they reinforce the idea of a superior way of picturing the world that isolates artistic knowledge from everything else. It is a position, however, that leaves out what Rose calls 'the social practices of visual images' (Rose, 2007: 58) and instead privileges artistic vision. In the case of the influential museum curator John Szarkowski, at the Museum of Modern Art, New York, artistic vision was an important criterion in his selection of work to be included in the influential exhibition entitled *The Photographer's Eye* in 1966:

> The vision they share belongs to no school or aesthetic theory, but to photography itself. The character of this vision was discovered by photographers at work, as their awareness of photography's potential grew.
>
> (Szarkowski, 1966: n.p.).

Szarkowski's formalism not only hinged on its separation from the other arts but also involved a narrowing of its poetics to an appreciation of the photographer. In other words 'artistic vision' transcends

HISTORIES AND PRE-HISTORIES OF PHOTOGRAPHY

any reality-bearing function carried by the photograph. The historian Beaumont Newhall, a forerunner of Szarkowski at the Museum of Modern Art, New York, anticipated the formalist approach when writing in the 1940s of the kind of photographer who was able to 'concentrate on aesthetic problems,' and 'his [sic] subjective interpretation of the scene' (Newhall, 1949: 166).

The formalist defence of the photographic 'eye' translates the documentary view of a subject, a fisherman for example (fig. 1.6), into a transcendent spiritual meaning wherein poetic meaning is divorced from 'the social practices of visual images'. Geoffrey Batchen has noted the salient features of photographic formalism articulated by Szarkowski in the 1960s and 1970s:

> In emphasising art photography above all other genres and practices, these histories tend to privilege the most self-conscious photographs, those that appear to be in some way about their own processes of production. In this sense these histories – and I refer to almost every recent publication that has attempted to cover the history of the medium – all contribute consciously or unconsciously to the general formalist project.
>
> (Batchen, 1999: 15)

Counter-Formalism: The Photographer as Postmodern Critic

In counter-formalist writing (including the work of Solomon-Godeau and other militant postmodernists) the hierarchical distinction between art and documentary forms of photography was quickly identified as an issue. When the American documentary photographer Walker Evans, strongly identified with 'social concern' photography in the 1930s, was given an exhibition at The Museum of Modern Art, in New York, his smooth transition to the art world raised major questions. As we noted above one difficulty is the value attached to the subject of the photograph. The English artist and theorist Victor Burgin called this kind of upgrading a 'recruitment of the subject in the production of the ideological meaning' (Burgin, 1982: 150).

To what extent does the cultural framing of the museum (or the 'art book') dominate the reading of a photograph? Some critics argued that the contextual meanings over-ride content and 'shared public meaning'. Burgin rejected what he called 'Romantic Formalism' as 'aesthetic luggage' (1982: 40), a wilful denial of social meaning; and Rosler directly attacked the American photographer Garry Winogrand:

> The line that documentary photography has taken under John Szarkowski … is exemplified by Garry Winogrand, who aggressively rejects any responsibility for his images and denies any relation between them and shared or public meaning … Images can yield any narrative, Winogrand says, and all meaning in photography applies only to what resides within the 'four walls' of the framing edge.
>
> (Rosler, 2003: 269–270)

We have seen that a particular brand of formalist writing on photography sought to relocate documentary photography in the museum alongside (or at least under the same roof as) a work of art. Whether this factor alone appears to deny the social content of the photograph is worth considering because it may not do so. What is more certain, however, is that the identity of the work is compromised by its contextualization. In the same way a religious painting, originally designed to occupy a place in an Italian Renaissance chapel, might be relocated to a museum. The change of location may affect its status as a devotional object and it might lose some of its spiritual value. Should we be tempted to see a Leonardo Madonna as a great 'masterpiece' or as document of sacred scripture? It can of course settle both accounts but its value as a cultural artefact is inevitably influenced by the change of context.

We have argued that theorists such as Newhall and Szarkowski turned the humble photographic documentary photograph into works of art. In her description of the Chicago Institute of Design in the 1940s Solomon-Godeau refers to 'a subjectivised notion of camera-seeing' (1997: 77) that had come to prevail in teaching methods and styles of photographic work emerging in the faculty at this time. The instrumental powers of social engagement characteristic of documentary photography in the 1930s had in any case come to look politically suspect in America at the beginning of the Cold War. In the changing political mood of the late 1940s 'agitational conceptions of "camera vision"' (Solomon-Godeau, 1997: 75) were reconstituted as artistic style. Solomon-Godeau notes:

> In a general way formalism had become a stylistic notion rather than an instrumental one, an archive of picture making strategies, that intersected with a widely dispersed, heroicised concept of camera vision.
>
> (Solomon-Godeau, 1997: 75)

This was a departure from the earlier leftist (European and American) model of artistic modernism that aligned artistic progress with wider social advancement. The camera had been seen in this context as a rational device that could be used for extending human perception. The militant avant-garde in the 1920s and 1930s had social aims that extended beyond the academy. Although art photography did not directly contravene these ideals the change in sensibility from an investigative, documentary and socially responsive outlook to the reflective and depoliticized styles by the end of the 1940s is histori-cally significant. This description defines the Cold War attitudes in America but there are equivalent trends in other parts of the West in this period.

The American brand of formalism we have described is centred on the idea that photography is an autonomous medium with a paradoxical claim to the status of art. Although the experience of art is heightened by the alienating culture that surrounds it, photography (for the formalist) is valued for its own sake. For the postmodernist, who is opposed to the American brand of formalism described above, photography belongs to every discipline and every institution. It is inescapably part of everything and its meanings are constantly shifting. In this view photographs have a productive (social) as well as an aesthetic value.

Thinking in a similar vein, Batchen says photography is a 'misleading fiction' (1999: 176) and has no identity of its own since it is widely dispersed in culture in general. The two views (formalist/ anti-formalist) are diametrically opposed and yet, as Batchen has noted 'they share some common approaches on the crucial question of photography's identity'.

> Both for example equate the origins of that identity with the unfolding of history (social history on the one hand, and art history on the other). More importantly, both presume that photography's identity can indeed be delimited, that photography is ultimately secured within the boundaries of *either* nature *or* culture.
>
> (Batchen, 1999: 176)

DISCUSSION: NATURE AND CULTURE

In critical theory a binary opposition refers to a pair of related terms judged to be connected in ways that determine understanding of what they mean. Nature and culture are terms that are conventionally defined by their opposition. Some examples of binary opposition are in fact influenced by historical roles the two terms have been made to perform. An example is the use of 'male' and 'female' as terms that define cultural difference. This opposition may create negative stereotypes that work to the disadvantage of women.

Binary opposition in social usage has been deployed to express power relationship as in 'high' and 'low', 'master' and 'servant', 'us' and 'them' or even 'art' and 'photography'. A postmodernist view on binary opposition allows for the contingent role of the concept of nature, which acquires a cultural meaning when it enters language. In this view nature/culture opposition is dissolved when a natural object (a landscape or person for example) is the subject of a cultural representation. This claim, however, is the beginning of a discussion rather than its end.

Nature versus Culture: Photography Theory as History

According to Batchen the formalist prioritzes the *nature* of the practice since its place in the world – what it *is* – is determined by this. The postmodernist, however, denies this *nature* – this inherent identity – and its claims to media autonomy. Both postmodernists (anti-formalists) and formalists construct an impossible binary opposition in which *nature* is opposed to *culture* and *essence* is opposed to *context*. Batchen argues that neither can be totally right as he looks back to the early days of photography – to the foundations of the photographic story – for guidance. In doing so he detects how the concepts of nature and culture were very much in the mind of early nineteenth-century pioneers of photography. Talbot's *The Art of Photogenic Drawing*, a privately published brochure of 1839, betrays a degree of uncertainty in its title. What is this thing, this drawing with light (shortly afterwards named photography) invented by Talbot? What is he announcing when he attempts to describe the purpose of his new process? It is, in his words, 'Some account of the Art of Photogenic Drawing, or the process by which natural objects may be made to delineate themselves without the aid of the artist's pencil' (cited in Gernsheim, 1971: 28). Is it invention or discovery? Is it art or science? Is the image automatically rendered or constructed by the hand of man? The lack of secure theoretical moorings for the new practice remains with us today and yet Talbot's ambiguous language (the title itself, 'photogenic drawing') captures the elusive identity of the medium. Batchen notes:

> Nature is simultaneously active and passive [in Talbot's formulation quoted above], just as photography itself is simultaneously natural and cultural. Taken as a whole, this description neatly embodies the conceptual paradox that pervades the discourse of all proto-photographers.
>
> (Batchen, 1999: 68–69)

The conflation of *nature* and *culture* in this statement suggests the photograph is a special kind of object. Talbot's choice of the word 'pencilled' suggests a cultural meaning since it refers to a traditional art medium. The 'pencilled' image is in effect made by the agency of light and the object it records is mysteriously still present. *Nature* is that part of the world that lives on in the photograph and *culture* is the conventional term that defines our way of reading it. The use of opposing terms ('art' and 'photogenic drawing') in Talbot's title is a play on words.

Louis Daguerre, eponymous French inventor of the daguerreotype, just like Talbot, attempted to describe the peculiarity of his creation. Batchen observes how he (Daguerre) accepts the impossibility of the nature versus culture dichotomy. Batchen comments:

> Daguerre claimed quite paradoxically, that the daguerreotype drew nature while allowing her to draw herself. Talbot spoke in similar terms of an 'art' that somehow is not a process of drawing … In other words where postmodern and formalists commentators want to locate photography within either culture or nature, the discourse of the proto-photographers consistently disrupts the very binary logic that underlies such choices.
>
> (Ibid.: 177)

We have discussed formalist and anti-formalist trends in the history of photography and have to some degree assumed their opposition is somehow definitive and irrefutable. This is in fact rather far from the truth since modernist photography and postmodernist photography are equally incorporated into the art establishment as if their differences are what make them important. So-called anti-formalist trends may well see themselves as closely connected with a 'widely dispersed culture in general', and opposed to the nostrums of high culture. They are, nevertheless, quite readily assimilated into the art market as any survey of contemporary photography will show.

There is irony in the realization that despite the critical attacks of its postmodern enemies investigative and journalistic photography continues its work. It is of course assimilated by museum culture and its message is diluted by the 'aesthetic framework' in which it appears. The work of the late Philip Jones Griffiths in Vietnam or Sebastião Selgado across the world relies on the founding attribute of photographic truth and the belief in the moral relevance of work that challenges authority and brings new material to receptive audiences. The modernist belief in the medium as provider of visual evidence survives in the work of socially minded and politically committed photographers around the world (Linfield, 2010).

Throughout the second part of this chapter we have followed the binary logic that separates 'nature' and 'culture'. We have, for example, aligned formalist approaches with the search for the nature of the practice and anti-formalist (or postmodernist) approaches with the view that photography is without a real identity since it is defined by a constantly changing world in which it operates. Following the photography theorist Batchen we have concluded that the pioneers ('proto-photographers') disrupted this opposition and, effectively, pronounced photography to be a hybrid practice that has both creative and social functions at the same time. This is not a pluralistic getout since the battles around social, artistic and political meanings (intellectual and real battles) are still raging. One of the reasons for reading histories of photography is to engage with sites of competing interest. All methods of historical writing have their own modes of ideological construction. It follows from this recognition that all methods might be (and most of them have been) open to challenge and opposition.

CONCLUSION

As noted above, the most vibrant histories are often combative and purposefully dedicated to extending the scope of photography beyond its established functions. Such histories form part of a growing field of critically engaged writing that is designed to encourage the reader to re-think photography and ask themselves where they position their own practices, or their own viewpoints, within it. Battles between art photography for its own sake and new forms of social, political, and commercial engagement continue.

What we have tried to show in this chapter is that there are contested historical approaches to photographic history. When cultural critics set the agenda they may strongly influence the kind of history that is written. Szarkowski for example had a major influence in establishing photography as a discipline with its own place in cultural history. This is a considerable achievement and yet according to his critics he detached photography from what they see as the inescapable contextual meanings it has to offer. In the next chapter we turn to a discussion of early photography and the unique potentialities of a new medium and the new professions it gave rise to.

SUMMARY OF KEY POINTS

- There is no single story of photography and yet key themes dominate studies of its past. Photography historians and contemporary theorists have studied the subject from different perspectives and have drawn different conclusions from its social and artistic applications.
- Readers should think deeply about how historians, theorists, practitioners and audiences have approached the subject.
- Histories of the subject are diverse and often multi-disciplinary in approach but most writers agree there is a specific object called photography. This may not guarantee its future as an independent practice but we have recognized the good health and vigour of scholarship in this area. Historical writing on photography is a well-established area of academic research.
- There are incalculable numbers of photographs in the world and most of them have a deadening familiarity about them. Rather than ignoring the proliferation of images historians and critics draw attention to social stereotyping, consumerism, and the increasing power of the creative and communication industries.
- Areas of photography have been routinely marginalized or ignored by historians. Neglected areas of photographic practice include recreational uses of the medium and diverse application in the creative and communication industries.
- Photography histories were influenced by the rise of cultural studies in the late twentieth century. This led to a widening of the field of study to include studies of photography and popular culture. We have underlined the importance of historical approaches that engage with cultural politics.
- The belief in photographic essence or medium specificity provided historians, critics and photographers with a powerful aesthetic credo operating under the banner of 'formalism'. Postmodernist critics challenged the formalist idea of photographic purity and the belief in the artistic autonomy of the medium. They argued that photographs mix freely with other media and are always mediated by contextual influences.
- Historians and critics surveying photography's past have struggled with the question of the medium's

identity. They have asked whether photography has its own nature or whether it is a cultural artefact. In our conclusion we have endorsed the argument that the photograph is a hybrid phenomenon which is uniquely capable of merging nature and culture.
- There are many different and competing interests in the field of study. The best examples of historical writing on photography encourage readers to reflect on their own perspectives and ideas.

REFERENCES

Barthes, Roland (1981) *Camera Lucida: Reflections on Photography*, trans. Richard Howard, New York: Hill and Wang.

Basalla, George (1988) *The Evolution of Technology*, Cambridge: Cambridge University Press.

Batchen, Geoffrey (1999) *Burning With Desire: The Conception of Photography*, Cambridge, MA: The MIT Press.

Beaumont-Maillet, Laure, Denoyelle, Françoise, and Versavel, Dominique (2006) *La Photographie Humaniste, 1945–1968, Autour d'Izis, Boubat, Brassaï, Doisneau, Ronis*, Paris: Bibliothèque Nationale de France.

Benjamin, Walter (1982) 'The Author as Producer', in Victor Burgin (ed.), pp. 15–31.

——(2009) 'Brief History of Photography' in Walter Benjamin, *One-way Street and Other Writings*, trans. J. A. Underwood, London: Penguin, pp. 172–192.

Best, Stephen and Kellner, Douglas (1991) *Postmodern Theory: Critical Interrogations*, Houndmills and London: Macmillan.

Bogre, Michelle (2012) *Photography as Activism: Images for Social Change*, Amsterdam: Focal Press.

Burgin, Victor (ed.) (1982) *Thinking Photography*, Houndmills and London: Macmillan.

Eder, Josef Maria (1978) *History of Photography*, trans. Edward Epstean, New York: Dover.

Edwards, Steve (2006a) *Photography: A Very Short Introduction*, Oxford: Oxford University Press.

——(2006b) *The Making of English Photography: Allegories*, University Park, PA: The Pennsylvania State University Press.

Ferres, Kay (2000), '"A sentiment as certain as remembrance": Photography, loss and belonging', in Jane Crisp, Kay Ferres and Gillian Swanson (eds), *Deciphering Culture: Ordinary Curiosities and Subjective Narratives*, London and New York: Routledge, pp. 174–188.

Fontcuberta, Joan (ed.) (2004) *Photography: Crisis of History*, trans. Graham Thomson, Barcelona: Actar.

Freund, Gisèle (1980) *Photography and Society*, London: Gordon Fraser.

Frizot, Michel (1998) *A New History of Photography*, Cologne: Könemann.

Garb, Tamar (ed.) (2011) *Figures and Fictions: Contemporary South African Photography*, Göttingham: Steidl.

HISTORIES AND PRE-HISTORIES OF PHOTOGRAPHY

Gelder, Hilde Van and Weestgeest, Helen (2011) *Photography Theory in Historical Perspective: Case Studies from Contemporary Art*, Malden, MA/ Oxford/Chichester: Wiley Blackwell.

Gernsheim, Helmut and Alison (1955) *The History of Photography: From the Camera Obscura up to 1914*, Oxford: Oxford University Press.

——(1969) *The History of Photography: From the Camera Obscura to the Beginning of the Modern Era*, London: Thames and Hudson.

——(1971) *A Concise History of Photography,* London: Thames and Hudson.

Greenberg, Clement (1960) 'Modernist Painting', in *Clement Greenberg (1986–93): The Collected Essays and Criticisms*', edited by John O'Brian, Volume 4, Chicago: University of Chicago Press.

Hall, Stuart (ed.) (1997) *Representation: Cultural Representations and Signifying Practices*, London/ Thousand Oaks, CA/New Delhi: Sage.

Hamilton, Peter (1997) 'Representing the Social: France and Frenchness in Post-War Humanist Photography', in Stuart Hall (ed.), pp. 75–150.

Ivins, William M. (1996) *Prints and Visual Communication*, Cambridge, MA and London: The MIT Press.

James, Sarah E. (2013) *The Common Ground: German Photographic Cultures Across the Iron Curtain*, New Haven and London: Yale University Press.

Larson, Jonas and Sandbye, Mette (2014) *Digital Snaps: The New Face of Photography*, London and New York: Tauris.

Lécuyer, Raymond (1945) *L'Histoire de la Photographie*, Paris: Baschet et Cie.

Lemagny, Jean-Claude and Rouillé, André (eds) (1987) *A History of Photography: Social and Cultural Perspectives*, trans. Janet Lloyd, Cambridge: Cambridge University Press.

Lentricchia, Frank and McLaughlin, Thomas (eds) (1995), *Critical Terms for Literary History*, Chicago and London: University of Chicago Press.

Lidchi, Henrietta (1997) 'The Poetics and the Politics of Exhibiting Other Cultures', in Stuart Hall (ed.), pp. 151–208.

Linfield, Susie (2010) *The Cruel Radiance: Photography and Political Violence*, Chicago and London: University of Chicago Press.

Marbot, Bernard (1987) 'Towards the Discovery (before 1839)', in Lemagny and Rouillé (eds), pp. 11–17.

Marien, Mary Warner (2002) *Photography: A Cultural History*, London: Laurence King.

Maynard, Patrick (1997) *The Engine of Visualization: Thinking Through Photography*, Ithaca and London: Cornell University Press.

Meggs, Philip B. (1992) *A History of Graphic Design*, New York: Van Nostrand Reinhold.

Memou, Antigoni (2013) *Photography and Social Movements*, Manchester and New York: Manchester University Press.

Merewether, Charles (ed.) (2006) *The Archive: Documents of Contemporary Art*, London and Cambridge, MA: Whitechapel Gallery and The MIT Press.

Mitchell, W.J.T. (1995) 'Representation', in Lentricchia and McLaughlin (eds), pp. 11–22.

HISTORIES OF PHOTOGRAPHY

Nesbit, Molly (1987) 'Photography, Art and Modernity (1910–30)', in Lemagny and Rouillé (eds), pp. 103–123.

Newhall, Beaumont (1949), *The History of Photography: from 1839 to the Present Day*, New York: Museum of Modern Art.

Newton, Kate and Rolph, Christine (eds) (2005) *Stilled: Contemporary Still Life Photography by Women*, Cardiff: Ffotogallery.

Patterson, Lee (1995) 'Literary History', in Lentricchia and McLaughlin (eds), pp. 250–262.

Phillips, Christopher (ed.) (1989) *Photography in the Modern Era: European Documents and Critical Writings, 1913–1940,* New York: Metropolitan Museum of Art.

Prosser, Jay, Batchen, Geoffrey, Gidley, Mick and Miller, Nancy K. (eds) (2012) *Picturing Atrocity: Photography in Crisis*, London: Reaktion Books.

Roberts, John (1998) *The Art of Interruption: Realism, Photography and the Everyday.* Manchester and New York: Manchester University Press.

Rose, Gillian (2007) *Visual Methodologies: An Introduction to the Interpretation of Visual Materials*, London/Thousand Oaks, CA/New Delhi: Sage.

Rosler, Martha (2003) 'In, Around, and Afterthoughts (On Documentary Photography)', in Liz Wells (ed.), *The Photography Reader*, London and New York: Routledge, pp. 261–274.

Rugoff, Ralph (2007) 'Painting Modern Life', in Ralph Rugoff, Caroline Hancock and Siobhan McCracken (eds), *The Painting of Modern Life*, London: Hayward Publishing, pp. 10–17.

Scharf, Aaron (1974) *Art and Photography*, Harmondsworth: Penguin Books.

Sekula, Allan (1989) 'The Body and the Archive', in Richard Bolton (ed.), *The Contest of Meaning: Critical Histories of Photography*, Cambridge, MA and London: The MIT Press, pp. 343–388.

Solomon-Godeau, Alison (1997) *Photography at the Dock: Essays on Photographic History, Institutions and Practices*, Minneapolis: University of Minnesota Press.

Spence, Jo and Holland, Patricia (eds) (1991) *Family Snaps: The Meaning of Domestic Photography*, London: Virago.

Szarkowski, John (1966), *The Photographer's Eye*, unpaginated, New York: Museum of Modern Art.

Taft, Robert (1964) *Photography and the American Scene: A Social History, 1839–1889*, New York: Dover.

Tagg, John (1988) *The Burden of Representation: Essays on Photographies and Histories*, Houndmills and London: Macmillan.

Wells, Liz (2009) *Photography: A Critical Introduction*, London and New York: Routledge.

Wollen, Peter (1982) *Reading and Writings: Semiotic Counter Strategies*, London: Verso.

Wood, Ghislaine (2007) *Surreal Things: Surrealism and Design*, London: V&A Publications.

Wright, Terence (1999) *The Photography Handbook*, London and New York: Routledge.

CHAPTER 2
PHOTOGRAPHY IN THE NINETEENTH CENTURY
With Andrew Golding

The photograph in Figure 2.1 is by Roger Fenton. He was an amateur British photographer using a wet collodion plate process invented in 1851. It shows Fenton's assistant quietly posing for the camera. It was taken in the Crimea before his more famous photograph of *The Valley of the Shadow of Death* (fig. 2.8). The enormously weighty and cumbersome nature of photographic equipment needed by travelling photographers in these early years of photography is one of the striking features of the image. The van carried a darkroom tent, chemical apparatus, cameras, distilled water and sundry materials. Photography was not for the technologically challenged or faint-hearted operator in the days before hand-held cameras. Fenton used glass plates treated with wet collodion which were prepared on location and developed as soon as a picture was taken. He travelled with five large cameras, and hundreds of glass plates carefully boxed to avoid damage in transit. Travel to distant lands combined military adventurism with photographic reconnaissance and reportage. Photography was invented at the same time as the railways and the two technologies facilitated the production of travel photographs. Exotic and faraway places became key subjects for early photographers. Europeans and Americans acquired a taste for monuments of ancient cultures or sublime images of the great outdoors. Pictures designed to please the tourist imagination were served by the camera from its beginnings.

2.1 Roger Fenton, *The Photographer's Van with Marcus Sparling in the Crimea*, 1855. © Sterling and Francine Clark Art Institute, Williamstown, Massachusetts, USA/Bridgeman Images.

HISTORIES OF PHOTOGRAPHY

INTRODUCTION

In this chapter we discuss photography in the nineteenth century. Specialists in a range of disciplines contributed to the study of photography. The first photographs were made in the early part of the century. They were the outcome of determined experimentation, guesswork, and skill. Dedicated efforts of specialists in various fields of scientific, technical and artistic work found a way of making a stable image on a sensitized surface through the action of light. The resources they drew from included drawing, optics, and chemistry and printing techniques. The process now called photography is rooted in the captured image and its successful multiplication. The invention of photography provided a way of making images without the labour of drawing and was also considered a spectacular new way of seeing the world. Early enthusiasts marvelled at the detail in the first daguerreotypes (a photographic method named after its creator, the Frenchman Louis Daguerre, in 1839) and for many years photography was seen as a new branch of the visual arts. In 1844 the English pioneer of photography William Henry Fox Talbot famously referred to the new medium as 'the pencil of nature' (fig. 1.1) as if to suggest the idea of a medium that allows nature to draw herself.

In their classic history of photography the authors Alison and Helmut Gernsheim address the old question of *who* invented photography and provide an answer:

> The invention of photography has been variously ascribed to Thomas Wedgewood, who conceived the original idea but was unsuccessful in practice, to Nicéphore Niepce [accent omitted in original], who first succeeded in taking a permanent photograph from nature; to Daguerre, who invented the first practicable process of photography; and to Fox Talbot, who introduced the first negative/positive process, the principle still employed in photography today. In our opinion, Niepce alone deserves to be considered the true inventor of photography.
>
> (Helmut and Alison Gernsheim, 1955: xxviii)

Whoever invented photography the question may now seem irrelevant and yet the discussion it gives rise to is fascinating in all sorts of ways. For example, we might want to know what photography actually *is*. This supplementary question may depend on who was the creator at its defining moment and this in turn begs the question: what is the defining moment? Daguerre made single pictures and William Henry Fox Talbot created the positive/negative system. Multiple prints could be made using Talbot's method. Which is the most important achievement? Which of the two men's discoveries helps us best define the medium? Is photography a word that defines a process or does it refer to the actual objects called photographs? If we accept that the process came before the distinctive results of Daguerre's famous pictures of the late 1830s does this make Niépce the inventor at an earlier time? What about Wedgwood, Bayard, Talbot and other contenders for the title? The debate forces us to think about the uniqueness of photography as we compare it with other media at the moment of its conception. Having done this, however, we may still struggle with the task of finding an all-purpose definition of what photography really is. On the question of photography's identity and in particular its 'realism' see Chapter 3.

This chapter outlines the some of the methods invented to enable the creation of photographs, considers the work of key figures and explores some of the ways in which photography developed. We trace the background and development of photography in the nineteenth century and the later emergence of new mass-production techniques. We also map the history of photography from its beginnings as a pursuit for gentlemen-scholars and amateurs to its later commercial and artistic absorption into the mainstream of modern life. We will also consider some of the social effects it had on representing the world to the public.

THE ORIGINS OF PHOTOGRAPHY

Historical Viewpoints

The account presented in this chapter is partial and represents a viewpoint amongst many possible viewpoints. For some historians photography was a logical end point of the historical search for an artistic or technical method that would accurately reproduce the look of things in the world. For others it is connected with the post-Enlightenment search for knowledge and truth. In both of these historical models the camera is an extension of human sense of vision and a means to make the world appear transparently to the human eye. The idea of establishing truthful contact with an external world is bound up with techniques for the enhancement of the eye including lens-based media such as telescopes or visual apparatus such as the camera obscura that prefigure what later came to be known as photography. In Western societies the faculty of sight is a privileged sense and a primary influence on the ways humans locate the relative position of things in the world. This way of thinking about perception is strongly rooted in a *spatial* sense of being in the world. The perspective systems used by artists created an illusory effect of bodies in space corresponding with some aspects of natural vision. Perspective in a picture, when convincingly applied, achieves power of illusion that is especially seductive in a photograph. Illusionism, a chief characteristic of Western systems of painting, had found in photography a consummate vehicle for its realization. This model of vision has been described as the 'unblinking eye of the fixed gaze' (Jay, 1994: 81) and suggests photographic seeing as an arrestment of time.

The discovery of photography in the early nineteenth century was a final staging post in a Western visual tradition that valued accuracy of vision and a complete imitation of the outside world. The pursuit of reality and the capture of its external features in painting and photography is a narrative that is easy to grasp. It is, however, an historical model that has its critics. Some theorists and historians see the emergence of photography in the nineteenth century as a product of less obvious but equally valid factors. At the beginning of the nineteenth century some theorists began to doubt the idea of 'reality' as a mirror reflection in the mind of an observer. The human subject, they argued, is active and vision is dynamic in its interaction with the world. This sense of active engagement with the world suggests interest in time as well as space. An action, it was argued, has duration as well as spatial significance. According to the photography historian Geoffrey Batchen 'time is important in discourses from which emerged the desire to photograph' (Batchen, 1999: 90).

Batchen's argument is that photography was invented in the 1820s (or thereabouts) at a time when Romantic poets reflected more deeply on the temporal nature of things. Talbot, for example, noted that 'the subject of every photograph is time itself' (cited in Batchen, 1999: 93). The concern with capturing, holding, fixing, stabilizing has a certain resonance in a period of change. Photography offers a means of stabilizing new experiences and giving legitimacy to desire in the picture of a loved one. The desire to 'fix' the transient image offered both intellectual and poetic satisfaction in a period of social and political upheaval. The temporal nature of the medium is explicitly one of its quintessential features. Batchen, paraphrasing Talbot, notes: 'A photograph explicitly directs our attention to the *temporal* implications of its own process of representation' (Batchen, 1999: 93. Our emphasis).

The argument is well made and reminds us that illustrated models of perception in old engravings of the camera obscura (fig. 2.2), and other pre-photographic apparatus, represent schematic and simplistic ways of seeing. It is, nevertheless, equally true that the camera obscura is a legitimate starting point for the study of early photography. Photography we might say is a name for a process that relies on the action of light striking a sensitized surface. The camera, box or chamber is an efficient means of establishing this objective and provides at least three of the basic requirements for registration of the photographic image: darkness, aperture, and a facing wall upon which it might appear.

KEY TERM: The Camera Obscura

This is the name given to a darkened room in a building in which you might imagine an artist searching for a way of making images without the labour of drawing and painting. It was known that surfaces are sensitive to light which discolours paper and darkens human skin tissue when the sun's rays are strong. Over time the effort given to exploiting this effect eventually led to the photochemical discoveries of the early nineteenth century. The importance of the camera obscura, however, lies in its ability to allow an image of the outside world to be projected through a hole, or more efficiently, through a lens in the wall of a chamber or a room. When the projected image appeared on a wall opposite the hole in the wall its main outlines could be drawn by hand. It was a short-cut way of drawing. In Figure 2.2 the artist is drawing an inverted tree. He has found a way into the room via the floor.

Smaller box-sized versions of the chamber made and widely used in the eighteenth century allowed artists to trace images reflected on a translucent glass panel. Portable camera obscura boxes were essential predecessors of the modern camera. All they lacked was a photochemically sensitized surface to 'capture' and 'fix' the reflected image in the next stage of the photographic process.

The Mechanization of Drawing

The earliest cameras were devised in the form of the *camera obscura* (which is the Latin name for darkened room) in a house. The term also applied to the box-like structures with a small hole to allow access of light. When light passes through a tiny hole into a darkened space an inverted image appears on the opposite wall. A sun-lit landscape, for example, could be projected on to a surface inside a darkened room as the artist carefully traced around its main features in preparation for making a painting (fig. 2.2). An early hand-held camera obscura was a box-like object that looked remarkably like early photographic cameras but, crucially, was lacking the means to capture and fix the projected image. Knowledge of 'dark room' technology and the principles of light projection were advanced by the late eighteenth century but the necessary alignment of optics and photochemistry was not yet in place.

2.2 Camera Obscura. From Athanasius Kircher, *Ars Magna*, Amsterdam, 1671. © Universal History Archive/UIG/Bridgeman Images.

The struggle to find a way of sustaining the life of a projected image adds drama to the historical narratives that map this early history right up to the 1820s and 1830s when the first photographs were made.

In the sixteenth century churches such as Santa Maria del Fiore in Florence and Saint Sulpice in Paris were both used as a camera obscura to make observations of the movements and eclipses of the sun. A small hole in the roof created a projected image of the sun on to the church floor. This effect was well known to several scholars, including the Renaissance painter Leonardo da Vinci and the Neapolitan scientist Giovanni Battista della Porta who announced in 1558 the possibility of using the camera obscura as an aid to drawing. The effect of light entering dark rooms had been an object of fascination for centuries before the experiments of Leonardo and Porto. In the sixteenth century it was studied in a manner that led to a more rigorous documentation in popular science and the decision to include a bi-convex lens, to replace the open aperture, facilitated the projection of a brighter inverted image on the opposite wall of the darkened room (Gernsheim, 1971: 10–11).

The custom-built camera obscura, much smaller than room-size, became popular in the 1700s and was used as a visual spectacle and as a form of popular entertainment. As noted they were also used for making accurate drawings of landscape and other subjects since the projected image could be copied and reversed. Convex lenses and mirrors were added to brighten and correct the otherwise reversed image, and in observatories on city hills, in Bristol and Edinburgh for example, the public continue to be able to witness projections of the outside world on to a white two- or three-metre dished surface. The images astonish spectators with their unexpected veracity of colour, rendition of details, and most impressively by the depiction of movement of people, of clouds and even leaves on the trees in the scene.

HISTORIES OF PHOTOGRAPHY

The camera obscura presages the invention of photography both technically and psychologically. In the technical sense we are following the conventional emphasis on scientific innovation as a key to understanding the pre-history of photography. We have also followed the view that the very mission of art, according to some historians, was to reach a point of perfection when the projected image could be 'captured' and fixed as if the *raison d'être* of Western art was the achievement of this objective. As we have noted this was a view premised on the idea that art aspires to the precise rendition of a single viewpoint perspective or that a photograph is merely a continuation of this objective. This way of thinking presents a mechanistic and impersonal model of visual perception. The approach is instructive but fails to account for the psychological motivation to own pictures of friends, family, and representative members of society. The desire to preserve the image as an investment in the signs of a successful life is at least as important in the early nineteenth century as the scientific rationality that led to the making of photography. A more expanded view of early photography that takes into consideration cultural factors (including the desire to preserve objects of affection) challenges the emphasis on the purely mechanical assessment of the motivation that led to its foundation.

Before the invention of photography wealthy patrons commissioned paintings depicting their own class in settings that reflected their social advantages. The emergent middle classes, rapidly gaining status and prosperity in the industrial period, used photography in a similar way as a means of establishing a sense of their place in the world. From the seventeenth century onwards painting and drawing were increasingly used in conjunction with the camera obscura, producing detailed images traced off with the minimum of interpretation by the artist controlling the pencil or brush. The drive to achieve likeness and truth to appearance, by means of artifice and labour-saving techniques, led to drawing machines in which optical devices and skilfully made apparatus seem, with hindsight, to anticipate the photographic camera. These included the pantograph, used to trace the face and to create silhouettes, and a portable drawing aid called the camera lucida (fig. 2.3). The latter allowed an image to be seen through an eyeglass supported at a regular height above the sketchbook of the artist. Like the camera obscura, it was a visual aid adopted by artists in need of a short-cut method of drawing.

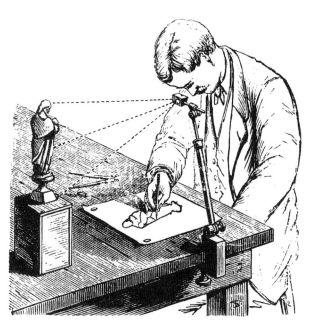

2.3 Unknown artist, *Camera Lucida in use drawing small figurine*, illustration from the *Scientific American* Supplement, 1879.

All the devices belonging to the pre-history of photography were used as labour-saving methods or as cheaper ways of procuring images. The pantograph silhouettes, for example, were cut-price portraits. The use of machines for drawing was not, however restricted to matters of convenience, and there is evidence that painters were fascinated by the prospects of achieving ever more convincing levels of naturalism in their work. Insofar as this objective could be enhanced by the use of optical aids they were judged to be legitimate means to an end. The principle was not universally welcomed by artists.

PHOTOGRAPHY IN THE NINETEENTH CENTURY

Many argued that a mechanized view of the world is lifeless and competes with imaginative interpretation of a subject (Scharf, 1974: 20–21). It is worth considering how far this clash of methods and ideas was reprised in the twentieth-century opposition between documentary photographers who favoured an impartial and objective view of their subject and the art photographers who would speak of the need for subjective interpretations of the world.

Niépce, Daguerre and Talbot

The 1939 announcement of the invention of photography was made on behalf of Louis Daguerre. He had refined a method devised by Joseph Nicéphore Niépce (1765–1833) who by most accounts had created the very first photograph demonstrated by his 1826 *View from the Window at Le Gras* (fig. 2.4). As with many inventions and discoveries during this period there is evidence that the kinds of experiments carried out by Niépce and Daguerre were paralleled by similar projects conducted by others during the same period. The equipment and chemicals required had been understood for many years and simultaneous developments were proliferating at this time.

Some accounts of early experimentation are widely known and yet some have been overlooked. For example, it is quite possible that the British manufacturer Thomas Wedgwood, of the Wedgwood china pottery manufacturers, might have been acknowledged as the inventor of photography if his early attempts to fix faint images from the camera obscura had succeeded. Humphrey Davy, famous inventor of the miner's safety lamp, who worked briefly with Wedgwood, actually succeeded in fixing photographic images but failed to stop them from continuing to darkness and so they were lost.

2.4 Joseph Nicéphore Niépce, *View from the Window at Le Gras*, 1826. Courtesy of the Harry Ransom Center, University of Texas.

49

HISTORIES OF PHOTOGRAPHY

BIOGRAPHY: PIONEERS

Joseph Nicéphore Niépce (1765–1833)

The historians Helmut and Alison Gernsheim have claimed 'the world's first successful photograph was taken by the Frenchman Nicéphore Niépce' (Gernsheim, 1971: 20). Niépce was an inventor and pioneer photographer. Following his death in 1833 his collaborator Louis Daguerre improved upon the great man's discoveries. Niépce was motivated to take up experimental photography (or heliography as he called it) when his interest in lithography, a flat-bed printing method, required a level of drawing skill that he lacked. His aim was to create images automatically by using photochemical methods. To begin with he took engraved images, made them translucent with wax, laid them on a light sensitive surface, and exposed them to sunlight. Having successfully completed this task he proceeded to fix images created in the camera obscura. The result of these experiments is the first ever photograph from nature entitled *View from the Window at Le Gras* of 1826 (fig. 2.4).

Louis-Jacques Mandé Daguerre (1787–1851)

The Frenchman Louis Daguerre is also often cited as the inventor of photography. He coined the word 'daguerreotype' (after his own name) to describe his technique, which was announced to the world in 1839 and patented in Paris in the same year. His invention is often compared with the contemporary achievements of the Englishman Talbot who independently created his own method of making photographs. Historians usually note the huge success of Daguerre who took full advantage of his widely proclaimed innovation and enjoyed the support of the French state and commercial success. Although Daguerre's invention was astounding and achieved amazingly sharp images it only produced one image at time and so became little more than an historical curiosity (fig. 2.5).

William Henry Fox Talbot (1800–1877)

William Henry Fox Talbot is credited with creating a negative-positive method of photographic duplication and in due course passed on this principle to successive generations and the world at large. His technique required a translucent paper negative from which could be taken multiple positive prints. This was his famous calotype method patented in 1841. Together with the advantage of being able to make any number of prints Talbot also reduced exposure time from hours to minutes. The daguerreotype has the advantage of sharper resolution but it was an opaque positive and could only be duplicated by re-photography. Frederick Scott Archer's wet collodion method of printing from a glass plate achieved a more sharply focused image and surpassed the calotype method in 1851.

PHOTOGRAPHY IN THE NINETEENTH CENTURY

The name Joseph Nicéphore Niépce figures prominently in standard histories of photography. He coined the term 'heliography' (which derives from Greek words for sun and drawing), and was intent on making images from the camera obscura. Widely acknowledged as the first inventor of photography, and like Davy, Niépce died before public recognition was officially granted to the new medium. Building on a scientific education Niépce's initial aim was to create an automatic approach to lithography. Lithography is an ink-based printing method in which the image is taken from a flat bed of stone. It was itself a new invention that inspired new ways of thinking about making and reproducing images. Lithography has an important connection with the early experiments of Niépce who placed engravings on paper (made translucent by the application of a film of wax) on lithographic plates covered with light-sensitive varnishes which were in turn subjected to sunlight. His approach was determined by a desire to find a graphic process that allowed the image to be made by photochemical methods (that is without the labour of drawing) and with a potential for image duplication from an inked surface. He believed his project had commercial potential. He was, it seems, half right insofar as Daguerre found great financial reward in the more advanced development of these experiments. Daguerre's improvements produced beautifully clear images but were incapable of duplication (Maynard, 1997: 39–40).

Niépce's great achievement was in progressing from the use of lithographic technology to the use of paper coated with freshly prepared silver chloride placed inside a camera obscura. The resulting exposure formed an image in which light and dark were reversed and temporarily fixed by nitric acid. He had created the first negative ten years before Talbot made the same discovery. One of the great wonders of this story is that after centuries of proto-photographic experimentation the discovery of the photographic process, including the tonal reverse image, the so-called 'negative' was made, independently by two men, in a very short space of time. These early results were unstable and the commonly agreed first photographic image of 1826 (fig. 2.4) is rather faint.

Niépce announced his aims and attempts an explanation of his photochemical techniques in his short essay entitled 'Memoire on the Heliograph' which was first published in 1839:

> The invention which I made and to which I gave the name 'heliography' consists in the automatic reproduction, by the action of light with their gradations of tone from black to white, of images obtained in the camera obscura … Light in the state of combination or decomposition reacts chemically on various substances. It is absorbed by them, combines with them, and imparts to them new properties. It augments the natural density of some substances, it even solidifies them and renders them more or less insoluble, according to the duration or intensity of its action. This is, in a few words, the basis of the invention.
>
> (Trachtenberg, 1980: 5)

His process required silver plates, vapour of iodine and bitumen, and exposures were very slow. The image taken at *Le Gras* shows crossed shadows of the sun as the light moved across the frame during the estimated 8- to 24-hour exposures. His meticulous scientific experimentation produced the first negative, then the first direct positive. Needing funding to push the process forward, he struggled to achieve his objectives, which included faster exposure times, greater clarity in the image and a marketable product. In 1827 he travelled to London to seek support from Francis Bauer, a fellow of the Royal Society, whom he had met along with Daguerre (Gernsheim, 1955: 42–43). The meeting came about through the Parisian optical instrument maker Charles Chevalier. At the time of their meeting Daguerre had been using the camera obscura to create highly detailed painted images for his Diorama.

51

HISTORIES OF PHOTOGRAPHY

A diorama is an illusionistic hand-painted, theatrical backdrop that exploits lighting and special effects for popular entertainment. It was a source of income for Daguerre before he achieved fame as a pioneer photographer. Daguerre had been experimenting with various methods to fix his camera obscura images but so far had had no success.

Niépce has a primary place in the early history of photography but was cheated by his early death and the later patenting of his discoveries by Daguerre. Niépce was hailed as the impoverished gentleman scientist who was forced to sell out his ideas to the brash, petit-bourgeois showman Daguerre. It seems clear, however, that Niépce attracted no meaningful investment or national interest and so a hastily drawn-up contract with Daguerre made available a much-improved camera and a sharing of knowledge and resources. When Niépce died in 1833 Daguerre began experiments with silver plates and iodine that led to the announcement of his eponymous 'discovery' of the new medium of photography in 1839.

The air of disdain for Daguerre in classic historical texts extends to his laborious experimental methods. But through strenuous effort and testing (and good luck when a partially exposed plate came into contact with mercury spilled from a broken thermometer) he refined a process, which was viable, both for the creation of highly detailed images and for commercial application. Whereas Niépce chemically enhanced a *visible* image with iodine fumes, Daguerre discovered the value of developing the *latent* image which, with mercury vapour, he used to develop the invisible trace of the image. The problem of fixing the image was solved by dissolving common salt in water. Relatively little exposure time was required to form the latent image. The captured image could thus avoid the blurring effects of moving shadows since the sun had not moved significantly. Daguerre's refinements avoided the extremely long exposure time evident in Niépce's *Gras* picture that reveals shadows at unnatural angles across the final image caused by movement of the sun. All subsequent film and paper processing has been based on the development of latent images and in more recent times, digital sensors functioning in similar ways with amplification of tiny electronic signals triggered by the reception of light. Daguerre had hit upon a key component of modern photography and his improvements were an essential progression from the Niépce process.

The histrionic announcement of Daguerre's method, made by a government deputy François Arago in Paris, 19 August 1839, was made simultaneously to the French Academy of Art and to the Academy of Science. It immediately placed photography into a hybrid role since it was unclear, at the time, whether its arrival was technological innovation or some kind of mystifying discovery. Arago was a distinguished astronomer and scientist, and in terms of social position and standing, a more convincing figure than Daguerre to the academies and the French government. The trumpeting of Daguerre's achievement was probably responsible for suppressing the contemporary achievements of Hippolyte Bayard and other photographic experimentalists of the time. Daguerre's success was widely celebrated and his fame extended beyond France. The discovery was greeted as a miraculous invention and the celebrations that attended its announcement suggest the arrival of a new phenomenon bestowed with a magical aura. For some it seemed that nature was reproducing itself in the photograph and that little or no human interpretive intervention was involved. Was it art? Was it science? Was it a magical emanation? *The Edinburgh Review* of January 1843 announced:

> From being at first a simple and not very interesting process of taking profiles of the human face, it [photography] has called to its aid the higher resources of chemistry and physics; and while it cannot fail to give a vigorous impulse to the fine arts, it has already become a powerful auxiliary

PHOTOGRAPHY IN THE NINETEENTH CENTURY

in the prosecution of physical science; and holds no slight hope of extending our knowledge of the philosophy of the senses. The art of *Photography*, or *Photogeny* as it has been called, is indeed as great a step in the fine arts, as the steam engine was in the mechanical arts…

(Goldberg, 2000: 52, italics in the original)

The art/science dichotomy had fundamental implications for the perception of photography. On the one hand it produced a direct transcription of the real, the photograph as a pure form of evidence, and on the other hand it aspired to be seen as art in its own right. One function is utilitarian and the other is aesthetic. The early period is marked by attention to these identity issues and yet these matters were swept aside in practical terms by the success of the medium.

Arago's announcement of the Daguerre process defined the arrival of photography. In England Talbot announced a prior claim to a photographic process. He immediately published his own paper and wrote to Arago to claim he had first invented a method of making 'photograms' in 1834. This was a method of sensitizing paper with sodium chloride, then silver nitrate to make silver chloride, then laying objects such as leaves, lace or feathers, on this paper before exposing them to sunlight. These 'salt prints' were fixed with potassium iodide and concentrated salt solution. By 1841 he had improved his process, called 'photogenic drawings', and finally patented this technique as the calotype – from 'kalos' the Greek word for beauty. As with the daguerreotype, the calotype exploited the latent image but most importantly it was a negative/positive method. The value of the negative is that it can then be printed through to make any number of positive reproductions.

The daguerreotype differs significantly in comparison with the calotype in being a unique process since the image created is a direct positive and cannot be reproduced except by re-photographing the original (fig. 2.5). The Polaroid latterly shared the same unique qualities. However the calotype could be reprinted and repeated. The calotype is the precursor to modern photography where any number of reproductions of an exposure can be made from film or digital file. It is also world-changing in its semiotic functions since many people can view the same image at different times and places. This effect was later reinforced by mechanical reproduction in print and online. Almost from the outset, reproducibility was a profoundly original attribute of the calotype since it meant that photographs, with their real traces of things, including celebrities, could be widely distributed. The phenomenon of the mass-produced *carte-de-visite*, the business or calling card, is a good example of the desire for public recognition and social status.

Talbot's creation had the greater promise for posterity. It was the daguerreotype, however, that defined the early- and long-lasting genres which persisted in the visual arts and which in many ways were invigorated by the invention of the new medium. These 'genres' (categories of artistic practices) included portraiture, landscape, still life, the nude, architecture, and a range of scientific, forensic and documentary applications.

Daguerre thought his process would be easy for others to adopt for their own use so he was keen to secure commercial rights to the method. Arago realized that the invention was of such moment that it could be used to raise national standing. He was particularly keen to stay ahead of the English. With a modest pension paid to Daguerre and to Niépce's son, the invention could be magnanimously given to the world. Daguerre's process was not, however, straightforward. A silvered-copper plate was placed silver side down over a container of iodine, iodine fumes thus creating silver iodide which forms a light-sensitive surface. The plate was fitted into the camera under cover and exposed to approximately four minutes of light. It is removed from the camera and placed in another box containing mercury that in turn develops the latent image. The plate and image are finally fixed by washing in salt then plain water.

As a unique object the daguerreotype quickly became a valued artefact and a market for this new type of product was established around the Western world. At first the middle classes enjoyed the affordable individual portrait or family portrait. Demand grew for staged studio images furnished with the kind of props to support the sitter through the long exposure time. Props used in the new portrait photography that followed the early inventions often included the sitter wearing fine clothes symbolizing affluence and social standing. This kind of image is closely connected with already-established picture making rituals that seek to enhance social profile and achieve this in the making of honorific portraits (fig. 2.5).

2.5 Daguerreotype of young woman about 1860. © Nancy Nehring. Courtesy of iStock.

From its inception photography seemed to imitate already-established pictorial and artistic genres such as portraiture, landscape and still life. It was, however, exceptional in its capacity to document the appearance of things and was accorded a unique position within the visual culture of the period in which it was invented. Photography was in other words a powerful new medium with a capacity for recording and documenting the existence of things in a manner well suited to the needs of an increasingly bureaucratic and scientific world. This clearly derives from the view that photography was a perfect tool for gathering information. The idea that photography is a direct transcription of reality is underlined in the terminology used by its founders – Niépce's 'sun drawing' (*heliographie*) and Talbot's 'pencil of nature' confirm a sense of unmediated, non-human contact with things. The argument for the unique powers of photography as a documentary medium is rooted in its proclaimed accuracy of observation and apparent neutrality in capturing whatever appears before the lens.

Photography and Society

The notion of photography emerging suddenly from the specific single technological cause of the camera obscura lineage is over-simplified. Whatever brought photography into existence its causes were a mix of social, cultural and scientific, material and technological influences and ideas. The social and political climate of the industrial age is marked not only by a search for visual truth, as an end in itself, but also by social change. One of the most conspicuous features of the period in which photography emerges is the rapid growth of cities and the perceived need for organization, structure and greater visibility in a world that was literally dark, unruly and in need of social reform. The transparency of the photograph was a social metaphor as well as a tool for closer investigation of things. Urban space in the rapidly expanding cities of the early nineteenth century was a danger. The historian Chris Otter notes: 'Here the built environment became a politico-visual problem precisely because it was perceived as blocked, gloomy, filthy, and demoralising' (Otter, 2008: 53).

The liberal response to this urban gloom was the provision of street lamps. An artificial supply of illumination offered security and improved techniques of visibility. The idea of *seeing clearly* captures the changing mood of early nineteenth-century England when reformist city planning and photographic experiment were both advancing their cause. Photography is one of many nineteenth-century technological innovations that played its part in the construction of modern ways of seeing. Photography contributed to the spread of knowledge and the formation of progressive and liberal societies. The availability of time, resources, and educational capital in the lives of gifted amateurs and experimentalists is also a contributory factor in the narrative of early photography.

Niépce, Daguerre and Talbot belonged to an intellectual stratum that grew up with industrialization and were, directly or otherwise, linked with its fortunes. Driven by scientific curiosity and practical objectives, their work formed the elementary stages of projects that had enormously wide applications. Niépce, as we have noted, wanted to find a mechanical means of circulating photographic images in processes linked with new printing technologies such as lithography. The importance of photography lies in its capacity for disseminating images rather than the uniqueness of the image itself. Maynard has noted that Talbot wanted to advertise 'a new set of technological procedures' rather than a 'new class of objects' (1997: 9). For many early photographers the commercial potential of the new medium and its potential for wide circulation were not the least of its attractions.

In the rapidly industrializing western world of the early nineteenth century there was an increasing demand for reproductions of the appearance of things in the world at large. This included new ways of making 'likenesses' of objects and images including new methods of printing; new approaches to illustration and printing are closely connected with the impetus to find ways of fixing projected images from a light source. There was a movement towards collecting and classifying things as if the complexity of modern life needed the imposition of a greater sense of order. Fastidious attention to detail, considered a virtue in the academic painting of this period, corresponded with the tendency to find ways of documenting observable facts. Scientific accuracy also corresponded with the invention of new instruments for recording time, the collection of anthropological data in the new 'sciences of man', the study of fossils and other specimens in the emergent fields of geology and natural history.

In a period when nation states were in the ascendancy, prestigious sites such as government buildings, stately homes and museums were conspicuous signs of power and wealth. The photographic documentation of these sites combined with the archival storage and dissemination of images of faraway dominions and outposts of empire. As noted in Chapter 1, a faithful rendition of the human subject was a sign of recognition and social position. Photographic portraits of the great and good continued a tradition of pictorial reinforcement of hierarchy and social order whilst also helping to cement family ties.

The formation of vast new global empires led to increased travel and a huge increase in the archiving of information and knowledge. Photography served the needs of an increasingly expansionist and imperial worldview. The affirmation of 'identity' and construction of a 'place in the world' for individuals and groups was assisted by new photographic genres. The availability of illustrated visiting cards, the so-called *carte-de-visite,* was a key factor in the early success of photography as a commercial medium.

PHOTOGRAPHIC APPLICATIONS AND THE DIVERSIFICATION OF THE MEDIUM

Photography Everywhere: An Expanding Field

Photography quickly became a viable profession and was adapted to a wide range of practices in its early years. From its inception the special powers of the medium recommended its prospective use in many areas of art and industry. Above all its capacity for recording appearances without omitting details combined with its reputation for impartial documentation guaranteed its advantages over painting, drawing and various engraving methods of representation. Broadly speaking its subject matter derived from the conventions of art including portraiture, landscape and still life. Its biggest challenge at the outset, however, was not so much *what* should be photographed but *how* to overcome the limitations of cameras and chemicals. The daguerreotype was relatively easy to apply to buildings since they keep still and, on a good day, are bathed in sunlight. It was also used for photographic portraiture but required heads to be clamped and groups encouraged to hold each other in an effort to remain steady. The stiff poses of the early photographic portraits are a result of these methods of image capture which struggled to avoid movement and the ensuing loss of detail. For expeditions and war documentation the reproducible techniques offered greater prospect of dissemination and commercial profit. The calotype, for example, was the favoured medium of Gustave Le Gray who was employed in the 1850s by the French Historic Monuments Commission (Marien, 2002: 58–60). This governmental group used photography to record intricate carvings in medieval French architecture with a view to ensuring its restoration and preservation. As noted, photography played a part in supplying the visual evidence for study purposes in emerging scientific disciplines. It also became an essential resource in academic areas of the visual arts including art and architectural history.

Photographs of great works of art could be studied at some distance from the original and also used in lectures and archiving of collections. Reproductions of famous objects, paintings, great buildings and monuments, were valuable aids to study. This kind of academic work is linked with the development of heritage cultures and movements dedicated to the preservation of landscapes, buildings and national monuments. This in turn has vital connections with new modes of cultural tourism and the travel industries. At one level the camera was a symbol of the growing enthusiasm for heroic exploration of distant lands. Transportation of heavy photography equipment for immediate processing required muscular effort and determination. In the late nineteenth century the invention of smaller, easy-to-use cameras became a symbol of tourism. In their more developed formations the tourist industries would be unthinkable without holiday snaps, photographic postcards and family albums.

PHOTOGRAPHY IN THE NINETEENTH CENTURY

In the 1930s the German literary critic Walter Benjamin argued that reproducibility of photographs would democratize high culture (Benjamin, 1936). In some ways this occurred, since national monuments, like the Athenian Acropolis, are widely known and admired. Photography democratized knowledge and allowed wider access to the world. It was also an effective promotional tool for the arts and wide dissemination of images reinforced the cult status of architectural monuments and rare works of art.

Travel photographers were often serious scholars or imperialist ambassadors of European nations when visiting distant lands. Such interests are now popularized and widely available but have acquired other meanings as consumerist extensions of the tourist and media industries. In its early days travel photography was an aid to study but its public display was limited to exhibitions and luxurious albums with 'tipped in' photographs.

Popularization of the medium was achieved in other ways including magic lantern shows. The projecting of images from hand-painted glass slides had been around for centuries and in the mid-nineteenth century photographic slides were used in popular entertainment, advertising, missionary work and education. Photographic slides were sometimes skilfully hand coloured for special effects. Slideshows were a precursor of the cinematic modes of viewing which involve the experience of collective viewing of projected images in darkened rooms. Audiences were attracted to photographs because of their exotic content but they also admired the 'good eye' and the skill of the photographer which they took to be evidence of worldliness and taste. Scenic photographs of mountains, deserts and pyramids (fig. 2.13) appealed to audiences living in cities. The wilderness appealed to the taste for sublime and myste-rious places and travel photographs of the Middle East had biblical associations for Western audiences already familiar with readings from the bible.

The growing popularity of photography was demonstrated in many ways. Photographs were appearing in shop windows, photographically derived illustrations were printed in newspapers and magazines, photographic societies were established in major cities around the world, specialist photographic journals consolidated the importance of the new medium and commercial photographic portraits were all the rage. Further, its reputation for accurate recording made it highly suitable for recording botanical specimens, microphotography, and new areas of social science such ethnographic photographs of the human subject where it was applied as an educational and therapeutic medium. The 'discovery' of new lands, wild places and exotic territories in the wider world was immediately followed by photographic documentation.

Photography was also used in campaigns for the establishment of national parks and the preservation of the land. These included petitions to the US government to isolate Yosemite in California and Yellowstone in Wyoming for social use by the non-indigenous Americans. Its use as a medium of surveillance often preceded colonial expansion. The visualization of news events contributed to the growth of the press in the 1850s and 1860s. Photographs were skilfully rendered as engraved images and used as a means of attracting readers and influencing public opinion as the medium was gradually incorporated into the new forms of popular and visually arresting journalism. One of its most distinctive applications in the second and third decades after its invention was its recording of war.

HISTORIES OF PHOTOGRAPHY

Landscape, War and the Collodion Process

In 1851 Frederick Scott Archer published the collodion process. The technique required the use of a light-sensitive emulsion applied to a glass plate. Great skill was required to make a usable plate as the emulsion of collodion and nitrate required even distribution over the hand-held glass in the dark, followed by immediate exposure whilst the emulsion was still wet. The benefit of Archer's method was greater sensitivity as the glass negative avoided the fibrous finish of the paper-based medium used in Talbot's calotype method.

> **KEY TERM: The Wet Collodion Process**
> This process was hugely important in the technical advancement of photography. The process, invented in 1851, succeeded and largely replaced the daguerreotype and the calotype methods. The wet collodion process achieved sharply focused images and was an improvement upon the use of paper negatives pioneered by Talbot. In the collodion process a glass plate is coated with a mixture of distilled water, light-sensitive salts and other chemicals. The photographer required skill and effort to achieve the right kind of result since the slightly wet plate was inserted into a camera before being exposed. Exposure time was long, as it had been with earlier methods, and the exposed plate had to be developed right away. Travel photographers not only had to carry heavy equipment, including glass plates, but they also needed to take some kind of dark room with them as well. The English photographer in the Crimea illustrates the use of a 'van' for this purpose (fig. 2.1).

The Frenchman Gustave Le Gray invented his own version of the collodion process in 1850. He started his career artistic career as a painter but abandoned this profession in favour of photography. He had also created a refinement of Talbot's calotype process. Using beeswax he created a finely grained paper negative capable of achieving a heightened rendering of detail. Le Gray was a pioneer of art photography and was disdainful of the kind of photography that appeared to achieve little beyond recording the appearances of things. The straight depiction of the material before the lens, in his view, lacked the intervention of the intellect and the emotions.

He typified the resistance to commercial trends towards mass production of stereographic images and the *carte-de-visite*. Le Gray's artistic training provided aesthetic ideas that he brought to photography including sensitivity to tonal variation and softness that parallels the brushwork of the French mid-century style associated with the Barbizon School of painting. The photograph entitled *Tree, Forest of Fontainebleau* of 1856 (fig. 2.6) is a study of shadows created by tall trees that rise out of the forest floor. Sensitively framed by dark edges, the picture contains a pattern of tree trunks and horizontal branches which echo the lines in the grassy surroundings below them. His landscapes capture the fleeting effects of sunlight falling on objects in the world and this quality together with humble subject matter anticipates the paintings of the French Impressionist painters. In his great enthusiasm for photography he argued that it would increase the study of nature.

PHOTOGRAPHY IN THE NINETEENTH CENTURY

2.6 Gustave Le Gray, *Tree, Forest of Fontainebleau, c.* 1856. Courtesy of Museum of Fine Arts, Houston, Texas, USA (Museum purchase funded by the Brown Foundation Accessions Endowment Fund), The Manfred Heiting Collection/Bridgeman Images.

The Great Wave, Sète of 1856–59 (fig. 2.7) by Le Gray is one of a series of seascapes produced near Montpellier on the Mediterranean coast where he was working from 1856 to 1859. In this work he devised a type of combination printing using two separate glass negatives to print the picture. Finding that a single negative could not achieve a satisfactory tonal balance between sea and the sky he made two separate exposures of the sky and the sea, combined them and retouched the join in the albumen salt print. Adapting painterly methods his approach to photographic aesthetics challenged purely optical notions of the 'real'. The outcome is a constructed view of the sea that, nevertheless, looks totally realistic. The technique is departure from the photograph as record of a single moment.

KEY TERM: Albumen Prints
The term albumen derives from the Latin word *albus* for white. The albumen process exploits the use of egg white combined with sodium chloride to form an emulsion that is applied to paper. The emulsion becomes light sensitive when allowed to dry in ultra-violet light. When placed in a frame with a negative and exposed it forms a positive image. This process was usually used in conjunction with a wet collodion negative. The hugely popular *carte-de-visite* pioneered in the 1850s relied on this method.

2.7 Gustave Le Gray, 1857, *The Great Wave, Sète*, 1856, albumen print from two collodion glass negatives. © Victoria and Albert Museum, London.

The English landscape photographer Roger Fenton, an early follower of Daguerre, adopted the collodion process to make the first ever official photographs from a war zone at the Crimea in 1855. Fenton was appointed by the British government to document the allied offensive against Russia in the Crimean War of 1853 to 1856. Some commentators suggest that it was the technical restrictions of the process that determined the nature of Fenton's images. He had the painstaking and difficult task of coating the glass plate with collodion in the sweltering heat of a horse-drawn wagon at the Crimea. The conditions in which he worked and the relatively primitive nature of the photographic process at that stage were unsuited to capturing battle scenes. The material, technological and chemical nature of the task might account for Fenton's tangential way of depicting traces of war and its aftermath in his famous image of *The Valley of the Shadow of Death* of 1855 (Fig. 2.8).

The barren valley strewn with cannonballs is a metonymic description of a terrible massacre of British cavalrymen made famous in Alfred Lord Tennyson's poem 'The Charge of the Light Brigade' of 1854. Simon Norfolk's recent work in Afghanistan draws firmly on this tradition where, at first glance, what appear to be picturesque images of ruins, photographed in the glow of the golden hour of sunset, actually shows the wreckage of bombardments and gunfire. Norfolk shares with Fenton a sense of the awesome beauty of desert and mountains strewn with the debris of war, and the paradoxical meaning of beautifully empty spaces disrupted by our knowledge of the tragic events that occurred within them. Figure 2.9 shows a discarded piece of military tank track that looks curiously like skeletal remains of an animal's vertebrae.

PHOTOGRAPHY IN THE NINETEENTH CENTURY

2.8 Roger Fenton, *The Valley of the Shadow of Death After the Charge of the Light Brigade*, 1855. © Private Collection/Ken Welsh/Bridgeman Images.

BIOGRAPHY: ROGER FENTON

Fenton was the first official war photographer. He studied at University College London and was awarded a Bachelor of Arts degree in 1840. Impressed by the photographs he saw at the Great Exhibition in London, 1851, he took up photography. He adopted the wax paper calotype methods of Fox Talbot and was sent to the Crimea in 1855 to report on the hostilities between Russia and the allied forces of France, Britain and the Ottomans. He is mainly remembered for his war photographs and the poignancy of his biblical reference to the 'Valley of the Shadow of Death' with its connection to the ill-fated 'Charge of the Light Brigade'. The images of the Crimea were intended to reflect favourably on a 'popular' war, but had the opposite effect. The squalid conditions of the war zone and the relative comforts of the officer class did not suit the intended propaganda objectives. The capacity for truth telling was clearly in evidence in Fenton's war photography. Fenton helped to establish the London-based Photographic Society and became its first honorary secretary.

HISTORIES OF PHOTOGRAPHY

2.9 Simon Norfolk, *Track of Destroyed Taliban Tank at Farm Hada Military Base near Jalalabad*, from the series *Afghanistan: Chronotopia*, 2002. © Simon Norfolk/INSTITUTE.

BIOGRAPHY: SIMON NORFOLK

Norfolk studied photography at Newport in South Wales. He worked as a photojournalist before taking up landscape photography in the 1990s. In 1998 he published a book entitled *For Most of It I Have No Word: Genocide, Landscape, Memory: Places That Have Suffered Genocide*. In 2005 he published photographs of the war in *Afghanistan: Chronotopia*. In 2005 his book *Bleed* reported the war in Bosnia. His work is predominantly related to the way war affects the physical shape of places, including human habitation and the natural environment. His work documents sites of atrocity and the social memories that accompany terror, suffering and loss. Contemporary war reporting is tightly controlled by the military and much of it is used for propaganda purposes. Norfolk eschews these methods and the restriction of 'embedded' photojournalism.

The heroics of war often characterized the military paintings of the past. Fenton's cumbersome equipment was not, however, suited to capturing battle scenes. The camera, at this stage in its evolution, was incapable of recording split-second action scenes. His alternative was the recording of the location of battle scenes and passive views of troops at rest that became the stock in trade of early war

PHOTOGRAPHY IN THE NINETEENTH CENTURY

photography. Matthew Brady, Alexander Gardner and Timothy H. O'Sullivan photographed the American Civil war in the 1860s with the same technology as Fenton and similar covered wagons. Unlike Fenton, however, they revealed the direct horrors of bodies on the battlefield (fig. 2.10). Fenton was much more constrained by governmental strictures and control of the 'message'. The Crimea campaign was badly organized by the British but much of Fenton's work is comparatively anodyne and shot at a safe distance from the battle lines or taken after the event.

In this period heroics of war were delivered by news reporters rather than by photographers. The photographs themselves were often reproduced as wood engravings (derived from drawings of photographs) in popular journals like the American *Harper's Weekly*, printed in limited edition albums, or circulated as cheap prints. Figure 2.15 provides an example of this kind of engraving. Some photographers owned galleries where prints were offered for sale. Uniformed soldiers in war zones proudly sent by post their own portrait photographs to families at home.

Harrowing images of dead soldiers, even at such historical distance, reveal the tragedy of the Civil War. The factual detail of the medium makes a quite different impression on the spectator than a painting or a verbal report. The American Civil War photographs of Brady, Gardner and O'Sullivan anticipate a genre of 'anti-war' photography in the twentieth century including Ernst Friedrich's published archive of mutilated victims of the First World War entitled *Krieg dem Kriege* (War Against War) of 1924 and the work of Philip Jones Griffiths who recorded horrific scenes in Vietnam in the 1960s.

Intriguingly Gardner's *Home of a Rebel Sharpshooter, Gettysburg* of 1863 (fig. 2.11) was a staged photograph in which the body and rifle were repositioned for a better visual effect. This type of falsification has become controversial but was not always seen in this way in the past. The staging in this example

2.10 Timothy H. O'Sullivan, *A Harvest of Death, Gettysburg, Pennsylvania,* July 4th, 1863. Courtesy of George Eastman House, Rochester, NY, USA, Bridgeman Images.

HISTORIES OF PHOTOGRAPHY

2.11 Alexander Gardner, *Home of a Rebel Sharpshooter, Gettysburg,* July 1863. © The Museum of Modern Art, New York/Scala, Florence.

is, arguably, unimportant since it clearly reports facts that were supported in written accounts of the war. The directness of the medium and the dreadful ordinariness of the scene are the salient features that make it disturbing.

War photographs were included in exhibitions or intended to be published as illustrations alongside written accounts of military events. Unlike war paintings, however, they have not usually been treated as works of art although Norfolk's work blurs this boundary. The identity of photography was in any case quite uncertain in the middle years of the nineteenth century. Already a viable profession by the 1850s it was still treated as mechanical art requiring high levels of skill but little artistic imagination. This limited view of the medium was, however, challenged by Le Gray in France and a small number of photographers throughout the world who campaigned for its recognition as a legitimate art form in its own right. Would-be art photographers, such as Le Gray, experimented with techniques in the hope of finding uniquely photographic effects whilst others emulated the conventions of painting. The two ways of working have influenced subsequent development in art photography up to the present day. Artistic interpretations of warfare at this time were restricted to painters and graphic artists who supplied heroic images of battle scenes and pageantry.

Art Photography

It is surprising how the central debates in photography and consideration of its key applications were forged in the early years following its invention. 'From today painting is dead' is a statement routinely attributed to Paul Delaroche, a popular French painter of historical tableaux. His outburst is intended to signal a turning point when the invention of photography in 1839 threatened the noble art of painting.

PHOTOGRAPHY IN THE NINETEENTH CENTURY

The prospect of photography actually replacing art loomed large. On the other hand there was deep scepticism, and expressions of doubt that photography could be anything more than a handmaiden to the arts. Against such scepticism generations of photographer-aesthetes have striven to establish the medium as an acceptable form of artistic expression in its own right. From its earliest days photographers were tempted by the fine arts and sought in many ways to learn from painting. In some cases photographers were intrigued by the poetic qualities of the medium and sought to exploit its specific qualities and effects.

The slow development of art photography demonstrates new ways of valuing photography at a time when it was relegated to instrumental functions or later when it was being adopted as a recreational pastime for the general public. The enormous success of photography in the nineteenth century was due to its impartial rendering of things and the suitability of this for illustration of scholarly and commercial projects. The medium was connected with 'the real' and its appropriation for documentary ends guaranteed its immediate success as the medium of accurate observation *par excellence*. The turn to photography as a fine art medium is a sharp counteractive response to photography as a functional mode of illustration. Some of the earliest attempts to assimilate photography to fine art were inspired by narrative paintings. These included constructed photographs that followed the technique of Le Gray's combinations printing method. Oscar Rejlander devised an allegorical tale entitled *The Two Ways of Life* in 1857 (fig. 4.3). The picture required 30 negatives combined in the single image and ambiguously mixes eroticism with moral censure. Two young men are faced with a moral choice: a life of vice or virtue? Using a similar technique Henry Peach Robinson's *Fading Away* of 1858 (fig. 4.4) is a contemporary genre scene in which a dying woman awaits her fate. She represents a stereotype and invites pity. This way of reading the image is reinforced by a dominant male figure in the room. As with the female nudes in Rejlander's work her physical condition defines her identity. The sentimental content of both pictures is aimed at the market for popular, narrative works of art.

Julia Margaret Cameron was an English photographer who is remembered for her expressive portraits of well-known figures including poets and scientists. Her imagery is romantic, nostalgic and steeped in the traditions of painting and challenges the idea of photography as a purely technical mode of representation. In soft-focus portraits she exploits the dramatic effects of light and the staging of visual effects. Staging was of course already widely practised in commercial photographic portraiture where the use of props and other fixtures was often contrived or banal. Cameron's work expresses the personality of the sitter through dramatic lighting effects, body language and pose (fig. 2.12). The shift is usually characterized as a move away from 'description' towards symbolism and poetic reading of the subject. Languorous female subjects, such as *Echo* of 1868, were influenced by similar qualities in the work of the artist Dante Gabriel Rossetti. The medieval-style gown worn by the model also evokes the idea of a distant pre-industrial age and the picture's title, 'Echo', is a classical reference to a beautiful nymph. Cameron's work is visionary and at odds with finely detailed and meticulously observed portraiture of this period. Although her source material is historical and literary she was experimental and innovative in the way she crafted the medium of photography to suit her own aesthetic ideas. In her struggle to find a signature style in a new medium she anticipates work of the Pictorialist school of photography later in the century. The soft out-of-focus photographs of Cameron showed how far the expression of feelings or ideas could be made to challenge the artisanal or functionalist role allocated to photography in the Victorian period.

2.12 Julia Margaret Cameron, *The Echo*, 1868. Courtesy of The J. Paul Getty Museum, Los Angeles.

Pictorialism is a label used to denote a late nineteenth-century movement in photography. The term describes the collective aims of an international group of photographers who broadly sought to privilege what they considered to be the artistic potential of the medium. The etymology of the term derives from the English noun 'picture' which forms an adjective as 'pictorial'. The French photography historian Marc Mélon has argued that the English word 'picture' refers to painting as a practice but is not restricted to this. It can refer to any kind of image and so photography is 'one image among others' (Mélon, 1986: 87) and has legitimacy outside the practice of painting. The Pictorialist style is, however, closely related to key movements in contemporary European painting including Impressionism. The movement also takes inspiration from the aesthetic ideas of the symbolist painters and poets also working in this period. The symbolists underlined the importance of feeling and inspiration as the integral element in a work of art. The Pictorialists adopted expressive techniques including image manipulation that often softened the image or made it less readable as a documentary image. They cropped figures and staged their subjects, favouring damp, misty and inclement weather for their landscapes and dark interiors for their portraits. The 1901 self-portrait, entitled *Solitude*, by the American photographer Edward Steichen (fig. 6.12) conveys the hermetic character of a style that places the creative artist outside the mainstream of life.

Pictorialism is a style associated with exclusive photography clubs and societies which attracted wealthy amateur photographers who wished to distance themselves from the applied technical functions of the medium and find a *métier* that aspired to the prestigious name of art. The invention of the affordable box camera in the 1880s and its commercial exploitation had the cultural effect of lowering the status of what had in many ways been a technically demanding practice. The invention of roll film and hand-held camera made photography popular and entertaining. This lowered the profile of the medium for specialists with high-level skills and a determination to find ways of aligning photography with progressive movements in painting. The reorientation of photography towards the fine arts was a particular response to its changing functions. The frivolous work of the Kodak snappers was anathema to the new members of august institutions such as the Linked Ring Brotherhood established in London in 1892, the Photo Club de Paris of 1894, and the New York Camera Club of 1896. The Pictorialists would have rejected William Ivins' later description of the photograph as an exactly repeatable image (Ivins, 1996: 118). Working against the principle of exact repetition they produced luxurious portfolio albums and ensured the rarity value of individual pictures (and their sense of 'aura') by destroying negatives. Their primary aim was to separate their work from the ordinary mass of images that were already in circulation at this time.

Campaigning figures such as Steichen and Alfred Stieglitz re-evaluated the potential of the photograph as a unique work of art and, more importantly, lifted the photographer out of the utilitarian doldrums and positioned him (and her, there were a few women Pictorialists) higher up the artistic scale. The subjective interpretation and personal expression are aesthetic ideas that reach back to the romantic painters and poets of an earlier period. The work of the Pictorialists and the critical debates they used to promote their position is a continuation of this earlier ideal. Stieglitz's photograph entitled *The City of Ambition*, of 1910 (fig. 6.13), connects the architectural power of the big city with his own spiritual response. His photographs of New York are unpopulated, empty looking images that avoid the rhetoric of street life that he associated with journalism.

Stieglitz's vision of modern city life, a legacy of French impressionist paintings of Paris, had been transported to New York City and his lyrical views of the city represented moments of poetic reverie and contemplation. Like most Pictorialist photographs they are wistful interpretations of modern life. By the early twentieth century a few revolutionary painters had begun to respond to this kind of urban subject matter very differently. The French cubists made fractured and alienating pictures of city life and the Expressionists in Germany produced bleak and dystopian visions of the modern world. These aggressively distorted views of the modern world contrasted starkly with Stieglitz's melancholy views of Manhattan in the early decades of the twentieth century.

Despite the efforts of the Pictorialists, photography still remained on the fringe of the art world in the early twentieth century. The coming of age of art photography was not fully established until it received the backing of important art institutions such as the Museum of Modern Art in New York. In the period after the First World War art photography was re-launched as an aggressively modernist style of 'straight' photography. Photographers such as the Americans Paul Strand and Edward Weston rejected Pictorialism as a dead end. Photography, they argued, should be a pure medium, avoiding any imitation of other art forms. The new direct approach underlined the importance of the camera's innate honesty and made a principle of the qualities intrinsic to the medium itself: its powers of accurate transcription of things in the world.

Faced with a contradiction between a straight view and a creative view photographers would traditionally resolve the matter by appealing to the idea of their heightened visual capacity. His contribution to history would be achieved in discovering new ways of seeing the world. The theoretical underpinning of this new kind of art photography was compelling for many of Strand's later followers. The negation of social meaning in any recording of a scene places greater value on the subjective interests of the recorder. This was an aesthetic suited to the growing market for art photography in the early twentieth century. In some cases it led to the misappropriation of documentary photographs whose social and political messages disappeared when elevated to the context of art.

Commercialism and the Mass Production of Photographs

Two factors explain the popularization of photography in the 1850s. First, photographic associations were formed with the intention to advance the study of the medium and disseminate ideas to a wider public. The Calotype Club was established in 1843 in Edinburgh by an associate of Talbot, the *Société*

HISTORIES OF PHOTOGRAPHY

Héliographique was founded in Paris by Gustave Le Gray in 1851 and The Photographic Society was founded in London in 1853 with Roger Fenton as its first honorary secretary. Pioneering photography societies organized exhibitions and published journals. Photography was popularized at the Great Exhibition of All Nations in the Crystal Palace, Hyde Park, London, in 1851, which had two different sections devoted to both scientific and fine art applications of the medium. Second, the invention of the *carte-de-visite*, which became a commercial and hugely popular mode of photographic portraiture, and the updating of an older technology, the stereoscope, as a kind of home entertainment, demonstrated the commercial potential of the new medium.

The technology for viewing stereoscopic images preceded the invention of photography. A device with two lenses for viewing two images of a scene created from two different viewpoints (the width of the eyes apart) produced an extraordinary three-dimensional view. Photographic stereographs became immensely popular in the 1860s and sets of commercially produced photographic cards made for this purpose were highly collectable. People amassed great numbers of these paired images, depicting a very wide range of subjects to be viewed as an entertainment in the home. The popularity of stereographic photography may be related to the variety of subjects available for purchase. In Figure 2.13 we see the New York-based firm of Elmer and Bert Elias Underwood's view of Egyptian pyramids. This type of image illustrates the fascination for Middle Eastern subjects in expeditionary photographs of this period, and appealed to Western taste for exotic and stereotypical views of the orient. The stereographic image was something of a novelty in an age before screened entertainment. Only one person could use the stereoscope at one moment but there was, in any case, pleasure in sharing images and delight in the effects of three-dimensional views of the world. It was an affordable middle-class entertainment that spread widely from the mid-1850s onwards and was still popular in the early twentieth century. A stereographic camera invented in the 1850s produced two simultaneous images. Demand for stereoscopic images led many photographers to carry stereoscopic cameras along with regular equipment.

2.13 A stereograph, Elmer and Bert Elias Underwood, *The Great Pyramid of Giza*, 1905. Courtesy of Getty.

PHOTOGRAPHY IN THE NINETEENTH CENTURY

> **KEY TERM: Stereoscopic Photography**
> The technology for viewing stereoscopic images preceded the invention of photography. A device with two lenses for viewing two images of a scene created from two different viewpoints (the width of the eyes apart) produced an extraordinary three-dimensional view. Translated into photography, stereographs became immensely popular in the 1860s and examples were highly collectable. People amassed great numbers of these paired images, depicting for example the landscapes of empire, to be viewed as an entertainment in the home. The stereographic image was something of a novelty in an age before screened entertainment. Only one person could use the stereoscope at one moment but there were pleasures in sharing images and delight in the effects of three-dimensional views of the world. It was a low-price form of photographic practice that spread widely from the mid-1850s onwards and was still popular in the early twentieth century. A new stereographic camera was invented in the 1850s that produced two simultaneous images.

The stereoscope and the *carte-de-visites* were trends that foreshadow later visual modes of home entertainment. André Adolphe Eugène Disdéri patented the *carte-de-visite* in 1854. His highly inventive technology included speeding up of exposure time and the multiple shooting of images on a single plate. More than any other early format this albumen print-based format massively increased the domestic consumption of photographs. Up to eight images on one plate, cut up to small postcard size, were then stuck to a visiting card. The creation of this personalized card was hugely popularized by distinguished clients. Disdéri's great fortune was having Napoleon III unexpectedly arriving at his studio requesting a portrait (fig. 2.14). The enormous prestige of this client helped him to promote the new format and marks the beginning of a demand for celebrity images. The biggest share of the market and the main output was staged portraits. Some providers of *cartes-de-visite* supplied smart and up-market clothing, hired out to the sitters, for the purpose of the shoot. The medium was available as a cheap form of self-promotion allowing the lower middle classes to emulate the fashionable and wealthy stratum of society.

2.14 André Adolphe-Eugène Disdéri, *Carte-de-visite of Napoleon III*, 1859. Courtesy of Private Collection/Bridgeman Images.

69

HISTORIES OF PHOTOGRAPHY

In the first decades of photography cameras and the processing technology required some level of affluence and technical expertise. This limited the practice to wealthy educated practitioners who were subsequently challenged by producers of *cartes-de-visite* and stereoscopic imagery. The invention of dry plates by Richard L. Maddox in 1871 also made photography significantly more convenient and began to make the process more accessible. Without the need for the complexity of the chemistry and coating of the plate just prior to the taking of the photograph, more people were attracted to take up the camera. The advantage of collodion was its ability to achieve fine detail. The disadvantage of this method was the need for elaborate apparatus including dark tents, quantities of glass and chemicals for fieldwork. The dry plate was a great labour-saving improvement especially for travel photography. On the spot chemical preparation was replaced by dry sensitized plates, commercially produced, and ready for use. The dry-plate method was eventually made to achieve rapid exposure time. This allowed for a new type of hand-held camera that marks the beginnings, in the 1880s, of modernized photography which was popularized soon after this period. By the late nineteenth century photography had become an immensely successful and commercially viable means of supplying the general public with portraits, mementoes, records and new kinds of entertainment.

The photographic professions were a component part of late nineteenth-century industrial capitalism. Manufacturing and marketing organizations spread widely as demand for cameras, chemicals, accessories grew. Popular illustrated journalism was an integral part of a growing leisure industry in late nineteenth-century in Europe and North America. By 1900 there were 2,328 magazines and reviews in circulation in Britain (Jobling and Crowley, 1996: 9). Areas of interest included fashion, arts, politics, and specialist literary and scientific publications. As we have noted engravings derived from photographs increasingly formed an important method of reproduction. This technique allowed the artist to make images that closely resembled the tonal values of the photograph. A wide range of techniques included lithography and other inventive modes of printing supported specialist branches of academic research including anthropology, criminology, geographical, antiquarianism and so forth. Photographs were often commissioned for books and appear in serial form in some of the pioneering texts of the period after the 1850s.

Charles Darwin famously used photographic illustrations for his book *The Expression of Emotion in Man and Animals* of 1872. Most of the publications in which photographs appeared in the early period of photography relied on the kind of image-text relationship established in Talbot's book *The Pencil of Nature*, published in instalments from 1844 to 1846. The important point to be understood is that before the invention of the halftone screen *actual* photographs had to be tipped in by hand. This meant that most books and portfolios were printed in limited editions and available to fewer readers (Brunet, 2009: 46). They were also costly and restricted to collectors and enthusiasts rather than the general public.

Photography for personal use was an affordable artefact in a market dominated by portraiture. By the end of the 1890s most big cities had hundreds of portrait studios and thousands of people were employed in the photography industries. Since its inception photography had been driven by technical, scientific, artistic and entrepreneurial ambitions. It had relied heavily on technical skill, physical effort and experimentation. There is no doubt these qualities continued in the new century but key changes led to the depersonalization of photographic practices (Freund, 1980: 86). Gradually photography became less craft-centred and more industrialized. One of the key practical outward signs of a change in the trade is the shift to hand-held cameras and the use of dry plates. These changes were quickly followed

PHOTOGRAPHY IN THE NINETEENTH CENTURY

by the development of smaller cameras supplied with roll film. Add to this the fact that towards the end of the nineteenth century cameras were much easier to operate and widely advertised as portable and easy to use.

The market for popular photography was firmly established by the American Kodak camera of 1888. This remarkable invention created a mass market in amateur photography. Advertising its products in the press and making full use of improved mail services allowed potential customers to send for and receive equipment. In 1891 a daylight loading camera was available. By 1900 photography products were affordable household commodities. The invention of the affordable box camera and its commercial exploitation had the cultural effect of lowering the status of what had been a technically demanding practice. The reorientation of photography towards the fine arts was one response to its changing functions. It is a response that reflected the taste and preferences of photographers alienated by the democratization of photographic products.

Professional portraiture continued to serve the needs of ordinary customers but the shift was towards weddings, baptism and photographs for special occasions. The inventive use of celluloid in the production of roll film made the camera more compact, relatively light and convenient for use. Jobbing photographers worked as topographers, social archivists, and suppliers of materials for professional, scientific and commercial documents. Others provided images for reproduction as wood engravings and, after 1900, were able to see photographs appear on the printed page in mass circulation newspapers and other graphic media. A new technique for printing intermediate tones from a photographic plate eliminated the need for drawing. This technique made it possible for photographs to be printed alongside typographical texts. The importance of the invention of the halftone screen process, as it was known, was immense.

Print media emerging after the turn of the century was increasingly reliant on photography as the primary source for pictorial illustration. Photomechanical reproduction replaced handmade plates and photography began to dominate factual modes of printed documentation. The graphic design historian Philip B. Meggs notes this had two effects. First, the appearance of the printed page was now strongly influenced by the 'textural and tonal properties of the halftone image', and second, illustrators were 'pushed away towards fantasy and fiction' (Meggs, 1992: 153). The strongly non-photographic look of art nouveau illustration in the period around 1900 is evidence of the split between hand-drawn and photographic methods of representation. It may be true to say they are reactions against each other.

> ### KEY TERM: The Halftone Process
> This is a process that allowed photographs to be printed in newspapers, periodicals, books and other publications, alongside written text. The technique produced a relief image usually mounted on a wooden block which raised the printing surface to the same height as letterpress type. Its great virtue was that it allowed the printing of text and image simultaneously and facilitated the kind of image-text juxtaposition familiar to all readers from the early twentieth century onwards. Its invention was a great boon for newspapers but made legions of wood engravers, that is the copiers of photographs, redundant. The method allowed a range of tones

between black and white. It derives from earlier experiments conducted by Talbot using a fine screen to simulate continuous tone when an image is re-photographed through a fine screen. The pattern and size of dots is determined by lightness and darkness in the print. The screened image is printed on a sensitized metal plate. The gelatine surface is hardened by light and the non-printing areas are etched with acid. The halftone method was patented in 1882 by the British printer George Meisenbach. He used his method secretively and it was not adapted more widely until the late 1880s (Wakeman, 1973: 139).

This was the second greatest invention in the field of photography after the great breakthrough work of the early nineteenth century. From the 1880s onwards the halftone block made it possible to print photographs alongside words and facilitated the growth of photo-illustrated documentation. The great pioneer of photography William Fox Talbot had noted much earlier that the tonal range of photographs could be reproduced in a method that translated the image into dots of different sizes. The principle relied on ink printed dots merging in the human eye and thus appearing as a photograph. The tonal range of the photograph is reproduced in a multitude of dots despite the even-ink application of printer's press. The halftone technique

2.15 *The Graphic: Arctic Supplement*, 'The Arctic Expedition', 1875, London. Courtesy of Private Collection/© Look and Learn/Illustrated Papers Collection/Bridgeman Images.

was founded by various experimenters. It relied on the use of a cross-lined screen that was deployed between a photographic print and negative. The cross-lined screen was used in making the plate for printing (see Phillip B. Meggs, 1992: 149–150; Geoffrey Wakeman, 1973: 138–139). The plate was mounted on wood to the height of letterpress type in a process allowing simultaneous printing of words and photographic image.

Before the period of published photographs line drawing was a standard form of Illustration and these had been made ready for printing by wood engravers using a hand-rendered method of block making, a highly skilled craft technique made redundant by the halftone block methods of reproduction.

Photographs were printed in newspapers by the early years of the twentieth century as mechanical reproduction of images was beginning to form the basis for mass communication in the print media. Early twentieth-century advertisers continued to rely on handmade illustrations which were widely used in the chromolithographic form made in large sizes for the early billboards and street posters of the late Victorian and Edwardian period. The profound importance of reproducibility for the making of a modern system of visual communication needs to be restated. The philosopher Patrick Maynard refers to the '*rei*nvention of photography around the beginning of the twentieth century (which electronic imaging's development may never rival in importance): the *ink*, or relief-impact, press-printing system without which even "the photograph" today would have a diminished historical significance' (Maynard, 1997: 18).

Figure 2.15 illustrates the wood engraving technique used for reproducing photographs *before* the invention of the halftone block.

CONCLUSION

Sifting through the complexities of nineteenth-century photography has required us to focus on some of the primary sites of its early discoveries and innovations. This has centred on pioneers in England and France. There are, however, parallel narratives of experimentation, artistic expression and commercial exploitation of the medium in all the great nations during this period. Nations with established cultures of painting and graphic art were ready to adapt experiments in printing technology, labour-saving methods of drawing, chemistry, and optics to the production of new media. Historians have shown this trend to be almost global during this early period, which is marked by a sudden rush to invent a way of capturing and fixing light impressions. One of the points we have stressed is that the emergence of photography in the early decades of the nineteenth century derives as much from social and cultural factors as it does from technology and science.

The camera obscura is a suggestive model for the instrumental tasks that would-be photographers needed to solve and there is no doubt that it 'explains' the optical side of the matter and yet it had been used for years without much advance. All the resources for photography were available in the previous century. This begs the question: why was it so late? What frustrated its earlier prospects for development? The answer is complex but some mention of the particular cluster of historical forces

HISTORIES OF PHOTOGRAPHY

in the industrial period, including the romantic impulses of the day, conspired towards the momentous achievement we have described. No single cause is in evidence and the ambitious movements in science, optics, precision engineering, literacy and travel play a part in this narrative. It is also true that a massive increase in the demand for documents and systems of classification which are part of mass society created the right conditions for the invention of the new medium. This does not explain why it arrived in 1839. To say the right conditions led to discovery is applying knowledge with hindsight. Nevertheless, photography captured the imagination of the Victorians and found a staggering range of applications from the outset. This might suggest that social needs provided some impetus for the inventions that actually took place.

The single greatest achievement might be the stabilizing of captured or reflected light and the formation of a permanent image. Equally important is the creation of the negative-positive system of duplicating the photographic image. Added to these innovations, the new technologies of the late nineteenth century which led to 'push-button' cameras and easy social use are equally important. Connected with the expansion of visual culture in domestic use is the widening public sphere in which mass reproduction of images in the press is highly significant. The introduction of the halftone screen in the 1880s is, arguably, the second great leap forward in the history of photography after its first announcement in 1839. The halftone screen allowed photography to be widely dispersed at low cost in a vast range of publications including the press, fashion catalogues and journals, and the mainstream graphic media that remained dominant before digital alternatives in the late twentieth century.

We have discussed different ideas about the identity of photography expressed in debates about high cultural and popular uses of the medium. The Pictorialist movement in photography was a provocation that forced photographers to think about the medium's relation to painting and the visual arts more generally. Without knowing it, the Pictorialists rejected the idea that photography has unique properties and started something that rolled over into the postmodernist ideas of the late twentieth century.

SUMMARY OF KEY POINTS

- The early nineteenth century was a fertile period in which new technologies combined with precision engineering, new printing techniques, and scientific experimentation to create revolutionary new methods of image capture and dissemination. Experimental methods in different places arrived at similar outcomes that came to be known as photography.
- The link between photography and earlier visual aids such as the camera obscura is taken for granted in historical studies. Historians also claim the search for new methods of visual communication is linked with industrial demand for mechanized forms of visual documentation. We accept both arguments as necessary but not sufficient as historical explanations for the birth of photography. The idea of marking surfaces with light and effectively arresting a moment in time was convergent with new philosophical and literary trends in the period of photographic invention. The camera/eye analogy is useful as a spatial model of visual perception but it fails to account for the temporal aspects of being. Photography satisfies a psychological need for a type of representation that preserves the past. It was born at a time of romantic fascination with the experience of time, memory and place. Recognition of this broadens the field of study beyond technological and economic causation.

PHOTOGRAPHY IN THE NINETEENTH CENTURY

- Contemporary debates about the future of photography, including its prospective absorption into new media, are productively informed by reflections on its early developments.
- In its early years photography was quickly adapted to a range of administrative, educational and commercial functions. When nation states were emerging sites of power and wealth, civic monuments, public buildings, stately homes and the outposts of empire were photographed for posterity. Royalty, heads of state and public servants were the subject of honorific portrait photography. The social and political consequences of this kind of mediation are an important aspect of photography history.
- As soon as it was technically available and ready for wider applications, photography was adapted to leisure and entertainment uses. The *carte-de-visite* and stereoscopic cards are important examples of the earliest commercial use of photography in the nineteenth century. In the 1880s the market for popular photography was determined by easy-to-use Kodak box cameras. Affordable daylight-loading cameras made photography products available as household commodities by the beginning of the twentieth century.
- Photography was invented at about the same time as railways and it is not surprising that travel and photography were connected from the earliest days of both technologies. Travel and expeditionary photographs are amongst the most distinctive images of the nineteenth century. Photographs made by travelling Victorians included grandiloquent sites and vistas, and scenes from everyday life. These subjects have continued into present times and yet modern tourism is greater in volume and often more informal or even intimate by comparison.
- War photography is a form of photojournalism intended for press publication. This follows the conventions of the earliest war photographers whose work was converted into drawings and published as wood engraving in the popular press.
- Photography was a restrictive technology until it was made widely available in the late nineteenth century. Two inventions in this period created wider accessibility and usage of the medium: the halftone printing process made photographs available to a mass audience and the portable 'snapshot' camera allowed photography to become a popular recreational activity.
- The late nineteenth-century Pictorialist photographers (perhaps unconsciously) challenged the autonomy of photography when their practice absorbed the influence of contemporary art. Early twentieth-century exponents of 'straight' (or 'pure') photography, including Paul Strand and Edward Weston, considered the idea to be in 'error'. The postmodern rejection of photographic purity in the late twentieth century is an historical reprise of this earlier schism.
- Photography is still one of the most powerful forms of visual propaganda. It is also an important means of documenting social concerns including physical cruelty and atrocity. Photographs can help audiences to confront injustice and act as reminders of what ought not to exist. Some of the earliest war photographs carried 'anti-war' messages.
- The main discoveries and inventions that define photography occurred in the nineteenth century. These discoveries and inventions were assimilated into media technologies that have remained dominant until the digital revolution of the late twentieth century.

HISTORIES OF PHOTOGRAPHY

REFERENCES

Batchen, Geoffrey (1999) *Burning With Desire: The Conception of Photography*, Cambridge, MA and London: The MIT Press.

Benjamin, Walter (1936) 'The Work of Art in the Age of Mechanical Reproduction', in Walter Benjamin (2009) *One-way Street and Other Writings*, trans. J.A. Underwood, London: Penguin, pp. 228–259.

Brunet, François (2009) *Photography and Literature*, London: Reaktion Books.

Freund, Gisèle (1980) *Photography and Society*, London: Gordon Fraser.

Friedrich, Ernst (1986) *Krieg dem Kriege* (War Against War), Franfurt Am Mein: Zwantausendeins.

Gernsheim, Helmut and Alison (1955) *The History of Photography: From the Earliest Use of the Camera Obscura in the Eleventh Century up to 1914*, London, New York and Toronto: Oxford University Press.

——(1971) *A Concise History of Photography*, London: Thames and Hudson.

Goldberg, Vicki (ed.) (2000) *Photography in Print: Writings from 1816 to the Present*, Albuqurque, NM: University of New Mexico Press.

Ivins, William M. (1996) *Print and Visual Communications*, Cambridge, MA and London: The MIT Press.

Jay, Martin (1994) *Downcast Eyes: The Denigration of Vision in Twentieth-Century Thought*, Berkeley, Los Angeles, London: University of California Press.

Jobling, Paul and Crowley, David (1996) *Graphic Design: Reproduction and Representation Since 1800*, Manchester: Manchester University Press.

Marien, Mary Warner (2002) *Photography: A Cultural History*, London: Laurence King Publishing.

Mélon, Marc (1986) 'Beyond Reality: Art Photography', in Jean-Claude Lemagny and André Rouillé (eds) (1986), trans. Janet Lloyd, *A History of Photography*, Cambridge: Cambridge University Press, pp. 82–101.

Maynard, Patrick (1997) *The Engine of Visualisation: Thinking Through Photography*, Ithaca, NY and London: Cornell University Press.

Meggs, Philip B. (1992) *A History of Graphic Design*, New York: Van Nostrand Reinhold.

Otter, Chris (2008) *The Victorian Eye: A Political History of Light and Vision in Britain 1800–1910*, Chicago: University of Chicago Press.

Scharf, Aaron (1974) *Art and Photography*, Harmondsworth: Penguin.

Trachtenberg, Alan (ed.) (1980) *Classic Essays on Photography*, New Haven, CT: Leete's Island Books.

Wakeman, Geoffrey (1973) *Victorian Book Illustration: The Technical Revolution*, Newton Abbott: David and Charles.

CHAPTER 3
PHOTOGRAPHIC REALISM: STRAIGHT PHOTOGRAPHY AND PHOTOGRAPHIC TRUTH

The Scottish photographer Alexander Gardner's portrait of Abraham Lincoln (fig. 3.1), sixteenth president of the United States of America, has strong historical associations with the American Civil War. This portrait pre-dates his Gettysburg Speech ('government by the people, for the people…') and for many people the image and the words Lincoln used at this time are connected. His austere looks had been revealed to the American public through *carte-de-visite* portraits they may have seen. These images had helped to establish his celebrity. The power of the image resides in its apparent truth claims as a photographic representation that captures a likeness of the man. It is, however, equally reliant on portrait conventions established in academic art. These include various ways of making the image correspond with the reputation and status of the sitter. He appears in the portrait as a mature man who knows the world. His posture is erect and he makes direct eye contact with the viewer. Light catches his forehead in a way that conveys intelligence and thoughtful reflection. It is a construction of iconic dignity and statesmanship. These are rhetorical devices well-known to the portrait artist and yet despite its staged effect the psychological force of the image resides in the knowledge that Lincoln was *there* in front of camera and now appears to us as a manifestation of the man rather than a mere picture.

3.1 Alexander Gardner, *Abraham Lincoln*, 1863. Courtesy of Private Collection/Bridgeman Images.

HISTORIES OF PHOTOGRAPHY

INTRODUCTION

The American philosopher Kendal L. Walton has noted how photographs of Abraham Lincoln 'are in some fundamental manner more realistic than painted portraits of him' (Walton, 2008: 21). Walton underlines the distinction between painting and photography in the following way: 'We don't see Henry VIII when we look at his portrait; we only see a *representation* of him. There is a sharp break, a difference of kind, between painting and photography' (Walton, 2008: 25, our emphasis). Both statements underline a key difference between photography and painting. Walton argues that photographs are different to other kinds of pictures because they relate to the world in a different way. Are photographs different? Are they realistic in a way that other methods of depiction are not realistic, or at least not realistic in the same way? The reference to painting is perhaps limiting in this comparison which leaves out other types of hand-made pictures or objects with marked surfaces including illustrations, drawings, watercolours and prints. As we saw in Chapter 2 there are halfway stages between photographs and handmade pictures that include traced silhouettes and camera lucida drawings. Much rests on the fact that photography is a mechanical process and photographs, unlike other types of pictures, and most types of marked surfaces, are not handmade.

There is a lot at stake in this discussion. Any claims made for the power of the photographic image (a widely expressed claim as we will see in later chapters) cannot be taken for granted. It is in any case a claim that presumes a higher level of effectiveness in comparison to other visual media. We will thus consider the following:

1 What it means to say that photographs are realistic
2 How the comparison with other ways of picturing the world helps to define the photograph
3 Challenges to the realist argument and the claims for photographic self-expression
4 Photography as a new (or special) way of seeing the world.

The describing word 'photographic' has many connotations. What does it mean to you? Perhaps you might think of other words to match it with such as realistic, detailed, sharp focus, and so forth. Photographs have other properties but there is a common tendency to think of ways in which they amplify what is normally seen by the unaided eye. The kind of visual clarity associated with sharply focused photographic images has a strong appeal to certain types of photographers (the exponents of 'straight' photography in the 1920s, for example, and the pioneers of the medium in the early nineteenth century were advocates of visual clarity).

If there is such a thing as photographic seeing it is often related to the idea of accurately fixing the look of things. It was this quality above all that audiences marvelled at when they first saw a daguerreotype in the early years of photography. The philosopher Patrick Maynard has observed that daguerreotypes were admired as 'almost as phenomena of nature rather than as human handwork' (1997: 46). The enhancement of human visual contact with things that appear in an image formed by light defines the special nature of photography. This is not a sufficient definition of photography since other media have strong depictive capabilities (painting for example). And yet 'depiction' suggests intentionality that might be lacking in the photograph. Maynard notes, 'in the case of photography it is the radiation that *forms* the image, whereas in painting it is not' (ibid.: 20). Photographs lack the kind of filtering of information typical of pictures made by other means. We have, possibly, an excess of detail in the photograph that might otherwise be edited out.

78

On the other hand the impartial or objective view of things (including excess detail) is often seen as one of the great strengths of photography since it confirms the idea of the truthfulness of the medium. We might say it is only from an aesthetic point of view that the indiscriminate fixing of the whole scene to include trivial or unimportant features is viewed as a weakness. It is in any case a key factor in our thoughts about what a photograph is.

The quantity of detail achievable in a photograph is an important consideration but the argument for the distinctiveness of the medium does not rest on this. We are concerned with a deeper issue: the mechanical transmission of 'information' (light waves) from something that exists in the world to the surface display we call a photograph. In other words we are concerned with the way photography allows nature to draw itself unaided by the hand.

REALISM DEBATES IN PHOTOGRAPHY AND ART

What it Means to Say that a Photograph is Realistic

There is a sense in which a photograph is not a representation in the normal sense of this word. What we see in a photograph has a link with the object to which it appears to refer. It is, however, a uniquely mechanical link and therefore lacks the kind of personal or subjective view of things that might be a factor in the way we see other kinds of pictures. This is not an argument for saying photographs cannot be works of art. All we are saying is that photographs are (arguably) different to other types of pictures and, furthermore, that a consideration of the word *representation* might assist our discussion.

Representation

Representation is a term that has been widely used in cultural theory since it draws attention to the degree to which social or artistic, or other, kinds of meanings are to some degree shaped by social context, manners of expression, and established ways of doing things. In other words the way an object or idea is *presented* or *re-presented* may tend to reinforce the way we see it. Representation is here taken to refer to conventional ways of making a thing stand for something else (such as a cartoon drawing that represents uncle Fred, or the name 'uncle Fred' that also represents him). The representation might take the form of habitually repeating what is already current or it might be more purposeful such as when an individual gloss is given to a certain way of saying things, or to a certain way of *re-presenting* things.

The notion of representation impinges on the discussion about realism in important ways. A consideration of this takes us into the wider debate about the singular qualities of the photograph when compared with other media. Insofar as the photographic process is mechanical it seems possible that it might bypass the kinds of choices made when we use language (using words to express what we wish to say) or the kind of choices made when a painter constructs an image. In the case of the photograph there is a suggestion that we see through the image as if it were a kind of window, as if it were transparent. In a photograph there appears to be no mediation or barrier to perceptual contact with the object – no words that stand for meaning (as in language), no brushwork or artistic distractions put there by the painter. There is a sense in which we are encouraged to think of the purity of photography as a provider of 'straight' access to the thing itself, the visual experience unsullied by construction. Practitioners who stress the creative potential of the medium are opposed to this extreme definition of the medium. The dualism of 'straight' and 'creative' approaches is at the centre of the debates on the true vocation of the medium discussed in this chapter.

The contention here is that photographs are not representations in the same way that spoken or written sentences, cartoons, or even realistic-looking paintings are said to be representations. There is a sense in which a photograph bypasses any feeling the photographer may have about a scene since the camera, a mechanical object, has no way of knowing what it is. Whatever is in the mind of the photographer is irrelevant since the details recorded by the camera have a degree of arbitrariness beyond his or her control. This is an extreme viewpoint and a caricature of the effortless work of the camera and its operator. It presumes a rigid divide between the photographic viewpoint and what actually appears in the image.

The photographer as human subject takes up a relationship with objects in the world. A photographer selects a landscape and establishes a relationship based on aesthetic ideas or other criteria that might influence the way the picture is taken. The selection criteria may determine whether the shot is a personalized subjective interpretation of a scene or objectively determined by a desire to make an accurate visual report. Some people say cameras capture the appearance of things objectively without feeling or human cognition. Others emphasize that camera viewpoint, technical strategy and poetic insight inform the way a photograph is made, that the camera is controlled and operates in accordance with the artistic aims of its user and in particular circumstances the picture is the equivalent of his or her state of mind. There is, nevertheless, a strong sense in which a photograph is a record of how an object looks rather than a realization of how the photographer felt when the shutter was released. How he or she felt may have nothing to do with the kind of picture they want to make. An example would be an advertising photographer making an image that looks like an advertising photograph. How he felt at the time may be irrelevant to the meanings his work creates. Subjective interpretation versus objective reporting is a stubborn opposition in cultural theory. In the case of photography the opposition is reinforced by the mechanical nature of the medium.

Objectivity versus Subjectivity

The discussion centres on binary oppositions between traditional positions. This is useful in establishing what is at stake. For example consider the following pairs of concepts:

Subjective	Objective
Personal Artistic	Mechanistic/impersonal
Artistic	Documentary
Representational	Non-representational
Painter	Photographer
Artistic truth	Prosaic truth
Interpretation	Report

PHOTOGRAPHIC REALISM: STRAIGHT PHOTOGRAPHY AND PHOTOGRAPHIC TRUTH

These are crude oppositions but they are widely used in the debates in photography circles. Such terms generate discussions that centre on the contest between reportage and aesthetic meaning in our assessment of photography. Photography is a term that refers to a range of technologies used in many different ways. We are reminded that it is a process and that its definition is not reducible to judgement based on photographs alone. This may explain the continued interest in the aesthetic status of photography and its comparative neglect in other intellectual fields such as philosophy and science. The tendency is to think in terms of photography's products rather than the over-arching issues about its uses and applications or the changing nature of these.

It is, nevertheless, true that discussion about the kinds of oppositions listed above are generated by anxieties about the occupational sites of photography. The globalization of electronic media and the concurrent rise of art photography in the late twentieth century have focused these issues but they go back to the perceived need to address the long-term dichotomy of art and industry. To the extent that photography belongs to industry (not least because it is one of the world's major industries) it was judged for many years to be an interloper in the academy and the museum. The idea that it is a mecha-nistic medium used for the transmission of information or combined with words to form a publicity tool has also ruled against it in the past. Over time this attitude has changed. To say that photography is in some way not as pure as art now sounds almost backward. Progressive artists have for a long time sought to blur the boundaries between technologies in the wider field of the arts, and photography has been important in defining the field of modern art (see Scharf, 1974, Campany, 2007, and Chapter 1 above).

The German theorist Siegfried Kracauer, writing in the middle years of the twentieth century, famously reversed the idea that photography is a mere recording device by pronouncing this property to be its great virtue – a virtue, moreover, that gives it an advantage over other media. All that is needed, he claimed, is an expanded definition of art. What this amounts to is a recognition that the realist recording powers of the camera are consistent with an observer's interpretation of the objects viewed and the two things are not opposed. In this formulation the common sense dualism (objective recording or subjective interpretation) disappears when photography and science are in pursuit of similar objectives: 'both probe an inexhaustible universe whose entirety forever eludes them' (1976: 20) and, for Kracauer, both confront 'unshaped nature itself, nature in its inscrutability' (ibid.: 20). Emphasis on the camera's 'revealing faculty' is faithful to what Kracauer call the 'photographic approach' (ibid.: 21), an approach that respects the limitations of the medium. This is an appeal to the medium-specificity of photography discussed in Chapter 1 above.

On the matter of the incidental detail Kracauer noted the charm of photographs is that they 'include things unknown to their maker, things which he himself must discover in them' (ibid.: 22) and underlines the importance of the 'realistic tendency', which he insists must be 'followed under all circumstances' (ibid.: 13). According to this view the 'photographic approach' is a refusal to assimilate photography to painting and an expression of commitment to a realist definition of the photograph as document. This definition was to an important degree modelled on an appreciation of documentary trends in Surrealism and street photography in the 1920s and 1930s which includes work by the Parisians Eli Lotar, Jacques André Boiffard and Brassaï whose photographs are documents of banal urban sites and unsightly body parts.

81

Realism, Photography and Art History

The phrase 'photographic realism' may sound tautological if we think of the medium's truth telling and realistic functions. There is, however, anxiety in contemporary thinking about the truth telling power of any medium including photography. Digitization, for example, has undermined confidence in the photograph as provider of visual truth. Postmodernist theory has also broadly, and sweepingly, denied the truth claims of all media. For the postmodernist photography lacks identity as a discrete practice since it is always dispersed across disciplines of art, commerce, science, journalism and any number of things. Photographs are always bound up with the context in which they circulate and constrained by the commercial, journalistic or more general narrative ends they are made to serve. Advertising and editorial photographs, tourism and propaganda forms, and most forms of documentary 'realism' or family snaps can be analysed as messages that reveal social values more deeply embedded in the social fabric.

All cultural products carry values beyond their innocent charms of self-reference or description. The photograph, however, has a kind of naturalness that makes it different. The critic Roland Barthes referred to 'the special credibility of the photograph' (Barthes, 1979: 21), a quality that gives it a certain power over other systems of representation. It is a power that captivates audiences and a quality that is widely exploited in the promotion industries where its persuasive powers are most effective.

The pursuit of visual accuracy in the arts is a defining property of Western traditions that stretch back to the ancient Greeks. It is tempting to think of the invention of photography as a culmination of this tradition. The art historian Ernst Gombrich makes the case for artists turning to visual representation of observable detail that, he claimed, marked the beginning of Greek naturalism (1987: 99–125). The desire to imitate or record appearances with increasing levels of accuracy has, nevertheless, always been accompanied by other aesthetic concerns. Gombrich notes: 'The very idea that it should be possible to observe without expectation, that you can make your mind an innocent blank on which nature will record its secrets, has come in for criticism' (ibid.: 271). Artists also rely on conventional ways of picture making and look to the work of other artists for guidance. Knowledge gained in this way is mapped on to what is interpreted in the study of nature. The idea of the mind as an innocent blank may well be inadequate. It does, nevertheless, provide a curiously useful model of the workings of the camera as a kind of blank plate awaiting the indexical imprint of nature.

The Concept of Realism in Art and Photography

Realism is an over-used and sometimes misleading term. It has wide currency in art and literature and is commonly taken to mean that a work of art 'is like' or 'resembles' reality. It is an approach that presupposes a world of real existence that can be known. Probably the most common usage of the term realism is connected to the everyday expressions of saying a picture is 'lifelike', 'realistic', 'true to life' and so on. In saying 'that picture is just like Uncle Fred' we are defining realism in terms of resemblance. There is a simple effect of recognition here that may not always be sufficient. One person may recognize the subject but another may not. Even photographic evidence is often unreliable and yet at the level of common sense the idea of resemblance has a certain appeal. What is important here is to think about the picture and its referent, the depicted object. The manner of the formation of this coupling (picture/

PHOTOGRAPHIC REALISM: STRAIGHT PHOTOGRAPHY AND PHOTOGRAPHIC TRUTH

referent), how it is made, is important for the way we think about it. The important thing, for the reality effect to happen, is that the connection between picture and referent is achieved. Consider the following:

> If we were to ask you, is a picture of a teacup more like a real teacup or more like a picture of a cereal bowl, you might agree that the two pictures are more like each other as flat objects with surface markings than they are like the things they appear to represent.

What do we mean when we say that a picture *of* a teacup is a like a teacup? What do we mean when we say a picture is true? What might be implied is that looking at these pictures is like looking at what they represent. For many people the issues of resemblance suggested by this are so obvious that it is never questioned. It is, nevertheless, the case that some kinds of 'realism' are superior to others in terms of their capacity to produce 'resemblances'. This is because some modes of visual representation have a more privileged status and this might to some extent be attributed to their capacity to create an effective look of reality. We include here those pictorial traditions that originate in fifteenth-century Italy.

Experimentation in fifteenth-century art and technology produced innovations in the mathematical formulation of perspective and rigorous new ways of denoting spatial depth. They developed in a period when mirrors were refined and new and more sophisticated uses of the camera obscura (see Chapter 2) reinforced the desire to copy nature accurately. Gombrich refers to a painter in this period as achieving the illusion of nature 'by patiently adding detail upon detail till his whole picture became like a mirror of the visual world' (1984: 178). Gombrich also refers to 'smooth transitions … letting colours shade off into each other … and miracles of accuracy' achieved through the radically new uses of oil paint to amazingly realistic effect (fig. 3.2).

The astonishment occurring in the fourteenth and fifteenth centuries to which Gombrich refers in this passage is indicated by the chapter title 'The Conquest of Reality' in his book *The Story of Art* (1984). A similar astonishment followed the invention of photography in the nineteenth century and perhaps for not dissimilar reasons. In the case of both innovations the surprised response is not so much to the image itself, but to the manner of its making. The miracles of invention and discovery that led to the creation of photography were optical and chemical in nature. Those of the Renaissance were a mix of mathematical perspective, new materials, and innovations in optical science. On the subject of the camera obscura, used as a mechanical aid, the painter

3.2 Jan van Eyck, *The Arnolfini Portrait*, 1434. © The National Gallery, London 2014.

83

HISTORIES OF PHOTOGRAPHY

Leonardo da Vinci notes: 'light entering a minute hole in the wall of a darkened room forms on the opposite wall an inverted image of whatever lies outside' (Newhall, 1949: 9). The photography historian Beaumont Newhall noted that a more brilliant image was later achieved by the substitution of a lens for the pinhole. The technological nature of these projects is at least in part a key to understanding their historical importance. The camera obscura image, for example, underlines the importance of a growing faith in purely optical experience. The development of perspective seemed to confirm a structured and rational basis for the way the world is seen. John Berger notes:

> The convention of perspective, which is unique to European Art and which was first established in the early Renaissance, centres everything on the eye of the beholder. It is a beam from a light-house – only instead of light travelling outward, appearances travel in. The conventions called those appearances *reality*. Perspective makes the single eye the centre of the visible universe.
>
> (Berger, 1972: 16).

In this schematic view 'everything converges' in the eye and the artist's view is that of a 'one-eyed, motionless, person' as Robert Hughes expressed it (1980: 17). Perspective creates a split between observer and the observed. In this sense the term realism has come to refer to a detached and analytical

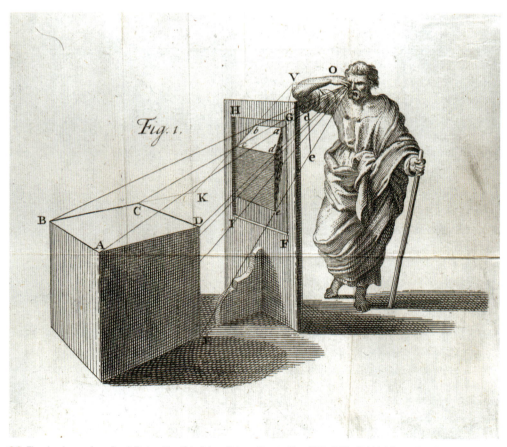

3.3 The visual cone, from Brook Taylor, *New Principles of Linear Perspective*, 1719. © The British Library Board.

PHOTOGRAPHIC REALISM: STRAIGHT PHOTOGRAPHY AND PHOTOGRAPHIC TRUTH

method of documenting the appearance of things. This division lends scientific authority to a structured and impartial way of seeing typified in the rigid geometry of the illustrations in the mathematician Brook Taylor's *New Principles of Linear Perspective* of 1715 (fig. 3.3). Earlier examples of the quest to find geometrically accurate models of visual perception are evident in depictions of architecture. Leonardo's *Study for the Adoration of the Magi*, *c.* 1481 (fig. 3.4), shows the outlines of steps converging on a vanishing point and the diminishing scale of things in the upper section of the drawing. It is a view with modern connotations and radical ambitions. In a classic text on the nature of realism Linda Nochlin writes: 'Its aim was to give a truthful, objective, and impartial representation of the real world, based on meticulous observation of contemporary life' (Nochlin, 1971: 13).

This statement describes an objectifying model of perception associated with the term realism. A dazzlingly impressive example of 'meticulous observation' is deployed in *trompe l'oeil* painting (fig. 3.5). Looking at objects in a *trompe l'oeil* painting is not, however, the same as looking at the objects themselves. We are beguiled by the illusion and enjoy a visual effect with magical denotative power. It is clearly possible to make pictures in a particular way, in particular conditions, that deceive the eye and allow the spectator to think a real space appears to exist (a hollowed out recessive space) where there is actually none. The illusionary effect is not, however, our normal experience of viewing this kind

3.4 Leonardo da Vinci, *Study for the Adoration of the Magi*, *c.* 1481. © 2014. Photo Scala, Florence – courtesy of the Ministero Beni e Att. Culturali.

3.5 Pere Borrell del Caso, *Escaping Criticism*, 1874. Courtesy of the Collection of the Bank of Spain.

85

HISTORIES OF PHOTOGRAPHY

of picture. The boy escaping from the picture in Figure 3.5 exploits the visual effects of illusion to good effect. It is, however, a type of pictorial mischief that equates with the antics of the boy. The deception is playful and easily seen for what it is: a sign for a boy rather than an actual boy.

Pictures often present us with an image of the world as if seen through one eye with a sharp focus, and, commonly, within a rectangular frame. They are usually encountered as objects in frames hanging on a wall and viewed by spectators who move around them. It is also true that in painting conventional perspective often denotes horizontal recession, but makes no allowance for vertical recession of the kind experienced when viewing tall buildings from the street. Equally we receive no effects of parallax when viewing a picture. The relative positions of *depicted* objects will not change when a person moves around them. Together with other factors this tells us (obvious though it may be) that pictures of things are not the things themselves. The realization does not, however, deny that realistic pictures have a particular and even quite uncanny relationship with their referent. The relationship between the image and its referent is constrained by the greater or lesser degree of truthfulness that obtains in the picture. The implications of this can be seen in portraiture that often provokes feelings of anxiety about likeness and truth not least for the sitter. This is perhaps more acutely felt in photographs since there is a sense in which the referent has a directly causal relationship with what appears in the image. The anxiety is of course connected with the belief that the camera does not lie.

> **KEY TERMS:**
>
> **Trompe L'oeil:** This is a French word that refers to a kind an illusionistic method of painting that attempts to trick the eye in a manner suggesting that the viewer is not looking at a representation, but is actually looking at the depicted object.
>
> **Parallax:** This term applies to the apparent displacement of objects caused by actual change of point of observation or the angular amount of this displacement of objects when we shift our position in a real spatial setting.

Resemblance or Denotation

The idea of a causal connection in photography that links the image and referent is central to our understanding of the medium. As we have seen, following Walton, our way of seeing images, possibly all images, is determined by this effect. Understanding of pictures changed after the invention of photography since it became the yardstick by which visual correctness was measured. It is, however, a measure that relies on the notion of resemblance and there is a dispute about this term. Gombrich (1986, 1987) and the American philosopher Nelson Goodman (1976) represent the two poles of the discussion. Gombrich argues that perspective and the techniques associated with it have a special connection to the way the human perceptual apparatus works in day-to-day experience. It is, for him, a way of recording what may be seen from a given position. Gombrich notes:

> Perspective is the necessary tool, if you want to adopt what I now call 'the eye-witness principle'. In other words, if you want to map precisely what anyone could see from a given point, or, for that matter, what the camera could record.
>
> (Gombrich, 1986: 281)

As we have noted, Gombrich accepted that paintings are never entirely natural signs since they are 'frequently made with conventions that have to be learned' (1986: 279) such as when drawing is determined by a system of representation that replaces actual observation. In his book *Art and Illusion*, first published in 1960, Gombrich emphasizes that 'all paintings ... owe more to other paintings than they do to direct observation' (1987: 268), which admits the way style and convention influence artistic performance, but he also recognizes the way perception plays a part in what he calls the 'closer rendering of the motif' (1987: 252).

In speaking of this 'close rendering' he was alluding to the way painters struggle to achieve a balance between intensely looking at the world (the motif) and composing the outcome as a picture. It is implicit in his argument that perspective, understood as a schematic way of depicting space, corresponds with human vision in certain ways. The composition is crucially determined by what is seen. Objects, for example, appear to decrease in size as they move away from the perceiving subject. The corresponding illusion of this effect in Figure 3.4 has a familiarity that corresponds with our experience of spatial effects and especially those in geometrically structured environments. Gombrich believes that certain kinds of images, including Western illusionistic painting and photographs, are 'natural' compared with early Egyptian forms of painting. When the classic realistic painting impassively *resembles* its referent it performs like an un-coded message.

The American philosopher Nelson Goodman advances a different view and argues that perspective is a purely conventional pictorial device. According to him the way pictures represent visual experience is through denotation and not through resemblance. Goodman argues that '[r]epresentational customs, which govern realism, also tend to generate resemblance. That a picture looks like nature often means only that it looks like the way nature is usually painted' (Goodman, 1976: 39). That is to say paintings are signs that *stand for* objects and no resemblance occurs. What we see is a denotation rather than a hole in the wall or an actual boy. It is true to say that, in fact, both Goodman *and* Gombrich reject the idea that painters mindlessly copy what they see. Both scholars accept that stylistic and conventional factors play a part in all forms of expression and communication. Artists copy each other and borrow ways of picturing the world and yet some turn more assiduously to the observation of nature. Painters such as the English landscapist John Constable trusted their own powers of looking and achieving a 'close rendering' of what they saw. For Gombrich, a painting and a photograph perform similar tasks and share similar audience response. They both, for example, conjure lifelike scenes in which making is replaced by matching. In the case of the photograph the matching is automatically obtained which, as we have argued, influences the way the viewer relates to what it shows.

In both painting and photography much can be said for the evidential force of the image over other systems of transcription. The naturalness of the image has advantages over verbal reports that rely on language and complex systems of representation. The power of the image has a certain universality that overshadows other systems of communication. The literary critic and culture theorist W.J.T. Mitchell observes how the picture succeeds where language might fail: 'the picture', he notes, 'reaches out to the object it represents, and to the viewer it addresses' (Mitchell, 1987: 79). This spatial model makes the object in the image accessible since it has no great dependence on reading skills or other kinds of acquired knowledge. Following Gombrich's argument we can now say that 'naturalness' in a painting is exceeded by this effect in a photograph. The objects we see in the photograph seem to have reached out to it. We trust the photograph as an accurate representation of what we see and yet it is not a representation in the way that realistic painting is representation. Gombrich actually fails to consider this difference. A photograph directly and automatically carries the imprint of its object to the viewer.

We may in any case conclude this point by adapting Gombrich's faith in the 'naturalness' of certain kinds of pictures and perhaps especially photographs. The argument is that realistic pictures correspond with human vision in important ways and may, therefore, be contrasted with conventional signs that 'stand for' or represent something without having any kind of direct contact with it.

The Example of Dutch Realism

The history of art offers many different modes of representing reality even within the Western perspective tradition. In the eighteenth and nineteenth centuries different models of 'realism' were determined by academic theory. The most exact and truthful style of representation was exemplified by the work of

3.6 Jan Vermeer, *View of Delft*, *c.* 1660–61. Courtesy of Mauritshuis, the Hague.

PHOTOGRAPHIC REALISM: STRAIGHT PHOTOGRAPHY AND PHOTOGRAPHIC TRUTH

Dutch painters of the seventeenth century. Two centuries later landscape painters such as Constable looked back at the 'natural' and down-to-earth quality in the work of landscapists such Anton Cuyp, and the French Impressionists' idea of painting urban scenes devoid of dramatic or narrative content had its roots in painting such as Jan Vermeer's understated *View of Delft* (fig. 3.6).

There are two connotations of the term 'realism' brought into play by Figure 3.6:

1   Dutch painting was highly prized by progressive artists and photographers in the nineteenth century because of its painstaking precision, its polished surfaces and detailed representation of textures and the effects of light falling on objects in space.
2   Subjects represented ordinary people engaged in ordinary activities. Domestic settings, still life motifs in domestic settings and simple figure studies.

In academic theory 'lowbrow' subjects were hardly considered acceptable as art. Art, it was thought, should convey elevated moral ideas through (imaginary) idealized forms. Thus the character of 'realism' was defined by different ways of representing the world. As Linda Nochlin has noted:

> But important though it might be fidelity to visual reality was only one aspect of the Realism enterprise; it would be wrong to base our conception on only one of its features: verisimilitude.
>
> (Nochlin, 1971: 22–23)

KEY TERM: Verisimilitude
Verisimilitude is a term that defines an idea of truthful appearances or accurate duplication in the representation of things.

What is clear is that fidelity (or truth) was a kind of technical aspiration that circulated widely in the arts of the nineteenth century but it was not an end in itself for its most crusading exponents. We have emphasized how far accurate representation is significant in the development of Western painting and faithful copying of reality by painters and in a different way by photographers. The pursuit of 'lifelike' effects was not an end in itself for most artists and the term 'realism' for progressive artists extended into ways of seeing the wider social context in which they worked. Sharp-focus views of the modern world increasingly drew artists (including photographers and writers) into the wider sphere of social comment.

Realism with a capital 'R'

Realism with a capital 'R' refers to a loose movement in art and literature that emerges in France in the period around 1850. Realism is thus not just an aesthetic idea but a name that represents a formation of artists and writers with a social and political agenda. They produced work of a kind that directed attention to aspect of modern life such as poverty, labour, or matter-of-fact locations in the city and suburbs – subjects that gained little support in the higher ranks of official high culture (fig. 3.7).

3.7 Honoré Daumier, *The Washerwoman (La Blanchisseuse)* c. 1860. Photo © RMN-Grand Palais (Musée d'Orsay)/Hervé Lewandowski.

Some of the more abrasive work associated with the Realist movement was directed at the audiences accustomed to cultural refinement. Works by French painters such as Honoré Daumier, Édouard Manet and Gustave Caillebotte (fig. 3.8) focused on themes of manual labour, sexuality, and even death as depicted in burial scenes. Places of entertainment also featured and often sought to capture the seedy glamour of the café concerts. Impressionist paintings later in the century sought to capture Parisian nightlife, depicting a mixture of social classes in a manner that challenged conventional notions of respectability and decorum.

In this context Realism was a militant and oppositional tendency that focused on the social atmosphere and the artists' own surroundings including street life, leisure and the pleasure zones of the city. Dutch Realism was an important influence on late nineteenth-century French painters. They also experimented with colour and tested their skills against the busy movement of the city. Inspired by the camera's direct approach to contemporary life painters looked around them for subjects that might express the poetry of city life. The capture of light and atmosphere has affinities with the work of the photographers and yet the excessive use of primary colour and loose brushwork adopted by the Impressionists signified an ambivalent attitude to photography. The main distinction of Realism as a new and modern movement in the arts is that it shunned the sentimental themes of narrative art and official modes dredged up from classical antiquity. The term Realism indicated a rejection of mythology and imaginary invention in the arts. It is also apparent from these examples that the Realists often shunned the slick finished surface of more traditional painting and the glossy look of the photograph.

Photography underlined the importance of scenes in modern life and a desire to keep a visual inventory of the world around the artists. This extended into a study of modern manners that was approached directly in documentary images of marginalized social groups such as laundresses (fig. 3.7) and street figures were a subject for the camera. It is also a time when department stores, exhibitions, public gardens and the spectacle of fashionable street clothes appear in the work of painters. Luxury sitting cheek by jowl with the filth and noise of the big city and the irony of this juxtaposition was seen by the observant stroller, the artist and the camera. The visual arts and the literature of the mid-nineteenth century responded to the immediacy of the photograph which allows for close inspection of things. The photograph provided a direct encounter with the world, an intimate view, rendered safe for inspection. It furnished the viewer with detail, substance, and materiality that could be shared by an expanding audience. The *carte-de-visite*, the stereograph, photo-engravings and photography exhibitions made a

PHOTOGRAPHIC REALISM: STRAIGHT PHOTOGRAPHY AND PHOTOGRAPHIC TRUTH

3.8 Gustave Caillebotte, *Raboteurs de Parquet*, 1876. Photo © RMN-Grand Palais (Musée d'Orsay)/Hervé Lewandowski.

cross-section of society available to public view. Viewers could imagine themselves within this larger picture of the social world and think of ways they might relate to this image.

In comparison with elaborate and contrived paintings of traditional subjects (saints, angels, and images of the social hierarchy, or sentimentalized narratives) the typologies of the modern city were sordid, exotic, revealing and invited comparison with the self-image of the spectator. The ecstasy of seeing things directly led artists and photographers to prosaic aspects of everyday life that were outside or even opposed to the rituals of high culture, a deliberate snub to the aristocratic distaste for the ordinary. In various ways and in various literary, artistic and photographic modes of expression the 'ordinary' is codified as a modern response to a changing social, political environment. The Parisian poet Baudelaire celebrated what he called the heroism of modern life with its cast list of itinerant vendors, idlers, the strolling *flâneur* and the bustling crowd reflect the glamour and the misery of the modern city. The early Impressionists painted marginalized figures, workers, concrete bridges, the places of industrial labour and bohemian sites of leisure and entertainment. The admixture of workman-like brush strokes and matter-of-fact description in the painting of the 1870s in France favoured truth rather than beauty. The analogy to the camera is evident in directness of approach and the choice of contemporary life. The new urban photography of Charles Marville and later Atget (figs 1.4 and 1.5) and the photographs taken by painters themselves are indications of the overlap between the two media in the period of the Second Empire and the Third Republic in France.

The truth telling powers of the photography answered to a growing demand for documentary images. Explicit images of sexuality in representations of the nude gained currency in painting and

91

3.9 Louis Mandé Daguerre, *The Artist's Studio (Intérieur d'un Cabinet de Curiosités)*, daguerreotype, 1837, Société Française de Photographie de Paris.

in photography. The photographic imitation of the Dutch still life is in evidence in the early experiments of pioneering photographers. Static objects made a good subject for a medium requiring long exposure times and the idea that they looked like paintings added a sense of legitimacy to their appeal (fig. 3.9).

The medium of photography easily lends itself to the idea of un-mediated engagement with everyday life and throughout its history great claims to its originality and truth have been determined by its documentary potential. This ignores the prospects for staging scenes and contriving subjects in front of the camera. As noted in earlier chapters the invention of the *carte-de-visite* (fig. 3.10) is an example of a deviation from the ignoble cause of capturing reality, warts and all, and a reminder that photography was made to serve commercial interests from the moment of its creation. The staging of visual effects in the *carte-de-visite* reveals a promotional function for the individual who used photography as a medium of self-presentation. Figure 3.10 shows an accurate record of the scene but follows the conventions of the studio picture with its props and contrived body language. It represents the antithesis of the Realist aesthetic.

There is some danger in conflating photography and Realist painting. Both were established in France in the 1840s. The mechanical nature of photography appealed to painters and the Realists admired its accuracy and direct link with contemporary life. Many copied photographs and other valued their immediacy and candid way of showing things. There is, however, more to 'realism' than the simplistic idea of showing things as they really are. If realism is simply a reflection of an object, a mirror of memory, or an unmediated transcription of an object it has no value as an aesthetic category. The term realism only takes on value when it is recognized as a critical method that engages with the social context in which the medium circulates. Its value as model of transparent denotation is only effective when it is made to say something and the various ways in which it achieves this are defined by its social mediation. In this sense we are referring to 'realism' as a type of critical understanding and a strategy for social intervention. The author and critic John Roberts underlines the importance of social context in this definition of the term:

> There is no such thing as realism of a photograph, even if we can talk about some photographs containing more iconic (indexical) realist information than another. A clear, well-defined photograph of an elm tree has greater iconic realism than a fuzzy photograph of the same tree. But this does not entail a value judgement. The 'realist effects' and cognitive and aesthetic merits of such a photograph will always be context determined.
>
> (1998: 5–6)

The context always acts on the way the image is understood and a photograph or a painting is an effective way of saying something when it draws attention to itself. It achieves this when its contents are challenging or when it demonstrates formal innovation in artistic and photographic techniques.

PHOTOGRAPHIC REALISM: STRAIGHT PHOTOGRAPHY AND PHOTOGRAPHIC TRUTH

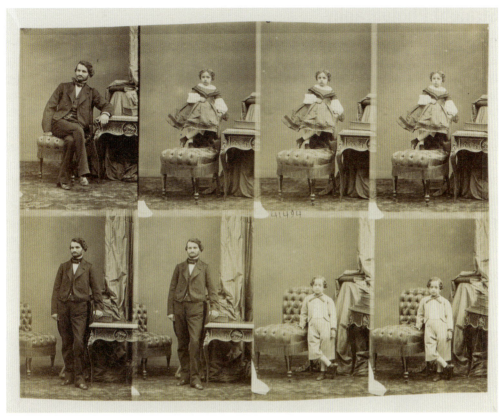

3.10 André Adolphe-Eugène Disdéri, *Portraits Sitting 41494: Docteur Magnan and His Son and Daughter*, 8 uncut *cartes-de-visite, c.* 1861. Courtesy of Art Gallery of Ontario, Toronto, Canada (purchase with donated funds in memory of Eric Steiner, 2003)/ Bridgeman Images.

Documentary photography adapted the interventionist taste for challenging subjects including occupational and social themes designed to raise the profile of the working class. In this regard the concept of documentary that emerges in twentieth-century film and photography was ideologically related to the Realist movement of the nineteenth century. 'Documentary' is a term that was invented in the 1930s to express a certain kind of campaigning journalistic approach to the medium and follows the social and political aims of the Realists. There is a direct line that connects the social orientation of Realist art and photography in America during the period of the Depression that reaches back to the grittiness of works by the French artists Daumier and Caillebotte. The campaigning and socially motivated photography that emerges in the 1930s also builds on the so-called 'straight' photography of Paul Strand and others after 1914. The sharply focused urban scenes of Strand demonstrate a desire to find a direct style that established a key orientation in twentieth-century photography. It also represented a conscious rejection of the artistic style of photography associated with the Pictorialists and a turning back to the realistic tendencies that had defined photography in its earliest years.

HISTORIES OF PHOTOGRAPHY

Straight Photography

The so-called 'straight' approach to photography is connected with a reputation for a type of work that is 'brutally direct, pure and devoid of trickery' (Stieglitz, cited in Newhall, 1949: 150). There are other defining properties determined by what theorists and practitioners regard as recognition of and loyalty to the true nature of photography. This meant avoiding Pictorialist styles of photography that now came to be associated with a misguided imitation of art. The kind of work associated with the label 'straight photography' seems to suggest a commitment to everyday life and the commonplace. There is a strong element of this in the work of Americans such as Ansel Adams, Imogen Cunningham, Strand, Walker Evans, Margaret Bourke-White, Russell Lee, Ben Shahn, Edward Sheeler, Dorothea Lange and Edward Weston – a generation of American photographers committed in their different ways to aesthetic ideals held in common. These ideas developed after 1914 included:

1 Sharp focus – a sought-after photographic effect signalled in Weston's short-lived photographic group entitled f/64, the group formed with Adams and Cunningham named after the smallest aperture size on the camera. 'f/64' gives good depth of field and sharp focus outcomes.
2 Close-ups of commonplace domestic objects, sculptural-looking vegetables which signify a preference for the mundane and the ordinary.
3 A studied avoidance of the slick imagery associated with advertising and studio portraiture.

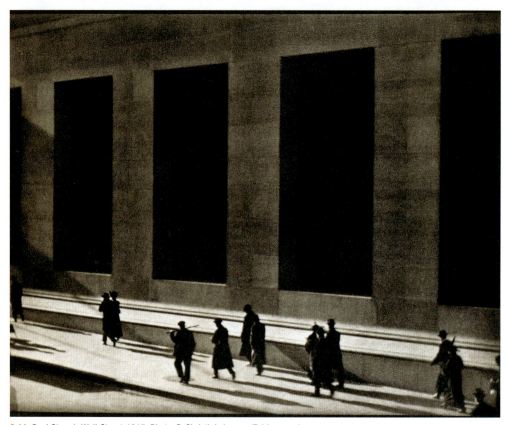

3.11 Paul Strand, *Wall Street*, 1915. Photo © Christie's Images/Bridgeman Images.

94

PHOTOGRAPHIC REALISM: STRAIGHT PHOTOGRAPHY AND PHOTOGRAPHIC TRUTH

4   A taste for American vernacular (for a discussion of the term 'vernacular' see p. 138) in the choice of subject matter to include geometrically-severe buildings, indigenous American styles of buildings as well as new technology (Sheeler's famous barns), monumental urban architecture (fig. 3.11), including skyscrapers, and sites of labour.
5   A self-consciously new and direct style that placed an emphasis on pre-visualization and 'photographic truth'; repudiation of manipulation and darkroom trickery.
6   Social engagement and political activism (fig. 3.12).

Social activism is more commonly associated with the government-led schemes of the 1930s in America in a period of economic recession, unemployment and social strife. Sharp-focused images and the American vernacular forms are important visual qualities in the photographs of Walker Evans in this period. His sharecroppers and Dorothea Lange's migrating agricultural workers have a strong anti-capitalist message that is largely ignored by later audiences. There are various ways of explaining this omission including historical distance, changing social attitudes, and the large-scale art-historical recuperation of works by leading documentary photographers from this period. When the evocative social content in a photograph is vivid and clear the process of assimilation to the aims of art often makes its imitative and didactic functions redundant. Bourke-White, Evans and Lange carried out government-supported fieldwork during the 1930s depression. Photographs made for social ends were later reconfigured as a work of art.

In his book *The Burden of Representation* the photography theorist John Tagg notes that American photography by the 1930s was rapidly becoming a tool of mass communication and notes how 'realist' images of unemployed cotton workers were made to serve political ends not in the interest of the subjects of the photographs. In Tagg's view the great iconic images of the Depression in America were exploited for short-term political ends and later recuperated as objects of reverie and nostalgia (Tagg, 1988: 182). By the 1950s images of Depression workers were often served up as 'old America' and 'true grit' reminders of lost community values (fig. 3.13).

In other words these classic images of rural America in a period of economic crisis were ultimately nothing more than sentimentalized images of an old frontier culture left behind in a rapidly changing world. The media used them to

3.12 Margaret Bourke-White, *Workers Leaving Jones & Laughlin Steel Plant at 3pm Shift*, 1936. Courtesy of The LIFE Picture Collection/Getty Images.

95

3.13 Margaret Bourke-White, *Portrait of a Sharecropper with a Bonnet on Her Head and Her Hands on the Handle of a Plow, Hamilton, Alabama*, 1937. Courtesy of The LIFE Picture Collection/Getty Images.

arouse sympathy for victims of a 'human tragedy' whilst ignoring their real aim to expose the capitalist greed that had actually caused the Depression. What looks like worthy photojournalism, designed to serve a good cause, was hijacked by the media and used as a form of government propaganda. In his book *The Burden of Representation* Tagg presents a narrative in which a politically motivated and original style of photographic reporting on a national crisis was largely defused. This perspective, however, is not the whole story. Roberts presents a counter-argument and claims that the reportorial style of photography in 1920s and 1930s America represented genuinely progressive ideals. He contrasts the documentary work of photographers like Bourke-White and Russell Lee with the rise of commercial imagery. Advertising in particular was at odds with the style and content of 'realist' trends that took inspiration from street life and oppositional working-class attitudes. As Roberts observes:

> Indeed, it is one of the distinguishing characteristics of construction of the category of documentary in the USA that progressive notions of the 'everyday' were contrasted ideologically with advertising and corporate cultural values generally ... It was not popular entertainment that was seen as the destroyer of communal working class identities, but a new voracious world of advertising, intent on replacing collective values with competitive individualist and cloyingly familial ones.
>
> (Roberts, 1998: 83)

Roberts emphasizes 'photography's powers of historical recall and remembrance' in this period, marks 'a strong sense of continuity with non-urban democratic ideals' (1998: 84) that are in some measure resistant to state paternalism and the neutralizing effect of media dissemination. Equally the work of modernist photographers like Weston sought to find a space for a kind of 'aestheticised realism' (the term is used by and Molly Nesbit, 1987: 110) that robustly avoided the stylized imagery of advertising in favour of more explicit subjects including sexuality, manual work and urban themes. It is a type of work that exploits what Roberts, in a memorable phrase, calls the 'troubling referentiality' (1998: 119) of photographs designed to debunk rather than flatter the self-image of a society in turmoil. The photographer Diane Arbus continued this counter-hegemonic tradition in the 1960s with her pictures of alienated individuals and 'freaks' which, Roberts claims, represent a later counterpoint to the sense of communality and good citizenship the photographers of the 1930s attempted to convey in America (fig. 7.5). Both are revealing in their directness and both, in different ways, offer a sense of critical engagement with the American establishment.

The Photograph as Document

The photographic document is a factual object but, as Abigail Solomon-Godeau has pointed out, 'documentary' is a term that usually carries with it a sense in which the work (photograph, film, or television programme) is designed to persuade or that it is 'animated by some kind of … humanistic impulse' (1997: xxvii). The term, 'documentary', described a kind of practice that avoids the staged artifice of advertising and publicity media. The persuasive power of the document is in its 'realism'. And yet the term documentary is not easily contained by the appearance of particular photographs. A purely factual document can find itself admired in other ways, as a 'decisive moment' or an example of poetic reverie. Documentary is an historical label for photographic and other practices connected with social and reformist projects. In most cases documentary media is endowed with a power to act as witness to the world in ways that make its content and its purpose an essential aspect of what it seeks to achieve. It is, however, an unstable category and the commitment to social reform shades into passive contemplation of the past. The documentary form's redeployment in other fields of interest including tourism, advertising, nostalgic picture postcards and art is evidence of its mutability. The grainy 'retro' look of American whisky ads is rooted in the documentary style of photography.

The documentary photographer Walker Evans, for example, presented a direct and unsentimental view of America in the period before the Second World War. The curator and author Emma Dexter has described his work as photographic realism 'that avoids romanticism, sentimentality, or nostalgia, in favour of a clear-eyed and dispassionate view' and represented an attack on the 'prevailing bourgeois money-making culture of the U.S.' at that time (Dexter, 2003: 15). The fact that his photographs express a strong anti-capitalist message did nothing to stop their assimilation into the American art market in the 1940s.

The argument against the artistic assimilation of documentary is a key issue in the history of photography since it splits practitioners, historians and readers into different groups. There are some who accept the artistic assimilation of documentary photography on the grounds of aesthetic merit (an abstract concept in any case) and those who say that documentary photographs are defined by their social imperatives, which normally lie outside the academy of art. A third position argues that social and artistic aims are not mutually exclusive and cite examples of campaigning photographers such as Mitch Epstein, Luc Delahaye and Simon Norfolk (fig. 2.9) whose museum work addresses social issues including environmental concerns and military conflict. The divide between aesthetics and politics is in fact misleading since the best documentary forms (in film and photography) rely on both elements. The dispute is not about the inherent qualities of a practice but rather more about its historical identity. From the middle years of the twentieth century onwards critics have minimized the information aspect of the photographic documentary form. The ascent of the documentary photography to high culture (and its reception in museums) promoted an aesthetic rather than a socio-historical reading of the work. Aesthetic assimilation has a powerful effect on audiences who, having no sense of its contextual meaning, see it as an historical curiosity or as an object that commands purely artistic interest.

HISTORIES OF PHOTOGRAPHY

Solomon-Godeau says 'a photographic formalist modernism (including the f/64 group and their followers) wanted to have it two ways' (1997: xxviii). First she observes: 'The privileging of so-called straight photography (no manipulation of the negative or print, no cutting or pasting, no invented tableau, no supplemental texts) mandates a photographic aesthetic that celebrates the camera's transcriptive capacities'. Second, she adds:

> But on the other hand, for photography to be art at all, it needs to be redolent of the artist's unique and exceptional subjectivity, his individual (I use the pronoun advisedly) and idiosyn-cratic *vision*. Hence the meaning of a title such as Szarkowski's homage to Garry Winogrand – *Figments from the Real World*, which attempts to render unto Caesar what is presumed to be his (the real world), and unto God the more elevated substance (Figments [of the imagination]).
>
> (1997: xxviii)

The 'transcriptive' capacities of the camera indicated in Solomon-Godeau's first statement underlines the reportorial functions of the camera. The second statement poses another way of seeing a photograph. What seems at first sight to be a photograph *of* something turns out to a tribute to the intentional act of taking it. The intentional act displaces what it seems to show: the landscape, the nude, the family gathering, etc. The 'artist' is privileged over what his picture presents. In this binary model the division between the 'real world' and the 'imagined world' is emphasized at the expense of a nuanced and flexible prospect for an interaction between to two positions. At one extreme there is an illusionistic depiction of the world and on the other hand there are the more abstract 'figments' discernible to the 'good eye' of the sensitive critic. One meaning is factual and the other is poetic and (arguably) can assume a higher value. At the heart of this dualism is the view that photographic transparency is in some ways a limiting quality when it comes to measuring the relative value of the medium. We look more closely at this issue in the next section and consider its consequences for the way we make aesthetic judgements about photographs.

TRANSPARENCY AND PHOTOGRAPHIC REALISM

Seeing the Picture or Seeing Through It?

The contemporary British philosopher Roger Scruton argues that because photographs are transparent the viewer sees only the object that it depicts (Scruton, 2008). This has two consequences: the photograph is invisible and therefore cannot (in itself) be an expressive object, and has no legitimate claim to aesthetic status. In Scruton's view manipulation is foreign to the medium and transforms photography into a kind of painting. When photography aspires to 'expressive' meaning it denies its identity *as* photography. This is an all-or-nothing position that reinforces the conventional separation between art and documentary forms of photography.

Needless to say there are challenges to this view. To argue that a photographic subject is by its nature without expressive power *as* photography is one thing. This, however, ignores the choices made in the production of the photograph including viewpoint, lens, focus, exposure values, selection and use of printing techniques. Subjectively minded and poetically inspired ways of seeing are tirelessly defended by art photographers. The 'expressive' factor is not easily dismissed since it is not opposed to the documentary objectives of photography. Photographic transparency productively assists ways of seeing the past and re-engaging with motionless objects of memory that are recalled in the image. It allows emotional attachment to lost objects, persons and the wider concerns of ancestry. There may be poignancy in the absent figure whose presence is felt in the photograph. It is an effect of memory and loss that is well known to artists, writers, or indeed anybody who visits places they used to know. There is expressive content in photography that emanates from what it shows. A well-crafted image can assist this feeling and yet an average print may achieve this equally well. On such occasions the object or familiar face manifests a feeling or an idea that is invested in what the photograph shows. The necessarily real thing that has been there before the lens carries an emotional value. The special nature of the medium may assist this kind of reading and suggest ways of reconciling the two views of the medium. A document may achieve this end as well as the work of art.

The two views of photography correspond with traditional oppositions in the arts generally such as the distinction between art-for-art's sake and art with a social purpose. As we have seen above photography can be viewed as an objective tool (a machine for looking) or a technology at the disposal of the wandering visual poet. The idea that photography has a 'special nature' is a mixed blessing for the medium. It underlines its purely mechanistic functions but leads doubters, such as Scruton, to deny its expressive efficacy. The argument that photography is not painting is, perhaps, now self-evident and we would underline this by saying that one of them is transparent and the other is not. Painting is always opaque and denies the viewer the option of looking through it. There are circumstances when an illusion occurs but the deception does not usually resist investigation. Even when painting is marvellously detailed and realistic (as in the *trompe l'oeil* example in Figure 3.5) it always turns out to be opaque. We might imagine some handmade pictures to be transparent but they are not.

Scruton's argument relies on the way a photograph stands in relation to a subject, a tree for example, that *causes* the image to come into being. The photograph is a curious object because it has a special relationship with its mechanically captured subject. This has advantages in many fields including courts of law, journalism and science, and underlines the detective content and investigatory

> ### KEY TERM: Epistemic
> The word epistemic is an adjective relating to knowledge. It derives from the word epistemology, a branch of philosophy concerned with the theory of knowledge. Through the exercise of sense or reason it is possible to gain knowledge that extends beyond what is assumed to be true or taken for granted. Knowledge of the world is derived from experience and this in turn is mediated by words and pictures (or other types of representation) used in the search for meaning. The word 'episteme' has its roots in the Greek word for 'meaning'. Meaning is not contained in pictures or in language in any simple way but it can be negotiated through a study of these things. Because of its mechanical nature the photograph is thought to have a higher level of veracity when compared with verbal or other kind of reporting. It has, we may say, an 'epistemic advantage' over other kinds of representation. Our simple faith in photographic realism can be challenged by artifice or manipulation but this is *atypical* and serves only to confirm the evidential power of the medium.

Direct and Indirect Seeing

We have emphasized the distinction between direct and indirect vision. Direct vision includes unmediated vision in the environment at large. Indirect vision includes the use of visual aids such as telescopes, binoculars and photographs. According to some theorists there is a tension between the two modes of vision. We argued in the first section of this chapter that the photograph is curiously close in some ways to un-mediated or 'ordinary' vision. We also claimed photographs may correspond with a memory of what was seen and may convincingly provide evidence for the imaginary reconstruction of the circumstances in which the picture was taken. These qualities make the photograph useful as evidence in support of a good cause, a contention or an idea expressed in words. On the other hand the photograph has limitations when compared with ordinary vision since it might be weak in conveying information about the spatial location of things in the environment. Ordinary vision is environmental and temporal, whereas the photograph is a framed object usually bound by four edges, possibly smaller than what it represents, and always influenced by its viewing context and its mode of dissemination (in a book, journal, screen or gallery).

There is little doubt that the photograph is a cultural object and yet its capacity for the mechanical harnessing of perceptual contact with things – 'no photograph without *something* or *someone*' (Barthes, 1981: 6) – influences how we see it in relation to other media. The denotative power of the photograph can be measured against other forms of depiction. Walton says 'photographic pornography is more potent than the painted variety' (2008: 14–15) and the idea of photographic witnessing, of negotiating what Barthes called something 'that has been', adds to the idea of the special nature of the medium. When it comes to the job of finding a realistic portrayal of something photography is a useful way of avoiding the slavish imitation of appearances that faced the artists of the past. That a photographer is able to do quicker and better what had been previously been done slowly by hand is important but misses the point. The French theorist André Bazin argued that the photographic image 'shares by virtue of its mode of becoming', which is essentially mechanical, 'the being of the model of which it is the reproduction: it *is* the model' (Bazin, 1980: 241). What Bazin means is that photography establishes a relationship between the viewer and the viewed that is profoundly new because the photograph has a ghostly contact with the past. Walton says photographs are not '*duplicates* or *doubles* or *reproductions* of objects, or *substitutes* or *surrogates* for them': 'My claim is that we *see*, quite literally, our dead relatives themselves when we look at photographs of them' (Walton, 2008: 22). This is a remarkable claim that he compares, quite playfully in our view, with seeing through a telescope an exploding star that died millions of years ago. But photographs are especially useful as visual aids precisely because they are transparent. The photographic picture, we are reminded, is like no other picture in at least one key respect: 'they are pictures through which we see the world' (ibid.: 24). It is way of thinking about looking at photographs shared with Roland Barthes, who wrote:

One day, quite some time ago, I happened on a photograph of Napoleon's younger brother, Jerome, taken in 1852. And I realized then, with an amazement that I have not been able to lessen since: I am looking at the eyes that looked at the Emperor.

(Barthes, 1981: 3)

We have established a view that photographs are uniquely capable of things that other ways of picturing the world cannot reach. In establishing this somewhat provocative view of the medium we have tended to play down the creative side of photography as we have foregrounded the 'transcriptive' and mechanical nature of the medium. We have shown how this established contact with the substantive object depicted in the photograph. Two things might be added as qualifiers:

1 There are persuasive arguments which challenge the claims that photography is a uniquely transcriptive medium. We will mention these below when we outline arguments that favour the idea of photography as a creative medium.
2 Not all photographs have the kind of charge that Walton and Barthes seem to claim in the quotations above. Most photographs are passed over in silence. They may be mug shots or advertisements – visual muzak – and, therefore, not the ones we collect and isolate from the mainstream. The mainstream, however, is an important object of study and sometimes the source of exceptional photography.

We have analysed the idea that photographs have a capacity to establish contact between the viewer and the viewed and followed the argument that transparency (in the photograph) is the condition that creates this.

From Transparency to Contact

Walton's discussion of photographic realism, with its privileging of transparency and contact, has both philosophical and aesthetic outcomes. The idea of contact for example is intended to establish a way of thinking about the way viewers relate to depicted objects. The suggestion is that a photograph can discharge a powerful sense of being in contact with something beyond the here and now. This is an effect that the photograph has in common with other kinds of things in the world such as holy relics (part of a saint's body or something that belonged to a saint), and icons. An icon is a type of religious picture traditionally associated with Orthodox Catholicism. It is a type of painting with a spiritual dimension and particular claims have been made for this kind of picture. The philosopher Cynthia Freeland (2008) has compared religious icons with photographs and argues that they have similar meanings and achieve similar *expressive* effects upon audiences.

In making this comparison Freeland is not saying that photographs are works of art. She argues that icons, having a purely spiritual purpose, are not aesthetic objects. Her argument is that an icon provides an important kind of contact with its referent that extends beyond description and provides a way of thinking beyond merely knowing what it is. What seems to be at stake here is the idea that pictures having such powerfully transcriptive resources allow access to deeper ways of thinking about the objects to which they refer. Freeland claims this is especially true in the case of photography which, she claims, like the icon, *expresses* rather than represents. On this view an icon functions as a *manifestation* of the depicted object to the viewer (acting in good faith) and the viewer experiences contact with it.

HISTORIES OF PHOTOGRAPHY

We take the meaning of the word 'manifestation', in this context, to mean having a power to reveal or disclose something that might otherwise remain out of reach or hidden. The claim that a photograph has this power is instructive. It enables us to think beyond the limiting idea that photographers lack artistic intention or spiritual depth, or that photographs are, in fact, nothing more than duplications of worldly things.

Realist definitions of photography have emphasized transparency and accuracy as keynote attributes of the medium. Freeland identifies a connected attribute in photography which she calls its 'psychological force' and which she defines as the capacity for 'emotional persuasiveness' in certain kinds of images. It is important to note that although this is a 'capacity' in photographs it is not restricted to the photograph and extends, in particular, to the icon. Religious studies scholar Georgia Frank has described the desire for contact with something beyond the physical senses:

> By the close of the fourth century, so many Christians had travelled to Jerusalem to see, touch and smell the holy places that it would appear that God was, indeed, visible and tactile ... These travellers drew the divine not only *in* their eyes, but also *before* the eyes, conjuring the biblical past.

(Frank, 2000: 98)

Although this statement refers to touch and smell it seems to give prominence to what Frank call 'devotional practices centred on vision'. We know, however, that our feelings and ideas are intimately connected with different senses and that photography appeals especially to tactile sensibility. Geoffrey Batchen, for example, has shown how the photo-album and other forms of domesticated photographic imagery forms 'an entanglement of touch *and* sight, that makes photography so compelling as a medium' (2001: 61).

As we have seen the traditional claim for photographic fidelity underlines a kind of mechanical view of things. This dispassionate and objective view of the medium is quite normal and most photographs are seen in this way. This view is not, however, common to all photographs and personalized, found, or selected examples have other meanings. A photo-album is an archive and as such it is a way of classifying and ordering reality. It also has a subjective and aesthetic function that provides access to the past in ways that extend beyond knowledge of family structure. It allows for everyday ways of addressing anxieties about the passing of time and the uncanny nature of things. The importance we might attach to an image is a function of personal and more general historical and material considerations. Freeland notes that we are accustomed to see pictures in a way that is determined by Westernized visual sensibility with its emphasis on accurate or realistic vision. She contrasts this with an Eastern tradition in which the beholder believes that she is in the presence of the object to which the picture refers. It is argued that we should consider a very specific and yet far-reaching idea: that a sense of presence of the subject, as a manifestation, is a component part of its value and meaning. The special nature of this view is peculiar to photography since it is normally presented in a secularist way. The religious aura that attaches to the icon is a counterpart to the psychological force of old photographs. A particularly vivid example of what we might call *a manifestation effect* is a photograph of a deceased friend or relative.

102

Depiction and Manifestation

We have argued that there are two kinds of realism: one is deceptively straightforward and relies on the idea of vivid images that look like what they represent. These are what we call realistic. The other kind is more difficult to describe since it relies on the idea of manifestation or disclosure produced by religious icons and photographs that provide a special sense of contact with the object to which they refer. The following table provides a comparative list of the two kinds of reality.

Depictive Reality	Manifest Reality
Depiction	Manifestation
Western visuality	Eastern visuality
Transparency	Opaque
Illusionistic depiction	Contact/presence
Epistemic value	Psychological force
Representational	Non-representational
Photograph	Icon

The table over-simplifies the two positions since it relies on a simple binary opposition. Following Maynard (1997) and other scholars, Freeland has in fact argued for the curious affinity of icons and photographs. Both have a capacity to engage the viewer in a way that extends beyond recognition of the depicted object. The table should allow a linking between the two when it gets to the bottom. Freeland admits that the linkage between photographs and icons is complex but provides, nevertheless, a basis for thinking beyond the assumed distinction between the manifestation functions of religious object and the depictive sense of the term realism. This link also signals ways of theorizing the contest of meaning between artistic and documentary functions of photography.

Facts and Feelings in Photography

We have relied on binary oppositions that make us think of straight or crooked pathways leading to different kinds of truth. Truth is a slippery concept anyway since it is dependent on a point of view that may change. The case of the photograph and its supposed differences with art is a central concern in art history and cultural theory. Art photographers have sought to dissolve the difference in different ways and their arguments are a mixture of special pleading and exacting debate. A simple way forward is to confront what Nelson Goodman called 'the domineering dichotomy between the cognitive and the emotive' in cultural debate (Goodman, 1982: 194). The word cognitive relates to the pursuit of hard knowledge and contrasts with the softer idea of the emotive. 'Hard' and 'soft' are suggested here with some irony since they form a conventional opposition like many others that have common currency such as truth and beauty, fact and feeling or communication and expression.

As we have seen the photograph and the icon are powerful communicators and to deny them expressive value would rely on word play. Goodman again notes

HISTORIES OF PHOTOGRAPHY

> In aesthetic experience the *emotions function cognitively* …The work of art is apprehended through the feelings as well as through the senses … Not as separate items but in combination with one another and with other means of knowing. Perception, conception and feeling intermingle and interact … How our looking at pictures and our listening to music inform what we encounter later and elsewhere is integral to them as cognitive.
>
> (Goodman, 1982: 194–199)

What we take from Goodman is the idea that art is a form of knowledge and as such relies on cognitive and technical skills. As we have seen in this chapter the struggle to define photography is centred on its medium specificity, or rather those specific characteristics that single it out. We have emphasized the mechanical nature of the medium and the photograph's causal relation to its subject. Some theorists (Scruton for example) argue this tends to repress the capacity for the medium to express ideas and feelings. Freeland on the other hand shows that photography has extraordinary psychological force and enormous resources as an expressive medium. This in turn is reliant on what she calls photography's *manifestation function* – a peculiar thing that is not undone by photographic transparency (as Scruton argues) but in contradistinction actually feeds on this. Transparency has the capacity to make us look through the image so that there is an uncanny sense of being in the presence of, say, Abraham Lincoln (fig. 3.1) in a way that no one will ever be in the presence of a painted image of Henry VIII. In the case of the Lincoln picture, or photographs in general, Freeland says 'this is not simply a likeness, but an actual appearing-before-us' (2008: 62). Transparency, however, is not an essential ingredient in pictures since the argument rests on the emotional persuasiveness of the icon that is painted and unrealistic. The key thing for Freeman is *contact* (between the depicted object and the viewer) which she claims is what gives the picture its psychologically realistic effect.

In this account the depicted object *caused* the photograph to be what it is. The viewer is really seeing something through the photograph. Freeland guides her reader away from a purely depictive model of photography since it falls on the transparency side and nullifies its psychological and expressive meanings. She accepts that we 'literally see' Abe Lincoln through the photograph, since the great man *caused* his portrait, and notes how this allows us to be in contact with him. As for the larger claim that the viewer might actually be in the presence of the man we are told this is a fiction. The subject of the portrait is instrumental in the causal history of the photograph. In the last analysis the 'special kind of seeing' that operates when we look at photographs allow us to see directly through it and establish a contact with its subject. On the other hand the idea of being in the presence of the subject is only fictional but, in the case of some photographs, may well be powerful and disarmingly affective all the same.

In shifting the weight away from the epistemic value of the photograph to an assessment of its psychological effect Freeland links the medium with the long history of the portrait. Since portraiture is an important genre in the history of painting this relocates photography in the domain of art.

The Formalist Defence of Photography as Art

The idea that photographs have a psychological effect on audiences emphasizes their emotional power. This is in addition to the descriptive functions of the photographic image, or more precisely, the psychological effect is a component part of its message. The comparison with religious icons seemed

PHOTOGRAPHIC REALISM: STRAIGHT PHOTOGRAPHY AND PHOTOGRAPHIC TRUTH

to confirm this idea of contact between the depicted object and the viewer. Freeland's undercutting of the importance of transparency in this discussion reduces what is unique to the medium – the satisfaction of seeing through the image – and returns it to more elevated way of seeing portraiture *as art*. On this view the photograph emigrates back towards painting as it did with the so-called Pictorialist photographers of the late nineteenth century who imitated painting in the hope that their work would be raised to the platform of art.

The claim that photographs have an expressive power in addition to their depictive functions is important in thinking of them as works art. This claim is a major concern for theorists and practitioners and has been since the beginnings of photography. The modernist tradition in the arts rests heavily on the claim that works of art are expressive and photographers adopting this should see the image as a projection of feeling rather that a report. The choice of subject becomes a poetic reverie and the formal properties of the print evidence of artistic sensibility. The *form* that makes up the work tends to be read on a more abstract level even though they are clear depictions of the world.

The term formalism arises out of this. It invites the viewer to dwell on the image and savour its aesthetic merits. It is of course an instructive and pleasurable way of thinking about photographs since it invites us to bring awareness of other types of pictures to the appreciation of the medium. The approach gave rise to the idea of 'pure' photography based on expressive and subjective interpretations through the eye of photographer *as artist*. The main contention is that the formalist approach tended to diminish the idea of photography as an art of social seeing ('to find the common in the everyday as a shared experience' as John Roberts puts it (1998: 76–77), whilst allowing a radical separation of form and content. In 'pure' photography theory the photograph demands to be seen as an aesthetic object in its own right. To say that a photograph is always a photograph of something and that the subject of the photograph has its own demands clearly becomes an issue. The formalist response to subject matter was to ignore or suppress its social value or significance. A photographic nude by Edward Weston (fig. 3.14) thus becomes a passive object of the aesthetic gaze

3.14 Edward Weston, *Nude*, 1936. Courtesy of Center for Creative Photography.

105

HISTORIES OF PHOTOGRAPHY

and an expression of patriarchal power. As such it reinforces a social message and yet this reading (our critical reading of the photographer's aims) is at odds with the formalist idea that as 'art' the photograph has no reference beyond the aesthetic. The artistic subject – the photographer – is placed in a higher position. John Pultz makes the point: 'Despite the clinical perfection and detachment with which Edward Weston's photography denied the subjectivity of women, his nudes were central to the construction of *his* subjectivity and *his* biography' (Pultz, 1995: 69).

The explicit meaning of the image is displaced in favour of art. In a similar way when Dorothea Lange's famous *Migrant Mother*, with its Holy Madonna comparison, became an art-historical favourite its social and political meaning gave way to the competing discourse of art. Diffusion of the social content of photographic messages is evident in the kind of photography teaching books that follow an ultra-formalist aesthetic in the middle years of the last century. The tendency was to think of photography as an unmediated aesthetic mode of seeing. In a photographic study of an apple the *Photography Magazine* publication of 1957 tells its reader that an apple can be 'seen visually'. What is meant by the tautology is explained:

> It is only how an apple actually looks. An artist knows what this means … He would not be interested in the taste, smell, or vitamin content, but only variations of shape, colour and texture. They are the visual qualities that describe the apple and the only ones he could possibly use…
>
> (Ray Bethers, 1957: 17)

In this example the apple is a prop to be used in a studio lighting class. A class in photographic technique may not be the place for analysing apple symbolism, and the entire statement is devoted to study of shapes, values and textures, pattern, abstract notions of space and movement, rhythm and the expressive effects of directional forces in 'good' photography. A text of this kind is only symptomatic and offered as a practical way of thinking about how pictures are made to function independently of what they depict as if the two dimensions of the photograph were innocently disconnected from the world outside the frame. Weston's treatment of the female nude is an example of this wilful separation of image and context. The following is a typical statement of this kind:

> Whatever advantages a photographer might possess in the way of technical skill and knowledge, first class equipment or the choice of a wide variety of subject matter, he is not likely to produce good pictures if he [sic] lacks the ability to 'see'.
>
> (Norman Hall in Bethers, 1957: 8)

Photographic seeing was an ideal for the European avant-garde who believed in photography as a kind of enhanced vision and means of gaining a closer view, experiencing unusual angles, thinking about frozen motion and a range of experimental effects including photomontage. The camera offered new ways of seeing the world and displaced painting as the medium of the avant-garde. Advanced artistic method was closely aligned with photography which in turn was linked with advanced or revolutionary politics. In the American context the formalist photographers such as Weston resisted this tendency and argued for a poetic and self-expressive approach to the medium. Subjects in his work, including desert landscapes and nudes, were artistic props made to serve the more serious purpose of art. In this approach the role of the artist as form-giver supersedes any value that attaches to the subject itself as the work becomes an exercise in self-expression.

Weston's tendency towards abstraction contrasts with Freeland's description of the way photographs can induce a sense of the subject being present to the viewer. In the example of the photo-album there is a

106

feeling of contact with the past. Barthes recalls the photographic image of his dead mother as a child 'caught in a History' (1981: 64), and speaks of photography giving him, 'for once … a sentiment as certain as remembrance' (ibid.: 70). And Walton speaks of his experience of seeing a photograph of President Lincoln, not as a study in form or expressive interpretation, but rather as if he is looking at the man himself.

The Strangeness of the Photograph

The idea of photographic seeing has two key meanings. The first meaning places an emphasis on the way photography, like other lens-based visual tools, aids vision through its capacity to capture detail not readily visible to the naked eye. The second meaning emphasizes the romantic idea of the photographer's eye which sees in a poetic or original way. One definition has a scientific emphasis and the other is more closely connected with the traditional idea of the artist as a kind of seer or mystical persona. Despite criticism in recent years the image of the art photographer as a romantic visionary is still dominant. We have tried in this chapter to qualify this as caricature or simplification. In discussing the concept of realism we noted photography as a direct way of showing things works against 'self-expression'. Photographs can create moods or feelings in the viewer but in general the message they transmit is contingent upon the object it captures. It is in this sense rooted in social expectation and common experience. This aspect of photography is in fact one of its great virtues.

Poetic reverie may intervene in the artificial construction of strangeness in photography but the photograph is essentially a product of the optical-chemical process. The photograph's strangeness results from the manner of its making and the power of the photographic image is a product of its causal origin. It is the photographic process that produces a contact with the past. This is how the strangeness is made. Anybody can achieve it! As we have argued, photography's unique way of picturing the world challenges its reputation for being an impassive mechanical process. The reality we are in touch with in the photograph is in the past. As Bazin said, the photograph is a means for the embalming of time (Bazin, 1980: 242) and it achieves this *because* it is an impassive mechanical process. It is exactly this matter-of-fact character in the photograph that disguises its twin properties: transparency and capacity for contact with its causal object. According to Bazin the Surrealists discovered in photography an image that is 'a reality of nature, namely, an hallucination that is also a fact' (ibid.: 243).

The Surrealists represented a romantic revolt against common sense reality and yet they embraced photography. It was not, however, the mere capture of facts that interested them but the strangeness of the factual. Their celebration of the 'straight' and inartistic work of Eugene Atget (figs 1.4 and 1.5) is evidence that whatever fascinates is to be found in the empty streets of Paris defamiliarized by the camera's gaze, as if they were crime scenes or places recalled in a dream. Utrillo's paintings, or anybody's paintings, of Paris had not yet done this. Roberts notes how the ordinary or the banal can be transformed into allegory by photographic means (1998: 102–103). The forensic objective gaze of the camera never exhausts its subject.

CONCLUSION

By its nature photography is always a kind of realism (with or without a capital R) and only ceases to be this when it merges with other practices. In this chapter we have asked the reader to consider

HISTORIES OF PHOTOGRAPHY

photography at two opposites ends of the spectrum of possible meaning attaching to the term realism. At one end the capture of the concrete look of things with an emphasis on the 'the world of things'. At the other end we have noted the formalist idea of the photograph as an aesthetic object which requires the viewer think more deeply about ways of looking that are particular to the medium itself. The first kind is good for noting how photography is a great social witness and an effective visual tool. The two kinds of realism are not, however, bound to be in opposition. Expression and communication have similar projects and often shape each other. The great beauty of Walker Evans's' famous tenant family prints from the 1930s is not lessened by their political content. Photography dissolves the gap between form and content. The idea of 'looking through' a photograph is partly metaphorical because we also see the framing edge and the textual or spatial context of the picture; and yet we always see the thing itself, the object that forms the image. It is usually a familiar flat form of a conventional size and it is transparent and so we actually see the thing that made it (the person or the scene). Whilst holding the photograph in our hand, or gazing at a screen, there is contact with the past. Take another look at President Lincoln (fig. 3.1). How do you see him? Is something there? Is it hallucination or a fact?

SUMMARY OF KEY POINTS

- Photographs are in a fundamental way different to paintings, drawings and all kinds of handmade images. The distinction is vividly experienced in a comparison of painted and photographic portraits.
- When photographs were first seen they changed the way audiences thought about pictures. Photographs correspond point by point with nature and have a physical connection with what they refer to. This in turn created a new level of pictorial accuracy, especially in the daguerreotype, and a measure of realism for all types of pictures.
- The invention of photography also made audiences think more deeply about the way pictures are made and how far they are determined by the skills of the artist.
- There is a sense in which a photograph is a provider of 'straight' access to objects in a process which is unmediated and direct. This has a strong bearing on its truth claims and its value as evidence in many fields including law, journalism and science. This property underlines the investigatory functions of the medium but arguably weakens its prospects as an expressive medium.
- The pursuit of visual accuracy in the arts has a long history and examples of naturalistic representation can be found in ancient Greek pottery and sculpture. The creation of photography in the nineteenth century is sometimes seen as a fulfilment of this Western tradition in the visual arts.
- Attempts to imitate the appearances of things have always been constrained by pictorial conventions and established ways of making pictures. The mind of the artist is never an innocent blank and artists always look at other paintings as well looking at nature.
- Reliance on conventional styles of picture making in the past was not always seen as an obstruction to the curiosity shown by artists who developed skills in copying the appearance of things in the world. Nature provided a starting point for the development of what the art historian Ernst Gombrich called the 'tricks of naturalism'.
- Mathematical perspective is a name given to the fifteenth-century pictorial methods that allowed artists to make a flat plane resemble objects in space. Combined with modelling in light and shade and the addition of strong foreground colour an illusion is often convincingly achieved. It created a visual effect sometimes called verisimilitude or fidelity to visual reality that is one aspect of the

PHOTOGRAPHIC REALISM: STRAIGHT PHOTOGRAPHY AND PHOTOGRAPHIC TRUTH

meaning we attach to the term realism. The term realism has thus come to refer to a detached and analytical method of documenting the appearance of things.

- In later definitions of the term realism (or Realism) in the nineteenth century the idea of objective or impartial ways of seeing shaded into closer investigation of modern life. The invention of photography in this period inspired painters and writers to explore modernity with scientific zeal. They rejected fantasy subjects in favour of social realities including 'low brow' subjects taken from 'ordinary' life.
- The staged techniques used in production of the *carte-de-visite* contrasted with the Realists' quest for truth and honesty. The use of photography as a form of social media anticipates later developments including its mass communication, advertising and entertainment.
- The so-called 'straight' photographers in America in the early twentieth century built on the Realist taste for commonplace objects and urban realities. Avoiding the slick styles of studio photography and the 'artistic' styles of the Pictorialists they restricted themselves to what they considered purely photographic methods. In other words no manipulation, cropping, or blurring of the image. There is strong social content in the work of this period and yet many demanded the photograph be treated as a purely aesthetic object. We have argued this was a negation of Realist methods and photographers such as Edward Weston undervalued the imitative and didactic potential of photography.
- Certain theorists have argued that the photograph is transparent and the viewer sees the depicted object but not the picture itself. The photograph is therefore invisible and lacks expressive meaning.
- It has been argued that this approach to the photograph ignores the way photographers exploit the technical properties of the medium and in so doing make aesthetic choices regarding viewpoint, exposure, lens, and printing quality.
- A more subtle form of the expression theory of photography emphasizes the way photographs uniquely establish contact between the viewer and the object viewed. The experience of direct contact with the past events allows a deeper way of thinking about the objects and people to which they refer. In this view the photographs bring back the past and establish emotional contact with objects and the histories to which they refer.
- The manifestation effect allows the viewer to enjoy a level of abstraction beyond the literal reading of the photograph.
- A manifestation effect also allows for a contemplative and aesthetic reappraisal of photography. It is a way of contesting photography's reputation for detached and analytical method of documenting the appearance of things.
- The term 'realism' clings to the medium but as we have noted it is an historical label rather than an ontological category. Nevertheless, the photograph is a special kind of image because it is an extension of its subject and is co-substantial with it. This factor might explain why it retains its independence as a practice. It is also a basis for a definition of what makes a photograph real.

REFERENCES

Barthes, Roland (1979) *Image-Music-Text*, trans. Stephen Heath, London: Fontana/Collins.

—— (1981), *Camera Lucida: Reflections on Photography*, trans. Richard Howard, New York: Hill and Wang.

HISTORIES OF PHOTOGRAPHY

Batchen, Geoffrey (2001), *Each Wild Idea: Writing, Photography, History*, Cambridge Mass., and London: the MIT Press.

Bazin, André (1980) 'The Ontology of the Photographic Image', in Alan Trachtenberg (ed.) *Classic Essays on Photography*, New Haven, CT: Leete's Island Books, pp. 237–244.

Berger, John (1972), *Ways of Seeing*, London: BBC and Harmondsworth: Penguin.

Bethers, Ray (1957) *Photo-Vision*, London: Photography Magazine.

Campany, David (2007) *Art and Photography*, Oxford: Phaidon.

Dexter, Emma (2003) 'Photography Itself', in Emma Dexter and Thomas Weski (eds) *Cruel and Tender: The Real in Twentieth Century Photography*, London: Tate Publishing, pp. 15–21.

Frank, Georgia (2000) 'The Pilgrim's Gaze', in Robert S. Nelson (ed.) *Visuality Before and After the Renaissance: Seeing as Others Saw*, Cambridge: Cambridge University Press, pp. 98–115.

Freeland, Cynthia (2008) 'Photographs and Icons', in Walden (ed.), pp. 50–69.

Gombrich, E.H. (1984) *The Story of Art*, Oxford: Phaidon.

——(1986) *The Image and the Eye: Further Studies in the Psychology of Pictorial Representation*, Oxford: Phaidon.

——(1987) *Art and Illusion: A Study in the Psychology of Visual Representation*, Oxford: Phaidon.

Goodman, Nelson (1976) *The Languages of Art*, Indianapolis: Hackett.

——(1982) 'Art and Inquiry', in Charles Harrison and Francis Frascina (eds) pp. 191–201.

Harrison, Charles and Frascina, Francis (eds) (1982) *Modern Art and Modernism: A Critical Anthology*, London: Harper and Row.

Hughes, Robert (1980) *The Shock of the New*, London: BBC.

Kracauer, Siegfried (1976) *Theory of Film: The Redemption of Reality*, Oxford: Oxford University Press.

Lemagny, Jean-Claude and Rouillé, André (eds) (I987) *A History of Photography: Social and Cultural Perspectives*, trans. Janet Lloyd, Cambridge: Cambridge University Press.

Maynard, Patrick (1997) *The Engine of Visualization: Thinking Through Photography*, Ithaca, NY and London: Cornell University Press.

Mitchell, W.J.T. (1987) *Iconology: Image, Text, Ideology*, Chicago: University of Chicago.

Nesbit, Molly (1987) 'Photography, Art and Modernity', in Jean-Claude Lemagny and André Rouillé (eds) pp. 103–123.

Newhall, Beaumont (1949) *The History of Photography: From 1839 to the Present Day*, New York: Museum of Modern Art.

Nochlin, Linda (1971) *Realism*, Harmondsworth: Penguin.

Pultz, John (1995), *Photography and the Body*, London: Orion.

Roberts, John (1998) *The Art of Interruption: Realism, Photography and the Everyday*, Manchester University Press.

Scharf, Aaron (1974) *Art and Photography*, Harmondsworth: Penguin.

Scruton, Roger (2007) 'Photography and Representation', in Walden (ed.) pp. 138–166.

Solomon-Godeau, Abigail (1997) *Photography at the Dock: Essays in Photographic History, Institutions, and Practices*, Minneapolis: University of Minnesota Press.

Tagg, John (1988) *The Burden of Representation: Essays on Photographies and Histories*, Houndsmills, Basingstoke, and London: Macmillan.

Walden, Scott (ed.) (2008) *Photography and Philosophy: Essays on the Pencil of Nature*, Malden, MA and Oxford: Blackwell.

Walton, Kendal L. (2008) 'Transparent Pictures: On the Nature of Photographic Realism', in Walden (ed.) pp. 14–49.

CHAPTER 4
THE CONSTRUCTED PHOTOGRAPH

In 1840 the French photographer Hippolyte Bayard developed a direct positive printing process, which required long exposure times, sometimes up to 12 minutes. Louis-Jacques-Mandé Daguerre's eponymous invention (*la daguerréotype*) made him instantly famous, whilst Bayard's similar process was largely ignored or rather overlooked by the *Académie des Sciences*, which favoured Daguerre. Lack of recognition motivated him to make a curious, staged photograph entitled *Self Portrait as a Drowned Man* (fig. 4.1). The extreme length of exposure suggests the figure must be dead and this is how he is humorously depicted. The picture is both a retort to Daguerre and a reflexive statement on the limitations of the medium at that time. Bayard posed himself for this picture with eyes closed (blinking would register as a blur) suggesting his own mock suicide. The title of the work creates a fictional reading for the image and reinforces its constructed meaning.

4.1 Hippolyte Bayard, *Autoportrait en noyé (Self Portrait as a Drowned Man)*, 1840. Courtesy of Collection Société Française de Photographie de Paris.

INTRODUCTION

In this chapter we concentrate on photographs that are constructed or staged. We trace the rise of the constructed photograph from the first staged images in early photography to the present-day use of seamless digital compositing in the work of contemporary artists. We also look at how the Surrealists constructed images out of found photographs, the influence of postmodern theory and the emergence of a new wave of artists using photography in the 1980s. The use of constructed photography within advertising imagery is analysed. This chapter examines the work of practitioners who prefer to 'make', or construct, rather than 'take' photographs. As Michael Köhler notes with this kind of photography: 'Scenes are staged deliberately for the camera and a fictional photographic reality is thus created' (Köhler, 1995: 7).

Defining Constructed Photography

To 'construct' means to build or make by putting together various parts. A constructed photograph is one that is formed by bringing together discrete elements to create a final picture. The photographer creates a scene for the camera, often carefully selecting location, actors and lighting just as a film director would. To the degree that the scene is constructed the idea of photography as a 'window of reality' is dispensed with. There are many types of constructed or directed photographs. For example it could be something staged in front of the camera, such as a performance involving the photographer or actors. The 'stage' could be a real place, or a 'set'. In some cases, constructed photographs are created within miniature sets, using scale models and figures. Another type of construction is photomontage, a type of composite image or scene created by collaging different photographs together. Early darkroom techniques such as combination printing and modern digital manipulation allow seamless montage photographs constructed out of tens if not hundreds of photographs. These differing approaches have one thing in common: a unique image results out of the construction of separate elements. Köhler in his book *Constructed Realities* summarizes the constructed approach:

> Practitioners of staged and constructed photography invent their motifs, freely combining the real and the invented, photography and painting, photography and stage design, weaving historical and mythological references into their works, and do not hesitate for a moment to manipulate reality. They do not behave destructively, however, but investigatively and analyti-cally. The question is not what reality is, but what modes of representing it are available.
>
> (Köhler, 1995: 8)

These practices are in principle directly opposed to the idea of 'straight' photography discussed in the previous chapter.

In this chapter the adoption of the various approaches to image construction is mapped onto socio-political and wider art world contexts. We also discuss relevant photographic technological developments or limitations, such as the invention and application of digital imaging in the wider field of photographic practice. The practice of constructing a photograph is important to consider as a key strategy in both art and commercial photography since photography's invention.

HISTORIES OF PHOTOGRAPHY

The First Constructed Photographs

The idea of constructing or making a photograph has been in practice since photography's invention. The long exposure times required in early photography dictated the type of subject matter that could be recorded. This explains why architecture and still life are widely represented in early photography. The earliest daguerreotype type process required an exposure of 3 to 15 minutes, which meant portraiture was impossible. The first daguerreotype was a constructed still life scene including plaster casts and wicker baskets lit by natural light (Louis Mandé Daguerre's *The Artist's Studio* of 1837 can be found in Figure 3.9). In his careful arrangement of the scene, and his selection of objects, Daguerre worked like a still-life painter as he considered the composition. The daguerreotype chemical process and lens technology was gradually improved to allow shorter exposures of less than one minute. This allowed for 'staged' portraiture, where the sitter was normally held still by an uncomfortable neck brace, which was always kept out of shot.

Henry Fox Talbot's first paper negative, the famous *Latticed Window* of 1835, is a depiction of inanimate objects. As he improved his calotype process to allow for slightly faster exposure times, he began to produce figurative work in which he posed models around the grounds of Lacock Abbey. We might call this turn to the figurative an example of early constructed scenes, since a degree of staging was involved. His subjects had to hold their pose for around one minute, which meant the poses were neither natural nor relaxed. In a manner of speaking we can say that Talbot became a director as well as photographer of these outdoor scenes.

Following the announcement of the first photographs of Daguerre and Talbot, the Frenchman Hippolyte Bayard also developed a direct-positive printing process. Figure 4.1 shows Bayard's constructed image, *Self Portrait as a Drowned Man.* This picture represents a reflexive statement on the limitations of the medium at that time. For example, the need for very long exposure times limited the types of subject matter depicted, most commonly to inanimate objects and staged scenes.

Post-mortem Constructed Photography

Bayard's staged picture of his own death brings to mind a popular practice of 'constructed' post-mortem photography in the Victorian era (1837–1901). Photographic technology improved greatly in this era, but early processes were expensive and few were able to take pictures of family members. The high infant mortality rate in this era inspired the strange practice of photographing the dead. Families considered a post-mortem photograph as a last chance to have a family group portrait taken, and often posed alongside the child's corpse. These photographs are further early examples of constructed images. The family group posed in the studio; living members of the family posed with the deceased child, or other family member, as if he or she were still alive (fig. 4.2). Sometimes eyes were even painted on the eyelids! This kind of fantasy reconstruction of the family relates to an earlier art-historical convention called the *memento mori.* The photograph preserves the memory of the deceased and yet reminds the viewer of his or her own mortality.

114

THE CONSTRUCTED PHOTOGRAPH

4.2 Typical Victorian-era post-mortem family portrait, private collection.

> **KEY TERM: Combination Printing**
> Early black and white film captured a narrow tonal range, and landscape photographs often suffered from loss of cloud detail in the skies. Victorian photographers frequently used a technique to combine two or more negatives with different exposures to get a wider tonal range. In the 1850s Gustave le Gray created perfectly exposed seascapes, using combinations of differently exposed negatives of the same scene. Combination printing involved the masking off of various areas of the print to allow selective printing of specific areas of the photographic paper. Using this method, early photographers soon saw the creative potential in combining not just different exposures of the same scene but different scenes entirely (fig. 4.3).

Constructing a Photograph from Multiple Negatives

Swedish-born photographer Oscar Rejlander (1813–1875), pioneer of the combination printing process, is considered to be the 'father' of constructed photography. We have described above the idea of staging or directing an image. In his most famous work, *The Two Ways of Life* (fig. 4.3), Rejlander took this strategy further by not only staging a scene but also combining scenes using a technique called combination printing. This image comprises over 30 separate negatives, arranged and printed on a single sheet of paper, so that the image appears as if it were one photograph. The scene is set on a stage, with hired actors and Rejlander himself role-playing as various characters in the scene, depicting both a

115

4.3 Oscar Gustave Rejlander, *The Two Ways of Life,* c. 1857, albumen silver print. © Photo: Moderna Museet, Stockholm.

virtuous life to the right of the image and a life of 'vices' to the left (Pauli, 2006: 20). It is a scene based on Raphael's sixteenth-century *School of Athens*, a famous wall painting in the Vatican. Rejlander's picture has an elaborate meaning that compares with the moralistic narrative art of the Victorian period. In taking his inspiration from a Renaissance 'masterpiece' Rejlander attempted to locate his picture in the best traditions of high culture. Queen Victoria liked the print so much she bought it.

In the Victorian period the *tableau vivant* ('living picture') was an artistic recreation enjoyed by the educated classes. Actors would stand in static poses on stage mimicking famous paintings. Rejlander's *The Two Ways of Life* is the first *tableau vivant* to be photographed in the specific manner of photographing the models separately and combining the negatives. This allowed Rejlander and the actors to play multiple roles. It was a process that allowed for the image to be photographed over a period of time and 'combined' in a way that imitates the addition of detail upon detail in the making of a painting.

Henry Peach Robinson is another Victorian photographer who used the combination printing technique. His *Fading Away* (1858) is composed of five negatives to make the whole scene (fig. 4.4). It shows a cloudy sky through a window. If the scene had been made through a single exposure, the window would have been out of the brightness range the film was capable of capturing. This example of a combination print is an early precursor to the later development of high dynamic range (HDR) techniques used in digital imaging in movie and stills formats. Advanced HDR imaging, much like combination printing, blends multiple digital exposures of the same scene to create an ultra-wide tonal range (a range that is still often impossible to capture even on the most expensive digital sensor). A detailed case study on digital imaging technologies is to be found in Case Study 2: 'The Digital Camera', pp. 141–8 below.

THE CONSTRUCTED PHOTOGRAPH

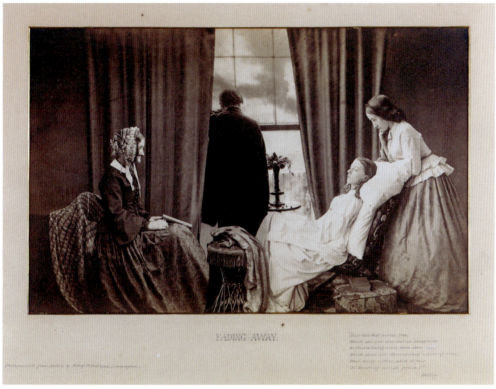

4.4 Henry Peach Robinson, *Fading Away*, 1858. Courtesy of the Royal Photographic Society/National Media Museum/Science and Society Picture Library.

Fading Away is interesting not only for its wide tonal range but also for its subject matter. A young girl is dying of a terminal illness. Audiences might have interpreted this as the common disease tuberculosis, and that would have been shocking to a mid-nineteenth-century audience because many families had suffered losses from the disease. For it to be made photographically 'real' is perhaps deliberately challenging. This work is different from Rejlander's theatrical rendering of *The Two Ways of Life*. *Fading Away* is a domestic scene rather than a 'stage', and there is an ambiguity as to whether the subjects are actors. It is vivid in a new way that makes the viewer see through the picture to what appears to be a real event. It is 'constructed' in two ways: first, it is a combination print, using different negatives for the sky and people, and, second, Peach Robinson appears to have instructed actors to play out their different roles.

Photographic Amusement Postcards

At the turn of the nineteenth century there was a craze for photographic amusements and trick photography, such as double exposures, 'spirit' photographs (where the trace of the previous sitter remained on the daguerreotype plate) and composite pictures (Ades, 1976: 7). The composite photographs were made using the same combination printing technique as described above, and became increasingly

117

4.5 William H. Martin, *Taking Our Geese to Market*, 1909. Courtesy of Wm. B. Becker Collection/American Museum of Photography.

popular for their comedy and entertainment value. The popularity of this kind of imagery led to numerous postcards being circulated with very strange juxtapositions. For example a postcard from 1905 depicts Piccadilly Circus, London, relocated to Venice. This is achieved by splicing two scenes together. At first glance the image appears like a standard tourist photograph, until Venice's waterways are seen flowing around the out-of-place London landmark. William H. Martin's 1909 postcard image *Taking Our Geese to Market*, depicts giant geese, as big as horses, being taken on their way to market (fig. 4.5). This kind of approach uses the same image construction technique as Rejlander and Robinson, but differs in its surreal depiction of reality. In *Photography: A Cultural History,* Mary Warner Marien describes how these types of amusement postcards suited social taste at that time. Marien notes: 'The postcard range originated a type of popular image that would not have seemed humorous in photography's first decade, when trifling with the appearance of reality was considered misplaced' (Marien, 2002: 171).

It is worth noting that the previous examples we have studied in this chapter require suspension of disbelief. In other words Rejlander and Robinson sought to disguise the constructed nature of their prints. Martin's goose picture is more playful in its reflexive use of the construction. There is a morbidly dark sense of humour in Bayard's *Drowned Man* (fig. 4.1), but early photography was earnestly committed to an accurate 'capture' of the moment rendered in detail. The established idea of photographic truth has a certain gravitas that was not seriously challenged by humour until the medium had become accessible to wider audiences in the early twentieth century. Photographic experimentation was used for comic effect at this time. The broadening of access and commercialization also caused a reaction amongst series practitioners. Many turned to image manipulation and artistic experimentation.

THE CONSTRUCTED PHOTOGRAPH

The Cottingley Fairies

In 1917 two young cousins, Elsie Wright and Frances Griffiths, from Cottingley, Bradford, in Yorkshire, made a series of constructed photographs (fig. 4.6). The series of five images are the famously faked Cottingley Fairies images. Wright and Griffiths cut cardboard illustrations of fairies and propped them up posed in the garden, as if they were real, and included themselves in the pictures. The author and spiritualist Arthur Conan Doyle published these photographs as illustrations for an article he had written on fairies. There was a mystery surrounding these pictures for many years until the cousins revealed the story behind their construction. To trained and cynical modern eyes these pictures immediately look faked. At that time, however, the photographic image was more readily accepted as truth, as were tales of the supernatural. Even famous authors were fooled.

The Cottingley Fairies images are an early example of constructing a photograph to create an alternative reality. They are also good examples of the way photographs, whatever their provenance, have an effect on audiences willing to be persuaded by their apparent truth-telling meanings. It may be worth considering how much, or how little, audiences have changed. As we will see below composite methods are widely used in art and commercial photography in the twenty-first century. How do we read digital images? This is an issue discussed later in the book (see Case Study 5, 'The Designed Photograph' in Part 4, pp. 357–68). It might, at this point, however, be worth thinking through this issue. To what extent do contemporary artists like Jeff Wall and Andreas Gursky assume that audiences will know their works (figs 4.12 and 4.13) are digitally enhanced?

4.6 Elsie Wright and Frances Griffiths, *Alice and the Fairies*, July 1917. Courtesy of SSPL via Getty Images.

HISTORIES OF PHOTOGRAPHY

Surrealism and Constructed Photography

The term 'constructed photograph' was first used by Walter Benjamin, in his 1931 essay, *A Short History of Photography.* In this text he makes a plea to 'straight' photographers to consider constructing a scene to be photographed. Benjamin quotes from Bertolt Brecht, a contemporary German playwright, theatre director and poet who had pioneered a new 'constructed' and anti-illusionist style of theatre. Benjamin observes:

> As Brecht says: 'The situation becomes complicated, because a simple reproduction of reality says less than ever about reality. A photograph of the Krupp works or the AEG says next to nothing about these institutions. True reality has slipped over into the functional. The materialization of human relationships, for instance in the factory, no longer offers the latter. And so something does indeed have to be *constructed,* something "artificial", "formed". And thus art is indeed just as necessary'. We must credit the Surrealists with having trained the pioneers of such photographic construction.

(Benjamin, 1931: 526)

Benjamin's point relates to the fact that photographs are made to produce meaning in specific contexts and in ways that are defined by that context. For example, a caption made of words directs meaning and provides anchorage or a thought for the picture. This may influence the way it is read. A photograph without a caption is a kind of open sign waiting for meaning to be attached to it. Its content will of course play an important part in constructing its meaning but it is always constrained by its potential use. This is a key point in a lot of so-called postmodernist theory that challenges the truth-value of all systems of representation, including photography. This point is discussed in Chapter 8.

Photography was an important vehicle for the Surrealists who experimented with the medium. They were captivated by the strange ambiguity of photographs that are both 'fact' and image at the same time. This duality makes them different to other pictures that are mediated by the hand because the photograph is mechanically produced: it takes the viewer back to the object in a uniquely original way of picturing the world. For many, this characteristic is a thing to be emphasized in 'straight' photographs. On the other hand some experimented with the 'facticity' of the photograph and sought to translate it into new kinds of picture construction. Facticity, the quality or condition of being a fact, was an inherent quality of early photography. The Surrealists Man Ray and Maurice Tabard used techniques such as photograms, solarization, double exposure, combination printing and photomontage to create dream-like and deviant images. René Magritte used photographic techniques such as staging and combination printing in the invention of ideas for his painting (see fig. 6.11). Hans Bellmer constructed dolls, which in turn became the subject of photographs. His photographic works are uncanny, like the Victorian *tableaux vivants*, with disturbing, ball-jointed dolls. Many critics have noted the inherent strangeness of photography. Susan Sontag, for example, notes that *every* photograph, whether constructed or 'straight' is 'surreal': 'Surrealism,' she claims, 'lies at the heart of the photographic enterprise: in the very creation of a duplicate world, of a reality in the second degree, narrower but more dramatic than the one perceived by natural vision' (Sontag, 1979: 52).

Sontag's comment is a powerful reminder that the terminology used in discussion about photography influences how we think about the medium. The categories of 'real' and 'true' are often used in quite relative ways, and as indicated above, we may be predisposed not to trust the reality effect of

THE CONSTRUCTED PHOTOGRAPH

photographs. We are, nevertheless, still very inclined to stick to common sense ways of talking about photography, and certainly the history of the medium is still effectively organized in ways that reflect this. For our purposes we are, therefore, agreed that in the century of photography's invention, and throughout the greater part of the last century, photographers were categorized into two camps: those who sought to replicate reality (as discussed in Chapter 3) and those who constructed a version of reality for the camera.

Photomontage as a Constructed Photograph

The Dadaists, an avant-garde art movement that pre-dates Surrealism, used the term photomontage to describe their collages made of found photographs. The Dadaists preferred to use 'found' material to create art works. They considered the photograph to be a readymade image, which they could in turn cut up and collage to construct 'a chaotic, explosive image, a provocative dismembering of reality' (Ades, 1976: 7). In the 1970s Martha Rosler began constructing politically charged photomontages. In her project *House Beautiful: Bringing the War Home* Rosler constructed collages from found photographs of the home cut out of lifestyle and design magazines and news photography from the Vietnam War (fig. 4.7). She carefully collaged the scenes to create alien and absurd spaces combining affluent Western-style interiors with the violence of war playing out through the window. Rosler often placed a female protagonist in the images which address the American taste for war and the domestic stereotype

4.7 Martha Rosler, *Cleaning the Drapes*. From the series *House Beautiful: Bringing the War Home [In Vietnam]*, 1967–72. Courtesy of Mitchell-Innes and Nash.

121

of Western women. By the mid-1980s Rosler, along with Allan Sekula, was part of a movement working within a genre called the 'new social documentary' that considered photography, specifically constructed photography, to have an important role in representing and questioning social issues (Marien, 2011: 438). This is an area of post-conceptual art practice that seeks to use photography to transmit ideas rather than as a medium of self-expression. In using found photographs Rosler draws attention to the medium itself and in so doing challenges the common sense idea of photographic truth. This kind of image has self-irony that is intended to make viewers think about how they read images as well as thinking about their ostensible subject matter.

The work of the New Documentarists relates closely to later developments including the work of photographers who photograph in war zones and exhibit their work in art galleries. For example Luc Delahaye and Simon Norfolk (fig. 2.9) create large-scale prints solely for the gallery wall. This raises issues about the ethical uses of photography and a consideration of the limitations of art practice. Rosler has recently made new work for her *Bringing the War Home* project which focuses interest on the war in Iraq and Afghanistan. War photography is discussed in Chapter 2 and further analysis of Rosler's work appears in Chapter 8.

Postmodernism and Constructed Realities

Postmodernism is a term that is notoriously difficult to define as it relates to a wide range of practices including architecture, design, literature and the visual arts. The term literally means 'after modernism'. It was a reaction against modernist values such as realism and formalism (for a discussion of these terms see Chapters 2 and 3). In literature, postmodernism is sometimes linked to the idea of 'intertextuality', a term that is used to describe the tendency of writers and artists to borrow images and ideas from existing texts. As an example of this we have discussed Rosler's photomontage technique, which is a kind of image redefinition. Earlier examples of one medium reflecting on another medium (often with a sense of irony and critical comment) can be found in the 'straight' photographs of billboards and signage in the work of American photographers such as Walker Evans and Margaret Bourke-White in the 1930s (see fig. 6.4). Intertextuality also refers to a reader's prior knowledge or memory of existing texts subconsciously referenced when reading new texts. This point also relates to the way the Surrealists understood that photographs contain layers of meaning which reach back into sometimes quite mysterious feelings about the past.

Many practitioners using photography in the 1960s to 1980s were informed by postmodernism and intertextuality as a way of consciously referring to other systems of representation or meaning, for example painting, literature and cinema. This was intended to have layers of personal, social and political references for the viewer. For many this way of working was in opposition to 'straight' or Pictorialist photography. The postmodern era made artists reconsider the strengths of constructed or staged photography as a method of knowingly referencing other systems of meaning. David Campany, in his book *Art and Photography,* notes: 'For many artists the overtly constructed image, owing as much to cinematography as photography, has allowed a depiction of the particular while alluding to more general social forces' (Campany, 2007: 29). Marien agrees with Campany and notes: '…the omnipresence of movies and television, in which a director orchestrates scenes, may have amplified photographers' desire to direct for the still camera' (Marien, 2011: 455).

Cindy Sherman and Staged Photography

Cindy Sherman is a contemporary American artist who uses the medium of photography. She is an example of a postmodernist who challenges the truth-value of photography. In her famous *Untitled Film Stills* (1977–80) project, Sherman photographed herself posing in costumes, including wigs and makeup. The project comprises 69 black and white photographs. She staged the scenes both on location and in the studio to look like film stills referencing the feel of cinema from the 1940s and 1950s (fig. 4.8). Sherman's early work was centred on the representation of women in film and included staged representations of the 'anxious housewife', the 'troubled heroine' and the '*femme fatale*'.

Marien comments on Sherman's film stills: 'Her *faux* film fragments played up the notion of the postmodern copy and its opposition to the ideas of invention and genius' (Marien, 2011: 444). As with Rosler the meaning of the work centres on the act of looking and what theorists in the 1970s began to call the politics of representation. Her later colour work still is staged, and she posed as fairytale princesses, 1950s 'pin-ups' and the subjects of Old Masters' paintings. In the 1990s Sherman took herself out of the picture and photographed the grotesque, combining body parts of mannequins, dolls and prosthetics in the manner of Hans Bellmer (ibid.: 444). Sherman has worked with herself as a model in a practice that now spans over 30 years. Her work is consistent with and influenced by postmodernist and feminist theory. What is common to all of Sherman's photography is that it is directed and staged. She has pre-conceived the whole shoot, much as a film director would do when making a movie. Sherman uses gesture, styling, setting, composition and lighting to tell a story. She is pictured as a gendered subject but since she is, herself, in control of the shoot the conventional way of reading the image is disrupted by the prospect of the audience's knowing this. The approach is a comment on the power of the photographic image to fix gendered meaning.

4.8 Cindy Sherman, *Untitled Film Still #58*, 1980. Courtesy of the artist and Metro Pictures, New York.

HISTORIES OF PHOTOGRAPHY

Narrative Tableaux Photography

Whilst Sherman stages and directs herself within scenes, the 1980s and beyond saw a trend for directing cinematic images with actors to construct narrative tableaux (pictures). Relevant practitioners, of that decade, working within this new genre included Joel Peter Witkin, Joe Gantz and Sandy Skoglund, all of whom were included in the show *Constructed Realities: The Art of Staged Photography* (1989, Germany). The following decades of the late twentieth century have seen many artists make narrative staged photographs. For example the work of Jeff Wall, Gregory Crewdson and Tom Hunter has been referred to as narrative tableaux. All three of these artists take on the role of directing staged/ tableaux photographs. We are again reminded of the constructed *tableau vivant* style used by Rejlander (fig. 4.3) and Peach Robinson (fig. 4.4) in the nineteenth century. We are reminded that if the camera never lies, it can always be used for fictional purposes.

Jeff Wall and the Painting of Modern Life

Jeff Wall is an artist who uses photography and is also an art historian. Rather than 'taking' pictures, he prefers not to carry a camera. His method relies on remembering and later recreating scenes by re-staging them (with actors) and photographing the reconstruction. Wall recreates scenes from everyday urban and suburban life in his native Canadian landscape. He has been constructing or directing photographs since the late 1970s and continues to work in a way that, he believes, reaches wider audiences: audiences that are used to film stills with narrative meaning. The constructed image is for Wall a return to the tableau, as found in nineteenth-century narrative painting. His manner of working is a deliberate retreat to an earlier narrative style of picture making and works in opposition to the conventions of modernist photography that privileges the 'visual effect'. He is keen to emphasize the prospect of a narrative reading that relates to everyday life. Wall is often quoted as saying he works as a 'painter of modern life', a phrase first coined by the nineteenth-century French poet Charles Baudelaire. Wall notes: 'Baudelaire managed to project a possible form of art into the future. The "painting of modern life" can be painting, photography, cinema, anything; it may be the most open model for art ever formulated' (cited in Lauter, 2001: 176).

Wall often makes references to historical paintings and prints. An example of this is found in his *Picture for Women,* a reworking of the French nineteenth-century artist Édouard Manet's painting *A Bar at the Folies-Bergères.* In composition and content it is directly comparable to the original painting, specifically in the depiction of the 'gazes' of the male protagonist and the viewer of Wall's picture. The large scale of nineteenth-century narrative paintings is imitated by Wall, whose backlit photographs on light boxes are often over 3 metres wide. His work is technologically adept and yet relates to an early modernist love of pictures that tell stories and are easy to read in a gallery context. They reference mass media advertising photography, such as backlit bus stop ad panels, but take their inspiration from nineteenth-century Paris and French cinema.

Near Documentary

Wall categorizes his work into three different modes: straight documentary, 'near' documentary and cinematography. Near documentary is a term Wall uses to describe images he takes that are not staged with actors, but are nevertheless taken in an environment or timescale dictated by Wall. In *Fieldwork* (2003) Wall arranged to photograph the site of an archaeological dig, as archaeologists worked on it over a period of one month. He believed that if he visited the site daily to photograph it, the workers would be accustomed to his presence and the resulting images would not appear 'staged'.

Cinematography

Those works in Wall's 'cinematography' category initially appear like a documentary photograph; only later do we realize the whole picture has been staged with actors. An example of a cinematographic approach can be seen in *Mimic* (fig. 4.9), one of Wall's first staged photographs to be set in a real urban environment. The scene depicts a moment of racial tension witnessed by Wall in a 'real life' street encounter in Vancouver. The central figure acts out his schoolyard racial gesture as the viewer is ideally placed to catch the 'moment'. This is not, however, a real moment. The three people in the photograph are actors. Wall directs and the actors follow a 'script'. When analysing the particular camera angle used in *Mimic*, David Campany notes:

> The subjects appear unaware of the camera positioned in front of the scene. The viewer sees more of the event than any of them. Such 'invisible' camerawork is common in narrative cinema but impossible in traditional documentary, yet the image has the feel of both.
>
> (Campany, 2007: 116)

4.9 Jeff Wall, *Mimic*, 1982. Courtesy of the artist.

HISTORIES OF PHOTOGRAPHY

Mimic is exhibited as a backlit photo-transparency measuring 198 x 229cm, rendering the figures life size. The presentation technique confirms Wall's idea of extending its reach beyond high culture as it looks cinematic and often uses dramatic content.

Other works by Wall in a cinematographic style include *Doorpusher* (1984), *Insomnia* (1994), *Milk* (1984), *Outburst* (1989) and *The Storyteller* (1986), which is influenced by Manet's famous painting *Le Déjeuner sur l'Herbe.* Most of Wall's tableaux are staged in real life settings, but occasionally he uses room sets (see fig. 8.6) (more on sets below). As noted, these works by Wall have in common both a link to narrative in early modern painting and to cinema. It should be clear that Wall is seen as an artist not a photographer. The conventional difference between the two practices is of course a matter of dispute (see Chapter 5 for a discussion of these boundaries). Wall's work is well known and typifies the kind of hybrid practice that defines postmodernism. His interest in narrative links him with other contemporary artists including the American photographer Gregory Crewdson.

Gregory Crewdson has been making photographic tableau narrative pictures since the mid-1990s. Like Wall his work has a cinematic look about it and often represents domestic scenes and small town life in provincial America. The films of David Lynch and Stephen Spielberg, as well as paintings by Edward Hopper, are influences on Crewdson's constructed photographs. Like Wall he pre-visualizes each scene and uses actors. Wall's pictures sometimes look like straight photographs, whereas Crewdson's are more obviously constructed, evidently shot on a set and more dramatically lit. Crewdson's pictures take days to photograph and, with a team of around 40 people, his approach is very much like that of a film director. His working method is elaborate and operates on an epic scale. Entire streets are closed down for a day in the making of his work, and sometimes his dissatisfaction with real environments requires room sets and fixtures built to his own specification.

Untitled (Ophelia) was photographed in a film studio, where the actual room set was flooded for the shoot. Crewdson's treatment of this subject is a modern, suburban telling of the death of Ophelia, a famous literary figure in Shakespeare's *Hamlet* (fig. 4.10). It is a subject that features in the work of many artists over the years such as, most famously, that of the English Victorian painter John Everett Millais. Crewdson provides clues to her suicide: a pair of slippers and pink dressing gown have been left on the stairs, a jar of pills and a glass of water sit on the table beside her. The stillness of the water in the image beautifully mirrors the female subject within the domestic interior. The composition, colour and lighting for this image have been carefully conceived, just as a painter or director of photography would do. As with Wall's work, this image, and all the production it entails, has been constructed solely for the one still image. No moment exists either before or afterwards. It is not a still extracted from a film sequence but an image that stands on its own. The viewer may not be familiar with the original Shakespearean narrative and may invent their own as they 'read' the story and relate it to their own film and TV references or even their own experience of the kind of scenario it represents. The image codifies the familiar, and it then disrupts this for psychological effect. In this way we can see the influence of the horror genre in film and literary fiction. When Crewdson finished this work the water was drained, the actors left and the set was dismantled. All that remains is the staged photograph that started out as an imaginary object in the mind of the photographer. Or should we say which started its life in the narrative that passed into the work of Shakespeare and continued in the many adaptations that followed?

British photographer Tom Hunter's narrative pictures draw on the lighting of Jan Vermeer. Hunter's 1998 image *Woman Reading a Possession Order* was an image of a female squatter by a window,

126

THE CONSTRUCTED PHOTOGRAPH

photographed with the same compositional elements as Vermeer's *A Girl Reading at an Open Window.* The type of work is only partially staged. Hunter makes the art-historical connection quite explicit to anybody with some knowledge of European art. Where this work differs from Crewdson and Wall is in the fact that the woman in this photograph is not a model but a real person who has been served an eviction notice. Hunter himself was part of the marginalized squatting community in Hackney, East London, for many years. His early work sits on a boundary between constructed and documentary practice.

Hunter's more recent work is more staged and constructed than *Woman Reading a Possession Order. Living Hell and Other Stories* was exhibited at the National Gallery,

4.10 Gregory Crewdson, *Untitled (Ophelia)*, from the series *Twilight*, 2001. © The artist. Courtesy of White Cube.

4.11 Tom Hunter, *Anchor and Hope*, from the series *Unheralded Stories*, 2009. Courtesy of the artist and Purdy Hicks Gallery, London.

127

London, in 2005. He is the first photographer to have a solo show at this major museum. This was an important moment in photography's acceptance as a medium within the academy. *Living Hell and Other Stories* consisted of a series of staged photographs retelling stories of poverty, violence and murder in Hackney. In his new work Hunter continues to explore his own locality. *Unheralded Stories* is a subtler retelling of the everyday lives of people living in his borough. However, he still continues to stage and borrow from painting. For example, in *Anchor and Hope* (fig. 4.11) a young woman is shown looking towards an Upper Clapton council estate in Hackney. Hunter made this photograph at a time when the residents of this estate were being threatened with eviction. *Anchor and Hope* mimics the composition and suggested narrative meanings in *Christina's World* of 1948 by the American painter Andrew Wyeth.

Seamless Digital Montage

Some cinematographic constructed photographs not only use actors, but also are further constructed and manipulated in the computer. This could be said to be a digital equivalent to the combination printing technique used by Rejlander in *The Two Ways of Life* (fig. 4.3) and photomontage (fig. 4.7). These digital collages merge backgrounds and different elements such as people and objects using post-production software, such as Adobe Photoshop, which allows a multi-layered image to be precisely edited.

Wall's photograph *A Sudden Gust of Wind* (fig. 4.12) is a digital-montage composite image of over 100 elements, shot in the studio and on location. It took Wall approximately one year to make this work. Much like the narrative tableaux discussed above, *A Sudden Gust of Wind* is influenced by Hokusai's woodblock print, *A High Wind in Yeijiri* (1830). At first Wall's picture looks like a snatched 'decisive moment' until we consider that a scene like this could only be accurately realized through shooting multiple photographs and stitching them together in the construction of a seamless montage. The technique here is important because the end result must *appear* to be seamless, like a single shot. The more we think about this process the less it becomes like 'straight' photography and more like painting. Wall notes:

> It has curious resemblances to the older way of painting in the way you can separate the parts of your work and treat them independently. A painter might be working on a large canvas and, one afternoon, might concentrate on a figure or object, or small area. Part of the poetry of traditional painting is the way it created the illusion that the painting is a single moment – the moment the shutter is released. Photography is based on that sense of instantaneousness … Things that could never coexist in the world easily do in painting. (Wall cited in de Duve *et al.*, 2003: 134)

A later work by Wall, *A View From an Apartment* of 2004, was photographed over 11 months in an apartment specially rented for the photograph. He asked one of the women who features in the final photograph to furnish it and live in it for that period. The final image is a digital composite of many images taken over the project. Without knowledge of this project, the viewer would assume it was just a 'straight' photograph of the inhabited apartment.

Andreas Gursky creates seamless digital composite images. Much like Wall's, the post-production on his combined photographs is faultless and the 'joins' are impossible to spot. *Shanghai* (fig. 4.13) merges multiple photographs taken from three different floors of the opposite balconies of a large hotel atrium. By taking images at various heights then merging to create one image, Gursky creates something away from

THE CONSTRUCTED PHOTOGRAPH

4.12 Jeff Wall, *A Sudden Gust of Wind (after Hokusai)*, 1993. Courtesy of the artist.

the traditional single-point or traditional Renaissance perspective. This construct is not so wrong that the viewer can tell immediately. This image would have been optically impossible to capture with one photograph.

In 2011 Gursky sold his photograph *Rhein II* (1999) for a record-breaking 4.3 million US dollars at Christie's auction house. It is a digitally altered photograph of the Rhine River in Germany. Gursky digitally removed the factories on the horizon and joggers and dog walkers in the foreground, to create a more abstract formalism. *Rhein II* is not so much a constructed photograph but moves into the genre of digital manipulation, which we discuss in more detail in Case Studies 4 and 5 in Part 4 below (pp. 342–68).

Both Wall and Gursky have been working with digital construction since the 1990s and have been discussed in this chapter to illustrate various concepts and discoveries. In the scope of this chapter it has not been possible to include an exhaustive list of practitioners working in this way. The following artists and photographers can also be researched in relation to digital compositing and manipulation: Pedro Meyer, John Goto, Tom Leighton, Loretta Lux, Paul M. Smith, Kelli Connell, Wendy McMurdo and Karen Knorr. Furthermore, the following artists can be researched in terms of staged photography: Sam Taylor-Johnson, Philip-Lorca diCorcia, Yinka Shonibare, Mitra Tabrizian (fig. 8.1), Melanie Manchot, Hannah Starkey, Justine Kurland, Anna Gaskell, Izima Kaoru, Trish Morrissey and Julia Fullerton-Batten.

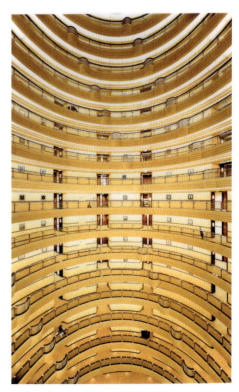

4.13 Andreas Gursky, *Shanghai*, 2000. Courtesy of Museo Nacional Centro de Arte Reina Sofía.

129

HISTORIES OF PHOTOGRAPHY

SETS CONSTRUCTED FOR THE CAMERA

The practice of building sets for the sole purpose of photographing them is an important sub-genre within constructed photography. It draws many theoretical parallels with the staged photography discussed above, including frustrations with the limitations of the 'real'. For example, Gregory Crewdson's *Untitled (Ophelia)* has already been discussed above and is shot in a room set. Photographing staged scenes on full size or miniature sets is a practice that can be traced back to the 1970s and 1980s. Laurie Simmons was a pioneer of this method. Her early black and white photographs of dolls within a doll's house setting questioned photography's representation and objectification of women. It is a socially engaged practice established at the same time as comparable work by Martha Rosler and Cindy Sherman. Simmons not only photographed found dolls' houses, but constructed domestic interior sets utilizing collage of found images from magazines.

David Levinthal photographed toy soldiers placed on hand-built dioramas of the battlefield in *Hitler Moves East* (fig. 4.14). He used extremely shallow depth of field to create blur in the image. This had the effect of hiding much of the detail in his images so they would almost resemble grainy war photojournalism. Some four decades later Levinthal continues to make work with miniature models and toys, including familiar American characters: Barbie dolls, action heroes, sporting figures and Wild West cowboys. In recent work Levinthal renders the miniature scale more obviously, and it has become his trademark. In the context of this chapter on the constructed photograph his early work *Hitler Moves East* is, arguably, more interesting, as it sits mysteriously between believable and artificial space.

Believability in a photographic space, and the question of how memory of place affects their reading, is a key concern for James Casebere, who photographs tabletop models. His structures resemble institutional places such as prisons, hospitals and schools, as well as internal architectural structures such as archways, corridors and tunnels. Unlike Levinthal or Simmons, Casebere photographs his models in sharp detail and exhibits his colour prints on a large scale. Casebere began his career as a sculptor and uses his skills to build intricate sets of architectural space. The construction quality of his models can withstand the photographic enlargement for the gallery wall, without giving the game away. Casebere often floods his sets with water and lights them dramatically; both have the effect of making the space strange and creating a tension between what is real and what is fake (fig. 4.15).

The German artist Thomas Demand constructs and photographs life-sized spaces out of coloured card and Styrofoam. Once photographed, the model is destroyed.

4.14 David Levinthal, *Untitled* from the series *Hitler Moves East*, 1975–77. Courtesy of the artist.

130

4.15 James Casebere, *Flooded Hallway*, 1998–99. © James Casebere. Courtesy of the artist and Sean Kelly, New York.

Like Casebere, Demand is meticulous in his construction of these models. However, he often chooses to reveal a small mark or tear somewhere in the model to expose its artifice to the viewer. Charlotte Cotton notes: 'It makes for a hyperconscious stance, as we look for narrative form despite the in-built warning signs that this is a staged, therefore unreal, place' (Cotton, 2004: 73). There is a back-story or intended narrative behind most of Demand's constructed images. He uses mass media images that are in the public collective memory, such as Saddam Hussein's bunker or the underpass where Princess Diana died in a car crash. He constructs models based on these news images. *Bathroom* (fig. 4.16) derives from a photograph of the scene of the death of Uwe Barschel, a German politician who was found dead in a hotel bathroom in Geneva in 1988. Demand decides not to exhibit or reveal the original photograph that inspired the scene and uses generic titling. His work is more concerned with how the photographic enlargement in the gallery allows the viewer to inhabit these spaces temporarily, before clues to the paper construct break the fantasy.

4.16 Thomas Demand, *Bathroom (Badezimmer)*, 1997. © DACS, London. Courtesy Matthew Marks Gallery.

Advertising photography

The art photographers discussed in this chapter have adapted methods used in commercial photography, especially in advertising photography. The constructed photograph is a common tool used by the advertising photographers to fulfil a creative brief. Commercial time constraints often dictate a limited timeframe in which to achieve the commissioned photograph. Therefore advertising photographers will often photograph parts of the scene separately, both on location and in the studio. After that, the art department within the commissioning advertising company will composite together these elements using post-production software such as Adobe Photoshop. The advertising photographer now often provides only the potential composite image as separate images. This practice differs from the art photographers discussed above who oversee the entire constructed photograph process: from capture through to the final image composition and rendering. Advertising images often include elements not shot by the commissioned photographer, such as stock imagery and even photographic elements simulated by computer generated imaging (CGI). Case Study 5 in Part 4 below discusses this concept further (pp. 357–68). See also Chapter 11 for an extended discussion of photography and advertising.

CONCLUSION

In this chapter we have considered photographs that are constructed or staged in some way. We have studied the rise of the constructed photograph from the first staged images to contemporary use of seamless digital compositing and set building. We have also analysed the work of practitioners who prefer to 'make' or construct photographs rather than 'take' photographs of a pre-existent reality. We learned that there are many types of constructed or directed photographs. Something can be staged in front of the camera, such as a performance involving the photographer or actors. The 'stage' could be a real place, or a 'set'. In some cases, constructed photographs are created within miniature sets, using scale models and figures. Additionally modern digital manipulation allows seamless montage photographs. These differing approaches have one thing in common: a unique image results out of the construction of separate elements. These practices are in principle in direct opposition to 'straight' photography. We also have seen how technological developments or limitations have led to different approaches for the constructed photograph.

SUMMARY OF KEY POINTS

- There are many types of constructed or directed photographs. A constructed photograph can be staged or require the use of seamless digital compositing and set building.
- The practices of constructing an image are in principle in direct opposition to 'straight' photography.
- Technical developments often combine with aesthetic ideas in the making of constructed photographic images. The idea that technique alone drives change or innovation should be resisted.
- The postmodern era made artists reconsider the strengths of constructed or staged photography as a method of knowingly referencing other systems of meaning.
- The constructed photograph is a common tool used by advertising photographers to fulfil a creative brief, often using discrete image elements that have been captured on location, in the studio and even using computer generated imagery.

REFERENCES

Ades, Dawn (1976) *Photomontage,* London: Thames and Hudson.

Benjamin, Walter (1931) 'A Short History of Photography', in Michael W. Jennings (ed.), trans. Rodney Livingstone, 2005, *Walter Benjamin: Selected Writings, Volume 2, Part 2, 1931–1934,* Cambridge, MA/London: The Belknap Press of Harvard University Press.

Campany, David (2007) *Art and Photography,* London: Phaidon Press.

Cotton, Charlotte (2004) *The Photograph as Contemporary Art,* London: Thames and Hudson.

de Duve, Thierry, Pelenc, Arielle and Groys, Boris (eds) (2003) *Jeff Wall,* London and New York: Phaidon.

Köhler, Michael (1995) *Constructed Realities: The Art of Staged Photography*, Zürich: Edition Stemmle.

Lauter, Rolf (ed.) (2001) *Jeff Wall. Figures and Places: Selected Works, 1978–2000,* Munich: Prestel.

Marien, Mary Warner (2002) *Photography: A Cultural History*, London: Laurence King Publishing.

Pauli, Lori (ed.) (2006), *Acting the Part: Photography as Theatre,* London; New York: Merrell.

Sontag, Susan (1979) *On Photography*, New York: Penguin.

CASE STUDIES 1 AND 2

The two case studies in this part of the book are specifically related to photographic techniques and processes. They are descriptions and commentaries on key moments in the technical development of photography and represent basic data that all readers, we feel, ought to know about. The first case study analyses the invention of the first hand-held, portable cameras and some of their social effects. The second case study describes the background and development of the digital camera and briefly considers its ramifications for the future of photography. Photography is viewed by some theorists as having become part of a new type of 'intermedia' (the world wide web for example). The issues raised in this case study are discussed in more detail in the final chapter of the book.

In Chapter 1, 'Histories and Pre-Histories of Photography', we confronted the question of what makes photography history distinctive and have concluded that there is no simple answer to the question. Photography is a practice that is embedded in wider histories and specific or particular histories. The latter include art history and media history but we also have noted that photography overlaps with related histories such as fashion, advertising, journalism and other subject areas. Photography does, however, have particularity in its technologies and we have emphasized portable cameras, image capture and dissemination. This explains the rationale for the two case studies in this part of the book. Our argument is that photography (however it is defined) is a practice, a manner of 'doing' things with particular technologies. When viewing photographs our thoughts are, perhaps unconsciously, influenced by the physical and technical processes that have led to their realization. We are more aware of this when we look at an early photograph since it has connotations of 'discovery' or 'invention' that may over-ride the denoted meaning of what it represents. Seeing oneself on CCTV may have a similar effect. This consciousness of 'the medium' is less obvious when we are smiling at a mobile phone snapshot and yet our amusement is partly created by casual usage of the technology.

CASE STUDY 1: SNAPSHOT PHOTOGRAPHY AND THE PORTABLE BOX CAMERA

From the mid- to late-nineteenth century, photography was an expensive, technically complicated and time-consuming affair. A photographer would need a considerable amount of skill in order to even expose a single image. A glass plate would have had to be pre-coated in light-sensitive emulsion. The plate would then have to be exposed for the correct amount of time and carefully transferred to a darkroom. A detailed list of materials and techniques associated with most of the standard processes during this period would have been extensive. Photography was restricted to professional photographers and rich amateurs. The only photographs found in the home would be formal studio portraits of family members taken by a professional photographer or the popular and collectable *cartes-de-visite* (small commercially printed photographs mounted on card) that were favoured by well-to-do classes. In this period of history a photograph was a precious thing. This case study explains how photography became accessible, affordable and popular.

Towards the end of the nineteenth century, and at the tail end of the second industrial revolution, the invention of new manufacturing processes allowed consumer products to be mass produced. This had a huge impact on the manufacture of cameras, which had previously relied on handcrafted production of individual cameras in small quantities. The Kodak box camera, invented by George Eastman in 1888, was made possible by the first commercial use of photographic roll film. It was the first mass-produced, hand-held camera. Family 'snapshot' photography with this new, affordable and easy-to-use camera quickly became a global phenomenon.

PHOTOGRAPHY SIMPLIFIED: THE KODAK BOX CAMERA

The Kodak camera was essentially a box, with a fixed focal length lens and an internal roll film holder (fig. CS1.1). Many of the techniques previously required with plate or stand cameras were simplified in the Kodak box camera. There was no glass viewing screen or

CS1.1 Kodak No. 1 box camera. Courtesy of National Media Museum/Bridgeman Images.

CASE STUDY 1

viewfinder; the user simply pointed the box in the direction of the subject. The lens was of a short focal length, which captured a relatively wide 60° angle of view, allowing for flexibility in the image composition. The lens had a fixed aperture, alleviating any need for the operator to manually focus on the subject, as everything from one metre onwards was in focus, due to the short focal length. The manufacturers calculated an average fixed aperture and shutter speed combination for normal outdoor lighting conditions. The Kodak box camera came pre-loaded with roll film. The film had wide exposure latitude to allow for different lighting conditions. Under or over-exposure caused by varying lighting conditions was corrected in resulting prints. The film roll was long enough to capture one hundred circular photographs. There were only three manual operations the user had to master, which were illustrated in one of the first Kodak advertisements (fig. CS1.2). '1. Pull the cord.' This was to reset the mechanical shutter to make an exposure. '2. Turn the key.' This advanced the roll film onto the next unexposed section. '3. Press the button.' The button on the side released the shutter to make an exposure. This simple three-step process was repeated until all of the one hundred exposures were made.

'YOU PRESS THE BUTTON, WE'LL DO THE REST'

CS1.2 An 1889 advertisement for the Kodak box camera. Courtesy of Kodak.

Eastman wanted to capture the general public's imagination and persuade people that they needed a camera. He was an astute businessman and mounted a strong advertising campaign designed to achieve a change in attitudes to photography. His campaign was hugely successful and had the effect of making photography popular and attractive as a leisure pursuit. The secret of his success is attributable to the radical simplification of the technology. His promotional methods placed a strong emphasis on the fact that he had simplified the previously complex techniques involved in the photographic process. Figure CS1.2 shows one of Eastman's earliest advertisements for the Kodak box camera, where the photographic process is 'reduced to three motions'. The ad claims comfortably in bold capitals: 'Anybody can use it'. George Eastman's gift to the operator of this new toy was the offer, promised in early Kodak advertising campaigns, 'You press the button, we'll do the rest'. This was a revolutionary idea since it meant that anybody could be a photographer as long as they could point the camera in the right direction. 'The rest' meant, in effect, that the camera could be posted back to Eastman's factory where the film would be developed and printed. The customer would then receive back one hundred circular prints and their original Kodak camera returned with a new roll of film pre-loaded, ready to use again.

SNAPSHOT PHOTOGRAPHY AND THE PORTABLE BOX CAMERA

Eastman democratized photography. Women, and even children, appeared in early Kodak adverts not just as photographic subjects but using the camera to capture everyday family events. Users were encouraged to capture 'memory pictures' for posterity. Formal professional studio portraits of family members were replaced with relaxed, candid snapshots. The era of snapshot photography began. Eastman also produced a promotional booklet *The Kodak Camera,* containing some helpful suggestions for photography subjects. These included:

Travellers and Tourists Use it to obtain a picturesque diary of their travels.

Bicyclists and Boating Men Can carry it where a larger camera would be too burdensome.

Engineers and Architects Use it to record the progress of work in hand, and to note details of construction as they pass by.

Artists Use it to save time sketching.

Parents Use it to photograph their children as they see them play, not in the stiff attitudes of a formal photograph…

Anyone can use it. Everyone will use it

(Coe and Gates, 1977: 18)

THE BROWNIE CAMERA

The Brownie camera was introduced in 1900 as an even more inexpensive version of the Kodak camera with the added improvement of a viewfinder. It was named after Palmer Cox's fictional children's character the Brownie, well known and loved in households across America and England. The new Kodak ads often included pictures of the Brownie characters operating the camera. These advertisements appealed directly to children and their parents. Like its predecessor, the Brownie was a phenomenal success. It cost only one dollar (or five shillings in the UK) and sold over 100,000 units in both America and England in the first year of production alone (Coe and Gates, 1977: 23). Advertisements for the Brownie often demonstrated its ease of use, portability and affordability (fig. CS1.3).

During the first half of the twentieth century the Brownie camera evolved from the original box format to a new, more compact folding design. The No. 2 Folding Brownie camera (from 1904) met growing demand for both portability and more creative control of the photographic process. The folding design allowed the user to set the focus by adjusting the lens distance and selecting different shutter speeds. Booklets were also provided with average settings for focus and shutter speed to accommodate those users who still shied away from the

CS1.3 Brownie advertisement, *c.* 1900.

CASE STUDY 1

technical side of photography. By this time other manufacturers had developed and produced similar cameras, such as the British No.1 'Scout' box camera made by George Houghton and Sons.

THE SNAPSHOT AND THE FAMILY ALBUM

The original Kodak box camera and the popular Brownie were important landmarks in the development of camera technology and manufacturing, as well as completely revolutionizing the public conception of photography. Imagine the delight a family would have experienced at receiving a hundred family snapshots back in the post, which recorded previously un-photographed moments. Family events and special occasions were memorialized in scrapbooks and albums. Manufacturers soon got the idea, producing black leather-bound albums, embossed with the word 'Photographs'. Albums were filled with these new snapshots of vernacular imagery: home life, holidays, family events, school events, and candid portraits. The snapshots were often more about the content than being technically perfect. Images were often annotated in the album with names of people and places, dates and humorous anecdotes. The album could also include the more formal school portraits and wedding photographs taken by professional photographers. Other paraphernalia such as tickets from special events and press cuttings could also be collaged into these albums. Compiling and archiving snapshots in the family album was a way of preserving and sharing memories of family life. In her book *Photographic Memory: The Album in the Age of Photography* (2011), art historian and curator Verna Curtin notes:

> When you hold a photo album, you sense that you are in possession of something unique, intimate and meant to be saved for a long time. As you turn the pages and look at the images, you imbibe the maker's experience, invoking your imagination and promoting personal memories.

(Curtis, 2011: 7)

VERNACULAR PHOTOGRAPHY

The term 'vernacular' is used to describe images whose form has evolved through common use, as opposed to those that have been consciously instigated by an identifiable artist. Vernacular pictures tend to be found in popular culture, rather than 'high' culture. Photojournalism and photographic documents used to record the look of things are obvious examples (Edwards, 2004: 248).

The term 'vernacular' also describes snapshots and everyday photographs taken for personal use. Some historians have remarked on the exclusion of vernacular photographs from 'official' histories. As Michel Frizot and others have noted this neglect has been addressed in recent histories. The growing interest in the everyday, in philosophy and social theory is a reaction against the privileging of high culture. This has been a feature of progressive trends since the 1920s and especially since the 1970s. Frizot's monumental history includes a section on vernacular photography. In a chapter entitled 'Rituals and Customs: Photographs as Memories' he notes how 'fragments of human life tell their own story and are still able to trigger an emotional response despite their veneer of ritual and custom' (Frizot, 1998: 747).

Another positive analysis of the family album emphasizes how photographs appeal to the sense of touch as well as sight. Geoffrey Batchen underlines the objecthood of the photo-album as something designed,

138

annotated and made uniquely personal (Batchen, 2001: 61). A more critical assessment of family snaps analyses the way in which conventional family albums often represent 'immaculate, happy families' (Spence and Holland, 1991: 5) that are influenced by advertising images. This approach in the writing of Jo Spence and Patricia Holland underlines the fact that advertising (perhaps unconsciously) teaches how to stage pictures and perform to the camera:

> The family group remains a centre of fantasy – of romantic social fantasy and those fantasies which spring from our earliest infant lives. Family pictures are pulled into the service of these overlapping dreams – hence the ambivalence of the pleasure they give. This is the warm, exclusive, perfected family which today's snapshots seek to put on record – just like the ads.
>
> (Spence and Holland, 1991: 5)

The success of Eastman's earlier monopolization of this market massively accelerated the sale of cameras and film. This had a lasting influence on the way leisure is structured in modern life. As the snapshot became an increasingly important component of leisure activities, it may now seem to reveal the separations in people's lives. The workplace for example is conspicuously absent in amateur photography, since it is a genre that ritually excludes the more repressive side of life. The conventional family album with family snaps, weddings and birthdays, represents life as it should be rather than as it is.

THE SNAPSHOT TODAY

The subject matter of an average family snapshot has changed very little in the last hundred years. However, the camera technology has developed considerably since the box camera. Kodak's invention certainly changed how we use photography in our everyday lives. Subsequently, our need for capturing family moments has given manufacturers a huge market to cater for. After the box Brownie, and its later folding model, cameras became increasingly portable and 'pocket-sized'. Though the Kodak box camera was the original 'point and shoot' camera, the twentieth century saw a huge increase in this market. In the 1960s Kodak produced the popular and inexpensive *Instamatic* compact camera range. This in turn led to other companies making compact cameras. In the 1970s Polaroid's SX-70, an instant camera with self-developing film, became popular. The next case study, on the digital camera, takes the story from this point, looking at the invention of the digital camera and its adoption by snapshot shooters as a replacement of the analogue compact camera.

KEY TERMS:

Box Camera: The box camera was a simple box, usually made of cardboard, with a fixed focal length lens on the front. Box cameras used roll film, which you could post off. The prints were posted back. It was the first commercially produced camera, which was so simple to use that the Kodak advertising slogan was 'Anybody can use it'.

Amateur: An amateur (from the French word 'lover of') is a person who is engaged in a skilled profession without any formal training. The craze of 'amateur photography' became possible for more people after the mass production of the inexpensive, and simple to use,

CASE STUDY 1

box camera. Prior to that it was only a wealthy few who could indulge their expensive hobby. Socially and professionally, 'amateurism' can be seen as a negative term.

Snapshot: The Oxford English Dictionary defines a snapshot as 'an instantaneous photograph, especially one taken with a hand camera'. The mass produced Kodak box camera allowed photographs to be taken out of a studio setting, with no tripod required. The resulting pictures by untrained amateurs were more concerned with capturing everyday life, than producing technically perfect images.

Vernacular Photography: Photography of the everyday world around us such as home life, family holidays and occasions. These are images of the commonplace moments throughout ordinary domestic life. Most snapshots can be described as vernacular photographs.

REFERENCES

Batchen, Geoffrey (2001) *Each Wild Idea: Writing/Photography/History,* Cambridge, MA and London: The MIT Press.

Coe, Brian and Gates, Paul (1977) *Snapshot Photography: The Rise of Popular Photography 1888–1939,* London: Ash and Grant Ltd.

Curtis, Verna Posever (2011) *Photographic Memory: The Album in the Age of Photography,* New York: Aperture.

Edwards, Steve (2004) 'Vernacular Modernism' in Paul Wood (ed.), *Varieties of Modernism*, New Haven, CT and London (in association with The Open University): Yale University Press, pp. 241–68.

Frizot, Michel (1998) *The History of Photography,* Cologne: Könemann.

Spence, Jo and Holland, Patricia (1991) *Family Snaps: The Meaning of Domestic Photography,* London: Virago.

CASE STUDY 2: THE DIGITAL CAMERA

Digital imaging is everywhere and the digital camera is taken for granted as an everyday accessory. Mobile phones take digital photographs and compact digital cameras make snapshot images. Printed photographs and documents are digitized on flat bed scanners and webcams transmit live digitized moving image footage. For millions of people around the world digital imaging is part of everyday life. New media has transformed communication in ways that have important implications for how we think about photography. In this case study we offer a brief historical survey of digital photography, to include:

- the background and development of the digital camera
- different types of digital camera
- the digital snapshot
- the dissemination of photographs and the changing nature of the family album.

THE DIGITAL EVOLUTION

Major advances in media technology in the late twentieth century contributed to the development of the digital camera. The invention of television in the 1920s and the first digitized photograph from a scan in 1957 by Russell Kirsch, and, in 1959, the printing of electrical circuits on silicon microchips heralded the start of the computer age. In the 1960s the development of the digital video camera also played a part in the evolution of the digital camera. Silicon image sensors were developed for video capture at this time. The making of the digital camera for stills photography was advanced further by some of the following innovations:

- Kodak was the first to experiment using CCD (Charge Coupled Device) sensors for still image capture. A CCD sensor is a silicon substrate that houses a grid of light-sensitive photo sensors (fig. CS2.2). The sensor has pixel sights, which record the light levels. Pixels are 'picture elements' that form a grid to capture a digital image.
- In 1975, Kodak engineer Steve Sasson made a prototype of the world's first digital still image camera using a commercially available 100x100 pixel black and white CCD sensor, made by Fairchild Imaging (fig. CS2.1).
- Later the Fuji DS-1P (1988), Fuji DS-X (1989) and the Dycam 1 (1990) were the first available digital cameras for the consumer market. At this early stage, the picture quality was very low and the unit price considerably higher than the average consumer could afford.

CS2.1 Prototype digital camera, Steve Sasson, 1975. Courtesy of Kodak.

CASE STUDY 2

It was over a decade before the consumer market embraced digital photography. The growth of the digital camera was initially driven by different needs in the professional sectors, which preceded the extension into the wider market for this new product. The digital camera rapidly seemed to make film cameras obsolete. This was good news for some manufacturers, since it meant that millions of cameras had to be replaced.

INDUSTRY AND PROFESSIONAL USES OF EARLY DIGITAL IMAGING

The space programme and newspaper industry were early adopters of digital still photography for different reasons. In the beginning the technology only allowed for very low quality images of a functional nature. Advertising and fine art photographers maintained the use of film when digital photography first became feasible because early digital images did not have enough detail for print reproduction. Certain types of images did not need to be of a fine resolution, since the higher necessity was to transfer the image wirelessly. An early example of the use of CCD sensors was the Hubble Space Telescope, which contains the Wide Field and Planetary Camera, manufactured in 1990. The CCD converts rays of light into electronic signals, and then the telescope radios data to an orbiting satellite relay system, which eventually reaches antennae on Earth. This would have been impossible with film photography.

News photographers also saw the benefit of capturing an image instantly since they previously needed to find a laboratory and darkroom for processing and printing. As early as 1920 news photographs were digitized using the Bartlane facsimile system and sent via submarine cable between England and America with cable picture transmission and greatly speeded up picture delivery times from over a week on a boat to three hours by cable. News agencies were early users of digital imagery as readers wanted to see today's news pictures today and not next week. When the means were available to first capture images directly on image sensors and to second send them immediately by satellite, news photographers grasped this new technology. These changes have transformed the gathering and dissemination of news.

DIGITAL SINGLE LENS REFLEX CAMERAS

CS2.2 CCD image sensor. © David J. Green – technology/Alamy.

Some of the main inventions and innovations include:

- The digital SLR evolved from the pioneering development of the CCD for the space programme and the need for instant digital capture with portable cameras in photojournalism.
- In 1991, Kodak released the DCS-100 dSLR, based on the popular Nikon F3 film body with a mounted CCD back plate to replace 35mm film capture. The photographer had to wear a rucksack containing a separate digital storage unit (DSU). The DCS-100 captured images with a CCD sensor, which converted the light values to digital numeric values, which were then fed down a connecting cable to the DSU in the rucksack. Modern professional digital SLRs no longer require a separate rucksack, but include a condensed DSU within the camera body.

142

THE DIGITAL CAMERA

- Digital SLRs used to predominantly use CCD sensors, but since 2010 less expensive CMOS sensors are now used. A CMOS (Complementary Metal Oxide Semiconductor) is a light-sensitive silicon sensor that works in a slightly different way to a CCD sensor. The CMOS has several advantages; it doesn't need a separate Analogue to Digital Converter (ADC), because it digitizes the light signal on board the sensor; they are less expensive to manufacture; they are compact and use less power than CCD sensors. CMOS are used in hybrid still and video cameras as they support 'live view'.
- A third type of sensor is the 'Foveon', which has three colour layers embedded into the silicon, mimicking colour film emulsion.

THE PROFESSIONAL USER AND PROSUMER

Digital SLR camera sensors differ in type and also physical size. Professional photographers who require high-quality images for enlargement for publication need to use a large sensor. The largest sensor in a digital SLR is termed 'full frame', after the equivalent size frame in 35mm. The majority of digital SLR cameras on the market do not have full-frame sensors and are aimed at a new market user type, the so-called 'prosumer'. These are users who fall between the professional and consumer or amateur categories; users who want to have the creative control of an SLR camera with interchangeable lenses, but without the high price tag of a professional camera. One of the first on the market of this type was the Canon Rebel in 1990. In this camera the sensor was approximately half the size of a full-frame 35mm and categorized as an APS sensor (after the short-lived APS small film format in pre-digital compact film cameras). The small APS sensors are what live inside most compact digital cameras, mobile phone cameras and 'prosumer' digital SLRs.

In media theory there is another definition for the term 'prosumer', referring to digital technology empowering the user to be both a producer and consumer. It is very easy for the average user to move from merely being a consumer of a digital camera, or a passive consumer of images online, to also being producer of content: a producer/consumer or 'prosumer' (Toffler, 1980). However, some new media theorists contend that amateur photographers have *always* been producer/consumers and photography itself was the 'original user-generated content' (Lister, 2014: 7). Digital cameras have nevertheless made dissemination possible to a global, networked audience.

DIGITAL CAMERA BACKS

Early digital imaging did not produce high enough quality files for photographers who produced images for reproduction such as advertising, fashion, catalogues and product photography. They chose to continue shooting in medium- and large-format film. The solution was to make the sensors larger, so that they exceeded the size of a 35mm film SLR and moved into the medium format realm. CCD sensors of near medium format size were subsequently manufactured at huge cost and placed in medium format digital camera backs (DCB). With the correct adaptor these backs can be attached to a traditional medium format body and lens, in place of a roll film back. The DCB can be either battery or mains powered and tethered to a computer to capture and store the images. Alternatively the image can be stored on a removable, compact flash memory card. At the time of writing the highest resolution of a single shot DCB is 80 million pixels, which would easily produce a billboard quality image. The flagship

143

CASE STUDY 2

Hasselblad digital DCB goes one step further capturing a 200 million pixels image using a multi-shot technique, for red, green and blue colour channels.

CONSUMER CAMERAS

In the early days of digital photography the average consumer, the amateur photographer, needed convincing. This compares with the arrival of the first portable cameras in the late nineteenth century. Most photographers were quite content with their 35mm film compact cameras and the routine of getting their prints back from the lab ready for the family album. When Steve Sasson first presented his prototype digital camera in 1975 (fig. CS2.1) his colleagues at Kodak had doubts about public demand for what appeared to be a new way of thinking about photography. Questions were asked such as how would the images be stored and what would an electronic family album look like? (Gustavson, 2009: 339)

Public demand for the new technology was initially low even though compact digital cameras were available to consumers quite early in the history of digital imaging. The Dycam Model 1 was released in 1991 but with a prohibitively high price tag. It was not until consumers had higher specification home PCs and access to the Internet that public interest in digital photography really took off.

The compact digital camera revolutionized the public use of photography. Like Brownie camera users in the past, consumers were convinced by advertising that the new compact digital camera would be easy to use, efficient, and, importantly, affordable. For example, Kodak ads at that time (*c.* 2001) for the EasyShare System (see fig. CS2.3) emphasized the ease of use of their new digital system. Their claim

CS2.3 Kodak EasyShare digital camera and dock system *c.* 2001. Courtesy of Kodak.

was that the product would provide: 'Fast picture transfer, easy emailing and printing and quick battery charging – all at the touch of a button'. The snappy use of language recalls George Eastman's slogan: 'You press the button, we do the rest'.

Kodak was not the only manufacturer to produce consumer compacts during this period. It was, nevertheless, the dominant force in the market until it ceased making digital cameras in 2012.

THE ONLINE ALBUM – A NEW WAY OF SHARING SNAPSHOTS

The name 'EasyShare' highlighted two key benefits of digital photography to the unconverted. First, it was fast and easy. Second, the consumer was encouraged to share their photography by emailing pictures direct from the camera via the computer. This was a completely new way of sharing images, particularly snapshots, with friends and family members. These so called 'Kodak moments', that had lived in dusty family albums for the last century, were now given a new home to be displayed on the computer screen. Initially this caused a period of disruption in the archiving of family snapshots. These images were seldom printed out and tended to be stored on users' hard drives. There seemed to be a collective desire to share these images and the idea of online albums grew.

In the last ten years the idea of having your own personal webpage or website dedicated to sharing photographs with and of friends and family has been increasingly popular. For many this is now the ideal way to share images. Early online photo gallery services were Picasa, Flickr and Photobucket. In 2004 Facebook combined the growing popularity of sharing images online with what is now well known as 'social networking', connecting with people virtually.

It is estimated that in 2014, at the time of writing, one billion photographs are uploaded each day to the Internet (Blodget and Danova, 2014). These figures are staggering and testify to the dramatic change seen in the photograph over the last hundred years. A photograph of a loved one is no longer something we hold in our hands, archive in an album or store in a wallet. It now floats in a virtual world, waiting to be viewed on computer screens and hand-held devices. It is possible to print digital photographs on home desktop printers, in high street labs and via print-on-demand websites, but this type of dissemination still falls woefully behind the billions housed on Facebook.

Facebook, in December 2011, launched a new way of presenting personal archived snapshots and key moments in personal history from birth to present day, called the 'Timeline'. It can be used to fill in the gaps in online albums and social networks and archive private moments. Critics suggest Facebook might be a ploy to target more specific advertising to users through these new data-rich profiles (Ulanoff, 2011). As a social networking site Facebook appears to create an interesting alternative to the traditional family album. Its registered users for example can create a chronological digital archive from baby pictures through graduation images and beyond. For a more detailed discussion of social networking and digital culture see Case Study 4, 'Digital and Mobile Phone Cultures' in Part 4 below (pp. 342–56).

PHOTO BLOGGING – PRIVATE TO PUBLIC

Photo sharing sites like Facebook allow the user to control who sees their images and 'status updates'. This is usually restricted to friends and acquaintances. Online photo albums are therefore relatively

CASE STUDY 2

private. Another method of disseminating digital photographs is by keeping a web log (a type of online journal) where the author writes about a subject of their choice and can include their own photography. A photo blog is a web log devoted only to images. Photo blogs are not normally private and can be viewed by anyone. They are uncensored and for the first time private, personal photography is common in the public domain. Fotolog was one of the first sites to encourage photo blogging. Users would upload one picture a day to create a unique visual diary and comments were attached to images by fellow users. This built up an online community, who encouraged and empowered each other to upload vernacular imagery from their everyday lives (Long, 2006).

MOBILE PHONE CAMERA

Many of the digital photographs that are uploaded to online albums, social networking sites and photo blogs are now taken with a mobile phone camera. The first mobile phone camera was available in 2002, but it was not until 'smart' phones were widely available, about half a decade later, with higher quality inbuilt cameras and faster Internet connectivity, that camera phone photography became feasible for the consumer. A smartphone is a mobile phone with high-resolution touch screen, Internet access, and inbuilt camera for still and moving image, GPS navigation, media player, as well as being a phone.

Apple is currently market leader with the iPhone, which has many photo-related 'apps' (applications) available. One popular app is 'Hipstamatic' (a play on words with the old Instamatic camera and 'hip', denoting its fashionable appeal). This app creates digital snapshots emulating the look of old analogue snapshots or Polaroids. 'Hipstamatic' had a huge cult following in 2010, though it was not only being used as a tool for snapshots but controversially for war photography.

In 2010 photojournalists Teru Kuwayama and Balazs Gardi were part of a small media team embedded

CS2.4 Teru Kuwayama and Balazs Gardi, collaborative 'Basetrack' photojournalist project using only a mobile phone (Apple iPhone with 'Hipstamatic' app). Basetrack was an experimental media project, chronicling the lives of 1/8–1st Battalion, 8th Marine Regiment, United States Marine Corps, throughout their deployment to southern Afghanistan in 2010. Courtesy of the artists.

THE DIGITAL CAMERA

with 1/8–1st Battalion, 8th Marine Regiment, United States Marine Corps, transmitting reports from Helmand province in Afghanistan. Using iPhones and social media platforms, they connected over a thousand Marines and Corpsmen to their families, and a broader public to one of the longest wars in United States history (see fig.CS2.4). 'Basetrack' was an experimental media project, chronicling the lives of the 1/8–1st Battalion, throughout their deployment to southern Afghanistan in 2010. Kuwayama and Gardi decided to leave their professional digital SLR kit at home and solely shoot with the iPhone Hipstamatic app. The photographers liked its ease of use in high-pressure situations and for practical reasons as the device is a sealed unit, ideal in the dusty desert environment (Kingsley, 2011). However, mobile phone photography in conflict areas is more normally taken by passers-by, not photojournalists, and is increasingly disseminated on websites like Twitter. It is an approach known as 'citizen journalism'. For a more detailed discussion of this term see Case Study 4, 'Digital and Mobile Phone Cultures' in Part 4 below.

THE FUTURE OF DIGITAL PHOTOGRAPHY

The future of digital photography is uncertain. Different users demand different technologies. Wearable technology such as the Google Glass is still undergoing development in 2015. There have been developments in digital cameras capable of refocusing images after capture. In 2011 Lytro released its first portable light field, or plenoptic camera, that uses micro-lenses to capture light field information. Other developments in commercial product photography, particularly of cars, are moving away from photography towards solely computer generating imagery (CGI). An extended discussion of photography and CGI appears in Case Study 5: 'The Designed Photograph: Computer Generated Imagery (CGI) in Car Photography' in Part 4 below, pp. 357–68.

KEY TERMS:

Analogue to Digital Converter (ADC): This is an internal device inside a digital camera which converts the analogue voltage received by a light sensor into digital binary code.

CCD Image Sensor: A CCD (Charge Coupled Device) sensor is a silicon substrate that houses a grid of light-sensitive photo sensors (see fig. CS2.2). The sensor has pixel sights, which record the light levels. Pixels are 'picture elements' that form a grid to capture a digital image.

CMOS Image Sensor: A CMOS (Complementary Metal Oxide Semiconductor) is a light-sensitive silicon sensor that works in a slightly different way to a CCD sensor. The CMOS has several advantages; it doesn't need a separate ADC, because it digitizes the light signal on board the sensor; they are less expensive to manufacture; they are compact and use less power than CCD sensors. CMOS are used in hybrid still and video cameras as they support 'live view'.

Digital Camera Back (DCB): A large CCD sensor housed within a camera back that attaches to a medium format camera.

CASE STUDY 2

> **Digital Storage Unit (DSU):** All digital cameras contain an internal Digital Storage Unit. Digital photographs are captured with a silicon image sensor, which converts the light values to digital numeric values, which are stored in a DSU.
>
> **Digital Single Lens Reflex camera (dSLR):** A digital SLR camera is based on a traditional 35mm single lens reflex camera body. A light-sensitive silicon sensor replaces 35mm film capture. Digital SLRs used to predominantly use CCD sensors, but increasingly less expensive CMOS sensors are now used.
>
> **Wide Field and Planetary Camera (WFPC):** The first generation digital camera using CCD image sensors on the Hubble Space Telescope. It was replaced by the WFPC2 in 1993.

 REFERENCES

Blodget, Henry and Danova, Tony (2014) 'The Future of Mobile', 22 March 2014. Available at: www.businessinsider.com Available: http://www.businessinsider.com.au/future-of-mobile-slides-2014-3#slide18-18 (accessed 19.04.2014).

Gustavson, Todd (2009) *Camera: A History of Photography from Daguerreotype to Digital,* New York, London: Sterling Innovation, Sterling Publishing Co., Inc.

Kingsley, Patrick (2011) 'War photography? Isn't there an app for that?', in *The Guardian* G2, 6 July 2011. Available at: http://www.guardian.co.uk/media/2011/jul/06/afghanistan-war-iphone-images (accessed: 10.12.11).

Lister, Martin (2014), 'Overlooking, Rarely Looking and Not looking', in Jonas Larsen and Mette Sandbye (eds) *Digital Snaps: The New Face of Photography*, London and New York: I.B. Tauris, pp. 1–23.

Long, Andrew, (ed.) (2006) *Fotolog Book: A Global Snapshot of the Digital Age,* London: Thames and Hudson.

Toffler, Alvin (1980) *The Third Wave*, New York: Bantam Books.

Ulanoff, Lance (2011) 'Facebook Timeline: Zuckerberg's Biggest Gamble Yet'. Available at: http://mashable.com/2011/09/22/facebook-timeline-zuckerberg%E2%80%99s-biggest-gamble-yet/ (accessed 10.12.11).

PART 2
PHOTOGRAPHY THEORIES

INTRODUCTION

In this part of the book we introduce readers to some of the key issues and debates in contemporary photography theory. We have indicated in the introduction to the book how far our thinking on the key changes occurring from the late 1960s to the early twenty-first century has been shaped by the influence of conceptual art. We have argued how this movement had a direct impact on the photography-centred trends in progressive fine arts during this period. We also show how far the political aims of key photographers, artists, educationalists, historians and others extended beyond the academy in a more focused critique of popular imagery and note the way photography circulates in society and achieves widespread social influence and ideological effects.

Chapter 5, 'The Rise of Photography Theory', includes a 'brief history of photography theory' and a critical discussion of the way periods are given an historical unity when they actually contain competing interests and ideas. We have noted that technical change and political struggles inform photographic ideas and practices. For example students had little direct affinity with high culture in the post-Second World War period and were attracted to photography as a medium that is closer to their everyday experience than painting and sculpture. We have noted how the 'ordinariness' of photography was adopted by conceptual artists using the medium to record performance work and other activities. A generation of students who were educated at art institutions in the 1960s and 1970s challenged the hierarchies of cultural knowledge that relied on a separation of artistic knowledge from wider social issues. The increasing use of photography by art students helped to establish the medium in the mainstream of contemporary art.

Case Study 3 in this part of the book introduces a semiological analysis of an advertising image. This study demonstrates one of the key intellectual methods that opposed contemporary forms of art criticism. Semiology was heralded as a more objective way of thinking about cultural production and its social effects. It was also judged to be a more democratic method of treating all signs, whatever their cultural status, in the same way. The techniques deployed in the work and ideas of key semiologists such Ferdinand de Saussure, Charles Sanders Peirce and Roland Barthes were a major influence on artists and theorist such as Victor Burgin in Britain and Allan Sekula in America. Burgin and Sekula are key contributors to what we have called New Photography Theory.

PHOTOGRAPHY THEORIES

Chapter 6, 'Photography and the Written Word', provides a closer investigation of the relationship between words and pictures. This builds on ideas discussed in the previous chapter in which we noted how artists and photographers bridged the gap between theory and practice and achieved this in various ways including mixing words with pictures in their gallery work and challenging the separation of writing and making works of art. Chapter 6 shows how photography relates to language and in a series of examples explores this relationship. One of the key points under discussion is the way photographs can be used in a 'language-like' way. We also investigate the relative autonomy of photography which has medium specific characteristics that make it resistant to the controlling power of language.

CHAPTER 5
THE RISE OF PHOTOGRAPHY THEORY

The British artist Hamish Fulton studied sculpture at St Martin's School of Art in London in the 1960s at a time when sensitivity to landscape was beginning to attract the attention of conservationists. Walking is a key aspect of the work and photography is used to record his journeys. This takes place in real time and the visual material and notes that follow it are a way of allowing the audience to engage with Fulton's experience of secluded and untravelled ways. Immersing himself in nature away from city culture and the world of art connects him with Romantic traditions in painting and poetry of the past. There is a link between the photo-text and the landscape to which it refers and yet its deadpan style of communication reads more like a documentary

5.1 Hamish Fulton, *A Hollow Lane on the North Downs*, 1971. Image courtesy Maureen Paley, London.

PHOTOGRAPHY THEORIES

report than subjective interpretation of the event. It is in some measure a critique of the common sense idea that art works provide access to private experience. Walking as a sensual and free activity is the real work. The few words he uses, like the black and white photograph, are objectively descriptive. We note also that the words are not merely a verbal supplement (as a separate title would be) but an integral part of the work inside the same frame. The journey along the ancient pathway between Winchester and Canterbury is recalled in the photo-text. The artist's experience is mediated by language.

INTRODUCTION

Photography has never been without theorists. The histories of photography are dominated by speculation on how it works and what it is. Photographers as disparate as William Henry Fox Talbot, László Moholy-Nagy and Jeff Wall have contributed to photography theory. This chapter discusses the rise of a particularly militant brand of photography theory in the period from the late 1960s to the 1980s. We underline the importance of French cultural theory, especially semiology, and the work of Anglo-American conceptual artists in this period. By the 1950s there was a growing interest in the ways images influence social behaviour and a critical backlash against commercial culture. Semiology was discovered by a new generation of artists interested in the way language impacts on the visual arts. The idea of artists working in a realm beyond language was questionable since audiences read catalogues and discussed works. They could see that photography and the visual arts are always surrounded by words. A key influence in the 1960s was the French theorist Roland Barthes who showed how images are coded in ways that underline their social use.

Barthes showed that signs are constituent parts of a signifying system which limits their meaning to socially agreed ways of reading them. He contributed to the development of a critical method of analysis called semiology, the science of signs. Barthes was interested in the way hidden rules (in language, in images, in objects themselves) have functions that suit established ways of seeing the world. He could see that meaning of words and other systems of representation (including photography) are suited to dominant social groups and made to seem a natural part of life. Glamour, wealth, power and consumerism are mediated by images or words and become part of our everyday reality. Barthes' method of analysis offered a critical method and a way of challenging what seems natural or taken for granted. An awakened political consciousness in the 1960s (amongst intellectuals, artists, and radicalized students in Western societies) encouraged a sceptical attitude to images generally. Photographs lost their innocence and were subjected to critical analysis by feminists, socialists and civil rights campaigners on the lookout for hidden social meanings.

High culture institutions assimilated 'art photography' from the 1930s in American and big name figures were the subject of monographs and exhibitions that gave them universal status by the middle of the last century. Edward Weston, Walker Evans, Ansel Adams are amongst this American elite and the Europeans include Henri Cartier-Bresson, André Kertész and many others. These figures represented what has been called 'serious photography' to distinguish it from the medium's industrial functions. They also represented a continuing belief in the autonomy of art photography prized for the originality of their work rather than the social meanings that might attach to their chosen themes. By the 1960s this kind of insularity came to be seen as conservative by those adopting a more critical social attitude to the medium.

THE RISE OF PHOTOGRAPHY THEORY

Two key factors contributed to the emergence of a new kind of photography theory in the 1970s and both were closely connected with conceptual art. The first, as we have noted, is the critical analysis of images and tendency to treat them as objects in common regardless of their cultural status. A photographic nude is therefore a treated as a way seeing women in general rather than an isolated aesthetic ideal. The second concerns a critical revaluation of cultural institutions including fine art museums and their ties with the market for contemporary art. Semiology and conceptual art widened the field of practice for artists and bridged the gap between words and images and between language and art. The artist Marlene Dumas said that 'words and images drink the same wine' (Dumas, cited in Morley, 2003: 9). Words and images are *signs* and both, in their different ways, are locked into ways of responding to and signifying meaning. Meaning is 'inscribed' – written – in images as well as in the words we use and our ways of using them are always constrained by social convention. Convention, however, can always be challenged.

THE FUNCTIONS OF THEORY

Photography as Knowledge

What are the functions of theory? What does theory do? Can it be avoided? Can the outcomes of theoretical work be achieved through the exercise of common sense? Can we steer round it and just *be* photographers? Photographers after all are intuitive and guided by their instinct and some of the best have avoided theory all their lives. We can generalize the idea that photography knowledge is a pragmatic mix of craft know-how and personal taste acquired in the learning process. Knowing *how* and knowing *that* are different kinds of knowledge. A skill might inform a way of thinking about photography as a social practice but it is not the same. Photographers have always talked about their practice and, arguably, whatever they think and say constitutes a kind of theory. How far this definition extends beyond the pragmatic demands of the practice itself is determined by the concept of theory itself.

What is Theory?

'Theorizing' is a name given to the quest for enlightenment. It often takes the form of confronting an issue, collating already existing points of view and measuring their relevance to the context in which we live and work. Photography theory surveys a vast area and includes everything from popular culture to a study of photography as high art. One of the key points in this chapter is to show that photographers engage with ideas in ways that inform their practice. It is equally true that practice produces knowledge (skills-based as well as intellectual and social knowledge) and this in turn passes into the words and ideas that are an integral part of the practice. Photography is a concept associated with its technology and its various applications. It is also a *discourse* – a network of regulated practices and ideas – which governs the way photographers go about their business. The common sense idea that photography is whatever we want it to be is an illusion. Photography is historically shaped by established ways of doing things and this in turn is always related to the language that surrounds it at a given historical moment. Theory is explanation of things in a field of study and is accompanied by a struggle to achieve an objective position on a given issue. 'Doing theory' is often little more than showing a level

153

PHOTOGRAPHY THEORIES

of engagement with issues and debates in the field of study. It presupposes knowledge of the field appropriate to the subject. A theorist contests or defends an established position.

Photographic Meaning and Common Sense

To what extent is common sense a product of handed down ideas and an established repertoire of techniques and methods in practical activity? It is often assumed that understanding a photograph is a matter of common sense but how far is this dependent upon assumptions or even prejudice? Stuart Hall and other theorists have argued there is always a 'preferred' or ideologically loaded way of reading a text (Hall, 1980: 134). *Ideology* – a key word in cultural theory – refers to sets of ideas that may appear to dominate the way people think. Ideology is a type of representation (including photographic representation) which reflects the interests of power. *Representation* is a general term for the way language (written and verbal), images, and discourse produce meaning. *Discourse* is a word that refers to the way structures of power (schooling, the family, the media) actually shape the way we represent the world. Terms such as ideology, representation and discourse are only useful insofar as they allow us to study the way the world is structured and organized.

Discourse is a term that refers to a body of ideas or practices which produce their own 'knowledge'. The theorist Kathryn Woodward says that 'discourses are true insofar as they are accepted as true, so that people act as if they are true' (1997: 253). When art historians talk of 'old masters' (or 'modern masters') their authority seems to confirm an accepted view that women are outside the official story of art. The art historian Linda Nochlin illustrates how 'discourse' (in its adjectival form) relates to photography in an art-world setting:

> Once the photograph is accepted as a unique work of art and the photographer as a creative artist with an interesting biography, a whole army of *discursive* practices and institutions spring into being: academic courses in art history departments, photography galleries and departments in museums, a supportive critical network, collectors and collections …
>
> (Nochlin, 1997: xiv; emphasis added)

A discourse is a set of ideas and practices sustained by the exercise of power. In this example Nochlin observes how critics and institutions validate what is acceptable (as art) and consolidate its status as a model of future practice.

Works of art are objects to be enjoyed but they also carry meanings that relate to already existing structures of meaning. Recognition of this is part of the pleasure of making connections with other works. Images are never innocent since they are informed by other images. A choice of colour in a dress code defines gender in real life as well as in its representations: pink for girls, blue for boys. The suggestion here is that *representation* works towards the construction of gender difference in particular circumstances (where patriarchy rules) and creates an opportunity for social ranking and discrimination. This is an illustration of 'theory' applied to a social situation in which photography plays an important representational role in art and commercial practices where social identity is at issue. It points towards one of the most fertile areas of contemporary photography theory that includes analysis of advertisements and popular illustrated magazines. There are, however, numerous areas of photography practice explored by contemporary theoreticians.

Current Sites of Photography Theory

Photography theory takes many forms that are informed by concepts and ideas in many different intellectual fields. They include art history, anthropology, Marxism, feminism, sociology and psychoanalysis to name some of the most closely connected academic disciplines. Photography theory is also closely linked with important trends in the visual arts and in particular the work of conceptual artists since the late 1960s. The work of theorists is found in specialist magazines, academic journals, exhibition catalogues, textbooks and online resources. This, in turn, can be separated into many branches including histories of the subject, technical references, monograph texts on single photographers and increasingly, in the present context, polemical and argumentative debates on key subjects which extend beyond appreciation and aesthetic issues to encompass controversial and politically inflected debates.

The applications of theory in photography are varied and wide-ranging. They include:

- histories of photography
- new technology: benefits and consequences. Some of the best theoretical work addresses photography in digital culture
- textual analysis: the study of single images, sequences or series, photo-essays, mixed media forms including art and advertising
- business and professional practice of photography, regulation and legal factors, the institutional framework of photography (societies, clubs, associations)
- changing uses of photography and modes of dissemination and reception and the widening of access; political interventionism, photography and digital cultures
- power and authority of the photographic image: ideology and political effect, the role of photography in consumer society
- photography in and around contemporary art and culture.

This list is far from exhaustive and new areas of investigation emerge in response to social and technological innovation. New and different ways of using photography invite theoretical revision and critical intervention. Recent developments include critical work on photojournalism and human rights activism and other struggles to find ways of making photography engage with social conflict and other global issues. The field of photography theory is expanding and has become a key area of contemporary literature in the arts and humanities. Before this period photography theory was a branch of art history. A wider discussion of photography education is offered in Part 3 of this book. By the end of the last century photography – theory and practice – had become a recognized field of study at university and a prolific area of academic publishing.

A Brief History of Photography Theory

The division of photography theory into historical sections is at best a convenience since it is often led by pre-existent historical categories outside the practice. Victorian Photography is usually followed by Early Modern (1901–1918), Inter-War (1918–1939), Post-War (1945–1960), the 1960s as a turning point in cultural history followed by a long, later twentieth-century (1970 to the present) known as Postmodernism. This generalizes periods as if they are represented by a single theme or idea. The fact is that all these periods encompass a wealth of ideas about photography and no single movement, style

PHOTOGRAPHY THEORIES

or idiom can easily be used to define them. What is significant, however, is that specific technologies emerge at precise moments and specific historical conditions influence the way photographers think about their practice. Photography in any case is part of related disciplines and practices which tend to assimilate it in ways that deny its autonomy. Resistance to incorporation, nevertheless, is part of the medium's folklore especially in higher education. All forms of reflexive discussion attaching to photography constitute 'theory' in its various formations. A history of photography theory, however, would normally address its most cogent and influential discourse rather than peripheral or ill-informed ones.

Photography theories are as old as the medium itself. Key issues and debates related to the birth of photography are discussed Chapter 2. The great debates in the Victorian period are governed by the partisan interests of those who sought in their different ways to exploit the medium in directions that suited their own interests. It was thus used as an 'art' medium by relatively small numbers of enthusiasts and by others as the most proficient way of documenting the appearance of the world in all its variety. It was for the most part, however, a documentary medium (before the word had any currency) and its great power of accurate transcription was its defining feature throughout the nineteenth century.

As we have seen, photography was a technically difficult and expensive medium which attracted amateurs with time and funds to support it. By the 1850s it was a commercial medium in Europe, Britain and America supported by the profits in studio portraiture, including the *carte-de-visite* and the craze for stereoscopic views. In addition it was widely used to document landscapes, the natural world, the built and the natural environment. Theories of photography were restricted to the work and ideas of photography societies and debate centred on technical matters and speculations about photography's relation to art. Most amateur themes in photography were related to the art-historical genres of landscape, still life and figure composition and especially portraiture. Picturesque views of pretty watercourses, rocky landscapes and suchlike dominated thinking about landscape.

One of the great anxieties for a nineteenth-century photography theorist was the mechanical nature of the medium and the tendency for it to be seen as an artisanal or craft practice. One of the most energetically promoted artistic styles of nineteenth-century photography was the movement called Pictorialism, which became an international movement in the late Victorian and Edwardian period (see Chapter 1). The first widely recognized body of photography theory produced by this generation is located in the exhibition catalogues, newspaper reports and personal correspondence associated with French, Austrian, German, American and British photographers loosely attached to the name Pictorialism (Doty, 1960). The work and ideas of the New York based German photographer Alfred Stieglitz provided a link between early modernist styles of Pictorialism and the high modernist trends of the 1920s. It is perhaps significant that photography theory at this stage, and later, is closely associated with the art world. The identity of the discipline is often most strongly contested by theorists with feelings about its status as art.

Producers as Theorists in the 1920s and 1930s

The venerated achievements of key figures like the Hungarian artist, photographer, writer and film maker László Moholy-Nagy or the Russian Constructivist photographers of the 1920s such as Alexander Rodchenko demonstrate that practitioners have always been active in generating debates, writing manifestoes and linking their practice to the radical and new ideas that surrounded them. It is

THE RISE OF PHOTOGRAPHY THEORY

significant that in this period we see the first real assimilation and application of photography into the mainstream of modern art. The f/64 group in the United States of America pronounced a commitment to photography 'as an art form' based on characteristics specific to the medium (that is, studied avoidance of techniques derived from art, preference for American vernacular subject matter, and sharply defined imagery). The argument that techniques of photography are themselves an important object of theoretical engagement for scholars and photographers is demonstrated in the history of the medium. The abundant faith in photography as a means of extending the limited powers of human visual perception is widely expressed by photographers. In his 1925 book *Malerei, Fotographie und Film* (Painting, Photography and Film) Moholy-Nagy sang the praises of photography: 'We have – through a hundred years of photography and two decades of film – been enormously enriched in this respect. We may say that we see the world with entirely different eyes' (Moholy-Nagy, 1980: 166).

'Theory' is not restricted to scholarship. Key concepts and ideas are always generated by practitioners. Insofar as photographers think about style, content, technique and potential audience response to their work they are engaging with theory. As the photographer and writer David Bate has noted 'there is no untheoretical way to see photography … all practices *presuppose* a theory' (Bate, 2009: 25) and yet some theories carry more weight than others.

The 1920s and 1930s were a period of economic recession and political unrest. It was also a period when techniques of reproducibility and dissemination of photographs had created a huge market for printed products. The widespread development of advertising and the availability of reproduced photography in journals and popular media generally inspired artists to question ideals of gallery art and high culture. Many turned to photography as a democratic medium and celebrated the idea of reaching a wider audience. The use of hand-held cameras with easy-to-use roll film encouraged documentary and photojournalism. Photographers found outlets for their work in popular illustrated periodicals, weekly magazines and avant-garde publications.

The close proximity between art and politics in the inter-war period led to intellectual speculation on the importance of photography as a method of mass communication. The German theorists Siegfried Kracauer and Walter Benjamin celebrated photography as a democratic tool with revolutionary potential. Benjamin, speaking at a meeting in Paris in 1934, envisaged radical new uses of popular media that would melt down traditional barriers between art and the general public. A key site for progressive politics is the newspaper, which allows the photograph to work in tandem with the written word: 'What we must demand from the photographer is the ability to put such a caption beneath his picture as will rescue it from the ravages of modishness and confer upon it a revolutionary use value' (Benjamin, 1982: 24).

The 'modishness' to which he refers in this statement was to be found in the type of contemporary art photography that he accused of turning social themes into stylish consumer products. In Benjamin's critical perspective the photograph easily becomes an object of consumption and loses its revolutionary potential when detached from its social use. For Benjamin photography was to be given a didactic role alongside writing in a popular medium that destroys the barrier between author and reader. He proposed the intellectuals find ways of engaging with new media, new techniques, and new audiences and cites the photomontage works of John Heartfield (fig. 7.8) 'whose technique made the book jacket into a political instrument' (ibid.: 23). Benjamin argued that stylish contemporary practice is limited by its appeal to the connoisseur. In his view advanced art and advanced politics work together hand in hand. This modernist principle guided the radical cultural politics of the inter-war period. It was an article of

157

PHOTOGRAPHY THEORIES

faith which survived the war and returned in radicalized art and politics of the 1970s. As we will see, photography once again becomes the favoured medium of the avant-garde as it had been in the 1930s. And once again, with Benjamin in mind, it is closely linked with the written word.

RETHINKING PHOTOGRAPHY: THE 1960S AND BEYOND

This part of the chapter draws on intellectual currents that have been formed in artistic and photographic practices from the late 1960s up to the present day. It is historical in its approach and concentrates on the British context in which influential links were established between theory and practice. This section provides an introductory guide to contemporary issues in art and photography. In various formations, methods and modes of address, photography increasingly occupied a central place within some of the most progressive trends in the visual arts. The rise to pre-eminence of avant-garde photographic practices is convergent with the rise of photography theory since the late 1960s. Radical confrontation with the institutions of art is one aspect of this story. Another major aspect is the historical lift in the cultural status of photography which was shaped by artists (first and foremost) turning to photography. It is also significant that this period (late 1960s to the present) has continued a remarkable symbiosis between art education and contemporary practice.

The growing interest in photography and the wider social context in which photographs circulate is related to the taste and values of a post-war generation whose interests were strongly influenced by the social and political context in which they lived. The influence of anti-war and anti-consumerist movements combined with the struggles for civil rights and women's liberation in the late 1960s. Photography also provided an alternative to painting and sculpture and a way of challenging the orthodoxy of established art practices. These changes can be summarized as follows:

- photography theory is closely connected with social radicalism
- photography is adopted by some conceptual artists who questioned the traditional nature of art
- art education is strongly affected by conceptualism which threatened the teaching of traditional methods of art.

Activism, Art and Ideas

The late 1960s and early 1970s saw the rise to prominence of key artists adopting photography as their principal medium of expression. In the wake of social protest movements and political activism in this period the author and critic John Roberts observed a 'radicalization of a younger generation of artists and intellectuals' (1998: 144). A few key institutions in England and Wales became the sites for the incipient forms of conceptual art. These included Lanchester Polytechnic in Coventry, Newport School of Art and Design, Nottingham Polytechnic and Regent Street Polytechnic amongst others.

Politicized students and a few art school teachers challenged some of the sacred cows of art education. The identity of art had been an issues since the Cubists and Dadaists had introduced non-artistic materials, found objects and written texts, into their studio practice and had challenged the rituals of high culture. In the later 1960s a sceptical and enquiring attitude began to define artistic practice and in some quarters this led to questions about its relations with social, political and intellectual life. The craft basis of existing practice failed to answer such questions. Some of the most demanding students

THE RISE OF PHOTOGRAPHY THEORY

turned to related areas of the curriculum including philosophy and the social sciences. Studio practice was displaced by research and the production of pamphlets and other writings which appeared in self-made journals and other formats. 'Theory' itself became a kind of practice. Roberts has noted how the widening of access to art education in Britain in this period led to an increase in the number of working-class students in Britain with 'little formal attachment to the virtues of higher education' (1998: 144). The questioning of hierarchies and the dominant role of the fine arts (painting and sculpture) influenced vocal dissent, refusal to follow convention, acquisition of skills and aptitudes not usually associated with art students and the rise of photography theory. The British artist Victor Burgin later commented:

> One of the things conceptual art attempted was the dismantling of the hierarchy of media according to which painting (sculpture trailing slightly behind) is assumed inherently superior to, most notably, photography.
>
> (1984: 18)

There is some irony in the fact that photography, after many years of struggle for acceptance in the academy, was ushered in, not by 'art photographers' in the old sense of the word, but instead by artists who admired its non-artistic and 'low-brow' documentary functions.

The study of photographs as mainstream media artefacts had been established by the theorists Roland Barthes and Stuart Hall. As we have noted, semiology provided an alternative to art criticism since it seemed to treat all sign systems, without discrimination, in the same way. This was its great appeal for some artists whose strategies were driven by a desire to question the institutional separation of art and society. Semiology was useful for theorists such as Burgin because, as a method of analysis, it offered an alternative to subjective expressions of personal taste and placed an emphasis on the way in which 'meaning' (in art, photography and in everyday language) is a normative, handed down, socially agreed fact of life in structured systems of social exchange. In other words 'taste' is a word that defines social refinement and the rituals of cultural consumption. The few proto-conceptual works of this period seemed to be always questioning themselves and their right to be seen *as* art. Much of it was ironic and humorous in examples such as Keith Arnatt's *Self Burial (Television Interference Project)* of 1969, which is a staged photograph of himself disappearing into the ground or John Hilliard's *Camera Recording Its Own Conditions* (fig. 5.2).

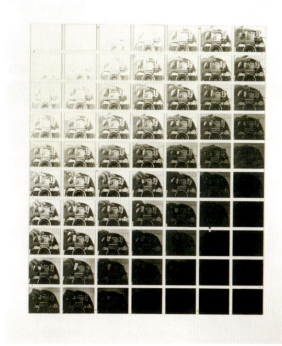

5.2 John Hilliard, *Camera Recording its Own Condition (7 apertures, 10 speeds, 2 mirrors)*, 1971. © 1972 John Hilliard. Digital Image © Tate, London, 2014.

Both works seem to show that 'art' is a product of the conditions in which it is made. It may have strong aesthetic appeal but this is always constrained by a multitude of competing influences and ideas. In other words art is governed by ideas that generate its production, circulation

PHOTOGRAPHY THEORIES

and consumption. Hilliard's *Camera Recording its Own Condition*, of 1971, explores the effect of isolating different combinations of shutter speed and aperture in mirror reflection. In this example 'photography' is the medium *and* the subject in the work. It presents a sequence of frames in which each is a version of reality pre-determined by the camera settings. Artistic intention is over-ridden by the determinations of the apparatus. Rather than seeing art as an expression of personal taste (as in a selective view of nature) we have a parody of self-expression. The work is invested with the *idea* of 'photography' and this is what makes it a piece of conceptual art.

Conceptual Art and Photography

According to the conceptual artist Ian Burn there are five progressive features in Conceptual Art that distinguish the movement:

- the reaction against the marketing of art
- the tendency for artists to use more democratic forms of media and communication
- greater attention to actual human relationships
- emphasis on collectively organized work methods
- an interest in education leading to demystification of art and increased awareness of its role in the social system.

These features were set out by Ian Burn, a member of the art collective Art and Language (see Paul Wood, 2002: 67). The crucial turn to language in the late 1960s was part of a tendency to confront what was seen as the privileged and class-bound mystique of high culture. The post-war consensus that allowed for upward class mobility produced some oppositional effects, not least in art education. Roberts comments:

> With the rise of photographic theory the 1970s and 1980s witnessed a substantive turn-around in critical agendas, attitudes and priorities in the practice and study of photography … as such, a confident theoretical culture of the image began to take hold in the academy and the photo-graphic workshop.

> (Roberts, 1998: 145)

The rise of theory in this historical moment is closely linked with the changing profile of photography as the medium of choice in progressive art. Steve Edwards has noted, 'Conceptual Art took language as its primary material, but its secondary form was the photograph' (Edwards, 2004: 137). The turn to language offered a way of diminishing art criticism as the domain of the connoisseur and the privileged 'educated' voice of the critic. The first order concept of practice (making things) and the second order level of commentary were combined in deliberate opposition to audience expectation. The conceptualists did the unthinkable: they exhibited words. These were often words about 'art' and/or the institutional context of the museum. When photography was assimilated into the work of some key figures in this period it might have looked like a compromise with the bleak intellectualism of the first wave of conceptual art. It was, however, a quite functional type of imagery that made no concessions to art photography. This was not the formalism of the earlier art photographers but an approach to the use of photography of a different kind. David Bate notes:

160

THE RISE OF PHOTOGRAPHY THEORY

Unlike fine art photography, where the craft value of the image production was itself part of the meaning-value, the use of photography by conceptual artists documented actions, installation work, performances and events or was part of an artwork.

(Bate, 2009: 29)

> **KEY TERM: The Vernacular**
>
> The word vernacular is often used to describe the kind of language or dialect associated with a region. It is often taken to mean a kind verbal expression that is down-to-earth and without any claim to distinction. Its value resides in its ordinariness as it has functional qualities and an absence of wilful self-determination. In regard to the design sphere, where it has been applied, it refers to the commonplace, anonymously made products such as houses or anything that is man-made without any claim to distinction. The water towers photographed by Bernd and Hilla Becher might be called examples of industrial vernacular. The attraction of these objects lies in their absence of any architectural self-consciousness. Vernacularism signals the existence of a style that derives from the vernacular.

The emphasis was on the photograph *as a document*, and as a means of *recording* transitional or temporary events. It was the ordinariness of the photographic document that appealed. Black and white photographs alongside modest looking written statements were submitted as a kind of 'art' that challenges traditional modes of aesthetic interpretation. A functionalist aesthetic was consistently used as a kind of foil. Edwards calls it an attempt to 'ruin high modernism's aesthetic' (Edwards, 2004: 146). This was a moment that echoed the anti-aesthetic turn to the vernacular last seen in the work of the Dadaists and the Russian Constructivists earlier in the century. It is worth considering how far this generation regretted the lost political idealism that marked the revolutionary aims of the 1920s.

> **KEY TERM: Dada**
>
> This is a style label that was coined by a group of dissident artists and poets during the First World War. Their work and ideas anticipate and strongly influenced the conceptual art movement that emerges in the late 1960s. The Dadaists challenged established notions of artistic practice, introducing non-art materials into the production of art works (pasted paper and found objects were childishly stuck to paintings); they exhibited found objects such as 'readymades' and adapted the techniques of popular illustrated magazines to their own subversive ends. The 'readymades' were commonplace objects nominated as art and made to challenge artistic expression as a defining attribute of the work of art.

PHOTOGRAPHY THEORIES

KEY TERM: High Modernism
This is a term that is often linked with theories of the American critic Clement Greenberg. His ideas were developed in the late 1930s and came to be associated with post-war New York School abstract art. He emphasized the importance of art that recognized and achieved its best outcomes when it exploited its own conditions. This is often taken to mean that a medium should find its own limiting or specific conditions and thus become a 'pure' example of its type. His ideas influenced the taste for large abstract colour field painting in the 1960s.

RUSSIAN CONSTRUCTIVISM

Russian Constructivism is a movement that emerged in the Soviet Union after the October Revolution of 1917. The term was coined in 1921 and refers to the way meaning in an art work can be reducible to its constructive features. The shaping and invention of a work are central to its valuation as a practical set of operations upon the specific qualities of materials used. It is an aesthetic that appraises the dignity of socially useful work. The Constructivists are associated with early forms of abstract art but quickly adapted their ideas to 'applied' art in graphic design, fashion, theatre and architecture. They saw themselves as the artistic fraction of the revolutionary avant-garde.

The ultimate aim of Russian Constructivism was to dissolve the gap between art and life. The movement was highly motivated to adapt new technologies to their cause. Using a small hand-held camera Alexander Rodchenko pioneered a dynamic use of camera angle shots that challenged traditional ways of seeing. Rodchenko attempted to make the audience more actively aware of looking by experimenting with multiple exposures and close ups that obscure the identity of objects recorded in the image. The technique was an attempt to 'defamiliarize' the object in ways that challenge conventional expectations. By the late 1920s he adopted a 'straight' style photography still informed by his use of spatial dynamics.

The Photograph as a 'Non-Art' Document

Before the 1960s the idea that art traditionally towered over other forms of visual expression (including photography) tended to make 'non-art' forms marginal or undistinguished. Thus graphic design, layout, illustration, political satire, photojournalism and so forth were treated as minor arts. Painting by contrast was privileged and especially abstract art, which seemed to appeal to the 'educated' eye. To the conceptualist this model of social preferment and privileged taste was unacceptable since it seems at several removes from the experience of everyday life. The new generation of the 1960s and 1970s adopted photography as a way of engaging with (and attacking) the framing conditions of art.

These changes can be explained in reference to Walter Benjamin's earlier writing on photography. Benjamin welcomed advances in photography that challenged and displaced traditional notions of art. The ideas of Benjamin were made popular in 1972 by John Berger in a television documentary entitled *Ways of Seeing*. This programme and the book that followed widened interest in sexual politics and the idea that art and photography exercise power as carriers of ideological messages. This had a wide influence in academic and artistic circles. Younger artists such as Victor Burgin established a way of using image and writing that seemed to ignore boundaries between disciplines and cultural levels that were taken as the norm in the period around 1970.

BIOGRAPHY: WALTER BENJAMIN (1892–1940)

Walter Benjamin was a German, Jewish philosopher and a critic. He is remembered for his critical essays on photography. His work is situated in a period of political crisis that included the rise of fascism. He committed suicide after fleeing the Nazis during the Second World War. His key works on photography include:

1 'The Author as Producer', 1934 (Benjamin, 1982)
2 'The Work of Art in the Age of Mechanical Reproduction', 1936 (Benjamin, 2009a)
3 'A Brief History of Photography', 1931 (Benjamin, 2009b)

Benjamin believed technology is a powerful reproductive force and argued that it had important consequences for the way we appreciate art. He was an original thinker and one of the first to address the way photographic technology and the printing press had become an inescapable part of all cultural practices in the age of mechanical reproduction. His writings in the 1930s confront the similarities and differences between art, photography, film and sound recording. His argument in the 'Author as Producer' essay is that revolutionary content (in art) must be presented in a progressive medium. His positive view of an intellectual and artistic alliance with revolutionary workers represents one side of his views on social and technological progress. On the other hand Benjamin belonged to a new generation of Marxist critics who diagnosed mass entertainment and commodity cultures as stabilizing features of modern capitalism.

The 'Invention' of Photography Theory

Burgin claimed that photography theory had not existed prior to the publication of his book *Thinking Photography* published in 1982. This was clearly a provocation. The book consists of a collection of essays written by Burgin himself with contributions from contemporaries and earlier key figures including Benjamin. It is a foundational document. In recalling this moment David Bate refers to 'the outbreak of theory' (Bate, 2009: 29) that has lasting importance for the emergence of photography as an important medium in late twentieth-century art. This proclaimed 'invention' of photographic theory in the 1970s (and early 1980s) is closely connected with conceptual art and in the English context it is an expression of unrest and agitation in art education. Burgin observed: 'The academic content of such courses tends overwhelmingly to take the form of an uncritical initiation into the dominant beliefs

PHOTOGRAPHY THEORIES

and values prevailing in the art institution as a whole' (Burgin, 1982: 3). Such beliefs include the search for a romantic inner-self, or the construction (in Burgin's words) of 'the familiar figure of the *artist* as autonomous *ego*' (ibid.: 145). It is a fashionable pathway that leads to glory for a few and yet the privileging of the photographer's personality ignores the photograph itself. Whatever motivation and design lies behind the making of a photograph it is always invested with meanings established elsewhere in the world at large. The artificial separation of photography from contingent fields of visual communication (such as news or editorial photography) represents, in Burgin's view, a special pleading for art photography. Photography reduced to 'pure form' invites a wilful suspension of contingent meanings attaching to the things it shows.

Burgin also notes how photographers adapt their work to 'prior texts' that are 'presupposed' by the photograph and 'serve a role in the actual text but do not appear in it' (Burgin 1982: 144). This refers to the way photographers are influenced by others but in Burgin's argument we find a more abstract sense of way images are formed. His interest in texts that relate to prior texts underlines the idea that all images are simulations of something else. This raises issues for the identity of the photograph and its truth claims that were denied or derided in the postmodern trends of the 1980s. In the postmodern view the artist is a manipulator of signs rather than their originator. This is played out in photographic strategies that rely on quotation, pastiche and parody – a tendency to appropriate earlier styles of art, photography and other media. It also involved staged photographs that imitate the production techniques of cinema and the narrative meanings of popular culture. The use of the still camera for fictional purposes has precedence in Victorian photography. In the 1980s it was a continuation of the conceptualist's attack on 'self-expression' and the cult of art.

Burgin's use of 'found' words and publicity photographs were designed in a way that makes a pastiche image out of the originals and invests an ironic reading of what might in other circumstance seem quite normal. In 1976 he designed and fly-posted a simulated advertisement that poses a question: 'What does possession mean to you?' (fig. 7.6). The poster literally uses a quotation ('7% of Our Population Own 84% of the Wealth' from *The Economist*) but also 'quotes' glossy styles of visual coding and intersecting symbols of gender and wealth. Being drawn to advertising as a site for critical deconstruction of popular imagery Burgin's poster was a pragmatic extension of his theoretical work.

> **KEY TERM: The Single Picture Aesthetic**
>
> This is a phrase used by the documentary photographer and theorist Allan Sekula to describe photographic images that obediently follow the art-institutional separation of words and pictures. Sekula criticized this tendency in art photography, especially in large works designed for museum installation. He condemned the 'single picture aesthetic' (with separate title and external discourse outside and beyond the work) as conservative because it accepts a return to the cultural hierarchies of the past that insisted on the separation of intellect (words) and intuition (pictures). The conceptualist photographers had of course challenged the dichotomy of criticism and practice. The delegation of intellectual authority to a self-styled 'expert' was anathema to the conceptual artist.

THE RISE OF PHOTOGRAPHY THEORY

The work of the photo-conceptualists offered a critical examination of the way signs are the carriers of sublimated messages in performance of their more obvious commercial functions. The straight photographer's separation of pictures and words (the so-called *single picture aesthetic*) was repudiated by the conceptualists who looked back to the interdisciplinary experiment in photomontage of the 1920s and 1930s. Like the Dadaists before them the conceptualists dissolved the traditional boundaries between art and the world around it. For both generations photography was closer to an industrial skill set which aligned it with the working class. The historical model for this link between artists and workers was found in writings of critics such as Walter Benjamin and the revolutionary avant-garde of the Soviet Union. Earlier in the century the Russian theorist Boris Arvatov had spoken of prospects for the 'melting of artistic forms into the forms of the everyday' (cited in Roberts, 1998: 26). For the artists of Burgin's generation it represented a high level of political idealism that was hard to sustain.

The words of artists expressed in typed statements and critical essays now joined photographs in a 'scripto-visual discourse' (Burgin's coinage in Godfrey, 1982: 9). This position represented a middling position between *language* and *pictorial* signs as signifiers. If the rupturing of disciplinary boundaries (of art, language, photography, 'theory' and politics) caused a major upheaval – and there is evidence that it did (see Godfrey, 1982) – it is nevertheless also true that these changes provided the inspiration for much of what was to follow.

In this context there was a turn to mixed media practices and a wide and varied use of new media. By the 1980s photography in particular had become a primary medium in the visual arts. This in turn led to an increase in political engagement amongst a generation of young artists influenced by identity politics and the semiotic guerilla warfare of the first generation of conceptualists. Indeed, the shift in intellectual and artistic fashion produced a new generation of multi-media practitioners and a spate of new university courses devoted to cultural theory. Many of these overlapped with art and photography degree programmes at key institutions in England and elsewhere.

5.3 Barbara Kruger, *"Untitled" (I shop therefore I am)*, 1987. © Barbara Kruger. Image courtesy of Mary Boone Gallery, New York.

Postmodern Trends and Second-Wave Conceptualism

Artists such as Cindy Sherman, Barbara Kruger and Richard Prince in America – all working in the now dominant medium of photography – represented a new generation of artists whose

165

PHOTOGRAPHY THEORIES

consciousness-raising projects fitted well with the glamour and exclusivity of the increasingly commercial art world that supported it during the international art boom of the 1980s. Kruger's word play art works demonstrate her skills in copywriting and graphic design. The philosophical pun: '*I Shop Therefore I Am*' (fig. 5.3) (lifted from René Descartes' rationalist principle: 'I think therefore I am') reflects the banality of consumerism in present times. Kruger's mix of words and photographs recall the agit-prop graphics of Heartfield, Daumier and the English satirists of the eighteenth century.

The work of this generation represents an explicit concern for the politics of identity. In particular we can see how far photographers and artists extended aesthetic interest into the wider fields of sexuality, gender, 'race', social class, Aids, and other discourses in which photography plays a role. Their work is a second wave of conceptualism rooted in photography and informed by a high level of political literacy. The turn to politics in the work of Burgin, Hans Haacke, Sherrie Levine, Allan Sekula, Martha Rosler, Sherman and others seemed to provoke audiences into critical engagement with repressive stereotypes and consumerist escapism. Specific sites of engagement included the human body (Sherman, and Levine), commodity culture (Burgin) and the city (Rosler) and corporate cultures (Haacke).

IDENTITY POLITICS

This is a term that defines social categories or alliances outside broad-based political parties. Affiliated groups and new social movements are shaped by a shared sense of social identity. Typical identity formations include gender, ethnicity, religion, sexual orientation, environmentalism and the politics of HIV and Aids. New social movement began to emerge in the 1960s with student unrest, anti-war activism, feminism and the struggle for civil rights. The most typical groups saw themselves in a marginalized or subaltern position by comparison with relatively privileged or traditional formations. Social class identity is often important to representatives of these groups without it being the most urgent or indeed the most central concern. Identification with a group offers sanctuary and a sense of belonging; it is also a platform that allows for organized political mobilization.

Identity politics has a strong presence in art and humanities teaching and learning and is closely aligned with issues in media and cultural representation. Academic methods used include textual analysis and studies of persuasion techniques in advertising, stereotyping, marginalization of minority groups and the social effects of institutional power. Identity politics has its critics who think that a group's proclaimed 'difference' (its identifying self-image) is celebrated as an eternal category that in turn reinforces separation. Its defenders claim that smaller, militant groups are dynamic and fluid. In other words they reject separatism.

Levine's work questions the conceptual framework of key work in the history of American documentary photography from the 1920s. One of her works is entitled *Untitled* (*after Edward Weston*), 1981. It is one in a series and is exhibited as a photographic print that is in turn a photograph of an original by Edward Weston from 1925. It is in other words a re-photograph or 'quotation' of a canonic work in the history of high modernist photography. To most people it is indistinguishable from the original and as an artistic gesture represents a critical assault on the very idea of authorship, subjectivity and authenticity. Whose work is it? Is it a 'Levine' or a work by Weston? Is it a plagiarism? What does the term 'original' mean in this discussion? Is the original a print or a negative? For the conceptualist the idea came first and the work, the material object, is merely a token presence. From a marketing and sales point of view the 'work' is a photographic print and unless the negative has been destroyed there can be any number of identical prints. Is the subject of the portrait (the photographer's son) the 'original'? Is the boy in the photograph the end point of the project? The photograph puts the viewer in contact with him, with his naked body, and this in turn recalls images from classical art and the idea of the idealized youthful body as art. This kind of reading locates its meaning as an aesthetic object in the history of art. Levine's intervention, however, makes us think again and reminds us how unstable photographic meaning can be. Think for example of photography as museum art and the contradictions that occur when, in the words of the photography historian Abigail Solomon-Godeau, 'a technology of multiples' is translated 'into one of originals' (Solomon-Godeau, 1997: xxv). Levine defiantly relocates 'the work' in a parallel history of artistic subversion that goes back to the ready-mades of Marcel Duchamp. Levine re-thinks photography as if to say: photographic meaning is never exclusive to the work itself.

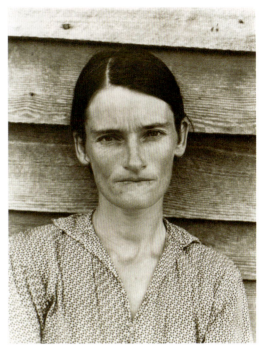

5.4 Sherrie Levine, *After Walker Evans: 4 (Allie Mae Burroughs)*, 1981. © Walker Evans Archive, The Metropolitan Museum of Art. © 2014. Image Copyright The Metropolitan Museum of Art/Art Resource/Scala, Florence.

KEY TERM: The Canon or Canonic (Its Adjectival Form)
The term derives from a Greek word that means 'rule' or 'rod'. It is generally used to assert the idea of a critical standard that is recognized by expert opinion. This in turn is related to 'great works' of authors and artists whose work is cited as examples of good practice. A canon is a list of works already received as genuine and the best of their kind.

Take for example her *After Walker Evans: 4 (Allie Mae Burroughs)* of 1981 (fig. 5.4). This image is a re-photograph of an Evans 'original'. The photograph taken by Walker Evans is a classic example of state-sponsored documentary photography taken during the Depression in the 1930s. And yet despite this knowledge the photograph, in Levine's treatment, is transformed by its changing institutional role as a valuable piece of artistic property. The act of re-photographing the original underlines its commodity status. This way of evaluating the image is compounded when Levine enters the market with her parasitical version of the image. The strangeness of this discourse around photographic meaning can be seen in a comparison of Figure 5.4 above and the 'real' Walker Evans reproduced below in Chapter 6 (fig. 6.19). Rarity value and celebrity often intrude in art appreciation. This point is highly relevant in Levine's practice.

PHOTOGRAPHY THEORIES

The work of this generation demonstrates an acceptance that there is no neutral space of pure aesthetic contemplation and that the spectator's and the artist's place in the world is always contingent and in some ways shaped by history. The reshaping of rural poverty into a fine art aesthetic disguises its original meaning as a Depression-era document. This is apparent in re-makes of Walker Evans' documentary photographs taken in the southern states of America during the 1930s Depression. Levine offers a critical response to the simplistic sense in which the image is supposed to represent the exact feeling the photographer experienced at the time of its creation. The oppositional view of Levine is that art is always a manipulation of artistic convention and is therefore measurable against the performance of others.

Levine presents a new idea for images already validated by the art world. They are now revalidated by different criteria. The feelings Evans had about sharecroppers in the 1930s are still relevant but the audience, when faced with a re-photographed version, is now obliged to think about what that actually means as a remediated level of communication. The audience is also asked to think about how Evans' photographs relate to the changing circumstances in which they are seen.

CONCLUSION

Conceptual art has had a major influence on key trends in photography. Looking back at this period it may appear paradoxical that, as a movement, it had the effect of sustaining photography as gallery art rather than extending its influence into a wider field of social and political activism. This may be a criticism that could be levelled at some of the key artist-photographers we have discussed but we should not leave the subject with a negative view. Conceptual photography was a transitional phase in the history of the medium and had a large influence in contemporary art, art education and publishing. Its legacy can be measured in rising standards of critical writing and the intellectual field it encompasses is wide and growing. Photography theory is closely connected with other disciplines including film and literary studies, philosophy, anthropology and media studies. It has become one of the most exciting areas of contemporary critical discourse. Conceptual photography has remained a powerful presence in the art world where the use of non-traditional materials and methods is now a legitimate and normal feature of contemporary art.

The rise of photography theory occurred in a period in which literacy-based images were a reprise of earlier attempts to challenge the 'single picture aesthetic'. The turn to mixed media in higher education, especially in the new universities, is symptomatic of key changes occurring in the recent past. Since the 1970s photography theory has raised standards of debate and maintained close contact with developments in contemporary art and culture. Photographers and theorists (often the same people) are in some measure united in the belief that they share a common desire to make sense of the world in which they operate and to continue to produce work that reflects this ambition.

SUMMARY OF KEY POINTS

- Photography has been theorized since its inception. It was invented by scholarly and experimentally minded individuals who were predisposed to speculate on how it works and what it is.
- We have provided a brief history of photography theory. The main purpose of the chapter is to underline the way art students and a younger generation of artists and critics developed a radical

THE RISE OF PHOTOGRAPHY THEORY

critique of photography in the post-war period, but especially in the late 1960s and 1970s. We have thus noted the rise of a particularly militant kind of theory in this period.

- Historical periods are often carved into manageable units of time. This creates a way of seeing periods as dominated by a spirit or ruling idea when in fact they are open to a range of competing interpretations. Technological change, political struggle and artistic innovation can be related to historical conditions at particular times.

- The institutional separation of theory and practice into scholarly and intuitive models of knowledge was challenged by conceptual artists.

- The relevance and legitimacy of traditional materials of art (painting and other kinds of handmade objects) was questioned as new material and techniques were deployed. Artists adopted photography as a useful medium for recording performance work and other activities.

- Artists stressed the 'ordinariness' of photography and disassociated their own use of the medium from 'art photography', photography as 'self-expression' and the cult of art.

- The increasing use of photography as an alternative to traditional media helped to establish the medium in the mainstream of contemporary art practice.

- Artists adopted semiology and other intellectual methods including philosophy and social science which informed their work and became part of their practice. Critical methods deployed by artists challenged the separate practices of art criticism. The latter was often motivated by social ideas of refinement and good taste. In contrast semiology is a more democratic method that treats all signs, whatever their social rank, in the same way.

- Semiology also showed how signs are social objects and can be understood to operate as coded messages. This also meant signs can be de-coded in ways that reveal their deeper social functions. This way of thinking about signs contrasted with the abstract and private meanings associated with art.

- Underlining the social embeddedness of the photograph, theorists such as Victor Burgin and Allan Sekula stressed that photographs carry meanings that are structured by the world that gives them currency. Audiences see images in different ways and thus play a part in the production of meaning. Seeing is obviously a private experience but is, nevertheless, social and historical too. In other words perception is structured by customary ways of relating to the world.

- Burgin and other theorists have shown that photographs are 'texts' which carry meanings deriving from an overlapping series of prior texts. Memory of other texts are therefore active when we view an image and productive in the construction of its meaning. This way of thinking about representation leads to the denial of *presence* (Barthes calls it an object 'that-has-been') in the photographic image. What seems to be real in the photograph is always a simulation of something else. We have shown how this way of thinking provided a theoretical basis for simulation methods in contemporary art and photography. The exploration of staging, quotation, repetition, copying and plagiarism typifies the postmodern trends of the 1980s. These anti-realist strategies found a rationale in the conceptual art movement's critique of documentary methods and the emergence of sceptical attitudes to the truth claims of photography.

- Identity politics is closely connected with the more combative forms of postmodern photography. Pressure groups and social campaigns inform photographic practices in the late twentieth century. The strategy of contesting stereotypes and social prejudice have characterized anti-war, feminist, gay and civil rights struggles: all these formations have representations in contemporary art and photography.

169

REFERENCES

Bate, David (2009) *Photography: The Key Concepts*, Oxford and New York: Berg.

Benjamin, Walter (1982) 'The Author as Producer', in Victor Burgin (ed.), *Thinking Photography*, pp. 15–31.

——(2009a) 'The Work of Art in the Age of Mechanical Reproduction', in Walter Benjamin, *One-Way Street and Other Writings*, trans. J.A. Underwood, London: Penguin, pp. 228–259.

——(2009b) 'A Brief History of Photography', in Walter Benjamin, *One Way Street*, pp. 172–192.

Berger, John (1972) *Ways of Seeing*, Harmondsworth: Penguin.

Burgin, Victor (ed.) (1982) *Thinking Photography*, London and Basingstoke: Macmillan.

——(1984) 'Absence of Presence: Conceptualism and Postmodernism', in Hilary Gresty (ed.), *1965–1972: When Attitudes Become Form*, Exhibition Catalogue, Cambridge: Kettle's Yard, pp. 17–24.

Doty, Robert (1960) *Photo-Secession: Photography as Fine Art*, Rochester, NY: George Eastman House.

Edwards, Steve (2004) 'Photography out of Conceptual Art', in Gill Perry and Paul Wood (eds) *Themes in Contemporary Art*, New Haven and London: Yale University Press in association with The Open University, pp. 137–180.

Godfrey, Tony (1982) 'Sex, Text, Politics: An Interview with Victor Burgin', in *Block* no. 7, pp. 2–26.

Hall, Stuart (1980) 'Encoding/Decoding', in Stuart Hall, Dorothy Hobson, Andrew Lowe and Paul Willis (eds), *Culture, Media and Language: Working Papers in Cultural Studies*, London: Unwin Hyman in association with Centre for Contemporary Cultural Studies, pp. 128–138.

Moholy-Nagy, László (1980), 'Photography', in Alan Trachtenberg (ed.), *Classic Essays on Photography*, New Haven, CT: Leete's Island Books, pp. 165–166.

Morley, Simon (2003) *Writing on the Wall: Word and Image in Modern Art*, London: Thames and Hudson.

Nochlin, Linda (1997) 'Foreword' in Abigail Solomon-Godeau (1997), pp. xiii–xvi.

Roberts, John (1998) *The Art of Interruption: Realism, Photography and the Everyday*, Manchester: Manchester University Press.

Solomon-Godeau, Abigail (1997) *Photography at the Dock: Essays on Photographic History, Institutions and Practices*, Minneapolis: University of Minnesota Press.

Trachtenberg, A. (ed.) (1980) *Classic Essays on Photography*, New Haven, CT: Leete Island Books.

Wood, Paul (2002) *Conceptual Art*, London: Tate Publishing.

Woodward, Kathryn (1997) *Identity and Difference*, London/Thousand Oaks, CA/New Delhi: Sage.

INTRODUCTION TO CASE STUDY 3

This case study includes an example of the kind of visual analysis that is informed by semiology and places an emphasis on the way technical codes adopted by photographers and designers often reinforce the values associated with the choice of theme or subject matter in an image. The case study also includes an introduction to the terminology and historical background of contemporary discussions of semiology.

CASE STUDY 3: SEMIOLOGY: HOW IMAGES MAKE MEANINGS

SECTION 1: INTRODUCTING SEMIOLOGY

Semiology is generally taken to be a study of signs. This gives it a wide area of operation. Signs might for example be visual or linguistic or a combination of the two things. They function as elements in wider systems of meaning production. Ordinary objects in the world also carry meaning when they are assimilated into the world of meaning. An oak tree can be made to stand for something when adopted as a corporate symbol of sturdiness and endurance. The selection of sites in landscape photography is often a clear illustration of 'meaning making' that may seem to be a straightforward and direct way to promote an idea. The semiologist will point out that the attribute we attach to an object is motivated by its place in an already existing structure which encourages a certain a way of seeing it. The oak tree stands for the qualities or ideas that are conventionally associated with it in advertising and other systems of representation. We might therefore accept the semiologist's claim that the actual sign is itself arbitrarily linked with its corporate meaning. Social custom and knowledge of its associated meanings developed over time allow us to connect the tree with its promotional significance.

Semiology is a powerful tool because it always stresses the *relational* value of a sign. It has been widely used as a technique in textual analysis of literary, artistic and commercial forms and is especially effective in detecting latent meanings in things that might pass unnoticed. As a technique it offers a way of exploring signs as part of organized social intercourse. As the theorist Daniel Chandler (2007) has noted, semiology (he uses the term semiotics) makes the coded meanings of signs more explicit and allows us to uncover their disguised or ideological effects. The suggestion here is that messages often have a deeper meaning that is obscured by what appears to be their most literal interpretation. As the theorist Margaret Iversen has noted, semiology is a useful technique in 'laying bare the prejudices beneath the smooth surface of the beautiful' (cited in Rose, 2007: 74). Semiology is one of the

CASE STUDY 3

key methods for understanding how meaning is constructed within a particular advertisement. Rose describes it as follows:

> Its prominence is due in part to the fact that semiology confronts head on the question of how images make meanings … semiology offers a very full box of analytical tools for taking an image apart and tracing how it works in relation to broader systems of meaning.
>
> (Rose, 2007: 74)

PHOTOGRAPHY AND SEMIOLOGY

Each sign is to some degree arbitrary because the meaning we attach to it is dependent on social custom and historical usage. 'Cat', 'chat' and 'kot' (English, French and Polish) are conventional signs for a furry creature that says 'meeow'. We could invent another term for a private language and it would suffice if we used it consistently. There are exceptions to this rule but most signs are arbitrary and can be subject to manipulation or used in special ways to shape meaning. For example a shouted use of a word is different to a softly spoken version. A large colourful sign for a product is different to a modestly scaled version it. The sign in these examples has an arbitrary relation to what it means and our way of understanding it is affected by cultural convention. Photographs, however, have a very special relationship with the object to which they refer. They appear to be causally related to what the semiologist Charles Sanders Peirce called the referent. In this case the sign is, arguably, not arbitrary because in its appearance it corresponds with what it shows.

In the estimation of Roland Barthes a photograph has a special status: it is an un-coded message with persuasive powers proportional to its reality effect. Some critics have doubted the idea of an un-coded or natural message. The act of perception itself, we are told, is a decoding operation and so a photograph, like any other sign, is equally constrained by the context which gives it meaning (Burgin, 1982: 63). In contrast to this view we have argued that photographs are different to other types of messages. The 'uncodedness' of the photograph allows it a measure of resistance to incorporation into wider structured meanings (see Chapter 6). It is an effect of 'innocence' that is exploited in advertising. It is also an attribute of the photograph that it provides evidence where other systems of verification are less convincing.

BIOGRAPHY: ROLAND BARTHES (1915–1980)

Roland Barthes was a French literary critic and a much-quoted theorist on the subject of photography. He was also a semiologist and his translated work began to exercise an influence upon photography theory in the English-speaking world in the 1960s. This influence was most widely effective with the publication of:

Mythologies (1972b) [first published in 1957]
Elements of Semiology (1972a) [1964]
Image. Music.Text (1979) [1977]
Camera Lucida: Reflections on Photography (1981) [1980]

> His work is important because it encourages readers to analyse commonplace objects including advertisements, popular novels, dress codes, cars, cookery, wrestling and photographs as if they contain messages, assumptions, beliefs and ideas. His reader is allowed to think how these objects are encoded by the words and images that surround them (and us) in everyday life. The cultural studies theorist Dick Hebdige said that Barthes set out to examine
>
> > The normally hidden set of rules, codes and conventions, through which meanings particular to a certain social group (i.e. those in power) are rendered universal and 'given' for the whole society.
> >
> > (Hebdige, 1979: 9)
>
> Following Barthes we might say that one of the tasks of the semiologist is to unpack these rules and reformulate our attitude towards them.
>
> *Camera Lucida: Reflection of Photography* is the English translation of Barthes' *La Chambre Claire*, which was published two months before his death in 1980. This short, semi-autobiographical book is a personalized account of the way certain photographs affected Barthes and includes a discussion of a photograph of his late mother. It is an influential book which builds on ideas developed in earlier writings on photography including the classic essays in *Image.Music.Text* first published in English in 1977. Barthes' key point is that photographs are irreducible to language since they are reflections on the presence and authenticity of the referent. This is a controversial idea since some critics believe there is no presence of anything 'real' in the sign but only chains of meaning, representations of representations, a procession of meaning or endless semiosis.
>
> *Camera Lucida* also famously differentiates between two ways of reading a photograph. At one level it performs as a *studium* which provides its abstract social meaning; at another level it performs as a *punctum* and conveys a message that might be personal, touching and even irrational. The discussion of 'photographic contact' and 'manifestation' in Chapter 3 of this book is related to ideas developed in *Camera Lucida* and other writing by Barthes.

Ferdinand de Saussure, the Swiss linguist and pioneer of semiology, argued that a sign is a two-sided entity:

The signifier

The signifier is an object or a shape on a surface. It is a sound-image, the word (spoken or written), or the picture that stands for something other than itself.

The signified

The signified is a thing that is inseparable from the signifier. All signifiers have a *signified*. It is what the *signifier* stands for. It is the concept, the idea, the mental image.

CASE STUDY 3

An example of a signifier is the word 'ketchup'. Another example is the image of a red bottle with a brand name on it. The signified in this example is a 'ketchuppy' thing in our head that we recognize from past experience as a sweet condiment that accompanies certain types of food.

For the purposes of analysis we might separate the two parts of the sign but in effect they are inseparable. The notion of the 'sign' in Saussure's semiological analysis needs to interact with other signs for it to participate in the production of meaning. We thus understand 'ketchup' as something that is not a signifier for a brown sauce. There is in this example a rather simple colour coding in the visual representation.

BIOGRAPHY: FERDINAND DE SAUSSURE (1857–1913)

Ferdinand de Saussure was a Swiss linguist and one of the pioneers of semiology. His principal interest was in the way meaning attaches to social practices, actions and modes of expression. He helped to promote semiology as a science of signs. His key textbook (*Course in General Linguistics*), first published in 1915, is based on lectures he delivered at the University of Geneva in the period before the First World War.

As we have indicated he pronounced on the two-part nature of all signs that are commonly expressed in English as *signifier* and *signified*. The importance of this idea is based on Saussure's proposal that the relation between the two parts of the sign is arbitrary or non-motivational. This is a key feature of language and forms the basis for the structural nature of all communication. There is in other words no natural link between the word 'egg' and the object it represents and no inevitable connection between the signifier and the signified. All terms of reference must be established in the speech community that uses them. Each language group has a different concept for objects that existed prior to their use. There are exceptions when words sound like what they stand for: 'splash' in English for example. Colour denotation presents a useful set of terms that belong to a sequence of red, blue, green, and so forth. An awareness of the sequencing of terms underlines a second important linguistic idea associated with Saussure: the capacity to hear and understand *differences* between verbal utterances and written concepts. When the English term 'red' is uttered we know what it refers to. Equally, we also know what it does not refer to. The value of language expression lies in what is not selected in particular utterance as much as what is selected. And every utterance relies on the entire system (*la langue*) from which the individual utterance (*la parole*) has been selected.

The production of meaning also requires that the listener has internalized the language. This analysis of language use extends into an awareness of the way signs operate more generally in society. When the sign is visual, for example in a body gesture such as a raised fist, we can 'read' it in certain ways that are familiar through its past uses. It may signal anger or social protest and the context in which it operates will help to determine what it means. There is a degree of arbitrariness between the gesture and what it represents and so its meaning will have been internalized by the receiver of the message. Saussure's approach to linguistics underlines the way meaning relies on social convention. It also recognizes that meaning is relative to changing contextual factors.

The question of how far pictures operate like language is a philosophical issue that we discuss in Chapter 6. Suffice to say pictures can be made to function in a language-like way and there is no doubting they rely heavily on social convention.

BIOGRAPHY: CHARLES SANDERS PEIRCE (1839–1914)

Charles Sanders Peirce (pronounced 'purse') was an American philosopher. He was a pioneer of 'semiotics' (or 'semeiotic' as he called it). 'Semiotics' is an Anglophone term. The French and Swiss have tended to use the term 'semiology' as we have throughout this case study. Both usages derive from the Greek word *sēmeion* for sign. Peirce is best known for his triadic theory of the sign discussed in this case study. Peirce identified three types of signs:

- *Symbols*, which are connected by convention to the object they represent
- *Icons*, whose significance derives from their resemblance to the objects they represent
- *Indices*, which have a causal relation with their objects. In this case the sign we might say has a physical connection with an object in the world. An example is a footprint in the sand or a photograph.

The conceptual value of the triadic theory is that it allows for important ways of thinking about the way signs relate to their objects. As we have argued the indexical sign (third in the triad listed above) has important implications for the values we attach to the photograph. Truth claims attaching to photography rest heavily on its indexical nature. Charles Sanders Peirce's writings are voluminous but a useful collection was published in 1955.

Peirce's idea that the sign has three levels (or classes) has been widely used in cultural theory. One of the three (the indexical) has special significance for the way we understand photographs. The three levels are:

Indexical Sign

In this class of signs there is a causal link between the object (or referent) and meaning. For example a death mask is an indexical sign, and smoke is a 'sign' for fire, or a black cloud in the sky signals that it will soon be raining. A photograph is said to have an indexical link with its referent because it is 'caused' by the referent and it is a trace of what it refers to. Because this relationship is quasi-mechanical and because the photograph is a registration of light rather human intention it is thought be un-coded. The photograph is not like other types of communication. It is for example very different to a painting or a drawing. An artist is involved in a coding procedure when she selects a particular type of line to draw, or when making a judgement about the choice of colour to represent what she sees. Roland Barthes argued, therefore, that in the case of the photograph we have the paradox of a message without a code. As we have argued elsewhere (see Chapter 3) this suggests that, as Trevor Millum has said, 'the photograph itself represents a total break with all previously existing types of signifying systems' (Millum, 1971: 38). It is a system that defines a particular kind of indexicality: it not only looks like what it represents, it was actually formed by it.

CASE STUDY 3

> **KEY TERM: What Is a Code?**
> A code is a sub-system of the sign: 'red' in a particular context means 'stop' because it has a consistent meaning in a sub-system of colour coding. Coding is a kind of designation that takes place in the process of naming things or adopting conventional meanings that have been handed down through social custom. A code is a form of socially constructed knowledge. Coded meanings are non-naturalistic and must be learned. Photographs are said to be *un-coded* messages.

The Iconic Sign

In the iconic sign the relationship between the signifier and the signified is a very specific one of resemblance. There is, for example, in this class of signs a uniquely important correspondence between the signifier and signified. This relationship is also called a denotation of the kind that we find in photographs or realistic paintings. Theorists have noted how in examples of this class of signs the meanings it produces have the character of appearing 'natural' as in a realistic painting. This predisposition to the natural can be misleading. An iconic sign is not causally dependent upon the object to which it refers. It is not an index. A painting may look like what it represents but it is not caused by it. It is mediated by style and the executive skill of the artist. The resemblance can, in fact, be approximate as in public signs for gender. There is a greater or lesser degree of conventionalization in the design of an iconic sign.

Symbolic Sign

In this case the link between the signifier and the signified is completely *arbitrary*. The link has no motivation. In every respect the symbolic sign is unlike the indexical and the iconic sign. Most words for example are symbolic signs. Flags are symbolic signs. For signs to be effective it is important that they express difference so that 'dog' and 'cat' cannot be confused. The Union flag (for Great Britain) and the *tricoleur* (the French flag) will never be confused. We should again note how colour coding (in tandem with other design features) facilitates the effectiveness of symbolic signs.

In the example of a national flag the link between the signifier and the signified is *conventional* and *arbitrary.* The word 'red' in English stands for the colour of London buses and UK letterboxes. There are socially accepted rules that dictate the meanings we attach to signifiers. The rules operate within a structure – if we make it up as we go along, and attempt a private language, we would literally cease to make sense. Different signs have different values and they rely on difference and opposition. For example signs might work by exclusion so that we get a system of binary opposites:

- black/white
- female/male
- active/passive,
- etc.

SEMIOLOGY: HOW IMAGES MAKE MEANINGS

Meaning is produced by the interrelationships between signifiers and their relations within the whole. The signifier does not produce meaning in isolation. Somewhere in the past the linkage of signifier and the signified was agreed or in some way established. In particular circumstances a white flag means 'surrender'. Saussure stressed that signification (the production of meaning) does not rely on an individual colour. What matters is *difference*. The significance of white is that it is *not* red (or anything else). The 'agreement' becomes a code when it comes into play and when it is sustained by use. Meaning is not, however, fixed. Because it is *arbitrary* it can be changed. 'Wicked' can be linguistically inverted to mean something else – possibly something good. This kind of inversion applies to the symbolic sign. The indexical sign cannot choose its signification. Smoke can mean a lot of things but it will always signal fire and the photograph (manipulation notwithstanding) will always have an indexical relationship with a non-negotiable referent.

The Importance of Semiology

Semiology has sought to expose hidden meanings in everyday objects and their representations. What appear to be natural and part of the general stock of things are in fact cultural constructions that disguise deeper truths embedded in a way of life. A signifying system like advertising, for example, requires a conformist audience that will accept its broadly ideological representations of modern life as perfectly natural to the order of things in the world that we know. These might include the classic distinctions between men and women or exclusion of particular groups as entirely in keeping with our worldview. When these conventions are idealized and made to seem glamorous they achieve a deeper hold on their target audience.

Ideology is a term that identifies the way in which ideas (in a social group at a particular historical conjuncture) are made to seem natural and perhaps even necessary. Advertising exploits existing values and makes them seem normal. It may use *stereotypes* that exaggerate social difference. For example an idealized body image relies upon the audience bringing previous knowledge and competencies to the task of 'reading' an image. The coding is familiar since we may have settled ideas about 'femininity' and the normality of seeing goods and services (anything from cosmetics to cars) linked with sexualized bodies. The linking of objects and 'desire' relies on the uncritical acceptance of the intended meanings inscribed in the advertising system.

Advertising has a double effect because it promotes products for sale and achieves this objective by establishing an association with something desirable or noteworthy. It is socially conservative rather than socially radical. To the extent that advertising fixes identity and confirms difference (active men/ passive women) it sustains and reproduces the order of the things in society as they stand. In the critical assessment of the social effects of advertising it is argued that ads create an imaginary (or delusional) place in the world which substitutes for our true condition.

Photography is an effective advertising medium because it takes us back to a primal scene in which something existed. It might be a pretty woman or a smiling baby, or both together, as a mother-child unit. In a typical example we see a photographic representation of a perfect mother and child conforming to the racial, generational, and social class stereotypes. The photographic denotation bestows on the image a 'truthfulness' that competes with its commercial aims. The naturalness of the photographic image (with its 'analogical plenitude') has every chance, however, of being mythical (see Barthes, 1979:

CASE STUDY 3

18–19) when it comes into contact with the viewer. In this example the image of mother and baby is reminiscent of the holy Madonna, which adds to its powers of persuasion. The meaning is double-barrelled as one level of meaning is constrained by the other: one is real and one is constructed. Barthes notes this as a paradox:

> The photographic paradox can be seen as the co-existence of two messages, the one without a code (the photographic analogue), the other with a code (the 'art', or the treatment, or the 'writing', or the rhetoric, of the photograph).

> (1979: 19)

Somewhat elusively Barthes says '… the connoted message [the mythical idea of the Madonna in our example] develops on the basis of a message *without* a code' (ibid.: 19). We take him to mean that the photograph in advertising or journalism is invested with values outside or beyond its analogical role and is thus made to serve supplementary or commercial ends.

It is clear that advertisements are designed with an audience in mind. Market research helps the industry to shape advertisements to audience expectation. Ads may include challenging materials but are often meant to please and achieve this by relying on traditional audience expectation. It is a world in which social attitudes are confirmed by signs that are easily processed. The signs for humans are standardized and conventional. They take their lead from other visual systems such as the fine arts or popular illustration from the past.

We might for example note how wisdom and knowledge might be encoded in the picture of an older person, sensuality and decorativeness in pictures of women, athletic black bodies in pictures signifying physical power, children connected to the idea of innocence and purity and babies may be used as a sign of the future.

It is important to note how the power of the photographic image (where the real body is there to be seen) reinforces the meaning transmitted in the linguistic message. As we will see in the next chapter verbal and visual codes have a complementary relationship in certain types of formats. Mainstream ads belong to this format.

KEY TERM: Ideology

The word ideology usually has negative connotations. For example we have described it as a set of ideas that may seem to dominate the way people think. It can also be used to describe the way unequal social power relations are made to seem normal or even inevitable. The taken-for-granted reality of quiz shows, art fairs, car styling, militarism, and 'styles of government' is sustained in the social rituals of modern life. Everything in the modern world that is dependent on representation can translate into what Barthes calls a mythology of everyday life. Semiology has many functions but in Barthes' writing it offers a way of criticizing dominant ideologies or, to put it another way, de-mythologizing their social effects.

Decoding Ads

A brief discussion about stereotyping is the first step in a process that might lead to critical engagement and analysis of advertisements and other 'signifying systems'. If the audience is aware that meaning is constructed and shaped to achieve a particular way of seeing it may be encouraged to resist its effects. Stuart Hall identifies three ways of reading signs:

- accepting the dominant or preferred meaning – that is the 'meaning' defined by the person who made it
- negotiating the dominant or preferred meaning
- refusing the dominant or 'preferred' meaning (see Hall, 1980: 128–138).

This is a simplified schema but it has the virtue of suggesting that all signs allow some measure of audience response and this may be relatively free. Some measure of sophistication and prior knowledge comes into operation. For example critical analysis is posed as an optional strategy in our way of dealing with advertisements. Analysis at this level has been described as 'decoding' – a process which is intended to reverse the construction of meaning and perhaps reveal a deeper truth about the nature of things. For an in-depth discussion of these issues see Judith Williamson's pioneering book *Decoding Advertisements* (1978). Decoding techniques rely on semiological methods. Two key terms used in semiology are denotation and connotation.

Denotation

Denotation refers to the literal meaning of a sign such as an image of the Eiffel Tower in a holiday brochure. It is sometimes called a *first order level of signification*. It is the level at which we identify something before attaching meaning. In reality there is no time delay before meaning becomes attached so that denotation is a theoretical term and its value is to help us think about the way signs (including photographs that function as signs) actually work. Denoting is a process of describing or recognizing what something is. We might for example attach a word, 'dog', to a denotative image of a dog. The denotation tells us it is a dog and not an elephant.

Connotation

Connotation is a much more interesting *second order level of signification*. We can *see* what the object is (since it is clearly denoted) but what does it actually mean? Connotation is the sign's capacity to *mean* something beyond its denotation. Whatever associations we attach to a dog (these are of course learned in childhood) have the effect of expanding our knowledge of its place in the world. When we infer a meaning from the image of the dog it has moved beyond denotation. This movement is in fact a spontaneous response to the sign.

The Eiffel Tower might serve as an example that explains connotation. It is a feat of engineering and yet has meanings beyond this. An image of the tower (in a holiday magazine) might trigger a sequence of thoughts about Paris and elegant city life. Connotation is a word that describes what happens when a sign is operating at a level beyond description. In the case of the Eiffel Tower we note how it is configured in a wider semiological scheme in which the reader brings a certain knowledge and sophistication to the project of looking. The image of the tower has connotations of 'Frenchness' – a complex signification mediated by tourism and other systems of representation. This is an example of a particular kind of connotation that is called *metonymy*.

Metonymy is a figure of speech that is used for convenience as in the example of something not being called by its own name. We might say 'the suits were out in force' when 'suits' stands for business people. The previous suggestion of a connection between children and innocence (in art or advertising) is a further illustration of this type of connotation.

Another type of connotation is widely used in advertising. This is called the *synecdoche*. This term is used to indicate the way a small part of something stands for the whole. Again the example of the Eiffel Tower can be used to stand for the whole of Paris or the whole nation of France in particular types of representation. Tourist literature with a picture of the famous tower illustrates this point.

It should be clear from this description of connotation that its effectiveness depends on the context in which it appears. An image of a naked human body has sexual connotations in a lurid magazine or a tabloid newspaper. Its powers of suggestion are dependent on the receptiveness of the audience to the message it conveys. Its semiological effect relies on its reception in a speech community that is familiar with its coded meanings. When the context changes the mode of reception may change with it. A picture of a naked body in a medical journal may not have the same value that it would have in another context since it would be an object of study and, in its way, a challenge to a reader's medical knowledge rather than a cheap thrill. Equally important are the purely textual characteristics of an image. These can be reduced to its purely visual properties when it is assessed as a creative object independently of what it represents in other terms. These aspects of an advertisement are an important part of what it means as cultural artefact. The technical or aesthetic characteristics of any kind of image are not, however, separate from what it represents as a social object since the style and content are related. In the next section we will consider a range of technical codes and show how they relate to conventional ways of reading them.

SECTION 2: TECHNICAL CODES

We have noted how photographs have a certain power of naturalness that distinguishes them from other types of signs. We have in other words underlined their status as indexical signs. We have also noted how this provides the viewer with a feeling of proximity to the subject that is not commonly found in other media. We will continue this line of thought in this section and show technical codes such as those found in the design of advertisements exploit this effect of photographic closeness to achieve powerfully erotic meanings that are made to work by association with marketable products. We will argue that technical codes assist the process of signification by producing meaning at the level of connotation.

As we have seen the choice of subject matter is important in the case of the advertising image. Equally important is layout, typography, and the design of the image. These are technical codes of composition that function as codes of connotation in audiences sensitive to their effects. The choice of black and white photography carries with it historical meaning linked with the 'truth-value' of the journalistic image. Other technical codes will come into operation and may form the basis of a more detailed visual analysis. These might include a study of some of the following:

SEMIOLOGY: HOW IMAGES MAKE MEANINGS

Information Value and Composition

The spatial location of elements (printed copy, the image, and the use of white or blank space) within an image is indicative of compositional meanings which influence the way the image is read. Consider some of the following properties in a perfume advertisement of the type we expect to find in a glossy fashion journal (fig. CS3.1).

In the *horizontal arrangement* we see a conventional placing of elements in the advertisements that correspond with a traditional way of reading a textual message – that is from left to right:

- Left side of the image presents given or familiar objects/ideas. In Figure CS3.1 the photographic representation of a female model is quite expected and normative in this kind of image.
- Right side of the image presents the new, or not yet known, object that is the product (a perfume). It may be a new name or brand, or else it may be new by virtue of re-branding. The 'newness' of the product is a selling point. If the product is established and unchanged the advertisement must be original in its approach. The position (bottom right) is normal for a pack shot and its visibility is clear.
- In a *vertical reading* of Figure CS3.1 we have have identified an established design methodology that has been scrutinized by the semiologists Gunther Kress and Theo Van Leeuwen in their book *Reading Images: The Grammar of Visual Design* (1999). These authors have noted how often press advertisements are structured by conventional ways of reading from the top of a page to the information below, that is from higher to lower levels of value.

In the upper part of the frame the viewer is given 'the promise', an object of desire, which provides the emotive content. In Figure CS3.1 the glamorous appearance of the model fulfils this function and is calculated to capture attention.

In the lower part of the image we see the pack shot which figures as the reward. This may be accompanied by the name of the product and below this any practical or actual information relating to the product. The latter may be expressed in small print in some advertisements.

Composition

Salience is a word used by the semiologists Kress and Van Leeuwen (181–229, *passim*). It is used to describe elements in images calculated to attract attention in differing degrees according to their *position* in the layout. Salient forms would for example be highly noticeable in the foreground or centre of a typical layout. The figure of the model is a clearly a salient elemental form in figure CS3.1.

Framing

The presence or absence of framing devices signifies connections or separation between different figures so that relative position, or *juxtaposition*, may carry an important message. The model in figure 1 appears in a pictorial mode that is reminiscent of a fine art print. The frame separates the image from the context in which it is seen. This privileges the image and influences our way of seeing it. This way of reading the image is confirmed by the abstract pictorial effects that surround the soft-focus view of the model. The classic pose of the reclining female nude also derives from art historical conventions. The

181

CASE STUDY 3

model's body conforms to coded ways of seeing the female subject as passive, sexualized and alluring. The bottle is caressed and its commodity status is changed by the narrative in which it appears.

Juxtaposition

Two images placed side by side may produce a relationship of unity or separation. In this case the model and the perfume are closely linked by their proximity.

Captions

An image without a caption may be considered to be a kind of 'open text'. This means it is open to interpretation. Captions function as an *anchor* that may reduce ambiguity in the reading of the image. Barthes claims that readers have a terror of 'uncertain signs' that is relieved by the addition of a linguistic message (1979: 37). For a discussion of this effect and the interrelation between words and images see Chapter 6 below.

Symbolic Codes

Audiences may be familiar with the connotative meaning of specific words or images. A dove is either a conventional sign for peace or in the context of Christian iconography it symbolizes The Holy Spirit. Symbolic signs may have more than one connotation so context is an important modifier in the production of meaning.

Body Language

Physical posture and pose are important signifiers that are often controlled by photographers in an advertising shoot. Equally relevant are decisions controlling body types such as thinness, fleshiness, and signifiers of ethnic or generational identity have connotations that are inscribed in the mindset of consumers. The facial expression of the model in Figure CS3.1 is expressively sensual and her outward gaze may suggest a private scene disturbed by an intrusion. The reader becomes a voyeur in a scene that relies on dramatic tension.

Clothing Codes

Identity issues are often controlled by the connotation of clothing. Occupation, nationality and religious belief are signalled in dress codes. Clothing may also be a signifier of social status and class difference. A uniform signifies exclusive membership of a social institution or group and has connotations of 'belonging' or respect for authority. Equally a deviation from a dress code may signify resistance to uniformity and rejection of authority. A loose school tie or a short skirt flouts the rules and has subversive connotations recognized by classmates and figures of authority.

Camera Angle

Camera angle is the implied angle of vision up or down, at an angle or straight on. It is a powerful carrier of meaning. A classic example is the downward gaze of the documentary camera that belittles and subjugates its subject. Another example is the upward camera gaze that allows a figure to tower over the viewer in a way that signifies the authority of its subject. An example would be a politician on a rostrum as seen by a press photographer from a lower position. Oblique angles can produce dynamic effects exploited in sports and dance photography. Camera position affects a viewer's point of view in literal and metaphorical ways. When a relative position is fixed in a photograph it conveys a social meaning.

Camera Distance

In a similar way the fixing of a relative distance between the viewer and the viewed can provide a strong social meaning. A key example is the proximity of the camera to its subject that often signifies intimacy. In Figure CS3.1 the model is seen in a way that would be socially unacceptable in everyday life for anybody except an intimate partner. The intrusiveness of the camera exploits what appears to be the staged innocence of the model. How far is the implied camera from the subject in this example?

CS3.1 Jimmy Choo fragrance advertisement, 2014. Courtesy of Advertising Archives.

Focus and Lighting

Soft-focus is often a technical code for romance. In Figure CS3.1 we can study the effects of soft lighting as an accompaniment to the sensuality of the image. What is highlighted and what is left in the shadows? The photographer has highlighted the uncovered parts of the body that are made to correspond with the product. An identity is thus established: they are both sensual objects. In other examples sharp focus brings salient forms into prominent view.

Colour

Colour can be used to suggest a mood of sorrow, gaiety or excitement. Colour may have the capacity to create abstract meaning such as romance or purity. Bright or dissonant colours may be used to suggest modernity, sepia range to signify tradition. Colour is also used to achieve a visual connection in advertising imagery so that a golden image of ripe corn in a field may correspond with a matching colour of the product itself in another part of the image. Cereals for example often rely on this kind of colour coding.

It is clear from these examples that the technical codes deployed in photography have a powerful influence on the social meanings of commercial images. In the example used above we have noted how

CASE STUDY 3

the photograph is connoted by the context in which it is used. We have argued that the special power of the photograph is an attribute of its naturalness and yet meaning is also created by technical codification. This is indeed a paradox that applies to the photograph which, uniquely, is natural and cultural at the same time. It is perhaps worth adding that whilst there are two messages at work its ultimate destination is to function as a part of what Barthes calls a traditional stock of signs. It is this that allows us to see the photograph, including the one we have used in Figure CS3.1, as something that is made to serve a commercial and (equally important) an ideological function. One of the reasons for studying signs is to achieve a better understanding of what lies behind them. Deconstructing the inner life of signs takes us back into the wider field of cultural politics.

CULTURAL POLITICS

All of the above rely on symbolic coding and may have an effect on a wide range of issues and concerns – especially perhaps in relation to the question of the effectiveness of design strategies in advertising and other systems of media representation. Some of the issues that might be activated by the use of symbolic codes include:

Branding

The word branding refers to the use of signs to construct an identity for goods and services in a marketplace where selling is driven by promotional techniques.

Celebrity

The placement of celebrities in advertisements alongside products may have particular effects: the latter gains status by association with the former. The product may take on connotations such as strength, elegance, or 'wickedness' by association with celebrity individuals.

Gender and Sexual Stereotyping

Gender stereotyping is a product of ideological fixations on gender roles that are widespread in all areas of cultural practice. Conspicuous examples of negative gender and sexual stereotypes are to be found in advertising, marketing and pornography. Photography is a key media and reproduces repressive social perspectives and yet materials used in this way are deeply embedded in the cultural life of signs that reach back through the centuries.

'Racial' and Ethnic Stereotyping

This can relate to exploitation of difference and the social construction of 'otherness' that take the form of presumed simplified, generalized, and negative views of 'exotic' figures in non-Western social groups. Equally widespread in Western media is the way ethnic minority groups are structurally excluded from media representation and made to feel outside the mainstream of contemporary life.

Objectification

Objectification is a word that relates to all the repressive modes of describing the human body as if it were a purely visual spectacle. It is often connected with close ups or body fragmentation and sexual attributes. The technique is often used in representation of women and also colonial photography. Objectification produces a negative reading against which its opposite is constructed. 'Masculinity', for example, is self-defined by its opposition to female stereotypes.

SUMMARY OF KEY POINTS

- Semiology provides a critical method for analysing how images relate to wider systems of meaning. We have noted how Barthes' essays on photography established new ways of thinking about the medium.
- Semiology has many functions but in Barthes' writing it offers a way of criticizing dominant ideologies or, to put it another way, it provides critical concepts that can be deployed in the study of their social effects.
- We have noted how the un-coded nature of the photograph can be exploited in the process of making meanings seem natural and true. This effect is productively used in advertising and press photographs where linguistic signs (captions and suggestive copy) determine the content of a message.
- We have argued that photographs have strong denotative power. This is a power that derives from the photograph's analogy with its referent and gives it a direct link with its object. When it reaches the level of connotation the message is reinforced by this direct link with the object.
- We have noted how mainstream images such as advertisements use rhetorical devices (including glamour and excess) to make lifestyle choices and consumer ideas seem natural. One of the effects of mainstream media practices is to achieve a match between audience expectation and a supply of images customized to this requirement.
- Decoding strategies used by semiologists have challenged negative stereotypes such as sexism, racism and class prejudice. Wider targets include the segmenting of society into consumer groups and the loss of occupation-related or other kinds of identity formation.
- Technical codes such as visual effects found in advertisements, especially those using photographs, carry meanings that influence the way we read the image. We have listed 'effects' such as compositional strategies that take account of conventional ways of reading from left to right and from the top of the page to the bottom. These structured ways of reading influence the designer's positioning of visual symbols and advertising copy. We also discussed the expressive meanings of image framing, juxtaposition of salient objects in an image, captions, body language, clothing codes, camera distances and camera angles. All these are ways of codifying the message contained in an advertisement.
- We have shown how visual effects transfer into social and cultural meanings.

CASE STUDY 3

Barthes, Roland (1972a) *Elements of Semiology*, trans. Annette Lavers and Colin Smith, London: Jonathan Cape.

——(1972b) *Mythologies*, trans. Annette Lavers, New York: Hill and Wang.

——(1979) *Image-Music-Text*, trans. Stephen Heath, London: Fontana/Collins.

——(1981) *Camera Lucida: Reflections on Photography*, trans., Richard Howard, New York: Hill and Wang.

Burgin, Victor (ed.) (1982) *Thinking Photography*, Basingstoke: Macmillan.

Chandler, Daniel (2007) *Semiotics: The Basics*, London and New York: Routledge.

Hall, Stuart (1980) 'Encoding/Decoding', in Stuart Hall, Dorothy Hobson, Andrew Lowe and Paul Willis (eds) *Culture, Media and Language: Working Papers in Cultural Studies*, London: Unwin Hyman in association with Centre for Contemporary Cultural Studies, pp. 128–138.

Hebdige, Dick (1979) *Subcultures: The Meaning of Style*, London and New York: Methuen.

Kress, Gunther and Van Leeuwen, Theo (1999) *Reading Images: The Grammar of Visual Design*, London and New York: Routledge.

Millum, Trevor (1971) 'Introduction to Roland Barthes's "Rhetoric of the Image"', in Centre for Contemporary Cultural Studies, *Working Papers in Cultural Studies* (Spring), University of Birmingham, pp. 37–39.

Peirce, Charles Sanders (1955) 'Logic as Semiotic: The Theory of Signs', in Justus Buchler (ed.) *Philosophical Writings of Peirce*, New York: Dover, pp. 98–119.

Rose, Gillian (2007) *Visual Methodologies: An Introduction to the Interpretation of Visual Materials*, London: Sage.

Saussure, Ferdinand de (1966) *Course in General Linguistics*, edited by Charles Bally and Albert Sechehaye in collaborations with Albert Riedlinger, trans. Wade Baskin, New York, Toronto, London: McGraw Hill Company.

Williamson, Judith (1978) *Decoding Advertisements: Ideology and Meaning in Advertisements*, London: Marion Boyars.

CHAPTER 6
PHOTOGRAPHY AND THE WRITTEN WORD

In his early writings on Semiology the critic Roland Barthes said that 'pictures become a kind of writing as soon as they are meaningful' (1972b: 110) which seems to express a subservience of the picture to writing. He later modified this view and accepted that photographs have a certain resistance to other structures of meaning including surrounding texts and language more generally. It is nevertheless true to say that images and words are often intimately connected and seem to co-operate with each other in the production of a unified message.

Most advertisements achieve effective interactions of verbal and visual messages in a shared space. This image is a parody of a pictorial style found in advertising imagery and reproduced in a book by Kalle Lasn, the founder of *Adbusters* magazine. The image belongs to a well-established multi-media format in which images and words are more or less equal in their semiotic value. It looks like it could be an ad for a baby product but the text subverts this reading. The anodyne message, 'she's got your eyes', is sabotaged by the montage image of a television set which offers the provocation: whatever you see in this life is mediated and controlled by mass culture.

The natural look of the baby enters into a symbolic level of meaning that is determined by the written message and the 'language-like' operation of the

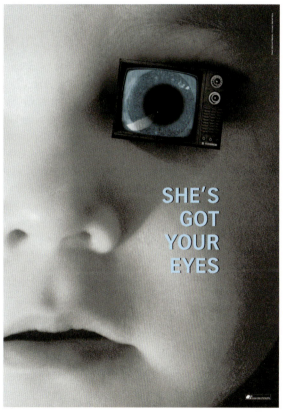

6.1 *She's Got Your Eyes*, concept by Warren Neily and photograph by Shannon Mendes. From Kalle Lasn, *Culture Jam: How to Reverse America's Suicidal Consumer Binge – and Why We Must*, 2000, New York: Harper Collins. Courtesy of Adbusters.

PHOTOGRAPHY THEORIES

photograph. Ads rarely encourage ways of breaking the media trance. This image humorously seems to be doing this.

INTRODUCTION

In this chapter we will address the way photographs relate to words. Photographs appear in many different formats and we will focus on some key examples which will enable you to think more deeply about the way they are used. The chapter questions whether photography is itself a kind of language with its own syntactic structures and powers of communication or whether it is something quite different, with a life of its own outside verbal discourse. Are photographs self-evidently different to other systems of communication? Is language intrusive or an unnecessary constraint upon the purity of the photographic image? Casual reference to photography as a language allows uncertainty: are we speaking literally or metaphorically? Does photography speak to us in a language-like way? Key concepts are explained as we study the way captions, titles and other verbal forms interact with photographs.

Photography as a Language

The term 'photography' may be taken for granted and so we begin this chapter with a reminder that it means 'light' and 'writing'. The Greek suffix 'graph' translates as writing (possibly 'written' or 'that writes') so we have light that *is written* or light that *writes itself*. The idea of writing with light (as if it were a medium) is a helpful way to think about it. This is perhaps fanciful since light is a phenomenon rather than a scribe. The etymology of the word photography is strange and yet it is hard of think of a better name for the practice. To speak of photography as a language is perhaps a tautology since the idea of writing is an in-built part of what the term actually means. It is, nevertheless, true that when we speak of photography as a language we don't usually mean it in a literal sense: it is a metaphor. What is often meant is that it operates *like* language without actually being one. On the other hand common sense might suggest that language and photographs are two quite different things. The photograph looks natural and true in a way that language does not. Despite this lurking doubt the association of 'photo' and 'graph' seems to insist that we analyse the linkage.

Photographers often refer to their practice as a 'language' as if it is 'saying' something. In the case of art photography the 'something' might be profound, or deeply felt, rather than merely a description of the world. This may in fact be a testing point in the case of photography when viewed as a quintessentially descriptive medium. Whether we think of the photograph as an expressive or descriptive medium (artistic versus documentary) the idea of *something* being transmitted is compelling.

Photographs transmit ideas and values as constituent parts of descriptive media. At this level we may think of a photograph as a something that operates like a linguistic sign. A photograph of a funny face may communicate 'humour' and is therefore comparable with a verbal joke. Insofar as the photograph's usage determines meaning it is made to behave like language. Photography has specific qualities that make it different to other media forms (including writing and speech). It is, nevertheless, always in the company of language and so it is necessary to consider some of the ways in which the two things interact. The least we can say about the interaction is that speech influences interpretation and affects the way photographs gain currency (value and meaning) in the world. Words in advertisements

188

or captions attached to press photos are obvious examples of the conventional juxtaposition of words and photographs.

In this chapter we explore some of the relationships between language and photography. Our strategy is to treat photographs and language as 'sign systems' and assume that they both transmit meaning.

When words and photographs combine, the meanings they produce are variable so that they may be (a) mutually reinforcing, (b) interchangeable, or (c) oppositional in the way that they communicate. In most cases one system of representation is an elaboration of the other as when a caption to a news photo directs our interpretation of it – as if it were telling us *what it is*. This function of 'anchoring' meaning, according to Barthes, has a repressive value: it 'counters the terror of uncertain signs' (1979: 39). Another example is a speech balloon that relays something as it stands in a complementary relationship with the image. In this case the image-text is a fragment of a story and the 'unity of its message' (its meanings) is embedded in a narrative (see Barthes, 1979: 41). The linguistic and visual signs belong to co-existent systems of meaning. As a strategy for understanding this 'co-existence' we return to Charles Sanders Peirce's semiological categories of indexical, iconic and symbolic signs (see Case Study 3 (pp. 171–86) for a discussion of these terms). Before attending to theoretical issues attaching to the way these categories relate to photography we will consider some of the standard formats in which visual and verbal signs interact.

Verbal and Visual Sign Interaction

There are several ways in which visual and verbal signs interact. These include:

The Illustrational or Supplementary Functions of the Photograph

First we note that books, newspapers and magazines rely on images that are supplements to the written text. Photographic illustrations in history books are of this type. Also titles to art works or photographs in an exhibition are written supplements. Generally one system is spatially separate from the other. We may call this a *supplementary* function of the photographic image which is often deemed to be secondary if not dispensable to the overall message of the text. In this case the image is tautological in the sense of repeating what is indicated in the written text. An example would be a verbal description of a beautiful person and a picture of the same.

Multi-Media Formats

Second, there are *multi-media formats* in which image and words are more closely interrelated in a shared space. In this format the image and the word are more equal in their semiotic value. Advertisements or recipe books exploit the potential of this kind of hybrid form. We may call them 'scripto-visual' formats to emphasize how two things (the written text and the image) compete for attention. The visual sign in this kind of format may have an open-ended range of meanings that seem to demand some kind of anchorage or directed meaning. This directed meaning is often

6.2 'Let Us Go Forward Together', World War II propaganda poster. © Victoria and Albert Museum, London.

6.3 Raoul Hausmann, *ABCD (self-portrait)*, 1923–24. © 2014. Image copyright The Metropolitan Museum of Art/Art Resource/Scala, Florence.

provided by the written text even when the image appears to be dominant as it is in Figure 6.2. As noted above the metaphorical idea of 'anchoring' meaning derives from Barthes (1979: 38) for whom a caption, title or advertising slogan reduces the potential for a merely arbitrary or random reading of the message. Barthes, in fact, argues that a linguistic anchor is 'repressive' because it dominates and controls the way the image is seen. In Figure 6.1 the image of the baby and the words have a reciprocal value since they 'conspire' to make the same political point about indoctrinated ways of seeing. Equally, the image of Churchill and the legend that it accompanies in the Second World War propaganda poster also 'conspire' to make the same political point. Compare these two 'multi-media' examples with the conflicting messages in Figure 6.3.

Mixed Media Formats

Third, there are *mixed media* formats in which the relationship with other kinds of media described above is dissolved so that we have a blurring of traditional boundaries. Simon Morley describes the mixed media dynamic in which he says: 'Here, word and image have less intrinsic coherence and are only minimally separated from one another' (2003: 12). An avant-garde art form such as photomontage is a mixed media form that seems to exploit the deliberate confusion of visual and written signs. The anarchic cut and paste images made by Dadaists in the early twentieth century frustrate the conventions of horizontal typesetting and segregated illustration (fig. 6.3).

Inter-Media

Morley uses the term 'inter-media' to refer to formats where typographical imagery has expressive value which equals or even supplements its semantic purpose. He notes that before the invention of moveable type the tendency in written communication was predicated on 'pictographic' forms in which the written sign has a schematic visual resemblance to its referent. An example would be a typeface or manuscript that conforms to a visual aesthetic. Decorative and expressive use of letters aspires to an aesthetic reading and underlines the fact that writing is a form of *visual* communication that, as Morley notes, 'appeals to the *eye* as well as the mind' (2003: 12). Handcrafted inscriptions and image making share a common history that reaches back to the earliest forms of writing. The rise of realistic techniques of visual representation in the fifteenth century created an intellectual distinction between writing and painting. Insofar as the invention

PHOTOGRAPHY AND THE WRITTEN WORD

of photography is a culmination of this 'realistic tendency' it is possible to say this separation was completed with the invention of photography in the nineteenth century. It is significant that modernist painters reversed this trend (as in fig. 6.3) and returned art to the inter-medial and mixed media formats of the past. The blurring of boundaries between typography and painting in the work of the Cubists and the Dadaists illustrates this point.

Environmental Media

There is a fifth type of interaction between the visual and the verbal that we have added to Morley's examples. We have called this *environmental media* where a written text is an objective part of the scene captured in photographs. We are thinking of topographical street scenes and photographic recordings of neon signs, billboards, shop signs, graffiti, Tee shirt logos and so forth with connotations of city life and modernity. The interesting thing about this kind of photograph is that it often uses brand imagery and publicity slogans as an ironical message or as a way of capturing the feel of a mediated world of commercial signs. There are many fascinating examples of the conjunction of the linguistic and visual signs in the environment including the work of 'straight' photographers whose use of 'found' linguistic signs contributes to the social meaning of the scenes they record. The photographer Margaret Bourke-White records a scene in Louisville, Kentucky in February 1937 (fig. 6.4). The photograph is a documentary record of people seeking food and clothing from a relief station following a flood. It is also an ironic juxtaposition of words and image and a statement about two ways of life: rich and poor and black and white.

6.4 Margaret Bourke-White, *At the Time of the Louisville Flood*, 1937. Courtesy of Time & Life Pictures/Getty Images.

191

PHOTOGRAPHY THEORIES

The photographer wittily sabotaged the copywriter's idea of 'The World's Highest Standard of Living'. Inverting its rhetorical meaning, ironic use of the message is expressed in the scene it depicts and in the title of the work. Found words provide an anchor for the whole street scene and yet in this example the linguistic and the visual messages are in conflict. At a deeper level the photograph plays on anxieties about the relation between words and pictures. As we will argue the intrusion of words is often a problem for visual artists and in this work Bourke-White gives us good reason to beware of them.

Photography as a Function of Language

Images and word combinations and formats are everywhere in the modern world. We rely on some of the above functions in our own lives (including professional usage of these functions) and yet may be ignorant of the way these signs interact. The intellectualist privileging of the verbal over the visual might also be taken for granted as images are often seen as an interesting but dispensable mode of communication. In many books the illustrations or pictures are supplementary or added when resources allow. This has changed to some extent since access to photographs in the media and widespread use of photographic technology has changed social attitudes to the medium. One of the outcomes of this change is the proliferation of popular media forms that are now more commonly a mixture of words and images. The changing character and use of visual media and its increasing juxtaposition with the verbal now makes the idea of a separate 'visual culture' seem old fashioned.

There is even talk of a 'new literacy' based on images (Kress and Van Leeuwen, 1996: 15–16). This may be a little over-determined and in danger of missing the point. Our concern is not to promote images over words but to analyse their interaction.

The assimilation of photographs in different media formats relies on interaction and mutual co-operation. In the case of the press photo Barthes (1979: 16) notes the 'totality of information is carried by two structures (one linguistic)' that are co-operative and interactive but separated by their different identities. And yet there are lots of ways in which photography can be assimilated to language and made to behave in a language-like way. When a photograph takes on a sequential role it behaves like language in the formation of narrative meaning. For example a photograph might illustrate a written narrative or form a narrative in its own right as the dominant message in a photo-essay. Any medium that is capable of communicating thought or constructing meaning behaves in a language-like way. In most cases thinking of verbal language as a universal type of communication prefigures other systems of human expression.

To say that verbal language is a defining and exclusive form of communication may, however, be somewhat contentious. Some theorists, including the sociologist Ruth Finnigan (1997), have argued that verbal language (with its privileging of linguistic meaning and cognitive content) may be only a specific formation of a more general phenomenon. In a more expanded definition of language it may be possible to make claims for the expressive power of non-verbal media (art and music for example) and their differences with written messages whose piecemeal structure consists of discrete bits of infor-mation and data such as words. The tendency to see the world mediated by text-based written notation defines a sequential and linear mode of thought. Finnigan says 'it can be misleading to assume a crucial element in songs – let alone other music – must necessarily be the verbal component' (1997: 135). Her view is that the grain of voice or the character of its delivery shows a resistance to the literal meaning of

PHOTOGRAPHY AND THE WRITTEN WORD

a musical message. The connotative meaning in any kind of message can be allusive and open-ended. A strictly verbal account of photographic message leaves its meaning incomplete.

An extreme formulation of this post-language view of meaning is developed in the writings of the philosopher Vilém Flusser. He has argued that a culture of the technical image foreshadows the end of linear writing, and the photograph is not a cognitive messaging system but something else: an irreducible symbolic object that turns away from the text (Flusser, 2007). In this formulation the photograph has a pre-linguistic, language-denying status.

Photography as 'Pre-linguistic'

The photograph is not built out of symbolic signs and is not normally presented as a system in the way that written language is presented. The photograph functions as an image, albeit a very special image. As a *record* of a past reality it presents the idea of an unmediated imprint. Its primordial effect is reference and its *emphasis* must be: 'this happened' rather than 'this image/text means'. The author Clive Scott has expressed this point in the following way: 'However conventionally (symbolically) readable a photograph may be, it cannot fully suppress a certain lack of mediation' (Scott, 1999: 24). Information contained in a photograph ('lines, surfaces and shades' as Barthes puts it [1979: 15]) is not straightforwardly representational in the normal sense of one thing standing for another. It is more like an emanation from the object towards which it seems to be pointing. This way of thinking about photographs leads into acceptance of photographic realism (see Chapter 3 for a wider discussion of this term).

The realist way of thinking understands the photograph as 'pre-linguistically' related to the world that defines it. It is a superimposition of reality, of a past that lacks intentionality. Its resistance to linguistic assimilation is at the very least a way of seeing the photograph's reluctant submission to another type of message. Its linkage with a past reality that produced it is a clue to its independence and its separation from language. The power of the photograph resides in this quality of attachment to the object in the frame: 'the necessarily real thing before the lens' as Barthes describes it in his book *Camera Lucida* (1980: 76). Its resistance is an inescapable part of the way we value it as a photograph. The photograph has the virtue of connecting the viewer directly with something that is always in the past. We *know* something or somebody stood before the lens and yet meaning is unstable and can easily be guided by language. Think of the way photographic meaning changes. A snapshot image of a family circle may become a news image when somebody dies. Context determines meaning and 'investment' or usage take control.

The photograph is in some ways a purely visual medium and its relationship to language can be discomfiting for photographers. This is partly explained by the sense of losing control of 'meaning' once the image is adapted for use. The assimilation of the photograph is an issue at another level (for example as an ethical issue) because its 'originating' contact with 'the real' is always compromised by the way it is seen. It is as if it has two sides: what it *is* and what it *means*.

As noted in the case study on Semiology (see pp. 171–86) Roland Barthes analyses what he calls the 'photographic paradox' in which we see two messages in the photographic image. One is the un-coded, analogical link with the object and the other is its development as a coded message. At one level it is a transparent photographic analogue and at another it is implicated by journalistic, commercial or other concerns. The photograph can of course be used to promote social and political agendas as well.

193

PHOTOGRAPHY THEORIES

What interests us at this point is the transitional nature of the photograph as its value changes from the pre-linguistic level of 'copying' the world to a condition in which it is 'invested' with meaning. According to Barthes the photograph 'is verbalized the moment it is perceived' (1979: 28) and yet it never loses its analogical value.

The Intrusion of Language

As an indication of the discomfort felt by a photographer on the subject of language the American photographer Lewis Hine noted: 'If I could tell the story in words, I wouldn't need to lug around a camera' (cited in Zakia, 2002: 258). The feeling of impatience with verbal discourse is often expressed by visual artists with a desire to privilege their own medium whilst perhaps wearily accepting the need to collaborate with writers, teachers, editors, or an inquisitive audience demanding a rationale for the style and content of their work. Traditional barriers between writers and practitioners may explain impatience with theory.

The question of the hierarchy of power in the language/image dichotomy is instructive. Amateur photographers might casually add a few words to an image in the family album ('Mum with Elsie, Margate 1982') and seem untroubled by the captioning of the image. Editorial control influences photographic meaning in the professional world of journalism. Captions may trivialize or mislead the reader and words written about photographs (especially art photographs) may be vexing in the case of a hostile criticism of an exhibition. A familiar response to the controlling effect of the written word is the viewpoint that claims photography is itself a language that has been learned and understood in professional execution of the practice. The idea of the photographer as a creative worker with something to *say* is comparable with an artist or poet who adds something to the stock images in the world. Control of the medium and high levels of craft technique in the work of the American landscape photographer Ansel Adams have been described as the equal of musicianship (Newhall, 1949: 166).

To speak of a 'language' of photography might suggest a practice that has some of the characteristics of a linguistic system that inclines towards poetry rather than description or the functional transmission of meaning. A documentary photographer might accept the descriptive language analogy and argue that photographs provide a visual supplement to the written word or the verbal description. A middling position is one that accepts that photographs *are* in some way independent but must collaborate with language, as if each had a degree of relative autonomy. For most photographers the use of words in professional practice is accepted as a matter of practical necessity rather than a theorized principle. There is of course the prospect of photographers co-operating with news media and advertising and the history of modern graphic design demonstrates this. The classic examples are to be found in the overlap between different media that characterizes the modernist trends of the 1920s.

Photography has, nevertheless, kept its distance from the interdisciplinary methods that dissolve its traditional boundaries. Institutional separation of photographers and art directors has continued in the advertising industry and other boundary lines are preserved in photography education. Resistance to photographic incorporation with other media is equally strongly expressed in the proudly separatist idea of 'pure photography' as a medium that 'speaks for itself'. From a postmodern point of view this plea for autonomy is a dogmatic and uncritical perspective associated with traditional forms of photography. The way a photograph is shaped by its subsequent dissemination and presentation may seem to the traditionalist to be irrelevant to what it really means. For the postmodernist these things are everything

PHOTOGRAPHY AND THE WRITTEN WORD

because, according to their point of view, photography has no identity. 'Its status as a technology,' in the immortal words of the art historian John Tagg, 'varies with the power relations which invest it' (1988: 118). And yet 'it' (photography) is a uniquely original technology that revolutionized the way we think about pictures and has philosophical interests that inform its practical applications and investments.

The exponents of the idea of 'pure photography' seek to defend the medium against its routine usage as a means to descriptive or functional ends. It is in some ways a defensible position and yet it seems to ignore what is inevitable: the wider context in which the image gains its value and meaning. It also ignores how far post-production interests, social and aesthetic, influence choices made in advance of any kind of photographic project. Our argument is that the photograph is *always* constrained by social and technical processes. A photographic image exists in the mind of the photographer before it is made. This fact alone guarantees its subjection to rhetorical use in contexts that include family snaps, portraiture, journalism and the various commercial applications that provide employment for the photographer. And yet the case for the autonomy of the medium persists and in some ways the paradoxical nature of the medium encourages this way of thinking.

The Paradoxical Nature of the Photograph

A defence of the photograph as an autonomous structure with its own properties is not restricted to die-hard practitioners. As we have seen the belief in the photograph as an autonomous structure, as something with its own properties (outside or beyond language), represents an important position in contemporary thinking about the ontology of the photographic image (see Chapter 3). Barthes notes the text is a 'parasitic message' (1979: 25) or a 'secondary vibration almost without consequence' (26). These statements are designed to ensure that we attend to the special qualities of the photograph as a 'pure and simple denotation of reality' (28). This is persuasive and underlines the great virtue of the medium and its famous truth-telling powers.

Barthes, nevertheless, is quick to point out that the 'unique structure that the photograph constitutes' is in communication with other structures including written texts. In the case of the press photo he refers to titles, captions, articles and headlines. The two 'structures' co-exist but they are heterogenous (they consist of different things) since, usually, they occupy different space but also one message consists of words and the other (the photograph) consists of 'lines, surfaces and shades'. Barthes calls it the paradoxical nature of the photograph. What he means is that the photograph (unlike any other medium) has two messages: one without a code (the analogical) and one that is coded (the 'art' or treatment, camera angle, subject matter). Insofar as we believe a photograph is a 'copy' of something it is always read as if it were the trace of an event. This is the un-coded message. The capacity in the photograph to achieve an existential connection with a past 'event' always influences 'reading' in a way that is never entirely banished by its treatment or style of presentation. This is why even manipulated or damaged prints may still evoke a strange sense of contact with something 'that has been' in front of camera.

What is important to our understanding of the way the photograph is seen (and understood) is that its power derives from what Barthes calls the prestige of its denotation. He notes that when 'truth' is called upon as a yardstick by which we measure the value of things then photographic denotation is effective since the claim to truth (in an advertisement or press photo for example) 'develops on the basis' of the un-coded photographic message. The transition from 'un-coded' existential event to 'coded' meaning

195

PHOTOGRAPHY THEORIES

is a shift from denotation to connotation. The photograph never keeps its innocence when (as it must) it takes on meaning and the 'exceptional power of denotation' (Barthes, 1979: 21) that exists in the photograph makes it a powerful tool when used in tandem with a linguistic image.

Barthes was nevertheless suspicious of what he calls 'the linguistic nature of the image' (1979: 32). Take an advertisement, for example, that includes a photograph (or several) and invites a consideration of its internal data and their interaction. It is a complex system of linguistic and photographic messages brought together to form a whole. The photograph, we might say, is a denotation: a copy of reality. Whatever it *means* is what we deduce. It is whatever we make of it. Its meaning will often depend on the linguistic message but other factors will enter the reading. These include compositional or technical codes influenced by aesthetic and logistical factors. These may well be highly conventional and subject to specific ways of presenting publicity forms. Gillian Dyer notes: 'Advertising, like language, is a system consisting of distinct signs. It is a system of differences and oppositions which are crucial in the transfer of meaning' (1982: 123).

There is a sense in which our reading of an image (including a photograph) is influenced by the feelings that are conventionally given to its objects in earlier experience of such things. The reader's response is learned. In this sense the psychological response to an image is not so different to the way we read linguistic messages. In advertising, art or news media, the response might be emotional so that the process of linking of products in ads with thoughts and feelings is an unconscious process.

A romantic couple on a sunny beach in a fashion advertisement (fig. 6.5) signifies a social and sexual identity as well as pleasure and escape from routine. The photograph's sense of being a copy of reality adds to its persuasive power. Although we call it an image, there is a sense in which we see straight through it to the scene it represents. It seems to be a transparent means of engaging with the world itself.

6.5 Couple sitting on a beach together in summer – stock image © Yuri. Courtesy of Getty Images.

PHOTOGRAPHY AND THE WRITTEN WORD

To the extent that we see a photograph as a transparent picture it ceases to be an intentionally expressive or artistic medium. It is appears to be natural and yet in seeing it we negotiate its meaning through the exercise of our own way of seeing 'beach', 'couple' etc. There is clearly a strong culturally inflected way of seeing as if it is driven by language, that is to say as if a voice were saying, 'beach', 'couple', and 'romance'. Our reading might be conventional and regulated by habit and custom. An advertisement for a holiday resort may use this kind of image to achieve an average or predictable response in the spectator. It is the equivalent of somebody saying 'nice couple, great beach, this could be you'. The picture is a supplement to this kind of reading. It is, nevertheless, a photographic picture and it has its own values that are not entirely reducible to words. We know this because it can be read in different ways, and has potential for more personalized or even abnormal reading of the image.

The Power of Photographic Authentication: *Studium* and *Punctum*

Contemporary photography theory has emphasized the importance of the photograph's reference to the world that takes priority over its ability to speak. This has two effects: one, it militates against the claims made for the expressive purpose of the medium, and two, it emphasizes the importance of its physical linkage with something outside itself. For Barthes 'its power of authentication exceeds the power of representation' (1981: 89). As we have seen this is an important realization which affects the way we see all photographs. As noted above, even the manipulated image stubbornly retains a sense of contact with the world. It is a power in the photograph that offers resistance to its use as a cultural rather than a natural sign.

6.6 Humphrey Spender, *Men Greeting in a Pub*, 1937. Courtesy of the Mass Observation Archive, Bolton Museum and Art Gallery.

197

PHOTOGRAPHY THEORIES

The tendency towards the creation of meaning is inescapable and yet the photograph is a curious thing that unites the world and the image. And since the world is held in suspense the 'pre-linguistic' moment of contact (the indexical sign function) remains. Humphrey Spender's photograph *Men Greeting in a Pub*, from his *Worktown Series* of 1937 (fig. 6.6) is a richly informative image. We can 'read it' as a statement about gendered space (the pub as refuge for men), and as a typical 1930s' view of northern working-class men. Much can be said about body language and interior design and the technical codes that define it as an effective piece of photojournalism conforming to the conventions of documentary photography. The man raising his hand may influence the way we 'read' the image. The title is a strong anchor and so we see it as a friendly gesture. We are familiar with body language and the gestural codes. The way we read the image is determined by coded meanings that we bring to the image.

This is a conventional reading. In *Camera Lucida* Barthes refers to this kind of conventional reading as a response to what he calls the *studium*, a Latin term, to define the coded meaning we find in the photographic image. Formal analysis might centre on a sociological or an aesthetic reading, that is to say the kind of readings that come within the system of codification that he calls *studium*. It is this aspect of the photograph that produces an *average* affect – a kind of predictable response. In contrast to this shared or collective way of defining the photograph Barthes coins another Latin term that he calls the *punctum*. This relates to what might be called a pre-linguistic or un-coded sense of what is in the photograph. It might be an irrelevent detail that sabotages analysis. For Scott this indicates a resistance to language: 'What we are left with, however, is a sense of photography's ability to disempower language, to be so undeniable that language cannot negotiate with it, cannot bend or belittle its evidence' (1999: 26).

As noted, the raised hand in the Spender photograph is striking. Without the title, which signals the benign nature of the gesture, it could be interpreted as a refusal to be photographed. In either reading it is an explicit gesture. It is a punctuation of the image that disturbs the *studium*. It is a gesture that is beyond the public knowledge we have about men, pubs, the 1930s, and so forth. It is a *punctum*. Barthes defines this term as a little stab, or punctuation, the viewer feels when seeing a photograph. It might be something that works against the conventional coding or the articulated 'language-like' working of the image. *Punctum* is a difficult and contentious term since it is a way of allowing a purely romantic or emotive response to the image, as if it is somehow beyond rational discourse. It opens up the possibility of an idiosyncratic or oppositional reading of the image. Barthes' use of the idea of a *punctum* allows a nostalgic reading and a subjective viewpoint. The Spender image may invite discomfort or class anxiety. The raised hand may even now be a reproach from the grave for nosey middle-class experts. The gesture takes us out of the framed composition to the wider world beyond. The *punctum* (in the Spender example) fantastically 'brings out' an ironic mix of humour and working-class pride.

A photograph's existential connection with what has been explains the special fascination for its illicit or forbidden subjects where a sense of witnessing something (through a lens darkly) is a force that resonates in the image. The abusive and surreptitious use of the medium is a product of this photographic effect. The dual theme of photo-voyeurism and murder is explored in *Peeping Tom,* a film directed by Michael Powell in 1960.

Reading the photograph against the grain is an involuntary action, a psychological response. This is what Barthes wants to indicate when using the term *punctum*. It is a way of seeing something that, for reasons of personal disposition, is vivid or disturbing. The emotional power of the *punctum* is an effect of its indexicality. The concept of indexicality indicates the way photographs are different to other types of visual representation and explains their candid link with reality.

From the Indexical to the Iconic

Indexicality is a term discussed in Case Study 3. It derives from the word 'index' which is a type of sign identified by the theorist Charles Sanders Peirce (1839–1914). He contrasts this type of sign with two other key signs identified as 'iconic' and 'symbolic'. Indexicality defines the conditions in which there is a physical or causal relationship between a sign and its object. We know that something occurred because there is a physical residue or marker that is a trace of its occurrence. The term 'indexicality' provides a way of thinking about the uniqueness of the photograph when compared with other systems of representation.

KEY TERMS:

Roland Barthes' Two Photographic Elements: Barthes' use of the terms Studium and Punctum, in his book *Camera Lucida*, has been widely discussed by photography theorists. For our purposes the terms provide a way of thinking about how photographs can resist conventional and structured ways of seeing.

The Studium: This term refers to the average effect or general meaning of a photograph that would be in agreement with the views of other people. It is the 'given' and conventional aspect of the photograph. This meaning might be influenced by a caption or other contextual factors.

The Punctum: This term refers to the unruly or unconventional effect that a photograph might produce. It is that aspect of the photograph that connects the viewer with the more random aspect of material reality which defines the photograph. Those parts of a photograph that might be excessive or, rather, supplementary to what it is taken to mean are characteristic of all photographs.

As we have noted above the photograph is *paradoxical* and possibly self-contradictory. It resists incorporation into the world of meaning and yet is inescapably bound in that direction. This, however, is a bit vague since the distinction between denotation and connotation (or between the photograph's appearance and its tendency to be read as a construction of meaning) is not a difference between temporally distinct phenomena. They are strangely interchangeable. If we see a photograph as an object that is informed by sense of taste for composition (or other technical codes) we are seeing it as something with its own properties. These might be thought of as additional properties with aesthetic connotations. These formal properties might have some independence from the subject of the photograph. We can think of this in the following way: an image appears when the world it represents disappears and the viewer sees a 'print' inscribed with visual codes. The world does not of course disappear. We have merely changed our way of reading the photograph as we attend to its visual properties. The photograph

PHOTOGRAPHY THEORIES

6.7 Fabian Cevallos, *French Philosopher Roland Barthes*, 1979. © Fabian Cevallos/Sygma/Corbis.

undergoes a shift from its indexical link with the world to begin its life as an image. It is no longer transparent and becomes a text-like object. As an image we might usefully think of the photograph as being subject to language. We should do this for two reasons:

1 The photograph is subjected to the influence of language as its conventional surrounding text in a publication (or other format) and forms an *illustration* of the written text. The text incorporates the photograph and produces a unified message in which the two types of signs (the linguistic and the non-linguistic) are complementary. For example 'Ways of Seeing … Barthes' is a caption to the French critic's photographic portrait in a copy of the *Guardian* newspaper on 26 March 2011 (fig. 6.7). The reference to John Berger's book and television series of 1972 (*Ways of Seeing*) links the portrait with a critical discourse about art. Our title to the same photographic portrait in Figure 6.7 provides another way of seeing Barthes.

2 Photographs behave (more strangely) as if conveying a symbolic meaning *without* the addition of words. In other words they behave in a language-like way or at least appear to do so in terms of having what Barthes calls their own connotation procedures (1979: 20). For example an Iraqi prisoner at Abu Ghraib is made to stand with arms outstretched in a Christ-like manner that has connotations of abuse and biblical cruelty (fig. 6.8). A description of this would be tautological.

We think of the photograph as having a double structure since it is conventionally anchored by the written word and yet simultaneously is capable of producing meaning by virtue of its own connotation procedures. These two modes of signification are used to achieve the same ends. They are mutually reinforcing or complementary. This mutuality is common in advertising and in the titles that accompany works of art (including photographs as art). Mutuality in the meanings of news photographs and their captions are also examples of this.

The key argument in this chapter is that photographs have a capacity to express meaning in a language-like way. This is not an attempt to deny the specificity of the photograph or to reduce it to something that it is not. Photographs express meaning in at least two different ways: first through their own internal codes and second in conjunction with the symbolic codes of language.

Photographs may also express meaning in conjunction with other images in the serialization and sequencing or in juxtaposition on the page or in other regimes of visual communication. Although the photograph is rarely isolated from other media it may in some circumstances be resistant to a systematic incorporation into language. The tendency to privilege the photograph as an aesthetic

200

PHOTOGRAPHY AND THE WRITTEN WORD

6.8 An Iraqi prisoner allegedly being tortured by American soldiers at Abu Ghraib prison, Iraq, between October and December 2003. Image published April 2004. Courtesy of Rex Features.

medium for example exemplifies this resistance. Language is an intentional activity and in this respect it resembles other modes of expression including photography. Indexicality as a term emphasizes a certain way of thinking about the photograph as a trace of something that existed in the past. What concerns us here is the way this 'something' is converted into speech and in so doing undergoes a change that expresses meaning in particular way.

Take the example of a news photograph of a smiling politician with troops which functions, in a media context, as a propaganda message. The fact that the photograph may not have been made for the purpose of propaganda is instructive since it demonstrates that the passage from indexical to the symbolic (through the iconic) is one in which a distortion takes place. It is a process of re-configuration – a chain of signification – that forms a message: '"Our boys" relaxing with senior politician; all is well in the art of politics and war' (fig. 6.9). There is a dynamic movement in the transition from the un-coded data of the image – the analogical content – to the symbolic or connotative meaning. This is not a one-way movement of meaning since the symbol reaches back to the denotational power of the photograph that underwrites its effect.

When the photograph gains currency as an image (when it is displayed, published or exhibited for example) it collides with language and appeals to the viewer's desire to know what it means, what it is, how it is to be 'read'. Whatever it means may seem obvious but the reading can be naive or wrong;

PHOTOGRAPHY THEORIES

6.9 Prime Minister Tony Blair addressing troops in Basra, Iraq, in May 2003. Courtesy of Rex Features.

it is easy to miss the deceptive logic of the propaganda image. The point is that *as an image* it loses its indexical innocence and now functions as an iconic sign. As Clive Scott notes: 'Photography leaves one world, in which it enjoys features not shared by the other arts, and enters another in which features are shared, although their specific modes of operation may be different' (1999: 34). The 'features not shared' are indexical. Features shared are the 'language-like' properties of the image and language itself that appears in verbal or written discourse. Scott shows how a documentary photograph can illustrate the shift from the iconic sign (where resemblance underscores the status of the image) towards the linguistic message. He notes how this 'drift towards the symbolic' (ibid.: 45) opens up a way of reading determined by its linguistic context (its title for example) and the prospect for a narrative interpretation that it provides. The drift to symbolic meaning is discussed below.

From the Iconic to the Symbolic

In photographs we see a captured 'reality' with a latent meaning that shifts from its purely analogical status into the production of meaning. It is a process in which a photograph – with the help of captions or titles – begins to work like a language. This is a progression in which it becomes a discrete object with a currency of its own. In her book *On Photography* Susan Sontag observed that the camera makes reality 'atomic, manageable and opaque' (cited in Scott, 1999: 106). What Sontag means is that the photograph is extracted from the flux of worldly things in a piecemeal way. It is a kinetic moment that endures *as* an image. We might even call it an artefact when it is prepared for publication. Barthes notes:

PHOTOGRAPHY AND THE WRITTEN WORD

'The press photograph is an object that has been worked on, chosen, composed, constructed, treated according to professional, aesthetic or ideological norms which are so many factors of connotation' (1979: 19).

When the transparency of the photograph gives way to opaqueness it loses its open-ness to variable interpretation. Semiologists refer to the polysemic properties of the sign – the viewer's personal or subjective reading. It may retain this function in any part of its life and the *punctum* can always arrest the audience in unpredictable ways. Photographs in use, in advertising, press photography or whatever, have an intentional role in which they are separated from their original 'nature' (as pure indexicality). As iconic signs they retain their link with the referent (which survives as resemblance) as they pass into an extended symbolic order and are *read* by an audience that consumes them.

Peirce's semiotic categories (index, icon and symbol) enable us to discuss the photograph as a medium constrained by the functions it is made to serve. Think of the photograph in movement (not literally but as its manner of being changes) as if it has an imperative to produce meaning. Photographs change their functions as signs in movement from the indexical to the iconic and from the iconic to the symbolic. The movement is one that emphasizes the fact that the sign is never stable and is always under pressure to move in different ways. We should also note that passage in our discussion is from the natural to the conventional sign; from the transparent to the opaque; and from the photograph as indexical sign towards 'language-like' symbolic use of the photograph in use.

As we have seen, language is a powerful, if not exclusive, influence on interpretation. Non-linguistic objects such as pictures have compositional structures modelled in a language-like way (see Kress and Van Leeuwen, 1996) and are contextualized by words. In his foundational text *Elements of Semiology* Barthes unequivocally states that 'every semiological system has its linguistic admixture' and, 'we are much more than in former times, and despite the spread of pictorial illustration, a civilization of the written word' (1972a: 10). As noted above some theorists have reason to doubt the certainty of this language-centred view of meaning. We live in a world in which images are an increasingly powerful means of communication. Barthes, however, may still be correct in his claim that there are no 'extensive systems of signs outside human language' (ibid.: 9). For our purposes we pragmatically accept the co-existence of words and photographs and the predisposition of the latter to behave, in particular circumstances, in a language-like way. Scott notes:

> The symbolic code is the code of language, and the more the visual becomes involved in the language system, the more it will be carried over into the symbolic, the more deeply it will be carried over into the semantic (not 'What is it?' but 'What does it mean'), and towards the abstract.
>
> (Scott, 1999: 40)

According to Saussure language is the most obvious symbolic sign since it relies on the arbitrariness of the relationship between the signifier and the signified. What does that mean? Well for example in the English language 'hat' stands for something worn on the head. The linguistic sign unites the image and the concept. 'Hat', in this example, is not motivated by resemblance and it is not 'caused' by anything outside itself. It is an arbitrary term that we agree to use. Insofar as a hat can be used to 'say something' then its appearance in a photograph can be language-like. In the old days a top hat, for example, was a widely understood code for 'gentleman'. This meaning applied to the wearing of a hat in real life

PHOTOGRAPHY THEORIES

6.10 Eamonn McCabe, *Ascot Racegoers*, 1977. © Eamonn McCabe/Getty Images.

and transfers to the image of the wearer in a photograph. A photograph of a top-hatted man might express something about social class. Indeed, this 'reading' might be supported by a written or verbal text: 'Here's uncle Tom in the Royal Enclosure at Ascot' (see fig. 6.10). The linguistic sign confirms the 'reading' of the photograph. A further example would be the photographic image of a nude that would normally carry a sexual connotation. In this case the language-like meaning may not actually require a linguistic message to confirm its 'reading'. It would hardly need the words: 'this girl is sexy: what do you think?' This, however, is what it appears to be saying.

It might be helpful to think of the transition from the indexical sign – via the iconic – to the symbolic as a process like translation. The photograph never loses its rootedness in the world – as we have noted, since it always functions as reference. It has at the same time a second meaning, described by Barthes as 'imposition' (1979: 20). The imposition comes into operation when we think of the photograph's aesthetic qualities which include its format, materials and style of presentation.

What concerns us here is the way the photographic analogue – its connection with the real thing that appeared before the lens – is subject to coding at some point in its production. We might think of this in the following way: the index becomes an icon when we see it as a picture (when it conforms to pictorial conventions or allows a pictorial reading) and slides into a semantic register or invites an aesthetic or social reading. To illustrate this we might think of the way a photograph generates values (for example 'family values' in a holiday snap) as if it were made for that purpose. If a photograph is not accompanied by written copy it will be a relatively open text with variable interpretations that might attach to it.

A certain freedom might thus be attached to a found photographic image with no name or data attached – and yet even this circumstance will not allow a completely arbitrary reading. Its open-ended visuality is not absolute. Constituent elements in the photograph would normally be sufficient to reduce possible ways of seeing it. Without a text to guide us we can expect a diversity of reading and yet normally there will be definite signification in the image itself. A nude for example is not a landscape or a family portrait. Human perception is governed by systems of classification that are themselves elements of social organization. A random image might thus be allocated a place in our overall view of the world and yet we normally look out for titles as a kind of official advice on what we are seeking.

> **KEY TERM: Visuality**
>
> Visuality is a term that has been used to describe the way we are conditioned by cultural circumstances to see the world in a certain way. In some accounts visuality is contrasted with 'vision' which refers to the purely physical operation of sight. The American critic Hal Foster has described visuality concisely as 'how we see, how we are able, allowed or made to see, and how we see this seeing or the unseen therein' (Foster, 1988: ix). The two terms (vision and visuality) are not opposed. The distinction is conceptual rather than actual since 'vision' is socialized and our way of seeing the world involves the body and the psyche. Fatigue for example determines how we 'see' things in both a literal and a metaphorical sense. The art historian Robert S. Nelson captured this way of thinking about seeing when he says:
>
> > Every viewer belongs to a society and subscribes in various degrees to the bodily convention and practices of society. In this sense, visuality is similar to sexuality. Both pertain to natural and universal human acts, but both are also learned, socially controlled, and organized, and therefore domesticated.
> >
> > (2000: 9).
>
> Visuality thus refers to ways of seeing within a cultural system and challenges the naive idea that seeing is a mechanical technique like that of the camera. What passes for the 'real' is something our visual culture has nurtured us into. It thus follows that repressive visualities may influence our way of seeing social groups in stereotypical or negative ways.

The Treachery of Words

The image always has a limitation to what it can stand for or represent. Its 'meaning' is always reduced to the language user's tendency to make the image fit his or her own frame of reference and in most circumstances this leads to a conventional way of seeing it. The matching of words and images begins when children learn to read. Some artists have sought to challenge conventional image–object relationships. Examples include the Surrealist mismatch of words and images. René Magritte's photo-realist style paintings attach 'wrong' words to depicted objects to create a 'coding disorder' (Wilden, 1987: 199). The realistic technique adopted by Magritte relies on an iconic reading that strains to look photographic so the coding 'disorder' gains maximum effect (fig. 6.11). Magritte's disruption of audience expectation in this example provides a humorous exception to the rules of naming. As such it is an exception that proves the rule.

PHOTOGRAPHY THEORIES

6.11 René Magritte, *The Key to Dreams*, 1930 (oil on canvas). Courtesy of Private Collection/Bridgeman Images. © DACS London.

The photographic image seems to presuppose translation (since that seems always to be its fate) into iconic meaning when influenced by a title or other kind of linguistic sign. At this level the sign is treated as if it is trying to say something about the object or person it represents. Its function is illustrational and, as we have seen, this is a short step from its operation as a 'language-like' symbolic sign. This 'translation' from a purely visual sign (which is iconic and indexical) to the symbol is an effect whereby the photograph is received into language. The photograph has ended its semiological journey when it functions as a symbolic sign. It is an effect that takes place when the photograph is accompanied by words such as titles, captions and so forth. It is an effect, however, that meets resistance as Magritte's perverse mis-naming of objects reminds us. A picture always contains more than what might be translated into words.

Captions, Titles and the Verbal Context of the Photograph

Captions, titles and the verbal context of photography (and by implication all systems of visual media) often imply a way of accessing an image that might otherwise seem indefinite or detached from conventional meaning. Words signify a desire to engage with an image. Mary Price makes a compelling argument for the importance of language in the production of photographic meaning. She argues that titles, captions and texts are implicated in the way a viewer sees a photograph (1994: 1). The titling of an image is a way of describing it and the addition of words directs our way of seeing. We are so used to captions and titles that the idea of a word-free environment is strangely utopian. Scott notes: 'Titles deliver the photograph from its inherent gratuitousness, incoherence, randomness and make it the instrument of design' (1999: 49). The attachment of titles to pictures is a normal aspect of most forms of graphic media. Some visual media are sensitively distanced from the intrusion of language. They include works of fine art and most kinds of museum or gallery installations where labels are supplementary forms of communication. In some examples the turn to language is coyly treated as an inescapable necessity and titling is understated and respectful. It is for example worth noting how the most aggressively subversive modes of modern art are supported by measured, objective and dispassionate use of language. We consider a small number of ways of using titles below. No matter how respectful, understated and non-coercive a title may be, it always produces an instrumental effect on the object to which it refers.

The 'Untitled' Title

Art works are sometimes untitled because the artist neglected to give them a title. In some cases the neglect is evidence of a reluctance to give the work a literary association. In this case the 'untitled' title

PHOTOGRAPHY AND THE WRITTEN WORD

is itself a kind of title that seems to be saying: 'The meaning is in the work itself; it is a "visual work" that functions independently of language'. If an art photographer wants the image to 'speak for itself' a title may be nothing more than a concession to rules of exhibiting.

The Poetical Title

The most rudimentary titles might do little more that confirm what is visually evident in something like 'Young Women in the Garden'. Others seek to transport the reader into a more poetic register such as, for example, in the American photographer Edward Steichen's *Solitude*, of 1901 (fig. 6.12). The word 'solitude', in this example, directs the reader's attention to a range of subsidiary connotations extending beyond the appearance of the subject. It is intended to suggest that we see beyond the bearded man and think of his psychological makeup or his status as 'artist'. Audiences may be familiar with the romantic figure of the artist isolated from a world that wilfully misunderstands him. The title secures this kind of sympathetic reading and invites us to reflect on the way it fits together with the visual codes contained in the image.

The body 'language', in this example, signifies a contemplative, reclining posture. The hand is a conventional sign for sensation of touch and placement on the head or face seems to point to his capacity for aesthetic contemplation. The dress code is bohemian (no top hat in this example) and represents

6.12 Edward Steichen, *Solitude (Portrait of a Man)*, 1901. Courtesy of Private Collection/Archives Charmet/Bridgeman Images. © DACS London.

207

PHOTOGRAPHY THEORIES

6.13 Alfred Stieglitz, *The City of Ambition*, 1910. Courtesy of Mary Evans/Everett Collection.

the dark and mysterious powers of art. Soft focus is a further codification of mystery. The artist's solitude is confirmed by the frame of the image which isolates him from the blind space beyond it. A glimpse of the photographer-artist's eye, a window on the soul, confirms his identity as a *visual* artist. His deportment (introspective and pensive according to the grammar of the image) defines his solitude.

Poetical titles are enabling and assist the viewer who may doubt the provenance of a photographic work. Alfred Stieglitz's photograph *The City of Ambition*, 1910 (fig. 6.13) is a homage to modernity and urban living and carries an indirect connotation: 'unlike most photographs this is not merely a document – it is a work of art'. Because of the mechanical mediation of the camera, photographers in the past (and especially during Stieglitz's period) had to work harder than painters to attract aesthetic appreciation. The title in these examples is an insurance against a descriptive reading.

Descriptive and Informational Titles

Descriptive titles supply information about the circumstances of the photograph's taking. Photographs belonging to different genres use descriptive titles. They have the tautological effect of re-stating what we can see in the picture. In general descriptive titles reinforce the desire to read the image as a document. The German photographer August Sander produced a body of work based on 'social types' defined by occupational and class status. The title *Handlanger* (Bricklayer), of 1928 (fig. 6.14) is an important 'anchor' for our reading of the individual image. It is obviously descriptive and normative. The deadpan style of the photograph is replicated by the factual nature of the title. Sander was not looking for a poetic reading of the image. He was slowly making an archive of occupational portrait images representing a cross-section of German society.

Few images are unbounded by language and it is unusual to be consciously faced with decisions related to word-free images. The peculiarity of this has been exploited in random-response experiments in clinical testing. Viewers faced with random images may allocate designation or meaning in a way that provides a way of understanding the associations linked with what they see. Random images may be subject to conventional classification. A photograph of a favourite aunt might be put away in drawer for safekeeping. Context and classification (perhaps at a later date) will determine its meaning and future usage. The addition of a title to an image is a clear indication of desire to communicate and is a way of attaching legitimacy to an image. A factual title (of the kind used by Sander) signals its place in a system of classification such as 'people in the twentieth century'.

PHOTOGRAPHY AND THE WRITTEN WORD

Sander's portraits serve a diversity of social functions. The linguistic anchor is an important part of the message and provides a rationale for the portrait's place in an archive or other system in which classification is required. Sander's method was consistent and the dress and props used indicated the subject's profession. His titles are not, however, always tautological since dress codes and context are sometimes non-specific and the addition of occupational description is essential to the archival purpose of the project. Photographs with captions and titles provide a convenient method of documenting and securing the placement of things in the world. Taxonomy is a word that defines the way things are classified, ordered and labelled.

Titling is an important stage in the allocation of meaning to a photograph and plays a part in its destination and future usage. The indeterminate nature of the photograph makes it vulnerable to the determinations of language which may subvert or exploit it. Andres Serrano's *Piss Christ* of 1987 (fig. 6.15) has a notoriety created by its irreverent title. Whatever we think about the aesthetic properties of the photograph its classification as a devotional crucifixion in a bubbly fluid is

6.14 August Sander, *Handlanger (Bricklayer)*, 1928. © Die Photographische Sammlung/SK Stiftung Kultur – August Sander Archiv, Cologne/DACS London/Tate, London 2014. Courtesy of Tate, London.

KEY TERM: Taxonomy and Photography

The word taxonomy refers to the science of classification and is historically associated with the identification, naming and systematic ordering of plants, animals and minerals in the world. We may also relate the term to the systematic ordering of photography into various categories of practices and applications. Needless to say this has been controversial and remains so. The Dewey system of book classification divides into two broad categories of fiction and non-fiction that approximate the vexing, and often confused, distinctions between art and documentary photography. Photography has an oddly unclassifiable character that makes it an interesting case for the taxonomist.

The issue of classifying and establishing boundaries between different types of photography becomes a central part of our thinking about the medium. It concerns the way books are classified by publishers and librarians. The art historian Steve Edwards notes that from its beginning, photography 'spilled across multiple sites of taxonomy' (2006: 199). Photography is closely linked with histories of the visual arts as a broad category and this divides into hierarchical categories which include the fine and the 'applied' arts. When photography is judged to have a technical or skills-based quotient it is grouped with the second category; when it aspires to a higher station it approaches the tertiary categories of printmaking and the graphic arts that are sub-divisions of art history. Movement in this direction links it with the fine arts and yet it retains strong links with media practices and the technical sphere. The matter is further complicated by the way advances in media technology threaten to subsume photography into digital arts or computer science.

troubled by its title, which made it a cause for public concern. A defining legend attaching to a picture will stay with it forever. In Serrano's case two words made him famous. In a similar way the notoriety of the words 'Myra Hindley', a child murderer, are now inseparable from her well-known and widely published 1960s press photograph (fig. 6.16).

The title (*Portrait of Myra Hindley*) connects the historical person and the photographic representation. The image, nevertheless, has such powerful connotations (because of its wide circulation) that any other caption would struggle to alter the defining legend that accompanies it. The Hindley legend is inscribed in the wider discourse that surrounds the image. In the case of Henry Hering's photograph of 1858 the addition of the words: 'Acute Mania' signifies mental illness that is undoubtedly its dominant reading (fig. 6.17). Hering was employed by the Bethlem Hospital to portray the mental states of patients. He appears to have followed the conventions of popular portraiture. The title, however, rules out any chance of a non-medical gaze. The exercise of power is inscribed in photographic codes and then firmly secured by the pseudo-scientific title. The photograph without words is a free-floating signifier. Its destiny is uncharted and seems to be passive and innocently waiting for directions. The photography historian and curator Russell Roberts has noted:

6.15 Andres Serrano, *Piss Christ*, 1987. Courtesy of the artist/Bridgeman Images.

The passivity associated with the photograph as evidence is subject to disruption through a recognition that its meaning is the product of relationships between cultural and historical forces that do not cling to its surface.

(Roberts, 1997: 51)

But nothing clings to the shiny surface of the photographic image better than words. Words mediate the image's potential and hold it in place long enough for the viewer to classify and put it – literally and metaphorically – in its right place. Its prospects are clearly variable and in some cases never certain or secure. Unlike more durable cultural objects photographs eventually fade away. Some live on in books, archives, museums, or as digitally retrievable resources. Their *entitlements* are a key to their survival and the gaining of status through authorship (author names combined with titles) relies on the use of words. As Scott notes, 'The route to authorship lies through the voice that can authenticate the image rather than through the image itself' (1999: 82). The status of the 'art photograph' depends heavily on its context and the title is one of the key indicators of its cultural status. As we have noted even the 'untitled' image has an allocated place in the world of titled objects. The title is one of several structures in a totality of information: others include its placement inside a historicizing textbook or an art world site such as an exhibition or museum catalogue. The linguistic context bestows recognition and value upon the image as it establishes its place

PHOTOGRAPHY AND THE WRITTEN WORD

in the symbolic order. The captioning of a press photo is less fraught since its function is a subsidiary one in a medium where writing is considered primary. The linguistic message attached to a press photograph not only adds information (including photographer's name and/or the agency that supplied it) but also, in the caption, controls the reader's interpretation of the image's meanings.

In all of these examples the title (and other types of textual addition) is part of the structural apparatus of the image and affect its transmission and its reception. Titles, captions, literary articles or other forms of written narrative are co-extensive structures and not merely things that follow the image. In the case of the press photograph there is inter-dependency between the verbal sign and the image. In news media the need for images to make a story run are often crucial. News media is increasingly driven by images. Images form an anchorage for news stories that often depend upon the availability of a suitable visual material. In some situations the visual mediation is itself the news event as in the case of celebrity images in the press (fig. 6.18). The photograph anchors language in a familiar visual discourse. In this case the written text is a supplement and the photograph is the anchor: the photograph is a compensation or reward for the more onerous task of reading written text.

6.16 Portrait of Myra Hindley, 1965. Courtesy of Rex Features.

Photographs and Narrativity

The stillness of the still photograph makes it resistant to sequential or narrative meaning. For example it is unlike film, which seems analogous to what we already see in real time, and unlike painting, which encourages an appreciation of brushwork and other constructive elements requiring time for evaluation.

A photograph can be understood in a glance. This may be an exaggeration since highly detailed photographs may seem to demand a longer and more concentrated look or 'gaze' as theorists have called it. The distinction is a troubling one since the photograph's truth telling powers and visual accuracy seem to undermine its prospects for artistic appreciation (see Chapter 3 for a discussion of this issue). What concerns us here is the difference between photographs and writing since one is an extract from the flow of time (the photograph)

6.17 Henry Hering, *Acute Mania – William Thomas Green*, 1858. Courtesy of Bethlem Art & History Collections Trust.

211

PHOTOGRAPHY THEORIES

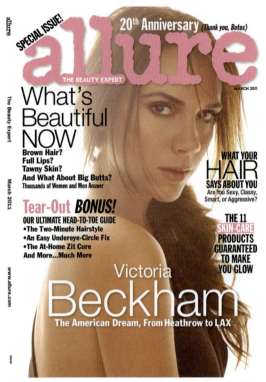

6.18 Cover for *Allure*, March 2011. © Allure Magazine/Michael Thompson/Condé Nast.

whilst the other is a construction that unfolds in the time of its making and in the time of its reception. The mode of language is one of sequential movement in time. The mode of the photograph is one of arrested movement. It is therefore resistant to a narrative reading. It is tempting, nevertheless, to say that since the photo has no narrative meaning in itself it can easily be adapted to other kinds of narrative structure. We have already discussed the potential for reading a photograph as it drifts into symbolic sign-hood earlier in this chapter. We might here note the potential for a narrative reading of photographs as they appear in some of the following formats:

1. Exhibitions that arrange photographs in a way that suggests a report on the development of a style, typology or theme. This includes exhibition literature and official 'histories' and other kinds of classification that conform to audience expectation such as national and regional schools, or photographs used to provide scientific evidence or confirm a didactic purpose.
2. The family album as an exclusive on-going narrative form confirmed by the words, 'mum', 'dad', 'baby Jane', and dated entries that confirm the chronological character of the document as a mixture of visual, linguistic and numeral signs.
3. Projects in which photographs provide an authenticating context for the written text as exemplified in crusading photo-essays such *Let Us Now Praise Famous Men*, 1939, by James Agee and Walker Evans (fig. 6.19). In this kind of hybrid mixture of image and text the evidential force of the image sustains the narrative through duplication and repetition of what has been said. Images may, however, have a degree of autonomy that works against the text and the non-caption photographs in *Let Us Now Praise Famous Men* are a deliberate break with the conventional mediating use of words. The images are, nevertheless, an essential part of the narrative (Smith, 2013).
4. Page layout offers a way of seeing photographs in a graphic and linguistic format that is designed for easy consumption. In newspapers for example the conventional nature of news itself conforms to pre-determined values (surprise, recentness, national or regional interests and so forth), and well-established aesthetic factors of layout, typeface and appropriate quantities of photographic or other types of visual message. A newspaper or magazine presents narrative structure designed to absorb the reader in a manner that detracts from the demands of the news itself. The latter is packaged for easy consumption and loses its value as a call to action. The press photograph is a powerful element in the transmission of news but its effectiveness is influenced by its mode of presentation. The effect is one that dilutes the photographic message which, as Sontag noted, becomes opaque when delivered to audiences as an easily digested read. This view clashes with the more positive view of the dangerous work carried out by campaigning photojournalists. Susie Linfield has defended the contribution of photography in the struggle for human rights. She poses the rhetorical question:

Why are photographs so good at making us *see* cruelty? Partly, I think, because photography brings home to us the reality of physical suffering with a literalness and irrefutability that neither literature nor painting can claim.

(Linfield, 2012: 39)

The explicit power of the image is in any case constrained by its manipulation for rhetorical effect. This way of thinking about the photographic image in context has led to case studies in 'visual rhetoric' that emphasize its *relational* position in the page or more broadly in the entire document. Rhetoric is the art of persuasion in a given situation and in the context of graphic media, legibility and coherence conspire to arrange the visual codes of the photograph in a way that conforms to editorial aims and objectives. The newspaper editor Harold Evans underlines the role of 'pictures' in the wider aims of the press during its mid-twentieth century heyday:

After newsprint rationing the Mirror reverted to more open design with one, two, or three, stories boldly projected on the front with a large picture … Directness of language is expressed in directness of design: no verbal equivocation, no gilded serif, no clutter of words, [and] no proliferation of display type.

(1982: 30)

6.19 Walker Evans, *Allie Mae Burroughs, Wife of a Cotton Sharecropper, Hale County, Alabama*, 1936 (gelatin silver print). Courtesy of the Museum of Fine Arts, Houston, Texas (museum purchase funded by the Caroline Wiess Accessions Endowment Fund, the Manfred Heiting Collection/The Farm Security Adminstration/Bridgeman Images from *Let Us Now Praise Famous Men*, 1941).

The question of photographic codes affecting the image itself is equally important. Stuart Hall noted: 'These compositional arrangements constitute a discourse of their own … composition in visual representation is a learned and historic practice, developed within the world of artistic production itself' (1972: 57). The interior space of the photograph can be organized expressively to carry meaning. Low-angle shots, for example, suggesting power invested in a public figure of authority, or the downward gaze of the camera that belittles the subject and makes it look weak. These conventions are the stock-in-trade of press photographers and sub-editors. As Hall noted, 'These are compositional arrangements constituting a discourse of their own' (ibid.: 57).

The Autonomy of the Photographic Image

It is now clear that photographic meaning is determined by structural determinations which include narration, captions, titles and surrounding texts. These determinations are often complementary and predictable. Photographs are also subject to internal coding and to the connotation procedures that in turn are influenced by staging or preparation of the reality itself prior to its capture. As Barthes noted, such prepared meanings also belong to the photograph's 'connotation procedures' because 'they too benefit from the prestige of denotation' (1979: 21). We have shown that the coding of the photographic

PHOTOGRAPHY THEORIES

analogue is realized in different ways as it passes into discourse and meaning. The movement is not simply one-way because our response to photographs always reaches back to their source, that is to say reaches back to the *something* or *someone* that stood before the camera. There is a sense in which the photographic message stubbornly clings to its place in the world.

There are two broad views on the subject of photography. One insists on 'contact' and 'record' as a primordial condition of the medium; the other allows for mediation and control. The first view tolerates the photograph as a site of resistance to later transactions that may claim to exhaust its meaning. The other routinely seeks to exhaust the image and present it nakedly as a constituent part of a signifying system. At this end of the argument the theorist may accept that the photograph is caused by something 'out there' but this takes second place to what Anne McCauley calls 'the uses that viewers subsequently make of the object' (McCauley, 2007: 417). The photograph in this view is always more than an index of past events. We have seen the photograph's causal connection with the world as its primary condition and yet accept this condition is not its only one. Skilful execution of the photographic process and thoughtful manipulation of technical codes in the processing of the image are valued as aesthetic considerations. McCauley rightly argues that they are often more interesting than the 'accidents of automatic recording' (ibid.: 419). And yet we have also argued that technique, however sophisticated, always relies on an appreciation of photographic transparency and the pleasure of seeing accidentally recorded detail. Such detail is not a trivial matter since it defines the image *as* a photograph rather than a subjective interpretation or journalistic 'story'. The non-intentional character of what appears in the photograph is important to the way we think about the medium. Without this value photography would have no claim to 'literalness and irrefutability'.

We have argued that the photograph has 'pre-linguistic' physical contact with the world that forms it. We have also said that the photographer's actions are intentional (i.e. directed and discriminating). There is something in the photograph as an object that precedes intention. Barthes says it is *a magic*, an untamed 'something' that is resistant to language. Verbal description has no physical link with the referent and is thus a weaker signal. The photograph, however, is inseparable from the object that stood before the lens. It has an indissoluble relation with the 'outside'; the probability of image manipulation is not an argument against this. The fact that the photograph is always mediated by language (or manipulated in other ways) does not deny its specificity. Language is self-evidently a representation but the photograph only *becomes* a representation when subject to use. The fact that it is *always* subject to use alters nothing: there is something special about the photograph that is anterior to its usage. This realist perspective, held by Barthes and others, naturally has its critics.

CONCLUSION

An ambiguity lies at the centre of the issues raised in this chapter: does the photograph manifest human intention or is it a manifestation of something else? At one end of the spectrum lie subjective intentions and desire. At the other lies mechanical reproduction. Clearly a bold text with a definite message will direct attention as will a verbal description attaching to an image. Pictures, nevertheless, have a way of resisting and this is especially true in the case of photographs. A bloody image will not easily lose its shock value by the addition of nice-sounding words. Mary Price says: 'What a picture is *of* limits meaning even while it encourages the exploration of meaning' (Price, 1994: 1–2). In this statement

PHOTOGRAPHY AND THE WRITTEN WORD

there is an indication that photographs seem to be independent of language and yet somehow they are blessed with a capacity to say something.

Titles, captions, literary articles and linguistic forms work together in the production of information. Barthes says that images and words are 'contiguous but not homogenized' (1979: 16) and yet the 'totality of information' (16) is achieved in the way the audience reads it. A press photo is a frozen moment seized from events occurring in everyday life and reconstituted by a story line that gives it an explicit and directed meaning. In a similar way Sander supplied individual photographs that unfold in a narrative about Germany and Victoria Beckham appears in a narrative about herself. Meaning unfolds like a story in which pictures and words co-operate in the production of meaning. In these examples the photograph behaves in a language-like way but is not reducible to language. One of the reasons it is included in a written text, a perhaps obvious reason, is due to its difference with language. A reader's interest in narrative is driven by a desire to see things directly and a photograph supplies *something* or *someone* that a written text cannot provide. It allows a closer contact with a subject (an otherwise absent body) than words can provide. We recognize that photography is couched in words and must negotiate its relationship with words. Nevertheless, the medium has an identity that is more sharply focused by its comparison with the written word and other forms of language use. This is a key issue and the debates that surround it influence the way we teach photography. In the next part of the book we address photography education as one of the principal sites for the understanding of photography.

SUMMARY OF KEY ISSUES

- Photography is a unique medium that expresses meaning independently and is not reducible to language. It is at least as important as language and other systems of communication in mediating social relations. Photographs may even resist language in important ways.
- Photography produces meaning in a language-like way and effectively achieves this when it co-operates interactively with linguistic signs.
- Photography has a dependency upon language which anchors its meaning and determines its future usage. In this view photography is always a passive object of linguistic determination. When photographs express meaning they do so as part of a narrative structure that tells a story in the symbolic realm of verbal language. The photograph may for example interact in a sequence of frames linked by verbal messages in captions or balloons. In some cases the two things are separated and their relations are relatively independent. James Agee and Walker Evans achieved this effect in their photo-essay *Let Us Now Praise Famous Men* of 1941.
- Photographs are rarely alone or separated from a context that frames their message. Barthes noted how captions are repressive and over-determining. He also noted that captions counter feelings of uncertainty attaching to photographs that might otherwise be seen as open texts.
- This chapter is consistently geared to a study of verbal and visual sign interaction. The idea of the co-existence of words and photographs is drawn from Barthes' pioneering essays on photography. More recent influences include Clive Scott, *The Spoken Image* (1999) and Simon Morley, *Writing on the Wall* (2003).
- We have noted the dominance of verbal discourse in semiological studies and cultural theory generally. We have also noted dissenting voices which have argued for a more expansive sense of language that encompasses art and music. The idea of meaning that derives from other kinds

PHOTOGRAPHY THEORIES

of structures is contrasted with verbal language. Photography as a medium that challenges the hegemony of the linguistic sign is indicated in this chapter.

- In most cases the press photograph is an extension of its surrounding text and a function of its narrative meaning. In other circumstances a photograph can assume an open or non-contextual meaning. A subversive or oppositional meaning can thus occur when its meaning lacks definition. The Surrealist detachment of images from their traditional moorings illustrates this point.
- Arguments in favour of 'pure photography' may challenge the intrusion of language. The distrust of words is influenced by their tendency to trivialize or mislead what is judged to be authentic, straight or free from rhetorical meaning. Rhetorical meaning is often thought to be 'fake language' or ways of disguising something for expressive effect.
- Purity in photography is at best a relative category. All photographs are, arguably, tailored to usage of some kind. A photograph in any case exists in the mind's eye of the photographer before it is made. This fact guarantees its assimilation to the generic function it is made to serve.
- Photographs serve many supplementary functions and can be highly rhetorical when used in publicity media and many other applications. This factor does not, however, deny the irreducible properties of the photograph and the possibility of its resistance to conventional or prescribed readings of an image.
- We have noted how Peirce's semiotic categories (index, icon and symbol) have enabled us to discuss the photograph as medium that is influenced by the functions it is made to serve. Think of the photograph in movement (not literally but as its manner of being changes) as if it has an imperative to produce meaning.
- Photographs change their functions as signs in movement from the indexical to the iconic and from the iconic to the symbolic. The movement is one that emphasizes the fact that the sign is never stable and is always under pressure to move in different ways. We should also note that passage in our discussion is from the natural to the conventional sign; from the transparent to the opaque; and from the photograph as indexical sign towards 'language-like' symbolic use of the photograph in use.
- In this movement the photograph moves away from the question of 'what it is' to 'what it means'.
- Without words it is a relatively open text but titles, captions and other types of commentaries locate the photograph in meaningful discourse which acts as a guide to its interpretation. We mention poetic and descriptive registers in which photographs establish their meanings. The linguistic anchor restricts the freedom of the image.
- A title is an indicator of cultural status and a way of classifying the image.
- Photographs are harnessed to narrative readings which form structured ways of seeing families, regions, nations, states and many other social formations. Photographs can also help to identify sub-cultural groups and oppositional formations. Contemporary social media practices provide examples of constructive and (sometimes) oppositional uses of photography.
- Structural formations that rely on pictures often take the form of sequential movement of framed images from left to right as in the photo-essay format.
- Photography is accorded a prominent place in popular media because its contact with its object is direct and unmediated by words or other kinds of structures.
- Photographs are at the same time mediated by compositional arrangements that constitute a discourse of their own. Captioning, titles and commentaries along with page layout and typographical features add to the totality of information in a given message.

- A photograph is inseparable from the object that it presents and the intervention of language and other forms of manipulation (up to a certain point of course) will fail to destroy its specificity. In the end a photograph is not a representation at all but an indexical link with its object. The fact that it becomes a representation when used alters nothing: there is something about the photograph that is anterior to its usage.

Agee, James and Evans, Walker (1965) *Let Us Now Praise Famous Men*, London: Picador Books.

Barthes, Roland (1972a) *Elements of Semiology*, trans. Annette Lavers and Colin Smith, London: Jonathan Cape.

——(1972b) *Mythologies*, trans. Annette Lavers, New York: Hill and Wang.

——(1979) *Image, Music, Text*, trans. Stephen Heath, London: Fontana/Collins.

——(1981) *Camera Lucida: Reflections on Photography*, trans. Richard Howard, New York: Hill and Wang.

Dyer, Gillian (1982) *Advertising as Communication*, London: Methuen.

Edwards, Steve (2006) *The Making of English Photography: Allegories*, Philadelphia: The Pennsylvania University Press.

Evans, Harold (1982) *Editing and Design: A Five-Volume Manual of English, Typography and Layout. Book 5: Newspaper Design*, London: Heinemann.

Finnigan, Ruth (1997) 'Music, Performance and Enactment', in Hugh Mackay (ed.), *Consumption and Everyday Life*, London, New Delhi, and Thousand Oaks, CA: Sage, pp. 113–146.

Flusser, Villem (2007) *Towards a Philosophy of Photography*, London: Reaktion Books.

Foster, Hal (ed.) (1988) *Vision and Visuality*, Seattle: Bay Press.

Hall, Stuart (1972) 'The Determination of News Photographs', in *Working Papers in Cultural Studies*, 3, Birmingham: University of Birmingham, pp. 53–87.

Kress, Gunther and Van Leeuwen, Theo (1996) *Reading Images: The Grammar of Visual Design*, London and New York: Routledge.

Lasn, Kalle (2000) *Culture Jam: How to Reverse America's Suicidal Consumer Binge – And Why We Must*, New York: HarperCollins.

Linfield, Susie (2012) *The Cruel Radiance: Photography and Political Violence*, University of Chicago Press.

McCauley, Anne (2007) 'The Trouble with Photography', in James Elkins (ed.), *Photography Theory*, London and New York: Routledge, pp. 403–430.

Morley, Simon (2003) *Writing on the Wall: Word and Image in Modern Art*, London: Thames and Hudson.

Nelson, Robert S. (ed.) (2000) *Visuality Before and Beyond the Renaissance: Seeing as Others Saw*, Cambridge: Cambridge University Press.

PHOTOGRAPHY THEORIES

Newhall, Beaumont (1949) *The History of Photography: from 1839 to Present Day*, New York: Museum of Modern Art.

Price, Mary (1994) *A Strange Confined Place*, Stanford, CA: Stanford University Press.

Roberts, Russell (1997) 'Some Notes towards the Histories of Photography and Classification', in Chrissie Iles and Russell Roberts (eds), *Invisible Light: Photography in Art, Science and the Everyday*, Oxford: Museum of Modern Art.

Scott, Clive (1999) *The Spoken Image: Photography and Language*, London: Reaktion Books.

Smith, Peter (2013) 'Photography, Language and the Pictorial Turn', in Warren Carter, Barnaby Haran and Frederick J. Schwartz (eds), *Renew Marxist Art History*, London: Art/Books, pp. 446–457.

Sontag, Susan (1979) *On Photography*, Harmondsworth: Penguin.

Tagg, John (1988) *The Burden of Representation: Essays on Photographies and Histories*, Houndsmills, Basingstoke and London: Macmillan.

Wilden, Anthony (1987) *The Rules Are No Game: the Strategy of Communication*, London and New York: Routledge and Kegan Paul.

Zakia, Richard D. (2002) *Perception and Imaging*, Boston: Focal Press.

PART 3
PHOTOGRAPHY EDUCATION

INTRODUCTION

Part 3 introduces readers to key issues and debates in contemporary photography education. Chapter 7, entitled 'Issue and Debates in Photography Education I: New Photography Theory', outlines the way a new generation of critical photography theorists re-evaluated the photography provision in Britain and elsewhere in the 1970s and 1980s. In this chapter we describe the ideas of a relatively small group of activists who challenged what they saw as uncritical, anti-intellectual and modish trends in commercial and fine art photography.

Reinforcing the view expressed by the American historian, Alan Trachtenberg in 1981, that photography lacked 'collective intelligence', artist-theorists such as Victor Burgin, Simon Watney and Jo Spence turned to photography as one of the key sites of contemporary cultural practice. They established a body of theory that was drawn from earlier critical work of writers such as the German Marxist critic Walter Benjamin and politically engaged styles of photomontage associated with the historical avant-garde in the period before the rise of fascism in Europe. As we have noted these New Photography Theorists launched themselves into an attack on complex issues of social class and the social construction of gender difference, and found ways of breaking down barriers between political theory and experimental artistic practice. Establishing a bridge between theory and practice, the new attitude encouraged photography students to form links with other areas of the academic curriculum including politics, social science, the fine arts, graphic design and philosophy. The idea that photography education at university level might be nothing more than a form of technical training for industry or a fast track into 'art photography' was displaced by critical engagement and a higher level of cultural and political literacy.

Chapter 8, 'Issues and Debates in Photography and Education II: The Return of the Real', acknowledges the positive educational outcome and the epochal changes that resulted from New Photography Theory. It also observes how far the socio-political influence of this moment in photography education impacted on photography-centred practices of contemporary art. This chapter additionally considers the limitations of this brand of critical theory and its academic assimilation into the university and the art market. We have argued that New Photography Theory became a victim of its own success, not least in its modish connections with postmodern aesthetic ideology. We also note how far the New Photography Theorists' attack on realism (mainly targeted at documentary photography) underrated the power of

PHOTOGRAPHY EDUCATION

photography, which was ultimately reduced in their eyes to an undifferentiated part of the mass media. In this chapter we revisit 'realism' as an aesthetic concept and relate this discussion to key examples of contemporary photographic practice. The motivation for this 'return of the real' for some practitioners is to find ways of working that are closely linked with audience taste for narrative forms of photographic expression and to provide a revaluation of empirical and archival work at the highest level. These approaches have enormous potential as areas for development in photography education.

Chapter 9, 'Teaching and Learning Photography', focuses on contemporary issues in photography education. The impact of New Photography Theory in the late twentieth century broadened the field of study and elevated its status in the academy. Photography courses have achieved academic parity with other arts and humanities subjects. The New Photography Theory, discussed in earlier chapters, has redefined the curriculum in ways that extend to critical evaluation of social contexts beyond the academy and the museum.

In Chapter 10, 'New Technologies and Photography Education', we look at how new technologies have impacted on photographic education. The chapter includes an overview of where photography education is now and highlights the plurality of vocations that now attach to photography. The impact of new technology on the learning experience is explored. Digital imaging is contrasted with darkroom teaching in a debate that pitches technical determinism against traditional craft skills. The oversimplified *either/or* nature of this opposition is challenged. The new reliance on virtual space is discussed, and new trends such as online and open courses. Chapter 10 addresses the need for new and old transferable skills and reference is made to Creative Skillset. Photography education now is experiencing a period of change, adapting to encompass new convergence technologies such as moving image and CGI. We raise some key philosophical questions: What is the future of photography? Are we in a post-photographic era? Can education keep up with technology?

CHAPTER 7
ISSUES AND DEBATES IN PHOTOGRAPHY EDUCATION I: NEW PHOTOGRAPHY THEORY

This image was analysed by the photographer-theorist Victor Burgin in his essay 'Looking at Photographs' (Burgin, 1977). He makes the point that the photograph is about social class and 'race' but goes beyond this reading in saying that it produces *visual* structures linked with *social* structures in the world at large. His concern is not just with specific meaning in a single image but images in general. He wanted to show that photographic meaning is influenced by socially agreed values and ideas (Burgin, 1982: 147–150). We may insist on seeing the photograph in our own way and yet *socially agreed values and ideas* still intrude. Burgin wants us to question what is taken for granted when looking at the photograph. In this way the reader is encouraged to think about the way interpretation of images is shaped by pre-existent ideas and perspectives. Burgin presents a model of analysis that challenges 'visual connoisseurship' or the tendency to like photographs for 'what they are' rather than what they 'say' or 'do'. His approach does not rule out artistic appreciation of photographs but it does argue that the aesthetic is never innocently separate from a world of meaning and ideas. This approach is characteristic of the New Photography Theory that emerged in higher education in the late 1970s.

7.1 James Jarché, *General Wavell Watches His Gardener at Work*, 1941.

PHOTOGRAPHY EDUCATION

Burgin's emphasis on the *social* meaning in Jarché's *General Wavell* demonstrates a politicized reading but it could easily figure in an art-based history of photography. Art and politics are not mutually exclusive but they can be, and have been, treated as separate categories. As a 'document' the photograph struggles to find a place in the world of art, except as an object of aesthetic contemplation. If this kind of prejudice against the camera was true in the past attitudes are now very much changed and a socio-political reading of the subject, in the manner of Burgin, is no longer a barrier to photography's acceptance as art. In fact the modern museum is now a commonplace site for documentary photography. Audiences can now address 'serious issues' in an artistic setting. *How far this works is a matter for further discussion*. Photography as a site for philosophical speculation has a long history but only in recent times has this approach found a place in the academy. The rise of photography education derives from a broad view of the discipline beyond its narrow claim to be seen as 'art'.

INTRODUCTION

In this chapter we present a history of photography education with particular reference to changes occurring in the period after 1970. It is a period in which Cultural and Media Studies challenged the independence of traditional subjects in the humanities. Art history expanded in this period as design subjects and photography were added to painting, sculpture and architecture as legitimate areas for advanced study in higher education. The coalescing of the social sciences with literary and other subjects marked out new boundaries and hierarchies of culture were questioned. Radical ideas were imported into art education and all of these changes impacted on the teaching of photography. From this point onwards the main change in photography education revolves around 'theory' and its relation to pre-conceptions and habits of thought that were common to the practice. Photography education in the past came to be seen as 'initiation into dominant beliefs and values' in matters of taste combined with technical instruction (Burgin, 1982: 3). The limitations of this educational model were intensely scrutinized by a loose formation of academics, artists and photographers whose work is connected with conceptual art in the 1970s (see Chapter 5). For convenience we have referred to this generation of scholars, artists and teachers as the New Photography Theorists.

NEW LAMPS FOR OLD

A Brief History of Photography Education

Photography education has an uneven history. In the past two centuries it was largely self-taught and to some extent had the character of an amateur pursuit taken up by enthusiasts. Unlike other areas of the visual arts the ascendancy of photography as a professional practice was not determined by the academies of art but largely took place in the margins of what we would now call the media industries. Publicity media such as newspapers and illustrated journals gave rise to a new generation of press photographers in the interwar period of the twentieth century. The increasing professionalization of photography was reinforced by rapidly expanding advertising and fashion industries turning to the use of photographic illustration in this period.

ISSUES AND DEBATES IN PHOTOGRAPHY EDUCATION I: NEW PHOTOGRAPHY THEORY

Photomechanical printing was invented in the 1880s but the technology for its wider dissemination was not generally economically viable until later. In the period around 1900 popular illustrations for books and other mass circulation formats used wood engravings that were often close copies of photographs rather than direct reproductions (see fig. 2.15). Photography remained during this period a hybrid medium, somewhere between art and technology but always distanced from education. It is significant that little has been written about how photographers are educated or more broadly how they acquire the specific skills and knowledge that constitute the practice. In many cases photography may have been little more than a peripheral area of craft training in art school courses before its establishment as a stand-alone academic subject in the late twentieth century.

Photography education may seem to have a motley history as the 'awkward child of higher education' and yet there is a view that a more substantial past is retrievable if only we look in the right places. Darren Newbury writes:

> Yet photography education has given rise to particular practices and identities that are not reducible to art or history or sociology. And if one surveys the history of photography, lying behind many major contributions, are formative educational engagements, often only quietly acknowledged at best.

(Newbury, 2009: 118)

Newbury sketches this history in the British context by listing important high-level photography courses with long histories and proud achievements. They include Newport, South Wales as a centre for documentary photography which has roots in the early twentieth century; the pioneering work in photography theory of Victor Burgin at Trent Polytechnic in Nottingham in the 1970s and later The Polytechnic of Central London, which forms a substantial area of discussion in this chapter. There are well-known names in photography associated with Manchester Polytechnic from the late 1960s and other major centres developed enduring courses including Derby College of Higher Education, and Ealing School of Art and Design in West London.

The Anglo-centric nature of our brief histories of photography education is a product of parochialism in contemporary debate and yet it also betrays the shortage of research in this field. Newbury rightly indicates a strong tradition of photographic modernism in Eastern Europe closely linked with film schools and other areas of visual arts provision. In the early twentieth century photographers in Europe were connected with photography clubs and associations which are also under-researched institutional parts of this history. We should mention the Bauhaus in the period that immediately precedes the Third Reich and later the Dusseldorf Academy of Art in Germany in the 1980s as key institutions. The latter has much influence in contemporary art photography and the former established high ambitions for the social use of the medium.

As we noted in Chapter 1 the histories of photography are varied and always shaped by the context in which they are written. Photography, for many people, is most easily assimilated to the traditions of art and it is assumed (often wrongly) that photographers have links with art institutions including schools, academies and museums. The historical boundaries between art and industry are well defined and collectors and historians discriminate against photojournalism and commercial photography. Discussions on the status and functions of photography have often focused on the ambiguous nature of the medium which hovers between the functional modes of image production (including printing and

PHOTOGRAPHY EDUCATION

the graphic arts) and the fine arts. A main concern throughout its history is the mechanical nature of the medium. The historian Alan Trachtenberg comments on this dilemma in the following passage:

> The earliest photographers of prominence in Great Britain seem to have been well-to-do amateurs, people interested in art as well as science. The Royal Photographic Society emerged early, giving a national focus to serious amateur work. Moreover, the great strength and influence of the Royal Academy and other institutions of 'fine art' placed amateurs in a peculiar position. Many strived for 'beauty' in their pictures, wishing to find a place for photography in the arts. But such a realm seemed founded upon a key principle in the larger idea of 'culture' that art distinguished itself from science and industry by its special quality of 'spirit'. And if 'spirit' was marked by a certain organization of feelings and sensibility – the mark of 'tradition' and personal 'genius' – then how could one achieve true art by use of a mechanical device?
>
> (Alan Trachtenberg, 1980: x)

KEY TERM: Academe

This is a poetic word for the garden near Athens where Plato, the ancient Greek philosopher, taught. It now means an academic place of learning, the scholarly life and its community.

Photography had a long wait for its elevation to academe. In the quotation above Trachtenberg underlines the cultural divisions and hierarchies that define photography. Photographs are made by a mechanical device and may be considered to belong to trade and the sphere of 'work', a relatively lower placement in the wider scheme of things. The quotation signals how far photography was reduced by this attitude to a subordinate role largely outside the educational establishment. Photography was slowly absorbed into art education but its true recognition was granted, as a medium for academic study, when 'theory' gained a more central place in the curriculum during and after the 1970s.

The familiar roll call of famous 'art photographers' often counts as the official history of photography. It is a narrative that marginalizes non-artists or recruits them retrospectively when collectors re-evaluate their status. The art world's assimilation of photography has paved the way for its entry into the academy as a mainstream subject in the humanities. Such change of fortune in the estimation of the medium has, nevertheless, been accompanied by a largely unmapped history of technical training in photography that still sits alongside its more elevated partner to this day. These historical divisions have been widely debated by the New Photography Theorists who launched an attack on the state of photography education in Britain in the 1970s. Un-theorized ideas of artistic expression and unbridled commercialism were key issues for critical investigation. The wider implications of this are discussed below.

KEY TERM: New Photography Theory

The New Photography Theory is a short-hand term for a movement in art and photography that emerges in the 1970s and extends into postmodern photography (sometime called post-conceptual photography) in the 1980s. As the name suggests it is primarily a term that relates to 'theory' but significantly, many people associated with this 'theoretical turn' were artists and practitioners whose favoured medium was photography. We speak in the past tense but many are still practising and building on ideas that originated in the period we discuss. The movement was closely connected with conceptual art and inherited the irreverent and critical cultural politics associated with that movement. Key figures in our discussion of the term include Victor Burgin, Jo Spence, Simon Watney and John Tagg in the British context. The work of the American artist, writer, photographer and film maker Allan Sekula is not discussed in this chapter but his contribution was highly relevant.

New Photography Theory energized critical debate on photography education. Two main areas of interest were:

- The claim that a photograph is an expression of artistic personality. This was challenged because meaning in any kind of expression is always a social construct. The idea that whatever a photograph is *of* should play second fiddle to the artistic ego that made it seemed unreasonable to most theorists who considered the issue.
- The idea that photographic transparency independently produces truth statements about the world – naive realism – was contested because it failed to take account of the social connotations that immediately attach to a photograph when it is viewed. Naive theories of realism, they argued, ignore language and other contextual factors. This line of thought was aimed at documentary photography that was scrutinized and remodelled by Sekula in particular.

New Photography Theorists were especially interested in the ideological functions of images and the way audiences read them. The political focus of their work centred on the way social identity is formed in dominant patterns of cultural representation of social class, racial and gender (and other) determinations. The favoured modes of expression of the artists associated with this formation were writing, teaching, essays, mixed media formats and a range of visual strategies that dissolved traditional barriers between language and images. New Photography Theory had a major influence on photography teaching in institutions of higher education.

Past and Present: The Re-Invention of Photography Theory

Conceptual art provided a foothold in the art world for photography and aided its rise to academic respectability. This turn of events was not immediately apparent and for some commentators photography still lacked what the historian Alan Trachtenberg has called a 'collective intelligence regarding the medium' (Trachtenberg, 1980: viii). Writing in 1980 he observed

A *formal* criticism, a set of analyses and arguments which attempts to delineate a general character of the medium, has yet to emerge. The canons of art history, of connoisseurship, are not likely to provide the necessary model. It is in the more venturesome and intellectually aggressive works of *cultural* critics like Walter Benjamin, William Ivins, and Roland Barthes that

PHOTOGRAPHY EDUCATION

the beginnings of a new seriousness of discussion, a synthesis of historical scholarship and aesthetic theory, might be found.

(Trachtenberg, 1980: xiii)

In this view photography was under-theorized and without a sense of its place in the kind of critical tradition that attached to other subjects such as literary studies and art. This state of affairs is now much changed and the rise of photography theory has broadened the field into a wider field of critical debate. Indeed, the avant-garde ideas of Benjamin combined with Barthes' semiological studies of the mid-century were amongst the key influences on the New Photography Theory. It was exactly this synthesis of aesthetic theory and leftist cultural politics that was revived in a few art schools and photography departments, mainly in England, in the 1970s.

One of the key changes in this period since the 1970s is that many of the writers contributing to 'a new seriousness of discussion' were themselves photographers. Discussion itself, however, was not at all new since Victorian and twentieth-century photographers have written eloquently on their own practices. More recently, however, conceptual photographers had combined writing with photography in art works and installations. Their intention was to challenge traditional barriers between mental and manual work that have in the past held sway. The transition from theory into practice and from practice into theory was radical because it challenged institutional boundaries and raised the intellectual bar. The upgrading of art schools to university status in the 1990s in England consolidated photography education at the highest level. Indeed, whilst we seek to emphasize the legitimizing effects of photography theory since the 1970s, the problems of sustaining high-level intellectual work (often laced with utopian ambitions) forms an important part of this narrative. We might, for example, note market pressures on academic life in the period leading up to the millennium and the changing experiences of students in this century.

Basic Photography Under Attack

Two positions are dominant in university education and more generally across other layers of provision in colleges and schools. There are the established disciplines such as History, English Literature and the sciences; other subjects are more eclectic and generalized. As we have noted photography is positioned between these extremes since it has often been taught in colleges as a branch of art and graphic design or alternatively as a skills-based subject area on media programmes. Once seen as a low-profile subject, its fortunes had changed. One of the reasons for changing attitudes to photography is its increasing role in mass communication.

Glamorization of media industries in the 1960s and the rising profile of the photographer in fashion and journalism created a demand for 'well-rounded' graduates with photographic skills and ideas. The growth of photography in both professional and domestic/amateur spheres underscores the enormous productive power of the growing market for cameras and easy processing in the 1960s and 1970s. The success of photography was driven in this period by market forces. Flagship courses in this period were often closer in spirit to a 'swinging sixties' escapism than they were to the lofty ideals of the connoisseur. Photography had a central role in the development of fashion, advertising and journalism and offered career routes for college-trained graduates.

ISSUES AND DEBATES IN PHOTOGRAPHY EDUCATION I: NEW PHOTOGRAPHY THEORY

Michael Langford used the term 'basic photography'. He was a photographer and influential teacher at the Royal College of Art in London. The term refers to a mixture of craft methods and artistic self-expression. His book *Basic Photography*, originally published in 1965, announced:

> From something which a previous generation had regarded as an old-fashioned, fuddy-duddy trade and would-be artistic occupation, photography became very much part of the youth cult of the 'swinging sixties'. New small-format precision SLR camera, electronic flash, machines and custom laboratories to hive off boring processing routines, and an explosion of fashion photography, all had their effects. Photography captured the public imagination.
>
> (Langford, 1995: 13)

Before the 1950s photography was taught in very few academic institutions. By the 1970s the subject was widely taught in technical colleges, art schools and in universities in America: 'Educational bodies recognised the value of including photography in art, design, cultural and social studies, English and communications' (Langford, 1995: 13). The formation of the new polytechnics in the UK in the 1960s created a more fluid interaction between technology and the arts in constructive ways that underpinned developments of photography as an academic subject. Langford noted the increasing recognition of the 'value' of including photography in the curriculum. This is instructive but vague since little is said beyond the recognition of a photography skill set (possibly a mix of technical training and contextual studies). The limitations of photographic textbooks to technical data and case studies on 'the nude', still life, landscape, 'people', portraiture, children, groups and so forth were standard. The cultural assumptions and stereotypical nature of illustrations in books by authors in this period may now seem strangely archaic and yet there seemed to be little else for students to read. There is little evidence to support the idea that photographic education provided any level of critical enquiry. The bias was in fact towards applied forms of photography including advertising, publicity, news media and entertainment in a period of full employment.

The broad aims of photography education in early courses were liberal and could bend in different directions. In some ways this was a great strength since it allowed students to find their own way in a vaunted 'learning by doing' approach. At its best this legacy of Bauhaus pedagogy was a success since it encouraged experimentation that linked photographic practice to progressive social thinking and artistic experimentation. For some students, and teachers, this allowed connections with a tradition of artistic radicalism that embraced social aims. It also fostered repetition of commercial subjects and techniques or uncritical acceptance of mainstream ideas.

Langford's excitement about the growing popularity of photography marks a high water mark for what was later castigated as an 'unthinking' approach to the subject. For a new generation influenced by the more revolutionary ideas of the late 1960s it seemed to offer little beyond technical training and artistic self-expression. It fostered little if any critical interest in what the art historian and photography theorist Simon Watney called a 'debate-based' photographic culture of the kind he promoted (with Burgin and others) at the Polytechnic of Central London in the 1970s and 1980s (Watney, 1986: 59). In response to the absence of critical debate workshops and groups were formed and new publications dedicated to photography were established. *Ten.8*, *Photography and Politics* and *Camerwork*, new journals at this time, offered a high level of critical discussion that extended into debates on popular culture and aesthetics. Pioneering studies in photography theory appeared in the film journal *Screen.* Special editions on photography were launched in mainstream art journals such as *Studio International* (Photography Special Issue, July/August 1975) in England and *Artforum* in the USA.

227

PHOTOGRAPHY EDUCATION

Radical and Oppositional Photographic Practices

The new photo-literature associated with these journals in the 1970s and 1980s was inspired by the advanced level of scholarship and critical engagement in film studies. Watney referred to the need for photography education to catch up with film theory, which had advanced levels of research and publications on authorship, audiences, the star system, genres and so forth. A growing awareness of how far this limitation extended into the framework of photography teaching was an issue for photographer-critics who established, or contributed to, the new photography journals. *Camerawork* (fig. 7.2) was founded in 1975 and continued into the 1980s. *Photography and Politics* appeared in two editions in 1979 and 1986 (fig. 7.3). Topics included worker photography movements in Scotland, Germany and the USA in the 1920s and 1930s; studies on the ideological functions of popular photography in pre-war popular photography magazines, and studies of contemporary socialist-feminist photography groups such as the Hackney Flashers' Women's Collective.

The first wave of conceptual art in the 1960s and early 1970s challenged the elitist forms of artistic consumption and education as technical training for the creative industries. Art education in its different modes throughout the world had fulfilled these objectives successfully for many years. The most progressive institutions had taken ideas from the German Bauhaus and sought to encourage students to engage with their practice in an experimental and reflective way. And yet the utopian ideas of Bauhaus and its commitment to social and political change were largely ignored or assimilated into the conservative or commercialized forms of modernism in the post-war period after 1945. Progressive and militant forms of avant-garde art had been neutralized and photography was part of this process.

7.2 Cover of *Camerawork*, November, 1977, Half Moon Photography Workshop.

A changing political mood in 1960s Western societies influenced social attitudes. Civil rights struggles and the war in Vietnam were key issues for a growing student movement campaigning for legislation against racism, sexism and exploitation in the workplace. Art students discovered the work and the ideas of an earlier 1920s generation of artists whose work had crossed over into politics and mass communication. Photography was adopted as a new technology with democratic potential by artists in the early twentieth century. Artists expressed similar attitudes in the 1960s. Painters cannibalized photographs and artists responded to an image-world dominated by photography. Many were pragmatic and opportunist in their appropriation of photographs – especially the Pop artists – and others were more circumspect and political in their desire to challenge mass culture as a site for critical intervention. One outcome of this tendency is evident in the way artists addressed matters of social repression, stereotyping and the commercialization of everything in modern life. Mary

ISSUES AND DEBATES IN PHOTOGRAPHY EDUCATION I: NEW PHOTOGRAPHY THEORY

Warner Marien has described this moment as a 'theoretical turn', a thinking person's approach to photography. She observes 'In the 1970s photographic practice became caught up in theoretical considerations of contemporary society, but also generated texts and images that addressed matters of gender, ethnicity and social control' (Marien, 2012: 188).

Photography/Politics: Two included articles on techniques such as pinhole photography and photography in secondary school education. This is alongside scholarly articles on the sexual politics of photography; Robert Mapplethorpe's controversial images of black male nudes; war photography and physical disfigurement; the social workings of photography in industrial environments; studies in young people's photographic self-representation; representations of children in advertising; and photography and eugenics (the bogus science of racial 'improvement').

Camerawork published theoretical essays and studies of individual photographers. It contained what appeared to be traditional documentary photography, descriptive commentaries on workshops (such as a one-day seminar entitled 'Kids and Photography' in *Camerawork* 3 July 1976); academic essays including Victor Burgin's 'Art, Common Sense and Photography' essay of 1976 and a reproduction of his street poster *Possession* (fig. 7.6). These journals were cheap, black and white publications with radical, abrasive and politically

7.3 Cover of *Photography/Politics: Two*, 1986, London: Comedia. Image courtesy of Patricia Holland.

challenging content. As with the DIY (Do It Yourself) aesthetic of punk music fanzines in the late 1970s the format was functional rather than slick and the studied avoidance of corporate graphics is evident.

Ten.8 (fig. 7.4), a quarterly journal funded by a regional arts association in Birmingham, England, published a report on phototherapy work by Jo Spence (Spence, 1991). *Ten.8* issued in spring, 1992, a special issue on ethnicity and British photography in the 1980s, claimed (in the words of the cultural theorist Kobena Mercer) to be 'part of a wider dynamic drive of cultural expression in the black community which can … be tracked through music and other visual and performing arts' (Mercer, 1992: 7). These journals represented a united front against negative social stereotyping and some of their contributors revived the techniques of the German photomonteur John Heartfield (fig. 7.8) as a bulwark against authoritarianism in the mass media. The wide array of materials presented in these publications, combined with a steady growth of books, formed the background to the development of new curricula and new approaches to photography education. Many of the writers and photographers associated with this type of radical literature were instrumental in the formation of new college and university courses.

We have reviewed the turn to theory in photography education from an English point of view. It was not, however, restricted to England and there were parallel movements and ideas elsewhere including the USA, Canada, the Soviet Union, Latin America, Wales and Europe and elsewhere (see Wood, 2002: 54–73). The international context of New Photography Theory overlaps with radical trends in

PHOTOGRAPHY EDUCATION

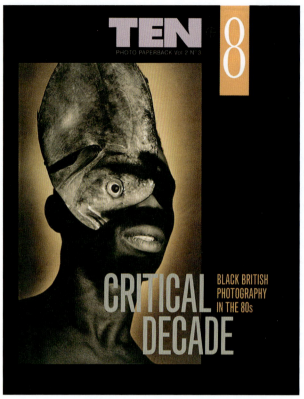

7.4 *Ten.8* Photo Paperback, vol. 2, no. 3, Spring 1992, 'Critical Decade – Black British Photography in the 1980s'. Birmingham: 10.8 Ltd.

contemporary art and in particular with conceptualism as an international movement in the visual arts. Some of the key new theorists emerging in this period were self-styled conceptual artists whose use of photography led to deeper philosophical engagement with the medium especially in relation to its influence on social behaviour and identity construction. The critic-photographer Victor Burgin followed this evolutionary passage from fine art student to artist and from artist to writer/critic/teacher. The photographer-artist was now also a critic. The old divisions (scholar/practitioner) were challenged in the making of new kinds of theoretical practice. This in turn led to an educational philosophy that gradually changed the way photography was taught at university by the 1980s.

As the subject established a stronger presence in higher education its integration with related academic territories (including media and cultural studies) seemed to threaten further expansion as a stand-alone subject. Advances in technology also contributed to the growth of new, non-analogue areas of 'imaging' and digital arts. As photography became a dispersed field of multi-media practice its identity as a discipline was questioned. Theorists welcomed a convergence of cultures and flexible image practices that seemed to extinguish photography as an autonomous discipline.

As early as the 1980s photography was thought not to really exist as a unified practice with its own identity. Its main interest for the theorist was in its role as mediator of social and political interest:

> What we begin to see is that the *so-called medium of photography* has no meaning outside its historical specifications … What alone unites the diversity of sites in which photography operates is the social formation itself … Photography itself has no identity … Its history has no unity. It is a flickering across a *field of institutional spaces*. It is this field that we must study, not photography as such.
>
> (Tagg, 1988: 63; emphasis added)

John Tagg, a key player in New Photography Theory, provoked a sense of crisis. His writing was an antidote to what he denounced as the 'unthinking' acceptance of truth claims of photography. In this view 'photographic truth' is structured by the context in which it gathers meaning and value. It has no independence or authority of its own. Tagg refers to 'the determining level of the material apparatus and the social practices within which photography takes place' (ibid.: 2).

The 'field of institutional spaces' to which he refers in the quotation (above) describes spaces or sites where the business of photography is carried out, how it is dispersed and made to act in the world. We might, for example, think of educational, commercial, legal and aesthetic operations of the medium

ISSUES AND DEBATES IN PHOTOGRAPHY EDUCATION I: NEW PHOTOGRAPHY THEORY

and consider how far photography reinforces identities in the wider fields of sexuality, status and social class. A 'social formation' (more commonly a 'discursive formation') is a term borrowed from the French poststructuralist Michel Foucault. It refers to the actual 'forms' of communication that make a practice visible or distinct. The photography section in the library, the 'department' in the college, the gallery that singles photography out from other artefacts, the archives and online resources are all constituent parts of photography as a discursive formation. In this sense a photograph, like any cultural artefact, is always framed by its place in the wider scheme of things. A photograph may be alone on the screen or isolated in the corner of a gallery but it is never detached from the anchoring effect of words and the cultural environment that defines it.

Tagg analysed the repressive surveillance functions of photography in the late nineteenth century which formed the basis for a wider perspective in which the medium is adapted to the commercial and political interests of the state. His historical research focused on repressive uses of police files, the pseudo-science of physiognomy, and stereotyping in photographic portraits of criminals. Together with other theorists, he showed how effects of lighting, pose, facial expression and the structured sameness of the genre were used in a systematic way to confirm hostile or beneficent modes of reception. The infamous press photograph of the criminal Myra Hindley (fig. 6.16) can be studied in the light of Tagg's views on photographic structure. 'Structured sameness' refers in this context to institutionalized victim photographs, the so-called 'mug shots', and vulgar stereotypes of the human subject. Tagg describes the photographic style thus: 'We have begun to see a repetitive pattern: the body isolated; the narrow space; the subjection to an unreturnable gaze; the scrutiny of gestures, faces and features' (Tagg, 1988: 85).

The systematic interrogation of criminals, patients, indigent families and colonial subjects produced archival photographic resources that were used as a basis for scientific work and bureaucratic social management. They served taxonomic functions and assisted in the identification and definition of 'social types'. The construction of subject groupings consolidated the need for their institutional regulation and control. This in turn provided evidence for the growth of new fields of knowledge and state institutions including medical, educational, legal and penal which, in their different ways, are constituent parts of the modern state coming into being during this period. The photography theorist David Green notes:

> Photography entered the field of the social sciences at a moment when the demand for modes of empirical observation and documentation, and techniques of quantitative measurement and analysis were uppermost.
>
> (Green, 1985: 6)

Tagg along with others writing on this kind of repressive photo-documentation (Sekula, 1989; Green, 1985) adopted an approach that was original and forceful and opened new ways thinking about photography as an instrument of social regulation. Emphasis on systems of power and regulation were an attack on the view that photographic meaning is value free or independent of operations it is made to serve. The critical assault on repressive use of photographic stereotypes was an important intervention in the naive realist view that a photograph provides an insight into states of mind and social being. Fabrication of social identity is not merely a reflection of its subject but a practice that says as much about the technique as it does about the sitter. Tagg's study of repressive methods of photo-documentation exemplified a way of extending photography discourse beyond the limited historical methods used in the past for the analysis of the portrait.

PHOTOGRAPHY EDUCATION

The critical engagement with portraiture now extended beyond assessment of its honorific and privileging functions to a wider assessment of poverty and social injustice. Photography is judged to be part of the social problem when it is used against the involuntary subject. Passive, coerced or unwary subjects are constrained by intimate observation and the subtle control of the camera. Documentary increasingly came to be regarded as a politically regressive mode. At its crudest it was accused of exploiting the photographic subject for its own professional ends. Sentimentalized images of the poor make good copy and sell newspapers.

Alongside John Tagg's virulent criticism of documentary photography Victor Burgin also launched an attack on what he called 'politically interested' photography practices that were current in the 1970s:

> At the time such practice ... was known as 'concerned photography'. This kind of photography had become frozen in a self-servingly pious sentimentality. The (middle class) photographer's narcissistic display of concern for the poor and oppressed took the place of any real analysis. The 'theory' we wished to bring to bear on this, and other photographic practices (especially advertising) took place in the gulf between then prevailing aestheticist and sociolinguistic attitudes. For aestheticism, the photograph was an occasion for 'purely visual pleasures', to which consideration of content was largely irrelevant. For sociologism, the photograph was a window on the world, a transparent means of access to the truth of experience, to which formal considerations were entirely secondary.

(Burgin, 1997: 74)

7.5 Diane Arbus, *A Young Brooklyn Family Going for a Sunday Outing, NYC*, 1966. © Tate, London 2014.

This comment has the virtue of breaking down issues and debates into manageable portions. The caricatured figure of an arty photographer 'doing his own thing' is contrasted with the 'concerned' documentary specialist raising consciousness and improving the world. One is a swooning aesthete and the other a 'do-gooder'. Neither of them, according to Burgin, has any real understanding of the work of politics in photographic representation.

The work of Tagg and the American artist Allan Sekula (amongst others) led to a rethinking of documentary as a more politically rigorous way of approaching social issues. This point notwithstanding, the campaign against documentary was, arguably, overstated and lacking in nuanced study of the genre. John Roberts and others have looked more sympathetically at the way photographs in popular use can express class solidarity, social unease, or wilful opposition to imposed social convention. For example photographers as different as Walker Evans in the 1930s and Diane Arbus in the 1960s (fig. 7.5) were both 'steadfast debunkers of the New America and the American Dream' (Roberts, 1998: 120).

Critical Approaches to Art, Common Sense and Photography

One of the dominant and perhaps inescapable themes in photography is its role as art. Even when photographs have no artistic pretentions whatever, there is a sense in which they may seem to be structured by aesthetic ideas. The New Photography Theorists were especially drawn to the way photography freely passed between levels of cultural signification. Attracted to its apparently 'non-artistic' qualities they enjoyed the way it appeared in the press, in the street, and randomly across the public spaces of the world. Burgin belonged to a generation of artists who challenged the traditional hierarchy of media which took for granted the relative importance of painting and its superiority to photography. The turn to photography was an oppositional gesture, and as Jessica Evans says, 'an assault on the decorum' of art. Evans:

> From this point onwards … Burgin made work which incorporated some of the tropes of mass culture … most importantly the integration of words with images, which replicate the 'scripto-visual' and intertextual social uses of photography.
>
> (Evans, 1994: 202).

KEY TERM: Intertextuality
The word 'intertextuality' is used in cultural theory to describe the way meanings migrate from one text to another. By 'text' we mean a piece of writing, image, advertisement, work of art, a film or television show, or magazine article. Intertextuality occurs when one text refers to another text. One text might 'quote' another text. Post-conceptual photography that mimics an already existing work is an example of intertextuality. For example, the early photographs of Cindy Sherman are called 'film stills' because they look like scenes from old movies. *The Simpsons* frequently references media events and personalities. The information flow between media forms is very much taken for granted and creates the illusion that we live in an integrated global culture.

A 'scripto-visual' work (a mixed media format that includes words and pictures) challenges the academic distinction between writing and pictures. In the past works of fine art were not supposed to have words in them. The mixing of words and pictures in the modern period suggested an affinity with popular media and a transgression of the ideals of art. There are further consequences: in the past criticism and history were physically and conceptually distanced from works of art. The inclusion of words in the work of conceptual artists was a provocation. Burgin's poster of 1975 that includes words and photograph is a quotation or parody in the style of an advertising image (fig. 7.6).

Photography (with words alongside) signalled a desire to intervene in the world beyond high culture. In appropriating the 'look' of advertisements and the rhetorical style of the copywriter Burgin attacked the primary sites and institutions of what he called 'official culture'. *Possession* (1976) directs attention

PHOTOGRAPHY EDUCATION

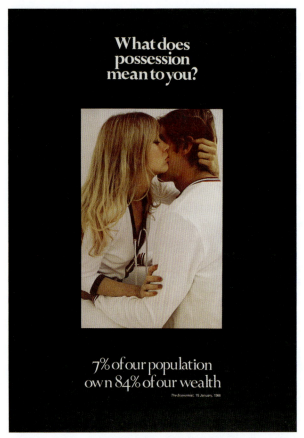

7.6 Victor Burgin, *Possession*, poster, 1976. © Victor Burgin, courtesy Galerie Thomas Zander, Cologne/Arts Council Collection, South Bank Centre, London.

to social and sexual ambiguities of words and imagery. A stock image and a found quotation play against sexual and economic uses of the word 'possession'. The slickness of the photograph corresponds with a centred composition and roman typeface. It could pass for a glossy ad in a fashion journal. An explicit link between 'desire' (for pleasure in its various forms) and economic privilege is suggested. The object of desire in most ads is not the product itself but its value as a status symbol. *Possession* is work of socialist art that seeks to educate. In an essay originally published in 1976 Burgin noted: 'A task for socialist art is to unmask the mystifications of bourgeois culture by laying bare its codes, by exposing the devices through which it constructs its self-image' (Burgin, 1993: 915).

The political temper of Burgin and many others at this time was directed against the media and cultural institutions. It marks a break with what some activists saw as the older Marxist struggles against the state or within the traditional sites of working-class activism in the manufacturing industries and the trade unions. This led to a widening of the field of social and political engagement to include consumerism and the manufacture of ideas in what came to be identified as the culture industries. Principal amongst these industries were advertising, fashion, the graphic arts and television. Visual communication was increasingly powerful in the creation of modern myths of daily life. For many critics, artists, photographers and teachers the broad task that lay ahead was that of unmasking ideological abuse in advertisements and other media products. The aim was to reveal what the theorist judged to be repressive social relations and oppose negative racial, sexual and class-based stereotypes systematically reproduced in the media.

The significance of photography criticism in the period around 1970 is that it was infused with the growing political militancy and oppositional youth culture at the time of the war in Vietnam. The radical turn to everyday photography as an object for ideological critique led to the study of *representation* more generally. The attraction of photography for this generation was not restricted to its expressive or aesthetic functions but included a greater sensitivity to its role in everyday life. As its political project extended into photography practice and scholarly publications its place in the university and college curriculum was consolidated by increasing numbers of courses. The prospect of its absorption into related fields remains a prospect in the future but the technological boosterism of the late twentieth century greatly exaggerated this outcome.

ISSUES AND DEBATES IN PHOTOGRAPHY EDUCATION I: NEW PHOTOGRAPHY THEORY

Vocational and 'Non-vocational' Approaches to Photography Education

The New Photography critique of institutions in the 1970s and 1980s was intended to broaden the outlook of students beyond what existed in higher education before their arrival. From the 1960s onwards, photography was divided into two blocks: vocational and non-vocational. Many institutions offered courses that veered towards the one or the other end of the spectrum indicated by this difference. They were never mutually exclusive but their differences were recognized. Vocational courses often identified a particular specialism or direction indicated in their titles. Fashion photography and photojournalism, for example, are now well-established vocational disciplines at key institutions. Non-vocational courses with non-specific titles often lean towards the fine arts. Writing in the 1980s Simon Watney characterized the role of theory in relation to the two sides of photography education. First he noted that what passed for theory was often little more than a supplementary form of applied studies within vocational and non-vocational courses which may vary from one institution to the next. Watney observed:

> For it is a fundamental requirement of all such courses that they provide the student with some kind of 'complementary' studies, since it is assumed that the photographer is a distinct type of person, fundamentally 'non-intellectual', whose manual and visual talents are in need of compensatory academic instruction. It is at this point that the two types of course begin to take on clearly definable and frequently incompatible characteristics.
>
> (Watney, 1986: 53–54)

There are compelling claims in this statement that may still ring true and yet it may now seem dated. The upgrading of art schools to university status and the enormous increase in student numbers on degree programmes has challenged the old *laissez-faire* educational model. The old distinctions between theory and practice, the division between 'applied' and 'main' studies has dissolved in many institutions and the academic ambition of courses in photography is now more highly calibrated than it was. Photography education has been strongly influenced by graduates with knowledge of New Photography Theory.

On the other hand many of the fault lines identified in the 1980s have in some ways remained. For example, old divisional boundaries are still in place. Vocational students are often more comfortable with the non-intellectual ethos of their course. For the non-vocational student the way ahead is less certain. Watney described what he judged to be the crudely instrumental role for 'theory' as it was applied to the kind of courses he saw in the early 1980s:

> The students on 'non-vocational' courses will thus be introduced to those historical and critical discourses which are to frame and make sense of his or her work. These are structured around the pivotal figure of the Fine Artist, and operate in such a way that the student will come to 'recognise' his or her work and identity in terms of the familiar aesthetic discourses of self-expression, innovation, and creativity ... This framework of complementary studies is matched in 'practice' by a curriculum which sets students endlessly in competition with one another around the familiar circuit of photographic categories in which he or she is expected to shine – documentary, landscape and portraiture...
>
> (1986: 54)

235

PHOTOGRAPHY EDUCATION

From a twenty-first-century point of view popular culture and high culture are still separate categories. Museums are no longer remote outposts of intellectual life but the old hierarchy still exists. The idea of 'art' as the gold standard for the assessment of aesthetic value reinforces distinctions based on taste and cultural knowledge. For Watney, the so-called 'vocational' was little more than a form of training:

> The vocational student is thus provided with a more frankly training-oriented education, and can expect at least a course in business studies of some kind … Such studio training is therefore unlikely to offer much in the way of oppositional analyses of say, 'News' photography, or Page Three pin ups, or Fine art practices. For behind all the discussions of style, lighting, and so on, the student's work will ultimately be judged in relation to client satisfaction and sales returns, in markets whose own values and practices remain unquestioned.

> (Ibid.: 55)

The lack of questioning was judged to be equally deficient in the case of non-vocational (fine art) photography since the student 'will be lucky,' Watney says, 'if he or she learns anything about the gallery system' (ibid.: 55). With few exceptions photography courses sustained a level of intellectual passivity that seemed to ignore the outside world except in terms of work opportunities it offered. In this view photography education in the 1970s was at best a form of technical training overlaid with an artistic gloss. A loose network of artists, art historians, photographers, social critics, teachers and writers shared this view. Almost all campaigners for integrated theory/practice curricula in higher education made writing an important part of their practice. Many contributed to the journals listed above. Others used the art world as a platform for their ideas and attempted to break the traditional barriers that separated theoretical work from image making. It is significant that production of art works relied heavily on the use of words. As noted in the last chapter, the professional boundaries between criticism and practice had been abandoned by conceptual artists who found they could think for themselves. Writing as the domain of the scholar and artistic practice coalesced in methods now promoted by the new theorists. One of the survivors from this period has recently noted:

> Teaching out of practice remains of central importance to photography education, and challenges the distinction between teacher, learner and researcher that dominate the discourse of higher education.

> (Andrew Dewdney, cited in Newbury, 2009: 123)

New Photography Theory and the Critique of Art

By the mid-twentieth century 'art photography' was an established section of art world interest and major museums had department and collections to reflect this. Stieglitz's photographs of cloud formations or sublime views of mountains and the great outdoors in the work of Ansel Adams were established styles of Western art photography. The photographer and critic David Campany describes this as a trend towards 'subjective photography' and the production of 'beautiful photographs' in a movement that kept its distance from popular culture and the affairs of everyday life. Mainstream art photography of this period, according to Campany, was 'insular and conservative … suggesting a reflex retreat into the opposite of the cheap colour images of post-war mass culture' (Campany, 2007: 16–17).

ISSUES AND DEBATES IN PHOTOGRAPHY EDUCATION I: NEW PHOTOGRAPHY THEORY

Historians and critics have underlined a tension in the period after the Second World War when art photography was widely valued by museum curators and collectors but out of touch with the growing interest in the wider economic and cultural effects of the medium. Mary Warner Marien notes the separation of art photography in this period from its wider social mooring: 'Meanwhile the growth of mass media, especially in the service of advertising, roused artists and critics to attend more closely to the effects of photography' (Marien, 2002: 370). One of the most conspicuous attempts to bridge the gap between art and everyday life was Pop art. By the 1950s mass culture attracted the attention of artists whose leisure interests overlapped with artistic practice. The artist Richard Hamilton in England recycled commercial photographs in screen-prints and paintings. His political satire *Portrait of Hugh Gaitskill as a Famous Monster of Filmland* of 1964 (fig. 7.7) demonizes a leading English politician in a mixed media work. A photographic image of Gaitskill is transformed into a film land anti-hero: *The Phantom of the Opera*. The blurring of high culture with Hollywood and press photography demonstrates opposition to the elevated poetics of art photography.

For later critics and innovators in the visual arts (including photographers and the emergent conceptual artist in the late 1960s) the photograph itself was an object of interest. Richard Hamilton's recycled photographs appeared to celebrate commercial culture. Pop was precursor of the postmodern idea that meaning is always a construction, mediation or *re*presentation of some kind. If you want to engage 'reality' look at the way it is *produced* in pictures, books, magazines, films, radio, and so forth. The sociologist and cultural theorist Stuart Hall explains: 'representation is conceived entering into the very constitution of things … not merely a reflection of the world after the event' (Hall, 1997: 6). Images are never merely reflections of things in the world because they always carry a higher meaning that supplants what the image shows us. Hall poses the question: 'Does visual language reflect a truth about the world which is already there, or does it produce meaning about the world through representing it?' (Hall, 1997: 7).

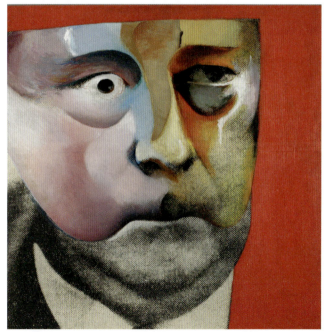

7.7 Richard Hamilton, *Portrait of Hugh Gaitskell as a Famous Monster of Filmland*, 1964. Oil and collage on photograph on panel. © The Estate of Richard Hamilton. Courtesy of Arts Council Collection, South Bank Centre, London.

To *represent* is an active verb and reflection is passive. The action of making something produces meaning. Communication is not a mirroring of meaning. It is constructive and the act of construction carries meaning. The glossiness of the photo-ad and its expensive looking shoot carries meaning. The artifice or style of showing something fascinated the Pop artists as if this carried greater meaning than what it attempted to show. The 'real' loses power in a world of simulated meanings. This way of thinking was central to New Photography Theory and its elevation of 'representation' above 'truth' about the world. Whereas the Pop artists loved artifice and exploited its effects, the New Photography Theorists saw it as deception, an allurement, with negative ideological effects. They

237

PHOTOGRAPHY EDUCATION

shared an interest in popular culture but their aims were diametrically opposed. Advertisements were treated by Burgin as the quintessential signs of capitalist culture.

The belief that photography plays a role in the construction of dominant ideas and beliefs in society is at the root of the New Photography Theory. The new wave of 1970s feminism had already targeted popular culture as one of the prime sites for revolutionary deconstruction. Burgin's thinking at this time was informed by a radical politics of representation that, amongst other things, produces ways of seeing women:

> One of the most generally influential achievements of the women's movement, in the field of cultural theory, has been its insistence on the extent to which the collusion of women in their own oppression has be exacted, precisely, *through* representations. They have argued that the predominant, traditional, verbal and visual representations of women do not reflect, 'represent', a biologically given 'feminine' nature (natural therefore unchangeable); on the contrary, what women have to adapt to as their 'femininity' (particularly in the process of growing up) is itself the *product* of representations [Burgin's emphasis].

> (1982: 8–9)

What passes for 'femininity' in street life photography is an artifice or construction. It is in other words a *re*presentation. Stereotyped pictures in the tabloid press correspond with their audience's expectation. They confirm an already established set of ideas and values that are repeated in the next edition. Photography plays a role in the construction of sexual, gendered and other kinds of social identity. In the case of a 'pin-up' the photograph anchors the written text. In simple terms a representation corresponds with ideas and beliefs that are taken to be true. However, since habitual ways of seeing are *constructed* they can be contested. The combative style of postmodernism associated with new photography theory underlines this idea of education as a critical practice engaging with the world and interrogating modes of representation. The aesthetic strategies of an earlier avant-garde inspired this approach.

AVANT-GARDISM RETURNS: THE WORK OF JO SPENCE

New Photography Theory and the Historical Avant-Garde

The publication of leading texts by Burgin, Watney, Tagg and others established a base for new approaches in education. As we have seen the main targets for this school of criticism were photography-as-fine-art and documentary photography. The first was judged to be elitist and backward looking and the second often based on naive ideas about transparency and truth. Earnest pictures of street life are negatively coded and politically weak and the idea of an un-coded reality beyond representation was attacked as naive. This led to the deployment of photomontage as a method that reveals its own reality as construction and thus negates the illusion of the real.

ISSUES AND DEBATES IN PHOTOGRAPHY EDUCATION I: NEW PHOTOGRAPHY THEORY

KEY TERM: Photomontage

Photomontage is a cut and paste technique that allows the construction of images from individual photographic prints. The technique pre-dates computerized techniques of image manipulation. In the past deceptively realistic 'photographs' were constructed to look like single images. The work of John Heartfield, in the early twentieth century, is a good example of a progressive use of photomontage and demonstrates a propagandist use of the medium. More generally photomontage is used in advertising and newspapers. The technique involves recycling existing images or using staged photographs, bringing different things together to create novel effects such as embarrassing or surrealist juxtapositions. The constructed image might be retouched and then re-photographed to give it a 'finished' or unified appearance.

A significant part of the new practices, in the 1970s and after, relied on a pre-existent repertoire of image use and borrowing from the historical avant-garde. The use of montage was an antidote to the photographic mainstream. The revival of interest in John Heartfield signalled a return to political satire made of cryptic slogans and found photographs (fig. 7.8). Photographers using constructed-image practices in the 1970s and 1980s adapted his methods. The representational strategies deployed by English photographers such as Jo Spence were linked with these influences and the perceived need to avoid the single picture window and the traditional separation of words and images.

BIOGRAPHY: JOHN HEARTFIELD

German political artist, belong to the avant-garde group of Dadaists. He adapted collage and photomontage to the purpose of subversive, anti-establishment propaganda in the period of the Weimar Republic. He is best known for his anti-Nazi propaganda and his famously irreverent, contemporary portraits of Adolf Hitler.

A combination of high art and low technology in the work of Barbara Kruger (fig. 5.3) and Jo Spence echoes Pop art but is now more politically directed and designed for mass circulation rather than the museum. Just as Heartfield had, in the 1920s and 1930s, published his photomontages in *Arbeiter Illustriete Zeitung* (*AIZ*) – Workers' Illustrated Times – the new work by Spence in the pages of *Camerawork* was an expression of ideas about identity, social class and politics.

Spence set out to find audiences outside the art world and was sensitive to the social effects of dissemination and reception. She claimed to be an educational photographer and channelled her writing, photography and teaching towards women's groups, secondary schools, adult education groups and the labour movement. In her written work she is attentive to the way context influences reception of the work:

> Ever since I have been creating images I've tried to get them used in different contexts so that it becomes clear that they don't have fixed meaning. It means that nothing is sacred and you can make your images mean what you want them to mean depending on where you place them.
>
> (Spence, 2006: 101)

PHOTOGRAPHY EDUCATION

7.8 John Heartfield, 'Mirror, mirror on the wall, who is the strongest of them all? The crisis'. Photomontage on the cover of *AIZ*, 24 August 1933.

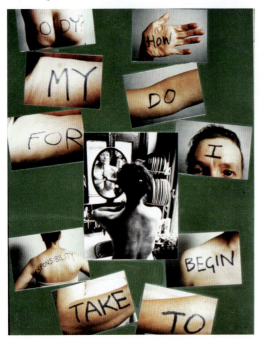

7.9 Jo Spence and Rosy Martin, *How Do I Begin to Take Responsibility for My Body?*, Creative Camera, No. 249, 'The Portraitive-Self in Context', September 1985. © The Estate of Jo Spence. Courtesy of Richard Saltoun Gallery and Terry Dennett.

Spence abandoned the single frame documentary image and found a range of formats including collaborative work with other photographers, sequential photographic displays, and didactic panels consisting of written data and photo-documents (including press cut outs). She created archives at The Photography Workshop that included some of the following: popular and ephemeral images, labour and trade union histories, technical history of photography resources and materials, postcards, cartoons, workers' films, and for historical record printed ephemera of a racist, sexist and class-bias nature. The building of archives and popularization of research is emphasized in Spence's overall project and the didactic function of this are realized in its dissemination.

She developed a complex practice that found expression in teaching, writing, photography and graphic media. The approach is didactic, propagandist, satirical, transgressive and avoids socially detached modes of art appreciation or sentimental images of the working class. It is the kind of work that was meant to provoke criticism and debate and reader-community participation. Like earlier German workers' photographs of the 1930s it was intended to have popular appeal especially for women (figs. 7.9 and 7.10).

Spence is best known for self-portraiture. In using a traditional genre she sought to draw attention to the politics of self-representation where the subject looks at herself. Artists and photographers have often made pictures of themselves working with a mirror or camera. It is a method for recording the ageing process (as in Rembrandt's self-portraiture) and recognition of the artifice involved in the 'capture' of a person's look (as in the staged photographs of the American artist Cindy Sherman). Both of these examples are relevant to our assessment of Spence. She condemned the social pressure on women to hide the ageing process and was clearly motivated by the artificial nature of a photo-shoot and the extent to which it might normally be governed by the gendered nature of the photographic gaze. She was interested in the way the subject revealed in portraiture relates to its 'social nature' and directed her own work towards this end. The editing out of the darker side of family life in advertising and domestic photography provoked Spence into finding disruptive and challenging roles for the camera:

> I want to cause a rift in how people see 'the real', but I don't want to leave the real behind. Thus when

ISSUES AND DEBATES IN PHOTOGRAPHY EDUCATION I: NEW PHOTOGRAPHY THEORY

BIOGRAPHY: THE PHOTOGRAPHY WORKSHOP

The Photography Workshop was formed in London in 1974 by Terry Dennett and Jo Spence and later combined with the Half Moon Gallery. Both Dennett and Spence were photographers and campaigning socialists. They promoted the idea that photography is a useful tool that can be used for educational and community purposes. They were committed to, as they put it, 'demystifying technology' (Bezencenet and Corrigan, 1986: 18). The workshop provided modest resources for technical training of young enthusiasts, women's groups, and others. It was connected with other start-up groups and institutions such the Hackney Flashers Collective, a women's photography group, the Half Moon Gallery, and photographic publications including *Photography and Politics* and *Camerawork*. The workshop had limited state funding and was mostly self-financed. Its founders regarded it as a research institution committed to building non-commercial archives and critical uses of photography. It was committed to local interests and community politics. As a radical organization it sought to challenge traditional photographic media. Spence changed direction as she addressed what she considered to be the limitations of reportage and photojournalism in general. Arguments in favour of the objective neutrality of the photograph were rejected and greater attention was given to the way the medium alienated its subjects and made them passive objects of the camera's gaze. She developed a method of staged self-portraits with interrogative self-written messages. The change of direction led to Spence's separation from the Half Moon Collective in the early 1980s.

I am dealing with fantasy, I am simply dealing with that which is suppressed in visual representation, that which is not normally shown.

(Spence, 2006: 100)

The idea of one's own history, one's own psychic reality, one's own makeup and desires, and one's gendered self-identity provided motivation for Spence's work:

7.10 Jo Spence and David Roberts, *Not of Our Class*, 1989, Jo Spence Memorial Archive. © The Estate of Jo Spence. Courtesy of Terry Dennett.

A lot of people are beginning to see that you can't teach theory without having some work in the first year on your own history; you just can't leap over the head of your own history. The problem is now to do that without going into straightforward reminiscence, or people inserting themselves into abstract texts without engaging with what is happening in their own lives. Of course in Adult Education where one's life experience is the basis for teaching, they often have problems with theory because they cannot move beyond the anecdotal and immediate needs of students, or beyond the question of bias. Phototherapy therefore attempts to work across the polarity of these two things: theory and experience.

(Spence, 2006: 92)

241

PHOTOGRAPHY EDUCATION

The self-portrait was a means of working something through image as an objective fragment of the interior self. The themes and motifs are not arbitrary but link to issues-based concerns made into dramatic self-exposure, in every sense of the word. In *Narratives of Dis-sease* (with Tim Sheard), a sequence of self-portraits carried out in 1989, Spence appears naked and presents the results of a mastectomy in a work (with Tim Sheard) entitled *Booby Prize* (fig. 7.11). In this work she attempts, in her own words, to deal with 'the "ugliness" of being seen as Other' (Spence, 2006: 374). It is, she claimed, a type of work:

> [d]one in one photo-therapy session ... This work is an example of the way in which it is possible, through the process of photo therapy, to distil feelings/events/ideas down to icons: these can be made public in the hope of disorienting the viewers' expectations, prompting ... an interior dialogue with themselves.

> (Spence, 1991: 12)

In *My Mother, ca. 1952*, she reinvents herself as her own mother. In this work she treats her life as though it were subject to external forces, self-regulation and personal choice. A powerful body of work develops out Spence's photo-therapeutic method. It is a self-questioning technique that has influenced other photographers and suggested useful methods for teaching and learning. Spence had strong connections with the cultural politics that emerged out of conceptual art and New Photography Theory in the 1970s. She was a student on the pioneering photography course at The Polytechnic of Central London run by David Faddy and Victor Burgin. She shared the accepted wisdom of her peers that all photographs carry messages between social groups and play a part in the reproduction of life. She could see that the production of knowledge was a site of contestation and her work was in this way confrontational and interactive. She was wary of the idea that photographs are neutral, 'just personal' or belonging to their own reality. She said:

> There seems to be a widespread assumption among photographers that their work is somehow 'neutral' or apolitical, that politics is something that goes on in parliament or the White House. How do we convince them they are mistaken? We have approached the problem by listing stages at which manipulation and bias can occur in the production of photographs.

> (Spence, 1995: 38)

The list includes reference to the photographer's *consciousness* which Spence regarded as a primary site for analysis and critical self-reflection. Choices made in the processing of an image are, she claims, determined by availability of resources and technical conventions and habits of procedure are taken into consideration as key factors in production. Spence also includes post-production determinations such as the addition of text to an image and wider questions relating to ownership and controlling effect of reproduction. She also raises 'the question of the beholder' (1995: 39) and the level of educational capital that he or she brings to interpretation of the image. And finally she asks: how far is a response to an image determined by social identity?

Photography itself was interrogated by Spence and subjected to critical analysis. One outcome was to think of new and subversive functions for the medium. Phototherapy deployed the camera as a recording device for performance and socially interactive sessions. The use of mimicry emulates the kind of processes that occur in all staged photography, portrait painting and other methods of portrayal

ISSUES AND DEBATES IN PHOTOGRAPHY EDUCATION I: NEW PHOTOGRAPHY THEORY

PHOTOTHERAPY

Jo Spence said phototherapy (photographic psychotherapy) is a word that suggests the idea of using the medium of photography as a strategy for self-healing. It is a type of photographic practice invented by Rosy Martin and Jo Spence in the 1980s. It has historical links with art therapy and clinical approaches to psychological disorder. For Martin and Spence it was a method based on re-enactment of past constructions of social identity. Spence adopted dress codes and body language that helped her to mimic and negotiate her past. Martin says she 'explores psychic and social constructions of identity within the drama of the everyday' (www.rosymartin.co.uk/Site/CV.html).

The psychological territory explored in phototherapy includes, gender, sexuality, social class, desire, memory and shame. Spence famously addressed her own pathology when she contracted cancer. Both Martin and Spence focus on the public-private duality that is particularly vivid in photographs of people. Domestic photography, for example, makes the body into a public display whilst it registers powerful thoughts and memories which have private meanings. Phototherapy accepts that psychic and social realities are convergent in everyday life.

7.11 Jo Spence in collaboration with Dr Tim Sheard, *Booby Prize*, 1989. From *Narratives of Disease*. This print appears in 'Cultural Sniper' in *Ten.8*, Vol. 2, no. 1, Spring, 1991. © The Estate of Jo Spence. Courtesy of Terry Dennett.

PHOTOGRAPHY EDUCATION

and image construction. Spence used photography as a technique for examining the lived world that might be inspected in closely observed images that mediate between the inner self and the outward appearance. John Roberts describes it as 'portraiture that takes a representation of the self into the area of *active* self dramatisation' (1998: 206). It is in any case a clear example of thinking about photography as practice that breaks through intellectual, artistic and professional boundaries. This was an aim of the New Photography Theorists. Photographic re-enactment of past events in her life provided a connection between performance art and portraiture. Studio-based practice foregrounds the performance which in turn provides a reflexive mode of self-examination.

The 'Lived World' and Student Experience

Spence's work has parallels with debates on teaching methods in media and cultural studies in the period from the 1980s to the present day. In particular the idea of 'self-research', 'self-representation' and its application to photographic practice, as 'a critical photography of the self' (Roberts, 1998: 206), opens up issues around social regulation and psychic constraints under which body management occurs. This trend was closely connected with identity politics which emphasized 'the personal' as a starting point for critical analysis of the social world. Although Spence's practice centred on human physical attributes (mostly her own), it was directed *outward* to the institutions in which they occur, including the family and its domestic setting, the medical profession, advertising and the press. Her 'self study' focuses light upon the way symbolic values attach to what we are, how we look, how we speak and conduct ourselves. In interviews she spoke with passion about her own consciousness of social class and gender, not as separate concerns but as intimately related aspects of her own self-image and social identity. Spence made her own body a site of resistance to the forces that shaped and influenced her life. It was a project that negotiated *self* and *social* identity.

The emphasis on the part played by the reader, the student, the audience in any kind of cultural project is central to cultural studies in the period of its ascendancy in the 1970s. Its subject field was youth culture, fashion, television and mass culture and close to student patterns of cultural consumption. The idea of cultural meaning inscribed in daily routines and pleasures was a refreshing alternative to the solemn study of high culture.

The quest was for theorists to sustain a level of critical thinking whilst recognizing that students may go in other directions. It had to overcome the traditional enemies of education including residual anti-intellectualism and the student perception that education is disconnected from the wider world. Other theorists have focused on students whose experience 'can be employed as the *scene* of theoretical analysis' (Roberts, 1998: 203). Spence's critical reframing of the family album is linked with theorist Greg Ulmer in John Roberts's discussion of these ideas:

> The communication of theoretical mastery is exchanged for a dialogic interaction between specialised discourses, popular and individual biography, allowing the life story of the student to become a vehicle for theoretical research. Ulmer calls this 'my-story': a form of discourse that replaces the process of critical distance involved in theoretical learning...
>
> (Roberts, 1998: 203)

ISSUES AND DEBATES IN PHOTOGRAPHY EDUCATION I: NEW PHOTOGRAPHY THEORY

Ulmer addresses the way *knowing* is translated into *telling*. Similarly Spence argued that photography is an object of study and not a 'master text' to be trusted on authority:

> For the photographer to place himself or herself into the picture is to immediately invert the place where the truth supposedly resides. Instead of the image serving as the object of study, it becomes a shared process of understanding between the photographer/subject and the spectator/subject.
>
> (Roberts, 1998: 204)

The student-centred approaches are calculated strategies to popularize research. We have argued that Jo Spence attempted a similar programme of photographic research which extended self-portraiture beyond its traditional truth telling or truth-fashioning techniques. Self-presentation thus becomes part of an argument or confrontation with the spectator. In this way the spectator has an active role in the assignment. There are successful examples of teaching that overcomes the polarization of intellectual thought and pleasure. Personal history, however, has its pitfalls since this often turns into uncritical autobiography or self-indulgent and confessional modes of photography.

There are weaknesses in the approach but research centred on student experience has been widely extended across higher education. It is one of the achievements of cultural studies to redirect the humanities towards what Raymond Williams famously described as the 'ordinariness of culture'. This approach might include a study of high culture but, as we have noted, it often means middlebrow art forms, the Internet, social media and popular forms of photography. The student-centred approach often foregrounds a common culture shared by teacher and student. The main point is to encourage students to look out from their own vantage point and from this position 'reconstruct the world in their own ways', as the cultural studies theorist Lawrence Grossberg has expressed the idea:

> It is a pedagogy which demands of students not that they conform to some image of political liberation nor even that they resist, but simply that they gain some understanding of their own involvement in the world, and in the making of their own future.
>
> (Grossberg, 1994, cited in Parham, 2002: 464)

The narrowing of critical distance between the student and the object of study challenges the old hierarchy of the student modestly looking over her tutor's shoulder at the great masters. One commentator has described 'an ethnographic turn to the lived world of their students' that recognises the sophistication and skills they bring into photography education (Dewdney, 2009: 109). New Photography Theory was closely aligned with a study of mass culture and from a student perspective it had a relevance to students who could see how the old divisions between theory and practice, art and industry, private and public, were played out. The more readable forms of semiology challenged these divisions from at least the 1950s onwards and, as an intellectual source, the ideas of the French writer Roland Barthes had a huge impact on the birth of an English brand of Cultural Studies in the 1970s. New Photography Theory was closely connected with these developments and the work of Burgin, Spence, Watney, Tagg and Sekula encouraged teachers and learners in the expanding field of photography education to think more deeply about their work.

245

PHOTOGRAPHY EDUCATION

CONCLUSION

In this chapter we have shown how the relatively unformulated practices of Basic Photography, in all its variety of forms, were re-shaped by New Photography Theory over a period from the 1970s to the present day. The English context has provided some of the key examples for this discussion. This does not restrict the debate to one social or national context since photography education has changed everywhere in this period. We have argued that photography theory played an important part in some of the key changes and especially in regard to teaching and learning of the discipline. The main change has been in the curriculum at university level.

One of the key changes has resulted from the proposals for levelling of the cultural field, which meant abandoning old divisions between high and low, and experimenting with hybrid forms of mass culture. As we have seen some hoped the arts would coalesce and a new politics of representation would rule. The field would create a new type of scholar-practitioner whose outlook would be ideologically correct, technically proficient and philosophically astute. It is debatable whether this has in any measure been achieved. The situation, nevertheless, is much changed in a way that Trachtenberg might approve.

We have argued that Victor Burgin and his allies played a key role in creating a wider and more expanded field in photography education. The struggle against entrenched anti-intellectualism might explain the confrontational style of the New Photography Theorists, especially in the early essays and related projects. It was, in fact, a rich period in cultural theory, tempered by feminist anger, class politics, and growing sensitivity to racial strife in the big cities. The leftist journal *New Times* announced, in the 1980s, an epochal change and the emergence of a combative form of cultural politics in education. It was a fertile period for the visual arts at a time when the level of debate across a range of institutions was at a new high. Burgin played an important part in these changes and the turn to photography theory spawned a wealth of new ideas for a wide range of new practices and growing literature in the field of study.

The key figures discussed in this chapter have presented important changes in the philosophy of photography in the world at large in the period from the 1980s to the present day. We have emphasized that ideas and politics have played an increasingly important role in questions about the functions of photography. We have stressed how the social and artistic functions of photography are seen as collusive in the formation of meaning. We have also seen how the old divide between documentary and art photography is no longer easily accepted. The art world has expanded and is no longer hostile to campaigning or propagandist work. Since her death Jo Spence has been made an art world figure and exerts influence on younger artists, photographers and teachers. The picture we have painted so far may not comprehensively represent all the changes and ideas that have emerged in this period. We have emphasized the school of Burgin and the influential turn to a 'politics of representation'. In the next chapter we address what some theorists, and some photographers, consider the limitations of this approach.

ISSUES AND DEBATES IN PHOTOGRAPHY EDUCATION I: NEW PHOTOGRAPHY THEORY

SUMMARY OF KEY POINTS

- Photography was lacking a 'collective intelligence' and a place within the critical traditions of the humanities. This view was noted by a new generation of critics and practitioners emerging in the 1970s.
- A new generation of critics saw established approaches to photography education as 'initiation into dominant beliefs and values' mixed with technical training. In other words photography education was uncritical and intellectually limiting.
- New Photography Theorists established a bridge between theory and practice, and established new methods of writing about photography that drew from contemporary cultural theory and identity politics.
- Photography aspires to and achieves wide recognition as an important subject across the field of education and forms important links with other subjects including journalism, advertising, fashion and art.
- Photographic practices are informed by and relate to key debates in humanities and social sciences.
- Phototherapy and other self-reflexive research methods offer new ways of making theory accessible and relevant to students.

REFERENCES

Bezencenet, Stevie and Corrigan, Philip (eds) (1986) *Photographic Practices: Towards a Different Image*, London: Comedia.

Burgin, Victor (1977) 'Looking at Photographs', in *Screen Education*, Autumn, 1977, No. 24, London: Society for Education in Film and Television. Reprinted in Burgin (1982), pp. 142–153.

——(1982) *Thinking Photography*, Houndsmill, Basingstoke and New York: Macmillan.

——(1993) 'Socialist Formalism', in Charles Harrison and Paul Wood (eds), *Art in Theory: 1900–1990*, Oxford, UK and Cambridge, MA: Blackwell, pp. 911–917.

——(1997)'Art, Common Sense and Photography' in Jessica Evans (ed.), *The Camerawork Essays*, London: Rivers Oram Press, pp. 74–85.

Campany, David (2007) *Art and Photography*, London and New York: Phaidon.

Dewdney, Andrew (2009) 'Editorial Statement: Special Issue on Photography Education', in *Photographies*, vol. 2, no. 2, September, pp. 103–115.

Evans, Jessica (1994) 'Victor Burgin's Polysemic Dreamcoat', in John Roberts, *Art has No History: The Making and Unmaking of Modern Art*, London and New York: Verso, pp. 200–229.

Green, David (1985) 'The Veins of Resemblance: Photography and Eugenics', in *The Oxford Art Journal*, vol. 7, no. 2, pp. 3–16.

Grossberg, Lawrence (1994) 'An Introduction to Bringin' It all Back Home – Pedagogy and Cultural Studies', in H.A. Giroux and P. McLaren (eds), 1994, *Between Borders*, London: Routledge, pp. 1–25.

PHOTOGRAPHY EDUCATION

Hall, Stuart (1997) *Representation: Cultural Representation and Signifying Practices*, London/ Thousand Oaks, CA/New Delhi: Sage.

Langford, Michael (1995) *Basic Photography*, Oxford: Focal Press.

Marien, Mary Warner (2002) *Photography: A Cultural History*, London: Laurence King.

——(2012) *100 Ideas That Changed Photography*, London: Laurence King.

Mercer, Kobena (1992) 'Critical Decade', Editorial in *Ten.8*, vol. 2, no. 3, Spring 1992, p. 7.

Newbury, Darren (2009) 'Image, Theory and Practice: Reflection on the Past, Present, and Future of Photography Education', in *Photographies*, vol. 2, no. 2, September, pp. 117–124.

Parham, John (2002) 'Teaching Pleasure: Experiments in Cultural Studies', in *International Journal of Cultural Studies*, London/Thousand Oaks, CA/New Delhi: Sage, pp. 461–478.

Roberts, John (1998) *The Art of Interruption: Realism, Photography and Everyday Life*, Manchester University Press.

Sekula, Allan (1989) 'The Body and the Archive', in Richard Bolton (ed.) *The Contest of Meaning: Critical Histories of Photography*, Cambridge, MA, and London: The MIT Press, pp. 343–388.

Spence, Jo (1991) 'Cultural Sniper', in *Ten.8*, vol. 2, no. 1, Spring, 1991, pp. 9–25.

——(1995) *Cultural Sniper: The Art of Transgression*, London and New York: Routledge.

——(2006) *Beyond the Perfect Image*, Barcelona: Museu d'Art Contemporani de Barcelona.

Tagg, John (1988) *The Burden of Representation: Essays on Photography Histories*, Houndsmills: Macmillan.

Trachtenberg, Alan (1980) *Classic Essays on Photography*, New Haven, CT: Leete's island Books.

Watney, Simon (1986) 'Photography-Education-Theory', in Stevie Bezencenet and Phillip Corrigan, (eds), pp. 53–59.

Wood, Paul (2002) *Conceptual Art*, London: Tate Publishing.

CHAPTER 8
ISSUES AND DEBATES IN PHOTOGRAPHY EDUCATION II: THE RETURN OF THE REAL

This photograph is part of a series called *Another Country*. The main focus in the image is on the Sunni and Shia Muslim communities in London. It represents a group of girls from the Shia mosque that stands in the background. Tabrizian says people look at this photograph and think it is a Middle Eastern setting (Sarah Phillips, 2012). The dress code of the girls may suggest this. The careful choreographing of the image creates a sense of hybrid social identity in a globalized context. It invites a narrative reading in a way that blurs boundaries between fact and fiction. The dilapidated building is reminiscent of the unloved architecture in Edward Hopper's realist paintings of American city life in the 1930s. Photography in this example is related to wider concerns beyond the image and forms a part of a wider investigation of cultural and political

8.1 Mitra Tabrizian with Andy Golding and Zadoc Nava, from the series *Another Country*, 2010. Courtesy of the artists.

PHOTOGRAPHY EDUCATION

dislocation. Undemonstrative body language contrasts with our expectation of children at play. Tabrizian notes her concern for a 'culture within' the minds of these girls. It is type of photography with strong social and aesthetic content. The image attempts to find something in the scene that suggests an imaginary world beyond it. In this chapter we discuss the term *realism*. Tabrizian's work is relevant to this discussion because it is investigatory and belongs to a wider field of social enquiry. Her work is included in this discussion because it represents a sharp contrast with the simulationist and constructed work of postmodern photographers discussed in previous chapters.

INTRODUCTION

This chapter provides a critical analysis of photographic projects including photo-essays from the 1930s and the more contemporary archival work that draws from earlier traditions. We underline attachments to social issues and engagement with photography as a social weapon. Photographers discussed include Walker Evans, Allan Sekula, Martha Rosler and Jeff Wall. In the previous section we have discussed the rise of the New Photography Theory and explained its radical approach to photography education. We have shown how the New Photography Theorists privileged the 'politics of representation' as a key principle in photography and all areas of communication and discourse. We now wish to question that approach and in doing so return to the notion of realism. We have focused on the changing curriculum in photography education and the return of the real as movement away from trends influenced by conceptual art and the feeling of theoretical overload experienced by students and teachers. We begin with a critical assessment of the school of Burgin.

DISCUSSION: WHAT IS REALISM?

John Berger answered this question in the following way:

Art cannot reproduce reality in its entirety. Instead it can do one of three things. It can accept our habits of looking (habits that have been largely formed by the art of the past and today by photography) and, building on these, it can remind us of what we have already seen, offering us at the most only new combinations. This is the way of Naturalism. Alternatively, it can build upon the belief that art is in some way superior to reality and so select, distort and simplify aspects of nature for the sole purpose of making a pleasing arrangement of form. This is the way of Formalism. Or lastly it can turn its limitations to advantage. It can select an aspect of reality and within its own artificial limits make a unity of that aspect, so that we are able to recognize its truth more clearly than we can in life itself and thereby extend and deepen our habits of looking. This is the way of Realism.

(John Berger, 1959, 'Problems of Socialist Art', in Lee Baxandall (ed.) 1972, *Radical Perspectives in the Arts*, Harmondsworth: Penguin, 216–217)

In this statement we have a guide to the language of art-photography criticism that still has currency. The argument in the chapter takes us back to the social argument for realism in the visual arts. Berger makes no special case for photography but we can adapt his commentary to recent trends in the use of the medium that 'select aspects of reality' and try to 'deepen our habits of looking'. Berger underlined the fact that all forms of representation rely on artifice and are therefore an act of reconstruction. A photograph is a still image and fails to duplicate movement and the sounds of everyday life. We enjoy this limitation and seek, perhaps, to make use of it. The photograph stops the world and invites a closer look. When we look thoughtfully at a photograph, or think about a photographic archive, we are, in effect, mapping this experience against our own worldview. The process might add to our knowledge of the situation or events to which it refers. This process might be edifying and even pleasurable. In this way our aesthetic appreciation will have evolved beyond 'pleasing arrangement of form' and mere description of things.

The New Photography Theorists collapsed realism into the more general notion of naturalistic representation. For theorists such as Tagg and Burgin, realism is always guilty of privileging the photographer or artist as an ideal observer, separate from or superior to what he or she observes. The critical opposition to realism denies the neutrality of the viewpoint (of the documentary photographer) since the image is always 'invested' with the subjective position or outlook of the observer. Berger also rejects naturalism as the pretence of neutrality when repeating a stereotyped view of things. Realism, however, avoids the stereotype and involves the spectator in a dialogue that challenges the familiar. This may be done with serious intention or humorously as in the work of a satirist.

The School of Burgin and its Critics

The school of Burgin is connected with the language-image hybrid and the mixed media format. There is in the various practices associated with Burgin and the New Photography Theorists a taste for montage, mixed media and a studied avoidance of the wordless photograph that we have called a 'picture window'. As noted in the last chapter theorists such Burgin distrusted documentary photography because it seemed to claim legitimacy on the basis of its visual evidence whilst ignoring contextual determinations of language. For Burgin and early Barthes language is the most systematic form of representation. Words for example stand for things or ideas in the world. Their function is to *relay* meanings. Some theorists claim all signs have a similar function and this includes photographs. Burgin, for example, is reluctant to allow the photographic image any degree of autonomy or any degree of difference when compared with language. And yet photographs, arguably, are different, and are not like words or sentences, since they are in some ways exactly like the things they represent and, therefore, strictly speaking are not *re-presentations* at all.

It is admittedly difficult *not* to think of a photograph as a *representation*, since we read it as a picture of things in the world. We may (unconsciously) adopt a way of seeing that derives from paintings and

PHOTOGRAPHY EDUCATION

illustrations when looking at a photograph. The tendency is to see it as a kind of *relay* when it operates like painting. Some kinds of manipulated and staged photographs exploit this way of seeing and seem to invite an aesthetic reading. These examples of mediation and construction are not uncommon and we normally see them for what they are. They are, we may argue, special cases that may weaken the denotative power of the photograph without necessarily denying its effect. There is something in the photograph about which we might say: no *relay* has taken place. It seems to resist mediation.

Photography is a different thing when compared with language since in the photograph there is a causal relation between the signifier and the signified. In comparison with language the photograph's 'message' seems transparent and natural. In Barthes' famous phrase, it is 'a message without a code'. Burgin, Watney and Tagg have always sought to play down this aspect of the photograph. Burgin thus argues: 'The naturalness of the world ostensibly open before the camera is a deceit. Objects present to the camera are already in use in the production of meanings' (1982: 47).

The idea of a pre-photographic object as something 'already in use' presents a pessimistic idea of a world in thrall to the image. The literal meaning of a photograph (say, a young woman smiling), and its ideological content (housework is fun because she cleverly bought the right product) are two things in a state of tension. For Burgin they are one thing only: the image is coded and so obviously 'in use'; the referent is also 'objects in use'. The anti-consumerist critic will unpack the deception (in the ad) whilst the unwary housewife might think it to be true. The advertisement (as Burgin notes) is openly fake and yet it invites a willing suspension of disbelief. But is the photograph in an advertisement entirely in league with the linguistic message? Are all images false and corrupting? Is its coding absolute? Can the photograph have any degree of autonomy? Is it in some way real? Is there life beyond the text?

Burgin struggled with the thought that the photograph is 'produced' by the referent. The photograph (he says) abstracts from and mediates the actual. His claim is that if the referent were a realistic dummy, not the 'actual' (a real person), we might be deceived. This is true but its use as an argument (against the real) is evasive since we do see *something* material that *was* there: a dummy, not an apparition. Photographs *can* deceive but this is not their defining character. Burgin's dogmatic anti-realism leads him to conclude that Barthes is wrong in saying the photographic message is un-coded or that photographs are different in important ways when compared with other kinds of visual images in the world (Burgin, 1982: 61–62).

The Realist's claim for the special nature of the photograph does not deny that photographs are devoid of coded meanings or that 'transparency' is their only salient quality. The photographer may, for example, exercise judgement in selecting the type of camera and its setting, and make important choices in selecting control of depth of field, focusing and so forth. The subject might be chosen in advance and the 'shoot' carefully designed and systematically directed. It will inescapably carry meanings that are determined by these factors. In saying this we are taking guard against the naive realist idea of gaining unmediated access to the thing we can see in the image. Indeed with Burgin's assurance we are rightly on guard against 'the pitfalls of an un-reflectingly naturalist attitude to photographs' (Burgin, 1982: 66). And yet despite the inevitable coding that enters into the project of making a photograph, arguably, something remains beyond the poetics of the medium, something *in itself* that defines it. Barthes famously returned to this question of what photography was 'in itself', and 'by what essential features it was to be distinguished from the community of images' (Barthes, 1981: 3).

Two Ways of Seeing the Real

For our purposes there are two ways of unpacking New Photography Theory. The first derives from Roland Barthes' subjective reading of the photograph in his book *Camera Lucida* (1981). In this book Barthes claims there is a way of seeing through the photographic image to the object and notices the way the object strikes him, not as a constituted site or a structured meaning, but as trace of an existential *something* that impressed itself into the mechanism that now retains it:

> Photography's Referent is not the same as the referent of other systems of representation. I shall call 'photographic referent' not the *optionally* real thing to which an image or a sign refers but the *necessarily* real thing which has been placed before the lens, without which there would be no photograph.
>
> (Barthes, 1981: 76)

And again:

> In photography I can never deny *that the thing has been there*. There is a superimposition here: of reality and of the past. And since this constraint exists only for Photography, we must consider it, by reduction, as the very essence, the *noeme* of Photography. What I intentionalize in a photograph (we are not speaking of film) is neither Art nor Communication, it is a Reference, which is the founding order of Photography.
>
> (Ibid.: 76–77)

The contest between late Barthes and Burgin presents two competing paradigms (Welch and Long, 2009: 12). Writing in the 1980s Burgin emphasized the explanatory value of analysis as a means to a political end. His ideas were informed by the early 'scientific' writing of Barthes. The later writing of Barthes centred on what has been described as a more personalized and subjective study of the photograph. In *Camera Lucida* he distinguishes between the two elements in the photograph. The *studium* defines its 'average effects' that might be studied by the semiologist. It is the field of 'unconcerned desire' deriving from 'ethical and political culture' (Barthes, 1981: 26). Barthes' second element, the so-called *punctum*, is the subjective thing that disturbs what the photograph might otherwise seem to be about. The *punctum* is 'that accident that pricks me (but also bruises me, is poignant to me)' (1981: 27). Consider for example a detail such as the period style of the lawnmower in *General Wavell Watches His Gardener at Work*, by the photographer James Jarché (fig. 7.1), as an interpretation that eludes the overt social dimensions of the image. *Camera Lucida* legitimized what appears to be an individualistic factor that influences what we might see in photographs.

Much has been made for and against the romantic inclination in *Camera Lucida*. It was a turning point for those who doubted semiotics as the final arbiter on photographic meaning. Barthes' earlier political reading of the photograph and his later emotion-laden reading of photographs (he speaks of his mother) is striking. It was not, however, a clean break since the two elements he famously describes (the objective/subjective division) are not mutually exclusive.

The so-called *studium* is not displaced by the *punctum* in *Camera Lucida*. Barthes reminds his reader the photograph must be 'reconciled with society' precisely because its functions are 'to inform, to represent, to surprise, to cause to signify, to provoke desire'. Like all forms of expression the photograph produces feeling and ideas that relate to our ways of seeing the world. The emotive and the informative are not separated spheres of meaning.

PHOTOGRAPHY EDUCATION

A recent commentator on *Camera Lucida* has noted the 'non-conventionalised relation a photograph might have with its referent' (Paul, 2010: 120). Paul argues that the non-conventional element in a photograph, if there is such a thing, establishes a personal attachment to 'what the photograph is *of*'. It provides a shock of proximity with something in the photograph. When it occurs in viewing old photographs, for example, an emotive reading is not at odds with its social or 'general' meaning. Some contemporary critics have seen Barthes as a realist seeking to find a place for memory, personal identity, ethical perspectives that counteract the instrumental and repressive uses of photography.

The second way of addressing the backlash against the more dogmatic forms of New Photography Theory emerged in the 1980s when theorists in film studies began to see the limitations in the monolithic view of audiences as passive consumers of dominant culture. Jessica Evans notes:

> It has been argued recently that the denigration of the classic form of illusionism and psycho-logical identification with characters has the effect of writing off mainstream cinema and popular 'realist' culture as retrograde – primarily because of its form.

> (Evans, 1994: 205)

The blanket dismissal of popular culture seemed to confirm the increasing separation from the communities that Spence had struggled to establish. The view that audiences are duped by popular cinema rather than engaging with it in a constructive way is not only elitist but overrates the propaganda effect of the image. A contrasting view showed that audiences know the difference between film form and the world to which it relates. More positively film and photography open up a vision of the world that reveals connections between the image and it referent. Film noir, a movement that originates in the 1940s, for example, remained popular for decades with urban audiences throughout the world who related to its gritty subject matter. The formal character of the realist text with its emphasis on narrative meaning, storytelling and character development has a wide appeal that extends beyond its capacity to entertain. The photographer Jeff Wall acknowledges the influence of popular cinema and the return of the pictorial and realist qualities in his own work:

> In my opinion the triumph of the avant-garde is so complete that it has liberated what had previ-ously to be seen as the anti-liberating element in art … There are transgressions against the institutions of transgression. I think the pictorial has come to occupy this position…

> (Wall, 1996: 17)

Wall turned to the conventions of transparency and illusion (the defining material properties of the photograph) as if the avant-garde opposition to it had completed its revolutionary cycle. What he claims is that montage and other modernist techniques of anti-realist transgression had become mainstream by (say) the 1970s if not before. His strategy, as we will see, was to transgress the transgression, and find ways of relating his own photographic work to the narrative forms of cinema and literary fiction. The democratic aim to reach a wide public through deconstruction of the ideological effects of photograph, in Wall's view, is a failure.

The conceptualist plan to make audiences think more deeply about the institutional uses of art (Sherrie Levine) or the attack on aesthetic contemplation as a mode of interpretation (Burgin) had not influenced its target audience: the working class. Roberts also notes a 'deep historical connection between repre-sentation and the possibility of a public' that was lost in the post-conceptual art milieu in which New Photography Theory developed. In returning to an earlier modernist tradition rooted in the everyday Wall

ISSUES AND DEBATES IN PHOTOGRAPHY EDUCATION II: THE RETURN OF THE REAL

adapted the naturalistic look of the world into 'the theatrical space of the staged photograph' (Roberts, 1998: 187). His creation of psychological tension and nostalgic subject matter in large-scale photographic works such as *A Ventriloquist at a Birthday Party in 1947* (fig. 8.6), a transparency in a light box, made by Wall in 1990, invites a narrative reading. This image is staged and highly constructed but makes no effort to admit this or reveal itself as a construction. The audience is expected to look through it and experience its troubling reference to things we know or imagine we know.

It is an approach that celebrates the audience's pleasure in seeing large-scale pictures of modern life. Roberts notes how the social power model, embraced by Tagg, underlines the negative and repressive effects of photography. It is a model that inserts the photograph in an 'inflexible regime of power and weakens the causal connection between the photograph and what it is *of*' (Roberts, 1998: 4). Wall, in contrast, strives to make the viewer interested in 'what the photograph is *of*'. He adopts the subjects of photojournalism (domestic or street life for example) and through the use of actors produces a staged, but highly naturalistic, back-lit photograph. The manipulation of the image combines with illusionistic aspirations of realism in a way that suggests knowledge of a painting. Many great works of art with enduring claims to realism have sought ways to address the look of things and proceed to engage a wider public. Engagement with the everyday and a commitment to report on the nature of things must also negotiate determining power relations. The picture does not speak truth without sensitive contextualization and many photographers, past and present, have found ways of connecting audiences with images that relate to their own lives or the lives of others.

The Return of the Real

The school of Burgin is representative of the mainstream political culture in photography education. Having said this we should observe that realism (in its different forms, and there are many) never went away. We are not referring to unreconstructed belief in the photographic truth. That had always been a legitimate target. What we are referring to is the idea that photographs are a way of comprehending the world. The French theorist Jacques Aumont says graphic images perform three functions: the aesthetic, the epistemic and the symbolic. The aesthetic is the sensual and pleasing effect; the symbolic represents an idea such as liberty or peace (or something to be feared); and the epistemic is about knowledge or information. All images might have a greater or lesser part of each of these functions (Aumont, 1997: 54–55).

> **KEY TERMS:**
> **Jacques Aumont's Three Categories of the Image:** Aumont argues that an image has three functions that define its relationship with the world. They are:
>
> **Aesthetic**
> Aesthetic ideas or objects create sensual and pleasing effects. The term sometimes refers to the appreciation or love of beautiful things. It is also used to define an artistic position or idea.

> ### Symbolic
> Symbolic refers to a type of communication in which one thing stands for another. In the case of the symbolic the meaning is socially recognized and agreed. For example rude gestures vary from one culture to another but some symbols are universal such as the dove of peace. A photograph of a man holding a white flag might be used to indicate surrender in a news bulletin.
>
> ### Epistemic
> Epistemic derives from the philosophical term epistemology which means 'theory of knowledge'. According to one school of thought the question of how we know the world is based on seeing or sensing the world. Other thinkers disagree and they consider thought to be prior to sensation. For the realist the empirical, or 'sensing' approach, is favoured and the existence of a concrete 'reality' is prioritized. In the case of a photograph visual information forms the basis of knowledge and, for the realist, understanding derives from this.

The English academic Malcolm Barnard claims that images provide a mix of these three functions, so that they may be decorative, persuasive or informative. An advertisement may achieve all three effects at the same time. Barnard also says that some images are sacred and have magical charm which may entrance the spectator (see discussion about photographs and religious icons in Chapter 3). This aspect of the image – especially the photographic image – may be a lure or trap. A photo-ad can magically transform a humble product into a lifestyle choice. The suspicion is that something is made to look real when it might not be so. Barnard notes:

> When Aumont says that symbolic images give access to the realm of the divine, he is describing the process by which the gods are made present, or appear to humans, but there is a secular version of the function. If this were not true, then we would not keep pictures or photographs of our loved ones in our wallets, on our desks and walls. Nor would we feel distinctly uncomfortable at the prospect of sticking a needle in the photograph of our mother, right in the eye.
>
> (Barnard, 2005: 16)

It is significant that Barnard's example is a photograph. Its physical connection with its referent intensifies its effect. In a photograph the symbolic is inextricably bound up with the epistemic since the 'information' it supplies is a trace or residue of something that was there. It has a poignancy that is similar to a recorded voice message. The link between the symbolic and the epistemic is, arguably, undervalued or ignored in some forms of semiotic analysis. The tendency to see all messages as part of a 'regime of power' reduces their causal connection with the world and their specific value for audiences for whom they may have positive value. The danger in this assessment is that it omits the epistemic power of the photograph and downgrades the dialogic and communicative part of the photographic message. One of the fascinations of realism, in a variety of media, but especially in film and photography, is the merging of knowledge about the world (the epistemic) with symbolic values and ideas. The return to realism and documentary in contemporary cinema and photography might be explained by its potential for harnessing symbolic as well as descriptive levels of meaning. Laura Marcus writes:

ISSUES AND DEBATES IN PHOTOGRAPHY EDUCATION II: THE RETURN OF THE REAL

> There has been a return to, or reinvention of, documentary cinema in North America and elsewhere, while 'reality TV' simulates 'real life' and the performance of reality in ways that raise new questions about spectatorship, voyeurism and participation, and truth and reality effects.
>
> (Marcus, 2010: 208)

We have argued that naturalistic properties of photographs have been adapted to social, commercial, artistic and political projects that are loosely connected with the label realism. The practices to which the label relates have connections with ordinary things: the street, the factory, the places of recreation and pleasure. The identification with recognizable places and the message they signal is vivid in the photograph. To say that it is coded and constructed misses the point in the case of a photograph. This kind of theory misses what is special in the photograph that invests it with a feeling reaching back towards something. The 'something that never really goes away' suggests a way of enabling audiences to exercise historical imagination in the productive use of photographs.

Just as the photograph album can have a comforting effect on its users, the photographic archive and the campaigning document have effects across a range of applications and social, scientific and artistic sites. This kind of positive interpretation of the photograph presents a challenge to the monolithic pessimism of the New Photography Theory. It is a counter-argument to the obvious claim that a photograph can lie. Manipulated images are an issue but they belong in a different discussion (see Chapter 4). Because something can be faked does not guarantee that it *is* faked. Photography had its enemies in the nineteenth century but, for many, it supported new systems of knowledge acquisition and was seen as a useful tool in the collection of accurate topographical and anthropological data. Ideological and political uses of the medium have been rightly condemned, but anti-realist theory has weakened the empirical and investigatory functions of photography and the critical use of the photographic archive. Recent scholarship on social media is far less judgemental and contrasts with the unsympathetic reading of family albums in the 1980s (Larsen and Sadbye, 2014).

The argument for a critical use of the photographic archive (or counter-archive in the subversive work of Spence) is determined by the idea of amassing documents for constructive social use. It might take the form of an art-book or a scholarly discourse. Writer-photographer collaborations include John Berger's work with the photographer Jean Mohr, *A Fortunate Man* (1967), John Heartfield with Kurt Tucholsky in the 1930s, and the work of Richard Wright and Edwin Rosskam, *12 Million Black Voices* in the 1940s, amongst many others. These word-image texts, in their different ways, are campaigning projects often linked with progressive political and artistic movements.

The common element in archival approaches is to treat the photograph in a positive way. Instead of seeing it as a distorting mirror or as a symbol of alienation, it becomes a useful tool in linking the past with a current climate of productive thinking. In these examples of the archive the desire is to make the photograph participate in a contemporary narrative so that it activates memory in ways that have a motivating effect on photographic spectatorship.

The special nature of the photograph as a trace or index of previous moments in time gives it a powerful role in environmental and architectural survival movements in the past. Such examples are forerunners to the examples given above. Elizabeth Edwards has emphasized how preservationist projects contributed to the salvaging of the past. She underlines the importance of photography as a dimension of the newly established surveys and archival projects launched in the Victorian period. This

257

was a period of rapid environmental change and the desire to record things before imminent destruction is noted. There is for example a socio-political ingredient when documentation is used in campaigns to preserve distinctive buildings, monuments and other artefacts. Edwards notes the work of organizations such the Society for the Protection of Ancient Buildings, founded in 1878, and the National Trust in 1895 which typified the campaigning attitude. The kind of photographic mapping associated with this trend constituted the beginning of major archival and survey work. Edwards echoes the enthusiasm of the Victorian archivists:

> The photographic surveys were based on the assumption that photography could, if properly regulated, deliver pure 'fact' without and beyond stylistic convention … it is impossible for the best written description to convey to the imagination so accurate an impression of a scene or an object that is given by a photograph.
>
> (Edwards, 2009: 69)

Edwards adds to this: 'The practice of photography at this period was saturated with anxieties of cultural disappearance' (ibid.: 70), and in support of photographic survey work she notes that 'Photography provided not only the evidential certainty of 'having-been-there' [Barthes's famous phrase], but a way in which the consciousness of an historical and cultural past could be revealed, reified, consolidated and projected into the future' (ibid.: 70). The question of 'cultural disappearance' and its anxieties have remained. It figures in the work of contemporary and recently past photographers such as Bernd and Hilla Becher's photo-documents of endangered winding towers, gas tanks and other types of industrial vernacular (fig. 8.2).

8.2 Bernd and Hilla Becher, *Winding Towers*, Belgium and Germany, 1983. 12 black and white photographs, 20 X 16 in. (51 X 41 cm).Courtesy of Sonnabend Gallery, New York.

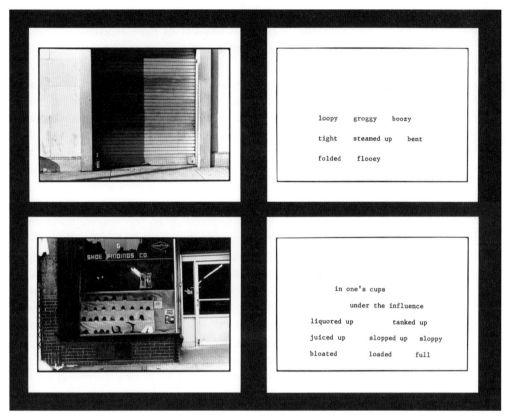

8.3 Martha Rosler, *The Bowery in Two Inadequate Descriptive Systems*, 1974–5. Forty-five gelatin silver prints of text and image mounted on twenty-four backing boards, each: 11 13/16 X 23 5/8 in. (30 X 60 cm). Whitney Museum of American Art, New York; purchase, with funds from John L. Steffens 93.4a-x. Photography by Geoffrey Clements.

Elizabeth Edwards notes that nineteenth-century archival work was thought to be 'useful and unselfish'. The American critic Hal Foster notes a growing interest in social documentation, sociological mapping, and geopolitical work that combines photographic fieldwork with written documentation and commentary. He calls it an 'ethnographic turn' and a departure from the inward-looking art simulations of contemporary photographic artists such as Cindy Sherman, Richard Prince and Sherrie Levine (Foster, 1996: 184). The work of Bernd and Hilla Becher is an example of an outward-looking survey of the changing nature of the industrial landscape that echoes the fieldwork of earlier ethnographic photographers. Foster also includes Allan Sekula and Martha Rosler as examples of contemporary artists who employ empirical research methods in the investigation of social issues. Martha Rosler's *The Bowery* (fig. 8.3) is a hybrid form of political documentary in a photo-text display directed towards social issues in a rough part of New York in the mid 1970s.

The ethnographical work of these artist-photographers has roots in photo-essays of the Americans Walker Evans and James Agee working at a time of economic recession in the 1930s. Rosler and Sekula returned to documentary in the late twentieth century, at a time when it was out of favour

PHOTOGRAPHY EDUCATION

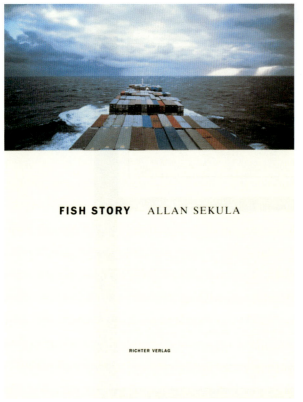

8.4 Allan Sekula, cover for the book *Fish Story*, Dusseldorf, Richter Verlag, 1995. Courtesy of Richter Verlag.

with other artist-photographers. Both had fiercely criticized the genre in its most exploitative modes and struggled to find ways of making it productive and relevant. Steve Edwards notes: 'Rosler's reaction to what she called documentary 'pornography' [the wilful photographic exploitation of the downtrodden] was to retain the vernacular forms of the documentary mode, but refuse its usual topics and points of view' (Steve Edwards, 2012: 11). She worked out possibilities for the reinvention of the genre and conspicuously left out the denizens of skid row, the wanton victims, whose 'juiced up' condition accompanies the photographic panels as a poetic reference rather than judgemental or moralistic sentiment. The complex interaction of words and imagery avoids the conventions of empirical description associated with ethnographic fieldwork. Sekula's *Fish Story* (Sekula, 1995) is descriptive and highly researched but it crosses boundaries between exposition and theory and has the character of a project that challenges easy classification (fig. 8.4). The work is scholarly and presented as a book and an exhibition dealing with maritime labour and the material forces that influence the lives of working people on the high seas.

Both Sekula and Rosler continue a tradition of engagement with contemporary events that have a strong political resonance. In the case of Sekula the historical link between the photo-essay books of the 1930 and 1940s and documentary text such as his *Fish Story* is noteworthy. In the American context this belongs to a tradition of photographing urban and regional subject matter, including abrasive subjects, presented in ways that experiment with the image-text relationship. One of the best examples, discussed briefly in Chapter 6, is James Agee and Walker Evans' photo-essay entitled *Let Us Now Praise Famous Men*, published in 1941 (fig. 8.5). The book is a powerful document portraying the hardships of rural workers and family members in the Great Depression. The text is an expressive component in its own right and not merely explanation or support for the images. The book consists of two distinct narratives, the visual and the verbal, that interweave with each other. The effect is to draw attention to the materiality and form of the text itself (pictures and words) whilst revealing a view of America that city-bound, Eastern audiences had not seen at this time.

The way the book is shaped and the interrelationship between text and photography is just as important as what it defines. *Let Us Now Praise Famous Men* is not transparently 'about' its theme since it has an aesthetic identity in its own right. The style of its presentation and the image-text connections do not form a traditional narrative structure. The photographs are commanding and direct. The American theorist W.J.T. Mitchell underlines the importance of photography in this kind of ethnographical work:

8.5 Walker Evans, *Sharecropper Bud Fields and His Family at Home, Hale County, Alabama*, 1935. Courtesy of Private Collection/Universal History Archive/UIG/The Farm Security Administration/Bridgeman Images.

> Pure denotation reaches all the way up to the most readable features of the photograph: the photograph is read as if it were the trace of an event, 'relic' of an occasion laden with aura and mystery…
>
> (Mitchell, 1994: 284–285)

The denotative, the descriptive, creates a powerful connection with rural families and their poverty. Roberts claims, optimistically, the special nature of photography as dialogism, as a two-way exchange of views and ideas, of the kind generally outlawed in repressive societies. The dialogic function of the medium is not crudely opposed to aesthetic reading. It does, however, place an emphasis on the evidential force of photography. This might take the form of giving presence to social protest movements, positive images of workers, women as forceful and dynamic organizers, the presence of activists at specific sites, and the use of photography in social network activism, confirming the conviction and the spirit of groups marginalized or ignored by the mainstream media. The recording of everyday life in the workplace and domestic environment is a commonplace of documentary photography but fails to cover the range and complexity of projects the term suggests. The archival work of Spence also, very knowingly, crossed the boundary from high theory into the gritty business of illness, surgery, and commitment to what remains untold or ignored in private and public life.

PHOTOGRAPHY EDUCATION

The turn to everyday life and reportage converged with the most combative and energetic artistic movements in the nineteenth century. The invention of photography underlined the potential for accurate transcription of the appearance of things. In a range of visual and non-visual media the development of new publishing houses, increased literacy, public exhibitions, new printing processes, and the growth of the public sphere added to the dynamic spread of new ideas. One of the most potent ideas was 'modern life' as the site of social change. Realism, one of the key style labels of the mid-nineteenth century, was linked with this progressive outlook. Some recent theorists have shown how the militant spirit of this movement has survived the twentieth century as a sub-current within some of the most progressive movements. We have used the photographic work of Spence and Wall to illustrate this point.

The audiences that turned to realism in the movies also have a taste for the 'show and tell' aspects of the photograph and the success of Jeff Wall is clearly a sign of this turnabout. Wall may not be the answer to the problems of photography education – what to teach and how to do it? The example, however, is instructive. His 'realism' offers alternative ways of thinking about photography as a narrative form with popular appeal and prospects for building a wider audience for the medium. *A Ventriloquist at a Birthday Party* (fig.8. 6) is a mixture of literary influence (Franz Kafka's short story 'The Cares of a Family Man'), film noir and a nostalgic image of the everyday. It has an affinity with the family album and unsettling childhood memories.

Rejecting the intellectual distancing of abstraction and high theory, Jeff Wall's work is entertaining and accessible. He is conscious of a need for dialogic address but mindful also that some distance, some remnant of the alienation effect, is a characteristic of all progressive art. In this sense his work is impressively reflexive in its references to art and cinema history. And yet despite these qualities his

8.6 Jeff Wall, *A Ventriloquist at a Birthday Party in October 1947*, 1990, transparency in light-box, 229 X 352 cm. Courtesy of the artist.

work offers light relief to the art school and the university photography department buckling under the oppressive weight of ideology critique and the tyranny of the photographic image.

CONCLUSION

The return of the real is epitomized in the few photographer-artists discussed in this chapter. We have shown it to be a revival of approaches to photography against the grain of sceptical theory. That is to say realism, as a concept, was judged to be the poor man of cultural history, left behind by abstract art, surrealist fantasy, the discrediting of documentary in photography, and the postmodernist idea of 'truth' as a relative term articulated by the discursive formations that use it. In the latter we note the turn to 'photography about photography', including for example the re-photographed photographs of Sherrie Levine (fig. 5.4), the widespread use of quotation in contemporary art, and a deepening of scepticism about the world beyond the supreme filter of all experience: representation. Anti-realist scepticism was extreme in the 1980s and for a while all forms of life were an illusion: 'No reality is known to us *outside* representations' (Burgin, 1986: 105).

In this chapter we have underlined the renewed importance of the term *realism* because it suggests ideas and methods beyond New Photography Theory. It is a word that has historical recall and deliberate attachment to past movements and ideas. It also suggests photography as part of a wider project that confronts social issues when it is put to work. This is why, as an aesthetic position, realism (in its concrete manifestations) is often part of work in serial formation as an archive or on-going projects. The 'return of the real' (Hal Foster's term) is a useful slogan and we have used it to profile ways of thinking about photography against the grain of postmodernism. It does not, however, represent a movement or even a cast iron defence of 'realism' which, after all, is only a label. What we have defended is a case for narrative forms of expression and documentation that can always be put to good use.

In the next two next chapters we look more closely at the teaching and learning environment for photography and consider, amongst other things, how far technical innovation is influencing image capture and dissemination. Digital manipulation of the photograph is traditionally presented as a threat to the realist aesthetic. The argument is that the predisposition to manipulate the photograph weakens its authority and accelerates the decline of its documentary effect. The prophets of 'post-photography' may have overstated this argument. Photography education has many issues to confront including issues around 'truth' and meaning that have followed in the wake of digital technology. It is, nevertheless, a buoyant area in the arts and humanities and respected in the wider field of visual communication.

SUMMARY OF KEY POINTS

- Anti-realist theory underrates the power of the photographic image and makes it a victim of structured meanings and regimes of power.
- The agency of photographers and audiences is often ignored in the anti-realist social power model. Photographers find ways of contesting mainstream media.
- The special nature of the photograph and its essential contact with the world is lost in the theoretical fog of New Photography Theory. The 'show and tell' aspects of the photograph can be used to entertain or enable audiences to negotiate their place in the world.

- The photograph is a link between psychic and material reality and exploits this to popular effect.
- Realism as an aesthetic has a tradition of directing the audience's gaze towards something obscured, marginalized or seldom seen. The task of unveiling and making things clear may be a way of expressing commitment to a pleasure denied or to the promulgation of a social ideal.
- Photographs are constructions but have other qualities. In being produced by the radiated light of objects in the world they have a degree of resistance to the textual functions that await them.
- The revival of realist modes of photographic practice in key examples of contemporary art and the supporting discourse in aesthetic theory may offer some relief to university and college photography departments. The monolithic pessimism of postmodernism and post-photography-ism may have passed.

REFERENCES

Agee, James and Evans, Walker (1941) *Let Us Now Praise Famous Men*, London: Pan Books.

Aumont, Jacques (1997) *The Image*, London: British Film Institute.

Barnard, Malcolm (2005) *Graphic Design as Communication*, London and New York: Routledge.

Barthes, Roland (1981) *Camera Lucida: Reflections on Photography*, New York: Hill & Wang.

Berger, John (1972) 'Problems of Socialist Art', in Lee Baxandall (ed.), *Radical Perspectives in the Arts*, Harmondsworth: Penguin, pp. 209–224.

Burgin, Victor (ed.) (1982) *Thinking Photography*, Houndsmills and London: Macmillan.

——(1986) 'Diderot, Barthes, *Vertigo*', in Victor Burgin, James Donald and Cora Kaplan (eds), *Formations of Fantasy*, London and New York: Methuen, 85–108.

Edwards, Elizabeth (2009) 'Salvaging Our Past: Photography and Survival', in Christopher Morton and Elizabeth Edwards (eds), *Photography, Anthropology and History: Expanding the Frame*, Farnham, UK and Burlington, VT: Ashgate, pp. 67–87.

Edwards, Steve (2012) *Martha Rosler: The Bowery in Two Inadequate Descriptive Systems*, London: Afterall Books.

Evans, Jessica (1994) 'Victor Burgin's Polysemic Dreamcoat', in John Roberts (ed.), *Art has No History: The Making and Unmaking of Modern Art*, London and New York: Verso, pp. 200–229.

Foster, Hal (1996) *The Return of the Real*, Cambridge, MA and London: The MIT Press.

Larsen, Jonas and Sandbye, Mette (eds) (2014) *Digital Snaps: The New Face of Photography*, London and New York: I.B. Tauris.

Mitchell, W.J.T. (1994) *Picture Theory*, Chicago: Chicago University Press.

Marcus, Laura (2010) 'Cinematic Realism: "A Recreation of the World in its Own Image"' in Matthew Beaumont (ed.), *A Companion to Realism*, Oxford: Wiley Blackwell, pp. 195–210.

Paul, Richard (2010) 'Re rereading *Camera Lucida*', a review of Geoffrey Batchen (ed.) (2009) *Photography Degree Zero: Reflecting on Barthes's Camera Lucida*, Cambridge, MA: The MIT Press, in *Philosophy of Photography*, vol. 1, no. 1, pp. 119–121.

Phillips, Sarah (2012) Interview with Mitra Trabizian, *Guardian*, G2, 18 October.

Roberts, John (1998) *The Art of Interruption: Realism, Photography and the Everyday*, Manchester University Press.

Sekula, Allan (1995) *Fish Story*, Dusseldorf: Richter Verlag.

Tagg, John (1988) *The Burden of Representation: On Photographies and Histories*, Houndsmills, Basingstoke and London: Macmillan.

Wall, Jeff (1996) in Thierry de Duve, Arielle Pelenc, Boris Groys (eds) *Jeff Wall*, London: Phaidon.

Welch, Edward and Long, J.J. (2009) 'Introduction: A Small History of Photography Studies', in J.J. Long, Andrea Noble and Edward Welch (eds) *Photography: Theoretical Snapshots*, London and New York: Routledge, pp. 1–15.

CHAPTER 9
TEACHING AND LEARNING PHOTOGRAPHY
With Andrew Golding

This photograph may seem to represent the traditional divide between an academic leader and a receptive student body. Such a literal reading of the image misleads since photography teaching and learning at college and university level is commonly interactive and socially informal. Courses at many institutions are often intellectually ambitious and yet the traditional boundary between theory and practice is challenged by courses, such as this one, which combine technical workshop teaching with contextual studies. The scholarly ambiance captured in this image is in keeping with key aspects of progressive photography education. On the other hand as a single image without further contextualization it fails to denote the wider aims of courses that allow for artistic invention and the acquisition of photographic skills. The woman facing the student group is a sign language interpreter translating for a deaf student.

9.1 Photography lecturer Nick Galvin teaching a BA Photography class at the University of Hertfordshire. The photograph is by Rebecca Thomas, 2013.

INTRODUCTION

This chapter focuses on contemporary issues photography education. The main focus is teaching and learning in universities with views and observations influenced by the authors' experience of educational provision in Britain. In Chapters 7 and 8 we analysed the rise of what we have called New Photography Theory in pioneering institutions such as the Polytechnic of Central London in the 1970s and the influence of The Photography Workshop and the publication of radical photographic journals including *Camerawork* and *Ten.8* in the same decade. In the present context the key issues and debates in curriculum development at institutions offering photography courses include the impact of digital technologies, specialization and training in occupational categories (advertising photography, photo-journalism, fashion etc.), the proportional mixing of theory and practice, and the more abstract issues that impact on questions of authorship and originality. The latter has important implications for the assessment of student achievement when some institutions value what they consider to be 'originality' and innovation whilst others are looking for intellectual sophistication and/or technical competence. Much of what had been said in the late twentieth century about the structural divide between industry and art is continued in current debates.

The institutional separation of art and industry is rooted in old divisions between the mythical figure of the creative artist (photographer) and the 'vocational' type geared up for 'applied' practice in the commercial markets of photographic work. The kind of contextual studies attached to photography education in the past were often technical and broadly mapped on to the achievements of named figures in 'canonic' histories of the medium. The New Photography Theory, emerging in the 1970s, displaced these conventions and is noteworthy in three ways. First, it challenged the autonomy of photography as an independent mode of self-expression. This was highly controversial since many courses encouraged students to 'cultivate their own visual style' whilst following the modern 'masters' of the medium. Second, photography education was extended into a wider field of social and cultural theory. Third, photography theory, despite its radical outlook, became a useful addition to university courses seeking academic legitimacy. In connection with this last point it is worth noting how far 'theory' contributed to the growth of photography provision in higher education. The accommodation of theory in photography education at university level has successfully achieved a balance between skills acquisition and critical reflection. There are drawbacks and inconsistencies in contemporary provision for photography in the universities and yet courses have multiplied. The prospects of employment might be an issue (see Chapter 12) and yet the wide range of intellectual, artistic and technical skills obtainable on progressive courses arguably gives photography an advantage over other areas of the arts and humanities curriculum.

ISSUES AND DEBATES IN PHOTOGRAPHY EDUCATION

Higher Education in the United Kingdom

Digital cameras focus and expose without user intervention and give instant feedback. They produce publishable images that can be immediately distributed across the globe. Such cameras require no handbook or skill to operate. As a consequence in some fields of photographic production citizen photographers using cheap, highly specified cameras are displacing trained photographers. At the same

PHOTOGRAPHY EDUCATION

time commentators note the over-provision of graduates chasing traditional occupations in photography and related fields of industry. Terence Wright notes:

> I think there is a danger that the photography boom could deflate. The UK seems to be producing far more students than a dwindling commercial photographic market can employ. This stresses the need to use the photographic medium as a vehicle for a broad-based education that can cope with the cultural and technological changes of the future.
>
> (Wright cited in Allbeson, 2012: 29)

Photography education is, nevertheless, an expanding field with over one hundred courses in the UK and growing numbers of short commercial courses. The range is from high-end courses with impressive resources and ambitious artistic and intellectual aims to 'hands on' training programmes. Higher education serves an enormous industry with over 50,000 employees according to a Skillset survey (Hirsch, n.d.). It is a changing field and is more susceptible to technological change than other areas of the academic curriculum. It may even be at the mercy of technologies that threaten its identity and its purposes, not withstanding that there are enduring characteristics in photography education which have enabled it to become an important part of the arts and humanities curriculum. These include, first, its adaptability to changing technologies. Photography has never had a period when its technical apparatus remained unchanging and in some ways it is a practice that is defined by change. As the philosopher Patrick Maynard observes: 'A history of photography could scarcely avoid a history of the technologies of photography' (2000, 15). Second, the harnessing of photography theory as a supplement and a matrix for practical work; and third, initiatives that allow photography to align itself with cognate areas of the academic curriculum. These initiatives include the formation of multi-disciplinary and experimental practices such as forensic science and photography, photography and moving image studies, fashion, advertising, journalism and fine art and many other disciplines in which photography is an essential part of the practice.

Photography Industries

According to Skillset experience is often valued more than vocational qualifications and there is evidence that prospective employers are interested in 'professional profile' rather than what he or she studied at university. Skillset also comments on skills shortage and gaps in key areas including use of digital technology, knowledge of digital workflow, business management, marketing and finance, intellectual property rights and related demands of the commercial and industrial workplace. Skillset report good prospects for qualified graduates in a sector that comprises 14,000 'photo-imaging' companies in the UK (Skillset, 2010: 74). The expansion of the creative industries gives further reasons for optimism: 40 per cent of employees in the 'photo-imaging' industries have a degree (ibid.: 74). According to a *Guardian* newspaper editorial, 'the UK's creative industries have been quietly outperforming the rest of British industry ... and accounts for almost 5.6% of all employment in the country' (*Guardian*, 2014: 26). A key factor in assessment of the 'imaging industries' is the predominance of small companies relying on freelancers drawn from a fragmented and highly competitive workforce.

Academic response to Skillset has promoted the idea of degree-level studies as resistant to the narrowly focused idea of education as training for the workplace. The chair of the Association of Photographers in Higher Education (APHE), responding to an earlier Skillset document, notes that 'we have difficulty with the whole idea of an "industry"' and proposed photography education to be a good example of a liberal arts education, preparing graduates with transferable skills:

> We explained that as educators we had to broaden students' worldview and prepare them for life where there were relatively few opportunities to become professional photographers. I asserted that we are doing a good job by our graduates and the specific skills deficits mentioned by our critics were the sort of things that could be learned relatively quickly on the job … a simple how-to-do-it photo education would disadvantage more students than it helped.
>
> (APHE, 2006)

The Association of Photographers in Higher Education (APHE) strongly defends the importance of cultural skills and the model of progressive photography developed in the 1970s and 1980s. Integrated courses allow students to take on a mixture of practical work and critical practice that stretches those who want something more than an apprenticeship. The crude distinction between training and critical thinking has largely dissipated in most areas of education. Recent industry-related training documents recognize the importance of intellectually creative ideals in the wider fields of the arts, entertainment and commerce. An Australian training document for the 'photo imaging industries', published in 2012, lists a range of skills including knowledge of 'theoretical and historical context for photo imaging practice' and 'critical thinking skills to identify work-based opportunities and to enhance technical and conceptual skills' (Australian Government, 2012: 5). Others have waved the flag for degrees that resist slippage into 'mechanistic, technically-based non-academic courses, besotted with work-based learning' (Golding, 2005).

Some recent observers of the media industries take a harder line. One of the pioneers of New Photography Theory, Victor Burgin, has recently noted the power (and interventions) of market forces in the public educational sector:

> The steady withdrawal of public funding for arts and education over the past forty years or so pitched museums and educational institutions alike into the marketplace to survive as best they can, with the result that a whole range of intellectual and cultural activities that were once valued according to their own criteria now have to look for their legitimation in market terms – in terms of 'contribution to economic growth' and 'impact on society', in terms of money and audiences.
>
> (Burgin, 2012: 13)

The historical challenge to academic convention, in this view, is replaced by a levelling down effect that blurs the boundaries of art and commerce. In contrast students struggling to meet the costs of higher education might take a more pragmatic view. There are in fact a growing number of courses tailored to the interests of students with specific career objectives who are aware of the needs of complementary skills in business management and marketing. Wider generic courses provide a range of skills and a body of knowledge that transfers into different forms of capital (social, economic, artistic) without guaranteeing a traditional career in photography. Specialist courses are more likely to provide profes-sional skills and the important networking contacts. And yet despite these pressures a recent survey show that photography graduates recommend their courses 'as an educational experience' in their own right and suitable for careers in other (possibly related) fields in industry and the media (Allbeson, 2012: 29). When designed as a 'non-vocational' or generic course (as it is in many institutions), photography

PHOTOGRAPHY EDUCATION

compares with other university courses such as English Literature or Fine Art. Students on such courses might not become novelists or artists but can, adeptly, apply their knowledge to other areas of life. There is still a strong attachment, not least amongst students themselves, to the benefits of broad-based generic courses that favour 'education for its own sake'.

Creative Resources

The consensus in the educational sector is broadly in favour of traditional social and cultural ideals of university provision. The absorption of critical theory and the harnessing of new technology have changed the most progressive areas of the curriculum and the market for images has expanded. Great advances have been made but the challenge of market forces creates anxiety in the academy. The expansion of higher education over the past few decades has widened the gate to allow for increasing numbers of students. There follows a debate about numbers and the struggle to maintain high standards when staff-student ratios increase, hours of work are longer, and technical resources are stretched to the limit. Mass access is not matched by increase in resources in higher education and the new universities have struggled to maintain standards. The introduction of the research ethos is encouraged across the whole of higher education. It is heralded by vice chancellors and embraced by academics and yet it can drive a wedge between those who teach and those do research. This often results in the making of a two-tier system of academic staffing in which students are distanced from a fraction of the academic community doing the most radical work. Writer and broadcaster Claire Fox makes the point:

> The belief that research and teaching must be closely linked reflected a view of universities, held in the not-so-distant pre-access past, as special places of scholarship and knowledge, where academics were at the cutting edge of social progress, expanding ideas and researching new areas. Undergraduates were educated by interacting with this atmosphere and with people who were pushing society's intellectual boundaries outwards. The education process lay less in the technical teaching of subjects and more in allowing the new recruits to academia, access to the greatest minds in the field. This was not school, but an apprenticeship to becoming independent thinkers.

> (Fox, 2000: 251)

Fox also notes the 'dead weight of utilitarian vocationalism' that, in her view, had replaced the 'search for truth, a desire to experiment, a sense of wonder and curiosity, an unapologetic interest in the irrelevant and the arcane' (ibid.: 252). The predisposition to treat students as customers paying for an educational service is at odds with the high-minded view of 'education for its own sake'. In reality the two extremes are somewhat caricatured since 'well-rounded' graduates with a creative initiative and knowledge of the subject still exist. Independent thinking, intellectual self-confidence, creative intelligence is evident in the work of successful graduates and these aptitudes transfer to the world of work. Whether or not 'well-roundedness' is achieved in spite of institutional policy or because of it remains an open question.

Photography education, as we go on to explore (see Chapter 10 below), may have some core values but its methods are variable and changing. It is increasingly dependent upon high-end technology that requires operating system updates and dedicated IT staff for everyday running of a department. The American academic Therese Mulligan notes:

TEACHING AND LEARNING PHOTOGRAPHY

Perhaps the most daunting barrier to the acceptance of best practices can be the lack of accurate, in-depth technical knowledge on the part of the faculty, students and photographers … there are many reasons for this including lack of administrative support and development opportunities, inaccurate information, inadequate facilities, or resistance to embrace a completely new paradigm in both technology and pedagogy.

(Mulligan, 2006: 12)

The demand for new forms of pedagogy driven by technological imperatives raises many questions. The temptation to allow technical apparatus to determine curriculum content might be resisted. The measure of a work of art or any kind of aesthetic project is not dependent on its suitability to the apparatus that makes it. We might, instead, judge the apparatus by its suitability to the work (Burgin, 2012: 13). Critics are often suspicious of '"upgrade" culture' (Lister, 2014: 15) and view the fetishism of new media as disabling when it replaces rational evaluation of its applications. Some courses celebrate the demise of their analogue foundations and rely on the 'born digital' image whilst others build new wet darkrooms to cater for the fashionable high-end market in film work and the well-crafted print.

At one end the post-photographic utopia of technological progress is seen as the next stage in history. On the other hand the danger of 'techno-avant-gardism' (Roberts, 1998: 223) is reminiscent of earlier wild-eyed theories of media globalism. Lister warned against a 'heady mixture of futurology' (Lister, 1995: 5) and Robins cautioned his readers against a 'false polarisation between past and future, photography and digital culture' (Robins, 1995: 33). The idea of technology as a causal factor in culture change is often generalized now as it has been in the past. Media panic has accompanied the history of photography since its foundation years. As Lister notes, the shaping influence of culture on media technology is an important part of the discussion. The debates on photography theory cannot ignore the question of technology since it affects the definitions of the practice and its institutional base. As we noted above photography has a history of its own reinvention and new ways of working co-exist with the old in hybrid forms adapted to new constituencies in a changing world.

It is clear that issues around the social value and meaning of new technology are just as important as the business of keeping up with it. The old question of how 'theory' relates to practice (or vice versa) has been important since the foundation years of photography. One of the important developments in photography education is the way some teaching methods establish links that make the connection more explicit. In the next part of this chapter we will consider examples of teaching practice.

APPROACHES TO TEACHING PHOTOGRAPHY

Theory into Practice

The emphasis on issues and debates in photography reduced the academic distance between the seminar room and the studio. The shortcomings of the old '*laissez faire*' art school system of teaching and learning were identified and denounced by a new generation of teachers. One critic argues that the art schools delivered very little education:

Indeed art students are put at a serious disadvantage (and ironically glory in it) vis-à-vis students in higher and further education … The rationale of art schools is to train rather than educate

271

PHOTOGRAPHY EDUCATION

> artists to become professional who must compete with each other and other professionals in a difficult market for jobs and sales … the school maintains a powerful sense of being an artist in total mystification of what working as one entails.
>
> (Pollock, 1996: 54)

The unreconstructed art student, in this view, is a limited figure relying on personal vision rather than knowledge acquisition or critical analysis. The change to integrated approaches to photography in which its technical aspects are considered alongside the social practice of picture making was a response to the limitations of an approach that relied on self-discovery and inwardness. In the unreconstructed model the student might talk about 'work' as limited by feeling and emotion as if language, context and social meaning were irrelevant. He or she might seem to be saying that if art is to be looked at it must be prior to language with its restrictive sense of rationality and convention. A student might read a technical manual but everything else was left to the free spirit of creation. Critics, such as the art historian Griselda Pollock, argued that wherever photography education followed this art school model it limited the field of study to art. As an antidote to the inward-looking aesthetic of mainstream modern art and museum photography there was a turn to engagement with the social meaning of commercial photographs, fashion, advertising, and documentary forms of photography. The photographers who confronted the limits of 'self-expression' raided commercial imagery (see fig. 5.3) and forced it into the domain of political argument and discourse. At a stroke the aesthetic was displaced by an interest in social effects. The critic Peter Wollen noted: 'Photography is not an "art-in-itself" any more than film, but an option within an inter-semiotic and inter-textual "arena"' (Wollen, 1982: 188).

> **KEY TERM:** *Laissez-faire*
> This term is translated in various ways as 'let them do as they will' or 'let it be'. It is used to describe an unregulated economic environment or one that is relatively free from government restrictions or subsidies. In social and aesthetic theory the term might equally relate to an absence of cultural authority and a relaxed attitude to, or rejection of, academic rules. We use the term to refer in this context to the idea of unfettered freedom of expression. It is an attractive principle except that freedom to make any kind of image often leads to stereotyped and highly conventional aesthetic practices. The stereotyped depiction of women favoured by the tabloid press, or the routinely downward gaze (upon the socially excluded) of the documentary camera, are examples of self-expression collapsing into cliché and banality. *Laissez-faire* in the arts is often a recipe for anti-intellectualism.

Photography as Social Practice

In its most routine uses photography may seem neutral and apolitical. In the next part of this chapter we focus on a particular studio exercise, recently carried out in a university photography department. The exercise is designed to encourage students to consider how strategic use of photographic equipment impacts on social meaning. Students participate in a group-based photographic exercise followed, in the same session, by an open-ended discussion of the results. The exercise is intended to show how camera format and other pre-production factors might influence the social meaning of photographs.

The question of 'approach' to the subject and the predatory nature of photography are addressed. The exercise is intended to make students think about the way camera settings influence the technical codes (and meanings) of the photographs. Students participating in this exercise will:

1 engage with the relation between camera design and other production factors and the interpretation of the visual outcome
2 understand the constructed nature of all photographs and challenge the 'common sense' notion of photographic truth
3 consider and engage with theoretical debates on representation and deconstruction of social difference
4 recognize how far the formal elements of the image determine meaning. The elements include framing, composition, and other technical codes.
5 understand how far technological limitations (self imposed or determined by the apparatus itself) act as expressive constraints on the content of the image. Conversely technological limitations can be used productively.

This exercise presupposes a group of photographers whose rather conventional use of the medium leads to class discussion of photographic meaning. The purpose is to introduce a reflexive and self-critical method of assessment in preparation for later work in which the production of social meaning might be considered in advance as it becomes part of the knowledge base of photographic practice.

The Activity

In a typical teaching session six digital cameras were placed in a room amongst 20 students. They were asked to photograph somebody in the room and informed that the resulting images would be projected on to a screen for discussion. Cameras were collected and a series of portrait photographs were made.

A male student requested the female student next to him to sit for him. She refused. Another male photographer took the female student's picture without her seeing him. Others sat, stood, and arranged themselves for the camera. After 15 minutes the cameras were returned. A check revealed that none of the camera settings had been changed from automatic exposure and focus, and only one or two of the zoom lenses had been adjusted. The presettings of camera controls were for the most part accepted as found.

Camera Bias

The female student who refused to be photographed wanted to avoid being objectified or discussed by the group. The photographer who had requested her participation moved to negotiate with other students. It was remarked that the second photographer had acted like a street photographer snapping randomly and assuming his subject's willingness to be photographed.

Cameras set to 'Automatic' or Programme mode become 'point and shoot' machines; their exposures are 'accurate' insofar as they conform to an internationally adopted standard. Normally the subject or object in the middle of the frame will be sharply focused and exposed as a mid tone. That is to say that the combination of the shutter speed, lens aperture and 'ISO' of the film or sensor will, without

PHOTOGRAPHY EDUCATION

intervention, produce an image where the point of focus and exposure will equate to a mid-grey tone, a tone that reflects 18 per cent of the light falling on it.

But the standard is not neutral and is not without consequences for the way people are reproduced on film or by digital cameras. The ISO is the scale fixed by the International Standards Organization, which brought together the 1930s DIN (*Deutsches Institut für Normung* – German Institute for Standardization) and ASA (the 1940s American Standards Association Camera). Cameras have a racial bias built into them and camera meters are set to best represent what some photography manuals describe as an 'average subject' and others describe as a 'skin tone'. Both match the dominant skin tone of the culture in which cameras were created (Lange and Golding, 2007).

The upshot of the 'pre-set' point-and-shoot mechanism is its suitability for certain types of subject (that is to say a white subject) assumed to be in social dominance. The camera setting codifies ways of seeing its subject. In other words the cultural effects of the apparatus parallel or anticipate already established ideas and beliefs. Some adjustment might counter crude technological determination. For example a technically adept photographer might want to adjust to the specific requirements of the shoot when and if the subject does not conform to the 'mid-tone' skin the equipment is expecting.

The female student who had refused to be photographed explained her reluctance to be objectified by the camera. The photographer who had requested her participation moved on to negotiate with other students. The question of trust and the sincerity of the photographer or other end users of an image were identified as important issues.

Further social implications raised by the exercise were taken up in the discussion that followed the exercise and this was extended to a wider debate about technical codes in photographs. The group considered questions such as the use of soft focus in advertising, close up intimacy, mid and long shots, the gendering effects of body position (high/low) in group portraits and bodily gestures, head tilting and other ritualized modes of subordination. Self-presentation and the highly conventional nature of 'looking good' were recognized as prime issues in portrait photography. It was noted that women historically have felt the burden of representation more than men. It was also noted how this inequality had shifted in recent years so that advertisements promoting the sale of beauty products for men have become more widespread. Men and women (and increasingly children) are constrained by social practices that have been codified in the apparatuses of photography (the limits imposed by the camera). This is an important aspect in the signifying process that includes photographic competence and knowledge.

The session was followed up with the tutor underlining how far the ritual nature of photography produces culturally imprinted visual effects. In other words the photographer, consciously or not, follows aesthetic conventions that in turn have social meanings beyond their descriptiveness. What appears to be 'natural' (in the photograph) enters a chain of signification and meaning. In other words it becomes a cultural object. The technology plays a part in the construction of meaning and the student is reminded that competence (or lack of it) affects the photographer's ability to produce the kind of visual effects the shoot requires.

Summary of key issues raised by the exercise

- the ethics of photographing people
- the purpose of making the images
- pictorial considerations including historical references and influences
- genre
- ownership of the image
- distribution and end users
- interpretation of meaning
- technological determination of meaning including cultural effects of the apparatus
- the image as commodity.

CONCLUSION

Photographic education is delivered in many different ways. It includes specialist distant learning and part-time modes (see Chapter 10 for a discussion of these), critique as a method of engaging students in a group discussion with peers and teachers (Doren, 2006: 16–19), and traditional lecture/seminar methods that encourage scholarship and writing skills. Integrated approaches on progressive courses are often led by tutors who see their practice as operating on a multiplicity of artistic and intellectual fronts. These include being a lecturer, a writer, theorist, and an artist using media forms such as conferences, exhibitions, books, journals and online resources. Courses that are concerned with practical work produced in a theoretical framework are widespread and yet older models survive. The academics Greg Lucas and Jane Fletcher offer the following provocation: 'It is currently possible to complete a photographic degree without fully understanding the medium's (historical) technological processes, social applications or cultural functions' (Lucas and Fletcher, 2012: 32).

There is perhaps exaggeration seeking to make a point in this statement and yet the marketing of courses and the market success of art photography often collapse into artistic cliché and the trumpeting of old-style expression theory. Perhaps the old divisions between theory and practice are now behind us even when some photographers, teachers and students pull one way or another. The positing of a nuanced and pluralistic way of doing things is better for students whose vocation is essentially practical and motivated by a love of photography.

Theory is often one-sided and misses the vital link between critical engagement and artistic innovation. The challenge is to make critical theory accessible and relevant to graduates anxiously approaching the world of work. Suffice it to say that critically informed education helps to shape photographic work, promotes enquiry, and allows students to question the traditional routes into artistic and industrial photographic practices. Teachers encourage students to broaden their knowledge so that cultural reference is built into their various projects. The anxiety about 'theory' (as an interloper) has been replaced by recognition that the experience of making things (including photographs) has its own dynamic (Harris, 2011). Recognition of this is not anterior to theory but one of its most important discoveries.

SUMMARY OF KEY POINTS

- The impact of New Photography Theory in the late twentieth century broadened the field of study and elevated its status in the academy. Photography courses have achieved academic parity with other arts and humanities subjects. Photography theory has redefined the curriculum in ways that extend to critical evaluation of social contexts beyond the academy and the museum.
- Technological change affects photography education more than other areas of the arts curricula. Skills shortages and gaps in knowledge are reported by external bodies such Skillset.
- Academics, practitioners and critics warn against a false polarization between photography and digital culture. Fear that photography is at the mercy of new technologies threatening its identity is exaggerated.
- Academics are resistant to 'how-to-do-it' approaches to education. Teaching and learning methods should allow for intellectual and artistic skills to exist alongside technical and applied modes of study.
- Photography education is delivered in different ways but there are common trends. For example we have noted the success of integrated courses where practitioners, teachers and students work on a number of artistic and intellectual fronts.

REFERENCES

Allbeson, Tom (2012) 'Photography Education 2: Career Prospects: Photography Education from the Student's Perspective', in *Source: The Photographic Review*, Autumn 2012, Issue 72 (special edition on photography education), pp. 27–29.

APHE (Association of Photographers in Higher Education) (2006) Feedback from Meeting with Skillset, Nottingham, 24 August.

Australian Government: Department of Education, Employment and Workplace Relations (2012) 'CUVPH1405A Develop self for photo imaging industry', ISC: Industry Skills Councils.

Burgin, Victor (2012) 'Limited Optimism', an email exchange with David Campany in *Source: The Photographic Review*, Autumn 2012, Issue 72 (special edition on photography education), pp. 12–23.

Doren, Mariah (2006) 'Critique as Method of Critical Engagement', in *Exposure: Journal of the Society for Photographic Education*, Spring 2006, vol. 39, no. 1, pp. 16–19.

Fox, Claire (2000) 'Education: Dumbing Down or Wising Up?' in Ivo Mosley (ed.), *Dumbing Down: Culture, Politics and the Mass Media*, Thoreveton: Imprint Academic, pp. 245–252.

Golding, Andrew (2005) personal email communication sent to chair of Association of Photographers in Higher Education (APHE).

Guardian (2014), 'Creative Economy: Standing Up For the Arts', Editorial, Monday 20 January.

Harris, Philip (2011) *Photographing Landscape: A Theory of the Experience of Making*, Birmingham: Birmingham City University.

Hirsch, Jonathan (n.d.), 'Skillset Photo Imaging Skills Strategy', in *The Sector Skills Council for the Audio Visual Industries*.

Lange, Silke and Golding, Andrew (2007) 'The Interactive Photograph: Photography's Role in the Acquisition of Creative Skills', in *The International Journal of Arts in Society*, 2007, vol. 1, no. 4, pp. 133–140.

Lucas, Greg and Fletcher, Jane (2012) 'The Empty Lens: Teaching Photography as a Dead Language', in *Source: The Photographic Review*, Autumn 2012, Issue 72 (special edition on photography education), pp. 32–35.

Lister, Martin (1995) 'Introductory Essay', in Martin Lister (ed.) *The Photographic Image in Digital Culture*, London and New York: Routledge, pp. 1–26.

—— (2014) 'Overlooking, Rarely Looking and Not Looking', in Jonas Larsen and Mette Sandbye (eds) *Digital Snaps: The New Face of Photography*, London and New York: I.B. Tauris, pp. 1–23.

Maynard, Patrick (2000) *The Engine of Visualisation: Thinking Through Photography*, Ithaca, NY and London: Cornell University Press.

Mulligan, Therese (2006) 'Putting the Digital in Photographic Education', in *Exposure: Journal of the Society for Photographic Education*, Spring 2006, vol. 39, no. 1, pp. 6–15

Pollock, Griselda (1996) 'Art, School, Culture', in *The Block Reader in Visual Culture*, London and New York: Routledge, pp. 50–67.

Roberts, John (1998) *The Art of Interruption: Realism, Photography and the Everyday*, Manchester University Press.

Robins, Kevin (1995) 'Will Image Move Us Still?', in Martin Lister (ed.) (1995) pp. 29–50.

Skillset (2010) 'Creative Media Sector', in *Skillset: The Sector Skills Council for Creative Media*. Available at http://www.skillset.org/photo (Accessed 20.04.2014).

Wollen, Peter (1982) 'Photography and Aesthetics', in Peter Wollen, *Readings and Writings: Semiotic Counter Strategies*, London: Verso, pp. 178–188.

CHAPTER 10
NEW TECHNOLOGIES AND PHOTOGRAPHY EDUCATION

Florian Einfalt, photographer and CGI artist, created this image when he was an undergraduate design student at Georg Simon Ohm University of Applied Sciences, Nuremberg, in 2011. Students on this undergraduate course specialize in creating images, which use both photography and computer generated imagery (CGI). This image comprises a traditional photograph of a desert scene with two additional elements, the tricycle and submarine, which have been simulated with computer software. Note that the tricycle is the same recognizable design from the cover of the influential 1976 exhibition catalogue *William Eggleston's Guide*. John Szarkowski, former curator at the Museum of Modern Art, New York and the American photographer Eggleston are recognized for having successfully relocated 'vernacular' colour photography in an art gallery context. Eggleston's iconic tricycle represents a particular type of colour documentary photography from America in the 1970s and 1980s. In Einfalt's work the tricycle, abandoned within a desert scene, provocatively implies the death of photography. The title *Desert Change* points to another reading: that of change. The photography industry is changing with the invention of new technologies and it is important to consider the question: where is photography now?

10.1 Florian Einfalt with Andreas Franke and Thomas Kapzan, *Desert Change*, 2011. Backplate photography: Andreas Franke (staudinger+franke). CGI and post-production: Florian Einfalt, Thomas Kapzan. Produced at Georg-Simon-Ohm University of Applied Sciences Nuremberg. Courtesy of the artists.

INTRODUCTION

In this chapter we look at how new technologies have impacted on photographic education. We concentrate on Higher Education at undergraduate level but the discussion is relevant for photography students at all levels including 'A' level, BTEC and post-graduate level. The chapter includes an overview of where photography education is now and highlights the plurality of vocations that currently attach to photography. The impact of new technology on the learning experience is explored. The new reliance on virtual space is discussed, and new trends such as online and open courses. The need for transferable skills is analysed and reference is made to Creative Skillset. We raise some key philosophical questions: What is the future of photography? Are we in a post-photographic era? Can education keep up with technology?

Are We in a 'Post-photography' Era?

In the early 1990s professional and consumer digital photography was in its infancy. Photography and media theorists William J. Mitchell (1992), Martin Lister (1995) and Kevin Robins (1995) wrote new texts, which heralded the birth of digital imaging technology as the start of a new era of so-called 'post-photography'. In his essay 'Will image move us still?' Robins notes:

> The death of photography is being widely reported. There is a growing sense that we are now witnessing the birth of a new era, that of post-photography. This, of course, represents a response to the development of new digital electronic technologies for the registration, origination, manipulation and storage of images. Over the past decade or so, we have seen the increasing convergence of photographic technologies with video and computer technologies, and this convergence seems set to bring about a whole new context in which still images will constitute just one small element in the encompassing domain of what has been termed hypermedia. Virtual technologies, with their capacity to originate a 'realistic' image on the basis of mathematical applications that model reality, add to the sense of anticipation and expectation.
>
> (Robins, 1995: 29)

Robins wrote this essay in the context of the excitement and fear that surrounded the new medium of digital photography in the mid-1990s. Just as nineteenth-century French history painter Paul Delaroche declared painting to be dead, when photography was invented, so the theorists predicted photography's demise upon the arrival of digital imaging and computer-generated imagery (CGI). Decades after Robins's essay all three media practices are still thriving: traditional silver-based photography, digital photography and, of course, painting.

Mitchell (1992), in *The Reconfigured Eye: Visual Truth in the Post-Photographic Era,* made an urgent case for a re-configuring or re-classification of the visual language of the photograph, underscoring the technological differences between the analogue photograph and the digital image. Some ten years after Lev Manovich (2003), a writer on new media and professor of Visual Arts at the University of California, in his essay 'The Paradoxes of Digital Photography', criticizes and questions Mitchell's description of 'post-photography'. Manovich analyses Mitchell's categories of traditional and digital photography and finds them to be outdated. Manovich instead does not think a photograph should be defined by its technology but the content, issues and ideas the image represents. This strategy is one most photography undergraduate students are encouraged to embrace.

PHOTOGRAPHY EDUCATION

After Photography

Photography academic Fred Ritchin's book, *After Photography* (2009), explores photography's role in the digital age and its social effects. Addressing technology and photography from a philosophical point of view he introduces extravagant new terms such as 'Hyperphotography' – a hybrid of photography and hypertext – and investigates prospective changes in habits of perception in a digital age. This kind of futuristic zeal has its limitations. Ritchin is aware of this and insists that his 'book makes no attempt at prophecy'. 'It is', he claims, 'an attempt to acknowledge the rapidly evolving present for what it is and what it might become' (2009: 10). Ritchin notes:

> We have entered the digital age. And the digital age has entered us. We are no longer the same people we once were … The changes in media, especially media as pervasive as the digital, require that we live differently, with shifting perceptions and expectations. Our cosmos is different, as is our sense of time … It's 8:17 now. Not a quarter past eight. Not a little past the first light. We live in the abstracted integers of the digital age.
>
> (Ritchin, 2009: 9)

This chapter focuses photography education in the digital age. The alarmist idea that everything is different now and all must change is treated with some caution. Like Ritchin and other media pundits we agree that new media presents great opportunities but we are aware of issues around obsolescence, new teaching methods, identity, and the relative place of the subject in the arts and humanities curriculum. As the technology of photography changes so does its pedagogy. Is one thing chasing the other? What comes first, philosophy of education or technical determination? These are concerns for both the learner and educator in what is hailed as a new era in photography.

Photography Education Now

As discussed in Case Study 2, the last 20 years have seen a revolution in new technology. In the last two decades the development of the home computer and the consumer digital camera has created new and ever-changing systems of communication. Now anyone with a camera phone or digital camera is potentially a photographer. Students of photography arrive at university already able to take photographs up to a certain level of competency. The programme of study might be influenced by this and take up the challenge of making them into critically informed and articulate practitioners. The skill-set of the average graduate in this field might be expected to provide knowledge that is specialist, extensive, and well beyond the amateur. And yet the enlightened amateur is increasingly adept and competitive in the chase for jobs and opportunities in the wider world. It is a much changed world compared with even the recent past. In 2013, 350 million photos were uploaded daily to the social networking website Facebook (Campbell, 2013: 269). The challenge for emerging photographers is to embrace the democracy of the image and use the tools given on a photography degree to stand out from the crowd. In an era of social networking, the Internet, camera phones, computers and digital cameras, photography students are privileged users of these technologies. Their privilege, however, may be a product of deeper engagement with the issues and debates that impact on the meaning of what they do, rather than its most obvious applications. Undergraduate photography courses in the UK encourage students to be critically engaged practitioners, adept at contextualizing their photographic brand within both contemporary culture and historical discourse.

NEW TECHNOLOGIES AND PHOTOGRAPHY EDUCATION

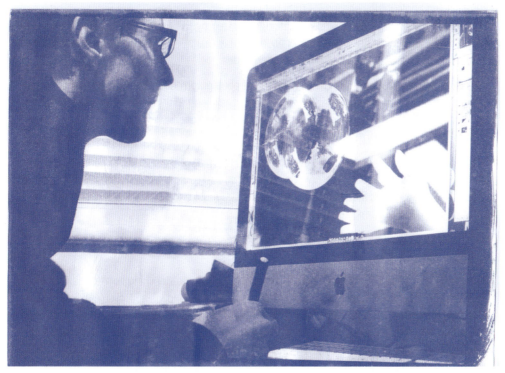

10.2 Trevor Coultart (undergraduate student at the University of Hertfordshire 2012–2015), *Retouching*, 2012. Cyanotype print created using an A4 acetate negative laid directly on treated cartridge paper and exposed with a UV exposure unit (negative was prepared using Adobe Photoshop). © Trevor Coultart 2012. Courtesy of the artist.

Developments in new technology have undoubtedly created significant change in photography curricula at all levels of education. The tools available to a student of photography far outweigh what was available in the recent past. Photography courses are now in a state of flux, where new skills in digital technologies are taught alongside traditional craft-based skills.

Change has been gathering pace and different institutions have responded in various ways. Some have closed darkrooms and become more fully digitally centred, embracing a kind of technological determinism. Most institutions, however, continue to offer a range of photographic technologies, from traditional to digital. At the University of Hertfordshire students on the undergraduate photography course explore a range of photographic techniques in a project-based approach to learning. In one module, first-year students take digital photographs in response to a set brief on the theme of 'Identity'. These digital files are then output as acetate negatives to create cyanotype contact prints. A cyanotype print is one of the earliest photographic techniques, invented in 1842 by scientist John Herschel, and later made well known by botanist and photographer Anna Atkins. The cyanotype print, a distinct blue colour, is exposed with UV light and as such these prints are often referred to as sun prints. Figure 10.2 shows a cyanotype print created by a photography undergraduate student at the University of Hertfordshire, which incorporates a digital self-portrait of the student absorbed in the digital workspace. This image exemplifies the hybrid output of today's students and professional photographers.

PHOTOGRAPHY EDUCATION

In 2009 leading photography academics from both the UK and other countries in Europe came together for a symposium on photography and education, organized by the journal *Photographies* and held at London South Bank University. In a paper entitled 'Identity Crisis', Anne Williams, Programme Director for Photography, London College of Communication, notes:

> We might equally well ask for how long specialist photography courses will continue to exist – the shift into multimedia increasingly requires multi-skilled multi-taskers who understand the interactions of media and modalities rather than just their specificities.
>
> (Williams, 2009: 133)

Williams makes a case for a broadening of classification for what constitutes photography now and what should be explored within contemporary photographic education. She accepts that medium specificity is still important but argues that education is an arena that must protect 'social and critical photography practice of all kinds' (Williams, 2009: 129).

Daniel Rubenstein, photography academic, presented a provocative stance on the current state of photography education. He notes:

> The tasks that photography education is committed to, those of teaching how to make photographs and how to interpret them, never seemed more redundant and obsolete than in the present moment … Photography education knows of no method with which to approach New Media image culture; instead, it attempts in vain to prolong its survival by clinging to the historical moment of photography, not realizing that this moment has passed and that it has nothing to offer to the present besides obsolete judgements and inadequate interpretations.
>
> (Rubenstein, 2009: 135)

Indeed, Rubenstein's argument is a timely one and offers what he considers urgent topics for debate including 'the crisis of the visual, the demise of the still photograph and the redundancy of authorship in photography' (Rubenstein, 2009: 138). Because the digital photograph exists 'both within and outside visual culture, photography education will have to consider the image as a holistic field' (ibid.: 141). The status of the image is at the centre of this concern but what are the main debates surrounding new technologies, photography and learning?

New Technology and Learning

New technology enhances the learning environment, making new techniques more accessible. For example, learning about photographic lighting is made simpler with new technology, as the tutor can shoot whilst 'tethered' to a computer and a data projector. Every time the tutor demonstrates a different lighting technique the result is instantly projected for the whole class to see. Likewise, probably a more obvious example, when a student photographer takes a digital photograph they are able to view their image instantly on the LCD screen on the camera, receiving instant feedback, which might improve their technique. If the student is shooting the same subject on a film (analogue) camera they have to go to the darkroom to process and print the negative, only to find out the shot is technically flawed. On the flip side of this process, shooting in analogue does slow photography down. Each decision technically, creatively and conceptually is indelibly written on a piece of film. If it is wrong hours are wasted in the darkroom and this can be financially costly. It could be said that shooting analogue tightens up and improves technique through trial and error.

The Traditional Darkroom as a Contemporary Learning Space

As noted some UK universities have decided to close down their darkrooms. With the obsolescence of silver-based chemistry, film and paper announced increasingly, it might be a trend that more universities follow. For the present time, darkrooms are still used for teaching in most universities. Here we look at why these spaces are potentially still important for the medium and what the main debates are around the maintained use of silver-based processes in the face of institutional and academic demand for technological advancement. It is therefore surprising and ironic that in last decade there has been a resurgence in the use of film. The return to film within fine art and fashion photography could be seen as a way of signalling a difference with amateur photography.

Jonathan Worth, photographer and lecturer at Coventry University, emphasizes the importance of the specialist craft skills or 'artisanal' skills, as a way of a professional photographer elevating their practice from that of an amateur. In this instance he defines an amateur as someone who uploads his or her digital snapshots to sites like Flickr or uses a photo filter app on a mobile phone. Worth believes the artefact produced using specialist craft skills, which could include digital and analogue skills, is something he contextualizes as a 'generative' experience.

> Such 'generatives' (as defined by Kevin Kelly) are experiences that cannot be digitised and transmitted virtually – a kiss or a smell cannot be recorded and broadcast. The value of these experiences is actually amplified by the digital. Even the most immersive virtual experience serves only to remind us of how much is lacking in comparison to the physical act.
>
> (Worth, October 2012)

Similarly, Conrad Tracy, course leader BA Commercial Photography, Arts University Bournemouth (AUB), agrees with Worth. In discussion with the authors for this chapter theme, Tracy reports the importance of the darkroom as a teaching space:

> Introducing students to traditional silver-based processes is a fantastic teaching tool. It underpins the fundamentals of what we do and it takes it away from 'point and shoot'. It aids an understanding of exposure, light and the precision and craft needed to be able to produce consistent and high quality silver-based output. We see it very much as a learning tool.
>
> (Unpublished statement taken from an interview with Conrad Tracy in October, 2012)

The approach at AUB, which runs both art-based and commercial photography courses, has been to integrate high-end traditional processes with new technologies. They invested in a professional industry standard digital c-type printer. A digital c-type is a silver-based archival print, which derives from a digital file. It is therefore possible to make a photograph with a digital camera and output an analogue print. The digital c-type printer exposes the light-sensitive paper to light, and develops and fixes with the same wet process traditionally used for c-type prints. This methodology echoes the approach at the University of Hertfordshire, mentioned above, where learners incorporate traditional craft activities with cutting-edge new technologies.

PHOTOGRAPHY EDUCATION

Technology and Resources

Photography is a resource-hungry specialism, in comparison to other humanities subjects, which are traditionally classroom based. Photography degrees need classrooms but also require darkrooms, a photographic equipment hire facility, photography studios for lighting people and still life, dedicated computer labs with imaging software, calibrated monitors and profiled print output. Photography students have access to a wealth of facilities and are encouraged to work in teams within shared workspaces. A professional photographer will often have to work as part of a team, but predominantly be responsible for their own time management, business affairs and branding. Similarly a photography student will spend half the week sharing learning spaces and resources with fellow learners and the rest of the time he or she will be alone, researching, reflecting and finishing creative work. Undergraduate photography students should be aware of this need for balance and make the most of learning communities and peer networks.

Learning Communities and Peer Networks

Generally the number of students enrolled on a photography course exceeds the number of cameras in the hire store and computers in the photography lab. It is therefore preferable for students to have regular access to their own equipment. Increasingly students are shooting digital, viewing their work on a home computer and are in a kind of closed feedback loop until they submit an assignment. This method of digital workflow can sometimes mean that student peer networks become fractured. Many courses are now relying on virtual spaces in which students can communicate with each other. Most universities now have a virtual learning environment (VLE). They have not yet become a genuinely used 'meeting place' for students to share work. Instead photography students are using external social networking and blogging sites to communicate with each other and share work. These forums, within sites like Facebook, Flickr and Twitter, are moderated by students, student-led, and a place to share views, work in progress, triumphs and disasters. Much as you would do as a group learning together in the darkroom or a shared base-room. The virtual world is becoming an additional learning environment outside of the university campus.

Student coursework may now sit on public blogs instead of the traditional method of using a paper-based sketchbook to collect research. The research blog has become a 'virtual sketchbook'. Photographer and academic Eti Wade uses blogging as a research tool and in an interview with the authors of the book, she explains why:

> We mostly research online now, looking for and looking at images and videos within the screen environment, so it makes perfect sense that students collate web (or screen) based work in the same environment. The whole process is more streamlined and the collation of the research outcomes becoming nearly one fluid activity. This is an activity that does not require the somewhat artificial break that occurs when a student has to print the images out, cut them up, and paste into a sketchbook. When photography students learn to blog, this makes their work processes public and generates a future audience for their practice.
>
> (Unpublished statement taken from an interview with Eti Wade in October, 2012)

The practice of blogging also gives students vital experience of publishing their work online. Many undergraduate photography courses teach web design skills to enable students to develop a professional web presence before they graduate. A photography graduate is now highly computer literate, opening further career opportunities such as website design and digital publishing. Through using the screen environment in curricula, photography is converging with other screen-based areas such as design and moving image.

Photography and Convergence

Photography has historically been a medium that 'converges' with other disciplines. For example, photography converged with science in 1843, when Anna Atkins' cyanotypes were published as botanical studies. Photography was the forerunner to motion pictures, when in 1878, Eadweard Muybridge's work *The Horse in Motion,* experimented with photography to record sequential shots of horses in motion. Even before photography was invented painters used the optical device of the camera obscura to aid their rendering of light and perspective.

In the twenty-first century notable convergences are with mobile phone imaging, moving image and computer-generated imagery. As noted at the start of the chapter, amateur photography has proliferated the digital realm now and many of those images have been captured with the ubiquitous mobile phone camera (see Case Study 4, 'Digital and Mobile Phone Cultures', pp. 342–56). Photography has 'converged' with everyday life and the recording of banal daily activities to share via virtual social networks. How do we analyse this within an educational context? The subjective and personal converges with the technical, artistic and professional discourses of photography. This provides opportunities for theoretical debate and analysis that centre on the photo-album, domestic photography and the displacement of older social functions of the medium, such as the family album (see discussion of family albums in Chapter 1). This line of thought also opens up opportunities for counter-culture group formation, events co-ordination, evidence gathering and new ways of social networking.

Photographic convergence with moving image technology began with Muybridge over a century ago. Today most digital SLR cameras now allow the user to capture High Definition (HD) video in broadcast quality. Developments in the technology have widened the skill-set required for professional photographers. Many practitioners are adapting their workflow to take on extra moving image commissions. Mirroring this identity shift of what it means to be a photographer in industry, most photography departments now incorporate moving image within their curricula. Assignments may be set that allow the learner to make either still photographs or moving image work for the same brief. Photography students wishing to pursue moving image will require a more lateral approach to skills acquisition, by seeking out the required expertise within their institution from peers in the film and video department. This is a reminder that we are moving in the direction of what Anne Williams describes as the shift in photography degrees towards a multimedia approach across visual arts, media and design disciplines (Williams, 2009: 133). This convergence is expanding to include computer-generated imagery of simulated photo-real scenes.

Computer-generated imagery (CGI) and photography

At the other end of the technologies spectrum, and closer to the ideas of Fred Ritchin, should photography curricula cover the use of computer-generated imagery (CGI) and photography? Commercially

PHOTOGRAPHY EDUCATION

10.3 Richard Kolker, *Around a Bodegon – after Juan Sanchez Cotan 1602*, 2012. Courtesy of the artist.

within advertising photography CGI elements already dominate. The image included at the start of the chapter (fig. 10.1) is student work produced on one of the few degree courses in Europe to teach photography and CGI to an industry standard. The undergraduate design course at Georg Simon Ohm University of Applied Sciences, Nuremberg, is run by Professor Michael Jostmeier. His students choose a specialism in three out of ten possible disciplines including: CGI, photography, interactive media, graphic design, film and animation. The CGI module has achieved global recognition in 2006 and 2012 at *Photokina*, an international photography trade fair in Cologne.

Figure 10.3 shows a CGI image created by London College of Communication, MA Photography graduate Richard Kolker, who has used CGI software to create *Around a Bodegon – after Juan Sanchez Cotan 1602*. In the Spanish seventeenth-century still life painting tradition, a *bodegon* is set within the humble, everyday kitchen and is usually composed of items from the pantry. Here Kolker has created a piece that at first glance is difficult to categorize as painting, photography or computer-generated imagery. Kolker has made a whole series of images created with CGI techniques, many of which appear like photographs. The idea of photographic practice converging with CGI is discussed in more detail in Case Study 5, 'The Designed Photograph: Computer Generated Imagery (CGI) in Car Photography', in Part 4, pp. 357–68.

INFLUENCE: PHOTOGRAPHY AND CGI

Interview with Heike Lowenstein, a professional photographer and Course Leader for Photography at the University for the Creative Arts, Rochester, on incorporating CGI in UK photography courses, October, 2012.

What are the problems involved in teaching CGI to photography students (pedagogically, logistically and technically)?

A lot of photographers have barriers towards engaging with this CGI. It's partially the interfaces of the CGI software which is quite complex and also because they are attached to the physical artefact of photography. Photographers are not used to thinking in three dimensions but understand the two-dimensional paradigm of photography. I believe that this paradigm of photography is disappearing.

Some students have a resistance to learning about CGI. My response is to insist on a need to understand what is possible today with new technologies and photography. It changes the way we read images, and that will change the way your images are read, even if you are a traditional documentary photographer (if that role can still exist).

The CGI work necessitates working in teams. Replicating the need to work well in a team in the workplace within a university course is a pedagogic strategy. The range of skills levels within a group of students balances out as some of the group might have already had experience of CGI software within a previous college course. The tutor needs to facilitate all elements of group work making sure that everybody works together and learns from each other.

In terms of teaching, what you have in most universities and art colleges is some sort of course that uses three-dimensional technology. It could be computer games design, architecture or product design. Those colleagues that teach on those courses will have the skills of operating the 3D interface and you could exchange teaching hours to facilitate teaching CGI within a Photography degree. This is a way to overcome the technical and logistical hurdle in terms of teaching. What is important here is to acknowledge with all of these new technologies there is a learning curve not only for the students but for the educator too. The educator who wishes to embed these new technologies into their teaching must learn along with the students.

What are your thoughts on the more philosophical debates around the idea of 'post photography' in relation to CGI?

The nature of photography is changing. Imagine that in the future you'll be able to take a 3D scan of a scene, then later in the computer take a photograph of any part of that scene. There is something happening here which is a complete paradigm shift. The shift from photography of reality to CGI is having the same impact as the shift from painting to photography. We can now photograph things after the event and before they even exist, in their physical manifestation. This is a big shift. We are all aware that images are potentially manipulated from magazines and advertisements. But are we aware that 98% of car advertising is done this way? CGI is

PHOTOGRAPHY EDUCATION

creeping into our environment and it does change how we read images and how we interact with our world. It provides fantastic opportunities for both commercial photographers and photographic artists who work with collage and image manipulation. It's not that far away from what Jeff Wall has been doing all along, it just goes into a slightly different dimension. In some ways I would say provocatively the future of photography is three-dimensional.

Should we teach CGI alongside traditional photography?

It is still important to teach both sides of photography alongside each other, both analogue and new technologies. I believe photography courses work best when students are given a breadth of photography teaching, an overview approach. They can then specialize and use the technologies they want to engage with, if they are analogue or digital, virtual or physical. It's a student's choice, and part of their journey which educators are there to facilitate.

Online and Open Learning

In a growing trend, starting in the USA, some UK universities are offering online versions of their on-campus courses, although predominantly in business studies. In 2011, the University of Hertfordshire, hosted by the Interactive Design Institute, piloted an online version of its BA Photography course, with exactly the same structure as their on-campus course. There is also now a growing trend to offer short courses as open and free. These are known as MOOCs (Massively Open Online Courses). Students do not receive any credits from the university, but enrol to learn and be part of a learning online community. The biggest providers of MOOCs are North American institutions, notability Harvard, MIT, Stanford and Princeton. Professor Sebastian Thrun, at Stanford, ran the first MOOC with a truly massive reach. In 2011 he taught a module in artificial intelligence as an open course and 160,000 students, from over 190 countries, enrolled for free. MOOCs have since become big business for advertising revenue within the module websites.

The Khan Academy is another type of open education, created in 2006 by Harvard and MIT graduate Salman Khan. The Khan Academy website provides over 3,000 video lectures from school to university levels. Subjects include mathematics, science, medicine, history, humanities and business. This is a non-profit company that relies on donations and has a global studentship. Many schools have now incorporated the Khan Academy tutorial into their classroom sessions. This open education model has been trialled at Coventry University, within an undergraduate photography context.

In 2009, Jonathan Worth and Matt Johnston at Coventry University released two of their photography modules as open classes. 'Open' effectively means that anyone, anywhere with an Internet connection can take part in the modules. The modules are: 'Photography and Narrative', shortened to 'Phonar' and 'Picturing the Body', shortened to 'Picbod'. All students taking the modules, whether fee paying on campus or as 'open/non fee paying' online students, can connect via social networking, specifically on Twitter using specific 'hashtags' (keywords that allow users to search/tap into various groups/themes) to share images. The online students receive no accreditation from the university, or formal feedback on their work from Worth. However, the online students have full access to course content. This is the major draw for the course as Worth has persuaded industry specialists from around the world to take part in video lectures for the course.

In an interview with the authors Worth explained the rationale behind the open course module and online teaching methods. Here he explains the benefits of interacting with students both in the classroom and in the virtual environment:

> The nature of student and tutor contact has changed from a traditional 'office hours' model. If they've got a question generally they'll need feedback straight away. I communicate via social media environments like Twitter and email. If somebody needs a face-to-face virtual conversation we can use a 'Google Hangout' or Skype video call. This is a much better way for students to get instant feedback and advice. If the digital camera has taught us anything, it's that quick feedback makes you better.
>
> (Worth, October 2012)

Worth also described how the fee-paying students interact with 'open' non-fee paying students:

> The fee-paying students understand that they are getting a premium product. They understand that the people online are looking in but they don't take away my time. What they do in fact is become this enormous resource and a great audience, and the students in the class become the centre of this focus. This becomes one of Jeff Jarvis's virtuous circles: the students value the classroom experience even more, they up their game because they know people are watching, and the people online feed into them. They [the online audience] are a resource that I can interact with, for example asking: 'What do we think about this' or 'Who knows more about this than me'.
>
> (Worth, October 2012)

Strengths and Weaknesses of the Open Class Model

The open class model offers potential for increased recruitment of photography students and is good news for universities seeking to expand this provision. The model also provides evidence that widening access to students and creative use of the medium is occurring. On the other hand the displacement of concrete teaching and learning environments and loss of personal contact with staff and students is problematic. The issue of shared resources and social environment is endangered by economic rationalism and the encroachment of educational pragmatism. The hybrid model preferred by educationalists, including some of those mentioned above, allows technology to support the community rather than offering a substitute that displaces it. Open classes reflect changes in society, whereby access to knowledge has been democratized and the Internet has become the virtual home of a community of learners.

Transferable Skills and New Technology

Transferable skills are 'skills used in one job or career that can also be used in another' (*Cambridge Business English Dictionary*). Photography graduates have a wealth of transferable skills which often relate to new technology. Photography more so than other subjects in the arts and humanities is

PHOTOGRAPHY EDUCATION

technology-reliant and produces students with a high-level skill-set. It is a learning outcome that meets the perceived values and ideals of prospective employers and fulfils the vocational re-orientation of education in this century. The industry focus of government-directed initiatives and emphasis on training is evident in Creative Skillset. This is an organization which provides a list of transferable skills relevant to the photo-imaging sector. Some of these transferable skills include: interpersonal skills, business skills, time management, ICT (Information and Communications Technology), literacy, visual literacy and creativity.

Creative Skillset is an organization within the Skills Sector Council. Funded by industry and government, it sets a benchmark for standards and skills in the photo-Imaging sector. Its research places a strong emphasis on transferable skills, new technology and photography. Creative Skillset strategy document notes:

> ICT literacy is increasingly important for an industry now so reliant on digital technology. Basic knowledge of computers and electronic equipment, and of general office and creative software, serves as a foundation both for the use of digital technology and for the lifelong learning necessary to maintain up-to-date knowledge and skills.

> (Hirsch, n.d.: 36)

Skills in digital technology and other transferable skills are vital to succeed in the photography industry. The argument is straightforward enough and states the obvious point that technical competency is important. This point, however, is not new. Most photography courses worldwide have always given prominence to the technical aspects of the discipline. Photography has always had a technical status and in some ways this has held it back (see discussions in Chapters 7 and 9). Many questions are evaded in the rush to promote new technology and these are questions that belong in the intellectual community of photographers, historians and theorists. Such questions could include the following, and are discussed in further detail in Part 4: Beyond the Academy:

- How do technical advances relate to wider questions about authorship?
- How does online distribution influence how we think about the photographic image? Is the paper print redundant and who owns images in a digital economy?
- Has the art market reinstated the value of art photography? Is this a reactionary turn back to an earlier aesthetic model?
- Is manipulation of photographs in keeping with the best traditions of journalism?
- Is photography education protected from absorption into other practices and will its future be determined by commercial or academic interest?

Careers in Photography

There are many vocations closely connected with the photo-imaging sector, including specialist areas, such as fashion and advertising, teaching, research, gallery sales, and in-house photography roles in the cultural and heritage industries. This provides a wealth of possibilities for twenty-first-century photography graduates. Many of these vocations have been around for decades, if not from the start of photography, but new technologies afford a widening of access for entry-level opportunities. For example, those students who acquire skills in digital technology at university can begin by working as

NEW TECHNOLOGIES AND PHOTOGRAPHY EDUCATION

a digital operator on a studio shoot. The Digital Operator is a studio assistant who is responsible for the setup of high-end digital cameras on a shoot and ensures digital files are being shot and stored on the computer correctly. Often the digital operator will command a higher day rate than the photographer's assistant.

The issue of funding for courses and the match between the perceived needs of students and prospective trades and professions goes to the heart of contemporary debates on photography education. The old art school model of *laissez-faire* teaching and learning had its strengths and weaknesses. As we noted in the discussion in Chapter 7, above, that model was weak on theory but allowed gifted students space and time to find ways of working. The outcome was often original and provocative. The overall effect of this was, arguably, better than the purely training model that is being offered in some parts of photography education. The mix of theory, history and innovation in practical work is widespread in many institutions. The discussion now, for many observers in photography education, is how to preserve the best of existing provision whilst moving forward. The question is philosophical and requires sensitive and thoughtful consideration. See Chapters 11 and 12 for a discussion of photographers and the world of work.

Career Opportunities

(Skillset Photo Imaging Skills Strategy, 2006, 14)

Professional photography specialisms:

Social Photography – for recording events such as weddings or producing portraits

Schools Photography – for large group or high-volume individual portraiture

Advertising & Editorial – for describing products or ideas, or illustrating stories or reports

Fashion – for illustrating or advertising clothes and accessories

Corporate, Industrial & Commercial (*Architectural**) – for company brochures, annual reports, records or marketing

Medical, Forensic & Scientific – for producing accurate and objective images that are recorded for measurement or analysis

Press & Photojournalism – for recording events and the people involved

Photographic Art – for galleries, communal spaces or fine art sales

Aerial Photography – for mapping, commercial or public sector use

Related photography activities

Earning a living as a self-employed professional photographer is not always easy, and many – especially those who prefer to focus on their own artistic, rather than commercial, work – undertake additional related activities to increase their income. Common examples are:

Photographic Research – typically funded by universities

Lecturing – typically in Further and Higher Education

Public Art Photography – typically grant-funded

Gallery Sales – an incredibly difficult area to get into

Book Sales – often more of a loss leader to gain exposure than a way of making money

Local Arts Sales – selling prints through local art fairs, markets, galleries, with the Internet as a popular way of starting out

PHOTOGRAPHY EDUCATION

Community Arts Photography – typically funded by local authorities, hospitals and charities

Stock photography *

In-house photography roles:

Police Forces – forensic photography

The Medical Sector, including hospitals, dentists and organizations such as the Wellcome Trust – medical imaging

The Ministry of Defence and Armed Forces – a wide range including corporate communications, industrial and commercial, portraiture, police work and intelligence gathering

The Creative and Cultural Sectors, including museums and organizations such as English Heritage and the National Trust – documenting the historical and cultural record

Publishers (including newspapers and magazines) – illustrative and editorial photography, photojournalism and press photography

Academic and Research Institutions – scientific imaging

The Leisure Sector, such as cruise ships – social photography

Support roles to photographers or the photo imaging sector:

Photographer's assistant (photography, lighting, production, transport, etc.)

Picture library roles: manager, picture library assistant, picture researcher, digital imaging specialist, sales

Professional photography laboratory (pro lab) roles: production manager, digital imaging technician, film processing technician, print finisher, photographic printer

Photography studio assistant or studio manager *

Photographer's PA (marketing, admin, bookings) *

Photographer's agent *

Digital Operator (studio assistant who is responsible for high-end digital cameras and monitors digital files) *

Digital retoucher/artist, 2D (Photoshop) or 3D (CGI software, such as Maya) *

Picture framer and mounter *

Web designer *

Magazine, newspaper and book publishing support roles: picture editor, picture researcher, graphic designer *

Archivist (analogue and digital) *

Gallery roles: curator, print sales, installation, education *

Photography Technician – in an educational institution *

Photography retail sales and professional hire *

* Italicized entries added by authors

New Types of Vocational Photography Degrees

Earlier we discussed some practical examples of how new technology impacts on pedagogy. We have signalled a slow drift towards technology-based approaches. In some educational institutions changes have occurred that are not merely technical but represent a change in the aims and objectives of courses; for example changes in the ethos of some photography courses from art-based to 'industry-facing' vocational courses. In the UK context a two-year Foundation Degree in Art (FdA),

NEW TECHNOLOGIES AND PHOTOGRAPHY EDUCATION

including the subject specialism of photography, was developed in 2001. This provided a new type of vocational qualification. This transition may be typical of broad changes in higher education in which critical skills are minimized. The struggle for an inclusive theory-enriched photographic education is therefore, it seems, in danger of replacement by more of a technical training approach to learning. This is a changing scenario in which the literate and engaged student with technical and intellectual skills is to become extinct. Most photography courses of distinction originated in art colleges or arts faculties in universities. Such courses struggled to sustain balanced critical and vocational learning objectives. The biggest challenge, however, in photography education is to retain independent status as an area of creative educational provision. The irony of this prospective change to educational functionalism is that it comes at a time when photography has become a fertile area of philosophical discourse with new journals springing up as the medium spreads itself across the art world. The art world is not a solution either and yet it provides the recognition the subject needs for academic survival.

Photographic Education and New Technologies TIMELINE

A timeline showing the key developments in photography education, photography technology and general global technological milestones.

	Education	Photography	Technology
1826		First photograph made – a 'heliograph' By Joseph Nicéphore Niépce.	
1835		First paper negative – The Lattice Window by Henry Fox Talbot	
1839	The Royal Polytechnic (which became University of Westminster) was the first UK institution to teach photography, and in 1841 opened the first photographic studio in Europe	Daguerreotype	
1842		English scientist and astronomer John Herschel invents cyanotype process	
1876			Telephone invented – Alexander Graham Bell
1878		Eadweard Muybridge's *The Horse in Motion,* forerunner of motion pictures	
1901		Kodak Brownie camera and roll film invented – Photography available to the 'masses'	
1903			First manned flight

PHOTOGRAPHY EDUCATION

	Education	Photography	Technology
1920s	First undergraduate degree in Photography at the Royal Polytechnic		
1925			TV introduced to public by John Logie Baird
1948		Polaroid Land camera	
1950s		First photograph used in an advertisement	
1957		First drum scanner – Russell A. Kirsch	
1964			Programma 101: first commercial desktop computer
1971	Open University begins		
1972	First chair in the history of photography at Princeton University		
1975		First digital camera invented by Kodak	
1982			Internet invented (not a publicly usable service until 1991)
1984			First Macintosh home computer with GUI
1987	Open College of Arts starts		
			First commercially available mobile phone
1990		Version 1 of Photoshop released	Hubble Space Telescope launched
1991		First commercially available digital SLR camera: Kodak DCS-100	World Wide Web available as a public service on the Internet
1992			First photograph uploaded to the World Wide Web.
1994		First consumer digital compact camera	
1995			Lynda.com – online software tuition videos
2000		Show Studio – Fashion Film website. New era for fashion photography	

NEW TECHNOLOGIES AND PHOTOGRAPHY EDUCATION

	Education	Photography	Technology
2001		First camera phone J-SH04, made by Sharp, released by J-Phone in Japan	
2001	FDAs in photography, industry facing		
2004		Kodak ceases production of film cameras	Facebook
2006	Khan academy – free online tutorials for school children		Twitter
2007			iPhone
2008		Polaroid ceases film production	
2008		Digital SLR hybrid Video HD (Nikon D90)	Broadsheet newspapers release online daily versions
2009	Coventry University releases to modules online as 'Open' courses: Pic bod and Phonar (see page 000)	Tate Gallery appoint first Curator of Photographs	iPad – tablet
2012	152 colleges and universities in the UK run undergraduate photography courses	250 million photos uploaded daily to Facebook	

CONCLUSION

The long struggle for academic respectability has largely been won. Photography is unique in many ways, as a large percentage of graduates will find employment within the photo-imaging sector or related creative industries. The career route is well mapped and available for students aspiring to the media industries. The old craft-based model of teaching and learning is no longer running effectively and yet technology is an expensive and unwieldy solution to the big questions in photography education. Short courses and technical training have much to be said in their favour but the well-rounded full-time programme still benefits students and has fostered high levels of scholarly and artistic work. Specialist courses offer opportunities as well but the overriding factor, arguably, in all areas is the need to sustain commitment to innovation and scholarly achievement. Without this photography is utilitarian and dull.

The rise in tuition fees and the expensive running costs in photography may drive students towards courses that advertise job potentiality. The trend to make courses vocational may be a worthy objective and it is an important consideration. This is not, however, an argument for an educational way forward more generally. Industry has its own resources for training young people and its needs belong to different areas of social debate. A good educational philosophy makes graduates employable because they have knowledge, skills and social attributes. It is hard to point towards a method or idea that fits all courses in photography but, arguably, the training academy is not the way to go. The theory-practice

295

PHOTOGRAPHY EDUCATION

dualism has been replaced in progressive photography everywhere. The future for photography courses is constantly evolving, encompassing new debates, new opportunities for dissemination and convergence with other disciplines.

SUMMARY OF KEY POINTS

- Photography education now is experiencing a period of change, adapting to encompass new related convergence technologies such as moving image and CGI.
- Wide-ranging philosophical debates have been raised throughout this chapter: what is the future of photography? Are we in a post-photographic era? Is education driven by the perceived need to keep up with technology?
- Digital imaging has been pitched against traditional darkroom teaching as a return to specialist craft skills in the face of technical determinism.
- As an important new trend virtual teaching space encourages the use of student research blogs and open courses in photography.
- The need for transferable skills is important in relation to Creative Skillset and the plurality of careers available to photography graduates.
- Vocational approaches to photography education provide an economic rationale for training academies that will not serve the best long-term interests of students.

REFERENCES

Cambridge Business English Dictionary, [online] Available at: <http://dictionary.cambridge.org/dictionary/business-english/transferable-skills?q=transferable+skills> (accessed: 13.09.2012).

Campbell, David (2013) 'Afterword: Abundant Photography, Discursive Limits and the Work of images', in Alexandra Moschovi, Carol McKay and Arabella Plouviez (eds) *The Versatile Image*, Leuven: Leuven University Press, pp. 265–270.

Hirsch, Jonathan (n.d.), 'Skillset Photo Imaging Skills Strategy', in *The Sector Skills Council for the Audio Visual Industries.* Available at: http://www.creativeskillset.org/uploads/pdf/asset_7722.pdf?1 (accessed: 13.09.2012).

Lister, Martin (1995) *The Photographic Image in Digital Culture*, London and New York: Routledge.

Manovich, Lev (2003) 'The Paradoxes of Digital Photography' in Liz Wells (ed.) *The Photography Reader*, London and New York: Routledge, pp. 240–249.

Mitchell, William J. (1992) *The Reconfigured Eye: Visual Truth in the Post-Photographic Era.* Cambridge, MA: MIT Press.

Ritchin, Fred (2009) *After Photography*, London and New York: W.W. Norton & Company.

Robins, Kevin (1995) 'Will Image Move Us Still?', in Martin Lister (ed.) (1995) *The Photographic Image in Digital Culture*, London and New York: Routledge, pp. 29–50.

Rubinstein, Daniel (2009) 'Towards Photographic Education', in *Photographies*, vol. 2, no. 2, pp. 135–142.

Williams, Anne (2009) 'Identity Crisis' in *Photographies*, vol. 2, no. 2, pp. 125–133.

Worth, Jonathan (2012) 'Coventry University: Opening Up the BA Hons. Photography Course', Available at: http://www.jisc.ac.uk/whatwedo/topics/opentechnologies/openeducation/coventry-university.aspx (accessed 13.09.12).

PART 4
BEYOND THE ACADEMY

INTRODUCTION

In this part of the book we extend the discussion of photography beyond the academy and focus more closely on the world of work. As we have noted in the chapters on photography education, courses in photography provide a mix of aesthetic and technical training that privileges interest in how photographs are made and how they look. The question of 'how images make meaning' (Rose, 2007: 74) has centred on what some theorists consider to be a scientific method for the study of signs called semiology. The semiological approach underlines the persuasive influence of images and yet spectators are sometimes resistant or indifferent to the message; what they bring to the image and their particular usage of it may be more revealing than the stereotype it presents. The relative power of images forms a key debate in the academy but it is also limiting. The cultural theorist Paul Frosh, for example, has strongly criticized the 'surprising absence of research on commercial and advertising photography'. The study of this field, he claims, is limited to 'textual (usually semiotic) analyses of advertisements or other cultural "texts", with little or no reference to the ways in which advertising images were manufactured' (Frosh, 2003: 3).

Frosh and other recent writers on photography have sought to extend the debate beyond the academic study of individual images. A narrow interest in photography as an independent technology has evaded its compliant use of Internet and mobile telephones. The 'everyday use of photography' (Larson and Sandbye, 2014: xxi) challenges the traditional borders between amateur and professional practices. In some ways this is consistent with established fields of recreational and personal photography centred on studies of the family album (Spence and Holland, 1991), tourism and friendship photography (Larsen and Sandbye, 2014). The two case studies in Part 4 of this book, in their different ways, address these issues. The family album is also discussed in Chapter 1.

We now talk about photography as an instant method of visualizing events for immediate dissemination. A mobile-phone image is a message for immediate use rather than something to be saved and, importantly, is often made by non-specialist, self-taught photographers, whose work may (in particular circumstances) be upgraded to news media or other widely accessible sites. Digital photography's impact on social behaviour and artistic meaning is addressed in Case Study 4: 'Digital and Mobile Phone Cultures'. We also include a case study that questions how far computer generated imagery (CGI) has displaced 'real' photography in car advertising. The study considers the displacement of traditional roles in photography and the perceived need for new skill-sets and possibly new definitions of the practice (see Case Study 5: 'The Designed Photograph: Computer Genererated Imagery (CGI) in Car Photography'.)

In the first chapter in this section, 'Photography, Advertising and Consumer Cultures', we discuss photographic advertising as a professional practice poised between art and commerce. Photographers will recognize the ambiguities of a world that confuses media demands with artistic aims. The splitting of the photographic identity between what appear to be disparate zones of social meaning is a key factor in these chapters. The study begins with a discussion of early commercial applications of photography and the close connections between progressive and experimental artists, designers and photographers in the inter-war period (1919–39). Modern art and advertising shared a sense of progressive idealism in the 1920s. Photography's potential for mass communication corresponded with ascendant technocratic ideals of the period.

Pioneers of modernist photography in the inter-war period saw themselves as contributors to a democratic and progressive social order. Experimental and creative innovation seemed to be well suited to the market for goods directed at enlightened consumers. Ideas promoted by progressive art educational institutions, most notably the German Bauhaus, confirmed this utopian outlook: progressive aestheticism was thought to be inherently good. That is to say: good for business and good for art. It was a view that carried some weight in the 1920s and set the pattern for later theorists of the so-called creative economies emerging in the late twentieth century.

The fact that photographers direct their skills towards lucrative employment comes as no surprise. The various levels of achievement in this field range from high-end photographic assignments with big name photographers employed on expensive campaigns. At the other extreme the massive growth of stock photography tells another story. In the chapter 'Photography and the Creative Economy' we diagnose the socio-economic imperatives against a background of artistic and cultural ambition. We also seek to throw light on the way photography (alongside art, fashion and popular music) has been inducted into the technocratic ideologies of the current period. John Hartley, a cultural critic, notes the emergence of a 'creative class' that will 'dominate economic and cultural life in the century to come' (Hartley, 2005: 2). In a similar vein the theorist Richard Florida describes a casual ambience in which 'creatives' – 'dressed in relaxed and casual clothes' – ease themselves into the 'no-collar' workplace (cited in Hartley, 2005: 2). Old-fashioned job security, Florida claims, is abandoned in favour of creative autonomy. The new breed of artistic innovator accepts risk as part of the deal. In the chapter 'Photography and the Creative Economy' we discuss the work environment, short-term contracts, and the social experience of 'portfolio' careers in the creative industries.

Frosh, Paul (2003) *The Image Factory: Consumer Culture, Photography and the Visual Content Industry*, Oxford and New York: Berg.

Hartley, John (2005) *Creative Industries*, Oxford: Blackwell.

INTRODUCTION

Larsen, Jonas and Sandbye, Mette (2014) *Digital Snaps: The New Face of Photography*, London and New York: I.B. Tauris.

Rose, Gillian (2007) *Visual Methodologies: An Introduction to the Interpretation of Visual Materials*, London, Thousand Oaks, New Delhi: Sage.

—— (2014) 'How Digital Technologies Do Family Snaps, Only Better', in Larsen and Sandbye.

Spence, Jo and Holland, Patricia (eds) (1991) *Family Snaps: The Meaning of Domestic Photography*, London: Virago.

CHAPTER 11
PHOTOGRAPHY, ADVERTISING AND CONSUMER CULTURES

This is a magazine advertisement published in the 1950s. It is highly conventional in style and content. The roman typeface gives the image a traditional look and the copy reads from left to right like a feature article. It is obviously a strongly gendered message. As a lifestyle image it links the product with glamour ('This delicate complexion glamour') and allurement (achieved within seconds). The naturalism of the photograph (note the intimacy of the close up) corresponds with the 'fresh, young, natural look' the advertisement promises.

In design terms the ad has no rakish angles or expressive lighting effects. It shows no taste for modernist influences in photography. It is a typical mainstream ad from this period. The model was more than likely posing for a professional photographer specializing in fashion advertising. The photographer and the designers are anonymous.

INTRODUCTION

This chapter focuses on the part played by photography in advertising. We evaluate how advertising, as an industry, relates to the career aspirations of its prospective workforce. We locate the discussion in an historical

11.1 Max Factor's creamy Pan-Stik make-up, 1950s. Image courtesy of The Advertising Archives.

framework that demonstrates the tensions between the artistic aims of photographers and the demands of a medium designed to sell things. The chapter shows how changing historical circumstances relate to changing approaches and brings the debate up to date in a conclusion that assesses the role of photography in contemporary consumer culture.

BEYOND THE ACADEMY

Commodity Aesthetics

Selling things is the main objective of most advertising practices. It is also a vehicle of social communication and works in tandem with a huge range of media resources. Indeed, it is often said that advertising not only appears in other media (the press, broadcast media, and the Internet) but finances them as well. In its choice of subject matter and the visual codes it commonly uses, advertising is closely connected with other cultural practices. For example it shares with popular cinema recognition of social interest in narratives of romance, family life, security and pleasure. Advertising and cinema both rely on realist techniques of storytelling that derive from popular fiction and early radio drama. The style and content of mass media forms of entertainment have had a strong influence on illustrated ads centred on home comforts and family life. Photography's famous truth-telling functions make it an invaluable tool of persuasion and this 'realist' imperative makes it highly suited to advertising's marketing and public service functions.

Photography's connection with kindred arts of painting and illustration was important but in the twentieth century it became closely wedded to graphic design and copywriting in industrial settings. Work carried out by illustrators was taken over by photographers in the early decades of the twentieth century. By the 1930s advertising had become a huge industry increasingly dependent on the skills of photographers. From this period onwards it was a key element in the creative parts of modern advertising practice (Lupton and Miller, 2006: 121).

Photographic Modernism and Advertising

In changing historical circumstance the question of individual talent and artistic ambition remains an important issue not least because this is often the motivation for individuals entering a profession that draws on this whilst exploiting it for commercial ends. The reader might note that social attitudes have changed as artists (including photographers) readily cross the boundaries between art and commerce in an environment where snobbish distinctions have been replaced by creative labour markets that ignore the old hierarchies of 'high' and 'low' culture. This freewheeling attitude was not, however, a new phenomenon. Already by the 1920s, artists (including photographers) were beginning to accept commission work for glossy magazines. The case of the American photographer Edward Steichen is often used to illustrate this point. He was closely connected with Alfred Stieglitz's pioneering art-photography journal, *Camera Work* and the Photo-Secession (an avant-garde group of art photographers in New York). Steichen turned to commercial work for fashion journals including *Vogue* and *Vanity* Fair (fig. 11.2), and was contracted to the well-established and famous advertising agency J. Walter Thomson in 1923 (Johnston, 1997). His example stimulated the trend for 'art photographers' to cross over to rewarding sectors which allowed artistic freedom and paid well. Apologists for creative advertising celebrate this connection and in many ways the old divisions survive and still impact on people working in advertising and the creative industries.

In Figure 11.2 we see the first *Vogue* cover printed in colour. The modernist aesthetic of geometrical simplicity and low viewpoint enhance its photographic effect. As this example demonstrates aesthetic value is not restricted to high culture or limited by traditional categories of taste and appreciation. Good popular culture (including advertising culture) wins justifiable praise and can rise above prosaic

304

market functions. The histories of photography have stressed the technical and aesthetic interactions with other media and some have noted the way alliances with painting and the graphic arts have opened up the prospect for a convergence of these practices. There have been cross-over trends between applied practices such as advertising and documentary merged with art photography in the avant-garde and progressive periodical publications that emerged in the 1920s.

Photography was little used in nineteenth-century advertising except in rare examples of photographs on trade cards and small half-tone reproduction in sales catalogues. Before the invention of the halftone process in the 1880s (see box on pp. 71–73) photographs were pasted into printed documents (mainly books). Huge efforts had been made to print photographs (alongside type) on printing presses without success. The half-tone block made this possible and revolutionized visual communication. Advertisers and newspaper editors quickly saw the commercial possibilities of photographic reproducibility. Its prospects for a new way of reaching large audiences emerged with photographically illustrated publications and other printed products in the 1920s and 1930s.

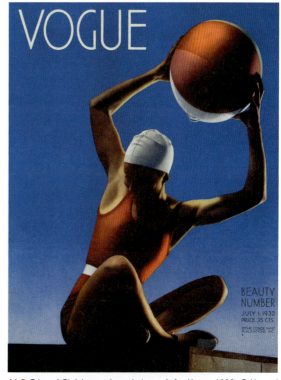

11.2 Edward Steichen, colour photograph for *Vogue*, 1932. © Vogue/Edward Steichen/Condé Nast.

Economic growth and improved distribution of goods led to the expansion of advertising in the 1920s. A mixture of consumer demand and new print technology helped to create a market for periodicals, retail catalogues and popular mass-circulation magazines. A shift in advertising psychology allowed consumers to be seen as suggestive to the creation of 'atmosphere' and social drama in a way that invites a comparison with similar tropes in pulp fiction and new media forms such as radio soap opera in the USA. Earlier advertising put emphasis on the 'reason why' a product should be purchased ('it is good for you, healthy, etc.'), proclaiming the real or imagined merits of a product. This was gradually changed by artists working with inventive photographers. Greater emphasis was now placed on the social context of consumption and the abstract and symbolic meaning of products begins to displace interest in their utility (Leiss, Klein and Jhally, 1997: 155). Ideas were codified in text and the choice of subject. Attractive and well-dressed figures denoting levels of social status and desirability surrounded the product. Sensuality and elegance of form conspired with laconic advertising copy. Lighting, camera position and the thoughtful use of visual effects was used to enhance the imaginary engagement and pleasures of looking. The deployment of visual codes explored in the early years of silent cinema – where image was of paramount importance – has parallels with the photographic innovations in some of the high-end advertisement for luxury products in the 1920s (fig. 11.3). The products shown in this image demonstrate a modernist sensibility directed towards a growing, fashion-conscious middle class consumer.

New camera techniques, inventive use of white space, modern-looking typefaces, and expressive layouts in book design, periodicals and posters were widely used across a range of commercial publications.

11.3 Anton Bruehl, *Art Deco Tobacco Jar, Pitcher, and Inkwell*, c. 1929. Condé Nast Archive/Corbis.

The employment of East European émigrés such as Martin Munkacsi and Alexey Brodovich revolutionized the look of the American fashion journals such as *Harper's Bazaar*. Using a hand-held Leica camera, the photographer Munkacsi achieved dynamic-looking figures in outdoor locations (Meggs, 1992: 315). The desire to create a sense of flow between text and pictures created a sense of movement that echoed the vibrancy of the modern city. This was a departure from the older ads in which the photograph sits above the text as if it were merely an accompaniment to the written message. In Anton Bruehl's photograph we may note the affinity between the appearance of fashionable consumer durables and new appraches to photography. Both trends typify the aesthetic ideals of the period.

Many of the photographers identified in the key histories of photographic modernism were part of a cultural elite closely connected with avant-garde art. Some of them contributed to the most advanced and forward-looking movements of the period. Photography and advertising were widely considered democratic practices which allowed artists to extend their work beyond the narrow sphere of easel painting and gallery art. The proliferation of new photo-journals connected with urban living in the early part of the century exemplifies this broadening of the field of high culture and the enthusiasm for artistic innovation, which had a wide appeal and marks the advance of international design and modernism in advertising (Sobieszek, 1988: 32)

Avant-garde artistic techniques adapted by designers and photographers included sharp focus, close ups, dynamic viewpoint, oblique angles, geometrical staging devices, raking light and dramatic shadows. Inventive camerawork corresponded with innovation in graphic design including off-centred layout, sans serif typefaces and striking, expressive use of white space, departures from the conventions of horizontal typesetting and centred composition. The graphic styles of the period were determined by radically new cut-and-paste methods of construction (derived from Cubist and Dada collage) making print media look radically different from the horizontal type and bookish illustrational conventions of the past.

In Figure 11.4 we see the cover of a book by Werner Gräff. It is a manual on how to execute close ups and other pictorial methods associated with the New Vision – a term used in the 1920s to denote optimism in Western societies before the Depression of the 1930s. The period is reshaped by the huge development of large-scale mass production, especially in the USA. It is also reshaped by a changing political landscape in which revolution in Russia had created the world's first workers' state. In the western world production of consumer goods intensified alongside advertising aimed at restless

PHOTOGRAPHY, ADVERTISING AND CONSUMER CULTURES

> **KEY TERM: The New Vision**
> The belief in photography as a new mode of vision was expressed in the 1920s. Progressives in the visual arts embraced photography as a way of extending human perception. Advances in printing technology and photo-reproducibility reinforced the prospects for new types of graphic media which incorporated the photograph with new styles of typography. Books, posters, handbills, pamphlets began to include photographs with a range of exciting new elements. These included sharp focus, close ups, dynamic viewpoint, oblique angles, geometrical staging devices, raking light and dramatic shadows. Inventive camerawork corresponded with innovation in graphic design including off-centred bold, sans serif typefaces and striking, expressive use of white space, departure from the conventions of horizontal typesetting. The emphasis on formal simplicity had an affinity with hard-edged abstract art emerging in this period.

11.4 Werner Gräff, *Es kommt der neue Fotograf (Here Comes the New Photographer)*, 1929. Courtesy of the Manhattan Rare Book Company.

audiences. The democratic shift towards the idea that good design (including good advertising) would serve all social classes did not, however, extend beyond this period.

The classic concept of artistic and political idealists marching side by side defines the highest social aims of the modern movement. The democratization of art would be achieved in the deployment of new media that would serve the needs of enlightened and progressive societies. Optimistic philosophies of this kind pre-dated the international economic collapse of 1929, the rise of National Socialism in Germany, and the hardening of Soviet Dictatorship. The historical catastrophes of the 1930s militated against the ideals of social-minded aesthetic ideas. Hope for the spread of an enlightened 'art for the people' was short-lived but its aesthetic properties were applied in later modes of visual culture.

The socialist principles embedded in some key aspects of European modernism were largely ignored or traduced in the corporate cultures of the mid-twentieth century. In the USA the tendency was to adopt the 'look' of modernism rather than its political ideals (Jobling and Crowley, 1996: 160; Solomon-Godeau, 1997: 52–84). The American historian Robert A. Sobieszek observes:

> To be fair, early modernist advertising in America, with its unthinking appropriations from Futurist or Cubist painting and graphics, was a passing fashion and not a serious threat. Nevertheless, what had been effected during the twenties was the permanent vitalization of advertising photography as a modern art form – progressive, intelligent, and in tune with international exchange of cultural influence.
>
> (Sobieszek, 1988: 33)

BEYOND THE ACADEMY

The idea of modern art as a *threat* is instructive. The political tone of European modernism, it seems, was not suited to the conservatism of the American establishment in the post-war period. This partly explains a return to a more traditional style of representation in advertising and other media in the 1950s.

11.5 Magazine advertisement for Kodachrome film, 1940s. Courtesy of The Advertising Archives.

New Naturalism and the Photograph

The 'new naturalism' in the content and style of advertising in the USA is linked with the influence of domestic themes in radio drama and the mood of the country at a time of economic depression in the 1930s. The realistic depiction of the 'ordinary' is reflected in family values and tradition (fig. 11.5).

Note the rich, tonal quality and lustrous hair of the bride and groom in Figure 11.5. Note also the absence of modernist 'photo-graphic' design thinking and a return to traditional image/text division in the layout of the image. The return to aesthetic conservatism in advertising denotes a widening of marketing strategies to reach audiences outside and beyond educated urban elites. This shift towards a more accessible and user-friendly photographic style in advertising parallels the rise of documentary photography. The latter appears as a distinct category at a time when photographic journals were part of a growing market for the portrayal of the everyday social life. Journals such as *Life,* in the USA, and *Picture Post*, in Britain, allowed for the production of cheap publications for mass consumption. In many ways the social themes in documentary produced a powerful sense of social identity for social groups that had never occupied a place of any distinction in the arts. This applies most conspicuously to working-class subjects who are made to seem an integral part of modern, democratic life.

The cultural theorist Stuart Hall praised the radical use of social realist photo-essays in *Picture Post* (in Britain, 1938–1957) informing a new kind of social vision (Hall, 1972). Instead of seeking to evolve the interests of consumer capitalism, *Picture Post* endorsed community values, rather than consumption. The historian Paul Rennie has written about Second World War safety posters as a 'socially progressive, politically engaged, mass produced and widely distributed form of graphic communication'. It was, he claims, the kind of legitimate use of new media by 'ordinary people to effect social change' heralded by the German Marxist critic Walter Benjamin in the 1930s (Rennie, 2004; Benjamin, 2009). Hall's comments on *Picture Post* and Rennie's view of safety posters (fig. 11.6) are framed by a sense of community values rather than consumption. Using similar strategies the commercial medium of advertising also seeks to persuade its audience 'to think and act in a particular way and for a particular persuasive purpose' (Welch, 2013: 2). The strategy is one that relies on easily understandable messages presented in a way that looks natural and in keeping with an established taste. Arguably *Picture Post* and wartime safety posters are more worthy than advertisements for luxury goods. Nevertheless, they both seek to persuade and arrive at their objectives in similar way.

Making it Believable: 'Story Appeal' and the Photographic Ad

Rising prosperity, especially in the USA, in the period after the Second World War secured the conditions for the growth of advertising agencies. The dominant style of print ads inclined towards middlebrow taste for story-telling narratives, sensuality and dramatic licence. These are aesthetic methods that connect it with the growing media and leisure industries. The authors Leiss, Kline and Jhally have noted how this shift is crucially dependent on visual media:

> The introduction of photography led to a greater emphasis on people and settings, thus preparing the ground for new dimensions of symbolic reference … As the emphasis moves from the efficacy of the product to the *personal consequences of consumption*, the advertising designer can explore the drama of consumer satisfaction rather than the prosaic facts of the product's effectiveness.
>
> (Leiss, Kline and Jhally, 1997: 279–280; emphasis added)

11.6 RoSPA World War II safety poster, 'Protect your eyes'. Designed by Manfred Reiss and G. R. Morris, 1942. Courtesy of Paul and Karen Rennie Collection.

The 'personal consequences of consumption' is a phrase that underlines the importance of emotional response to the advertising message. The illusory ideals of symbolic power (invested in the look of things) and the promise of things to come were represented in fashionable dress codes, attractive locations, relaxed body language and playfulness. The shift towards the *meaning* of the product, rather than its performance or utility, was connected to social perceptions and anxieties. The shift to lifestyle advertising is closely connected with the idea of socially identifiable groups or 'consumption tribes' and this was increasingly reflected, from the 1960s onwards, in new theories about consumers and pronouncements on how advertising works. The advertising figurehead David Ogilvy noted:

> The kind of photographs which work hardest are those which arouse the reader's curiosity. He glances at the photograph and says to himself, 'What goes on here?' He then reads your copy to find out. Harold Rudolph [author of *Attention and Interest Factors in Advertising*, 1947] called this

BEYOND THE ACADEMY

magic element 'Story Appeal,' and demonstrated the more of it you inject into your photograph, the more people look at your advertisements.

(Ogilvy, 1983: 76)

The capacity for the photographic advertisement to suggest narrative readings is a central factor in its arsenal of visual effects. Narrative is a story and storytelling is common to time-based media such as drama, novels, television shows and so forth. Narrative meaning relies on a sense of time unfolding and yet the photographic image is still. It is a frozen moment but is not limited by this. As soon as it enters the world of meaning (as soon as it is seen), it relates to an imaginary structure of events 'before' and 'after' the shutter release. This allows for a narrative reading that might be aided by the headline and copy that accompanies it. A photographic representation of a young, attractive woman applying makeup to her face invites a conventional reading not so different to 'soap opera' versions of the same subject. The more pictorial trends that emerge in the mainstream advertisements of the post-war period rely heavily on narrative reading of the text (fig. 11.1).

The illusionistic look of the photograph is adeptly used in this kind of ad in a manner that will appeal to readers of magazines. The photo-ad is often seen alongside editorial pictures and the similarity in content is important. The narrative meaning and substance of essays and articles is absorbed by adjacent advertising material in a continuous line of visual meanings. Words provide anchorage and guide the reading when the image has aroused curiosity. Humour, surrealism and conventional embodiments of beauty or masculinity are often used. Pictures of children are widely used because they symbolize caring and deeper feelings about future life. The famous art director Henry Wolff notes how the

> ...photograph became an ideal tool for making believable representations quickly and inexpensively. The inference was that since the object had been in front of the camera to be photographed the camera could not lie. The photograph thus became *the* believable image.

(Wolff, 1988: 14)

'*The* believable image' clearly privileges the photograph as the transparent window that does the job of telling the audience something, convincingly, or making fantasy realistic. The integration of image and text in the ad connect the format with ancient manuscripts and illustrated typographic books of the past. The latter were often religious documents in which the pictorial offered an imaginative rendering of its subject. In saying this we are stating two aspects of the picture: its factual meaning (man, women, home interior etc.), and its expressive meaning. The former is closely connected with language (the linguistic message in the copy) and the latter is to a degree guided by what the photographer or the art director brings to it (Panofsky, 1970: 55–56).

Photography as a Defining Practice in Print Advertising

We have argued that advertising was strengthened by its connections with the modern movement in the arts. Innovation in the crossover practices such as painting, graphic design and typography ensured that advertising kept pace with other aspects of the visual arts. We have also said that much of this remains an essential aspect of its aesthetic outlook and evidence of these influences informs the practice at the level of visual presentation. We have also noted how photography became the defining practice in print

PHOTOGRAPHY, ADVERTISING AND CONSUMER CULTURES

media and the main vehicle for the lifestyle-oriented narratives used in mainstream advertising. Critics take the view that mainstream cultural forms such as these are essentially conservative in the sense of reproducing fixed ideas about social life.

It has been suggested that photographic ads often seem to make claims (such as the generalized notion of the vanity of women) that would not be acceptable in words. Insofar as the photographic image functions as an 'open text' it is available for interpretation. The ad's meaning is undoubtedly circum-scribed by the framing power of the context in which it is presented, the glossy magazine format or the billboard, and yet photographs allow some room for interpretation. It is a more open text (compared with linguistic text) and the viewer can playfully interpret what it means. The theorist Paul Messaris argues that the relative indeterminacy of the photograph 'plays a central part in processes of visual persuasion … in ads this "deficiency" is one of its strengths' (Messaris, 1997: xiii). In other words the photograph's openness, and its ability to say what the copy fails to say, helps to sell the product. This argument underlines the spectator's strong reaction to imagery where sexuality, visual puns or humour disguise its real aim: to establish contact with the reader.

Capturing the appearance of a 'real person' the realistic photograph elicits an emotional response. In the mind of the reader a psychological predisposition is linked with the product (Messaris, 1997: vii). The truth effect is reinforced by the photographic proof that something (possibly staged) actually happened. Indeed, as with pornography, the pleasure of the staging is, arguably, the main attraction. The aesthetic code of realism is a central factor in market segment advertising. Youth culture was an important segment and consumption of new products such as vinyl records, concert tickets, fashionable clothes, fast food and holidays led to a massive growth in packaging, graphic products and advertising that targeted young people. The socialist outlook of the high modernist photography and design had, by the 1950s, largely disappeared.

The highly personalized and expressive work of the action painters for example was a riposte to commercial cultures and repudiation of photographic realism. In the late 1950s and early 1960s Pop art emerged as an antidote to the high seriousness of the Expressionists. Artists such as Richard Hamilton created collages that seem to make ironic reference to films and advertising. Art and advertising had converged once more but this time the mix was more like a playful overlap. In this sense it had no connection with the political hopes of the earlier modernists' aim of combining fine art principles with commercial and industrial design.

Pop Art and the Advertising Image

Pop art was primarily a new trend in painting that took its material from popular culture. Its detractors called it 'copy cat' art and yet, arguably, it addressed the nature of the photograph as an inescapable part of present-day reality. The preoccupation with visual properties of the photograph, the mechanical and glossy shine of its printed surface and its democratic availability made it interesting for artists attracted to its commonplace look and everyday associations. The collaboration between the Beatles and the fashion photographer Robert Freeman resulted in the *With the Beatles* album of 1963.This project, and many like it, underlined the prospects for media interactions that seemed positive for the growing ranks of art school graduates seeking employment in the creative industries (fig. 11.7). Freeman's work has 'retro' qualities that recall the portrait photography of the Victorian photographer Margaret Cameron. The

BEYOND THE ACADEMY

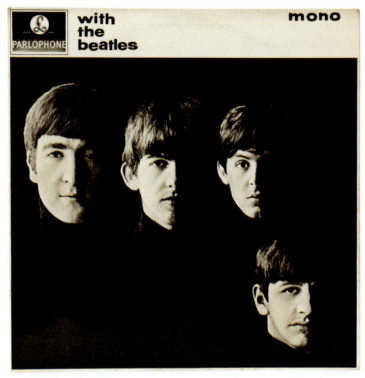

11.7 Robert Freeman (photographer), *With the Beatles*, long playing record sleeve, 1963. © Marc Tielemans/Alamy.

'artistic' reference mixes freely with the contemporary feel of the music. Similarly the Beatles' *Sergeant Pepper* album also has 'retro' Edwardian style. Pop celebrated youth culture but, unlike modernism, it sometimes looked back.

The enormous success of Pop art as an art world phenomenon is in need of explanation. It was closely aligned with the demonized forms of mass culture. It appropriated the kitsch products of capitalist serialized production methods and yet it seemed ironic and critical of the affluent society developing in Western economies after the Second World War. It had in many ways the anarchic pretensions of rock music and seemed to present a challenge to the great divide between elevated form of cultural consumption and the less exalted kinds that lay outside it. For audiences that had grown up with commercial television, cheap-but-stylish clothing, packaged food, and improved standards of living Pop seemed to be a strategy in a taste war between the old and new. It was, in short, a democratic turn in a world of intellectual and artistic elites that seemed, to those in the know, related to the activism of the pre-war Dadaists and Surrealists, and shared their enthusiasm for the camera and the dazzling visual effects of montage. The use of unexpected combinations such as the fur-lined cup and saucer (Meret Oppenheim, 1936) or the soft sculptures of Claes Oldenburg in the 1960s, the use of words in pictures, vivid colour, humour, explicit sexuality, represent some aspects of the kind of visual codes used in Pop. In some ways these are a survival of earlier modes of the avant-garde transgression of official taste and good manners.

With hindsight the democratization of art by Pop was only a semblance of this, a moment of excitement

PHOTOGRAPHY, ADVERTISING AND CONSUMER CULTURES

11.8 Still from a TV advertisement for Vauxhall, *c.* 2010. It is a repeat photo image of a car in the style of Andy Warhol. Image courtesy of The Advertising Archives.

that quickly passed into art-historical myth-making and the big business art of the present day. It was an anti-intellectual and apolitical movement with a low-threshold level of cultural access (Lander, 2013: 50). Its associations with commercial culture were actually limited to the occasional crossover links with graphic design assignments such as Long Playing record sleeve design (Blake, Warhol) and yet its influence in the wider field of design is enormous.

The continuing success of Pop in the present century is confirmed by the frequency of its display in the great museums and the vast sums of money still being paid for it. The emphasis on superstar artists undermines the prospects for their inclusion in a progressive or democratic visual project beyond the art world. Pop was a dead-end except for the commercial success of its founding figures and the handful of later artists and photographers who adapted its taste for the subaltern to their own purposes. This criticism can be moderated by the recognition that Pop had a wide cultural currency and was hugely influential in advertising, fashion and in some of the more eccentric areas of architecture. Advertising, flattered by the attention of painters, repaid the compliment in adapting its own 'artistic' aims to youth culture, consumerism, aspiration, excess and celebrity (fig. 11.8). The key influence on this image is Andy Warhol's screen-printed canvases from the 1960s. The Pop 'quotation' would be understood by prospective consumers of fashionable products – young people with some knowledge of recent past movements in art and culture.

Repetition, snapshot photography, supermarket colours, strange juxtaposition of abstract forms and photographs led to the creation of ads that looked like Pop Art. The advertising specialist and author Barry Hoffman observes:

Pop signalled the total triumph of the selling state of mind in American Culture ... while

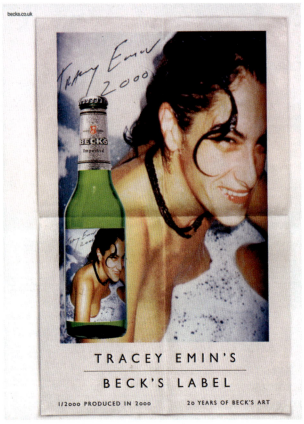

11.9 Beck's beer advertisement featuring Tracey Emin (c. 1998). Image courtesy of The Advertising Archives.

critics, intellectuals and moralists ... inveighed against materialism, capitalism, corporatism, and Mammon, consumerism barrelled forward.

(Hoffman, 2002: 101)

The successful merging of art and advertising is the theme of Hoffman's book. Two things arise from the merger: first, crossover activities of artists and photographers validate ads as a credible site for aesthetic intervention. Second, corporate institutions are aware of their own symbolic standing and association with the visual arts provides social and cultural legitimacy. Art places advertising above what Chin-tao Wu calls the 'shabby cut and thrust of the business world' (Wu, 2002: 11). The alliance of art and advertising in the late twentieth century is ironical and wry in its correspondences. Inter-textual referencing and sophistication are widespread so that little if any difference exists between advertising and art. They imitate and quote each other. The postmodernist practices of the artists Barbara Kruger (fig. 5.3) and Richard Prince (fig. 11.10) pose questions about consumerism and social identity. They appeal to audiences with knowledge of political discourse. In Figure 11.10 Prince 'quotes' a well-known cigarette brand in open recognition that art is seen by him as inseparable from the accumulated knowledge of visual data. It looks like an ad but is something else. The picture raises conceptual issues about the limits of art. The work of Kruger and Prince has a political edge. Advertising in some of its more conspicuously progressive modes adopts similar tactics 'to stay contemporary and to target niches' (Hoffman, 2002: 115). The demarcation lines between advertising and cultural forms such as art, movies, music and fashion are not evident in the (audio)-visual product itself. As Mica Nava says 'the visual codes used in ads operate across cultural forms' (Nava, 1997: 42) and seem to deny any qualitative difference between, say, a Tracey Emin gallery work, and an advertisement in which she appears (fig. 11.9). This is an attempt to use celebrity as a marketing device. Emin's reputation as an artist and socialite transfers to the product as a drink for people in her age group.

By the same token the notoriety that attached to Benetton or Diesel advertising is closely aligned with the shock tactics of modern art. Both fields are defined by the need for their products to make themselves visible and arresting. The work of Oliviero Toscani (fig. 12.2) for Benetton is informed by the confrontational logic of contemporary art. It belongs (perhaps uncomfortably) to the visual discourse of advertising but is qualitatively indistinguishable from what passes for contemporary art. A section of an existing ad for Marlboro cigarettes displayed in a museum seems to cancel its commercial value and

PHOTOGRAPHY, ADVERTISING AND CONSUMER CULTURES

11.10 Richard Prince, *Marlboro Man* series: 'Untitled (Cowboy)', 1989. © Richard Prince. Courtesy Gagosian Gallery. Photography by Robert McKeever.

turns its attention (or our attention) to the institutional structures of art. In other words it challenges the identity of 'art' and the aesthetic disposition of the viewer.

Works by Prince and Kruger seem to ask the same questions raised by Warhol: why are there two kinds of things (art photography and publicity photography) and how do we negotiate their affinities and differences? The photography historian Abigail Solomon-Godeau refers to a range of contemporary postmodern artists whose work simulates publicity and advertising:

> Postmodernism, as style on the other hand, eliminates any possibility of analysis insofar as it complacently affirms inter-changeability, if not co-identity, of art production and advertising, accepting this as a *given* instead of a problem.
>
> (Solomon-Godeau, 1997: 143; emphasis added)

Hoffmann comments on the American artist Jeff Koons making identical copies of print ads (as Levine made identical copies of art photographs) as evidence of one field collapsing into the other (Hoffman, 2002: 135). Our view is that the two domains are interchangeable but, as Solomon-Godeau observes, they do not share the same identity. Indeed, it is important to note that the separation of art and advertising is a key factor in the life of both fields. It is a separation that has important implications for the professional photographer. In the next chapter we look more closely at the so-called creative economy and the place of photography within it.

CONCLUSION

Advertising photography gained widespread currency in the 1920s. Before the invention of techniques for reproduction of the photograph it was not widely used in commercial media. With rapid development

315

BEYOND THE ACADEMY

of modern marketing techniques in the period after the First World War, advertising photography was in great demand. New techniques for reproducing photographs in specialist magazines created commercialized forms of leisure. Early advertising emphasized the 'reason why' a product was good for its user and photography was often little more than an effective illustration. Art directors and other cultural intermediaries such as psychologists, copy writers and business managers transformed the newly emerging advertising agencies. The prospects of a more suggestive style of imagery with lifestyle connotations gradually came into being. The romantic and soft-focus look of pictorialist styles (originating in the Victorian period) or the sharp-focus industrial look of modernist photography demonstrated the increasing role of visual expression as a marketing device.

The aesthetic style of ads changed in relation to the historical context in which they gained currency. We have underlined parallels between advertising photography and the fine arts. On the one hand advertising photography corresponds closely with progressive style and seeks to promote the feeling of modernity and enlightened thought. On the other hand the turn to naturalistic styles that centred on traditional family and gender roles marked a reaction against modernism. The conservative styles of the 1950s relied on easily readable photo-ads that targeted lifestyle groups ('consumption tribes') centred on the symbolic meaning of goods. We have noted how the accessible style of advertising paralleled enormous interest in documentary photography in periodicals such as *Picture Post*, *Life* and *Vu* in France. The huge expansion of the illustrated press in the middle years of the last century created new conditions in which ordinary people – perhaps for the first time – could see themselves as staple subjects of new kinds of media. Before the arrival of television the vibrant mixture of publicity and marketing with entertainment media was generated by photography. We have noted the importance of the cultural mix of editorial and advertising as a key factor in the style and content of the illustrated press. For example stereotypes in ads were often continuous with features and story lines in popular culture.

We have stressed the way ads, like soap opera, present drama and meaning as if the efficacy of the product were a secondary concern. The overlap between entertainment and art is a theme that runs through advertising. Saleability and pleasure also converge in the more playful aspects of modern art. In particular we have noted how Pop art 'signalled the triumph of the selling state of mind'. Finally, we have underlined how far popular artistic movements in our lives abandoned the modernist ideal of artistic and social improvement working in tandem. The postmodernist period (after Pop) is marked in many ways by interdisciplinary cultural practices. Photography, film and graphic design are classic examples of a crossover practice between commerce and art. We have cited examples of artists working for advertisers (Warhol, Koons and Emin) but have noted that, unlike the idealists of the 1920s, their careers are positioned firmly in the art world. Despite the overlap the two domains remain separate. The art world itself is closely connected with (and increasingly dependent upon) corporate sponsorship and publicity services. Nevertheless, it jealously guards its higher status. Where does this leave the photographer working in the creative industries? Is he or she an artist or a hired worker? If the distinction is necessary will it influence the style and content of the work? In the next chapter we address these issues.

SUMMARY OF KEY POINTS

- Advertising photography gained widespread currency in the early twentieth century and became the dominant form of illustrated advertising by the end of the 1920s. The combined influence of new

marketing techniques with photography underpinned the development of advertising agencies and the formation of new professional skills including copywriting, art direction and account management.
- The technology for mechanical reproduction of photographic imagery (and the widespread dissemination of photography) made goods and services visible and attractive to large audiences. The visibility of goods and services led to increased sales. This created a chain reaction when sales led to increased levels of manufacturing and further promotion. Innovations in photographic dispersal created new markets in which consumer taste began to influence the production end of the business cycle. Cultural intermediaries such as advertising photographers and art directors came to play an important role in the formation of consumer societies.
- Progressive aesthetic codes are adapted to ambitiously new kinds of advertising in the period between the two world wars. Avant-garde artists and photographers turn to advertising as a source of income. Many also approach the demands of assignment photography as a new and inclusive approach to visual communication.
- Conservative styles of advertising paralleled modernist trends. Some were influenced by the escapist dramas of soap opera in the Depression era of the 1930s. Easily readable (anti-modernist) styles of advertising were designed to appeal to mainstream groups. The taste for highly naturalistic methods of representation and the construction of gender stereotypes and family life were dominant – especially in the USA – in the 1950s. This trend in advertising is convergent with the consumption of photo-documentary publications including books and magazines. The period from 1920–1970 is the golden era of print media and photography was the key to its success.
- Early ads focused on the 'reason why' a product is worth buying ('washes whiter'). Later ads were more sophisticated and relied on abstract meanings associated with the product. This kind of ad offers viewers ways of thinking about themselves and their social worth ('You know you are worth it'). In other words astute modes of advertising avoid the hard sell and offer lifestyle connotations.
- Pop art 'signalled the triumph of the selling state of mind' and renewed the link between advertising and art. Photography was adapted by painters (such as Warhol) and translated into a new kind of art rooted in commercial culture. The linking of commerce and art is an essential aspect of some important postmodernist practices and yet the line between high and low cultural practices is sustained by the autonomy of the art world.
- The ambiguous role of the advertising photographer (artist/hired hand) is explored in the discussion of the creative industries in the next chapter.

REFERENCES

Benjamin, Walter (2009) 'The Work of Art in the Age of Mechanical Reproduction', in *One Way Street and Other Writings*, trans. J. A. Underwood, London: Penguin.

Hall, Stuart (1972) 'The Social Eye of *Picture Post*', in *Working Papers in Cultural Studies*, no. 2, pp. 71–120.

Hoffman, Barry (2002) *The Fine Art of Advertising*, New York: Stewart, Tabori and Chang.

Jobling, Paul and Crowley, David (1996) *Graphic Design: Reproduction and Representation*, Manchester University Press.

BEYOND THE ACADEMY

Johnston, Patricia (1997) *Real Fantasies: Edward Steichen's Advertising Photography*, Berkeley: CA: University California Press.

Lander, Tobias (2013) 'Just What is It That Makes Pop Art So Different, So Appealing? A Success Story', in *Pop Art Design*, Weil am Rhein: Vitra Design Museum, pp. 34–51.

Leiss, Willliam, Kline, Stephen and Jhally, Sut (1997) *Social Communication in Advertising*, London and New York: Routledge.

Lupton, Ellen and Miller, Abbott (2006) *Design Writing Research*, London and New York: Phaidon.

Meggs, Phillip B. (1992) *A History of Graphic Design*, New York: Van Nostrand Reinhold

Messaris, Paul (1997), *Visual Persuasion: The Role of Image in Advertising*, Thousand Oaks, CA/London/Delhi: Sage

Nava, Mica (1997) 'Framing Advertising: Cultural Analysis and the Incrimination of Visual Texts', in Mica Nava, Andrew Blake, Iain MacRury and Barry Richards (eds), *Buy This Book: Studies in Advertising and Consumption*, London and New York: Routledge, pp. 34–50.

Ogilvy, David (1983) *Ogilvy on Advertising*, London and Sydney: Pan Books.

Panofsky, Erwin (1970) *Meaning in the Visual Arts*, Harmondsworth: Penguin Books.

Rennie, Paul, (2004)'RoSPA's WW2 Safety Posters Challenge Orthodox Views of British Modernism', in *Eye Magazine*, Summer 2004. Available at: http://eyemagazine.com/feature/article/socialvision (accessed 23.03. 2014).

Sobieszek, Robert A. (1988) *The Art of Persuasion: A History of Advertising Photography*, New York: Harry N. Abrams.

Solomon-Godeau, Abigail (1997) *Photography at the Dock: Essays on Photographic History, Institutions and Practices*, Minneapolis: University of Minnesota Press.

Welch, David (2013) *Propaganda and Persuasion*, London: British Library.

Wolff, Henry (1988) *Visual Thinking: Methods for Making Images Memorable*, New York: American Showcase, Inc.

Wu, Chin-tao (2002) *Privatising Culture: Corporate Art Intervention since the 1980s*, London: Verso.

CHAPTER 12
PHOTOGRAPHY AND THE CREATIVE ECONOMY

This is a typical stock photograph made by a photographer in the expectation of licensed use in a mainstream advertising or editorial format. The mobile phone in the image – a 1990s model – would make the picture unusable in a contemporary media setting. This is a key factor since in order to be saleable stock images must keep up with contemporary trends and ideas. This is good news for stock photographers since the market for new images never fades and demand for new work is guaranteed. A contemporary ad might use this as a humorous comment on old phones. Old ads have currency in 'retro' style ads and might appear in historical and editorial narratives.

Notice other factors that define the image as an aesthetically conservative example of commercial photography. It is a location shot with city buildings in the background providing contextual meaning. It suggests a busy working environment. The model is smiling in a way that suggests her life and work are balanced. She dresses in a business (almost masculine) way and firmly holds on to the brick-like phone and a briefcase. This type of stock image is meant to convey the feeling of seriousness and trustworthy values that would attach to the company (or product) it is intended to promote. It is a slick image intended to convey a progressive corporate outlook.

12.1 Businesswoman outdoors using mobile phone. Bart Geerligs. Courtesy of Getty Images.

INTRODUCTION

Commenting on what he calls the photo-imaging industry Jonathan Hirsch has noted 'low awareness amongst many new entrants of its different sub-sectors and opportunities they offer, with many people simply "falling into" jobs rather than taking a planned approach to their careers' (Hirsch, n.d.: 11). Most professional photographers are freelance and opportunities for 'staff jobs' or salaried employment are

BEYOND THE ACADEMY

limited. On the one hand freedom and creativity is linked with self-employed modes of work (Florida, 2002). On the other hand sceptical commentators underline the precarious nature of temporary and part-time work (Standing, 2011; 2014).

Specialists in the field of business offer important guidance notes on setting up as a photography business (Pritchard, 2011). Commentators on the creative industries can be divided into two groups: those who connect 'entrepreneurial flair' and creativity in a highly positive way, and those concerned about the problems of low pay and the uncertainty of contract work. Specific questions relating to business practice and conditions of employment are beyond the scope of this book. We are concerned with broader issues surrounding organizational models of photographic work and the bearing this has on the self-image of practitioners and the social meanings that attach to their work.

Radical change in graphic media is a crucial factor in the growth of consumer societies. Improved techniques for the wide dispersal of visual messages, the inception of information technology and education and training had a great impact on economic growth in the twentieth and twenty-first centuries (Flew, 2005: 345). Opportunities for employment in what theorists have called the creative economy have increased widely. The conjunction of 'creative' and 'economy' underlines the concept of 'innovation' in particular forms of work (often seen as glamorous or progressive) in consumer societies. One of the key factors in the advance of the creative economy is the role of intangible assets such as innovation, research and development. The cultural critic and author Charles Leadbeater notes: 'Knowledge sharing and creation is at the heart of innovation in all fields – science, art, business – and innovation is the driving force for wealth creation' (Leadbeatter, 2005: 127). Fashion, advertising, news, publishing, public relations are examples of major creative industries in which photography plays a key role. In some accounts the traditional distinction between the art museum and the wider field of 'applied' photographic practices is replaced by the image of a more unified field of 'creative labour markets' (McRobbie, 1999: 3) in which the categories of 'high' and 'low' culture have, arguably, disappeared. Business and art are seen as related projects blended into new forms of creative and economic activity. This is described as a widening field of culture in which artists, in the broadest sense of the word, are viewed as 'new economy pioneers' (McRobbie in Sholette, 2004: 262).

> **KEY TERM: Creative Economy**
> The term 'creative economy' has been used to define the changing role of art and industry in modern society. A creative economy is dominant in societies where the arts have a primary role and might be contrasted with older industrial economies. In older industrial societies production (especially factory production) was a central and defining condition of the modern way of life. This has been replaced by a new way of life in which consumption has a more defining role. Proponents of the term 'creative economy '(Flew, 2005; McRobbie, 1999) have shown how artists (in the widest sense of the word) have a powerful influence on the social and economic character of modern societies. When a society is structured around the distribution and exchange of goods this dynamic becomes a strategic part of the economic system. When the system is defined by this kind of 'dynamism' rather than by technical innovation or production it becomes more reliant upon its creative industries. The creative industries in turn now require

PHOTOGRAPHY AND THE CREATIVE ECONOMY

a standing army of creative labour that shapes cultural preference (through advertising and other promotional methods) in a marketplace geared to the consumption of symbolic goods. In other words the creative industries sustain and drive the economic life of the society.

A creative economy is one in which the image of things has a power over the production process. For example a constant re-fashioning of products requires industrial methods adapted to rapid turnover and short life expectancy of products. As an efficient means of instant visualization photography is well suited to the promotional side of the creative economy.

THE NEW ECONOMY PIONEERS

Art and Advertising

The work of photographers is in some measure defined by the client area or market in which they work. Historically, photographers have attached themselves to a single-field specialism allowing them to establish contacts with other professionals and develop a signature style. The alliance of photography, art and popular culture is evident in the period described by the cultural theorist Angela McRobbie. She notes the backlash against 'political art and photography of the 1980s generation' (1999: 6) which had taken critical aim at fashion and advertising. Artist-photographers such as Victor Burgin and Jo Spence appropriated advertising imagery in ways that challenged its common sense or uncritical reading (see Chapters 5 and 7). McRobbie observes a counter movement against the political ideals of the Burgin generation in the 'low brow' exhibits of Sarah Lucas including 'soiled mattress with phallic shaped fruit pieces casually thrown on top' (McRobbie, 1999: 6), the sexual revelations of Tracey Emin or the Goya-influenced mutilated figure sculptures of the Chapman brothers. The advertising figurehead and art collector Charles Saatchi brought these artists together. It is a kind of work marked by its intellectual indifference:

It self-consciously staged itself as shocking but was also completely unintimidating. In this respect art has come down from its pedestal … The new 'lite' art also means the blurring of the boundaries between where art stops and where everyday life commences.

(McRobbie, 1999: 7–8)

McRobbie uses the term cultural populism to describe some of the more accessible forms of postmodern art that overlap with the design and media industries. Late twentieth-century cultural theory and popular journalism (in the English context magazines such *ID* and *The Face*) provided evidence of increasing employment in this sector. Inspired by an attack on 'old cultures' and *passé* modes of industrial labour the 'no-collar' working environment was to be a 'dynamo for growth and change' in the new century (Hartley, 2005: 2). McRobbie adeptly links avant-garde art with design, photography and music in a creative *mélange* that over-rides cultural boundaries. The 'real' world beyond the academy allows increasing opportunities for 'creative' workers in market-led economies. Artists were able to make money and more graduates were finding jobs in the creative industries. Even museums began to feel like the 'real' world with blockbuster shows, corporate events, cafés and shops. The

321

BEYOND THE ACADEMY

major art institutions seemed to be closely connected with everyday life in their choice of artists and exhibitions. The *Sensations* show at the Royal Academy (1997), curated by Saatchi, is a paradigm case of cultural levelling in which punk attitudes and high art converged. Cheerleaders for the new spirit of enterprise advised '… emerging creatives… to grasp opportunity and fashion themselves towards the new economy, and to adapt a more entrepreneurial and business-like approach to creative production' (Cunningham, 2005: 288).

Our assessment of the creative economy is more circumspect. Artists work in advertising and exhibit their work in prestige art galleries but the key institutions are unchanged. The elite crossover advertising campaigns in the past included Edward Steichen, László Moholy-Nagy, Salvador Dalí, Andy Warhol, and Richard Hamilton. More recent ones include Jeff Koons, Tracey Emin and Damien Hirst amongst others (see Hoffman, 2002). In many ways it looks like business as usual. There appears to be a co-identity between advertising and art yet the old hierarchy stays in place. What is genuinely new, however, is the pragmatic change in artistic outlook. McRobbie notes:

> While creativity has traditionally been nurtured in interiorised, slow and quiet mental physical spaces, in the new cultural economy it is encouraged to be increasingly populist, noisy, easy, thin … Where there is little or no time for thinking, the art-work itself can hardly be thoughtful.
>
> (McRobbie, 2001: 3)

Photography is of course a medium that can transfer across practices and institutional spaces without substantive alteration to the material object in the process. The taste codes and visual properties in advertisements and museum photography are often very similar and artists exploit the common properties of artistic and commercial imagery. Indeed, much is made of the fact that photography is a great social leveller since it has visual properties that are not tied to an institutional base in the way that painting might be. The tendency to ignore the cultural distinctions between advertisements and art has strategic value. Cultural theorists can admire the promiscuous mixing of different levels of cultural meaning when museums celebrate ad-art mixtures in Warhol, Koons and others. Photography was the favoured medium of the avant-garde artist in the past. It was thought to be a progressive medium without high-cultural connotations. It has a similar appeal in the present age but, arguably, now lacks any sense of democratic earnestness associated with the early twentieth-century avant-garde.

Photography as a Common Denominator

The photograph is common to advertising and contemporary art. There is no discernible difference between technical standards except where one deliberately avoids academic standards of perfection for aesthetic effect. The exchange of aesthetic ideas between art photography and commercial imagery reinforces their common properties. In basic design teaching the artistic level of an assignment was often ignored in favour of technical and aesthetic factors such as drawing technique, photographic method, layout and other visual effects. Mastery of these things came before social questions about application. Assignments in art, photography and design presented similar challenges. In some teaching institutions the key tenets of basic design education developed in the last century still survive. These include the use of expressive visual effects that are still taught in photography courses despite their different vocational orientations. The ideas and principles of the renowned art director Allan Hurlburt in his book *Photographics: The Interaction of Design and Photography* are informed by what he called

PHOTOGRAPHY AND THE CREATIVE ECONOMY

the 'uncanny blend of photography and graphic design' (Hurlburt, 1983: 42). The book discusses the skill-set of would-be designers, art directors and photographers. Hurlburt's schematic lessons on contrasts of scale, value and shape, and general sensitivity to page layout are purposeful and convincing. The guileless innocence in the view that 'good work' transcends genres derives from an earlier generation of artists and designers including the Russian Constructivists and the artists, designers and photographers at the famous German art school, the Bauhaus in the 1920s. The revolutionary ideals of these 'pioneers' had largely disappeared by the 1950s but the assimilated knowledge of basic design continued along with embedded notions of teamwork and 'standards' common to the artisanal work of the older 'creative' occupations.

How far the principles of 'basic design' and the older photography skill-set have continued into the new economy is not clear. McRobbie notes that the end of 'fixed location, duration of employment' leads to individualized approaches that open new 'possible spaces' for the development of art and culture (2001). The increased possibility of working remotely in new media formats creates changes not only to the skill-set but also the traditional idea of the working day. In some ways the changing time-disciplines of the new creative economy are a throwback to older industrial models of subcontracted work where 'The capitalist distributed work on a piecework basis to workers for manufacture in their own homes, through the medium of subcontractors and commissioned agents' (Braverman, 1974: 61). Home-based working routines and the prospect of isolation or networking contact with on-going and prospective employers is a mixed blessing. It offers flexibility and creative, rewarding work but is open to exploitation and periods without work. There are wider questions about the quality of photographic work in the creative economy and the related issue of the status of practitioners.

Privileging the Aesthetic in Photography

Photographic work in most of its professional aspects is a matter of routine and habitual practice. Making a living is a priority and artistic recognition an added value. As the sociologist Howard S. Becker noted: 'Most participants in any art world are not concerned with being enormously expressive or creative; they are content to work within quite conventionalized formats' (Becker, 1978: 877). The constraints of established working practice may limit the expressive choices available to the photographer. Equally the requirements of a brief must shape the outcome of an assignment. The work setting imposes stylistic conventions and 'ways of doing things' that a novice practitioner must dutifully learn. The acceptance of routine and socialization is a requirement in most areas of working life. Adjusting to a system may be challenging and even a rewarding aspect of work especially in those fields that allow some measure of personal expression.

A key aspect of work in photography, in all its various practices, is the acquisition of skill and familiarity with methods of work. A mastery of technique and familiarity with style (including knowledge of recognized practitioners) is, arguably, a necessary part of professional advancement in the field. For most practitioners, including successful ones, the budget, the brief, the chain of command, are normal aspects of the work routine. To say that most photographic work is unexceptional is perhaps stating the obvious. The world is glutted with commonplace images and yet the struggle to stand out and make an impression is part of the folklore of the visual arts. Fashion and advertising photography are closely related to painting and high culture. Despite this close relationship practitioners in these areas are

BEYOND THE ACADEMY

notoriously sensitive to their social standing since photography in these categories is arguably more directly linked to the mass-production of commodities and waste. Photographic work in fashion and advertising might, however, share the characteristics of the fine art genre of portraiture. Such work might be admired for its technical proficiency and the subtlety in the use of lighting, composition and other visual effects. It may also draw upon conventional ways of thinking about beauty and the ideal.

The dividing line between craft skills (artisanship) and art (creativity, originality, expressiveness) is hard to establish. If credit is due to the skills that are clearly in evidence in the best photographic work it is equally valid to note the over-use of the term 'creative' for most kinds of ordinary photographic work in circulation. The ordinariness of photography is, nevertheless, belied by its alignment with the fine arts. Despite the ordinariness of what they create photographers, cultural intermediaries, art directors and clients adopt the label 'creative' and apply it to anything that is published. As Becker notes, 'they [the practitioners] and those who support their art world as patrons and customers generally orient themselves to ideas of expressiveness and creativity' (1978: 877) in circumstances where this component is possibly absent. Photographic work of the most subsidiary and banal kind collapses into a generic category of the 'creative'.

A summary of the above might suggest a crude distinction between art photography and all other forms of photographic practice. We see on the one hand photographs made for appreciation, collection and display, and on the other photographs subject to the wilful imposition of an employer's requirements. The deployment of virtuoso skills for the satisfaction of patrons and prospective audiences might be a real constraint on the aesthetic choices available to anybody. This applies to the fine artist whose work is meant to satisfy the interests of the art establishment. Artists have traditionally relied on patronage of the church or wealthy clients which often specified and directed the nature of their work. Contemporary artists are free to express themselves and yet the legitimization of their work is only tentatively assured by the art world. They must in some way conform with the bureaucracy of the public art world if they wish to exhibit in recognized galleries, make their work available to collectors and accessible to critical debate. In the first case they worked by commission and in the second they rely on collectors buying work that is already made. Commissioned commercial work has similarities with older forms of patronage. Photographers finding scope for creative intervention *within* assignments generated by commercial interest has historical precedent. The struggle for *expression* against the grain of commercial interest is a precondition of professional photography. How photographers deal with this 'precondition' is addressed in the second part of this chapter.

We have argued that the fine art world, despite commercial overlap and hybrid styles of practice, remains largely independent of the fashion industry, advertising, media practices and the crafts. This is broadly true and the art establishment is sustained by its aristocratic standing in relation to the 'applied arts'. Museum art might be seen as an object of pure contemplation whereas an advertisement, like a religious work, has 'extra-aesthetic' interests (Bourdieu, 1994: 30) that include marketing products and sending a messages to a wider audience. There are, nevertheless, important examples of free movement in art photography across the lines of art, fashion and advertising. The work of Oliviero Toscani for Benetton had all the outward signs of a rebellious art form as it adopted the shock tactics of contemporary art. His advertising images of new born babies and burning cars were an antidote to the banality of family life or gender stereotypes still dominant in mainstream clothing advertisements in the late twentieth century (fig. 12.2). Replacing fantasies of consumption with a kind of

324

12.2 Burning car advertisement for United Colors of Benetton. Photography by Oliviero Toscani (c. 1992). Image courtesy of The Advertising Archives.

pseudo-documentary image of street fighting and terrorism were amongst the various shock tactic used by Toscani. This approach has connections with the challenging subject matter in work by contemporary artists such as Damien Hirst and the Chapman brothers.

In a similar vein recent photographic theorists (Gelder and Westgeest, 2011: 188) have noted a 'critical strategy from within' advertising and fashion in work that draws on Surrealist influences. Again the strategy of discomfiting the spectator is achieved in novel ways including body transformations, human bodies merging into the wall (fig. 12.4) for example, and strange visual effects of chest hair printed on T-shirts in Walter Van Beirendonck's *Finally Chesthair* of 1997 (fig. 12.3).

Erwin Olaf's digitally manipulated images present glamorous and expensive *haute couture* dresses worn by strangely faceless/headless women (fig.

12.3 Walter Van Beirendonck's 'Finally Chesthair' T-shirt, 1996. Courtesy of Museum Boijmans Van Beuningen, Rotterdam/Photographer: Bob Goedewaagen, Rotterdam.

12.4 Erwin Olaf for *The New York Times*, 'Style: Couture Collection: Grand Illusions', 10 August 2006. Christian Lacroix, haute couture, lace ruched blouse over long taffeta and moiré flounced skirt and shoes. Courtesy of Hamiltons Gallery, London, UK/The artist.

12.4). The idea is a reprise of the German Surrealist painter Max Ernst's collage novel, *La Femme 100 Têtes* published in 1929. The title is deliberately ambiguous and a play on words. '100' or 'cent' sounds like 'sans' ('without') in spoken French. The inter-textual referencing of Surrealism in the work of Olaf establishes a link between art, fashion and social ideas. Olaf's *Haute Couture Collection* photographs were published in *The New York Times* with an epigraph that reads: 'Wearing a dress that costs as much as a house, a girl can't be blamed for losing her head' (cited in Gelder and Westgeest, 2011: 187). As with many of his surrealist forebears Olaf's work challenges traditional boundaries between fashion and art.

As noted above the traffic between high and low is increasingly busy with successful artists 'placing themselves at the very heart of consumer culture' (McRobbie, 1999: 6), as they enjoy the spoils of celebrity culture. The ambiguous identity of Olaf's commercial work (as hybrid forms of art, fashion and advertising) allows commercial interests to mix with the arts. The art historian Chin-tao Wu comments on this type of relationship:

> Alert to their symbolic standing in people's (consumers'?) minds, companies utilise the arts, replete with their social implications, as another form of advertising or public relations strategy … striving to gain an *entrée* into a more sophisticated social group through identifying with their specific tastes.
>
> (Wu, 2002: 9)

The idea of a status group outside the world of business is conjured in this statement. Wu emphasizes the contract between art and commerce whilst noting the survival of traditional separations and distinctions. Her argument is that the 'status group' is compromised by its increasing dependence on the private sector. Again the bridging of high and low is highlighted but, unlike McRobbie, Wu reveals the commercial interests at stake in this alliance. We have argued that expansion of the creative industries increases opportunities for artists and photographers. How far working conditions in the commercial sector, and the somewhat haphazard methods of entry to it, influence the nature of the work is not so clear. In the next section we look more closely at the vocational status of photography.

ON THE VOCATIONAL STATUS OF PHOTOGRAPHY

The Paradox of Creative Labour

The paradox at the centre of the discussion about the vocational status of photography can be expressed as follows. On the one hand a photographer holds firmly to the romantic aesthetic. In other words she espouses the aesthetic of spontaneity and adopts the traditional role of the visionary artist, struggling to find a signature style. On the other hand she works within a market system that demands standard products, efficiently and repeatedly made to order. These extreme poles seem to define the opposition between rewarding and alienated labour. For the artist who enjoys her work there is no obvious divide between work and leisure so long as provision is made for sufficient rest and material reward as essential aspects of the vocation.

To say that advertising photography, or any of the key practices such as news or editorial photography, is constrained by the world that contains it is an obvious point to make, and yet the privileging of artistic individualism is very much part of the discourse of creativity that sustains the image of professional photography. This is perhaps most evident in fashion and advertising photography, where 'vision' is a legitimating principle of business and artistic life. What concerns photographers, whatever their rank, is whether the structure allows expression that might in some way to be surplus to the commercial message it contains, or alternatively whether that message itself has meaning that justifies its expression.

Style and Innovation

The idea of the romantic artist may be intellectually unfashionable but it has a professional coinage in the creative industries. More importantly it sustains artistic labour when the pay is bad and the work is boring. The idea of what might be achieved is often a way of sustaining the routine of working life. Successful photographers repeatedly urge ambitious learners to 'think outside the box', 'find your language and your voice', 'be confident about your work and stick to it', 'be true to yourself', and generally follow the dream of all artists: 'it's a way of expressing some inner need to be "creative"' (cited in Pritchard, 2011, *passim*). The idea of 'making a mark' and 'fitting in' sums up the contradictory demands of style and innovation in all creative occupations. Finding a market in which a photographer can work normally precedes their creative intervention. It can of course work the other way around when 'personal style' coincides with market requirements. The success stories of artists centred on 'genius' and struggle underrate the mundane networking skills and other aptitudes essential to progression in the arts. The successful photographer finds a place in the system and achieves this in different ways.

Reliability and skill are important but in the more colourful accounts of upward mobility, rule breaking and some measure of attention-seeking behaviour might be necessary. The market is said to thrive on innovation and the discourse of creativity sustains its mythical value. Innovation is a high-risk business and sometimes leads to fame and fortune. Corinne Day and Juergen Teller working for *The Face*, in the 1980s and 1990s, challenged the up-market styling of *Vogue* with a grungy 'chic' style of photography. The photography agent Lisa Pritchard argues that the key to success is to match a target client area with an identifiable subject matter and style (Pritchard, 2011: 26–27). In the creative economy the market

BEYOND THE ACADEMY

itself is driven by consumer taste which generates the cycle of supply and demand. The photograph may seem to be independent of the world that surrounds it but its value is measured in a system that celebrates its claim to originality.

The art historian Richard Shiff underlines the saleability of artistic difference. He notes how 'originality' can be imitated and used by fellow artists or cultural intermediaries:

> To seek originality by stressing one's deviation from others has consequences in the social realm; it encourages a certain personal competition which in turn has economic implications. Artists sell their unique difference, but not always easily.
>
> (Shiff, 1996: 108)

The artist Paul Gauguin noted the irony of struggling for market recognition in a world ruled by fashion:

> Nobody wants my work because it is different from that of others … Strange illogical public which demands the greatest possible originality from a painter and yet will not accept him unless he resembles others …
>
> (cited in Shiff, 1996: 108)

Gauguin's paradox is familiar to anyone who thinks about individual identity and authorship. As we have noted elsewhere in this book postmodern photographers, such as Sherrie Levine (see Chapter 5), made imitation of past work into a comment on the mediated nature of all human expression. If all human expression is mediated and nothing is new we are condemned to repeat ourselves. The art critic Harold Rosenberg noted the creative absurdity of newness following itself repeatedly: 'In the arts an appetite for the new is now a professional requirement' (Rosenberg, 1962: 11). The contempt for the 'professional requirement' – coded words for the 'marketplace' – signals a familiar divide between art and industry. Most photographers, however, rely on the market for employment and adopt strategies that allow them to rise above this kind of scepticism. They may continue to believe there is truth and meaning in their work. Accommodation with the market is not enough to prevent innovation and surprise in the production of the most utilitarian objects regardless of their provenance or destination. We might, nevertheless, consider more exactly what is often meant by the word 'creativity' and comment on the structural forces that shape its definition.

Artistic Conformity in the Workplace

We have noted a conflict between creative innovation and the demands of fashion and popular taste. The tendency to privilege the fine art notion of individual creativity contrasts with commercial work conducted in an occupational community such as an advertising agency or newspaper. In her book *Photographers at Work* the sociologist Barbara Rosenblum emphasizes the changing ways of working that come with experience in the workplace. She notes how photographers entering the world of work change individualistic ways of working to ones that are socially complex and collective. She compares the role of assistant photographers in advertising with the apprenticeship systems for newspaper photographers, and emphasizes skills acquisition and professional practice. More importantly, however, Rosenblum's study focuses on work organization, the importance of shared understanding between co-workers, and the stages between different operations in the process of advertising image production. The key point that runs through the book is that *style* is a product of work organization. In the case of the

PHOTOGRAPHY AND THE CREATIVE ECONOMY

advertising photographer, we are told, 'he must please art directors and advertisers when he is an established photographer' (Rosenblum, 1978: 28). A chain of command in the workplace regulates aesthetic decision-making as the principle of artistic autonomy (independence, self-expression) is challenged by the administered nature of the work.

Rosenblum's book is a sharply-worded caution for starry-eyed graduates or photography trainees embarking on a lifetime of self-expression and creative labour. How closely it relates to current practices leaves scope for critical examination. As we have noted, short-term contract work has made photography professions more precarious, but markets have expanded and opportunities for ambitious workers have increased. Rosenblum's book, written several decades ago, focuses on assignment photography and neglects the widespread media usage of stock photography. Nevertheless, much of what she says has continuing relevance to the discussion of the term 'creativity'. For example she comments on psychological aptitudes for professional photographic work:

> For most students, the end of art school training means entering the commercial marketplace …
> [where]… they have the special set of problems of reconciling their 'purist' art school ideology
> with the practical exigencies of financial survival.
>
> (Rosenblum, 1978: 39)

Rosenblum also notes how the neophyte photographer becomes a *type* of photographer according to their vocational orientation. This signals the importance of choosing a professional pathway and developing a distinctive portfolio. Photographers may not restrict themselves to a single client area or market but expertise in a single genre, say portraiture, landscape or still life, is often a sign of professional identity needed for specialist types of assignment work. The person an agency wants to select may have a recognized area of specialization. Individuals often become 'specialists' because they have purposely restricted themselves to one particular area of practice. Having acquired a recognizable style they have made themselves known to buyers who associate them with a genre or specialist subject matter. As Pritchard says specialists have 'more chance of being remembered when a suitable job comes up' (Pritchard, 2011: 27), and better prospects for continuing employment. In some ways this sounds like a way of beating the system. The more personal the work becomes, the more employment comes their way. And yet, creative control of assignments and self-expression are compromised by the commercial objectives of the task and the divided nature of the process.

On the one hand the market (or rather the intermediaries who represent it) has pre-conceived ideas about image production. On the other hand photographers have their own ideas and find ways of working that sustain professional and artistic identity. Others compromise in accepting work that allows them to remain in the market where employment is uncertain. Some degree of stealth may be an accepted aspect of the working life of the photographer.

The Unity of Conception and Execution

Rosenblum's argument is centred on her description of the work of commissioned assignment advertising photographers at the time that she carried out research in the 1970s. The division of labour in the process of making ads at this time might typically reduce creative input of the photographer to that of 'technical translator' of the art director's design. Rosenblum notes how far the art director limits the

329

BEYOND THE ACADEMY

aesthetic choices made by a photographer. In advertising assignment photography, as described by Rosenblum, the key social constraint is the hiring of the photographer *after* the art directors and client have agreed on the proposed look of the ad.

The photographer thus sought to maximize 'control over this limited area' in the deployment of what Rosenblum calls 'technical variation … focus, lighting, distance, scale and distortions' and so forth as evidence of the photographer's aesthetic input. The 'visual unnaturalness of advertising', she claims, results from the creative elaboration of what is deemed to be a secondary role of technical manipulation (1978: 82). In a key passage of her book Rosenblum characterizes advertising photographers as storytellers, concerned to get the right shot, and yet reduced to the ranks of hired labour. The photography theorist Paul Frosh, in his comments on Rosenblum, has noted the importance of the limited role of the photographer in the assignment shoot:

> Indeed, Rosenblum argues, for assignment advertising photographers, the separation of conception from execution, the norm of illustrating a concept not of their own choosing, is a key factor in distinguishing between the world of work and its products and that of the art photographers, *for whom the unity of conception and execution is paramount.*
>
> (Frosh, 2003, 51; emphasis added)

Both Frosh and Rosenblum present a bleak picture of the photographer whose creative role is diminished by art directors and clients where 'technical virtuosity is constituted as the entire space of creativity' (Frosh, 2003: 50). Economic and social constraints confirm the piecemeal aspect of commercial photography and the enforced separation of conception and execution. The role of the photographer, when presented with a graphic design image, is to turn it into a photograph. The artistic and conceptual work is complete before the photographer joins the assignment. The photographer might then seem to be 'filling in' a photographic image where the sketch indicates it should be in the overall design. In other words the photographer is deprived of control of the conception of the image and pessimistic conclusions about the creative role of the medium are made to follow this.

KEY TERM: Assignment Photography

When a photographer is hired to capture a specific event or represent an idea the term 'assignment photography' is used to describe the activity. Assignment photographers are contracted by an agency, a client or other kind of end-user to carry out specific photographic shoots as required. A typical example would be an assignment for a Company Annual Report that included executive portraits, pictures of staff and the workplace. Further examples include product imaging in advertising, architectural illustration in books and other publications, fashion shoots and so forth. In other words assignment photography is used when generic or stock images are unsuited to the particular needs of a promotion or visual communication project.

Frosh's interest in the division of labour in commercial photography relates mainly to his discussion of what he calls the 'visual contents industry'. One of his main concerns is the changing role of photographers in a system that encourages the renting of 'ready-made' or vintage stock images. Changing approaches to capture, storage, retrieval, dissemination and new techniques for image manipulation

PHOTOGRAPHY AND THE CREATIVE ECONOMY

have changed the identity of the photograph and affected the way people see it. In the next section we consider some of the following questions: when a stock photograph is made for an archive or a photo-library (in advance of its possible selection for commercial or other usage) can we say the conceptual part of its meaning and its execution (now re-united) is freely made by the photographer? Has the increasing demand for stock photographs helped photographers to find a new creative role? Alternatively has the demand for stock photographs increased prospects for wider dissemination of 'visual ordinariness' (Frosh, 2003: 26), and stultified imagination in the media at large?

> **KEY TERM: Visual Contents Industry**
> The term 'visual contents industry' has been used by Paul Frosh (2003) to describe the growth of 'super agencies' whose main business is the sale and leasing of stock photographs and other images. The two largest agencies, Corbis and Getty Images, and numerous others, acquire photographs from various sources including libraries, archives and individual photographers. Agencies make a profit from reproduction rights. The visual contents industry produces and distributes millions of images used in a wide range of marketing sites, advertising, editorial, websites and media platforms. Key agencies own important photographic archives and have rights to important historical and fine art materials. Photographers have a share of the profit on sales of their stock images. Frosh has emphasized negative effects of the centralizing and monopolistic influence of super agencies. These include
>
> - As human creativity becomes an economic resource it loses its status as intellectual property.
> - Erasure of distinctions between separate media forms and the capacity to know and understand the historical conditions that enabled their origination – fine arts, painting, drawing, illustrations, photographs, film stills, news formats etc., are treated as 're-cyclable, transferable, detachable, "content"' (Frosh, 2003: 199).
> - Decontextualization of stock imagery reduces it to a new role as a commodity. Its value is established in circulation and repeated usage. In this regard it resembles 'money itself' (ibid.: 198).

What is Stock Photography and is it Good or Bad?

In our comments above (see the description of fig. 12.1 at the beginning of this chapter) we noted how the most typical stock images made for commercial use are shaped by socially constructed beliefs and historical conventions. We also noted stock images may be digitally adjusted to match current standards of beauty and taste. The first point to be made about stock photography (or more broadly stock images) is that they have a long history. In the past they were often cheap alternatives to assignment photographs. They were often taken from the surplus or un-used materials made in the more traditional way for assignments. They may have been out-takes or secondary material not suitable at the time and stored up or sold on for extra revenue by needy photographers. By the end of the last century they had become a speciality practice in their own right made by freelance photographers to be licensed for later use.

331

BEYOND THE ACADEMY

The second point is that most people are not aware of stock photographs and rarely actually see them for what they are. They are of course everywhere and huge quantities of visual materials are stored in monopolistic agencies such as Getty Images and Corbis. The third point is that they are often de-contextualized images with predictable meanings ('happy families' or 'busy office workers' for example) available, at a price, for on-going distribution and further use. Stock photographs have what Frosh calls 'profitable polysemy' (usable for different ends) and 'formulaic predictability' (2003: 16–17). They provide a rich source of promotional materials for editorials and ads: 'The perfect image to fit your brief' (Tony Stone Images, 1995: n.p.). The advantage of stock photographs over assignment work, apart from their relative cheapness, is their availability. They can now be found at online databases, purchased and easily adapted for particular use.

Most commonly stock photographs are professionally made photographs that rely on the use of hired models and props. They might be studio or location shots, street scenes, landscapes, single or group portraits, landscapes and so forth. In some cases they might be elaborately staged and manipulated images that seem to challenge conventional categories. The conception and execution of a task are unified aspects of the creative process in stock photography. In this sense he or she defines the aesthetic character of the shoot and exercises a sense of artistic autonomy that compares with the practices of art photography. Many contemporary photographers see stock as a legitimate field that provides creative opportunity and financial rewards. Indeed, there is a cadre of named photographers celebrated by the top agencies that sell their work. The name 'stock', however, signals the idea of a standardized product in a supply chain. In this sense photo-libraries and photographers may veer towards aesthetic conservatism in the choice of style and content of their images. Proliferation of sentimental and traditional themes is determined by a perceived need for the saleability of the product.

12.5 Stock image, caption: 'View from the top', 2013. © BeachcottagePhotography. Courtesy of Getty Images.

PHOTOGRAPHY AND THE CREATIVE ECONOMY

Stock photographers also build into their 'concept' the end-user's (the advertiser's) addition of typographic and other features. For example leaving space at the top or to the side of the image for a heading is a design feature that prefigures the shoot (fig. 12.5).

The organization of stock photography websites and catalogues by *subject* (science, sport, business, tourism etc.) marginalizes the photographer who might not be mentioned at all. Finally, the artistic integrity of the image is always at the mercy of manipulation or re-combination with other images further down the line.

KEY TERM: Stock Photography

Stock photographs have been described as 'pictures for rent … a form of currency that funds advertising, text books, real estate pamphlets, greeting cards … and innumerable forms of visual communication' (Lupton and Miller, 1999: 121). They are *already-existing* images offered for sale or lease to end-users. The provider might be an individual owner, but more generally they are stored and licensed out by a library, an archive or an agency. Stock photography, originally a sub-genre of assignment photography, has grown into a huge business in its own right and provides vintage and contemporary materials to all kinds of outlets. In the past stock largely consisted of recycled out-takes and secondary material. Today photographers set up in business and build up collections of specially made stock images to generate income.

Clients are attracted to the use of stock images because they are often much cheaper than hiring a photographer to promote an idea, product or service. The client can browse a catalogue of images structured into genres such as sport, travel, nature, animals, architecture or broad categories such as 'people' with sub-sections of 'couples', 'babies' etc. The great advantage is being able to see a wide range of images quickly and easily before or during the development of an assignment.

Licensing of images is complicated but there are two basic ways of offering photographs for sale. Rights Managed is when the customer buys the right to use the image once. If they want to use it again they have to buy the right to use it again. Royalty Free is when a customer pays once and is allowed to use the image as many times as he or she likes.

In many ways the stock photograph is enmeshed in a system of highly conventional image production not very different to the more established assignment work of the past. Much of it relies on gender, class, and race stereotypes that confirm 'pre-existing systems of differences' (Williamson, 1983: 27). Stereotyped and conservative styles of imagery are the aesthetic norm in most stock photography although some agencies encourage an 'edgy' style of work for specialist markets. We have noted Toscani and Olaf (above) as examples of niche trends and target audiences 'with disposable incomes' (Frosh, 2003: 5). Frosh notes the emergence of a 'consumption-driven, flexible, small batch production' market for goods and services that challenge the old stereotypes. As we have seen, this kind of development has been rated as a site for adventurous new work in the arts. Whether or not it can be seen as genuinely subversive is doubtful and yet these examples might in some way signify what might be called the struggle for expression against the grain of commercial interest and artistic mediocrity. For example the stock image in Figure 12.6 has an affinity with contemporary topographical styles of photography.

333

BEYOND THE ACADEMY

12.6 Stock image, caption: 'Pittsburgh, Pennsylvania, USA. Cars parked in front of suburban houses at dusk'. Photographer: Lynn Saville. Courtesy of Getty Images.

Creative Photography in the World of Work

In the final section of this chapter we challenge the sceptical view that all forms of commercial photography are compromised by the demands of an economic system that discourages experiment and rewards conformity. The average stock photographer might, for example, be tempted to raid stock agency catalogues for ideas or else, more ambitiously, develop a signature style that builds on established practice in some way. This presents a traditional hierarchy of those who comply with the system in copying standard work and those who form a vanguard of experimental practice. What seems to be at stake in this kind of discussion is the degree to which 'personal style' is subordinated to the employer's or the consumer's requirements. The idea of the commercial photographer's conformism is thus frequently contrasted with the relative freedom of expression in the work of the art photographer. In a typical example the 'commercial' photographer relies on skill and technical virtuosity at the expense of originality and expression.

Frosh accepts that some level of aesthetic experiment can be found in advertising but argues that activities other than art define its ultimate purpose. It is, in other words, an inescapably compromised medium. His most astringent comments are in fact directed at the kind of marketing rhetoric that seeks to legitimize stock photography by underlining its putatively 'creative' value. He expresses the dilemma in the following way:

> 'On the one hand it ['creativity'] is based on a romantic aesthetic that privileges spontaneity and the personal vision of the artist, and on the other it must work within a stock system dominated by marketing and product formatting.
>
> (Frosh, 2003: 64)

PHOTOGRAPHY AND THE CREATIVE ECONOMY

In a similar statement, Rosenblum emphasizes how far advertising photographers are dominated by the organizational structure in which they work: 'Definitions of creativity function in the service of organizational needs, not necessarily according to the needs of individual photographers' (Rosenblum, 1978: 129). Rosenblum and Frosh are equally sceptical about the creative potential of advertising photography. With a keen eye for the saleability of their work, Frosh notes, stock photographers rely on 'technically competent variation on an already successful formula' (Frosh, 2003: 59), and, similarly, Rosenblum criticises assignment photography as a 'formulaic aesthetic' (1978: 117).

A system that relies on systematic re-cycling of stock images might well encourage photographers to 'expect a steady income from repeated sales of the same image' (Frosh, 2003: 4). The routine work of the commercial photographer might be little more than hackwork carried out in accordance with market needs and yet this kind of view is monolithic and simplistic. It fails to account for the complexity of photography across a range of practices that overlap, operate at different levels, and appeal to audiences in different ways. An obvious comparison might be made with motion film that in its various forms is equally compromised by the demands of studio conventions, budgeting, producers and audiences. Film is valued by its artistic merit but this is always constrained by how far we judge it to be tailored to the market for this kind of product. We might note the commodity character of all contemporary art production but that is the beginning of the discussion, not its end. Film genres are highly formulaic and tailored to audience expectation. Just like advertisements they are conventionalized in their use of sentimentalized family situations (the romantic comedy for example) and yet they may be inventive and pleasurable. Film theorists Lehman and Luhr argue that film genres (such as an action movie or a western) allows for a trade off with audiences:

> Film makers include, for example, a certain amount of sex and violence in some genres, which they feel will fulfil their audience's expectations, in exchange for which they have the opportunity to present them with serious food for thought.
>
> (Lehman and Luhr, 2008: 104)

Hollywood allows progressive social ideas in commercial movies such as Tarantino's anti-slavery film *Django* (2013). Creative tension between convention and invention exists in all forms of artistic expression and the idea of working against a formula or seeing what happens in the process of making something is a vital part of what it means. The element of risk-taking is sometimes favoured when least expected. In a current television ad a beautiful women turns to the camera and reveals a missing tooth: glamour mixes with comedy in the promotion of mouthwash. The charge of escapism and 'easy listening' leaves a sense of intellectualist guilt that mediates the pleasure of popular culture. In the 1940s the German cultural theorists T.W. Adorno and Max Horkheimer expressed the view that industrial capitalism creates 'pseudo-individualistic' forms of pop music and jazz (1979: 128–154). Their attack on the industrial model of culture is based on an analogy between mass-produced objects (such as cars) and different forms of commercial culture. The limitations of this analogy have been argued by the cultural theorist Bernard Gendron (1997) who notes the failure to appreciate important differences between the production of a musical text and the production of a functional object on an assembly line. Mechanical production has its consequence but is it always the enemy of art?

335

BEYOND THE ACADEMY

Standardization as Pleasure

Pop songs and ads rely on repeatable elements that carry over from one unit (one song or ad) to the next one that might be very similar. The idea of the mindless repeatability of component parts is what enforces recognition of the genre. Gendron says

> Part interchangeability results from the drive to minimize the cost of production; pseudo-individualization results from the imperative to maximize sales. The system of advertising seduces us into believing that differences in packaging reflect differences in essence. Pseudo-individualization glamorizes style over the real inner content.
>
> (Gendron, 1997: 112)

Adorno and Horkheimer held strongly to the idea that cultural products such as popular songs are constructed out of interchangeable parts. Songs, advertisements (or cars) vary only slightly in ways that attracts sufficient attention to effect sales. Gendron refers to the 'pseudo-individualising' hook of the pop song that disguises its 'part interchangeability' (Gendron, 1997: 113). The illusion of novelty, so the argument goes, disguises its lacks of the quality of 'serious art', which in turn leads to boredom and further consumption. The argument is convincing and yet Gendron shows that the reproducibility of a sound recording is not the same *as the recording itself*. Serial production might influence the meaning of the object and the manner of its reception but the experimental effects that were tried out on the day of the recording, and any number of variables that led to its making, are not standardized in the music industry as in other areas of mass production. Gendron is perfectly aware that creative practice is often 'technically rationalized to maximize the power of management' (ibid.: 116) but we are, he claims, mistaken to think that functional artefacts (cars for example) and musical texts can be treated as the same kinds of things.

The analogy between cultural products (such as advertising photography) and the mass production of consumer durables is not without its importance. Frosh argues, convincingly, that stock photography is invariably made as a pre-digested object for popular consumption. Rosenblum has also shown how patterns of work in advertising and news photography 'shape and limit the types of aesthetic choices that can be made' (1978: 5) by the photographer in these industries. She also shows how 'fine art' photography is constrained by art world consumption of fashionable goods. And yet the notion of standardization in photographic practice is often exaggerated and fails to account for the actual performance of practitioners in their working lives. Standardization may not be the demon anyway since all cultural practices rely on 'tried-and-true paradigms' (Gendron, 1997: 114) handed down or creatively transformed in the making of artistic goods.

Photographs (like hit records) are both functional objects in some measure and have qualitative differences when compared with the standardized component in a car. Car parts are necessary for production and maintenance of the vehicle. Films, songs, and photo-ads are not made (or maintained) in the same way. They may have standard or generic components but they are qualitatively different to the absolute uniformity of automobile component parts. The repetition of elements in cultural products may be aesthetically pleasing. The use of dramatic lighting and other visual effects are standard components of photographic meaning and often have strong and pleasurable connotations. Conventions of scale, layout, texture and other design issues influence the meaning of an image just as much as subject matter. Design is often predictable and routine. This is not always a sign of artistic failure since routine

PHOTOGRAPHY AND THE CREATIVE ECONOMY

offers a framework in which originality may occur. The assembly-line model of cultural production draws attention to important aspects of the debate but in fact it is merely a caricature of occupational groups such as photographers in the different fields of their practices.

Segmentation

The sociologist Howard S. Becker (1978; 1982) has noted the complexity of occupational groups in the visual arts. His analysis of the cultural boundaries between different types and levels of art and craft leads him towards an awareness of the 'worlds' in which art (in the broadest sense) is made. He underlines the important identity of groups with shared ideas and conventions that unify and co-ordinate their activities. Becker places a strong emphasis on the value of the creative environment as an important factor in the production of the visual arts in much the same way that McRobbie characterizes the influx of young, freelance artists and designers as a flexible workforce in the burgeoning creative industries springing up in major cities in the 1990s.

Becker's writing indentifies propensity for movement of practitioners between different 'worlds' of art and craft. He notes the boundary lines between practices that have different aims: one group emphasizes aesthetic criteria whilst for the other utility is paramount. As we have seen this is a foundational distinction but Becker is equally mindful of the movement of practitioners across these boundary lines. For example the distinction between the *craft* worker and *artist-craft* worker relies on the latter's 'more ambitious goals and ideologies' (1978: 866). The boundary lines are well established and yet they are porous enough to allow the crafts to invade art. Becker describes the formation of 'segments' that allow the hidebound craft worker some advance toward a more liberal expression of artistic ideas:

> A craft world, whose aesthetic emphasises utility and virtuoso skill and whose members produce works according to the dictates of clients or employers operating in some extracraft world, develops a new segment. The segment's members add to the basic aesthetic an emphasis on beauty and develop some additional organizational elements which in part free them from the need to satisfy employers so completely.
>
> (1978: 867)

In this statement Becker tries to capture the image of craft workers moving around organizational settings in an effort to gain support for their work. It presents a picture of struggle for some measure of independence and artistic freedom. The variable practices of artists, designers and photographers whose practice is 'flexible' enough to publish work online, or in recognized print media, exhibit work, sell work to stock agencies, and do a bit of teaching might constitute a 'segment' in Becker's terms. He notes:

> These artist-craftsmen develop a kind of art world around their activities; we might reasonably call it a 'minor art' world. The world contains much of the apparatus of such fully-fledged 'major arts' as painting and sculpture: shows, prizes, sales to collectors, teaching positions, and the rest.
>
> (Becker, 1978: 867)

In some individual practices skilled craft workers produce work of their own independently of employment. For others the paid work and artistic pleasure is achieved in day-to-day work and in

337

BEYOND THE ACADEMY

professional accreditation that goes with successful performance. Becker's idea of a 'segment' is dependent on a critical mass of people rather than individuals acting independently. The idea of social networking and finding regular work through contacts has always been an aspect of the cultural occupations in their various forms. Belonging to recognized sites of work and establishing a good reputation is valued by industry professionals.

We might note that professional categories that are used as markers of social distinction – such as art versus craft – are increasingly arbitrary. As Becker notes, most high art practices started out as craft practices (1978: 887) and, in any case, there is nowadays some evidence of 'co-existence' between different levels of practice. The history of photography is full of arbitrary shifts of meaning between levels when, for example, older forms of documentary (as in the work of Atget) are elevated to the museum or when self-proclaimed 'artistic' photography (Rejlander's artistic composites) is dismissed by later generations. Becker is keen to underline the fact that the experience of work for the photographer (and his or her place in the world of work) might not be secondary to an assessment of the work itself. The work is obviously important but the social value of occupational groups in which the photographer 'finds a position' is a significant part of the practice.

CONCLUSION

We have identified different cultural zones and traditions as sites of employment in the visual arts. The fine arts, associated with museum culture, are increasingly occupied by art photography. Alongside this we find industrial and commercial traditions that treat cultural products as commodities to be sold to consumers. Both zones are occupied by photography which contributes in different ways to the creative economy. We have also noted how these zones are increasingly interdependent and how far the historical distinctions between them have faded. A discussion about occupational categories forces us to think about the nature of the actual work itself, what it looks like and what it means, as well as the practices that generate its making. In these terms the conditions of work have an impact on what we might make of it. As we have seen there is a degree of celebration of the creative economy and the prospects it offers for creative labour.

There is no shortage of pundits singing the praises of acceleration in the cultural realm with an expanded workforce in the arts. Photographers have enjoyed high-profile status in cultures that thrive on celebrity and yet the greater part of the visual contents industry relies on practitioners responding to the demand for stereotyped and conventional imagery. Social theorists have described the shift towards self-employment, freelancing and casualization of creative labour in a system that favours short-term contract work. The show business model of hiring workers for specific tasks has been adapted in other areas of cultural sector employment. This might involve working as part of a creative team on short-term projects. The prospect of independence and variety of opportunities is a defining aspect of this kind of work. Freelance workers develop networking and business skills in the kind of fluid environment in which they work.

The theorist Richard Florida (2002) has identified the creative industries as the new engine of the economy (Harney, 2010: 432). New forms of production and investment are linked to a changing approach to work discipline. McRobbie notes the paradoxical nature of changing work. She sees the prospect of creative labour bypassing the boredom of nine to five working routines: 'There is a utopian thread embedded in this wholehearted attempt to make over the world of work into something closer to a life of enthusiasm and enjoyment' (McRobbie, 2005: 380). This optimism is moderated by the changing nature of work in the present century. Self-exploitation, long hours and low pay, argues McRobbie, are a reality for many workers in the creative industries (McRobbie, 2001; 2005). Other writers have noted the precarious nature of work especially in the early stages of a career. It is also the case that many of the new kinds of work taken up by self-taught creative workers or graduates trained in the art schools or universities demand high levels of technical skill in rapidly changing and unpredictable working situations. Multi-skilling and acceptance of diversity of occupation are replacing the old specialisms that defined the craft elements in photography. We have noted the utopian side of photographic work and the extent to which photography offers scope for rewarding employment. Successful practitioners often underline the enormous pleasure of the discipline. We have also noted that diversification of working practices presents a challenge that skilled and resourceful photographers accept. Following Becker (1978: 880) we note prideful opposition to exploitation in the workplace when workers take satisfaction in a job that is well done despite the odds against it.

SUMMARY OF KEY POINTS

- A new creative class of workers has been invented, dependent on new forms of employment in a rapidly changing workplace. Photographers continue to find work in the creative industries of advertising, fashion, news and a wide range of new and developing occupations.
- The market for symbolic goods (including clothes, transport, holidays, restaurants, new media products and so forth) is sustained by a 'talent-led' or creative economy. Self-taught, and art school/ university educated graduates form a reserve army of artistic labour. Photography is a central practice in the creative fields but employment requires supporting artistic, social, managerial and technical skills.
- The convergence of high art cultural and commercial practices is celebrated by theorists and real world opportunities exist for crossover between levels of practice. Evidence shows that high and low cultural practices interact but prestigious art institutions and established practices in the commercial sector are largely sustained by elite culture.
- The creative industries sustain a large working population of photographers and designers and yet it is a highly competitive market with social consequences such as long hours, low pay, and enforced diversification of working practices.
- Commercial work is normally tailored to client expectation. This often makes it predictable in style and content. Some stock agencies, however, favour experimental and oppositional styles of work.
- Photography is constrained by the division of labour that separates execution and conceptualization in the workplace. Traditional boundaries have been displaced by the widening of prospects for self-expression in some areas of stock photography. Photographers find other strategies for self-expression and social identity in occupational groupings and diversification of working practices.
- The pleasure of professional photographic work as experienced by successful photographers outweighs negative factors raised in this chapter.

BEYOND THE ACADEMY

REFERENCES

Adorno, Theodor and Horkheimer, Max (1979) *Dialectic of Enlightenment*, London: Verso.

Becker, Howard S. (1978) 'Arts and Crafts', in *American Journal of Sociology*, vol. 83, no. 4, pp. 862–889.

——(1982) *Art Worlds*, Berkeley: University of California Press.

Bourdieu, Pierre (1994) *Distinction: A Social Critique of the Judgement of Taste*, trans. Richard Nice, London and New York: Routledge.

Braverman, Harry (1974) *Labor and Monopoly Capitalism: The Degradation of Work in the Twentieth-Century*, New York and London: Monthly Review Press.

Cunningham, Stuart (2005) 'Creative Enterprises', in John Hartley (ed.), pp. 282–298.

Du Gay, Paul (ed.) (1997), *Production of Culture/Cultures of Production*, London/Thousand Oaks, CA/New Delhi: Sage.

Flew, Terry (2005) 'Creative Economy', in John Hartley (ed.), pp. 344–360.

Florida, Richard (2002) *The Rise of the Creative Class*, New York: Basic Books.

Frosh, Paul (2003) *The Image Factory: Consumer Culture, Photography and the Visual Content Industry*, Oxford and New York: Berg.

Gelder, Hilde Van and Westgeest, Helen (2011) *Photography Theory in Historical Perspective: Case Studies from Contemporary Art*, Oxford: Wiley Blackwell.

Gendron, Bernard (1997) 'Theodor Adorno and the Cadillacs', in Paul du Gay (ed.), pp. 111–118.

Harney, Stefano (2010) 'Creative Industries Debate – Unfinished Business: Labour, Management, and the Creative Industries' in *Cultural Studies*, vol. 24, no. 3, May 2010, pp. 431–444.

Hartley, John (2005) *Creative Industries*, Oxford: Blackwell.

Hirsch, Jonathan (n.d.) 'Skillset Photo-Imaging Skills Strategy', in *Sector Skills Council for the Audio Visual Industries*.

Hoffman, Barry (2002) *The Fine Art of Advertising*, New York: Stewart, Tabori and Chang.

Hurlburt, Allan (1983) *Photographics: The Interaction of Design and Photograph*, New York: Watson-Gupthill.

Leadbeater, Charles (2005) 'Delia not Adam Smith', in John Hartley (ed.), pp. 126–132.

Lehman, Peter and Luhr, William (2008) *Thinking About Movies*, Oxford: Wiley Blackwell.

Lupton, Ellen, and Miller, Abbott (1999) *Design Writing Research: Writing on Graphic Design*, London and New York: Phaidon.

McRobbie, Angela (1999) *In the Culture Society: Art, Fashion and Popular Music*, London and New York: Routledge.

——(2001), 'Everyone is Creative: Artists as New Economy Pioneers'. Available at: http://www.opendemocracy.net/node/652 (accessed 06.05.2014).

——(2005) 'Clubs to Companies', in John Hartley (ed.), pp. 375–390.

Pritchard, Lisa (2011) *Setting Up a Successful Photography Business*, London: A & C Black.

Rosenberg, Harold (1962) *The Tradition of the New*, London: Thames and Hudson.

Rosenblum, Barbara (1978) *Photographers at Work: A Sociology of Photographic Styles*, New York and London: Holmes and Meier.

Shiff, Richard (1996) 'Originality', in Robert S. Nelson and Richard Shiff (eds) *Critical Terms for Art History*, Chicago and London: University of Chicago Press, pp. 103–115.

Sholette, Gregory G. (2004) 'Welcome to the Desert of the Real Art World', a review of Chin-tao Wu (2002) *Privatising Culture*, in the *Oxford Art Journal*, vol. 27, no. 2, pp. 257–262.

Standing, Guy (2011) *The Precariat; A New Dangerous Class*, London and New York: Bloomsbury.

——(2014) *A Precariat Charter: From Denizens to Citizens*, London and New York: Bloomsbury.

Stone, Tony (1995) *Tony Stone Images*, volume 14, Worldwide House, 116 Bayham Street, London, NW1 0BA.

Williamson, Judith (1983) *Decoding Advertisements: Ideology and Meaning in Advertising*, London and New York: Marion Boyars.

Wu, Chin-tao (2002) *Privatising Culture: Corporate Art Interventions Since the 1980s*, London: Verso.

CASE STUDIES 4 AND 5

The two case studies in this part of the book are specifically related to contemporary photographic practices 'beyond the academy'. In Case Study 4 we focus on the everyday use of photography and the widespread use of photography in social and recreational media. In Case Study 5 we analyse new approaches in photographic manipulation and radical new techniques in the design and commercial promotion of cars.

CASE STUDY 4: DIGITAL AND MOBILE PHONE CULTURES

CS4.1 World Press Photo of the Year 2013. John Stanmeyer, VII for *National Geographic*, 26 February 2013. © ANP/Alamy. African migrants on the shore of Djibouti City at night raise their phones in an attempt to capture an inexpensive signal from neighbouring Somalia.

DIGITAL AND MOBILE PHONE CULTURES

The winning image of the World Press Photo of the Year 2013 taken by John Stanmeyer (fig. CS4.1) is a beautifully symbolic image of the mobile phone in contemporary culture. The picture depicts African migrants attempting to get a cheaper mobile phone signal at the shore of Djibouti city. However, more than this, Stanmeyer's picture also describes the new phenomenon of global connectivity. In 2014 it is predicted that 40 per cent of the world's population is online, a statistic that suggests media theorist Marshall McLuhan's idea of a 'global village' is becoming a reality (Internet World Stats, 2014). Both computers and mobile 'smart' phones now access the World Wide Web. A recent headline predicted that 'Mobile internet devices will outnumber humans this year' (Arthur, 2013). At the time of writing over six billion mobile phones are currently in use and half of these devices are purported to include in-built cameras. More than ever before, photography has become an accessible, democratic medium. In the developed world, many people have a camera with them at all times, as part of the functionality of their mobile phone. In an earlier case study on the digital camera (in Part 1, pp. 141–8) we described the development of the digital camera and introduced the idea of the mobile phone camera. In this case study the effect digital and mobile phone photography has on our culture is examined. We also consider the implications for both amateur and professional photographers. We will discuss three main areas: personal or snapshot photography by amateurs; photojournalism and the rise of the 'citizen journalist'; and the influence of digital and mobile phone cultures in contemporary art practice.

A Tsunami of Images

It is estimated that in 2014, one billion photographs were uploaded to the Internet each day (Blodget and Danova, 2014). Contemporary writing on the new realm of the networked image and mobile photography usually begins with mind-boggling statistics for the numbers of images uploaded globally to the Internet on a daily basis. When discussing several of the online platforms for photography below, we will mention statistics to give the reader a sense of the volume involved. However, these figures are often hard to grasp, bearing little relation to the individual and most often are superseded by more phenomenal statistics by the time the article has been published.

Media historian Martin Lister describes this new era of digital culture as producing a virtually 'incalculable' amount of circulated photographs, creating a 'tsunami of images' (Lister, 2014: 1, 16). Elsewhere, in other recent related articles, further metaphors abound in an attempt to bring a sense of the enormous scale of images now shared online: an 'avalanche of images' and an 'inexhaustible stream' (Rubenstein and Sluis, 2008: 18, 22). Critics such as Andrew Keen critique this new freedom of sharing user-generated content online, as 'an endless forest of mediocrity' (Keen, 2008: 2). Keen's book *The Cult of the Amateur* condemns the freedom of publishing the Internet now affords: a stance many professional photographers may have in response to the ever-rising amount of photography flooding the Internet.

Writer David Campbell, in discussing image 'abundance', concedes that more photographs are in circulation in digitized culture but argues that image upload statistics are misleading. Using Facebook as a case in point Campbell points out that statistics quoting 350 million daily image uploads actually equate to 'one picture uploaded every three days per Facebooker' (Campbell, 2013: 269) which does not sound so much like a 'tsunami of images' flooding virtual space.

343

CASE STUDY 4

Web 2.0: The Age of Online Participation

When Tim Berners-Lee proposed the World Wide Web in 1990 he dreamt of a platform for the democratic sharing of information, with readers creating new material and a culture of 'collaborative authorship' (Berners-Lee and Cailiau, 1990). However, the first websites were mainly 'read only'. Users needed specific technical skills to upload new content to websites. In 1999 Darcy DiNucci predicted a new age for the World Wide Web as 'Web 2.0' (DiNucci, 1999). Often referred to as the age of the amateur, the term Web 2.0 came into prominence in 2004 with a conference presentation by Tim O'Reilly, 'The Architecture of Participation' (Moschovi, McKay and Plouviez, 2013: 20). Web 2.0 is not a new operating system or coding language but rather a new media conceptualization of the Internet in the twenty-first century. The Internet has become an increasingly participatory experience: anybody with access to a computer and an internet connection can make their own blog, edit a Wikipedia page or add to various social networking websites. This has been dubbed 'user generated content'. The increased capability of mobile phones to act as small, personal networked computers has certainly aided the journey of the Internet from a passive transmission of information, to a place that encourages participation. Mobile internet users can take a photograph with their phone and instantly upload to multiple web platforms. The Internet is now an inclusive arena for image sharing.

There are many positive attributes of Web 2.0: it is open, collaborative, participatory and democratic. Opponents of Web 2.0 such as Keen, mentioned above, worry that it encourages amateurism and is diluting culture. Keen notes the blurring of the boundaries between author and audience and worries that Web 2.0 is in danger of 'transforming culture into cacophony' (Keen, 2008: 14).

A Brief History of the Camera Phone

A huge driving force in this change in digital culture in relation to photography was the widespread global adoption of the camera phone. The Japanese company, Kyocera, released the first mobile phone with an in-built camera called the 'Visual Phone', in 1999. Adoption of this type of image capture device grew in popularity in Japan alongside another type of cult image making: the *puri-kura* or 'Print Club'. This is a youth culture craze of posing in specialist public photo booths with groups of friends. The resulting images are output as stickers and often stuck onto mobile phones as a method of customization. The practice of *puri-kura* and the use of mobile phones to take snapshot photographs of friends became part of the Japanese youth cultures' way of expressing their identity (Goggin, 2006: 144–145).

As cameras became an integral part of users' mobile phones, initially in Japan, then globally, many users began to take more photographs than previously with a traditional film compact camera. They took photographs of their family and holidays but also more banal moments of everyday life. This type of 'pervasive' photo taking was, of course, in part because users would always have their mobile phone camera easily at hand, as part of their everyday belongings (Goggin, 2006). The mobile phone, a device to speak to people with, became a camera. At the turn of the twenty-first century, users could send their mobile phone photographs to other mobile users via a Multimedia Messaging Service. In 2006 this type of photography became networked by the widespread adoption of 3G, or third generation, mobile broadband Internet (and since 2013 an even higher speed 4G connection) enabling mobile users to directly upload their photographs from their mobile phones to the World Wide Web. In 2007

Apple released their first 'smartphone': the iPhone. Although other smartphones or PDA ('palm sized' Personal Digital Assistants) existed beforehand, Apple developed many in-phone software programmes ('apps') that complemented photography. This popularized the use of the iPhone for both amateur and occasional professional use, and ease of sharing images online.

Use of the iPhone and similar smartphones for taking photographs has become a universal practice. Few amateur photographers now use film cameras, with only a niche market remaining for a minority of professional photographers and vintage enthusiasts. Analogue practices, however, retain a strong presence in documentary and art photography output for the gallery or book publication market. For the amateur and everyday vernacular photographer, digital capture is now the easiest method for the majority. For many that now means using a small compact point and shoot digital camera or increasingly a mobile phone camera.

The Apple iPhone embodies the massive changes that have taken place within this new landscape of photography. It is a device that integrates three important activities: 'the making, processing, and distribution of images' (Gómez Cruz and Meyer, 2012: 203). Comparisons have been made to the Polaroid camera, but this could not *distribute*, and the *user* could not control processing. Some digital cameras could connect directly to a printer, but the iPhone was one of the first all-in-one devices. This functionality made it very easy for the average user to move from merely being a consumer of the iPhone, or a passive consumer of images online, to also being producer of content: a producer/consumer or 'prosumer' (Toffler, 1980). However, some new media theorists contend that amateur photographers have *always* been producer/consumers and photography itself was the 'original user-generated content' (Lister, 2014: 7). Photographers, unlike musicians, filmmakers and authors, have always been able to produce and output their work. Whereas consumer video cameras and desktop music production software only became available in the 1980s, photography could be seen as being a precursor of user-generated developments by over a century (ibid.: 8).

Photography academic Nicholas Muellner explores the relationship between consumerism and photography further. Once the image is captured, he notes, it is immediately uploaded to a social networking platform for further consumption:

> Our images are rated, analyzed, inventoried and aggregated. We claim our individuality and worth through the very gesture of offering ourselves up for ever more public and immediate consumption, and photography is a central agent of this quickening exchange.
>
> (Muellner, 2013: 79)

Muellner makes a further philosophical observation that the camera phone or digital camera has increasingly removed the photographer from the experience. The world is viewed through the screen of their camera, and not in first person: it is a mediated reality. After each capture the photographer will check the image, in a repeated circuit of: 'viewing, shooting, editing, viewing, shooting, editing' (ibid.: 78).

Lister notes instant processing habits are to do with the tactile physicality of cradling these palm-sized devices in our hands (Lister, 2014: 17). The camera becomes an extension of our body, where 'the human hand, mobile imaging device, screen and eye come into a new relationship' (ibid.: 18). An early report on mobile culture by communications researcher Carole Rivière describes the mobile phone as a 'prosthetic' object and as such is part of its owner (Rivière cited in Goggin, 2006: 146). Everywhere you look in urban spaces people are 'glued' to their mobile phones: using a navigational device, reading

CASE STUDY 4

social media updates, typing on the go, occasionally making voice calls, taking photographs and shooting video. A natural progression is to make the mobile 'hands-free' and wearable, for on-the-go use. In the 1970s, engineering professor Steve Mann pioneered wearable computer technology, most notably the EyeTap Digital Eye Glass and a WearCom2 device, a precursor to the connectivity and geo-positioning capabilities of modern smartphones (Goggin, 2006: 154). In 2014 Google released 'Google Glass', a head-mounted smartphone. This device is worn like a pair of glasses and gives the wearer a digital display via a prism in front of the right eye (Corbyn, 2014).

The Google Glass is a device that, just like the iPhone, is multi-featured. The Google Glass user can take a photo by blinking the eye; shoot moving image by a voice command; utilize mapping capabilities as a GPS device; as well as it being a micro-computer for emails, internet access and running many apps, such as video cookery demonstrations (very useful for hands-free cooking). Some critics worry about the potentially sinister or creepy uses for this device and Google have even published an etiquette guide for their tribe of 'Glass Explorers'. Users of the device are advised not to be 'creepy or rude (aka, a "Glasshole")' (Google.com, 2014).

Other manufacturers have now also started producing and marketing prototype 'smart glasses' (Hussain and Kelion, 2014). However, Google Glass is still the only product available and yet at the time of going to press can only be obtained on eBay. Google Glass, as noted in Case Study 2 above, is in development. A version entitled Google Glass 2 is yet to come. Other types of wearable technology include smart watches. The Apple Watch is the market leader and incorporates many smartphone features including a camera into a hand watch device. It was made available as a consumer product in 2015.

Networked Photography – 'Photo 2.0'

The mobile phone camera is essentially a networked camera. Andy Adams, a web producer and photography publisher, popularized the term 'Photo 2.0', which references Web 2.0 culture (Adams, 2011: 69). Photo 2.0 means for many photographers that they have an instant output and audience for their work. Increasingly smartphones are the only device needed for online image sharing. They are now outselling compact digital cameras globally, although growth in digital SLR purchasing continues to increase (Robinson, 2012). On Flickr, the image-sharing website, the Apple iPhone is the most popular camera (flickr.com, 2014). Most professional photographers and keen amateurs adopt a workflow of shooting on a professional standard digital SLR, then uploading images to various online platforms. Increasingly many digital cameras now have wifi to allow direct image upload.

Photographers who shoot on analogue cameras using film also engage in online image sharing to promote their latest project. Often complementing their 'slow' analogue workflow, film photographers shoot 'out-takes' or sneak previews of their current work using an iPhone and then upload it to Instagram, an online mobile photo-sharing service. The documentary photographer Anastasia Taylor-Lind, for example, regularly posts iPhone 'snaps' on Instagram whilst on assignment or shooting personal work, on medium format film. In 2014 she had over 57,000 followers on this platform alone (http://instagram.com/anastasiatl). Social networking has provided an instant market for her future publications and prints. Professional photographers also use crowdfunding websites as a way of fundraising for live projects and book print runs. Crowdfunding initiatives also raise the profile of a photographer and their project, often turning a once passive online audience into active participants and indeed funders or stakeholders in the project. Crowdfunding usually takes place on dedicated online platforms, where creative practitioners can pitch new projects that need financing. This also means new work is made in a participatory culture, whereby photographers involve their audience in the actual creative process, helping fund projects as well as suggesting locations and subjects (Adams, 2011: 70).

Author and critic Fred Ritchin anticipated and identified this change in the nature of photography as being a 'paradigm shift' and proposed a new name of 'hyper-photography' (Ritchin, 1990: 132). Hyper-photography has not yet been fully realized, but the idea has been incorporated into the new digital storytelling methods of professional photojournalists who use multimedia strategies such as video, slideshows and sound, with photographs. At the other end of the scale, a photograph on the website Flickr.com could be described as a 'hyper-photography', because of the capability to add clickable descriptive text labels on the image. Ritchin goes further to even suggest that the term 'photograph' might be outdated, and that 'image' might be more encompassing for the Internet age. Ritchin notes:

> If the last century was the century of the Photograph, this century is that of image-branding, surveillance and sousveillance, geo-positioning, sexting, image wars, citizen journalism, happy slapping, selfies, photo-opportunities, medical imaging, augmented realities, video games, snapchat, and within it all, photography.

(Ritchin, 2013: 160)

Ritchin's list portends a bewildering environment for the emerging photographer to enter into and make sense of. This list is so broad that it illustrates the wide gamut of imagery captured in mobile and digital culture. In the final section of this case study we look at personal photography (selfies, photo-opportunities, snapchat), citizen journalism (sousveillance) and art photography (which might appropriate any of the genres identified by Ritchin).

Personal Photography

It has never been easier to take photographs. Historically, personal photography may have been limited to significant moments in family life, such as births, weddings and holidays. Now we live a 'life more photographic' with constant access to a networked camera phone (Rubinstein and Sluis, 2008). The main output, and impetus, for personal photography is social networking online platforms. Social networking platforms and photo blogging websites provide the reason and 'occasion for taking photographs: for walking, for wandering, for being alert to opportunities' (Lister, 2014: 19). Media analysts have branded this type of user as part of 'Generation C', a label that describes consumers who *create content* and share within a *connected* online community (Rubinstein and Sluis, 2008: 18).

One of the biggest subjects of personal photography for Generation C is the self-portrait or 'selfie', a term that Oxford Dictionaries online heralded as word of the year in 2013. Oxford Dictionaries online defines a 'selfie' as 'a photograph that one has taken of oneself, typically with a smart phone or webcam and uploaded to a social media website'. The term derived from a trending social media hashtag and has now spilled into common language as a well-known phrase for a self-portrait photograph (bbc.co.uk, 2013). A 'selfie' is generally taken with a smartphone that has a front facing camera. This technology makes it easier to capture a self-portrait, as the user is given a real-time view of their image whilst composing, to enable the most flattering shot. This is an example of the

CASE STUDY 4

technology driving a new cultural trend, just as the invention of affordable roll film and the box Brownie impacted on photography in its infancy. Celebrities and politicians have jumped onto this craze as a tool for self-promotion. Arguably the reason for taking these photographs is to share them, as a performative practice for online communities watching from virtual screens (Larsen and Sandbye, 2014: xx). Everyday personal photography is no longer private, but performed, almost live. These individual personal photographs lose value as 'mementoes' for a treasured family album and become transient 'moments' to be communicated, then forgotten (José van Dijck quoted in Larsen and Sandbye, 2014: xx).

The online platform, Snapchat, is a service that allows users to send photographs to individuals or groups, literally chatting with snaps. These images only appear on the recipient's mobile phone screen for a few seconds before being automatically deleted. At the time of writing Snapchat is the most popular social networking platform for sharing photographs, on which users currently share 400 million images a day (Knibbs, 2013). The trend in personal photography is moving towards using images as a kind of visual small talk or 'visual chit-chat' (Villi, 2013: 89). Another photo sharing platform, Instagram, allows users to share or perform live moments from their private lives. Instagram images can also be modified by vintage photographic 'filters'. This makes the instant mobile image appear more like an old faded photograph in the family album.

Platforms such as Snapchat, Facebook and Instagram are very much about sharing the 'now' and allowing images to speak for themselves. Other web platforms, such as Flickr, encourage archiving images using tags to describe qualities of the image for helpful retrieval. 'Within this avalanche of images, the practice of tagging one's photos acts as a strategy for preventing them from disappearing from view' (Rubenstein and Sluis, 2008: 18). This could be described as a system of classification called 'folksonomy', a combination of the two terms: folk and taxonomy. Added to that, digital images now include geo-placement data. All of these markers make digital images more appealing and useful for a future audience of anthropologists or ethnographers. This is a new kind of digital archaeology, where even banal photographs bear witness to the past (Shanks and Svabo, 2014: 240).

Citizen Journalism

In early 2014 the Kiev street riots generated a wealth of citizen journalism images, which were shared on social media instantaneously. One such user was featured on the Esquire website, showing Instagram users' images before and after the riots (Joiner, 2014). Figure CS4.2 shows two mobile phone photographs taken by Natalia Ukolova, a Ukrainian citizen caught up in the riots. The first picture shows a typical 'selfie' taken on 15 February 2014. The image on the right, which Ukolova took on her phone only four days later, captures a riot scene. This diptych illustrates the stark contrast in subject matter captured by citizens in times of crisis or atrocity.

In his recent book *Bending the Frame: Photojournalism, Documentary and the Citizen,* Ritchin discussed the phenomenon of the citizen journalist:

> The more fluid, participatory images coming from the owners of cellphones, rather than staking a claim to being definitive, can often be easily supported or contradicted by contrasting them with the many others made at the same scene ... Rather than claiming a doctrine of

DIGITAL AND MOBILE PHONE CULTURES

CS4.2 Two mobile phone photographs taken by Ukrainian Instagram user nata_original. Real name: Natalia Ukolova. From the article by James Joiner, 'Before and After: Kiev on Instagram'. 21 February 2014. Available at http://www.esquire.com/blogs/news/life-in-kiev-before-and-after.

journalistic objectivity or neutrality, the very subjectivity of non-professionals, their transparent self-involvement and lack of financial incentive, can be reassuring – many viewers may empathise with the motivations of these ordinary citizens, which are probably similar to their own.

(Ritchin, 2013: 11)

In 2003 Steve Mann coined the phrase 'sousveillance' from the French words for below, *sous,* and to watch, *veiller* (Mann *et al.,* 2003: 332). Where *sur*veillance represents organizations observing people, *sous*veillance is the inverse, a new tribe of citizen journalists reporting 'from below'. This becomes 'watchful vigilance from underneath', with citizens and activists recording atrocities as a 'technologically mediated practice of bearing witness' (Goggin, 2006: 154). Three types of people produce this wealth of journalistic image content: ordinary citizens, politicized activists and military personnel. Citizens and activists could be said to capture images 'from below'. However, the photography taken by military personnel is altogether different.

In 2003 mobile phone photographs taken by US military personnel evidenced the torture and abuse of prisoners detained at the Abu Ghraib prison (see fig. 6.8). Some of these photographs were leaked to the press and the officers were subsequently charged. The mobile phone photographs and videos, taken by military personnel to document criminal behaviour, were later retrieved and used as evidence against them. Arguably these images describe the atrocities of war more faithfully than an embedded professional photojournalist (Ritchin, 2013: 71). Military personnel also capture more everyday photographs of training exercises and their daily lives off duty to send to their families back home (ibid.: 71).

CASE STUDY 4

The images of the infamous Abu Ghraib tortures were subsequently published with one even appearing on the front cover of *The Economist* in March 2004. But how are the other kind of images of atrocity taken by citizens and archivists shared and published, either online or in print? This is a new area for the major international news organizations and regulations have yet to be standardized. News reporting, in print, online and on TV, is increasingly reliant on the photographs and videos captured by citizen journalists to cover stories (Patrick and Allan, 2013: 109). It has been suggested that amateur producers understandably shoot footage from a position of wanting to voice their suffering, as opposed to official or government sourced footage which might seek to tell a different story (ibid.: 113). This often very raw, 'shaky and grainy' footage helps provide a watching and waiting media audience with an almost live feed of scenes of war and rioting (ibid.: 112). When these photographs or videos are used they are normally captioned with 'anonymous footage' or 'amateur footage'. There are issues attaching to the validity and provenance of citizen-generated footage and news agencies are often careful to label this content appropriately.

What are the implications for professional photojournalists? For Ritchin this is no simple discussion of amateur versus professional, because the environment for a professional photojournalist has changed so dramatically in recent years. Editorial and commissioned opportunities have diminished and pay rates have shrunk. Photojournalists are both borrowing from the language of the citizen journalist by shooting on mobile phones (see Case Study 2, 'The Digital Camera': Kuwayama and Gardi are photojournalists who use mobile phone photography) and at the other end of the scale borrowing from the language of staged art photography (for example, Simon Norfolk's large format *Afghanistan* series, fig. 2.9). Photojournalism is constantly evolving and will continue to borrow from other genres and embrace the power of the 'connected camera'.

Art Practice

Some contemporary artists appropriate and curate selections of digital *found* photographs. Many are lifted from social networking platforms and photo sharing websites. The idea of the 'found photograph' and, more broadly, found objects stems from the artist Marcel Duchamp's 1915 notion of the readymade. Throughout the twentieth century artists have continued to 'appropriate' everyday objects and re-classify them in an art context. In the 1960s Gerhard Richter began his 'Atlas' collection including thousands of found photographs. Since the 1980s Joachim Schmid has been trawling flea markets and antique fairs to hunt for old photographs and represent them in a gallery context. More recently artists, including John Stezaker and Julie Cockburn, have used vernacular photographs in collages. Photo historians Michel Frizot and Cedric de Veigy published examples of *Photo Trouvée* in 2006 to celebrate the genre of the found photograph (Frizot and de Veigy, 2006).

Penelope Umbrico has developed a practice of collecting images found on image sharing websites often using image tags to trace certain themes. This is an example of the 'folksonomy' classification system giving new life to a digital image. In 2006, intrigued by the repetition of similar subject matter online, she typed the word 'sunset' to the search box on the photo sharing website Flickr.com. This search yielded 541,795 results. She printed a selection of these as 4 X 6 inch machine prints and exhibited them in a grid format installation. In this work each sun is cropped in a regular and consistent manner. This gives an absolute uniformity to the installation. Each time she exhibits this series she updates

DIGITAL AND MOBILE PHONE CULTURES

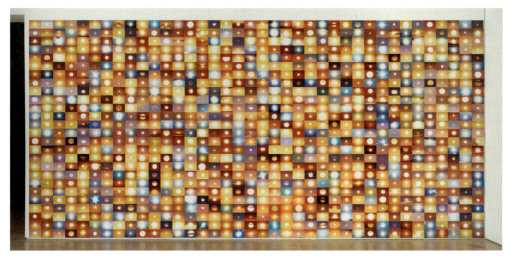

CS4.3 Penelope Umbrico, *5,377,183 Suns from Flickr (Partial) 4/28/09*, 2009. Courtesy SF MOMA. © Penelope Umbrico.

the work by conducting a new Flickr search. Figure CS4.3 shows '5,377,183 Suns from Flickr (Partial) 4/28/09'. On Umbrico's website the project is listed as 'ongoing' and the present count of sunsets on Flickr is currently over eight million. Umbrico notes that the title of the work makes a comment on the ever-increasing number of images being shared online (Palmer Albers, 2013: 12).

Joachim Schmid is another artist who has used Flickr as a source for image appropriation. Between 2008 and 2011 Schmid created 96 photobooks in a series called 'Other People's Photographs', exploring collective patterns in digital personal photography by amateurs. In a recent panel discussion at Tate Modern Schmid explained that he was fascinated why people take the same sorts of subject matter (Schmid, 2013). He would sit for hours, days and weeks at his computer trawling Flickr searching for themes. A selection of themes discovered by Schmid include: Airline Meals, At Work, Cleavage, Coffee, Collections, Dogs, Drinks, Encounters, Eyes, Faces in Holes, Feet, Food, Fridge Doors, Hotel Rooms, Maps, Objects in Mirror, Parking Lots, Self, Sunset and Television.

Figure CS4.4 shows *Another Self,* a collection of pictures of people's feet, a very common type of image circulated on social media platforms. This type of image is an example of how the mobile phone camera is always at hand to photograph every moment, as discussed above. Schmid initially exhibited these themed groupings as a

CS4.4 Joachim Schmid, *Another Self,* from the book series *Other People's Photographs,* 2008–11. Courtesy of the artist.

351

CASE STUDY 4

projected slideshow in a gallery setting. However, he found that visitors would grow impatient and not spend time viewing the show for very long. He then printed these collections as books and installed long tables in the gallery to display them. After this he found visitors would spend much longer, in some cases hours, poring over each page of his books (Schmid, 2013). The act of printing these images, like Umbrico's *Suns from Flickr*, forces the viewer to have a physical encounter with an object. This kind of imagery also blurs the conventional boundaries between art and vernacular, everyday, or social media. It underlines the fact that 'art' is always mediated and circumscribed by the processes that generate it.

In 2011 curator Erik Kessels printed out all of the one million photographs uploaded to Flickr in a 24-hour period, and installed them in piles around the FOAM gallery in Amsterdam (fig. CS4.5). Much like the metaphors described above, Kessels uses such terms as an 'avalanche' of photographs uploaded daily and describes his installation as literally 'mountains' of photos (Kessels, 2014).

Increasingly artists are choosing to work with mobile phone technology to generate new work. The American artist Nina Katchadourian makes work using her mobile phone camera. Katchadourian started her on-going project, *Seat Assignment,* on a flight in 2010. She had become increasingly frustrated with the amount of time she wasted on long-haul aeroplane flights for work. Katchadourian began taking playfully creative shots on her mobile phone camera; initially, of the things in her immediate environment, such as the inflight magazine as the backdrop for an avalanche created from smashed pretzels. She enjoyed the anonymity that using a small mobile camera afforded and its portability. If Katchadourian had tried setting up a large professional digital SLR camera more questions would have been asked. But with the mobile phone being such a ubiquitous device now, Katchadourian can work virtually unnoticed (Somerset, 2011). In over 150 flights only three people have taken an

CS4.5 Erik Kessels, *24HRS IN PHOTOS*. Photograph by Carsten Rehder. © dpa picture alliance archive/Alamy.

DIGITAL AND MOBILE PHONE CULTURES

interest in what she was doing. Figure CS4.6 shows her image *Lavatory Self-Portrait in the Flemish Style #12* (2011) from *Seat Assignment* (2010 and ongoing). In her project *Seat Assignment* Katchadourian adopts poses and styling inspired by fifteenth-century Flemish portraits. She uses whatever is at hand in the aeroplane toilet: such as tissue, toilet seat covers and paper towels.

In 2013 five international curators and photographers launched the show 'From Here On: Post Photography in the Age of Internet and the Mobile Phone', at the *Rencontres d'Arles*. In his foreword to the catalogue for this show Vincenç Altaió, Director of Arts Santa Mònica, describes this as a radical new time for 'Photography 2.0':

> The creative implications of this new technological potential are still incipient, but it has already modified and put in crisis such key concepts as authorship and the original work, as well as multiplying the possibilities of reproducing and circulating images to an unexpected extent.
>
> (Fontcuberta, 2013: 7).

CS4.6 Nina Katchadourian, *Lavatory Self-Portrait in the Flemish Style #12*, 2011, from *Seat Assignment* (2010 and ongoing). Courtesy of the artist.

CONCLUSION

We have explored the effect digital and mobile phone photography has on our culture and the implications for both amateur and professional photographers. We looked at the implications of 'Web 2.0' for photographers and image-makers. We examined three main areas: personal or snapshot photography by amateurs; photojournalism and the rise of the 'citizen journalist'; and the influence of digital and mobile phone cultures in contemporary art practice.

The camera is no longer a stand-alone device: it is networked. Cameras are owned by increasing numbers of people and they are often ready to hand and used playfully and quite randomly. The age of online participation alters the nature of photography, which could be referred to as 'photography 2.0'. Photographs taken with a mobile phone are often made for instant dissemination, typified by platforms such as Snapchat, rather than being made for an archive. Technology is driving social change, as friendship photography becomes a social norm. This has created a seemingly vast amount of circulated photographs, creating a 'tsunami of images' (Lister, 2014: 16).

Citizen journalism serves competing ideologies when used by ordinary citizens, political activists and authority figures such as military personnel. Artists are now appropriating and curating selections of digital 'found' photographs mined from social networking platforms and image sharing websites. As the technology races ever forward and the ease of image dissemination continues, there is a place for culture amid this apparent image abundance. Photographers will continue to make powerful work and be mindful that photography itself was the 'original user-generated content' (Lister, 2014: 7).

353

CASE STUDY 4

REFERENCES

Adams, Andy (2011) 'Photo 2.0 – Online Photographic Thinking (Revisited)', in Louise Clements and Alfredo Cramerotti (eds) *Format: Right Here Right Now. Exposures from the Public Realm*, Derby: Quad, pp. 69–70.

Arthur, Charles (2013) 'Mobile internet devices will outnumber humans this year', 7 February 2013. Available at: http://www.theguardian.com/technology/2013/feb/07/mobile-internet-outnumber-people (accessed 19.04.2014).

bbc.co.uk (2013) '"Selfie" named by Oxford Dictionaries as word of 2013'. Available at: http://www.bbc.co.uk/news/uk-24992393 (accessed: 20.04.2014).

Berners-Lee, Tim and Cailiau, Robert (1990) 'WorldWideWeb: Proposal for a HyperText Project', Available at: www.w3.org/Proposal.html (accessed: 19.04.2014).

Blodget, Henry and Danova, Tony (2014) 'The Future of Mobile', 22 March 2014 www.businessinsider.com Available: http://www.businessinsider.com.au/future-of-mobile-slides-2014-3#slide18-18 (accessed 19.04.2014).

Campbell, David (2013) 'Afterword: Abundant Photography, Discursive Limits and the Work of Images', in Alexandra Moschovi, Carol McKay, and Arabella Plouviez (eds), *The Versatile Image*, Leuven: Leuven University Press, pp. 265–270.

Corbyn, Zoë (2014) 'Google Glass – wearable tech but would you wear it?', *theguardian.com*, 6 April 2014. Available at: http://www.theguardian.com/technology/2014/apr/06/google-glass-technology-smart-eyewear-camera-privacy (accessed: 20.04.2014).

DiNucci, Darcy (1999) 'Fragmented future', in *Print*, April 1999, pp. 32 and 221–222. Available: http://darcyd.com/fragmented_future.pdf (accessed 19.04.2014).

Flickr.com (2014), 'Most Popular Cameras in the Flickr Community'. Available at: https://www.flickr.com/cameras/ (accessed 20.04.2014).

Fontcuberta, Joan (2013) *From Here On: PostPhotography in the Age of the Internet and the Mobile Phone*, Barcelona: RM Verlag SL.

Frizot, Michel and de Veigy, Cédric (2006) *Photo-trouvée*, London: Phaidon.

Goggin, Gerard (2006) *Cell Phone Culture: Mobile Technology in Everyday Life*, London and New York: Routledge.

Gómez Cruz, Edgar and Meyer, Eric T. (2012) 'Creation and Control in the Photographic Process: iPhones and the Emerging Fifth Moment in Photography', in *Photographies*, vol. 5, no. 2, September, pp. 203–221.

Google.com (2014) Available at: https://sites.google.com/site/glasscomms/glass-explorers (accessed 20.04.2014).

Hussain, Zarina and Kelion, Leo (2014) 'Computex: Google Glass Rival and Other Wearable Tech Seek Sales', 5 June 2014. Available at: http://www.bbc.co.uk/news/technology-27701933 (accessed 22.10.2014).

Internet World Stats (2014) Available at: http://www.internetworldstats.com/emarketing.htm (accessed 19.04.14).

Joiner, James (2014) 'Before and After: Kiev on Instagram'. Available at http://www.esquire.com/blogs/news/life-in-kiev-before-and-after (accessed 20.04.2014).

Keen, Andrew (2008) *The Cult of the Amateur: How Blogs, MySpace, YouTube and the Rest of Today's User-Generated Media are Killing our Culture and Economy,* London and Boston: Nicholas Brealey Publishing.

Kessels, Erik (2014) '24 HRS OF PHOTOS'. Available at: http://www.kesselskramer.com/exhibitions/2014/24-hrs-of-photos (accessed 20.04.2014).

Knibbs, Kate (2013) 'Snapchat users share 400 million images a day, as the app surpasses Facebook photo uploads', 19 November 2013. Available at: http://www.digitaltrends.com/social-media/comes-photo-uploads-snapchat-facebook-beat/#!Eniec. (accessed 19.04.2014).

Larsen, Jonas and Sandbye, Mette (eds) (2014) *Digital Snaps: The New Face of Photography,* London and New York: I. B. Tauris.

Lister, Martin (2014) 'Overlooking, Rarely Looking and Not Looking', in Jonas Larsen and Mette Sandbye (eds) *Digital Snaps: The New Face of Photography,* London and New York: I. B. Tauris, pp. 1–23.

Mann, Steve, Nolan, Jason and Wellman, Barry (2003) 'Sousveillance: Inventing and Using Wearable Computing Devices for Data Collection in Surveillance Environments', in *Surveillance & Society,* vol. 1, no. 3. Available at: http://library.queensu.ca/ojs/index.php/surveillance-and-society/article/view/3344/3306 (accessed 20.04.2014).

Muellner, Nicholas (2013) 'The New Interval', in Alexandra Moschovi, Carol McKay and Arabella Plouviez (eds), pp. 75–82.

Moschovi, Alexandra, McKay, Carol and Plouviez, Arabella (eds) (2013) *The Versatile Image,* Leuven: Leuven University Press.

Palmer Albers, Kate (2013) 'Abundant Images and the Collective Sublime', in *Exposure: Journal of the Society for Photographic Education*, Autumn 2013, vol. 46, no. 2, pp. 4–14.

Patrick, Caitlin and Allan, Stuart (2013) '"Humane Truth-Telling": Photojournalism and the Syrian Uprising', in Alexandra Moschovi, Carol McKay and Arabella Plouviez (eds).

Ritchin, Fred (1990) *In Our Own Image: The Coming Revolution in Photography,* New York: Aperture Foundation.

——(2013) *Bending the Frame: Photojournalism, Documentary and the Citizen,* New York: Aperture Foundation.

Robinson, Oliver (2012) 'The Evolving Landscape of Photography'. Available at: http://www.gfk.com/magazine/techtalk/techtalk-disruptive-technologies/the-changing-landscape-of-photography (accessed: 20.04.2014).

Rubinstein, Daniel and Sluis, Katrina (2008) 'A Life More Photographic: Mapping the Networked Image', in *Photographies*, vol. 1, no. 1, March, pp. 9–28.

Schmid, Joachim (2013) 'Everyday and Everywhere: Vernacular Photography Today'. A talk and panel discussion organized by Tate Modern in partnership with UCA Farnham and the journal

CASE STUDY 4

Photography & Culture. Speakers included: Geoffrey Batchen, Ben Burbridge, Kathy Kubicki and Joachim Schmid, 26 November 2013.

Shanks, Michael and Svabo, Connie (2014) 'Mobile-Media Photography: New Modes of Engagement', in Jonas Larsen and Mette Sandbye (eds) pp. 227–246.

Somerset, Guy (2011) 'Nina Katchadourian Interview', http://www.listener.co.nz, 28 April 2011. Available at: http://www.reframingphotography.com/sites/default/files/user/Katchadourian_NewZealandListener_1.7.12.pdf (accessed 20.04.2014).

Toffler, Alvin (1980) *The Third Wave*, New York: Bantam.

Villi, Mikko (2013) 'The Camera Phone as a Connected Camera', in Alexandra Moschovi, Carol McKay and Arabella Plouviez, (eds) pp. 87–106.

CASE STUDY 5: THE DESIGNED PHOTOGRAPH: COMPUTER GENERATED IMAGERY (CGI) IN CAR PHOTOGRAPHY

CS5.1 Press image for Porsche Cayenne. Courtesy of Dr. Ing. h.c. F. Porsche AG. The car in this image is fully computer generated. The landscape is a real photograph.

Car photography has been a thriving and lucrative specialism for public relations, advertising and product photographers since the early twentieth century when half-tone blocks began to be widely used to reproduce photographs alongside printed text. This case study looks at a growing trend in car advertising[1] both for print and screen, to incorporate computer-generated imagery (CGI) together with or instead of photography. How has this new technology influenced the specialism of car photography?

---

1   Whenever in this case study the term 'advertising' is mentioned, it includes 'press and public relations'.

CASE STUDY 5

Does this have further implications for the photography sector as a whole? Should we broaden the definition of photography or what it means to be a photographer in the twenty-first century?

Increasingly car companies are publishing press pictures and advertisements that offer for sale a car that is not yet in production. If no physical model of the car exists to purchase and drive on the road as shown for example in the press picture in Figure CS5.1 how has it been photographed? The answer frequently lies in using a computer simulation of the new car. The use of simulated photo-real images of objects raises issues around the authenticity of the image (for a more in-depth discussion of 'The Constructed Image' see Chapter 4). Such questions form a significant part of the history of pictorial representation. Photography is haunted by the question of 'the real' and in the case of advertising the collaborative work of the art director and photographer compounds the sense of not really knowing what is there. One is tempted to say that advertising photographs are 'designed' or constructed. For product and car photography the production team has evolved to include a digital artist incorporating computer-generated imagery (CGI) into the photograph.

In 2012 approximately 80 per cent of car advertisements and press pictures contained CGI elements, in contrast to 20 per cent in 2002 (Southern, 2012). To date this percentage of CGI content is increasing with automobile advertising. Most commonly the CGI element is the car and not the surrounding background. Figure CS5.1 shows a Porsche Cayenne speeding through a landscape. In this image the car is computer generated and composited into a photograph of a real landscape. Experienced car photographers David Breun and Martin Grega, who work together, photographed this landscape. They were commissioned to shoot this backdrop for a car not yet in production. The landscape shoot took place in December 2009, where an older model of the Porsche was used to give the photographic duo an idea of placement. The production of the Porsche Cayenne featured in Figure CS5.1 began in March 2010. The car in this image was created in the computer. Breun and Grega supervised the final CGI production of this image, ensuring that the car appeared photo-real.

Technological expertise has risen to such a high level of proficiency that it is difficult to tell whether the car in this example is real (a manufactured product available for sale) or a computer simulation. In examples such as this simulations are carefully crafted to look like photographs rather than computer models. This kind of practice seems to have advanced so far beyond normative levels of retouching and manipulation that the photographer may now seem to be displaced by new kinds of image making processes. It also asks you to think about the wider implications for the future of photography.

CGI makes the future of assignment photography look uncertain at least in some of its applications – such as the one we are discussing in this study. It may seem that it has, in some ways, exceeded the limits of photography. The image that is a fully rendered CGI entity is neither painting nor photography. It is a strange kind of thing in search of a name. The ontological question might be ignored if we ask what it does rather than what it is, and yet it is important to know what we are looking at. Despite its novelty the CGI image, in the examples we are using here, relies heavily on the old sense of photographic truth to achieve its narrative aims. As a perfect illusion it suspends disbelief and from an advertiser's point of view the consumer sees the Porsche (fig. CS5.1) in all its splendour as it was meant to be.

THE DESIGNED PHOTOGRAPH: COMPUTER GENERATED IMAGERY (CGI) IN CAR PHOTOGRAPHY

Simulation of the 'Real'

The use of photo-real CGI components in car advertisements derives partly from technological developments in the movie industry and partly from the growing importance of computer-aided design (CAD) in the car design process itself (see table in Figure CS5.2). CGI has been used extensively in films since the early 1980s, but came into the public eye with ground breaking full CGI animations such as *Toy Story* (1995) and incorporated with live action in feature films such as *The Abyss* (1989), *Terminator 2* (1991) and *Jurassic Park* (1993). In the case of *Jurassic Park* the viewing public came to realize it cannot always believe that images derive from an actual object or person (Staud, 2010). *Jurassic Park* is highly realistic in its creation of what appear to be 'live action' dinosaurs. The illusion is astonishing and yet the extinct creatures are obviously simulated.

The media historian and theorist Martin Lister defines a simulation as 'an artefact that can be experienced as if it were real, when no corresponding thing actually exists outside of the simulation itself' (Lister, 2009: 114). The CGI elements in *Jurassic Park* were painstakingly rendered to match the look of live action. The techniques deployed in CGI moving-image technology have parallels in still photographic practice where objects photographed in the world are seamlessly combined with CGI elements. The media theorist Lev Manovich suggests a completely new language for the photograph in an era of computer-generated imaging.

> The paradox of digital visual culture is while all imaging is shifting towards being computer-based, the dominance of photographic and cinematic looking images is becoming even stronger. But rather than being a direct, **'natural'** result of photo and film technology, these images are constructed on computers … And the reason we may think that computer graphics has succeeded in faking reality is that we, over the course of the last hundred and fifty years, *have* come to accept the image of photography and film as reality. What is faked is only a film-based image. Once we came to accept the photographic image as reality, the way to its future simulation was open.
>
> (Manovich, 2001: 180–200)

Manovich argues that CGI artists are aiming to make the final rendering appear like photographs, not the real world. New Media theorist and academic Sarah Kember notes in her book *Virtual Anxiety* that the veracity of the photograph is not threatened by this paradigm shift since, in her view, any representation constructs nothing more than an 'image-idea' of reality (Kember, 1998: 17).

Kember's postmodernist view favours the idea that photographs are like other kinds of visual images and as such they are always constructions. As we have seen in Chapter 4 this 'anti-realist' view has its opponents. Barthes (1981: 88–89) for example argues that a photograph is not a copy or simulation of reality but is, rather, 'an emanation of a past reality'. The Barthian argument is that a photograph has a causal relation with its referent. Other kinds of pictures (non-photographs) do not have this relation with the object to which they refer. Simulation for example merely enjoys an analogous relation with the object it appears to represent. For Barthes the photograph, in its traditional sense, is not a representation at all. It is a trace of something that appeared before the lens. The 'designed photograph' referred to in the title of this case study is not a traditional photograph, having only a limited causal relationship to the real. The designed photograph, it might be said, occupies a new liminal state between the real and the simulated.

CASE STUDY 5

For most viewers this photograph of a car in a landscape (fig. CS5.1) matches their expectations. They see the scene as if it had been photographed in a traditional way. For it to be seen in another way (as constructed) the viewer would need to be (literally) disillusioned before he or she could see it as something other than what it appears to be. In other words they would need to 'theorize' it as a computer-generated image. This might involve a degree of scepticism about how it was made leading to a re-conceptualization of its meaning.

CGI and the Uncanny Valley

Film directors and CGI artists are no longer constrained by what a moving image or stills camera can capture. It is now possible to bring extinct creatures back to life or at least to create convincing screen versions of them, and yet animators and CGI artists have not been able to produce a believable human in CGI. Computer generated technology can achieve exceptionally high levels of photo-likeness but, in most cases, it is more economically viable to take an actual photograph of a human subject, rather than creating it with computer software. A side note to this is that audiences are arguably not ready for realistic CGI photographs or moving images of simulated humans. There is a view that hyper-real human constructions can trigger reactions ranging from distrust to repulsion. In 1970 robotics professor Masahiro Mori described this phenomenon as the 'Uncanny Valley' and published a graph, illustrating a dip in empathy for near-realistic humanoids (Lucas, 2012). The limit of human likeness audiences can endure before they are repulsed has more recently been called the 'uncanny wall' (Tinwell *et al.*, 2011: 327). In this new analogy the 'wall' is the idea of an impenetrable uncanny wall, representing the viewer's evolving shrewdness for distinguishing imperfections in simulated images of humans, and keeping up with advances in new imaging technologies.

The movie *The Adventures of Tintin* (2011) portrays a near lifelike rendering of the human character, Tintin. The construction is so convincing that film critics have noted the eponymous figure was let down only by the rendering of his glassy, 'dead' eyes (Rose, 2011). In this example a peculiar level of uncertainty occurs when photography merges with animation. The strange hybrid that results seems uncanny or at least difficult to place. For some people perverse pleasure might result from this ambiguity. For others the effect is unsettling.

In 2009 London-based CGI specialists, Saddington Baines, received an ad agency commission to create a photo-real human face. Managing director Chris Christodoulou commented:

> You would think that with all the people in the world it would be easier to shoot someone but we get asked by agencies all the time, eager to avoid the issue of model release fees. With CGI you could design exactly the person you wanted. There's an incredible amount of work to be done in CGI, both for print and interactive media. We've been working with it for five years and we've only scratched the surface.

(Smith, 2009)

KEY TERM: The Uncanny

Sigmund Freud, the inventor of psychoanalysis, used the term 'the uncanny' (*das unheimliche*) in 1919 (Freud, 2003: 123). It is a word that translates as 'unhomely' and is often used to refer to persons, objects or events that appear to lose their familiarity and in so doing become uncomfortably strange. When human features and movements are duplicated and appear in the form of a cyborg or life-like copy – so that it is simultaneously familiar and alien – it might cause revulsion in some observers. In the case of mainstream advertising this effect is rarely sought since ads are generally very conservative. The kinds of visual effects achieved through increasingly sophisticated methods of simulation may, however, have parallels with the darker side of entertainment media.

Product Photography and CGI

The idea of audience resistance or the building of walls to keep out uncanny versions of the human subject might be good news for the commercial portrait photographer. However, there appears to be little psychological resistance to CGI representation of the non-human realm of things. CGI specialists such as Saddington Baines (mentioned above) and Taylor James (London and New York) mostly specialize in creating CGI photo-real simulations of material products, spaces and places.

Material products such as cars and all manner of saleable objects can be simulated from their computer-aided design (CAD) data into believable photographic renderings. This short-cut method of image creation is changing how companies now choose to 'photograph' new products for marketing purposes. For example, the Ikea product catalogue in 2013 is estimated to contain 25 per cent CGI content. It is noteworthy that the 285 in-house photographers, carpenters and interior designers, at Ikea's European photography studio have been retrained in CGI skills (Hansegard, 2012).

Increased Use of Computer-generated Images of Cars

The rationale and need to use CGI simulations of new car models instead of photographing the actual car is tied up in the timescale, economics and technology of the car design process. From the initial pencil sketch through to the final showroom model, the car design process takes three to four years. Images of cars for marketing purposes and pre-sales are needed well before the showroom completion date. These pre-release-date photographs were often in the past created by photographing a top-secret prototype of the newly designed car. Great lengths would be taken to shoot the prototype car at secret locations to prevent new designs being leaked to the press or stolen by competitors. To avoid this happening, photographers were ushered into car design studios to photograph these prototypes in the safety of a closed set or a windowless studio.

Figure CS5.2 shows the workflow of the main stages of car production. The car design process incorporates CAD using 3D computer graphics software, most commonly from the Autodesk package. All cars begin as paper sketches, which are then translated into 3D computer models. The next stage is to make a scale model using specialist clay. The scale is most often in the ratio of 1:4 or 1:1. The most successful

CASE STUDY 5

STAGE 1: Product planning and concept design (2D)
Initial design sketches on paper and/or using a stylus and
graphics tablet, with graphics software, such as Photoshop.

STAGE 2: From 2D to 3D – Testing designs in CAD and clay
Various designs translated into 3D Computer Aided Design
(CAD) models and 1:4 or 1:1 scale clay models.

STAGE 3: Design refinement
Final design selected and refined, using the clay model and CAD.

STAGE 4: Design completion
Design finished. CAD data available for advertsing CGI.
Prototypes are built (for testing, advertising and trade shows).

STAGE 5: Vehicle production
The final car is manufactured in the factory.

CS5.2 From concept to factory floor – the main stages of car design.

of these clay model designs are then scanned. The scanned data is recombined with the computer data to create a 3D wireframe (a virtual structural model) of the car. CAD modellers now continue to sculpt and refine the design, under the guidance of the exterior and interior car designers. Once the design process is nearing completion, the 3D wireframe can be rendered either as still photographs, animated for TV advertisements or website marketing footage.

This process can also help the designers improve the design, by viewing the car with visual refinements such as reflections and shadows (as shown in figure CS5.3). The CAD and visualization process also has the more obvious advantage of creating a number of design variations of the virtual car before its final look is established.

Synthetic Shading

Once the car has been designed the CAD data needs to be rendered to display different surface materials such as glass and metal. This is a technique called 'synthetic shading' which transforms the wireframe into a simulation of a realistic photograph of a car (Mitchell, 1992: 137). Lighting algorithms, including reflections and highlights are applied to the virtual 3D model. In the early days of CGI the placement of the lighting and shading was subjective and decided by the CGI artist. Now photography is used to provide this information. Two different photographic elements are combined with the 3D CAD data to create a photo-realistic image of a car: the photographic backplate and the CGI sphere.

THE DESIGNED PHOTOGRAPH: COMPUTER GENERATED IMAGERY (CGI) IN CAR PHOTOGRAPHY

CS5.3 Stages in the creation of a CGI 'designed photograph'. René Staud.
A: The photographic backplate (a real landscape photograph)
B: The CGI sphere (a full spherical HDRI photograph – 360° horizontal x 180° vertical)
C: The wireframe is manipulated into its correct position in relation to the backplate with 3D visualization computer software
D: The rendered car without the surface textures
E: The finished blended CGI car and photographic backplate

Image and caption text source: Staud, René (2010) 'Straight talk – Interview with René Staud' in *Designers Digest* CGI Special, volume 110, 2010, p. 24–35. Courtesy of the artist.

The Photographic Backplate

Most car advertisements are now created by placing a computer-generated image of the vehicle in a real photographic scene. The 'real photographic scene' is known as a 'backplate' (fig. CS5.3). Unless the car company or advertising agency demands the car is placed in an unreal or fantastical environment, an actual photograph of a real landscape or cityscape can be used. Car companies no longer need to ship their delicate and top-secret prototypes out to be photographed: all that is required is the backplate

CASE STUDY 5

photograph. For a high-profile campaign this will be a commissioned backplate shoot. Car photographers are increasingly finding themselves working on location, but without the actual car. A new genre within the stock photography industry has arisen because of this specialist type of image. Companies have now been set up to specialize in supplying these backplate images from locations all around the world. Moofe is one such a company, set up in the UK by photographers Carl Lyttle and Douglas Fisher. They were car photographers and needed to change their business model if they were to survive (Smith, 2009). Lyttle and Fisher shoot landscape backdrops around the world and display them in a specialist stock library on their website for use with CGI cars.

The CGI car can then be placed into these backplate photographs. Then the CGI artist can match the lighting, lens focal length, depth of field, etc. However, because a car is a highly curved and reflective object, the CGI artist needs to know *what* will be in the reflection. More image data is required. It could, of course, be synthesized but as the backplate is taken in reality, this reflective data can be also recorded in reality as a 'CGI sphere'.

The CGI Sphere

The next stage in the CGI workflow is to use a full spherical, panoramic photograph taken at the scene (when the backplate was captured, in same lighting conditions). The CGI sphere provides the CGI artist with even more information to use as realistic reflections and lighting data for the surface of the car. This image can be captured with a custom-made panoramic camera, which captures 360° horizontally and 180° vertically. This specialist image data is captured as a high dynamic range image (HDRI), a photograph with an extended tonal range. An example of a specialized camera for this purpose is the SpheroCam HDR manufactured by German company, Spheron CGI. A sphere or dome can also be captured using a standard digital SLR camera, photographing multiple shots, which can be merged to create a panoramic image. Image B in Figure CS5.3 shows an example of a CGI sphere.

3D Visualization Software

A 3D visualization of the digital prototype car can now be viewed and manipulated in specialist software such as Autodesk Showcase. 3D visualization software combines the three ingredients listed above: the car wireframe CAD data, the backplate and the sphere. Reflections from the sphere image can be used to create a believable final rendering. This software also assists designers even at early stages in the car's design, as well as being used at the final stage of the design process for outputting images for advertising. The CGI elements, once rendered, look and behave like an actual photograph. Using an industry standard graphics editing software such as Adobe Photoshop, the image can be enhanced and retouched ready for publication.

Categories of Car Images – The Implications for Photographers

Figure CS5.4 shows that there are four main variations of a designed car photograph. The category of using real photographs for the whole image is becoming increasingly rare. Only around 20 per cent of car advertising is done in this way now (Southern, 2012). However, actual photographs of cars already in production are still in demand for car magazines such as *Top Gear*. The three other variations in Figure CS5.4 all incorporate CGI. The categories of 'CGI car and real photo backplate' and 'real photo of a real car and CGI backplate' provide ample opportunities for car photographers. However the final category of 'Full CGI image – simulated car and background' has a limited role for a photographer other than as a potential CGI supervisor.

The Photographer's Role

In the past the photographer took pictures of a car on location or in a studio. In a CGI workflow the photographer takes the location 'backplate' photograph and then the CGI sphere. In an interview for *Designers Digest* (2010) the car photographer Werner Deisenroth proposes that the photographer can become a 'visual lead' for the CGI artist. He suggests the specialist lighting and photographic knowledge of the car photographer can be transferred into the CGI environment (Deisenroth, 2010: 20–21). He can also advise on correct depth-of-field lighting and reflection control. In this way a car photographer becomes like a director of photography. Breun and Grega, who shot the photo backplate and CGI sphere for the image in Figure CS5.1, also acted as CGI supervisors for the car's insertion into the scene. It might be quite telling of the diversity necessary for survival as a car photographer in this climate of change: it is significant that Breun and Grega describe themselves as photographers, videographers and CGI supervisors. The diversification in the photographer's role is clearly a factor in the work now being carried out in car advertising.

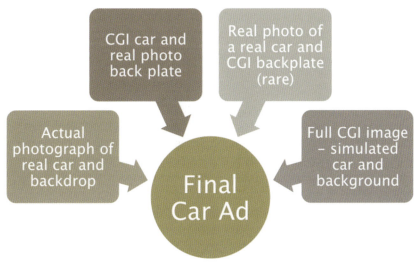

CS5.4 Variations on the make-up of a designed car photograph.

CASE STUDY 5

Towards a Broader Definition of Photography

Certainly in the realm of car and product photography the use of CGI will continue to rise. The whole design process incorporates CAD data from an early stage, so it makes perfect sense to use this data to create digital photographic prototypes before the product is made. Digital artists incorporating these computer-generated elements strive to achieve the natural look of a single shot photographic image. Here the photographer can transfer his or her skills to behave as a creative lead or director of photography. For photographers wishing to have a fruitful career in product photography, an understanding of the idea of CGI is now essential. For other areas of photography, only time will tell. We have discussed how the idea of the 'uncanny valley' may be psychologically disturbing and noted it is usually economically more viable to photograph a model or actor. An exception to the use of an actor would be the case of a posthumous shoot, for example the 2013 advertisement for Galaxy chocolate featuring Audrey Hepburn, brought back to life with CGI technology.

This case study begins to suggest a broadening of the definition of photography and what it means to be a photographer in the twenty-first century. Despite the resistance of the realists, the term 'photography' might for example now be a construct of light, data and pixels. Manovich (2001: 180–200) outlined a key argument: CGI artists are aiming to make the final rendering *appear like* photographs, not the real world, which suggests the visual language or ontology of a 'photograph' has not changed, but only the way we construct or design it.

The term photography may still be used for practices that seem to deviate from the kind of productive process that relies on the action of light on a photosensitive surface. The union of optics and chemistry – one for projection and the other for making surfaces 'ready' for the capture of it – is a defining property of photography. This account has a way of underlining the essential event in photography that connects the image and its referent in the world. Once this 'event' is short-circuited the image rendering process becomes a different (and arguably less profound) kind of practice that has many names including constructed imagery and CGI. It is a matter for speculation whether these practices are in some way photographic ones. This case study is not intended to appraise new media or even to measure its comparative worth as a component part of what has been called photography in the past. It is, however, our concern to reflect on the limits of the term photography since this is what the book seeks to define.

CONCLUSION

We began this study by asking to what extent the car in Figure CS5.1 is constructed. We noted that the background is a landscape photograph made with a camera so that the image is only partly constructed away from the scene as it were. The advertising image is of course deceptively like a photograph but our investigation has revealed it to be a composite of photographs of reality and photo-realistic computer simulations. We might be tempted to say that whatever it is, it is not a photograph or at least that it does not conform to the definitive 'event' described above. Photographers are instrumental in this rapidly evolving technology and yet readers may have reason to note the passing of skills and techniques pioneered and developed over time. Car photographer roles are constantly changing with this new technology, often taking the role of CGI supervisor.

THE DESIGNED PHOTOGRAPH: COMPUTER GENERATED IMAGERY (CGI) IN CAR PHOTOGRAPHY

We have suggested that the 'designed car photograph' occupies a new liminal state between the real and the simulated. The photographer has to develop new skills to continue to have a role to play in this ever-evolving branch of product photography.

GLOSSARY OF NEW TERMS:
2D – Two-dimensional
3D – Three-dimensional
Algorithm – A process to be followed in calculations by a computer. E.g. add a texture or shadow to an object
Backplate – A photographic or CGI backplate is a traditional photograph of a real environment
CAD – Computer Aided Design
CAD modeller – Creates computer 'virtual' models of a car design in process using specialist software
Clay modeller – Creates models of a car design in process from specialist clay
CGI – Computer generated imagery
Composite – A photographic-looking image, constructed in the computer comprising several photographs and/or CGI elements: Also referred to as a Seamless Photographic Montage.
HDRI – High Dynamic Range Imaging
Rendering – The processing of the computer model to make it appear solid and three-dimensional, with appropriate lighting and reflections
Simulation – A computer model that accurately imitates the appearance of a person, object or place
Sphere – The CGI or HDRI sphere is a full spherical, panoramic photograph taken at the scene (when the backplate was captured, in the same lighting conditions). The CGI sphere provides the CGI artist with even more information to use as realistic reflections and lighting data for the surface of the car.
Wireframe – A virtual structural model, which has the appearance of a wireframe. No surface renderings appear on a wireframe. A wireframe only displays the 3D shape of the model.

REFERENCES

Barthes, Roland (1981) *Camera Lucida: Reflections on Photography*, trans. Richard Howard, New York: Hill and Wang.

Deisenroth, Werner (2010) '3D Visualisation – Dream or Drama: Interview with Werner Deisenroth, BFF, Photo-designer, Co-publisher of Designers Digest', in *Designers Digest* CGI Special, volume 110, 2010, pp. 12–21. Available at: http://issuu.com/designers-digest/docs/cgi_2010

Freud, Sigmund (2003) *The Uncanny*, London: Penguin.

Hansegard, Jens (2012) 'Ikea's New Catalogs: Less Pine, More Pixels: Computer-Generated Images Aim to Save Money on Marketing Costs as Photographers Are Retrained to Apply Skills to 3-D Scenes', in *The Wall Street Journal*, 23 August 2012. Available at: http://online.wsj.com/article/SB10000872396390444508504577595414031195148. html?mod=WSJEUROPE_business_LeadStoryCollection

Kember, Sarah (1998) *Virtual Anxiety,* Manchester University Press.

Lister, Martin; Dovey, Jon; Giddings, Seth; and Kelly, Kieren (2009) *New Media: A Critical Introduction*, London and New York: Routledge.

Lucas, Gavin (2012) 'Beware the Uncanny Valley', *Creative Review*, June, pp. 49–54.

Manovich, Lev (2001) *The Language of New Media,* Cambridge, MA and London: The MIT Press.

Mitchell, William J. (1992) *The Reconfigured Eye: Visual Truth in the Post-Photographic Era*, Cambridge, MA: MIT Press.

Rose, Steve (2011) 'Tintin and the Uncanny Valley: When CGI Gets Too Real', in the *Guardian* newspaper. Available at: http://www.theguardian.com/film/2011/oct/27/tintin-uncanny-valley-computer-graphics

Smith, Diane (2009) 'The Traditional Studio Photographer Is About to Die', in *Creative Review,* July 2009. Available at: http://www.creativereview.co.uk/back-issues/creative-review/2009/july-2009/the-traditional-photographer (accessed: 22.10.2014).

Southern, Alex (2012) 'Real or Rendered? How 3D Imagery Is Changing the Way You Shop', in *Forbes Magazine,* October 2012. Available at: http://www.forbes.com/sites/techonomy/2012/10/15/real-or-rendered-how-3d-imagery-is-changing-the-way-you-shop/

Staud, René (2010), 'Straight talk – Interview with René Staud' in *Designers Digest* CGI Special, volume 110, 2010, p. 24–35. Available at: http://issuu.com/designers-digest/docs/cgi_2010

Tinwell, Angela, Grimshaw, Mark and Williams, Andrew (2011) 'The Uncanny Wall', *International Journal of Arts and Technology*, vol. 4, no. 3, pp. 326–341.

INDEX

3D visualization software 364

Abstract Expressionism 34
abstraction 106–7
academe 224
activism 158–60
Adams, Andy 346–7
Adams, Ansel 94, 152, 194, 236
Adobe Photoshop 132
Adorno, T. W. 335, 336
advertising 4, 17, 31, 96, 132, 164,
  196–7, 256, 299, 303–18; cars
  299–300, 313, 357–68; CGI
  299–300, 357–68; constructed
  photographs 132, 139; creative
  economy 319–41; digital images
  142; Kodak 135–7, 144–5; New
  Photography Theory 238; parody
  233–4; semiology 177–9, 181, 185;
  standardization 336; written word
  187–8
aesthetic function 255
Agee, James 212, 259, 260
agit-prop 166
albumen prints 59, 69
Allbeson, Tom 269
Altaió, Vincenç 353
amateurs 139–40, 143, 222, 285, 299,
  344, 345
Analogue to Digital Converter (ADC)
  143, 147
anchoring 189
Arago, François 52–3
Arbus, Diane 96–7, 232–3
Archer, Frederick Scott 50, 58
architecture 56–7, 114
archives 210, 241, 257–9
Arnatt, Keith 159
Art and Language 160
art nouveau 71
art photography 12, 18, 22, 36, 49,
  64–7, 104–7, 152; context 210; New
  Photography Theory 233–4, 236–7;
  origins 58; realism 81–6
art school system 271–2
Arvatov, Boris 165
assignment photography 330

Association of Photographers in Higher
  Education (APHE) 268–9
Atget, Eugène 18, 19, 91, 107
Atkins, Anna 281, 285
Aumont, Jacques 255–6
authentication 197–9, 212
authorship 210, 344
autonomy 213–14
avant-garde 14–15, 28, 32, 36, 106,
  121, 158; advertising 306, 321–2;
  New Photography Theory 226, 228,
  238–44; techno 271

Barnard, Malcolm 256
Barthes, Roland 33, 82, 100–1, 107,
  152, 159, 175, 198, 199, 200,
  225, 252; anchoring 189, 190,
  200; authentication 197; biography
  172–3; Cultural Studies 245;
  imposition 204; meaning 213; photographic paradox 175–6, 193, 195–6;
  pre-linguistic 193; press photos
  192, 202–3; realism 253; semiology
  177–8, 185, 187; *studium* and
  punctum 198–9, 253; words 215
Bartlane facsimile system 142
Basalla, George 11
'Basetrack' 147
basic photography 226–7, 246
Batchen, Geoffrey 9, 35, 36, 37, 38,
  45–6, 102, 138–9
Bate, David 157, 160–1, 163
Baudelaire, Charles 91, 124
Baudrillard, Jean 31
Bauer, Francis 51
Bauhaus 223, 227, 228, 300, 323
Bayard, Hippolyte 44, 112, 114, 118
Bazin, André 100, 107
the Beatles 311–12
Becher, Bernd 258, 259
Becher, Hilla 258, 259
Becker, Howard S. 323–4, 337–8, 339
Beck's beer advert 314
Bellmer, Hans 120
Benetton 314, 324–5
Benjamin, Walter 15, 19–20, 57, 120,
  157–8, 163, 165, 219, 225, 308

Berger, John 15, 84, 163, 200, 250–1,
  257
Berners-Lee, Tim 344
Best, Steven 29
Bethers, Ray 106
bias 273–4
binary opposition 37, 38, 80–1, 103
blogging 145–6, 284–5
bodegon 286
body language 182, 207
Bogre, Michelle 13
Bohrmann, Horst Paul Albert *see* Horst
  P. Horst
Boiffard, Jacques André 81
Bourdieu, Pierre 324
Bourke-White, Margaret 94, 95, 96,
  122, 191–2
box camera 66, 71, 75, 135–40
Brady, Matthew 63
branding 184
Brassaï 81
Braverman, Harry 323
Brecht, Bertolt 120
Breun, David 358, 365
Brodovich, Alexey 306
Brownie camera 137–8
Bruehl, Anton 306
Burgin, Victor 2, 35, 159, 163–4,
  165, 166, 169, 172, 219, 221–2,
  223; advertising 321; concerned
  photography 232; funding 269;
  New Photography Theory 229, 230,
  233–4, 238, 242, 246, 251–3; repre-
  sentation 263
Burn, Ian 160

Caillebotte, Gustave 90, 91, 93
calotype 50, 56, 114
Calotype Club 67
camera angle 183, 213
camera distance 183
camera lucida 48, 173
camera obscura 46–8, 49, 51, 54, 73,
  74, 83–4, 285
Camera Work 22, 304
Camerawork 228, 229, 239, 267
Cameron, Julia Margaret 12, 65–6

INDEX

Campany, David 81, 122, 125, 236
Campbell, David 343
canon 167
Canon Rebel 143
captions 120, 182, 194, 202, 206, 211, 215, 216
car advertising 299–300, 313, 357–68
careers 290–2, 319–20
carte-de-visite 11–12, 53, 56, 58, 68, 69–70, 75, 77, 135, 156; realism 92, 93
Cartier-Bresson, Henri 152
Casebere, James 130, 131
celebrity 184, 314, 348
Cevallos, Fabian 200
Chandler, Daniel 171
Chapman brothers 321, 325
Charge Coupled Devices (CCD) 141–3, 147
Chevalier, Charles 51
Christodoulou, Chris 360
cinematography 124–8, 254, 335
citizen journalism 147, 267, 348–50, 353
clothing codes 182–3, 203–4, 207–8
Cockburn, Julie 350
codes 305, 314; definition 176; *see also* semiology
colonial photography 185, 231
colour 183–4
combination printing 115–17
commercial art 4
commercialism 67–73
commodity aesthetics 304
common sense 82, 154, 233–4
Complementary Metal Oxide Semiconductor (CMOS) 143, 147
composite pictures 117–19
composition 181
computer-aided design (CAD) 359, 361–2, 364, 366
computer generated imaging (CGI) 132, 147, 278, 279, 285–8, 299–300, 357–68; sphere 362, 364, 365, 367
Conan Doyle, Arthur 119
conceptual art 153, 160–1, 168, 228
conceptualism 165–8, 230, 254
conformity 328–9
connoisseurship 29
connotation 179–80, 185, 193, 196, 200, 201, 213
Constable, John 87
constructed photographs 3, 112–33
Constructivists 14, 161, 162, 323
consumer cameras 144–5
consumer cultures 303–18

contact 2–3, 32, 100–2, 104–5, 109, 214
context 210, 215; connotation 180; pre-linguistic 193
contextual meaning 35–6, 39, 82
convergence 285, 286
Cottingley Fairies 119
Cotton, Charlotte 131
Coultart, Trevor 281
counter-formalism 35
craft workers 337–8
creative economy 319–41
creative labour 327
creative labour markets 320–1
Creative Skillset 220, 290
Crewdson, Gregory 124, 126, 127, 130
critical theory 37, 219, 270, 275
crowdfunding 346–7
Crowley, David 70
Cubists 158, 191
cultural disappearance 258
cultural politics 184
cultural populism 321
cultural theory 152, 299
Cunningham, Imogen 94
Curtis, Verna 138
cyanotype 281, 285

Dadaists 14, 121, 158, 161, 165, 190–1, 312
Daguerre, Louis 38, 44, 49–54, 55, 92, 112, 114
daguerreotypes 44, 50–1, 53–4, 56, 78, 112, 114
Dalí, Salvador 322
darkrooms 281, 283
Darwin, Charles 70
Daumier, Honoré 90, 93, 166
Davy, Humphrey 49, 51
Day, Corinne 327
decoding ads 179, 185
Deisenroth, Werner 365
Delahaye, Luc 97, 122
Delaroche, Paul 64, 279
Demand, Thomas 130–1
democratization 307
Dennett, Terry 241
denotation 87, 179, 185, 195–6, 213
depiction 5, 78, 98, 100, 103–4, 109
Descartes, René 166
descriptive titles 208–9
de Veigy, Cedric 350
Dewdney, Andrew 236, 245
Dexter, Emma 97
digital camera backs (DCB) 143–4, 147–8

digital cameras 139, 141–8, 267–8, 345; auto setting 273–4; single lens reflex (DSLR) 142–3, 148, 285, 346
digital c-type printer 283
Digital Operator 291
digital photography 116, 119, 279–82, 284–96; case study 342–56; the future 147; seamless montage 128–9, 132; *see also* computer generated imaging (CGI)
digital storage unit (DSU) 142, 148
digitization, truth 82
DiNucci, Darcy 344
direct vision 100–1
discourse 153, 154
Disderi, André Adolph-Eugène 12, 69, 93
documentary photography 18–22, 28, 31, 35–6, 49, 65; language 202; photo-essays 259–61, 308; realism 91–2, 93, 97–8; repressive 231–2
Doisneau, Robert 21, 22
Doren, Mariah 275
double exposures 117
dry plates 70
Duchamp, Marcel 167, 350
Dumas, Marlene 153
Dusseldorf Academy of Art 223
Dutch realism 88–9, 90, 92
Dyer, Gillian 196

Eastman, George 135, 136–7, 139, 145
Eder, Josef Maria 9
education 3, 158–9, 219–97; New Photography Theory 221–48; return of the real 249–65; teaching and learning 266–77; technology 278–97
Edwards, Elizabeth 257–9
Edwards, Steve 9, 10, 12, 32, 138, 160, 161, 209, 260
Eggleston, William 278
Einfalt, Florian 278
Emin, Tracey 314, 321, 322
emotion 103–4, 253
environmental media 191–2
epistemic function 99–100, 104, 256
Epstein, Mitch 97
Ernst, Max 326
'essential being' 10
Evans, Harold 213
Evans, Jessica 233, 254
Evans, Walker 31, 35, 94, 95, 97, 108, 122, 152, 167–8, 212–13, 233, 259, 260–1

370

INDEX

f/64 group 94, 98, 157
Facebook 145, 280, 284, 343, 348
facticity 120
Faddy, David 242
Fairchild Imaging 141
falsification 63–4, 257
family albums 25–6, 138–9, 194, 212, 244, 257
family values 26–8, 308
fashion photography 16–17
feminism 27–8
Fenton, Roger 43, 60–2, 68
film noir 254
film theory 335
fine art photography 142, 161, 236, 336
Finnigan, Ruth 192
Fisher, Douglas 364
flâneur 91
Fletcher, Jane 275
Flew, Terry 320
Flickr 283, 284, 346–8, 350–2
Florida, Richard 300, 320, 338
Flusser, Vilém 193
focus 183
folksonomy 348, 350
Fontcuberta, Joan 8–9, 353
formalism 32–6, 37–8, 39, 104–5; counter-formalism 35
Foster, Hal 205, 259, 263
Foucault, Michel 231
found photographs 350–1
Foveon 143
Fox, Claire 270
Fox Talbot, William Henry 7, 11, 37–8, 44, 50–1, 53–4, 55, 70, 152; fine screen 72; *Latticed Window* 114
framing 181–2
Frank, Georgia 102
Freeland, Cynthia 101–2, 103, 104–5
Freeman, Robert 311–12
Freud, Sigmund 361
Freund, Gisèle 9, 70
Friedrich, Ernst 63
Frizot, Michel 9, 23, 24, 138, 350
Frosh, Paul 299, 330–1, 332, 333–5, 336
Fulton, Hamish 151–2
funding 269, 291, 346–7

Galvin, Nick 266
Gantz, Joe 124
Garb, Tamar 25
Gardi, Balazs 146–7
Gardner, Alexander 63–4, 77
Gauguin, Paul 328

gaze 211
gender 184; New Photography Theory 238; objectification 185; social pressure 240
Gendron, Bernard 335–6
Generation C 347
Gernsheim, Alison 9, 23, 44, 47
Gernsheim, Helmut 9, 23, 44, 47
global village 343
Golding, Andrew 249, 269, 274
Gombrich, Ernst 82, 83, 86–8
Goodman, Nelson 86, 87, 103–4
Google Glass 346
Gräff, Werner 306–7
Green, David 231
Greenberg, Clement 34
Grega, Martin 358, 365
Griffiths, Frances 119
Griffiths, Philip Jones 38, 63
Grossberg, Lawrence 245
Gursky, Andreas 119, 128–9
Gustavson, Todd 144

Haacke, Hans 166
Half Moon Gallery 241
halftone process 71–3, 74, 75, 305
Hall, Norman 106
Hall, Stuart 25, 154, 159, 179, 213, 237, 308
Hamilton, Peter 20–1
Hamilton, Richard 237, 322
Harper's Bazaar 306
Harris, Philip 275
Hartley, John 300, 321
Hasselblad 143–4
Heartfield, John 15, 157, 166, 229, 239
Hebdige, Dick 173
heliography 51, 54
Hering, Henry 210, 211
Herschel, John 281
High Definition (HD) video 285
high dynamic range (HDR) 116
High Modernism 156, 161, 162, 166, 311
Hilliard, John 159–60
Hindley, Myra 210, 211, 231
Hine, Lewis 194
Hipstamatic 146–7
Hirsch, Jonathan 268, 319
Hirst, Damien 322, 325
historiography 30
Hoffman, Barry 313–14, 315, 322
Holland, Patricia 139, 299
Hopper, Edward 249
Horkheimer, Max 335, 336
Horst P. Horst 16–17

Hubble Space Telescope 142
Hughes, Robert 84
humanist photography 20–2
Hunter, Tom 124, 126–7
Hurlburt, Allan 322–3
hyperphotography 280, 347
hyper-reality 31

iconic sign 176, 189, 199, 202–5, 216
icons 101–2, 103, 104–5
identity politics 166, 169, 244
ideology 154, 178
Ikea 361
illustration 71, 73
imposition 204
indexical sign 175, 189, 199, 202–4, 216
indexicality 199
indirect vision 100–1
information value 181
informational titles 208–9
Instagram 346, 348, 349
Instamatic camera 139
inter-media 190–1
intermedia 134
Internet: global village 343; Web 2.0 344
intertextuality 122, 233, 314
iPhone 345, 346
Iversen, Margaret 171
Ivins, William M. 11, 66, 225

James, Sarah 13
Jarché, James 221–2, 253
Jay, Martin 45
Jhally, Sut 309
Jobling, Paul 70
Johnston, Matt 288
Johnston, Patricia 304
Jostmeier, Michael 286
journals 227–8, 229
juxtaposition 182

Katchadourian, Nina 352–3
Keen, Andrew 343
Kellner, Douglas 29
Kember, Sarah 359
Kertész, André 152
Kessels, Erik 352
Khan Academy 288
Kirsch, Russell 141
Kline, Stephen 309
knowledge: photography as 153; sharing 320
Kodak 71, 75, 135–9, 141, 142, 144–5
Köhler, Michael 113
Kolker, Richard 286

371

INDEX

Koons, Jeff 315, 322
Kracauer, Siegfried 81, 157
Kress, Gunther 181, 192, 203
Kruger, Barbara 31, 165–6, 239, 314–15
Kuwayama, Teru 146–7
Kyocera 344

laissez-faire 271, 272, 291
Lander, Tobias 313
landscape photography 47, 54, 58–62, 151–2, 156, 171; picturesque 156
Lange, Dorothea 94, 95, 106
Lange, Silke 274
Langford, Michael 227
language 152–3, 165, 251; conceptual art 160; photography as a function 192–3; pre-linguistic 193–4, 198, 214; see also semiology; written word
Larson, Jonas 13, 299, 348
Lasn, Kalle 187
Leadbeater, Charles 320
learning communities 284–5
Lécuyer, Raymond 9
Lee, Russell 94, 96
Le Gray, Gustave 56, 58–60, 64, 65, 68, 115
Lehman, Peter 335
Leibovitz, Annie 26
Leiss, William 309
Lemagny, Jean-Claude 9
Leonardo da Vinci 47, 84, 85
Levine, Sherrie 31, 166–8, 254, 263, 328
Levinthal, David 130
licensing of images 333
Lidchi, Henrietta 25
lighting 183, 282
Lincoln, Abraham 77–8, 104, 108
Linfield, Susie 13, 212–13
Linked Ring Brotherhood 66
Lister, Martin 143, 271, 279, 343, 345, 347, 353, 359
lithography 51, 70
'lived world' 244–5
Lotar, Eli 81
Lowenstein, Heike 287–8
Lucas, Greg 275
Lucas, Sarah 321
Luhr, William 335
Lupton, Ellen 304, 333
Lytro 147
Lyttle, Carl 364

McCabe, Eamonn 204
McCauley, Anne 214

McLuhan, Marshall 343
McRobbie, Angela 320, 321–3, 326, 337, 338–9
Maddox, Richard L. 70
magic lanterns 57
Magritte, René 120, 205–6
Manet, Édouard 90, 124, 126
manifestation 101–3, 104, 109
Mann, Steve 346, 349
Manovich, Lev 279, 359, 366
Mapplethorpe, Robert 229
Marbot, Bernard 10
Marcus, Laura 256–7
Marien, Mary Warner 9, 118, 122, 123, 229, 237
Marlboro advert 314–15
Martin, Rosy 243
Martin, William H. 118
Marville, Charles 91
Marxism 155, 234
mass production 67–73
Massively Open Online Courses (MOOCs) 288
Max Factor advert 303
Maynard, Patrick 11, 24, 73, 78, 103, 268
meaning 154, 214–15, 299; advertising 309; anchoring 189; contextual 35–6, 39, 82; language 206; narrative 211–13, 309–10; semiology 171–85; social 221–2; written work 189–90, 192
media panic 271
Meggs, Philip B. 71
Meisenbach, George 72
Mélon, Marc 66
memento mori 114
Memou, Antigoni 13
Messaris, Paul 311
metonymy 180
Miller, Abbott 304, 333
Millum, Trevor 175
Mitchell, W. J. T. 31, 87, 260–1
Mitchell, William J. 279, 362
mixed media formats 190, 233, 237, 251
mobile phone cameras 146–7, 299, 342–53
modernism 14–16, 30, 31–2, 38, 67, 96, 105, 157–8, 300; advertising 304–8, 317
Moholy-Nagy, László 152, 156, 157, 322
Mohr, Jean 257
montage: digital 128–9, 132; photo-montage 121–2, 157, 165, 219, 238–40, 254

monuments 56–7
Moofe 364
Mori, Masahiro 360
Morley, Simon 190
Muellner, Nicholas 345
Mulligan, Therese 270–1
multi-media formats 189–90
multi-perspectival histories 28–30
Munkacsi, Martin 306
Museum of Modern Art in New York (MOMANY) 29, 34–5, 67
mutuality 200
Muybridge, Eadweard 285

narrative meaning 211–13, 309–10
narrative tableaux 124–8
nationhood 25–6
naturalism 82, 108, 251; new 308–9
nature versus culture 37–8
Nava, Mica 314
Nava, Zadoc 249
near documentary 124–5
Nelson, Robert S. 205
Nesbit, Molly 32, 96
new naturalism 308–9
New Photography Theory 149, 219–20, 225, 250, 267; definition 224–5; issues and debates 221–48; realism 250–4, 257, 263–4
new social documentary 122
New Times 246
New Vision 306–7
New York Camera Club 66
Newbury, Darren 223
Newhall, Beaumont 9, 35, 84, 194
news photography 201; digital images 142; see also war photography
Niépce, Joseph Nicéphore 44, 49–54, 55
Nochlin, Linda 85, 89, 154
'non-art' documents 162–4
non-vocational approach 235–6, 269–70
Norfolk, Simon 60, 62, 64, 97, 122

objectification 185, 273, 274
objectivity 80–1, 109, 253
Ogilvy, David 309–10
Olaf, Erwin 325–6, 333
Oldenburg, Claes 312
online albums 145
online learning 288–9
open learning 288–9
Oppenheim, Meret 312
O'Reilly, Tim 344
O'Sullivan, Timothy H. 63
Otter, Chris 55

372

INDEX

page layout 212
Panofsky, Erwin 310
panorama 364
pantograph 48
parallax 86
Patterson, Lee 10, 31
Paul, Richard 254
peer networks 284–5
Peirce, Charles Sanders 149, 172, 175, 189, 199, 203, 216
The Pencil of Nature 7, 11, 44, 54, 70
permission 273, 274
personal style 327–8, 334
perspective 84–7, 108–9
Phillips, Christopher 14
Phillips, Sarah 249
Photo 2.0 346–7
photo blogs 145–6
Photobucket 145
Photo Club de Paris 66
photo-essays 259–61, 308
'photograms' 53
photographic amusement postcards 117–18
photographic backplate 362, 363–4, 365, 367
photographic paradox 175–6, 193, 195–6
The Photographic Society 68
Photography and Politics 228
Photography/Politics: Two 229
Photography Workshop 241
photojournalism 17, 95–6, 146–7, 350
Photokina 286
photomontage 121–2, 151, 157, 165, 219, 238–40, 254
Photo-Secession 22–3, 304
phototherapy 241, 242–3
Picasa 145
Pictorialism 66–7, 74, 75, 93, 94, 105, 109, 156
Picture Post 308–9
'picture window' 251
plenoptic camera 147
poetical title 207–8
Polaroid 139, 345
political-sociological approach 28
politics 95–6, 157; cultural 184; identity 166, 169, 244; New Photography Theory 228–9, 232, 234; satire 239; social meaning 222
Pollock, Griselda 272
polysemic properties 203
Pop Art 228, 237, 239, 311–15, 316–17
popular culture 254, 304–5, 335–6
popularization 67–8, 135–40

Porta, Giovanni Battista della 47
portfolio careers 300, 329
portrait photography 11–12, 54, 55–6, 65–6, 70–1, 104; conventions 77; daguerreotypes 54; official 26–7; self 240–4, 245, 347–8; *see also carte-de-visite*
postcards, photographic amusements 117–18
postmodernism 30, 31–2, 33, 35–6, 37–8, 39, 120, 155, 164, 263, 314, 321; autonomy 194–5; CGI 359; constructed photographs 122–3, 132; New Photography Theory 237; trends 165–8; truth 82
post-mortem photography 114–15
post-photography 263, 271, 279–80, 287
Powell, Michael 198
preservationist projects 257–8
Price, Mary 206, 214
Prince, Richard 31, 165, 314–15
printing 305
Pritchard, Lisa 320, 327, 329
propaganda 15, 24, 75, 96, 190, 201–2
Prosser, Jay 13
prosumers 143
Pultz, John 106
punctum 198–9, 203, 253
pure photography 105, 194–5, 216
puri-kura 344

racial stereotyping 184
radicalism 32
Ray, Man 16, 120
realism 34, 77–111, 193; New Photography Theory 219–20; return of the real 249–65
Rejlander, Oscar 65, 115–16, 118, 124
Rennie, Paul 308
representation 79–80, 86–7, 154, 234, 237–8, 251–2, 263
Richter, Gerhard 16, 350
rights managed images 333
Ritchin, Fred 280, 285, 347, 348–9, 350
Rivière, Carole 345
Roberts, John 34, 92, 96–7, 105, 107, 158–9, 160, 232–3, 244–5, 254–5, 271
Roberts, Russell 210
Robins, Kevin 271, 279
Robinson, Henry Peach 65, 116–17, 118, 124
Rodchenko, Alexander 156, 162
Ronis, Willy 20, 21, 22

Rose, Gillian 34, 171–2, 299
Rosenberg, Harold 328
Rosenblum, Barbara 328–30, 335, 336
Rosler, Martha 28–9, 35, 121–2, 130, 166, 259–60
Rosskam, Edwin 257
Rothko, Mark 34
Rouillé, André 9
Royal Photographic Society 224
royal photographs 26–7
royalty free images 333
Rubenstein, Daniel 282, 343
Rudolph, Harold 309–10
Russian Constructivism 14, 156, 161, 162, 323

Saatchi, Charles 321, 322
Saddington Baines 360, 361
safety posters 308–9
salience 181
Sandbye, Mette 13, 299, 348
Sander, August 20, 208–9, 215
Sasson, Steve 141, 144
Saussure, Ferdinand de 149, 173–4, 177, 203
Scharf, Aaron 9, 49, 81
Schmid, Joachim 350, 351–2
Scott, Clive 193, 198, 202–3, 206, 210
scripto-visual formats 165, 189, 233
Scruton, Roger 98, 99, 104
segmentation 337–8
Sekula, Allan 18, 28, 122, 149, 164, 166, 225, 232, 245, 259–60
self-portrait 240–4, 245, 347
self-research 244
selfie 347–8
Selgado, Sebastião 38
semiology 149, 152–3, 159, 169, 177, 187–9, 203, 216, 299; case study 171–86; New Photography Theory 245
Serrano, Andres 209–10
set construction 130–1, 132
sexual stereotyping 184
Shahn, Ben 94
Sheard, Tim 242
Sheeler, Charles 94, 95
Sherman, Cindy 123, 130, 165, 166, 233, 240
Shiff, Richard 328
signifiers/signified 173–4, 252
Simmons, Laurie 130
simulation 359–60
'single picture aesthetic' 164, 165, 168
Siskind, Aaron 33
Skillset 268–9

373

INDEX

Skoglund, Sandy 124
Sluis, Katrina 343
smartglasses 346
smartphones 146, 345, 346, 347–8
smart watches 346
Snapchat 348
snapshot photography 135–40
Sobieszek, Robert A. 306, 307
social activism 95
social behaviour 299
social codes 25
social formation 231
social identity 166, 225, 231, 238, 242–4, 249, 308, 314
social meaning 221–2
social networking 145, 280, 343, 345, 346–7
social power model 255
social practice 272–4
Société Héliographique 67–8
sociological approach 28
Solomon-Godeau, Abigail 17, 18, 35, 36, 97, 98, 167, 315
Sontag, Susan 120, 202, 212
sousveillance 349
Spence, Jo 28, 139, 219, 225, 229, 238–44, 245, 246, 254, 261, 321
Spender, Humphrey 197–8
'spirit' photographs 117
staged photographs see constructed photographs
standardization 336–7
Standing, Guy 320
Stanmeyer, John 342–3
status group 326
Steichen, Edward 22, 66–7, 207, 304, 322
stereoscopic photography 68–9, 75, 156
stereotypes 179, 184–5, 231, 333
Stezaker, John 350
Stieglitz, Alfred 22, 67, 94, 156, 208, 236, 304
still life 54, 92, 114
stock photography 300, 319, 331–6, 364
straight documentary 124–5
straight photography 23, 67, 75, 78, 80, 93–8, 107–9, 120
Strand, Paul 23, 33, 67, 75, 93, 94, 98
strangeness 107
structured sameness 231
studium 198, 199, 253
subjectivity 80–1, 253
supplementary function 189

Surrealism 16, 81, 107, 216; advertising 325–6; constructed photographs 120–1
survey work 258–9
symbolic codes 182, 184
symbolic function 256
symbolic power 309
symbolic sign 176–7, 189, 199, 201–5, 216
synecdoche 180
synthetic shading 362–3
Szarkowski, John 34–5, 39, 278

Tabard, Maurice 120
tableau vivant 116, 120, 124
Tabrizian, Mitra 249–50
Taft, Robert 9
Tagg, John 28, 95–6, 195, 225, 230–2, 238, 252, 255
taxonomy 209
Taylor, Brook 85
Taylor James 361
Taylor-Lind, Anastasia 346
technical codes 180–5
technology 220, 268, 271; education 278–97
Teller, Juergen 327
Ten.8 229, 230, 267
Thomas, Rebecca 266
Thrun, Sebastian 288
titles 206–11, 215, 216
Toffler, Alvin 143, 345
Toscani, Oliviero 314, 324–5, 333
tourism 56–7
Trachtenberg, Alan 51, 219, 224, 225–6, 246
Tracy, Conrad 283
transferable skills 289–90
transparency 34, 55, 98–102, 104–5, 108–9, 196–7, 203, 225, 238, 254; realism 252
travel photography 43, 75
triadic theory 175
trompe l'oeil 85, 86, 99
Tucholsky, Kurt 257
Twitter 147, 284, 288

Ukolova, Natalia 348
Ulmer, Greg 244–5
Umbrico, Penelope 350–1, 352
Uncanny Valley 360–1
Underwood, Bert Elias 68
Underwood, Elmer 68
'untitled' title 206–7

Van Beirendonck, Walter 325
van Gelder, Hilde 18, 325
Van Leeuwen, Theo 181, 192, 203
verisimilitude 89, 108–9
Vermeer, Jan 88, 89
vernacular photography 95, 138–9, 140, 157, 161
video, HD 285
video cameras, digital 141
virtual learning environment (VLE) 284
visual connoisseurship 221
visuality 205
vocational approach 235–6
vocational qualification 290–6
vocational status 327–8
Vogue 16–17, 304–5, 327

Wade, Eti 284
Wall, Jeff 119, 124–6, 128–9, 152, 254–5, 262–3, 288
Walton, Kendal L. 78, 86, 100, 101, 107
war photography 56, 57, 60–4, 75, 349–50; mobile phones 146–7; propaganda 201–2
Warhol, Andy 313, 315, 322
Watney, Simon 219, 225, 227, 235–6, 238, 252
Web 2.0 344, 353
web design 284–5
Wedgwood, Thomas 44, 49
Welch, David 309
Westgeest, Helen 18, 325
Weston, Edward 23, 33, 67, 75, 94, 96, 105–7, 152, 166
wet collodion plate process 43, 50, 58, 60, 70
Wide Field and Planetary Camera (WFPC) 142, 148
Williams, Anne 282, 285
Williams, Raymond 245
Williamson, Judith 179
Winogrand, Garry 35
Witkin, Joel Peter 124
Wolff, Henry 310
Wollen, Peter 15, 272
Wood, Paul 160
Woodward, Kathryn 154
Worth, Jonathan 283, 288–9
Wright, Elsie 119
Wright, Richard 257
Wright, Terence 268
written word 150, 187–218, 233–4
Wu, Chin-tao 314, 326